Natural Reason and Natural Law

Natural Reason and Natural Law

An Assessment of the Straussian Criticisms of Thomas Aquinas

JAMES CAREY

RESOURCE *Publications* • Eugene, Oregon

NATURAL REASON AND NATURAL LAW
An Assessment of the Straussian Criticisms of Thomas Aquinas

Resource Publications
An Imprint of Wipf and Stock Publishers
199 W. 8th Ave., Suite 3
Eugene, OR 97401

www.wipfandstock.com

PAPERBACK ISBN: 978-1-5326-5774-0
HARDCOVER ISBN: 978-1-5326-5775-7
EBOOK ISBN: 978-1-5326-5776-4

Manufactured in the U.S.A. SEPTEMBER 23, 2019

To Lisa, with gratitude immeasurable

Contents

Preface | xi
Abbreviations | xii

Introduction | 1

Part 1 The Teleology of Natural Reason | 9

Chapter 1 Preliminary Considerations | 11

Section a. The Theological Context | 11
Section b. Natural Reason | 20
Section c. Prudence, Judgment, and *Synderesis* | 31
Section d. Law and the Ends of Human Action | 33

Chapter 2 The Case for Natural Law | 38

Section a. The First Principle of Practical Reason | 38
Section b. The Precepts of Natural Law | 42
i. The order of natural inclinations | 42
ii. Primary and secondary precepts | 44
iii. Self-evidence | 53
iv. Love of one's neighbor | 55
v. Natural law and the moral precepts of the Decalogue | 58
vi. Application of the precepts of natural law | 61
Section c. Obligation Explicated | 63
i. Freedom of choice | 64
ii. Is and Ought | 69
iii. Conditional obligations | 72
iv. Unconditional obligations | 74

Chapter 3 Reason Commanding | 80

Section a. Natural Law and Roman Catholicism | 80

Section b. The New Natural Law Theory | 84

Section c. Thomas Aquinas and Kant | 97

Section d. The *Bonum Rationis* | 111

Part 2 Straussian Criticisms | 123

Chapter 4 Criticisms Advanced by Leo Strauss | 125

Section a. Medieval Philosophy vs. Christian Scholasticism | 125

Section b. The Criticisms in *Natural Right and History* | 137

Section c. The Criticisms in "On Natural Law" | 147

Chapter 5 Criticisms Advanced by Harry Jaffa | 152

Section a. Thomas's Departures from Aristotle | 153

Section b. The Natural Desire for a Supernatural End. | 159

Section c. Natural Law and the American Founding | 163

Chapter 6 Criticisms Advanced by Ernest Fortin | 168

Section a. Providence and Natural Law | 168

Section b. The Promulgation of Natural Law | 172

Section c. The Question of Punishment | 174

Chapter 7 Criticisms Advanced by Michael Zuckert | 180

Chapter 8 The Precept Commanding the Love and Worship of God | 193

Chapter 9 The Scope of *Synderesis* | 204

Section a. *Synderesis* as Natural | 204

Section b. *Synderesis* as Universal | 214

i. Seth Benardete on obligation in Greek antiquity | 215

ii. Douglas Kries on the acquisition of *synderesis* | 220

iii. The feeling of right and wrong | 225

iv. *Synderesis* in moral education | 227

Section c. Synderesis as Inerrant—Moral Absolutes | 230

Chapter 10 Rational Sociability | 240

Section a. Exotericism | 242

Section b. The Good of Others | 245

Section c. Philosophy and the Catholic Faith | 252

Part 3 Beyond Natural Law | 257

Chapter 11 Inconsistencies and Other Aberrations | 261

Section a. The Denial of Universal Rules | 261

Section b. Circumventing the Practical Syllogism | 272

Section c. Competence and Conscientiousness | 276

Section d. Science and Values | 279

Chapter 12 Philosophizing in the Shadow of Heidegger | 284

Section a. Nature and World | 284

Section b. Strauss's Struggle with Heidegger | 286

i. Choice of ends | 287

ii. Historicism | 288

iii. The Struggle with Heidegger in *Natural Right and History* | 292

iv. The Struggle with Heidegger in "Introduction to Existentialism" | 301

Section c. Toward a Thomistic Response to Heidegger | 305

i. Problems in the Husserlian background | 306

ii. The ontological difference between Being and beings | 309

iii. Metaphysics and mysticism | 312

iv. Logic, ontology, and *theoria* | 321

v. Conscience phenomenologically considered | 325

Chapter 13 Natural Teleology Revalidated | 329

Chapter 14 Objections and Replies | 353

Conclusion | 361

Bibliography | 367

Index | 381

Preface

THE PRESENT STUDY EVOLVED out of a paper that I presented in 2006 at the 41st International Congress of Medieval Studies, held at Western Michigan University. I thank Professor R.E. Houser of the Center for Thomistic Studies at the University of St. Thomas for affording me the opportunity to present that paper in one of the sessions he organized.

I have learned much from conversations with Thomists and Straussians over the years. It is possible that, in commenting on this or that book or article, I have spoken of someone as a Straussian who does not want to be identified as such. If so, I apologize. No harm was intended. I am sometimes identified as a Thomist. But I am not a Thomist. I am not a Roman Catholic either. I am an Orthodox Christian who, unlike most of my co-religionists, happens to be an admirer of Thomas Aquinas. I do not agree with him on all points. But I agree with him on a great many points.

I am indebted to my home institution, St, John's College, Santa Fe, for granting me a sabbatical for the 2015–2016 Academic Year. During that year, I was able to make considerable progress towards bringing this project to completion. I am also indebted to Col. James L. Cook, Chair of the Department of Philosophy at the United States Air Force Academy, where I have served as a visiting professor off and on for a number of years. Col. Cook encouraged me to offer courses in medieval philosophy, and in these courses I was able to deepen my understanding of Thomas Aquinas and other medieval thinkers. I wish to thank members of the Colorado Springs Philosophy Reading Group for their critical observations on an early version of one of the chapters included in this study. I also thank blind reviewers for their comments. I am particularly indebted to Bruce Sanborn for commenting helpfully and in detail on an early draft of the manuscript.

My greatest debt by far is to my wife, whose intelligence, sound judgment, and patience I have relied on continuously. It is to her that I dedicate this book.

Abbreviations

AMPLT	Finnis, *Aquinas – Moral Political and Legal Theory.*
ATAP	Fortin, "Augustine, Thomas Aquinas, and Natural Law."
CCPO	Fortin, *Classical Christianity and the Political Order.*
CM	Strauss, *The City and Man.*
DEE	Thomas Aquinas, *De Ente et Essentia.*
FB	Zukert, M., "The Fullness of Being."
GS	Strauss, *Gesammelte Schriften.*
HA	Caputo, *Heidegger and Aquinas.*
HSPPh	Velkley, *Heidegger, Strauss, and the Premises of Philosophy.*
IE	Strauss, "Introduction to Heideggerian Existentialism."
KRV	Kant, *Kritik der Reinen Vernunft* (*Critique of Pure Reason*).
LSPPPh	Zuckert, C. and M., *Leo Strauss and the Problem of Political Philosophy.*
NBFr	Jaffa, *A New Birth of Freedom.*
NLNR	Finnis, *Natural Law and Natural Rights.*
NRH	Strauss, *Natural Right and History.*
PAWr	Strauss, Persecution and the Art of Writing.
PNL	Kries, *The Problem of Natural Law.*
PR	Strauss, "Progress or Return?"
RR	Strauss, "Reason and Revelation."
PSP	Armstrong, *Primary and Secondary Precepts in Thomistic Natural Law Teaching.*
SCG	Thomas Aquinas, *Summa Contra Gentiles.*
SNRH	Kennington, "Strauss's *Natural Right and History.*"
ST	Thomas Aquinas, *Summa Theologiae.*

STANLT	Goyette et al, eds., *St. Thomas Aquinas and the Natural Law Tradition.*
SZ	Heidegger, *Sein und Zeit.*
ThAr	Jaffa, *Thomism and Aristotelianism.*
WhPPh	Strauss, *What is Political Philosophy?*

Introduction

Natural law consists of precepts of action constituted by a fundamental power of the human soul. Natural law is not derived from convention, and it is not derived from the claims of revelation either. Its source is natural, human reason. If the concept of natural law is sound, it is the standard for assessing positive laws, both of one's own political community and of other political communities, and it is the standard for guiding the choice and actions of individuals as well as communities. Natural law is the canon with which positive laws, choices, and actions must agree if they are to be rational, and its articulation and defense are necessary at all times. Its articulation and defense are of particular urgency in our times, characterized as they are by the ascendancy of relativism and misology, a chaos of flaccid hedonism and forceful decisionism, and general moral confusion.

The concept of natural law emerged in late antiquity. But it is generally acknowledged by both its admirers and its most thoughtful critics that "the classic form of the natural law teaching" finds its expression in the writings of Thomas Aquinas.[1] Thomas's teaching is criticized at present from several perspectives. Some critics hold that reason, though it may have something to say about facts, is simply silent when matters of good and bad—what these critics prefer to call "values"—are in question. Some hold that the concept of rights, of fundamental human rights in particular, pertains more evidently to human nature than does any concept of law. Others hold that there is actually no such thing as human nature, man being an essentially historical being and more or less indefinitely malleable. In spite of disagreements among the critics of natural law, they all agree in denying that there is a trans-political and rationally accessible law that commands and prohibits. They deny this most vehemently when the commands and prohibitions in question are repugnant to current sensibilities. Their criticisms are rarely informed by a close engagement with Thomas Aquinas's natural law teaching.

The case of the political philosopher Leo Strauss is quite different. He read and reflected seriously on what Thomas had to say about natural law. Though impressed, he was not persuaded, and he employed his remarkable intellectual powers to launch an attack against Thomas's teaching at what he understood to be its foundations. Some

1. Strauss, "On Natural Law," 143.

of his followers have attempted to press this attack further. The attack has gone unnoticed by many Thomists, in part because it has been understated. But it has also gone unnoticed by them because of a vague sense that, since both they and the Straussians greatly admire Aristotle, have little use for Kant, and are about equally critical of modernity, they and the Straussians are in essential agreement regarding the ultimate principles of choice and action.[2] Some misperceptions could be further from the truth than this one, but not many. It is a misperception of which the Straussians themselves are not guilty.

Strauss and his followers allege that Thomas's natural law teaching presupposes belief in revelation, or a discredited cosmology, or both, with the consequence that it cannot provide adequate moral guidance for those who accept neither.[3] At first glance, the criticism does not seem to be exactly devastating, for it dovetails in part with a tendency among many who share Thomas's faith to advertise his natural law teaching with understandable pride as a Roman Catholic teaching. As should be expected, however, such an advertisement raises the suspicion among unbelievers that natural law is not so much natural as it is revealed, or, more precisely, based on what is believed to be revealed. This suspicion is reinforced by occasional pronouncements by Roman Catholics that "the church teaches" or "the Pope says" that such and such an

2. For a book that exhibits a good understanding of both Thomas Aquinas and Leo Strauss, see Mary Keys's *Aquinas, Aristotle, and the Promise of the Common Good.* Hereafter cited as "Keys." Keys's interest is somewhat different from mine. Whereas she focuses on Thomas's political thought, I focus on his ethics and, in connection with this, on his rational theology as well. Keys does not examine the logical structure of Thomas's case for natural law, she does not respond to the Straussian criticisms, except obliquely, and she does not examine the consequences that follow from the denial of natural law. But there is much to praise in Keys's balanced treatment of her subject, and I shall have several occasions to refer to it in the present study.

3. See Leo Strauss, *NRH* 157–8, 163–4. According to Strauss, "the term 'Natural Law'. . . is open to grave objections." See, "Law of Reason," 95–98. In *The Political Philosophy of Hobbes*, which was originally written in German in 1936 and translated into English in 1952, Strauss uses the expression, "natural law," somewhat more loosely, or less critically, than he does in his later works. See pages vii-viii in the first Preface to that work. Strauss also appears to endorse something that he can call "the natural law" in Chapter 4 of *NRH* (127, 150). But what Strauss is apparently endorsing there is a far cry from Thomistic natural law, as he makes unforgettably clear on the last two pages of that chapter. (See Part 2, Ch. 4, Section b, below.) Strauss says that for "the classics," i.e., especially the Greek and pre-scholastic political philosophers—with whom he typically concurs and from whom he does not dissociate himself here—"[t]he *politeia* [i.e., the civil polity or regime] is more fundamental than any [!] laws; it is the source of all [!] laws" (136). In "The Problem of Socrates" (1970) Strauss says, "Nature is here [i.e., in Hobbes's state of nature] only a negative standard: that from which one should move *away*. On the basis of this, the law of reason or the moral law [as it was called] ceased to be *natural* law; nature is *no* way a standard" (326; the first clause in brackets is mine; the second is in the original). I do not understand Strauss in this passage to be endorsing the concept of natural law, as distinct from natural right, but only contrasting the pre-modern conception of nature, which can function at some level as a positive standard for ethics, with the modern conception, which cannot. Regarding the latter, Strauss likely has in mind Kant, Fichte, and Hegel, and not just the first generation of moderns. See his observation a few lines later regarding a "non-miraculous overcoming [of human particularization through nature and customs] . . . visualized in modern times by means of the conquest of nature and the universal recognition of a purely *rational nomos*." (Emphasis in the original.)

act is mandated, permitted, or prohibited by natural law. Such pronouncements, when insufficiently qualified, carry with them the implication that it is religious tradition or authority that determines something that, if it is really a matter of natural law, is supposed to be evident to natural reason, that is, to ordinary human reason, without reliance on religion. Roman Catholics who argue that natural law is ultimately a matter of belief are comfortable in their faith. They are not troubled by a criticism that moral convictions presuppose belief in God. To them this sounds less like a criticism than a confirmation of a view that they would like to see gain credence, namely, that only believers can give good reasons for why they try to be moral. If, however, Thomas's case for natural law is logically dependent on the claims of revelation, two problems arise.[4]

The first and more obvious problem is that if moral precepts derive their binding force from religious belief then they cannot be reasonably presented as binding on unbelievers. Those who say that we ought to refrain from certain acts simply because they are prohibited by God should not be surprised when those who do not believe in God employ related reasoning to excuse or celebrate engaging in these acts. When someone in an officially secular political community, especially one such as ours in which religious belief is on the wane, appeals to natural law in moral, legal, or political deliberations, he can count on hearing objections to the effect that he is not exhibiting due deference to the hallowed principle of "the separation of church and state." What Thomas presents as a genuinely rational teaching cannot get a hearing. And it very much needs to get a hearing if he is right in his claim that the precepts of natural law derive their evidence exclusively from human reason and ordinary human experience. For then his teaching is just what is needed to buttress morality in our increasingly profane times. If, however, he is wrong in his understanding of whence the precepts of natural law derive their evidence, then unbelievers are justified in refusing to put any stock in them.

A second, less obvious, but much graver problem arises for Thomas's natural law teaching if it turns out to presuppose revelation. For Thomas explicitly says that divine law, by which he means revealed law, presupposes natural law.[5] If there is no natural

4. A claim, argument, or teaching, is logically dependent on another claim or set of claims if it derives any of its evidentiary force from the latter. If the case for natural law were logically dependent on the claims of revelation, then, since assent to revelation is an act of faith and not of knowledge, natural law would not be—as Thomas says it is—knowable by natural reason. When I speak in what follows of a claim or set of claims as dependent on, based on, relying on, deduced from, or presupposing another claim or set of claims, I have in mind this relation of logical dependency. What *motivates* the forming of a theory sometimes gets called, loosely and misleadingly, a "presupposition" of the theory, and sometimes, even more loosely and misleadingly, a "premise" of the theory.

5. "*Sicut enim gratia praesupponit naturam, ita oportet quod lex divina praesupponat legem naturalem.*" *Summa Theologiae, Prima Secundae* (First Part of the Second Part), Question 99, Article 2, reply to argument 1. The questions, articles, etc., from the *Summa Theologiae* will hereafter be abbreviated such that the above citation would read as "*ST* 1–2, q. 99, art. 2, ad 1." *ST* 1 stands for "*Summa Theologiae, Prima Pars.*" 1–2 and 2–2 stand for the "*Prima Secundae*" and the "*Secunda Secundae*," respectively. The abbreviation "ad 1" stands for "Reply to argument 1; the abbreviation "co.," refers to the *corpus*, i.e., the body or central part, of the article. The abbreviation "arg." stands

law distinct from divine law, then the status of divine law itself becomes problematic according to Thomas's own reasoning. Thomas tries to show that, prior to revelation, we possess moral knowledge by nature, that the primary precepts of natural law are the content of this knowledge, and that the giving of divine law through revelation presupposes this knowledge and either reinforces or supplements it. Thomas's claim that divine law presupposes natural law parallels his claim that "faith presupposes natural cognition, as grace presupposes nature, and perfection the perfectible." [6] If he is wrong in his claim that natural law is accessible to natural, human reason, but right in his claim that divine law presupposes natural law, then the concept of divine law itself is impossible to defend, as he understands it. Not all Thomists have a sufficient appreciation of how much Thomas's case for the possibility of divine law, if not for the very possibility of revelation itself, relies on his conception of natural law as something that is antecedently present in the evidence and operation of human reason.

The concern of the present study is with Thomas not as a proponent of Christian ethics, though he is surely that, but as a proponent of rational ethics. There is, however, not the slightest opposition between Christian ethics and rational ethics, least of all in Thomas's teaching. Rational ethics is by no means the whole of Christian ethics. But it is, for Thomas, an indispenaible constituent of Christian ethics.[7]

Strauss and his followers criticize Thomas's rational ethics, the core of which is his case for natural law, from a number of angles. The most conspicuous criticisms are the following:

1. That Thomas departs, on grounds that have nothing to do with reason, from his Aristotelian model by grafting onto a supple teaching regarding natural *right* a

for a so-called "objection" situated by Thomas at the beginning of an article. Most short quotations from the *Summa Theologiae* in Latin are taken from the version contained in the *Biblioteca de Autores Cristianos*; citations from the *Prima Pars* are taken from the fourth edition (Madrid, 1978); citations from the *Prima Secundae* and the *Secunda Secundae* are taken from the third edition (Madrid, 1962). A number of passages from *ST* and other works are quoted according to the on-line *Corpus Thomisticum*. Translations from these and other works are usually, though not always, my own. In some cases my transations depart only slightly from the English translations given in the bibliography; in other cases they depart significantly. I have made use of *The Basic Writings of Thomas Aquinas*, Volumes I and II, edited by Anton Pegis, and *St. Thomas Aquinas—Summa Theologica* Volumes I –V, translated by Fathers of English Dominican Province, typically altering passages from these translations in the interest of greater literalness or consistency with other passages. Though Thomas treats natural law elsewhere, especially in the relatively early *Commentary on the Sentences*, I speak primarily to his treatment in *ST* 1–2.

6. *ST* 1 q. 2 art. 2, ad 1: *sic enim fides praesupponit cognitionem naturalem, sicut gratia naturam, et prefectio perfectible.* See 1–2 q. 94 art. 6, ad 1. Thomas is not saying here that faith presupposes a perfect understanding of the world and man's place in it. But if one did not possess some cognition of what is typical, ordinary, or natural, one would not be able to recognize or believe that something is atypical, extraordinary, or supernatural.

7. For a comprehensive account of Christian ethics from a Catholic perspective, see Pinckaers, *The Sources of Christian Ethics*. Hereafter cited as *Sources*. See also Porter, *Moral Action*.

rigid teaching regarding natural *law*, thereby depriving his ethics of the latitude characteristic of its classical antecedents.

2. That Thomas's natural law teaching depends on the claims of biblical revelation.
3. That Thomas's natural law teaching has little of importance to say to those who are not Roman Catholics, and virtually nothing of importance to say to those who are not believers at all.
4. That Thomas's case for our knowledge of the precepts of natural law presupposes his natural theology, and thereby also presupposes a discredited teleology and defunct cosmology of Aristotelian provenience.
5. That more genuine freedom of thought occurred in Medieval Jewish and Islamic philosophy than in Christian Scholasticism, where the church, by institutionalizing philosophy, effectively clipped its wings.
6. That natural law, as understood by Thomas, derives its obligatory force from belief in, or presumed knowledge of, the existence of a providential God.
7. That natural law need not be appealed to in dealing with concrete ethical problems, since such problems are adequately managed by prudence and practical judgment.
8. That natural law does not allow statesmen sufficient discretion for dealing with political exigencies in extraordinary circumstances.
9. That law as such—natural law included—is essentially a matter of convention rather than reason.
10. That natural law is not really law because it is not really promulgated.
11. That natural law is not really law because infractions of some of its most important precepts are not punishable, except perhaps by God.
12. That there are no moral absolutes, since all precepts of natural law must admit of dispensation in extreme situations.
13. That there is no natural desire for a supernatural end.
14. That even if natural reason could establish that God exists, it cannot establish, except when informed by faith, that God is to be loved.
15. That *syndereis*, the habit of which conscience is the act, is not a natural *habitus* but a Patristic construct only.
16. That even if something like *synderesis* exists, it varies from individual to individual.
17. That the so-called common good is not truly common, due, among other things, to differences in the types of human beings, in particular, to the difference between philosophers and non-philosophers.

18. That there is no genuinely common good because the good is essentially one's own good.
19. That the concept of moral freedom is ultimately incoherent, all so-called choice being naturally necessitated by what appears to be best when the choice is actually made.

Not all of these criticisms are advanced by all Straussians, and not all of them are advanced by Strauss himself. But every one of them has been advanced by a Straussian either in writing or orally in my presence, or both. They all get addressed in the course of the present work. All of them will be shown to be inconclusive. Most of them will be shown to be based on serious misunderstandings. Some of them will be shown to be entirely off the mark.

Before assessing and responding to these criticisms, it is necessary to revisit and make the case anew for the foundational principles of Thomas's natural law teaching. I do this in Part 1, in the course of which I also consider contemporary questions pertaining to the ultimate ground of natural law and how Thomas would respond to them. It should go without saying that there is much more to Thomas's teaching on natural law than what he has to say about its foundational principles and that there is much more to his ethics than what he has to say about natural law. But it is the foundation of his natural law teaching that is the principal target of the Straussian criticisms. How this foundation is to be understood, however, is a matter of some controversy, even among thinkers who are highly sympathetic with Thomas. There are two tendencies in the interpretation of his ethics that unintentionally distort what he has to say about natural law. Some Thomists, as I noted above, are so determined to make sure that the theological context of Thomas's teaching does not get overlooked that they give the impression that natural law is as much a matter of divine revelation as it is of natural reason. Others are so determined to make sure that his perceptive and thorough account of the virtues does not get overlooked that they give the impression that what he has to say about natural law is little more than an appendix to what he has to say about virtue. I shall argue not only that these two tendencies are misguided but that they reinforce the central thrust of the Straussian criticisms, which is that the knowledge of natural law as Thomas presents it, namely, as consisting of properly *obligating* precepts, is not accessible to man as man. Because not only Straussians, but many Thomists as well, fail to appreciate how rational, how *radically rational*, Thomas's natural law teaching is, I have found it necessary in the course of this study to restate, in a range of contexts, the foundational principles of this teaching.

Though I concur in Strauss's claim that it is Thomas to whom we must turn in order to find "the classic form of the natural law teaching," I think that Kant needs to have a larger voice in the defense of natural law than most Thomists have been willing to give him. That Kant speaks of "the moral law" rather than "the natural law" is certainly significant, and I have something to say about this. There are a number of places in their respective teachings on the principles and operation of practical reason, not to mention their divergent accounts of what speculative reason can know, where Thomas and Kant simply cannot be reconciled. But there are also some points, some crucial points, on which the two thinkers are in remarkably close agreement. Accordingly, I have not hesitated to introduce observations and arguments advanced by Kant when I think they support observations and arguments advanced by Thomas. I do realize that pointing out where these two thinkers are in agreement is not likely to win me many friends among Thomists, even among those who may find themselves otherwise sympathetic with my attempt to rebut the charges of Thomas's Straussian critics. But that Kant was not right about everything of importance does not entail that he was wrong about everything of importance. He is not in the Catholic Church to be sure, not on any interpretation of the word "catholic." But that fact actually counts in favor of bringing him into the conversation. For Kant can serve as a secular ally of those who defend natural law as a foundation for rational ethics. And it is secular allies, most of all, that the beleaguered defenders of Thomas's natural law teaching need in the current disputations taking place in the public forum, where the very concept of natural law is commonly derided as little more than a medieval relic. Still, lest my occasional mention of Thomas and Kant in the same breath leave the impression that I do not know how much they differ from each other, I devote an entire section in Part 1 to the differences, as well as the similarities, between the two thinkers.

Whereas Part 1 consists mainly of what could be called a mobilization of forces, Part 2 is a defense in depth. There I consider the Straussian criticisms in detail, and I attempt to show where they go awry. I begin with Strauss's distinction between Jewish and Medieval philosophy, on the one hand, and Christian Scholasticism, on the other, and I argue that he exaggerates the extent to which freedom of thought was stifled in the latter. Strauss's account of Thomas's natural law teaching in *Natural Right and History* and in his essay "On Natural Law" is given especially close attention, and his criticisms in these two works are analyzed sentence by sentence, occasionally word by word. The criticisms advanced by Harry Jaffa, Ernest Fortin, Michael Zuckert, and others working in the Straussian tradition are considered as well. A recurring defect in these criticisms is confusion about what motivates an argument and the actual premises of an argument. Thomas Aquinas and the other great scholastics are not confused about this distinction, which is as elementary as any in the whole sphere of logic.

I assume the offensive in Part 3. There I probe the inconsistencies and other aberrations that are bound up with the denial of natural law, and I expose their implications for Strauss's own teaching. His unavoidable reliance, and that of his followers, on incontestably moral concepts, even in their criticisms of what they call "moralism," is a central target of my counter-critique. Another target, equally central, is the Straussian reluctance to acknowledge that judgment, including practical judgment, is not a way of circumventing or dispensing with universal rules but is, always and of necessity, the application of universal rules to particular cases, even in those extreme cases to which universal rules are alleged to be inapplicable. In Part 3, I also show that, though Strauss and his followers frequently appeal to reason, they do not sufficiently spell out what they think reason is, what its principles are, or how it operates. I argue that Strauss's attempt to vindicate the classical conception of philosophy against the challenge of Heideggerian historicism falls short of its goal, largely because this attempt relies on a concept of nature that is not adequately explicated, much less validated. I also argue that an incontestably teleological principle, namely, the purposiveness of nature for our rational investigation of it, is implicit in Thomas's conception of the eternal law, of which natural law is the participation in the rational creature. This particular teleological principle is knowable, in fact self-evident. It is, moreover, invulnerable to the criticisms of teleology put forth by modern natural science. I argue that anyone who wishes to attempt an adequate response to Heidegger must avail himself of this teleological principle.

In the Conclusion, I return to the question of the relationship between our knowledge of natural law and rational theology. I argue that, precisely because the former is not derived from the latter, it can serve as a premise of an independent argument that powerfully reinforces the claims of the latter.

Straussians might be tempted, understandably, to skip Part 1 and hasten to see what I have to say about Strauss and his followers in Parts 2 and 3. But although the third chapter of Part 1 consists largely, though not exclusively, of an account and appraisal of intra-Thomist disputes that Straussians may not find especially interesting, the first two chapters of Part 1 advance an interpretation of Thomas's natural law teaching that withstands the Straussian criticisms while being true to this teaching in both letter and spirit. It is not possible to evaluate what I have to say in Parts 2 and 3 without reading these two chapters of Part 1.

What is most fundamentally at issue in the Straussian criticisms is not the definition, nor even the context, of Thomistic natural law, each of which is admittedly theological: natural law is indeed defined in the terms of rational theology, and it is indeed related to the revealed theology of the Roman Catholic Church, though the character of this relationship is easily misunderstood. What is most fundamentally at issue in the Straussian criticisms is the nature of our awareness of the precepts of natural law. This awareness, according to Thomas, is both natural and rational. And it is not belief. It is knowledge. It presupposes neither rational theology nor revealed theology. Knowledge of both the first principle of practical reason and the primary precepts of natural law is immediately evident in the very operation of natural reason. This is Thomas's understanding of the matter. The present study attempts to exhibit the clarity, the comprehensiveness, and the depth of his understanding.

Part 1

The Teleology of Natural Reason

The criticisms that Leo Strauss and his followers advance against Thomas Aquinas are focused most pointedly on his natural law teaching. Their criticisms cannot be adequately assessed unless one has a firm grasp of that teaching. However, as is manifest in the varied and incompatible interpretations that one finds in the literature, there is considerable disagreement regarding Thomas's natural law teaching, even among those who are sympathetic with it.[1] Many claim Thomas to be an exemplar of what these days is called "virtue ethics," while a few others stress the "deontological" dimension of his teaching, though rarely using this word, perhaps because of its associations with Kant, who, as far as I know, did not use this word either. There are disagreements as to whether natural law takes precedence over prudence, or vice versa, or whether they are equally primary. There is disagreement about what, in the theological context of Thomas's teaching, is a matter of reason and what is a matter of revelation. And there is disagreement about what nature has to do with natural law. Some hold that Thomas's teaching is inextricable from an Aristotelian conception of natural teleology, even from the essentials of Aristotle's cosmology, while others hold that Thomas's teaching can be harmonized with the claims of modern, anti-Aristotelian natural science. Finally, a relatively small but slowly growing number of scholars who have written on Thomas Aquinas show the influence of Strauss and his followers. Some of these scholars argue that what Thomas says about natural law has to be significantly modified in light of the Straussian criticisms. Others suggest that there is, between the lines of Thomas's express teaching, a secret teaching that Strauss overlooked, or maybe only pretended to overlook, but which in either case closely corresponds to Strauss's own teaching,[2] about which, however, there

1. For an account, by no means exhaustive, of the multiple interpretations of Thomas's teaching, see Fergus Kerr, "Natural Law: Incommensurable Readings."

2. Consider the following observation, revealing on several levels, made by George Anastaplo: "The remarkable astuteness of Thomas Aquinas, in dealing competently with one subject after another across decades, might even make one wonder what he 'really believed.' I myself somehow gathered that Leo Strauss, in his last years, came to suspect that the remarkably intelligent and learned Thomas Aquinas he had come to know must have had more reservations about the religious orthodoxy of his day than he considered it responsible to make explicit." "On the Thomas Aquinas of Leo Strauss." It would have been helpful if Anastaplo had spelled out concretely why he thought one might wonder

is as much disagreement among Straussians as there is disagreement about Thomas's teaching among Thomists.

For these and other reasons it is necessary to revisit and restate the foundational principles of Thomas's natural law teaching. In the course of doing so, I shall have to speak, sometimes at length, to current controversies in the interpretation of this teaching. They have a significant bearing on how the Straussian criticisms are to be assessed. Because the same errors frequently recur in the interpretations and criticisms I shall be considering, the same corrections will have to be repeated, more than once. In Chapter 1 of this part, I examine the context and the presuppositions of Thomas's natural law teaching. My intention is to clear up some common misunderstandings and set the stage for a consideration in Chapter 2 of the actual case that Thomas makes for natural law. Chapter 2 is the core of this part. In Chapter 3, I consider some of the implications of Thomas's case for natural law, and I tie up a few loose ends. The interpretation of Thomas's natural law teaching that emerges in this part is faithful to the relevant texts and to the reasoning that animates them. It has the additional merit of being the interpretation that most effectively blunts the Straussian criticisms.

what Thomas really believed, rather than just suggest that remarkable astuteness, intelligence, and learning are incompatible with assenting to the articles of the Catholic faith. A sustained attempt to show that the careful reader, by paying attention to Thomas Aquinas's manner of writing and to what might appear to be subtle hints here and there, can gain access to a secret and heterodox teaching that expresses Thomas's deepest intention more clearly than what one finds on the surface of his texts is Thomas West's *Thomas Aquinas on Natural Law: A Critique of the "Straussian" Critique* (see 3, 72–88). There is much that is interesting in West's study. I shall, however, have several occasions in what follows to say why I am not persuaded by his suggestions regarding Thomas's intention.

Chapter 1

Preliminary Considerations

SECTION A. THE THEOLOGICAL CONTEXT

THOMAS'S NATURAL LAW TEACHING is clearly situated within the context of theology.[1] The definition of natural law that Thomas gives is "the participation in the rational creature of the eternal law."[2] But, contrary to what many of Thomas's critics and even some of his supporters think, Thomas's natural law teaching does not logically depend on belief in revelation. It does not appeal to the claims of revelation either to establish the existence of natural law or to identify its precepts.

Thomas makes a major distinction between what he calls the preambles to the articles of faith and the articles of faith proper. The latter concern such things as the Trinity, the incarnation, the sacraments of the church, and the like. These articles cannot be demonstrated by natural, human reason. They are held to be supernaturally revealed, and assenting to them is an act of faith. And yet, though it is not possible to demonstrate the articles of faith by reason alone, it is possible to show that they are

1. Thomas Smith, in "The Order of Presentation," gives a good account of how Thomas's pedagogically motivated placement of the "Treatise on Law" in the overall structure of the *Summa Theologiae* has to be distinguished from how he understands us to know natural law. But though Smith says much about the former, he has relatively little to say about the latter. He thinks, in fact, that Thomas himself has relatively little to say about the latter, and that what he does say is "murky at best" (623). This is an overstatement, as the present chapter and the following one will bear out.

2. *ST* 1–2 q. 91 art. 2, co. ". . . participatio legis aeternae in rationali creatura lex naturalis dicitur." See John Finnis, *NLNR*, 398–403, for an explication of this expression. Finnis points out (400) that, in *ST* 1 q. 79 art. 4, co., Thomas refers to the "documents of our faith" in identifying the "supposed 'separate intellect' [mentioned in Aristotle's *De Anima*, Book 3, ch. 5] as God." But Thomas also says there that it "will become evident (*patebit*) below" (in *ST* 1 q. 90 art. 3) that God is the creator of the [rational, or intellectual] soul. In the later article, Thomas argues, on the basis of natural reason, that God is the sole and immediate creator of the rational soul. Regarding Thomas's definition of natural law, it should be noted that it pertains not just to man but to all rational creatures. That is, natural law pertains to angels too. *ST* 1 q. 60 art. 5, *sed contra*. However, Thomas's focus in his treatment of natural law in *ST* 1–2 q. 90, art. 2, and q. 94 is clearly on man. Since that is my focus as well, I shall be speaking in this study only of how natural law pertains to human beings.

not self-contradictory, that they do not contradict each other, and that they are not contradicted by anything that man truly knows.[3] The preambles, on the other hand, are demonstrable, according to Thomas. These preambles consist of the existence of God and everything else that can be known about him by natural, human reason.[4] There is then, for us, a dual truth (*duplex veritas*) regarding divine matters, consisting both of what can be known by reason and of what must be accepted on faith.[5] Thomas does not use the expression "dual truth" to suggest even the slightest opposition between what is naturally knowable and what is exclusively a matter of faith. Truth is a consistent whole. Revelation *adds* to what can be known through natural reason.[6]

The first three books of Thomas's *Summa Contra Gentiles* treat what can be known by reason; the fourth book treats what can be accepted only on faith.[7] The organization of his *Summa Theologiae* is different. Question 1 of the *Prima Pars* is introductory. Questions 2–26 treat what can be known about God through natural reason. Questions 27–43 treat the Trinity, which is a matter of faith. Afterwards, Thomas proceeds to treat what pertains to creatures, including man, and he argues in certain articles from the standpoint of reason alone, in others from the standpoint of faith. In the *Summa Theologiae* the line of division between what Thomas treats as knowable by natural reason and what he treats as an article of faith in the strict sense is not a straight line, as it is in the *Summa Contra Gentiles*, but a winding one. With a bit of effort, however, it can be traced, even when Thomas shifts, as he occasionally does, from one side of the line to the other in the course of addressing a given question.[8] In the

3. *SCG* liber 1, cap. 9; see cap. 7; *ST* 1 q. 1 art. 8, co. The following formulation, by James Schall, S.J., states the matter well. "The test of whether a presumed revelation is 'unbelievable' is not simply that it claims to have arisen from outside human reason, but whether it specifically contradicts reason. If what is said to be revealed is irrational or contradictory, it cannot be believed even according to revelation." *At the Limits*, 191.

4. *ST* 1 q. 2 art. 2 ad 1: ". . . quod Deum esse, et alia huiusmodi quae per rationem naturalem nota possunt esse de Deo, ut dicitur Rom. 1, 19, non sunt articuli fidei sed praeambula ad articulos." See 1 q. 1 art. 6, co., where Thomas contrasts what is knowable about God through creatures, which is how the philosophers knew about him, with what is known about God by God himself and communicated to others by revelation. Both belong to "sacred doctrine," broadly speaking. Compare 1 q. 1 art. 7, co., where Thomas calls the articles of faith (as distinct from its demonstrable preambles) "principles of this science," i.e., of sacred doctrine, with 2–2 q. 1 art. 4 on the distinction between faith, knowledge, and opinion.

5. *SCG* 1 cap. 4.1; cap. 3.2; cap. 9.1. Truth is dual only for us, not for God. See cap. 9.4. See *Quaestiones Disputatae de Veritate* (hereafter cited as *De Veritate*) q. 14, art. 9, co.: "impossibile est quod de eodem sit fides et ratio;" cf. *sed contra* 2. See *Super 2 Tim.*, cap. 1, l. 4; *ST* 2–2 q. 1 art. 5, ad 4.

6. *ST* 1–2 q. 19 art. 4, ad 3.

7. *SCG* 4 cap. 1 n. 13.

8. Although Thomas is arguing almost invariably from natural reason in *ST* 1 qq. 2–27, there are a small number of *responsiones* in these questions where, because of the subject matter, he brings revelation into the picture, e.g., in q. 12, art. 1, art. 13, and in certain passages in qq. 23 and 24. Nonetheless, the arguments that Thomas makes for his main points—namely, the existence, simplicity, unity, eternity, goodness, omnipotence, omniscience, freedom, providence, liberality, and justice of God—can be shown not to presuppose in any logical sense his occasional references to the claims of

sed contra of an article that deals with something that can be known by natural reason, Thomas will often cite sacred Scripture or one of the church fathers. And in the replies to the counter-arguments that he places at the beginning of his articles he will answer citations from Scripture and sacred tradition with his own citations from Scripture and sacred tradition. But in the *Respondeo* of articles dealing with matters accessible to natural reason, Thomas argues in his own name. He cites Scripture in a *Respondeo* only to supplement a sound argument, which he also gives, or to show that this argument is not at odds with what the church teaches. Thomas's conception of a dual truth regarding divine matters, consisting of what we can actually demonstrate and what we can take only on faith, is the elemental distinction that shapes his whole conception of theology. The distinction between what is accessible to natural reason and the claims of revelation is a distinction that he is as sensitive to as any thinker in the Western intellectual tradition. I shall call what Thomas treats as accessible to natural reason "rational theology," and what he treats as a matter of faith "revealed theology."[9] It will become clear in what follows that Thomas does not derive his precepts of natural law either from his rational theology or from his revealed theology. But because Thomas's natural law teaching occurs in the context of his rational theology, and in fact strengthens it, it is worth looking briefly at the foundation of this theology. Most of his critics are unaware of it, while the few who are aware of it underestimate it.

In the *Summa Theologiae* we are presented with five distinct ways to prove that God exists.[10] These five ways make no mention of the claims of revelation, nor do they covertly rely on them. Of equal importance, only the First Way relies on an Aristotelian theory of motion, which has been repudiated by modern natural science; and only the Fifth Way relies on a teleological conception of the operation of subhuman entities, which has also been repudiated by modern natural science. The Second, Third, and Fourth Ways rely on neither of these things.

The Second Way to prove the existence (or being—*esse*) of God, Thomas says, is from the concept of an efficient cause (*ex ratione causae efficientis*). By an efficient cause Thomas does not mean a moving cause only, for then there would be no

revelation in this section of the *ST*. Hence these references do not in any way compromise the purely rational character of the arguments he makes for his main points.

9. What I call "rational theology" is traditionally called "natural theology." The latter expression, properly understood, means what we can know about God solely through natural reason and ordinary human experience. It is, however, sometimes taken as meaning what we can know about God on the basis of an Aristotelian conception of nature and especially on the basis of an Aristotelian theory of motion. Since, as will be shown above, Thomas has a powerful argument for the existence of God that does not presuppose either of these things, I prefer the less ambiguous expression "rational theology." By "revealed theology," on the other hand, I mean a theology that assumes, without any attempt at a demonstration, that the basic claims of revelation are true and then attempts to show their internal consistency and what follows logically from them. Revealed theology, especially as we find it in Thomas Aquinas, appeals to natural reason and ordinary human experience, as does rational theology. But, unlike rational theology, revealed theology does not appeal only to natural reason and ordinary human experience.

10. *ST* 1 q. 2 art. 3, co.

distinction between the First Way and the Second Way. An efficient cause produces an effect, but not every effect is a motion. In the Second Way, Thomas argues for a first efficient cause that is not itself the effect of another efficient cause. But he does not give us any examples of efficient causality. However, in his early treatise, *De Ente et Essentia*, Thomas argues for a first efficient cause, not of motion, but of being (*esse*).[11] His argument, if sound, enables him to prove not only that God exists, but that he is the ultimate cause of everything else that exists, including both the matter (or material) of things and their form. The argument, though concentrated in a few paragraphs of *De Ente et Essentia*, is prepared at some length. The refined metaphysical distinctions that Thomas makes in this work would have been out of place at the beginning of the *Summa Theologiae*, where they would have had to be introduced. We should keep in mind that the *Summa Theologiae* is announced by Thomas in the *Prologus* as intended for—hence composed in such a way as is conducive to—the education of beginners (*ad eruditionem ad incipientium*).

Some Thomists discount the proof in *De Ente et Essentia* because Thomas says in the *Summa Theologiae* that there are five ways to prove the existence of God. But he does not say that there are only five ways. And even if Thomas did say that, what he presents in the *Summa Theologiae* are, to repeat, only *ways* to prove the existence of God. One of these is the way to prove the existence of a first efficient cause, and it is precisely the proof of such a cause that Thomas advances in *De Ente et Essentia*, though in a form that is both different from and more rigorous than that of the Second Way as presented, or rather sketched, in the *Summa Theologiae*. Moreover, there is an ambiguity in wording of the Second Way that can impede an adequate understanding of what Thomas is saying there.

> Neither is there found, nor is it possible, that something be the efficient cause of itself, because it would thus be prior to itself, which is impossible. But it is impossible to proceed to infinity in efficient causes . . . Therefore it is necessary to posit a first efficient cause; which all men call God."[12]

11. See *DEE*, especially pages 34–42. [English trans., 55–65. When I provide my own translation of a given passage, I often refer to a published English translation so that the reader can locate the passage and the context in which it occurs.] Thomas explicitly speaks of the cause of *esse* as an efficient cause on page 35 [56]. For a thoughtful analysis of the argument in *DEE*, and for a comparison of that argument with the argument of the Second Way in the *ST*, see John Wippel, *The Metaphysical Thought of Thomas Aquinas*, 405–10; 459–62.

12. "[N]ec tamen invenitur, nec est possibile, quod aliquid sit causa efficiens sui ipsius; quia sic esset prius seipso, quod est impossibile. Non autem est possibile quod in causis efficientibus procedatur in infinitum . . . Ergo est necesse ponere aliquam causam efficientem primam: quam omnes deum nominant." *ST* 1 q. 2 art. 3, co. In addition to the ambiguity noted above, there is a further problem with the Second Way. An order or series of efficient causes does culminate, necessarily, in a first efficient cause when such a series is construed, as Thomas construes it, as a series of essentially ordered causes. In such a series, all the causes are operative at once. They do not extend indefinitely backwards in time as happens in a series of accidentally ordered causes. (The terminology of "essentially ordered causes" and "accidentally ordered causes" is Duns Scotus's. The distinction itself, however, is Thomas's as much as it is Scotus's.) But the Second Way as presented in the *ST* does not, by itself, preclude the

At first glance it could appear that by "prior" Thomas means prior *in time*. But if that were the case, the Second Way would lead to the conclusion that there must be a first efficient cause bestowing existence, or being, way back at the beginning of time, when the world, motion, and time were created all at once. On this reading, the Second Way would purport to establish that the world is not eternal. But Thomas expressly teaches that the non-eternity of the world is a matter of faith and cannot be demonstrated.[13] So the word "prior" in the Second Way can only mean prior in a causal order in which the cause is *simultaneous* with the effect.[14]

The instance of an efficient cause that Thomas focuses on in *De Ente et Essentia*, where the cause *is* simultaneous with the effect, is the cause of an entity's being (*esse*). Why it is that the entities that we are familiar with need a cause, not only of their motion, and not only of their coming into being at some point in the past either, but also of their *continuing* to be in the present, is not made clear in the Second Way as it is presented in the *ST* 1 q. 2, art. 3, but only afterwards, beginning in *ST* 1 q. 3, art. 4, where the reasoning that motors the proof in *De Ente et Essentia* is succinctly summarized.

Thomas is struck by the fact that, in the case of worldly entities, knowing *what* something is is not the same as knowing *that* it is. That such an entity actually exists cannot be attributed to what it is. Thomas's argument for a first efficient cause in *De Ente et Essentia* turns on this distinction. The being (*esse*) of a worldly entity (*ens*) is not a part of, much less the whole of, its essence or what-ness (*quidditas*). It is for this reason that the being or existence of a worldly entity never enters into its definition. This is particularly clear in the case of a member of a species that is on the verge of extinction, say, a northern white rhinoceros.[15] We can know, partially if not entirely, what a northern white rhinoceros is even if, unbeknownst to us, it has recently ceased to exist. This consideration alone establishes a distinction between its *esse* and its *essentia*. Worldly entities are, in Thomas's language, always composed of *esse* and *essentia*.[16] The composition of *esse* and *essentia* in an intra-worldly entity cannot be due to that entity itself but is due to something else. No entity can be responsible for its

possibility that the first efficient cause at the "top" of every particular series of essentially ordered causes is nonetheless a *caused* cause within a series of accidentally ordered causes extending indefinitely backwards in time. Accordingly, the Second Way as presented in the *ST* cannot, without further elaboration than Thomas gives there, count as a demonstration of the existence of an efficient cause that itself has no cause of *any* kind, i.e., as a demonstration of the existence of God. The criticisms of the Second Way that I have made here have no bearing at all on the argument in *DEE*. (I have spoken at greater length to this matter in an unpublished lecture, "Thomas Aquinas's Second Way to Prove the Existence of God," a copy of which will be provided on request.)

13. *ST* 1 q. 46 art. 2, co.

14. *ST* 1 q. 46 art. 2, ad 1.

15. Thomas, who presumably did not know about species on the verge of extinction, gives as his examples a man and a phoenix. (*DEE* 34 [English translation: 55]).

16. The composition of *esse* and *essentia* is more elemental than the composition of matter and form, as it holds both for immaterial creatures, i.e., angels (assuming they exist), and for creatures that are also composed of matter and form. See *ST* 1 q. 50 art, 2, ad 3.

own composition. Its coming into being may well take place through the operation of another worldly entity or multiple worldly entities, as in the case of natural generation and production through art. But its continuing in being, and also the continuing in being of whatever worldly entities played a role in generating or producing it, is due to something of a different order.

According to Thomas, an entity composed of *esse* and *essentia* owes its being, *at every moment of its being*, to an efficient cause, a cause of being that is distinct from that entity.[17] If this efficient cause is not composed of *esse* and *essentia*, then it is an absolutely first, or uncaused, efficient cause. If, however, this efficient cause is also composed of *esse* and *essentia*, then either we are left with an infinite regress of ordered efficient causes, all exerting their efficient causality simultaneously—an unsustainable view of things according to both the medieval philosophers and the medieval theologians—or we are led inexorably to an absolutely first efficient cause.

As Thomas sees it, an absolutely first efficient cause is an entity whose being (*esse*) does not depend upon the being of another entity. It is not composed of *esse* and *essentia*, but is simple. Its *essentia* is *esse tantum*, that is, its essence is simply to-be.[18] Moreover, because Thomas conceives being as an act,[19] indeed as the most fundamental act that an actual entity (as distinct from a merely potential entity) engages in, the essence of an absolutely first and uncaused efficient cause is pure act (*actus purus*).[20] Because its very essence is to *be*, it exists with unqualified necessity and for all eternity.[21] There can, moreover, be only one absolutely first efficient cause, so conceived, because the identity of its *essentia* with *esse tantum* rules out any way in which two or more such causes could differ from each other. The first, sole, and necessarily existing efficient cause is, of course, God.

17. Though Thomas argues that the temporal eternity of the world can be neither conclusively proven nor conclusively disproven by natural reason, he also argues that, even if the world were eternal, it would still be a creature in the technical sense of owing *everything*, including its very materiality, *throughout* its eternal existence, to the free choice of God. For a lucid analysis of the opusculum, *De Aeternitate Mundi*, and other texts by Thomas that deal with the question of the eternity of the world, see John Wippel, *Metaphysical Themes in Thomas Aquinas*, 191–214.

18. That God's essence, uniquely, is *esse tantum*, and hence that he alone exists of necessity, is *declared* in the Bible (Exod 3:14; see John 8:58). But it is *argued for* by Thomas, without reliance on this declaration as a premise of any kind.

19. *Scriptum super Sententiis* (hereafter cited as *Super Sent.*) liber 1, distinctio 8, quest. 5, art. 3; *De Veritate* q. 1 art. 1 co; *ad sed contra*. 3; *Quaestiones Disputatae De Potentia* (hereafter cited as *De Potentia*) q. 7 art. 2 ad 1.

20. *Super Sent.*, lib. 1 d. 2 q. 1 art. 1 ad 2–3. See *Quaestiones de quolibet* 3 q. 2 art. 1, co.; *SCG* lib. 1 cap. 44 n. 8; lib. 2 cap. 52 n. 4.

21. It should be kept in mind that, whereas the proposition, "God's essence is to be," is a *premise* in some versions of the so-called "ontological argument" for the existence of God, it is the *conclusion* of Thomas's argument for the existence of God. For Thomas's criticism of the "ontological argument," see *Super Sent.*, 1 d. 3 q. 1 art. 2; *SCG* 1 cap. 1; *ST* 1 q. 2 art. 1.

Thomas argues that God is *freely* responsible for the existence of worldly entities.[22] For worldly entities, by virtue of the distinction between their *esse* and their *essentia*, do not exist with unqualified necessity.[23] God is therefore the free creator of the world *ex nihilo*. Even if the world has always existed, it nonetheless owes its existence, *at every moment of its existence*, ultimately to the will of God alone. The world is then a creature in the precise sense of the word.[24]

The demonstration of an absolutely first efficient cause is the solid basis for Thomas's rational theology, which includes arguments that go far, very far indeed, beyond anything that Aristotle says, or is able to say, about God.[25] In addition to establishing that God is the sole first cause of the existence of worldly things (including even the matter of material things), Thomas argues, again by appeal solely to natural reason and ordinary experience, that God is perfect, good, omniscient, free, loving, just, merciful, providential, and omnipotent.[26]

22. *SCG* 2 cap. 15–16; cap. 23; *ST* 1 q. 3 art. 2, co.; art. 4, co.; q. 15 art. 4, ad 1; q. 19 art. 1–3; art. 8, art. 10; q.22 art. 2, ad 4; compare q. 44 art. 1–2 with q. 46 art. 1–2; q. 104 art. 1. The fundamental disagreement between the medieval philosophers, on the one hand, and the scholastic theologians, on the other, does not concern whether God, an absolutely first uncaused cause, exists. It concerns, instead, whether God is freely responsible for the world's existence. Does the existence of the world follow only contingently from God's existence, as the scholastic theologians argue. Or does the world follow necessarily from God's existence, as the medieval philosophers argue. (The scholastic theologians argue that God would have been able to create freely even if he had never created. Put somewhat differently, God could have refrained from creating; but he could not have refrained from choosing either to create or not to create. He had to choose one or the other.) Leo Strauss recognized more clearly than anyone else in the last century that the crucial disagreement between philosophy and theology does not turn on the alternatives, atheism or theism, but on radically different assessments of contingency, or freedom, as an "ontological" principle. See *PR* 117, beginning of the second paragraph. Few of Strauss's followers have given adequate attention to the distinction that Strauss makes in this most important passage.

23. Though Thomas understands God to be the only being who exists with unqualified necessity, he speaks of certain created beings as necessary too, although in a qualified sense. These are entities, such as angels (if they exist) and the intellectual soul of man, that though created cannot undergo *natural* generation or corruption. They owe their existence immediately to the divine will, by which alone they can also be destroyed, i.e., annihilated. See Patterson Brown, "St. Thomas's Doctrine of Necessary Being," in Kenny, ed. *Aquinas*, 157–174. In what follows, I shall speak of all creatures without distinction as contingent inasmuch as their existence depends on the free choice of God. When I speak of God alone as necessary, I mean necessary without qualification.

24. Thomas's First Way to prove the existence of God purports to establish that there is a first unmoved cause of *motion*, not, as the argument in *DEE* purports to establish, that there is a first uncaused cause of *being*.

25. *ST* 1 q. 3–26. Consider especially q. 3 art. 3; art. 4; and q. 19 art. 3; art. 10.

26. *ST* 1 q. 4; q. 5; q. 6; q, 14; q. 19, art. 1; art. 3, co.; ad 5; art. 8; art.10; q. 20; q.21; q. 22; q.25. In q. 21 art. 1, co. Thomas cites Paul only by way of showing that commutative justice cannot be attributed to God. The quotation from Paul is actually a compressed argument, and one that Thomas could have easily made in his own name on the basis of what he has already demonstrated about God. Thomas does argue in his own name that distributive justice can, and must be attributed to God. This argument is a component of the rational theology that he has been developing over the preceding nineteen questions, beginning with q. 2 art. 1. Regarding divine providence and divine omnipotence, see the note appended to this section,

Like all proofs, Thomas's proof for the existence of God as the first efficient cause of all worldly entities, and thereby the first efficient cause of the world itself—a proof which I have only adumbrated here—depends on premises. The premises are (1) that for anything that exists there must be a sufficient reason accounting for why it exists, and this reason is either intrinsic to its essence or distinct from to it; [27] (2) that no worldly thing, understood as composed of *esse* and *essentia*, is the ground of, the cause of, or the reason for its own being at any and every instant of its being;[28] and (3) that there cannot be an actually infinite chain of ordered efficient causes, all operative and efficacious *at an instant*. From these premises, Thomas argues to the conclusion that there must be something, a first efficient cause, whose own reason for being is intrinsic to it. Such a being, God, is necessary without qualification. He cannot *not* be.

One can, to be sure, dispute Thomas's argument for a first efficient cause, though in doing so one is under an obligation to exhibit the formal invalidity of his demonstrations or to propose alternative and more evident premises, as, for example, Spinoza and Heidegger try to do, in diametrically opposed ways. Whereas Thomas argues that God is *the* necessary being and that the existence of the world is contingent upon his will, Spinoza argues that the world is *itself* the necessary being and that there is no God distinct from the world. God and nature are one and the same. Heidegger, on the other hand, argues that the world is *radically* contingent; it has no ground, cause, or reason at all for its existence; and that there is no necessary being, period. A comprehensive defense of Thomas's rational theology requires coming to terms with the counter-claims of these two thinkers.[29] It also requires coming to terms with the thought of Avicenna, with whose philosophical theology Thomas agrees on some crucial points and disagrees on others equally crucial. But, however one assesses the metaphysical claims of these thinkers, and of other thinkers who have taken issue or would take issue with Thomas's rational theology, any unbiased consideration of the demonstration that Thomas presents in *De Ente et Essentia* will show that it is a properly metaphysical demonstration, a demonstration that is independent of both revelation and an Aristotelian (or any other) theory of motion. Confusion on this

27. Saying that for anything that exists there must be a reason why it exists does not imply that this reason must in all cases be located outside or distinct from what exists. Quite the opposite: it ultimately implies that something exists by reason of its very nature and is, moreover, a self-determining cause of other things, something that is both necessary in its being and free in its causation (see *ST* 1 q. 19 art. 3, ad 5). The principle that there must be a reason for why something exists is not self-evident, as are the properly logical principles such as non-contradiction. That there is *no* reason why things exist is a proposition that can be entertained, by a Heideggerian for example. This proposition, however, is at odds with the teleology of human reason, which of its very nature aims at finding, in Thomistic language, a *causa prima* (*SCG* 1 cap. 15.5; *ST* 1, q. 2, art. 3 co), or, in Kantian language, an unconditioned ground of what is conditioned (*KRV* B xx; 364–365).

28. See *ST* 1 q. 46 art. 1, co.; q. 75 art. 6, ad 2; q. 104 art. 1, co.

29. I have spoken to Spinoza's metaphysical claims in a lecture entitled, "Spinoza's Response to Christian Scholasticism," presented at Tulane University on March 20, 2014. I speak to Heidegger's conception of being (*Sein*) in Part 3, Ch. 12, below.

point is the chief obstacle that prevents non-believers from giving Thomas's teaching on matters that he thinks are accessible to natural reason the close consideration it merits. Thomas rational theology can be contested, but it cannot in good conscience be dismissed with the unsupportable allegation that it is just revealed theology in masquerade.[30] Any disputation with Thomas regarding his argument for the existence of God as first efficient cause and what follows from that argument has to be conducted on the plane of natural reason, since this is where he situates his demonstrations.

Note: Divine Providence and Divine Omnipotence

Though the claims that God is provident and that he is omnipotent are not part of Thomas's case for our actual knowledge of natural law, that is, of its precepts and their obligatory character, these claims do play a role in his broader teaching on natural law. Some of Thomas's critics wonder not only whether these claims can be validated by natural reason, but even whether Thomas himself thought they could be validated by natural reason. The former question can be decided only by a thorough examination of the arguments that he advances for these claims. I speak in this note only to the latter question.

In the first three articles of the *Summa Theologiae* 1, q. 22, Thomas argues progressively for God's *providence*, for his providence over *everything*, and for his *immediate* providence over everything. These arguments appeal to natural reason alone, though they need to be isolated from appeals to authority that Thomas makes in the interest of showing that what he says accords with Catholic tradition.

Thomas explicitly argues, solely on the basis of natural reason for divine omnipotence, in the following texts: *Scriptum super Sententiis*, liber 1, dist. 42, q. 1, art. 1; art. 2; *Summa Contra Gentiles*, liber 2, cap. 22; *Compendium Theologiae*, cap. 19; *De Potentia*, q. 1, art. 2; art. 3; *Summa Theologiae* 1, art. 25. These arguments, the context in which they occur, and the reasoning that prepares them, are nicely summarized and helpfully commented on by John Wippel in his article, "Thomas Aquinas on Demonstrating God's Omnipotence."[31] Fr. Wippel also considers two passages, one from *De Veritate* and another from the *Summa Theologiae*, where Thomas seems to say—surprisingly, at first glance—that divine omnipotence and divine providence *cannot* be demonstrated. [32] As Fr. Wippel points out, these two passages speak of divine omnipotence and divine providence in the context of what is included in the

30. As Strauss dismisses it in *NRH* 164. See Part 2, Ch. 4, Section b, below.

31. *Metaphysical Themes in Thomas Aquinas* II, 194–217.

32. *De Veritate* q. 14 art. 9, ad 8; *ST* 2–2 q.1 art. 8, ad 1. In the former passage, consider the distinction between "quod Deum esse unum prout est demonstratum" and "unitas divinae essentiae talis qualis ponitur a fidelibus." In the latter passage, note the word "de" in "multa per fidem tenemus de Deo" and the word "circa" in "circa providentiam eius et omnipotentiam." Catholics hold by faith many things *about* God, many things *about* his providence and omnipotence, that natural reason cannot know. Natural reason's knowing *that* God is providential and omnipotent is perfectly compatible with natural reason's not knowing all that Catholics believe *pertaining* to God's providence and omnipotence.

Catholic faith, that is, in the context of revealed theology rather than of rational theology. Fr. Wippel's attempt to reconcile the apparently conflicting passages is, I think, persuasive. Note that when Thomas argues for divine omnipotence and providence from the perspective of natural reason, he does so first of all in a general way: God can do whatever is non-contradictory (he cannot make the past not to have occurred) and whatever does not conflict with his essence (he cannot sin). Thomas also argues more specifically for divine omnipotence: God is able to create a world *ex nihilo* (and to annihilate it in an instant, too), and he provides his creatures, including man, with what is indispensable to their reaching the ends to which they are naturally inclined. Still, natural reason cannot gauge the full range of what falls under God's omnipotence and providence. It suffices to think of the Incarnation and all that it effects. The Incarnation is a manifestation of God's omnipotence and providence, of which natural reason, without the assistance of revelation, has not an inkling.

Thomas is walking a fine line here. For he holds that the same proposition cannot be properly a matter of knowledge and of faith.[33] And yet he also holds that the articles of faith, as they are expressed in the Nicene Creed, have been suitably enumerated.[34] The Nicene Creed begins *Credo in unum Deum, Patrem omnipotentem* . . . ("I believe in one God, the Father almighty . . .") Thomas's position, as I understand it, is that the way faith regards "omnipotentem" differs from the way natural reason regards "omnipotentem." For example, faith regards God, not just as almighty, but as the *Father* almighty. It is with such a qualification that God's omnipotence can be said both, in one sense, to fall within what natural reason can know, and, in another sense, to lie beyond what natural reason can know.

When I speak in this study of Thomas's demonstrations of God's omnipotence and providence, I am speaking of the arguments that he advances in his rational theology, apart from any appeal to revelation. I agree with Fr. Wippel that Thomas regarded these arguments as properly demonstrative. Those who think that Thomas did not regard them as properly demonstrative need to show where, in Thomas's eyes, they fail to prove what they set out to prove.

SECTION B. NATURAL REASON

According to Thomas Aquinas, natural law is a rule of reason, of natural, human, reason.[35] It is, in fact, something actually constituted by reason.[36] Thomas does not think that one can account for natural reason, either speculative or practical, without invoking a divine, intelligent, and providential being as its cause. So God is ultimately the cause of natural law. But he is the cause of natural law because he is the cause of

33. *De Veritate* q. 14 art. 9, co. *ST* 2–2 q. 1 art. 5.

34. *ST* 2–2 q. 1 art. 8, co.

35. *ST* 1–2 q. 90 art. 1, co., ad 2. q. 91 art. 2.

36. *ST* 1–2 q. 94 art. 1, co.: "lex naturalis est aliquid per rationem constitutum."

natural reason itself. Thomas's arguments in support of his claim that God is the cause of natural reason are included in his rational theology, not in his revealed theology.[37] What he says there is no more, and no less, essential to his teaching on the nature and proper exercise of practical reason than it is to his teaching on the nature and proper exercise of speculative reason.[38] The question of where our reason comes from, then, lies outside Thomas's natural law teaching proper. But if, as he argues, natural law is rooted in natural reason itself, then its precepts depend no more, and no less, on the existence of God for their authority than do the principles of speculative reason, such as the principle of non-contradiction.

According to Thomas, man could not be rational, that is, he could not be what he is, without knowing natural law, just as he could not be rational without knowing the principle of non-contradiction, granted that he only rarely formulates either in explicit terms. If the primary precepts of natural law and the principles of speculative reason are self-evident (*per se nota*) to human reason, as Thomas holds them to be, it follows that God could keep man from knowing them only by annihilating or mutilating his reason, that is to say, only by dumbing down human nature to something sub-rational.

Thomas draws an analogy, to which he repeatedly adverts, between speculative reason and practical reason. The fundamental and most universal precepts of natural law are to practical reason what the first principles of demonstration are to speculative reason.[39] Thomas follows Aristotle in holding that speculative reason operates on a foundation of indemonstrable principles, the truth of which is self-evident to all;[40] and he attempts to show that the same is true of practical reason.[41] Reason by its very nature is oriented toward determining both what is and what ought to be (or what should be), and it effects this determination through the application of self-evident

37. Thomas argues that the rational soul is directly created by God in *ST* 1 q. 90 art. 2 and 3. See q. 75 art. 2.

38. In *ST* 1–2 q. 97 art. 3, co. (cf. ad 1), Thomas says that both divine law and natural law proceed from the reasonable will of God (*a rationabili Dei voluntate*). They proceed, however, in different ways, the former immediately from God's reason and will as divine positive law, the latter ultimately from God's reason and will, but through the natural reason of the rational creature. Natural reason, including the invariable rules of its proper operation with respect to both what *is* and what *ought to be*, is created by the will of God (and his will is reasonable, not capricious): "tota communitas universi gubernator ratione divina." *ST* q. 91 art. 1, co. If divine law and natural law did not proceed in these two quite different ways from the reasonable will of God, there would not be any meaningful distinction between them, contrary to what Thomas explicitly teaches.

39. *ST* 1–2 q. 90 art. 1, ad 2; q. 91 art. 3, co.; q. 94, art. 1, co.; art. 2, co.

40. Aristotle, *Prior Analytics* 64b35–65a25; *Posterior Analytics* 71b20–34; 72b6–19; 99b15–100a18; *Nicomachean Ethics* 1139b26–35; 1140b35–1141a8; *Metaphysics* 1005b13–15; 1006a15; 1008b13; 1011b16. See Thomas Aquinas, *Super Sent.* 1, d. 24, q. 2 art. 3; dist. 39, q. 3, art. 1; *In Duodecim Libros Metaphysicorum Aristotelis Expositio*, Lib. 2 Lect. 1.277; see Lect. 5.333. See *Expositio libri Posteriorum Analyticorum* Lib. 1 (Prologue), for Thomas's understanding of the various themes of Aristotle's *Organon*. The claim that people disagree sharply about moral principles is addressed in Part 2, Ch. 9, Section b, below.

41. *ST* 1–2 q. 58 art. 4, co.; q. 91 art. 2, ad 2; q. 94 art. 2, co. See q. 91 art. 3, ad 2.

principles to the particular content of experience. As we know the first principles of speculative reason by means of the "understanding of principles" (*intellectus principiorum*) so, Thomas holds, we know the primary precepts of natural law by means of an analogous understanding.[42] The name for this understanding is *synderesis*. Thomas argues that it is a natural understanding.[43]

Knowledge of what is self-evident is not the result of demonstration but the starting point of demonstration, in the practical sphere no less than in the speculative.[44] As Thomas sees it, neither the principles known by the speculative understanding nor the precepts known by *synderesis* are "innate" to the human mind, as though they were known apart from experience of any sort. On the other hand, this knowledge is not colored by even a tincture of the uncertainty that necessarily holds for the inductively inferred generalizations from the particular content of experience that constitute the empirical sciences, such as physics. Whether oriented toward knowledge solely or

42. Thomas sometimes includes the habitual knowledge of the precepts of natural law within the "understanding of principles" broadly considered, i.e., as the self-evident principles of both speculative and practical reason, e.g., *ST* 1–2 q. 59 art. 5 co; q. 62, co.; also *Super Eph.*, cap. 4 l. 6: "In homine enim est ratio iudicans de particularibus agendis; item, intellectus universalium principiorum, qui est synderesis." But sometimes he reserves the expression *intellectus principiorum* for the understanding of the principles of speculative reason, which he distinguishes from the principles of practical reason. This is how Thomas speaks in *ST* 1 q. 79 art. 12, which is devoted to clarifying what *synderesis* is. In *ST* 1–2 q. 57 art. 2, ad 1, he speaks of *intellectus* as a habit of the *speculative* intellect. In what follows, I shall for clarity's sake reserve the expression "understanding of principles" for the habitual knowledge of the principles of *speculative* reason proper, in order to distinguish it from *synderesis*, the habitual knowledge of the principles of *practical* reason. But it should be remembered that both, according to Thomas, are knowledge, or understanding, of principles, even of self-evident principles, and that, moreover, the speculative and practical intellects are not distinct powers of the soul but a single power directed in the former case to the consideration of truth, in the latter case to operation, or doing.

43. *ST* 1 q. 79 art. 12; 1–2 q. 94 art. 1, ad 2. Considering these passages in conjunction with 1–2 q. 58 art. 4, co., we can infer that *synderesis* is reason itself, though as knowing the self-evident principles of its practical, as distinct from its speculative, operation.

44. In his short but influential study, *Aquinas and Natural Law*, D. J. O'Connor expresses reservations about Thomas's (and Aristotle's) understanding "that some propositions must be known by intuition (*intellectus, intuitus*)" (66). O'Connor is more impressed by the procedure of modern logicians. "We must have *some* set of axioms as our starting point . . . But as long as these axioms and rules satisfy certain conditions, we may use now one set and now another. What propositions we take as primitive will be relative to the system of logic or geometry in which we are operating" (66; emphasis in the original). Thomas would undoubtedly find this procedure interesting. He would insist, however, that unless some axioms are known as self-evident we do not have demonstration but syllogistic merely, a rule governed procedure, to be sure, but not demonstrative knowledge in the strict sense of the word. On this matter he is in agreement with Plato and Aristotle (see *Republic* 533b1-c7; *Posterior Analytics* 71b22–24). O'Connor states Thomas's position clearly but, aside from deferring to the authority of modern logicians, he does not show what is wrong with it. "[W]e cannot know that the conclusion is true unless we are assured that our premises are so. There are complexities here into which we need not go . . ." (67). After this statement, O'Connor proceeds to speak about the different ways in which various kinds of propositions are said to be true. But he does not answer the question of how we are able to *know* that indemonstrable premises or axioms are true. And so he does not answer the question of how we are able to *know* that the conclusions deduced from them, however so rigorously, are themselves true. Disagreeing with great philosophers from Aristotle to Husserl, O'Connor thinks that this question pertains not to logic but to psychology. He does not spell out why he thinks that this is so.

toward choice and action as well, reason has direct insight into the necessary truths that govern its own operation.[45]

Thomas sometimes uses the terms reason (*ratio*) and intellect (or understanding—*intellectus*) interchangeably. But sometimes he distinguishes between them, not as two different powers, but as one power of the soul related to intelligible truth in two different ways.

> To understand (*intelligere*) is to apprehend intelligible truth simply. However, to reason is to advance from one thing understood to another . . . In this way, reasoning is compared to understanding as moving to resting, or as acquiring to possessing; one of which [i.e., understanding] pertains to the perfect while the other [i.e., reasoning] to the imperfect . . . Now it is manifest that resting and moving are not referred to different powers but to one and the same power . . .[46]

Since man, unlike God, does not possess perfect, or immediate and fully intuitive, knowledge of the whole of truth, his thinking proceeds discursively from one thing to another. Reason, as Thomas puts it, advances from what is simply understood by the intellect, namely, the first indemonstrable principles, to particulars; and it returns by analysis to first principles, in light of which it examines what it has found. Reason, as distinct from intellect, proceeds or advances. It *moves*. It moves both from something as its principle and toward something as its end. Indeed, Thomas says, it is by virtue of this manifest movement of advancing from one thing to another that man is called "rational"[47] And though man does not have immediate knowledge of all the truth that he is able to know, he does have immediate knowledge of some truths, namely, the first principles of the understanding, such as the principle of non-contradiction, on the one hand, and, as shall see, the first principle of practical reason and the primary precepts of natural law, on the other.

The movement of man's reason then, both in its speculative and in its practical application, is guided by the simple apprehension of principles; and it is guided toward the true and the good respectively. But the true and the good (or, if one prefers,

45. Because these truths are constitutive both of what is and of what ought to be, they are not themselves powers or habits of the human mind, though they are known by the human mind. It is as an object of knowledge, rather than as the act of knowing, that law is an extrinsic principle of human acts. (ST 1–2 q. 90 introd.; see 1–2 q. 49 introd.) It is through law in general that, as Thomas says, God instructs us regarding our acts. In the case of natural law (as distinct from revealed law) God instructs us *through our own reason*, which, though natural, nonetheless has its origin in God, who is the author of nature and whose reason is the original of which ours is only a faint image and likeness, but an image and likeness nevertheless.

46. *ST* 1 q. 79 art. 8, co.: "Intelligere enim est simpliciter veritatem intelligibilem apprehendere. Ratiocinari autem est procedere de uno intellecto ad aliud . . . Patet ergo quod ratiocinari comparatur ad intelligere sicut moveri et quiescere; quorum unum est perfecti, alius autem imperfecti . . . Manifestum est autem quod quiescere et moveri non reducuntur ad diversas potentias sed ad unum et eandem . . ." See q. 79 art. 9–11; q. 58 art. 3, co.

47. *ST* 1 q. 79 art. 8, co.

what is true and what is good) are not disparate, much less opposed. "The true and the good include one another; for the true is something good, otherwise it would not be desirable; and the good is something true, otherwise it would not be intelligible."[48] Practical reason must be guided by the principle of non-contradiction: its conclusions about what is to be done cannot be self-contradictory, nor can they contradict other things that are known to be true. This is immediately obvious. What is less obvious, but becomes equally obvious with slight consideration, is that speculative reason is guided by the recognition that the pursuit of truth is good. Otherwise, man would make no attempt to understand the truth. Speculative reason and practical reason, though distinct as regarding their objects, or rather the two different aspects of the same object, are nonetheless absolutely inseparable as regarding their operation.[49]

As a Christian and from the perspective of revealed theology, Thomas holds that a fuller apprehension of what is true and what is good than anything reason can naturally achieve on its own is supernaturally and externally provided for in this life by divine revelation, which is accepted on faith; and he holds that in the next life this apprehension is supernaturally perfected in the beatific vision, which is knowledge. But, on the basis of his rational analysis of human nature alone, Thomas holds that the human soul is oriented and directed toward the true and the good through natural reason itself, independently from, though not in the slightest opposition to, divine revelation.

From these considerations we can conclude that, according to Thomas,

Reason is man's natural guide toward what is true and what is good.

This guidance is based on universal principles; and it proceeds *via* rational analysis (*ratiocinatio*) and judgment of diverse matters, including temporal matters, in light of these principles, which are themselves, Thomas says, eternal.[50] Natural reason is teleologically oriented toward the true and the good. It is not a mere calculator or any other kind of machine indifferent to the principles of its own operation. It has an *interest* in the true and the good. And this means that, whether directed toward speculative or practical matters, natural reason has an appetite (or desire—*appetitus*) of its own. That there is an appetite of reason should come as no more of a surprise than that there is an appetite of the senses. A clear sign that reason really does have an appetite proper to it is that there is a pleasure associated with its activity, a pleasure distinct from pleasure of the senses merely, as philosophers are usually the first to insist on.[51]

48. *ST* 1 q. 79 art. 11, ad 2.

49. The object of both speculative reason and practical reason is being. But in the former case it is being as intelligible, i.e., as true, whereas in the latter case it is being as (properly) desirable, i.e., as good.

50. *ST* 1 q. 77 art. 3, ad 4; q. 79 art. 8, co.; art. 9, co.; art. 12, co.; 1–2 q. 91 art. 2, ad 2.

51. See, e.g., Plato, *Republic* 580d4; 583a1; *Philebus* 51e9–b8; 66c3–7; Aristotle, *Nicomachean Ethics* 1173b11–19; 1174b20–21; 1176a2, 24–29. In my article, "The Pleasure of Philosophizing and Its Moral Foundation," I argue that one would not take pleasure in philosophizing unless one understood

One might object that it is not reason that has an appetite, even for knowledge, but rather the individual human being or the human soul that has this appetite, and that reason is only the means used to fulfill the appetite. [52] But the individual human being has this appetite only because he is rational, and the same is true of the human soul. The formulation that reason has an appetite of its own has the advantage of making sense of the traditional formulation that one should submit the lower faculties of the soul, and their appetites or desires, to the rule of reason. Reason could not rule unless it had an appetite of its own—minimally, an appetite for order—as distinct from the appetites of the other parts of the soul. It would not be possible to "follow the *logos*" if the *logos* (which can be translated as *ratio* or "reason") were not *of its own nature* headed toward or at least oriented toward something.[53] And being headed toward something or oriented toward something by nature is just what is meant by having a natural inclination to (*inclinatio ad*) that thing. The natural inclination of reason toward something is properly called its natural appetite for that thing. Man, or the human soul, has such an appetite only because reason itself has it. Otherwise, it would be thinkable that man or his soul could have this appetite even if, *per impossibile*, he did not possess reason, in which case the appetite, though actually present, would not be even partly satisfiable. He, or his soul, would long for knowledge but would not have the means to move towards it at all. Thomas would say that such a view of things makes no sense.

For Thomas, the name for the appetite or desire of reason or the rational desire (*appetitus rationalis*) is the will (*voluntas*).[54] He does not regard the will and free

philosophizing to be *inherently* good, that is, good independently of the pleasure, which may be great or slight, that it undoubtedly gives rise to. Aristotle speaks of the object of appetite as the good or the apparent good, not as the pleasant or the apparent pleasant, at *De Anima* 433a27; *Nicomachean Ethics* 1113a15–b2. Philosophizing, like other intellectual activities, can involve considerable effort and thereby some measure of pain as well. One makes the effort not because one calculates that, on balance, more pleasure than pain will be felt while philosophizing, but because one understands this activity and the knowledge at which it aims to possess *intrinsic* worth. The pleasure accompanying it is secondary. See Leo Strauss, *On Tyranny*, 204. See also *NRH* 126: "The thesis of the classics is that the good is *essentially* different from the pleasant, that the good is *more fundamental* than the pleasant" (emphasis added); cf. *NRH*, 126–129.

52. For a reply to this objection, see Alan Donagan, "Thomas Aquinas on Human Action" 654.

53. There is then a dual implication in the Socratic formulation, "to follow the *logos*." (*Phaedo* 107b7; see *Republic* 604c8–d4.) I take the simile "*hōsper pneuma*" at *Republic* 394d9 as indicating the difficulty of the task—also indicated in the passage just cited from the *Phaedo*—and not the pointlessness of the task.) One implication, the familiar one, is that we should subordinate what is *not* rational in us what *is* rational in us, i.e., to reason, or the *logos*. The other implication, related but insufficiently appreciated, is stated above: the *logos* is of its very nature headed or oriented toward something, whether we choose to follow the *logos* or to ignore or even resist it. I have treated this issue in "Socrates' Exhortation to Follow the Logos." Consider, in this connection, Heraclitus, Fragments 2 and 50 in *Fragmente der Vorsokratiker*, by Hermann Diels, edited by Walther Kranz (Zürick: Weidman, 1972), Vol. 1, p. 151 and p. 161. See also Aristotle *De Anima* 433a9: "Those who are self-controlled . . . follow the intellect" (*hoi gar egkrateis . . . akolouthousi tōi nōi*). The teleology of natural reason is not a fabrication of Christian scholasticism.

54. *Super Sent.*, lib. 2 d. 30 q. 1 art. 3, ad 4; *ST* 1–2 q. 6, prologue; q. 8 art. 1, co.; q. 30 art. 3, arg. 3.

choice (*liberum arbitrium*) as simply identical. We *necessarily* will happiness as our last end; we *freely* will, or choose, only the means to happiness.

The conception of an appetite specific to reason or the intellect, an appetite or desire for ends that are not sensuous or corporeal but are specifically rational, is not unique to Thomas. It can be found in Plato and Aristotle, and it reappears in Kant.[55] The conception of an appetite of reason in both its speculative and its practical operation is central to Thomas's understanding that "reason is the first principle of human acts."[56]

Now, Thomas says not only that, as the first principles of demonstration are to speculative reason, so are the primary precepts of natural law to practical reason; he also says that, as the first principles of demonstration are to speculative reason, so are ends to human acts.[57] These two proportions enable us to infer a third: ends are to human acts as the primary precepts of natural law are to practical reason. Since there is a most intimate connection between human acts and practical reason, we can infer that there is an equally intimate connection between ends and the primary precepts of natural law. And this is exactly what Thomas teaches.

The concept of an end (or end-goal, *telos*) is central to the thought of both Aristotle and Thomas Aquinas. But, as Strauss and his students point out, natural law (Gr. *nomos*), as distinct from natural right (Gr. *dikē*), does not figure into Aristotle's ethics.[58] It is anachronistic, then, to speak of Aristotle as "a natural law philosopher."

See *In Duodecim Libros Metaphysicorum Aristotelis Expositio*, Liber 12, Lectio 7, 2522: "Sed non potest esse huiusmodi diversitas in primo intelligibile et primo desiderabile. Sed oportet quod primum intelligibile et primum desiderabile sint eadem. Et hoc ideo, quia concupiscibile quod non est intelligibile bonum, est apparens bonum. Primum autem bonum << opportet quod sit voluntabile >>, idest appetibile appetitu intellectuali. Nam voluntas in intellectu est, et non in appetitu concupiscentiae tantum."

55. See. e.g., Plato, *Republic* 580d5–583a9; *Philebus*, 67b5–8. See also Aristotle *Nicomachean Ethics* 1139b5–7; and *De Anima* 432b5–433a31, where Aristotle says that spiritedness (or anger—*thymos*) and impassioned desire (*epithumia*)—these are the irascible and concupiscible desires, respectively—are in the irrational part (*tōi alogōi*) of the soul, but that *boulēsis* (cf. *Metaphysics* 1072a28) is in the ratiocinative part (*tōi logisitōi*). Aristotle speaks of all three as making up the faculty of desire (*to orektikon*), and he suggests that each is a desire (*oreksis*). There is no reason not to translate *boulēsis*, the desire of the ratiocinative part of the soul, as "will" here, other than the worry that doing so would imply that Aristotle believes in freedom of choice. But, as indicated above, demonstrating that someone has will (*voluntas*), or a rational desire, does not by itself demonstrate that he also has free choice (*liberum arbitrium*), not for Thomas anyway. *ST* 1 q. 19 art. 1; art.10; 1–2 q. 6 art. 1; q. 10 art. 2; see 1 q. 62 art. 8, ad 3. Kant distinguishes between a lower and a higher faculty of desire, the latter being the will (*Wille*) or practical reason itself. *Kritik der Praktischen Vernunft*, *Werke*, Band 6, 129–32 [English translation: 20–22.]. Kant's distinction between *Wille* and *Wilkür* is roughly parallel to Thomas's distinction between *voluntas* and *liberum arbitrium*.

56. *ST* 1 q. 90 art. 1, co. To say that reason as such has an appetite for, and hence aims at, ends is not to say that all consciousness is appetitive and aims at ends. For free association and reverie are usually if not always experienced as aimless. It is the rational, rule governed, activity of discursive cogitation and of deliberation that aims at ends, at determining what *is* and determining what *should be*, respectively.

57. *ST* 1–2 q. 57 art. 4, co.; see 1 q. 82 art. 1, co.

58. The general law (*koinos nomos*) that Aristotle in the *Rhetoric* (I. xiii) says is according to nature

To be sure, Aristotle does distinguish between merely conventional and natural right, with the former varying from community to community, and the latter retaining the same force (*dynamis*) everywhere.[59] But the much broader range of natural right is not equivalent to, nor does it imply, unchangeability of natural right. According to Aristotle, natural right and political (or conventional—*nomikon*) right are *both* changeable.[60] Thomas, however, argues that the primary precepts of natural law, and the first principle of practical reason that lies at their foundation, are unchangeable.[61] The difference between Thomas and Aristotle on these points is not minor.

In fact, Thomas's natural law is more akin to Kant's moral law than it is to Aristotle's natural right. Thomas, no less than Kant, argues that law in this sense is a rule of practical reason itself, not a mere convention, and that its first principles are absolutely unchangeable.[62] It is true that Kant's replacement of "natural" with "moral" reflects a major reinterpretation of nature, which according to the "Transcendental Analytic" of the *Critique of Pure Reason* is merely the complex of phenomena standing under laws prescribed to it *a priori* by the human understanding.[63] Kant contrasts

(*kata physin*) is problematic. The examples he gives, reflecting a common justice that all men somehow "divine" (*manteuontai*), namely, burying the dead and not killing what is alive (*empsychon*), are odd. Concerning the former, Aristotle would surely have known that not all peoples bury their dead (see Herodotus, *Histories*, 3.38). And, concerning the latter example, Aristotle himself teaches that even plants are alive, to say nothing of sheep and cattle. It may be significant that Aristotle does not cite these examples in his own name but in the names of Antigone and Empedocles respectively. He also cites Alcidamus as an authority on the matter of general law but without citing any precept of Alcidamus's. The Scholiast thinks that Aristotle may be referring to Alcidamus's claim that "nature has made no one a slave," (see"*Art*" *of Rhetoric*, 140–141, fn. b), a claim that Aristotle himself denies in the *Politics* (1252b1; 1254a14–1255a2). From the Greek perspective, the very expression "natural law"—*nomos ho tēs physeōs*—is odd, given the frequent equation of "law" with "convention" in the single word *nomos* and the contrast drawn in Greek philosophy between nature and convention. See Leo Strauss, "On Natural Law," in *SPPPh*, 139–40; "The Law of Reason," 95–98; and Ernest Fortin, "Augustine, Thomas Aquinas, and Natural Law," 181–2. Callicles' formulation, *kata nomon . . .ton tēs physeōs*, in Plato's *Gorgias*, 483e3, has virtually no relation to *lex naturae* as Thomas uses this expression and its equivalent, *lex naturalis*.

59. *Nicomachean Ethics* 1134b20. Consider Helmut Kuhn's analysis of Aristotle's argument in "Naturrecht und Historismus," reprinted in *The Independent Journal of Philosophy*, Volume II, 1968. Kuhn's article is a review of *Natural Right and History*; and Strauss's letter to Kuhn, also contained in the same volume, is a response to the latter's review. Strauss is given the last word, but Kuhn's article, which is not translated, merits consideration.

60. *Nicomachean Ethics* 1134 b29–33; see 1140a35.

61. *ST* 1–2 q. 94 art. 5; art. 6; see 2–2 q. 57 art. 2, ad 1; ad 2.

62. *ST* 1–2 q. 94 art. 2; art. 3.

63. This a central claim of the *KRV*: B xix; B 163–5, B 198, B 263, B280; cf. B 720–2; *Werke*, Band 3–4. (All references to the *KRV* are in accordance with the standard "A" or "B" designations of the first or second edition of this work, both in German and in most translations.) Compare *ST* 1–2 q. 1, art. 3, co.; ad 3. Thomas, having identified moral acts with human acts, argues that two distinct acts can be the same in their *natural* species—his example is the killing of a man—but diverse in their *moral* species; and that the converse can happen as well. See also 1–2 q. 94 art. 3, ad 1. See *ST* 1 q. 60 art. 5, co., where Thomas briefly distinguishes between reason and nature, but where he also makes clear that in this distinction—which he by no means uniformly adheres to, even in this very article—"nature"

nature, as a mechanistic system of thoroughgoing determinism, with the realm of a-temporal and a-spatial things-in-themselves. Only the latter can be thought of as a moral order constituted by rational and, indeed, teleological laws of freedom.[64] But Kant also speaks of nature in an older sense, not as a teleologically constituted cosmos, but as essence.[65] The nature of man is the essence of man.

Thomas, of course, puts much more stock in natural teleology than does Kant, even in the latter's *Critique of Judgment*. Thomas's teleology is subtle, and it has not been totally refuted by modern natural science. It has not even been adequately understood by modern natural science. Thomas's natural law teaching proper does not presuppose the existence of a cosmos in which every body that is naturally in motion is headed toward a *telos* construed as the very place where it is meant to be. His natural law teaching does not presuppose that a rock forcefully belched into the air by a volcano naturally aims at returning to the earth construed as the center of a finite and spherically shaped cosmos; or that the forward motion of a projectile is sustained only by disturbances in the air around it that the projectile itself is responsible for; or that a rock dropped from the mast of a rapidly moving ship will fall some distance behind the mast; or that the stars move in diurnal and perfectly circular motion around the earth; or that the other heavenly bodies move in paths that can be reduced by way of epicycles, and epicycles upon epicycles, to perfect circles also having the earth as their ultimate center. Thomas's natural law teaching is not compromised in its essentials by the scientific revolution of the 16th and 17th centuries.

Moreover, so far from appealing to an Aristotelian theory of motion in his account of natural law, Thomas says that "every entity (*substantia*) seeks the preservation of its own being" and that this natural inclination in us pertains to natural law.[66]

means only subhuman nature. See *Quaestiones de quolibet* 1.4.8 for a similar distinction.

64. *Grundlegung zur Metaphysik der Sitten*, *Werke*, Band 6, 60–61 [English translation: 35–36]; *Die Metaphysik der Sitten*, Band 7, 508–20 [English translation: 145–53].

65. See, for example, the distinction between sensible and supersensible nature in the *Kritik der Praktischen Vernunft*, *Werke*, Band 6, 156 [English translation: 38]. See also the *Grundlegung zur Metaphysik der Sitten*, *Werke*, Band 6, 51 [English translation: 30]; *Die Religion innerhalb der Grenzen der blossen Vernunft*, *Werke*, Band 7, 665–694 [English translation: 69–89]. Even the *KRV* occasionally employs the term "nature" to represent something other than the complex of phenomena merely. See, e.g., B 21; B 446; B 829 fn. b; B 858 fn. a; B 859. Compare Aristotle, *Metaphysics* 1015a1–19 and Thomas Aquinas, *DEE* 3–4. [English translation, 31–32]; *ST* 1–2, q. 10 art. 1, co.

66. *ST* 1–2 q. 94, art. 2, co (I translate "*substantia*" as "entity" rather than "substance" here because in current English parlance the latter term typically names only a kind of matter, with the result that "an immaterial substance" sounds like a contradiction in terms.). See 1–2, q. 85, art. 6, co.; 2–2 q. 25 art. 7, arg. 2; q. 64, art. 5, co.; art. 7, co. *De Potentia* q. 5 art. 1, arg. 13. In these passages Thomas does not explicitly connect self-preservation with self-perfection as he does at *SCG* 1 cap. 72 n. 4. Compare *Compendium Theologiae* 1, 103, co. with 115, co. Compare also *ST* 1 q. 60 art. 5, ad 3: ". . . natura reflectitur in seipsam non solum quantum ad id quod est ei singulare, sed multo magis quantum ad commune, inclinatur enim unumquodque ad conservandum non solum suum individuum. Et multo magis habet naturalem inclinationem unumquodque in id quod est bonum universale simpliciter." In the article in which he articulates the foundational principles of natural law (*ST* 1–2 q. 94 art. 2), Thomas does not need to make so broad a claim, which in some quarters would be regarded as

Thomas's reference to self-preservation is, as far as it goes, consonant with the claims of inertial mechanics, and even Spinoza would not quarrel with it, though he would surely quarrel with many other things that Thomas has to say.[67] Thomas's good sense kept him from grounding his natural law teaching in questionable theories about the motion of inanimate bodies; and little justice is done to this teaching by nailing it to a physics, many if not all particulars of which have been discredited by modern science, even if modern science has failed to offer a coherent account of its own, either of nature as a whole or of man in particular.

What Thomas's natural law teaching does presuppose is that there is an unchangeable *human* nature, or essence, and that *it* is teleologically constituted.[68] How and to what extent subhuman nature can be understood as teleologically constituted is a question of considerable interest to Thomas but one that, like the question of where our reason comes from in the first place, lies outside his natural law teaching proper.[69] We shall return to the theme of a general teleology of nature in Part 3, Chapter 13, below. For now, suffice it to say that the indirect evidence that post-Aristotelian natural science appeals to in support of its claim that subhuman nature is *not* teleologically constituted can hardly nullify the immediate evidence we human beings have that we *are* teleologically constituted. It is, after all, as self-evident as any law of logic that we move through life by orienting ourselves towards ends of all kinds, ends that we understand to be goods in some sense of the word, that we pursue them as goods, and that we take satisfaction and pleasure in attaining them. Many contemporary "neuro-philosophers" argue that reason is, at most, only an epiphenomenon floating

questionable. There he limits himself to saying "quaelibit substantia appetit conservationem sui esse secundum suam naturam. Et secundum hanc inclinationem, pertinent ad legem natualem ea per quae vita hominis conservatur, et contrarium impeditur."

67. According to Spinoza, "Unaquaeque res, quantum in se est, in suo esse perseverare conatur" (*Ethica* 3, Prop. 6). If Spinoza were to take issue with Thomas's figurative use of the term *appetitus* in relation to inanimate entities, Thomas would respond by asking Spinoza what he thinks is gained by replacing *appetitus* with *conatus* (endeavor, undertaking, or striving). Thomas uses the word *conatus* in the same *general* way that Spinoza does, though there are signal differences between the two thinkers regarding how *conatus* functions. See, for example, *SCG* lib. 3 cap. 2 n. 4: "Non est igitur possibile quod actiones in infinitum procedant. Oportet igitur esse aliquid quo habito conatus agentis quiescat. Omne igitur agens agit propter finem."

68. R. A. Armstrong, after noting that there are "many hundreds [of texts by Thomas] which assert that human nature is immutable," gives careful consideration to three texts from which one might be led to infer the opposite. He shows in each case that such an inference is unwarranted. *PSP* 174–7. Armstrong treats the secondary literature (up to 1966) on natural law exhaustively and fairly. Though I have some minor disagreements with him, which I shall be expressing occasionally in this study, I recommend his book to anyone who aims at more than a superficial understanding of Thomas's natural law teaching.

69. D. J. O'Connor raises a doubt about how we can "argue from what is natural—in whatever sense of the very ambiguous word—to what is morally obligatory." *Aquinas and Natural Law*, 62. I address this question in the sequel, along with other concerns that O'Connor expresses on the same page about how the primary precepts of natural law are related to the secondary precepts, and whether "Thomas's concessions about the variability of the natural law destroy the basic character of his theory." These concerns will be shown to be groundless.

above bio-chemical processes in the brain that are not teleological at all. But, as Aristotle warns, one should not attempt to explain the more evident by appeal to the less evident.[70] The "neuro-philosophers" actually do something worse. They deny the self-evident by appeal to generalizations from experience that necessarily fall short of the evidence found in immediately lived experience, as they also fall short of purely logical and mathematical demonstrations.

Direction toward ends through the evidence and operation of reason pertains to the very sense of human action. This claim might seem to be at odds with the fact that we do some things accidentally and others habitually, if not automatically, apparently with little if any thought. But accidents, such as slipping and falling on an icy sidewalk, are not human actions properly so-called.[71] If, in some unusual situation one slips and falls on purpose, in order to trick someone or make a point, then one does so for the sake of an end that one judges to be in some respect good. And the judgment that something is good is an act of practical reason. Regarding habits, if their initial formation was intentional, then their ongoing, apparently automatic performance are effects of which practical reason is at least a partial cause. If their initial formation was unintentional, as is the case with tics and the like, then they are no more human actions properly so-called than mere accidents are. In general, if one can give a reason for why one does something, then one can be sure that practical reason is playing a role in one's doing it, however automatic or even "unconscious" doing it might seem to be.

Man, who is a finite being and, unlike God, does not possess his whole good all at once, is directed by his reason toward ends that specifically pertain to his nature as a rational being. Though knowledge is not the only end of reason, it is the most obvious end of reason, and it is the end of reason most difficult to contest. Certain kinds of knowledge can of course serve as means to ends other than knowledge. However, as Thomas and his classical predecessors argue, knowing is a good that is eminently desirable in itself quite apart from its utility. In the pursuit of knowledge for its own sake reason aims at its own fulfillment or perfection. That human action proper is characterized by rational orientation toward ends and by the rational pursuit of them is then most definitely a teleological presupposition of Thomas's natural law teaching. But it is not a mere presupposition. It is an incontestable teleological fact.

70. *Physics* 193a5. Cf. Plato, *Phaedo* 98c3–99b4.

71. Butera, "The Moral Status of the First Principle," 621–3, and note especially the important distinction, to which Butera draws attention, between *actus hominis* and *actus humanus* (622).See *Quaestiones Disputatae de Malo* (hereafter cited as *De Malo*), q. 2, art. 5. In this connection, consider Plato, *Gorgias* 468b1–4, and *Meno* 99a1–5.

SECTION C. PRUDENCE, JUDGMENT, AND *SYNDERESIS*

Thomas agrees with Aristotle that prudence is an intellectual virtue. It is a *habitus*. There is no need to refrain from translating *habitus* (or the Greek word *heksis*) as "habit." We use the word today more narrowly than Thomas and Aristotle did, but the broader sense of the word is worth recovering. A habit stands between a mere potentiality and an act. A mere potentiality (potency, power—*potentia*, Gr. *dynamis*) to do one thing or another is, as such, indifferent to which of these two, or more, acts emerge out of it. A habit is like a potentiality in that it is not an act (*actus*). But, unlike a mere potentiality, a habit is not indifferent to the act that emerges out of it. Instead, it is disposed toward that act. The virtue of courage, for example, is not the act of courage; but it is not the mere potentiality for acting courageously either, since the potentiality for acting courageously is at the same time the potentiality for acting cowardly. The virtue of courage is, rather, a *readiness* to act courageously. [72] The way in which a *habitus* is situated between *potentia* and *actus* reminds us of Aristotle's threefold distinction between potentiality and two degrees of actuality, and even of his definition of motion.[73]

Prudence is the virtue that manifests itself in intelligent deliberation about the means to an end. Thomas speaks of *prudentia* more generally as "right reason about the things that are practicable" (*recta ratio agibilium*). Good counsel and judgment are "annexed" to prudence in this more general sense.[74] Thomas identifies two virtues of judgment (*iudicium*), namely, *synesis* and *gnome*. They are distinguished according to the different rules (*secundem diversas regulas*) by which actions are judged. *Synesis* judges them according to common law (*lex communis*), which is part of positive human law, while *gnome* judges them according to a higher law, namely, natural law, in situations where the common law does not achieve its purpose.[75] In both cases correct

72. The translation of *habitus* (or Gr. *heksis*) as "state"—a common rendering—is misleading, because a *habitus* is not static. The word "capacity," suggested by Armstrong (*PSP* 29), is also misleading since a capacity is only a potentiality, and a *habitus* is more than a potentiality. "Disposition" and "readiness" are much better, but can sound unnecessarily forced in certain contexts. I shall use the word "habit" for *habitus* (and likewise for the Greek *heksis*), except when I leave *habitus* untranslated, because it is much the most literal translation of this word.

73. *De Anima* 417a 21-b1. Cf. Thomas Aquinas, *Commentary on the De Anima*, Lect. 11, n. 3, where a *habitus* is in act when compared to potency, but in potency when compared to act. See *Physics* 201a12; Thomas Aquinas, *In Octo Libros de Physico Auditu sive Physicorum Aristotelis Commentaria*, p. 132, § 561: ". . . unde neque est [motus] potentia existentis in potentia neque est actus existentis in actu, sed actus existentis in potentia."

74. *ST* 1–2 q. 57 art. 4, co.; art. 5, co.

75. *ST* 1–2 q. 57 art. 6, ad 3: "Distinguuntur autem synesis et gnome secundum diversas regulas quibus iudicatur: nam synesis est iudicativa de agendis secundum communem legem; gnome autem secundum ipsam rationem naturalem." E. A. Goerner notes that Anton Pegis (actually the English Dominican Fathers whose translation Pegis reproduces here) translates *ipsam rationem naturalem* as "natural law," and that this translation is not literal ("The Good Man's View of Thomistic Natural Law," 405–6). But that Thomas is in fact referring to natural law with this expression is implied by his use of the word *regulas* earlier in the sentence. (On *lex communis*, which is here opposed to *ipsam rationem*

judgment takes place in accordance with rules, indeed, with law. Whether directed to speculative or to practical matters, judgment necessarily makes use of univeral rules. The rules are universal because they embrace within their scope all the individuals of the class under consideration. There is no such thing as a rule that does not hold for all the members of some class, however large or small that class may be. The principle of non-contradiction is a rule so universal that it holds for anything that can be thought. A private maxim, on the other hand, is a rule of much narrower scope. Even so, a private maxim, for example, to memorize one poem per month, is intended to function with a certain universality: one poem every month without exception, until the maxim is modified or suspended. Judgment and universal rules go together in both speculative and practical reasoning.[76]

There is a close analogy between judgment and prudence, which is hardly surprising inasmuch as judgment, Thomas says, pertains to prudence.[77] Judgment is the application of a given rule to a particular case. This application can be made only with a rule in sight, but it is not a logical deduction from that rule. Good judgment is ultimately a matter of discernment, of determining which individuals fall under the rule. Judgment can be sharpened by experience. But some will always have better judgment than others. Similarly, prudence is the virtue that enables one to discover the means appropriate to a given end. This discovery can be made only with the end in sight, but it is not a logical deduction from that end. Prudence, just like good judgment, is ultimately a matter of discernment, of determining which means are most appropriate to the end. Prudence can be acquired, up to a point, by experience. But some will always be more prudent than others. In brief, though judgment is not a logical deduction from a rule and prudence is not a logical deduction from an end, judgment and prudence necessarily take their bearings from a rule and an end, respectively. Practical judgment is then exactly the opposite of a wily calculation of how an exclusively private interest, even the private interest of a purportedly superior human being, can be pursued by ignoring or circumventing rules.

Thomas goes so far as to call prudence the perfection of practical reason.[78] But it is, so to speak, a founded perfection. For besides the *habitus* of practical reason that is prudence, which is concerned with the means to an end, Thomas recognizes another *habitus* of practical reason, one concerned with the end itself. This is *synderesis*, the very *habitus* whereby we also know the precepts of natural law.[79] Thomas uses a Pa-

naturalem, as part of *human* law, see 1–2 q. 96 art. 1, ad 1; 2–2 q. 80 art. 1, ad 4.) Goerner does give sufficient attention to the *rules* whereby *gnome* judges. See *ST* 1–2 q. 90 art. 1, co.; q. 91 art. 2, co.; art. 3, ad 2.

76. *ST* 2–2 q. 47 art. 6, co.; compare Kant, *KRV* B 171–173.

77. *Super Sent.*, lib. 3 dist. 33, q. 1 art. 1 qc. 3, co.

78. *Super Sent.*, lib. 1, dist. 1, q. 1 art. 2, ad 2.; lib. 3, dist. 33, q. 2 art. 1 qc. 3, arg. 6. See *Sententia Ethic.*, lib. 1, l. 1 n. 1.

79. Michael C. Crowe, in *The Changing Profile of Natural Law*, says that "[B]y the time he came to write his *Summa theologiae*, St. Thomas no longer regarded *synderesis* as a term of importance" (139).

tristic term here, but only to *name* a natural faculty of discernment that, as rational, is apparent to reason when it reflects carefully on the principles of its own operation. "Natural reason, which is called [!] *synderesis*, appoints the end to the moral virtues . . . but prudence does not do this."[80] To the extent that prudence is an intellectual virtue concerned with determining the means to an end, it has an intrinsic relation to *synderesis*, to which it is subordinate just as means are subordinate to ends. As the perfection of practical reason, prudence is relatively uncommon. *Synderesis*, on the other hand, is as common as our natural, if only occasionally articulated, knowledge of the principle of non-contradiction. Conscience is the act of which *synderesis* is the habit.[81] Because of the essential correlation of *synderesis* and conscience with natural law—as distinct from natural right—neither *synderesis* nor conscience makes an appearance in Aristotle's ethics. But conscience does play a role in the moral philosophy of Kant.[82] The elements of Thomas's ethics, then, consist of concepts inherited from Aristotle and concepts anticipatory of Kant, two philosophers who are, so to speak, worlds apart. To understand how such heterogeneous elements form a coherent whole we need to attend to Thomas's claim that "it is fitting that the first direction of our acts to [their] end be through natural law."[83]

SECTION D. LAW AND THE ENDS OF HUMAN ACTION

The ultimate end of our acts and the ultimate perfection of our rational nature is happiness (*beatitudo*).[84] Happiness is not a mere state, much less a feeling. It is essentially

This is an overstatement, unless Crowe really means only the "term" itself, as distinct from what the term designates. As Crowe himself notes, Thomas devotes an article to *synderesis* in *ST* 1; and he employs the term substantively in 1–2 q. 94 art. 1, ad 1 and in 2–2 q. 47 art. 6. Because Thomas had written extensively on *synderesis* in his *Commentary on the Sentences* and in *De Veritate*, there was no pressing need for him to treat the matter at any length in the *Summa Theologiae*, especially in light of its purpose and targeted audience—*ad eruditionem incipientium*. Crowe suggests that the role played by *synderesis* in the earlier works is replaced by law, or "the first principles of the practical order," in the *ST* (138–9). With this suggestion Crowe blurs the distinction between the precepts of natural law and the *habitus* whereby one knows these precepts (see *ST* q. 94 art. 1, co.; ad 2), though he does not always blur this distinction (see, e.g., 175). If the precepts of natural law are *per se nota*, there must be a *habitus* whereby they are known. Its *name* is of no special importance. See the following footnote.

80. *ST* 2–2 q. 47, art. 6, ad 1: "ratio naturalis quae *dicitur* synderesis . . ." See 2–2 q. 47, ad 3; also 1 q. 79, art. 12: "principia operabilium nobis naturaliter indita . . . pertinent . . . ad specialem habitum naturalem, quem *dicimus* synderesim" (emphasis added in both quotations). Thomas insists on the natural character of this habit, by whatever name it happens to be called. Cf. *ST* 1–2 q. 63 art. 1, co., and *Quaestiones Disputatae* Vol. 1, *De Veritate* q. 16, art. 1, co; and Vol. 2, *De Malo* q. 16 art. 6, ad s. c. 5: "synderesis est cognoscitiva universalium principiorum operabilium, quae naturaliter homo cognoscit, sicut et principia universalia speculabilium."

81. *ST* 1 q. 79 art. 12; art. 13. See 1–2 q. 19 art. 5, *sed contra*.

82. *Die Metaphysik der Sitten*, *Werke*, Band 7, 531–2, 572–6 [English translation: 160–1, 188–91].

83. "Et sic etiam oportet quod prima directio actuum nostrorum ad finem, fiat per legem naturalem." *ST* 1–2 q. 91 art. 2, ad 2; compare art. 4, co.

84. ". . . nomine beatitudine intelligitur ultima perfectio rationalis seu intellectualis naturae." *ST* 1

an operation; it is an act in the highest grade of actuality.[85] For Thomas, perfect happiness, were we ever to attain it, would consist in an act of the intellect in which we would behold the essence of the first cause or causes of things.[86] Thomas thinks he can prove, and that he does not have to just take it on faith, that there is a first cause, that it is one, and that it is God. Still, beholding the very essence of God is a supernatural end, according to Thomas, and so we need supernatural assistance to attain it.[87]

Apart from the supernatural end of perfect happiness, however, there is the natural end of imperfect happiness. "Imperfect happiness, such as can be had here, consists first and principally in contemplation but secondarily in an operation of the practical intellect ordering [or setting in order—*ordinans*] human actions and passions."[88] We are directed to our natural end of imperfect happiness by natural law which, like all law, is a rule of reason.[89] If there were no divine, or revealed, law directing us to a supernatural end, natural law would still direct us to the end that we are capable

---

q. 62 art. 1, co. See *ST* 1–2 q. 1–6.

85. *ST* 1–2 q. 3 art. 2, co. See Aristotle *De Anima* 412a23–28; *Nicomachean Ethics* 1098a4–20. In *Sources*, Servais Pinckaers, OP, rightly emphasizes the centrality of happiness in Thomas's ethics. According to Fr. Pinckaers, Thomas places "[t]he stress on happiness over obligation" (18). It is indeed significant that Thomas begins his ethical teaching in *ST* 1–2 with a "Treatise on Happiness," and that he refers to what he says there repeatedly in what follows. However, as I shall argue in the next chapter, the concepts of obligation and imperatives are as central and indispensable to Thomas's ethics as is the concept of happiness. Fr. Pinckaers qualifies the above statement when he writes a few pages later that "the moral theory of beatitude [= happiness], if properly understood [i.e., *not* as it understood by Kant or by Mill], can perfectly well include the question of obligation and accord the Commandments a fitting role within its structure" (22).

86. *ST* 1 q. 12 art. 4.; art. 11; 1–2 q. 2 art. 8, co.; q. 3 art. 5–8; q. 62 art. 1, co. *In Duodecim Libros Metaphysicorum Aristotelis Expositio*, Lib. 1 Lect. 1.4.

87. *SCG* lib. 3 cap. 150 n. 5; *ST* 1, q. 63 art. 2, ad 3; q. 75 art. 7, ad 1; 1–2 q. 2 art. 3; q. 3 art. 8; q. 5 art. 6; 1 q. 12 art. 11. We need divine law in addition to natural law. 1–2 q. 91 art. 4, co.; see q. 3 art. 2, ad 4. Concerning the desire to know the essence of the first cause as a natural, and rational, desire, see Part 2, Ch. 5, Section b, below.

88. *ST* 1–2, q. 3 art. 5, co. (emphasis added). The whole passage reads, "Et ideo ultima et perfecta beatitudo, quae expectatur in futura vita, tota consistit in contemplatione. Beatitudo autem imperfecta, qualis hic haberi potest, primo quidem et principaliter consistit in contemplatione; secondario vero in operatione practici intellectus ordinantis actiones et passiones humanas . . ." See *Super Sent.*, lib. 4, dist. 49, q. 1 art. 1 qc. 4, co. Following Aristotle, Thomas elevates contemplation, even in the case of imperfect this-worldly happiness, above action. (Contemplation of revealed mysteries is, to say the least, not ruled out by Thomas as a component of this-worldly happiness. But this-worldly happiness need not depend on belief in revelation, since there is plenty in the natural order of things to contemplate and marvel at.) However, the ordering of actions and passions is an actual *component* of worldly happiness and not just a *means* to worldly happiness. We shall return to this component and consider it a greater length later on. For now we note that, according to Thomas, a human being needs friends in order to be happy. *ST* 1–2 q. 4, art. 8, co. (Cf. *Nicomachean Ethics* 1155a2–6.) Friends are necessary, he says, for the sake of good operation (*propter bonam operationem*). One needs friends in order that one might *benefit* them, *delight* in seeing them do well, and *be helped* by them in one's own worthy endeavors. The third of these three reasons could be interpreted as implying a merely instrumental need for friends, e.g., in one's trying to understand things that they already understand (though see the beginning of the *corpus* of this article). The first two reasons cannot be interpreted this way.

89. *ST* 1–2, q. 90 art. 1.

of reaching through our natural powers.[90] Even if one were to contest, on whatever grounds, the possibility of a law revealed by God, natural law would still retain its evidentiary force.[91]

Thomas argues on the basis of natural reason and ordinary human experience alone that there is an eternal law whereby the world is rationally governed. This is the supreme reason (*summa ratio*) existing in God. "The whole community of the universe is governed by divine reason." This governance extends to the very existence of things, and hence to their motion as well. "Nature is immediately from God." [92] The whole cosmic order is freely created, sustained in its being, and governed by God. Nature, most remarkably in its rational structure and hence in its intelligibility and purposiveness for our investigation of it, reflects the *summa ratio* that is eternal law. All this, Thomas argues, is demonstrable without appeal to the claims of revelation.

Thomas also argues, again on the basis of natural reason and ordinary experience alone, that in addition to eternal law there is natural law and, of course, that there is human law.[93] However, he cannot argue by appeal to natural reason and ordinary experience alone that there is a *divine* law, but only that it *was necessary that there be* a divine law.[94] The necessity of which Thomas speaks here is not absolute necessity but what he calls "necessity of the end," which could also be called "hypothetical

90. *ST* 1–2, q. 91 art.4.

91. *ST* 1–2 q. 100 art. 11, co. See Romans 2:14–15, which is the authoritative text that Thomas cites at 1–2 q. 91 art. 2, *sed contra*, not to prove his case, but to show that his rational teaching does not contradict revelation. (In his commentary on this passage, *Super Epistolam B. Pauli ad Romanos lectura*, Caput 2, Lect. 3, Thomas suggests two different ways in which this passage can be interpreted, only one of which accords with the use he makes of it in q. 91 art. 2.) Ernest Fortin says that "Paul himself never uses the word 'law' save in reference to the Mosaic law or, by analogy, to what he calls elsewhere the 'law of Christ' (1 Cor. 9:21; Gal. 6:2) or the 'law of sin' (Rom. 8:2)." (*Classical Christianity and the Political Order*, 227.) In the sentence preceding this one, however, Fr. Fortin quotes Paul as saying, in Romans 2:14, "When the Gentiles who are without the law [presumably the Mosaic Law] do by nature what the law requires, they are a law unto themselves, even though they do not have the law." The law (*nomos*) that the Gentiles "are unto themselves" is not reducible to any of three ways in which alone, according to Fr. Fortin, Paul uses the word "law."

92. *ST* 1–2 q. 93 art. 1, co.; art. 4, ad 1; q. 91 art. 1, co. (The reference to Proverbs in the *corpus* of the latter article is not essential to Thomas's argument since he has previously demonstrated, by appeal to natural reason alone, that the divine reason has an eternal awareness of things, an awareness that is not subject to time: 1 q. 10 art. 1–3; q. 14 art. 7; art. 8, ad 2.) At *ST* 1 q. 62 art. 6, ad 2, Thomas says that though it pertains to the nature of the rational creature to be the author of its *acts*, the rational *nature* comes directly from God.

93. *ST* 1–2 q. 91 art. 2 and art. 3.

94. *Utrum fuerit necessarium esse aliquam legem divinam.* 1–2 q. 91 art. 4, title. Though Thomas distinguishes divine law from eternal law in the "Treatise on Law" section of the *Summa Theologiae* (1–2 q. 90–108), earlier in *ST* he occasionally uses the term *lex divina* not to name divinely *revealed* law, but eternal law itself (which is "divine" in the broad sense of the word, but of much wider scope than revealed law: q. 91 art. 4, arg.1, ad 1; q. 93 art. 4; art. 5). For example, at 1–2 q. 63 art. 2, co., Thomas subsumes what is ruled by human reason under what he there calls *lex divina*. But he justifies the subsumption by referring back to 1–2 q. 19 art. 4, co., where he subsumes what is ruled by human reason not under *lex divina* but under *lex aeterna*, the latter being, he says, divine reason itself. Cf. q. 19 art. 4, ad 3, where he makes distinctions that reappear in the "Treatise on Law."

necessity."[95] Divine law, that is, revealed law—which, for Thomas, is not equivalent to eternal law—is necessary in addition to natural law *if* man is to reach the supernatural end of wisdom that he naturally desires. But we cannot know by reason alone that man will in fact reach this supernatural end, in which perfect happiness consists, or that he ever has been offered or ever will be offered the supernatural assistance without which he cannot reach it. That there is a *need* for divine law, and hence for revelation, is a matter of reason for Thomas. That this need has actually been met is a matter of faith. Natural reason can recognize its own limits. In so doing, it can, and should, become open to the *possibility* of assistance coming from beyond those limits. But natural reason cannot claim to know what can only be taken on faith. Natural reason can establish that in its speculative operation it needs to be supplemented by revelation, without which we could have no awareness whatsoever of the essence, as distinct from the causality, of the first principle of things. And natural reason can establish that in its practical operation it needs to be supplemented by divine law, without the revelation of which we could not reach the supernatural end of perfect happiness, but could only long for it.

Revelation, whether one grants or denies that it has actually occurred, is according to its very meaning an un-anticipatable irruption of the divine into human history, at the initiative of God rather than man. Since natural reason by its own efforts cannot establish that revelation has actually occurred, it cannot establish what has been revealed. Were natural reason able to demonstrate conclusively that revelation has occurred, it would have to do so through exclusively rational arguments built on evidence accessible to man as man at all times. Were natural reason able to demonstrate conclusively that revelation has occurred, it would have been able to do so both before as well as after the historical event, real or alleged, of revelation itself—which is absurd. Unlike natural law, neither the Old Law nor the New Law, which together comprise divine or revealed law, is coeval with man as such.[96]

In the *Summa Theologiae* Thomas uses the expression "divinely given" (*divinitus data*) for divine, or revealed, law as distinct from natural law.[97] Natural law is no more "divinely given," that is, it is no more revealed, than is the principle of non-contradiction. Unlike divine law, the principle of non-contradiction and natural law are, according to Thomas, self-evident to human reason. To be sure, he holds that natural reason, like everything else in nature, has God as its ultimate source, and so in

95. *ST* 1 q. 82, art. 1, co.

96. In *Sources*, Fr. Pinckaers gives a rich account of the New Law as the "high point of St. Thomas's moral teaching" (172–90). The New Law deepens immeasurably everything in the "Treatise on Law" that comes before it. Needless to say, what Thomas says about the New Law occurs in the context, not of his rational theology, but of his revealed theology.

97. *ST* 1–2 q. 91 art. 4, co. See Thomas's use of this expression in *Super Sent.* lib. 3, dist. 23, q. 3 art. 2; lib. 4, dist. 43, q. 1 art. 2; and also his use of this expression at *ST* 1 q. 100, art. 1, co; 1–2 q. 83 art. 2, ad 2. In his much shorter treatment of law in *SCG* Thomas does not highlight and develop the distinctions between the four kinds of law as he does in *ST* 1–2 q. 90 ff.

that way whatever pertains to it could also be said to be "divinely given," though not in the more precise sense of this expression, namely, "given through an act of grace."[98] Man's knowledge of both natural law and the first principles of speculative reason is an immediate consequence of his having been created as a rational being. "[T]he very light of natural reason is a certain participation of the divine light."[99] This light of natural reason, however, is not the effect of grace elevating man above his nature.

But why, one might ask, do we need *law* of any kind to direct us to the natural *telos* of happiness in this world? Thomas's answer is that unlike the lower animals we act not by instinct merely but by reason and by will. Law in general is "a certain rule and measure of acts whereby one is induced to act or restrained from acting: for law is named from binding (*ligando*), because it obligates [one] to act." [100] To this observation, Thomas adds at once that "the rule and measure of human acts is reason," and that "it belongs to reason to direct to the end." Thomas does not say here that the rule and measure of human acts is God, or that it belongs to God to direct to the end. But he holds this to be true as well, in light of both what he thinks natural reason can establish and what he believes as a Catholic Christian. God directs man to his supernatural end through revelation. But God also directs man to his natural end through natural law, though he does the latter simply by endowing man with reason, which of its own nature is directive and teleological. [101]

98. See 1–2 q. 19 art. 4.

99. *ST* 1 q. 12 art. 11, ad 3; *SCG* 1 cap. 11, ad quintam. 7. Cf. Aristotle, *De Anima* 430a14–16.

100. *ST* 1–2, q. 90, art. 1, co. The entire passage is as follows. "Respondeo dicendum quod lex quaedem regula est et mensura actuum, secundum quam inducitur aliquis ad agendum, vel ab agendo retrahitur: dicitur enim lex a ligando, quia obligat agendum. Regula autem et mensura humanorum actuum est ratio, quae est primum principium actuum humanorum, ut ex praedictis patet: rationis enim est ordinare ad finem, qui est primum principium in agendis, secundum philosophum."

101. *ST* 1–2 q. 90 art. 4, ad 1: "God instilled it [i.e., the natural law] into the minds of men so as to be naturally known." ("Deus eam mentibus hominum inseruit naturaliter cognoscendam.") This sentence should not be taken to imply that natural law is merely adventitious content that God happened to deposit in human reason. For on that interpretation natural law would not be something actually constituted by reason, as Thomas says it is, *ST* 1–2, q. 94 art. 1, co.; ad 3. God instilled natural law into the minds of men by endowing them with natural reason. Accordingly, it is *naturally* known, rather than supernaturally revealed and assented to in an act of faith. See q. 90 art. 1, co.; q. 91 art. 2, co.

Chapter 2

The Case for Natural Law

We have not yet considered the question of exactly how natural law can be understood as a rule of reason. Does practical reason really employ universal principles of action that are analogous to the universal principles of speculative reason? Thomas Aquinas gives his answer to this question in the *Summa Theologiae, Prima Secundae*, Question 94, Article 2 (hereafter referred to simply as q. 94 art. 2).

SECTION A. THE FIRST PRINCIPLE OF PRACTICAL REASON

The first principle of practical reason," Thomas says, "is founded on the *ratio boni*, which is, 'Good is what all things desire.'"[1] When Thomas uses the expression *ratio boni* he means what pertains to the very concept or meaning of good or the good, just as when he uses the expression *ratio veri* he means what pertains to the very concept or meaning of true or the true.[2] We have already seen that the intellect and the will are closely related, and their proper objects are the true and the good respectively. The true is being, or what-is, though under the aspect of intelligibility (or in terms of its character as knowable—*ratio cognoscibilis*); and the good also is being, or what-is, though under the aspect of desirability (or in terms of its character as appetible—*ratio appetibilis*).[3] That Thomas sees the good as being, albeit with the qualification of *as desirable*, precludes his regarding the good as a mere subjective value or preference. For he recognizes that some things are occasionally valued, preferred, or desired that are not *intrinsically* desirable. Thomas's conception of the relation between the true and the good as two aspects of being is an architectonic principle that, like the distinction

1. *ST* 2 q. 94 art. 2. "[P]rimum principium in ratione practica est quod fundatur supra rationem boni, quae est, *Bonum est quod omnia appetunt*."

2. *ST* 1 q. 16 art. 1 co; ad 3. See 1–2 q. 64 art. 3, co.

3. *De Veritate* q. 22 art. 10 co; *ST* 1 q. 5 art. 1, co.; q. 16 art. 3–4. The *ratio veri* and the *ratio boni* presuppose, at the most fundamental level, the *ratio entis*. See *ST* 1 q. 16 art. 4, ad 2, for how these three *rationes* are at work in the order of knowing.

between demonstrable preambles to the articles of faith and the articles of faith themselves, informs his entire intellectual project, down to its finest details.[4]

The formulation that Thomas gives for the *ratio boni* is a condensation of what Aristotle says at the very beginning of the *Nicomachean Ethics*. "Every art and every investigation, and likewise every action and choice, seem to aim at some good. Therefore the good has been well declared to be that at which all things aim."[5] But, after echoing Aristotle, Thomas does something that Aristotle does not do, certainly not explicitly. Thomas transforms the *ratio boni*, a simple declarative, "Good is that at which all things aim," into a gerundive: "Hence this is the first precept of law, that good is to be done (*est faciendum*) and pursued, and evil avoided (*vitandum*). Upon this are founded all the other precepts of natural law." [6] Aristotle's indicative statement, an expression of speculative or theoretical reason, describes action.[7] Thomas's

4. Compare *ST* 1 q. 16 art. 4, ad 2, with q. 27 art. 1, 3, and 5; also with q. 45 art. 6, co.; art. 7, ad 3.

5. *Nicomachean Ethics*, 1094a2. See 1097a30; *Politics* 1269a4. (Cf. *Republic* 505d5–e2.) Cf. *Primae Redactiones—Summae contra Gentiles*, lib. 1: "Bonum definitur quod omnia appetunt." See *Expositio De Ebdomadibus*, l. 2. This definition of *bonum* is correct, as far as it goes. It is, however, incomplete inasmuch as it does not make clear exactly *what* it is that that all desire. This turns out to be God—who is *the* good (*SCG* lib. 3 cap. 17 n. 6; *ST* 1 *ST* 1 q. 3; 5–6). Of course, many people do not realize that God, or closeness to God, is what they desire. But the same is true of happiness when it is defined, as Aristotle defines it, as an activity of the soul in accordance with virtue. On the other hand, all or almost all people see, or can be brought to see, that they desire something because they understand it, rightly or wrongly, to be somehow good.

6. *ST* 1–2 q. 94 art. 2, co. The entire passage reads, "Et ideo primum principium in ratione practica est quod fundatur supra rationem boni, quae est, *Bonum est quod omnia appetunt*. Hoc est ergo primum praeceptum legis, *quod bonum est faciendum et prosequendum, et malum vitandum*. Et super hoc fundantur omnia alia praecepta legis naturae . . . ." I have emphasized the gerundive phrase to set it in relief against the previously emphasized simple declarative, the *ratio boni*. My intention in rendering *malum* as "evil" here, rather than "bad," is not to endow *malum* with a specifically moral sense. My intention is only to respect English idiom. We can say "evil is to be avoided." But "bad is to be avoided" is not English. Regarding "*ergo*" in the above quotation, I interpret it as meaning "accordingly," not as introducing the conclusion of a logical demonstration. There is no way to logically deduce the first principle of practical reason from the *ratio boni*. And if there were such a way, the first principle of practical reason would not be *per se notum*, as Thomas says it is. Still, though the first principle of practical reason cannot be deduced from the *ratio boni*, it must accord with the *ratio boni*. Compare *De Anima* 431a16, where Aristotle says—and this too is only an indicative statement—that the thinking part of the soul (*hē dianoētikē psychē*) avoids or pursues (*pheugei ē diōkei*) what it takes to be [respectively] bad or good.

7. Consider *Nicomachean Ethics* 1139a22: "What affirmation and denial are in thought, pursuit and avoidance are in desire." Aristotle makes use of gerundive-like expressions, though with a range of significations, some of which are ambiguous. See, in particular, the use of "choiceworthy" (*haireton*) at *Nicomachean Ethics*, 1176b3–29, and Terrence Irwin's discussion of this term in the Glossary to his translation of the *Nicomachean Ethics*, p. 319. See also the contrast of *haireton* and *pheukton* that Aristotle makes, when speaking of Eudoxus, at *Nicomachean Ethics*, 1172b19–20. We cannot know what Aristotle would think of Thomas's move from the indicative statement that expresses the *ratio boni* to the gerundive that expresses the first principle of practical reason. Strauss and his followers might say that, since Aristotle does not himself make this move (though see *De Anima* 432b27-29), he tacitly rejects it. But then the question can be put to them: if all human beings pursue the good (real or apparent), then what initiates and propels, or animates, them to do so? "Nature," they might respond. And that response would be correct. But it would be insufficient. For man is *by nature* a rational

gerundive, an expression of practical reason, indeed its first expression, initiates and propels action.[8]

Thomas does not attempt to demonstrate the first principle of practical reason, that good is to be done and pursued, and evil avoided. But this does not mean that he understands it to be an inscrutable edict issued from on high. Neither this precept nor the principle of non-contradiction can be demonstrated. That, however, is only because both, according to Thomas, are self-evident, even if they are only rarely formulated and thematized.[9] These highest principles are, as is said today, underivable.[10] But, though the first principle of practical reason is not derived or deduced from the indemonstrable principles of speculative reason, it does depend on them inasmuch as it conforms to them. Without the principle of non-contradiction in particular, one could not meaningfully distinguish between "to be done" and "not to be done," between good and bad, or between pursuit and avoidance. Without the principle of

animal. If it is nature that initiates and propels human beings to seek a specifically *human* good, it can only do so through their *reason*. The first principle of practical reason, because it is a gerundive with practical import, serves this initiating and propelling function. The *ratio boni*, because it is a simple declarative, cannot, by itself, initiate or propel any *action* at all.

8. The significance of the gerundive in Thomas's account of natural law is addressed in Germain Grisez's ground-breaking paper, "The First Principle of Practical Reason: A Commentary on the *Summa theologiae*, 1–2, Question 94, article." Hereafter cited as "Grisez." Though Grisez clears up a number of common misunderstandings, he introduces a few misunderstandings of his own, which I shall address in the following chapter.

9. In q. 94, art. 2, Thomas calls the gerundive we have been considering both the *primum principium in ratione practica* and the *primum praeceptum legis*, with the implication that there is only one such thing deserving this designation. (See Grisez, 178, fn. 21 on the equivalence of these two expressions.) Although Latin does not possess a definite article, we can call this gerundive *the* first principle since, as Thomas tells us, all the other precepts of the law of nature are founded on it. And yet Thomas argues in this very article that there are several precepts and that they too are self-evident. Thomas's usage of *principia* and *praecepta* varies. At *ST* 1 q. 79, art. 12, ad 3, he uses the plural expression *prima principia operabilium*; and at 1–2 q. 94, art. 5, co., he speaks in the plural of *prima principia legis naturae*. In q. 94, art. 6, co., he contrasts *praecepta communissima*, which he shortly afterwards refers to as *illa principia communia*, with *secundaria praecpta magis propria*. Following Grisez, I shall reserve the expression "the first principle of practical reason," in the singular, for the foundational gerundive, "Good is to be done, etc." The *praecepta communissima* that are identified at the end of *ST* 1–2 q. 94, co. (on the interpretation I propose above), I shall call "the primary precepts of natural law," or just "the primary precepts," so as to distinguish them both from the first principle of practical reason and from the secondary precepts. In what follows, I shall argue that whereas precepts, both primary and secondary, are properly obligatory, and can be disobeyed, the first principle of practical reason does not obligate in this sense, but naturally necessitates. It cannot be disobeyed, i.e., we cannot choose to do something that does not appear to be good in *any* respect.

10. Grisez, 195; See John Finnis, *NLNR* 33–36. At the beginning of the *corpus* of q. 94, art. 2, Thomas speaks of principles of demonstration, in the plural. A bit later in the *corpus* he says, citing Aristotle, that the indemonstrable principle of non-contradiction is the one on which the others are founded. The single principle, "Good is to be done . . . etc.," is to practical reason what the principle of non-contradiction is to speculative reason. We shall see in the following chapter that the first principle of practical reason is at work within the primary precepts of natural law, and that the latter are informed and animated by this principle, though, in Thomas's presentation, they are not deduced from it.

non-contradiction the first principle of practical reason would not be intelligible, and hence could not be acted upon rationally. Still, because the latter cannot be deduced from the former, or from any other declarative proposition or combination of such propositions, it has to count as a first principle as well. Human reason guides both thinking and acting, and it does so by employing principles of its own. Thomas would find it odd were someone to concede, say, on the authority of Aristotle, that natural reason operates in the light of its own self-evident and exceptionless principles in the speculative sphere but were to deny that it operates in the light of its own self-evident and exceptionless principles in the practical sphere.

It is not difficult to show that, although the highest principles of speculative and practical reason cannot be demonstrated, unwelcome consequences follow from the denial of either. One can vocally deny the principle of non-contradiction, for instance, but one cannot think without implicitly affirming it. In denying the principle of non-contradiction—the principle that one cannot meaningfully affirm and deny the same proposition at once—one assumes that one is not, in the very act of denying this principle, also affirming it. Much the same is true, though less obviously, of the principle of excluded middle and, more obviously, of the principle of propositional identity.[11] Similarly, one can vocally deny the principle that good is to be done and pursued, and evil avoided, but one cannot act either well or badly, or at all, without relying on it. Thomas would say that one cannot use terms such as "should" and "ought" without some reference, if only implicit, back to this principle, without which these terms would be deprived of all sense. The natural interest of reason is then twofold: what is *simpliciter* and what is to be done, in theory and practice respectively, and the truth pertaining to each.

It might seem that acting in accordance with the first principle of practical reason is a matter of obligation. But it is not. For one cannot freely choose to act in opposition to this principle; and free choice pertains to the very nature of obligation. Man is no more obligated, strictly speaking, to act in accordance with the first principle of practical reason than water is obligated to flow downhill. It is a matter of natural necessity in the former case as much as it is in the latter, though in the former case the necessity is not, so to speak, blind.[12] It is simply how man's natural reason has to operate when

11. What I am calling "propositional identity" is sometimes called "reiteration." The principle of propositional identity is the always taken-for-granted principle that a proposition, throughout its multiple iterations, remains identical to itself whether the proposition happens to be true *or* false. A new context may invest one or more of the terms in a proposition with new meaning, and when this happens in the course of an argument the result is a paralogism. But one can recognize a change in the meaning of a term, or a proposition, only if the original one remains available in its self-identity for consideration and comparison.

12. Thomas's formulation that *dicitur enim lex a ligando, quia obligat ad agendum* holds most obviously for natural law, human law, and divine law. It is clear from the context of this formulation (ST 1–2, q. 90, art. 1, co.) that Thomas has the rational creature principally in mind. The way in which eternal law governs sub-rational creatures is different. They are bound to be sure, but they are not obligated in the way Thomas typically uses the expressions *obligare* and *obligatio*. See the definitions

applied to action. We cannot aim at anything unless it presents itself to us as in some respect good. Even people planning to commit suicide, whether or not they believe in a hereafter, have been known to say that they would be *better* off dead than alive. It is hardly imaginable that anyone planning to commit suicide has ever given as his reason for doing so that he thought he would be *worse* off dead than alive. In starting with the *ratio boni*, "Good is what all desire," Thomas grounds himself in the tradition of Plato and Aristotle, who understand human choice and action to aim of necessity at something good, whether it is truly good or only appears to be good.[13]

When Thomas immediately transforms the *ratio boni* into the first principle of practical reason, "Good is to be done and pursued, and evil avoided," he does not move straight from what is actually the case (the so-called Is) to what is properly obligatory (the so-called Ought). He only begins to move in this direction.

SECTION B. THE PRECEPTS OF NATURAL LAW

i. The order of natural inclinations

Because we naturally desire what is good, we cannot choose anything for ourselves unless it presents itself under the aspect of the good, whether it is good or bad in reality. If there were only one good, it would be done or pursued as a matter of necessity.[14] Similarly, if there were only one evil, it would be avoided as a matter of necessity. However, as Thomas says in q. 94 art. 2, we have a multiplicity of inclinations coordinated with a multiplicity of goods. And these have the character of ends: according to the nature we share with inanimate entities, the inclination to self-preservation; according to the nature we share with sub-rational animals, the inclination to sexual union and the bringing up (*educatio*) of our offspring;[15] and according to the nature

and citations for these terms that Roy Deferrari gives in *A Lexicon of Saint Thomas Aquinas*, 753–4. Consider *ST* 1 q. 19 art. 10, co: "Non enim ad liberum arbitrium pertinet quod volumus esse felices, sed ad naturalem instinctum." We will happiness, according to Thomas, not freely but as a matter of necessity. And since we cannot will anything unless it appears good to us in *some* respect, we also will good, whether real or only apparent, as a matter of necessity. (See 1–2 q. 8 art. 1, co.; and compare q. 10 art. 2, co.). Such willing is for us a matter of *instinctus naturalis*. It is a matter of *natural* necessity; and, as we shall see, it is distinct from what is sometimes called "moral necessity." In understanding the will as the appetite of reason, we can see how a rational being could will some things necessarily and other things freely. For Thomas this is true of both God and man. *ST* 1 q. 19 art. 3, art. 10; q. 82 art. 1; art. 2; q. 83 art. 1. Speculative reason can entertain possibilities, even without regard to action. Practical reason can not only entertain possibilities, but can command the actualization of some to the exclusion of others.

13. *ST* 1–2 q. 1 art. 6; Plato, *Meno* 77b-e; see *Republic* 438a; Aristotle, *Nicomachean Ethics* 1097a19; 1114a30–b25; 1145b21–1147b18.

14. *DeMalo* q. 6 art. 1, co. Because real happiness, as Thomas (unlike Kant) understands it, is an end that is good in every respect, we will it not through free choice but necessarily (even if, as is often the case, we do not adequately understand it). It follows that if we could discern only one means to this end, we would also will it necessarily.

15. No matter how successful molecular biology might become in understanding organic

of reason itself, which is proper to our humanity. Inclinations are always inclinations *toward* something. The "toward which" of an inclination is its end.[16] That end may also be a means to something else, or it may be an end absolutely and not a means to anything else whatsoever.

The various natural inclinations that we have can come into conflict with each other. When this happens, we have to choose which ones to follow. But these inclinations are not a mere multiplicity. Thomas says that they have an order (or rank, *ordo*) and that the order of the precepts of natural law reflects this order.[17] At the top of this order, and higher than inclinations such as self-preservation and procreation, which we share with sub-rational beings, is our inclination to know the truth about God and to live in society.[18] This inclination is natural as well, though it is specific to us as rational animals.

processes in non-teleological terms, to deny that sub-human animals have ends is to deny that they have inclinations, and that means to deny that they have desires of any sort. We have an immediate awareness of our desires and we have an immediate awareness that we are oriented towards ends as the objects of these desires. Nothing natural science would ever be able to find out could cast the slightest doubt upon this immediate awareness. We do not have the same kind of awareness of the desires that we understand sub-rational animals to possess. We infer, after a fashion, that they—the higher animals, anyway—have desires analogous to some of our desires, from behavior that is analogous to some of our behavior. This inference cannot be seriously undermined by what biologists observe to be taking place at the level of bio-chemistry and neurophysiology. We could be confident that sub-rational animals have no desires at all, and are not oriented toward ends in any way, only if we could enter into their modes of awareness exactly as they possess them—which would mean leaving behind all of our own experience, including our thinking and our discourse—and, on doing so, discover the absence of all desire; and then report this finding back to human beings, in the form of a proposition, no less. Such a thing is both unthinkable and unimaginable since apart from other considerations there would, on this hypothesis, no longer be even a desire to report back our "discovery."

16. On the epistemological question of how we know the natural inclinations and their order, see Brock "Natural Inclination and the Intelligibility of the Good." For a comprehensive account of the natural inclinations themselves see *Sources*, 400–456. Fr. Pinckaers stresses that the inclinations to self-preservation and sexual union, which we share with sub-rational beings, can take on a distinctively human character, and thereby become ennobled (423–6 and 437–47). While not disagreeing with Fr. Pinckaers on this point, I stress the other side of the matter, namely, that acting on these inclinations can on occasion come into conflict with acting according to reason. As I shall argue in the sequel, it is the possibility of a conflict in certain situations between the inclinations that we share with sub-rational beings and the inclinations that are proper to us as rational beings that gives rise to obligation in the strict sense of the word.

17. "Secundum igitur ordinem inclinationum naturalium, est ordo praeceptorum legis naturae." *ST* 1–2 q. 94 art. 2, co. The order of the one follows the order of the other. But what is ordered, i.e., inclinations and precepts, are not the same. For some other places where Thomas relates precepts to inclinations without identifying them, see *SCG* lib. 3 cap. 136 n. 14; *ST* 1–2 q. 101 art. 3, co.; q. 108 art. 3, arg. 5; 2–2 q. 22 art. 1, arg. 1; ad 1; q. 79 art. 2, ad 2.

18. When speaking in what follows of the inclination to know the truth about God and to live in society, I shall occasionally have to speak of them as two distinct inclinations. But it should be noted that Thomas sees them as intimately related. For at the end of the *corpus* of q. 94 at. 2, he speaks of them, repeatedly, as one inclination to good: "inest homini *inclinatio* ad bonum secundum naturam rationis . . . homo habet naturalem *inclinationem* ad hoc quod veritatem cognoscat de Deo, et ad hoc quod in societate vivat . . . ea quae ad huiusmodi *inclinationem* spectant . . . et cetera huiusmodi quae ad hoc spectant." (Emphasis added.)

The inclination to know the truth about God does not presuppose that God actually exists, only that we want to know whether he exists or not. Even the committed atheist has to concede this much. At the most elementary level, the inclination to know the truth about God is simply the inclination of a rational being to know the ultimate cause or causes of things. If a rational being concludes that God does exist, then he also wants to know how we and our world are related to him. But the inclination itself presupposes neither a demonstration of God's existence nor belief in God's existence. It is present in all rational beings, granted that in many of them it does not give rise to much in the way of serious and sustained inquiry.

Regarding the inclination to live in society, we note that, for Thomas, it must mean more than a mere inclination to procreate, for we share the latter inclination with sub-rational beings. And, for the same reason, the inclination to live in society must mean more than a mere inclination to congregate in herds with others of the same species. In what follows, we shall return more than once to the question of what Thomas means by living in society.

From our natural inclination to know the truth about God and to live in society, Thomas derives the content that enables him, at the conclusion of the *corpus* of q. 94 art. 2, to transform the otherwise merely formal gerundive, "Good is to be done, etc.," into two concrete precepts that he regards as *per se nota*, and these are characterized by genuine moral obligation as distinct from natural necessity of any kind. They are (1) that one avoid ignorance, and (2) that one not offend others with whom one is bound to live.[19] These two precepts I shall speak of as "primary precepts," in order to distinguish them from what Thomas later calls "secondary precepts."

ii. Primary and secondary precepts

In one of the best books on the subject, R. A. Armstrong's *Primary and Secondary Precepts in Thomistic Natural Law Teaching*, the author writes as follows.

> We have indicated the different categories of inclinations possessed by man and shown that corresponding to each category there exists a principle of a very general kind, the truth of which is able to be grasped by all normal

19. Thomas West writes, "From the point of view of reason, as Aquinas describes it, the natural law comes to be known not as a series of commandments, but only as natural instincts or inclinations observed by the human mind and then turned into precepts or rules of action by practical reason" (*Critique of the 'Straussian' Critique*, 28; see. 29–30). West does not explain how practical reason turns inclinations into actual precepts; nor does he explain how he understands a precept (*praeceptum*) to differ from a commandment (*imperium*). See *ST* 1–2 q. 90 art. 2, ad 1: *praeceptum importat applicationem legis ad ea quae ex lege regulantur*; q. 108 art. 4, co.: *haec est differentia inter consilium et praeceptum, quod praeceptum importat necessitatem, consilium autem in optione ponitur eius cui datur.* (The necessity that Thomas speaks of here is moral necessity, not natural or irresistible necessity.) See 1–2 q. 90 art. 2, ad 1; q. 17 art. 1, 4–6. See also q. 92 art. 2, arg. 1: *Sed idem est imperare quod praecipere.* Thomas Aquinas does not take issue with this formulation in his reply. He employs a similar formulation in the *corpus* of this article, as he also does in q. 90 art. 1, *sed contra*.

> people. These principles we listed as follows; "One ought to respect and preserve not only human life, but where possible, all life," "the sexual relationship requires some form of regulation," "the family group ought to comply with some fixed pattern" and "We ought to live together in obedience to certain rules and regulations." These, we suggest, comprise the class of self-evident, natural law precepts.[20]

I do not take issue with Armstrong's claim that the precepts he lists here belong in some sense to natural law. But I do not think that they can be simply read off the natural inclinations listed in q. 94 art. 2. Perhaps Armstrong does not think this either, though I infer that he does because the order in which he lists these precepts follows the order in which Thomas presents the natural inclinations. In any case, Armstrong does not undertake a close examination of q. 94 art. 2. His focus, as he says, is on q. 94 articles 4–6, because he is mainly concerned with the question of how primary and secondary precepts are to be distinguished, rather than with the question of what constitutes a precept as such.[21] Armstrong's treatment of the former question is thorough and convincing, and we shall consider his findings shortly. But the passage quoted above is somewhat misleading. For if we ignore the last precept that Armstrong mentions, which is a kind of restatement of the second of the two precepts that Thomas presents at the end of the *corpus* of q. 94 art. 2,[22] and if we restrict our attention to the inclinations we have with sub-rational beings, the precepts most directly corresponding to them would seem to be not the ones Armstrong has listed but something like the following: "Preserve thyself," "Procreate," and "Train thine offspring." And yet these precepts cannot be primary precepts since they admit of exceptions. If the only way one could preserve oneself were by, say, deliberately killing an innocent human being, then the precept pertaining to self-preservation would get eclipsed by the precept forbidding offense against another human being.[23] The precept pertaining to

20. *PSP* 50; see 125–9; 181–2. Armstrong sometimes reformulates the beginning of the first principle of practical reason as "good ought to be done" (e.g., 91; 129; 181; cf. 98). I think that "ought" is not the best word here since, as I argue above, pursuing the good in general is not a matter of moral obligation but of natural, though not blind, necessity. This pursuit is intrinsic to the very operation of practical reason. In spite of the use of the word "ought" in his reformulation of the first principle of practical reason, Armstrong recognizes that the force of this principle differs from that of the concrete precepts of natural law. "[W]hile there is a necessity for the good in general, there is no necessity (as exists at the natural level) to seek for this or that particular good" (*PSP* 29). Thomas A. Fay in "The Development of St. Thomas's Teaching on the Distinction between Primary and Secondary Precepts of Natural Law," 262–72) gives a list of principles (269) similar to the list that Armstrong gives.

21. *PSP* 87–89.

22. Because the first of the two primary precepts that Thomas presents at the end of the *corpus* of q. 94, art.2, namely, the precept commanding us to avoid ignorance, is based on the natural inclination to know the truth about God, Armstrong thinks—wrongly, for reasons I give above—that it presupposes the actual existence of God. He therefore concludes that it cannot be self-evident (*PSP* 49), contrary to what Thomas explicitly says about primary precepts. A more difficult problem, which I address in Part 2, Ch. 8, below, concerns the precept commanding us to love and worship God.

23. See *ST* 2–2 q. 69. See also Schrock, "Resistance to Punishment," 91–126.

procreation is similarly subordinated to this precept forbidding offense. To take an extreme example, one is not permitted to rape even if, in a particular case, this happened to be the only way in which one could procreate. Nor, according to Thomas, is one permitted to procreate through adultery. And, of course, an entirely celibate life dedicated to the service of God is permissible in Thomas's eyes, and hence not contrary to natural law. Finally, the precept pertaining to the upbringing or training of one's offspring cannot be rationally complied with by offending others, as, for example, by stealing textbooks to use for the education of one's children. The sub-rational inclinations do not generate genuine precepts except when ruled by reason. As Thomas says, "[A]ll the inclinations of whatsoever parts of human nature, for example, of the concupiscible part and the irascible part, *insofar as they are ruled by reason*, pertain to natural law, and are reduced to one primary precept."[24]

That there is an order of the natural inclinations to self-preservation, to sexual procreation, and to education of offspring does not mean that, though ranking below the inclination to know the truth about God and to live in society, they are not also inclinations to what is good for us as human beings. All these inclinations aim at goods, at goods that are naturally knowable to us and perfect human life. But the goods at which the sub-rational inclinations aim are not unqualified goods. Only the goods at which the rational inclination aims are unqualified goods.

But how do the actual, concrete precepts of natural law, as distinct from both the first principle of practical reason and the natural inclinations towards goods as ends, make their appearance in Thomas's presentation? In q. 94, art. 2, Thomas says, regarding the natural inclination to preserve oneself, that "those things that preserve human life and impede the contrary pertain to natural law."[25] But he does not at this point name anything that could be called a precept or that could even be converted immediately into a precept. Similarly, he says, regarding the inclinations to procreate and train one's offspring, that "those things are said to be of the natural law that nature teaches all animals, such as the conjunction of male and female, and the education of

24. 1–2 q. 94 art. 2, ad 2 (emphasis added in the above translation): "omnes inclinationes quarumcumque partium humanae naturae, puta concupiscibilis et irascibilis, secundum quod regulantur ratione, pertinent ad legem naturalem, et reducuntur ad unum primum principium."

25. *ST* 1–2 q. 94 art. 2, co.: "Et secundum hanc inclinationem, pertinent ad legem naturalem ea per quae vita hominis conservatur, et contrarium impeditur." Armstrong's formulation, "One ought to respect and preserve not only human life, but where possible, all life" (*PSP* 50), is a bit ambiguous. We destroy the lives of animals and plants in the process of preserving ourselves—most obviously when we eat them. I assume that with his qualification, "where possible," Armstrong means that we should not destroy even sub-human life thoughtlessly and wantonly. There is nothing to quarrel with about that.

children."[26] Again, he does not at this point state anything like a precept. [27] Things are different, however, when he speaks of the inclination proper to our rational nature. There he says "those things pertain to natural law that refer to the [aforesaid inclination]: such as *that* man avoid ignorance, *that* he not offend others with whom he is bound to live, and other such things that refer to this."[28]

One might respond that the formulations "that man avoid . . . etc." and "that he not offend . . . etc." are not exactly precepts either. True. But they do not name an inclination merely; they have a propositional form that permits them to be transformed immediately into precepts, either in the gerundive or the imperative mode, and that is not true of the previous statements regarding our natural inclinations. The formulations "those things that preserve human life," "the conjunction of male and female," and "the education of children" do not have a propositional form. It is not possible to transform them immediately into precepts. The propositional form, needless to say, is the work of reason.

The two precepts mandating, first, that one avoid ignorance and, second, that one not offend others with whom one is bound to live concern the operation of speculative and practical reason respectively, and hence reflect the two constituents of natural, or this-worldly, happiness that Thomas has earlier identified. Of the two precepts, the former rationally governs one's relation to oneself, that is, to the operation of one's speculative reason.[29] The latter rationally governs one's relation to others. The latter

26. *ST* 1–2 q. 94 art. 2, co: "Et secundum hoc, dicuntur ea esse de lege naturali *quae natura omnia animalia docuit* . . . ut est coniunctio maris et feminae, et educatio liberorum , et simila." Thomas does *not* say here, or even imply, that sub-rational animals are governed by natural law; for doing so would be at odds with his definition of natural law. What nature teaches all animals, it necessarily teaches human beings. But only in the case of human beings does what nature teaches all animals pertain to natural law. See ST q. 91 art. 2, ad 3.

27. A blurring of the distinction between natural inclinations and precepts of natural law recurs with some frequency in the scholarship. For example, Fergus Kerr writes, "Though Thomas sometimes speaks of 'precepts' it is more usual for him to refer to 'inclinations'. . . . When he considers the 'content,' or the 'extent' or 'the order of the precepts of the natural law' he equates it with the 'order of the natural inclinations . . . '" "Natural Law: Incommensurable Readings," 255. Fr. Kerr is surely right that, for Thomas, the order of the precepts of natural law follows the order of man's natural inclinations. But a precept is something quite different from an inclination, and Thomas does not use them interchangeably. Moreover, it is not more usual for Thomas to refer to inclinations than to precepts. In *ST* 1–2 q. 90–97, Thomas uses *praecepta* about five times as frequently as he uses *inclinationes*. In his *oeuvre* taken as a whole, there are (according to the Index of the on-line *Corpus Thomisticum*) some 2000 occurrences of *praecepta* and 63 occurrences of *inclinationes*; and there is a comparable ratio between the occurrence of these two words in the other cases of the plural and in the singular. Clifford J. Kossel also seems to misidentify the precepts with the inclinations themselves. ("Natural Law and Human Law," 75, bottom of left hand column to top of right hand column). Fr. Kossel's oversight on this matter does not keep his short essay from being as clear a *précis* of Thomas's natural law teaching as any available in English.

28. *ST* 1 q. 94 art. 2, co. (emphasis added): Et secundum hoc, ad legem naturalem pertinent ea quae ad huiusmodi inclinationem spectant: utpote quod homo ingnoratiam vitet, quod alios non offendat cum quibus debet conservarsi, et cetera huiusmodi quae ad hoc pertinent.

29. Avoiding ignorance or, put positively, pursuing knowledge is, *qua* operation, an action in the

precept appears to be the more problematic of the two, since acting in accordance with it could cause one to forgo the single-minded pursuit of self-interest, narrowly understood; and in extreme situations it could require one to act in opposition to other natural inclinations specifically mentioned by Thomas, most obviously self-preservation. Thomas's Latin reads, "*quod homo . . . alios non offendat cum quibus debet conversari, et cetera huiusmodi quae ad hoc spectant*." There are three points here that need some clarification.

(1) The word *offendere* (literally, "to strike against") does not mean simply to offend in the contemporary sense of to annoy or irritate, but to commit an *offense* against, as I have used the expression above: to harm, or attempt to harm, without provocation or out of proportion to prior harm received. The English legal expression, "the offender," preserves this sense of *offendere*.

(2) The phrase "*alios non offendat cum quibus debet conversari*" has been translated by some as "to avoid offending those with whom one has to live."[30] The rendering of *alios* as "those," rather than, more literally, as "others," is misleading because it gives the impression that the following "*cum quibus*" clause is restrictive rather than non-restrictive. But in a similar passage, where Thomas speaks of man as ordered to the rule of reason, to divine law, and to other men, he writes of the last of these, "*ideo necesse . . . quo homo ordinetur ad alios homines, quibus convivere debet.*"[31] Since the "*quibus*" clause here is clearly non-restrictive, the "*cum quibus*" clause in q. 94 art. 2 can plausibly be inferred to be non-restrictive as well. For not only does "*cum quibus . . .* etc." make more sense as a non-restrictive clause when modifying *alios*, but, more importantly, an obligation not to offend others, including those among whom one does *not* live, is required for Thomas's defense of the concept of just war.[32]

(3) I translate *debet conversari* as "is bound to live." But it is also possible to translate the phrase as "ought to live." In fact, that is the first translation of *debet conversari* that comes to mind, though "has to live" and "must live," along with "is bound to live," are possible too. If *debet conversari* is translated as "ought to live," then the whole clause would read: "that one not offend others with whom one ought to live." On this reading, the most fundamental precept regarding our relation to our fellow men would appear to be that we live with them, rather than that we not offend them. And yet, in the preceding sentence, living in society is said to be a matter, not of precept, but of inclination. This fact does not by itself preclude living in society from

---

broad sense of the word. Otherwise, it could not be mandated by a precept.

30. The English Dominican Fathers in *St. Thomas Aquinas—Summa Theologica* Volume II, 1009–10. Anton Pegis retains this translation in *The Basic Writings of Thomas Aquinas*, Volume II, 775.

31. *ST* 1–2 q. 72 art. 4, co. I take *conversari* and *convivere* as meaning essentially the same thing, i.e., not just to live physically *surrounded by* others, but to live *with* others, that is, to have to substantive relations with them.

32. *ST* 2–2 q. 40 art. 1; compare with art. 3. See my article, "Christianity and Force: The Just War Tradition." (The word "philosophies" on page 246 is the publisher's or the editor's modification; it should be "forces" instead.)

being both something we are inclined to do and something we are commanded by a precept to do. However, as I see it, a significant parallelism holds in the articulation of the two primary precepts presented in q. 94 art. 2. The inclination to know the truth about God, in combination with the first principle of practical reason, constitutes the precept that one avoid ignorance.[33] The inclination and the precept are closely related. But they differ in concept (*ratio*), as tendency and proposition, respectively. An inclination is not obligatory; a precept, on the other hand, is obligatory. Similarly, as I interpret this passage, the inclination to live in society, in combination with the first principle of practical reason, constitutes the precept that one not offend others with whom one is bound to live. Here, again, inclination and precept differ in both concept and content. This parallelism, which I think Thomas intended, would be lost if the second of the two primary precepts identified in q. 94 art. 2 were, not that one not offend, but that one live with others. The inclination and the precept would still differ in concept. But they would not differ in content, since to live (*vivere*) in society and to live (*conversari*) with others mean essentially the same thing. It is for this reason, and for others that will become clear in what follows, that I regard to the two primary precepts of natural law presented in q. 94 art. 2 as mandating (a) avoidance of ignorance and (b) not offending others, rather than as (a) avoidance of ignorance and (b) living (*conversari*) with others. Nothing really critical turns on this, however. For if a primary precept of natural law mandates living with others, then it mandates not offending them as well, since *offendere alios* is incompatible with *conversari cum aliis*. A precept mandating that one not offend others would follow at once (*statim*) from a precept mandating that one live with others.[34] So whether *debet*, in the clause *quod homo . . . alios non offendat cum quibus debet conversari, et cetera huiusmodi quae ad hoc spectant*, is translated as "ought" or as "is bound," Thomas is articulating a primary precept of natural law that refers back to a fundamental and natural inclination proper to us as rational beings.

There is, however, a further consideration that weighs, decisively I think, in favor of regarding the second of the two primary precepts presented in q. 94 art. 2 as mandating, not that we live with others, but that we not offend them, and against regarding the latter as following even *statim* from the former as from a yet higher precept. For a few questions later, Thomas presents *quod nulli debet homo malefacere* ("man ought to do evil to no one") as a precept and, moreover, as something that is *per se notum*.[35]

33. I shall have more to say in this section and the following section about the way in which the first principle of practical reason is combined with a natural inclination so as to constitute a precept of natural law. I shall show that it is not a matter of simple logical deduction from premises to a conclusion, but of explicating the meaning of an obligatory precept, itself *per se nota* and, hence, not demonstrable.

34. *ST* 1–2 q. 100 art. 1, co; art. 3, co.; art. 5, ad 4. See 1–2 q. 95 art. 2, ad 4.

35. 1–2 q. 100 art. 3, co. See q. 95 art.2: "*nulli esse malum faciendum*." I understand these two formulations to be equivalent both to each other and to the formulation in q. 94 art. 2: "*quod homo . . . alios non offendat cum quibus debet conversari*."

Since being *per se notum* is what distinguishes a primary precept of natural law from a secondary precept, *quod nulli debet homo malefacere* is clearly a primary precept of natural law. But it does not differ substantively from the precept *quod homo . . . alios non offendat cum quibus debet conversari*, unless one takes the clause, *cum quibus debet conversari,* as restrictive, in which case the precept, *quod nulli debet homo malefacere,* removes the restriction.[36] So we can infer that in q. 94 art. 2 Thomas is presenting the precept *quod homo . . . alios non offendat cum quibus debet conversari* as a primary precept of natural law, and not as derived from a higher precept. When I speak of the two primary precepts presented in q. 94 art. 2 in what follows, I shall always mean the precept that one avoid ignorance and the precept that one not offend others among whom one is bound to live.

Regarding Thomas's distinction between primary and secondary precepts, Armstrong concludes, on the basis of his investigation of the relevant texts, that they can be ordered as follows:

1. Primary precepts—*per se nota.*
2. Secondary precepts.
    a. Not *per se nota*, but arrived at by a logical *demonstratio.*
        i. deduced after slight consideration (*modica consideratione*).
        ii. deduced after much consideration (*multa consideratione*).
    b. Neither *per se nota* nor arrived at by *demonstratio*, but arrived at by *determinatio.*[37]

I have argued that the primary precepts include the negatively formulated but nonetheless concrete precepts presented at the end of the *corpus* of 1. 94 art. 2, namely, to avoid ignorance and not offend others; and I shall soon argue that they include positively formulated expansions as well. These two precepts declare moral obligations in spite of their breadth. The very fact that the primary precepts of natural law can serve as premises for *demonstrationes* of secondary precepts is a sign that their breadth is not equivalent to emptiness.[38]

36. If, taking the *cum quibus* clause in the earlier formulation as restrictive, one were to hold—quite mistakenly I think—that the formulation there expressed not so much a moral obligation as a "merely prudential" directive only, the later formulation, *quod nulli debet homo malefacere,* is unequivocally moral.

37. *PSP* 124–138. On the distinction between *demonstratio* and *determinatio,* see also Robert George, "Natural Law."

38. Thomas calls the primary precepts *praecepta communissima* (1–2 q. 94 art. 6, co.). Though they are already concrete, in a way that the first principle of practical reason is not, they are the basis for expansion and for derivation of secondary precepts by way of both *demonstratio* and *determinatio.* (Cf. q. 94, art. 4, arg. 2; co.; ad 2.) According to Daniel Mark Nelson, "prudence and virtue have priority over natural law in Thomas's account of moral understanding." *The Priority of Prudence*, 70. This claim is false except as regards the actual sequence of Thomas's presentation, where virtue in general is considered prior to natural law (though it should be remembered that he treats *synderesis* in *ST* 1,

The secondary precepts that are arrived at by *demonstratio* are divided into those that can be reached with slight consideration and those that require much consideration. *Demonstratio* is a logical procedure. The more remote the secondary precepts are, the more particular and varied are the circumstances in which they are operative. These circumstances, and the manifold contingencies with which they are bound up, must be taken into account, and the possibility of occasional exceptions to the more remote secondary precepts arises. At that point, practical wisdom, including experience, judgment, and prudence, must come fully into play.

Armstrong concludes that the secondary precepts arrived at by *determinatio* are the precepts of human positive law. They include such things as "Drive on the right side of the road," "Register for the draft at age 18," "File your income taxes by April 15," and so forth. Because such precepts have something arbitrary (though not simply irrational) in them—right side of the road, age 18, April 15—they cannot be strictly deduced from the primary precepts or even from the secondary precepts arrived at by *demonstratio*. Secondary precepts that are arrived at by *demonstratio* are often codified in human positive law. But only those arrived at by *determinatio* are specific to human positive law.

It is frequently said that Thomas does not present his natural law precepts as propositions in a formally deductive system. This is true in the literal sense: he does not simply state the indemonstrable primary precepts and then at once set about demonstrating all the secondary precepts that can be derived from them, expressly supplying the pertinent minor premises in each case. But, though Thomas does not give us a deductive system of moral principles, he does give us a way of distinguishing between the various precepts of natural law that is as true to the evidence and operation of practical reason as one could ask for. He does not relativize, in the least, the primary precepts that are known by *synderesis* and the secondary precepts that are derivable from them *modica consideratione*. Nor does he inordinately absolutize those secondary precepts that are derivable from the primary precepts only *multa consideratione*. Much less does he inordinately absolutize precepts arrived at by *determinatio*.

Derivation of secondary precepts by way of *demonstratio*, as distinct from *determinatio*, is manifestly a deductive process. Thomas says, for example, that "one should not murder" may be derived as a conclusion from the principle "evil is to be done to no one."[39] This enthymeme can be expressed as a syllogism:

but the virtues, including prudence, in *ST* 1–2 and 2–2 .). Nelson says that knowledge of the primary precepts of natural law is "insignificant with respect to guiding action" (103; see 65), that they "provide no guidance for our conduct" (100), and that they "do not help us know what to do" (114). Nelson depreciates the concept of natural law more than anyone I know of who seems to be otherwise in general agreement with Thomas Aquinas, with the possible exception of E. A. Goerner, whose interpretation of natural law I shall speak to in Part 2, Ch. 3, below.

39. *ST* 1–2 q. 95 art. 2, co: "Derivantur ergo quaedam a principiis communibus legis naturae per modum conclusionum, sicut hoc quod est non esse occidendum, ut conclusio quaedam derivari potest ab eo quod est nulli esse malum faciendum."

One should not do evil (to anyone).
To murder is to do evil (to someone).
One should not murder.

The major premise is *per se notum* and known by *synderesis*.[40] The minor premise is a subsumption that is accomplished in an act of judgment. The conclusion is a necessary inference accomplished by discursive reasoning from the two preceding premises. It is through this procedure that *synderesis* is applied to action. And since conscience is the act of which *synderesis* is the habit, Thomas can say that the conclusion of this deductive process is known by conscience.[41] The only questionable element in the deductive process is the judgment that gives us the minor premise. If a person cannot see that murder, the deliberate slaying of an innocent human being, is a case of doing evil to someone, Thomas would rightly say that there is something wrong with his intellect. But, though this judgment can be made by everyone who has reached the age of reason and whose intellect is not grossly compromised, other judgments are not so easy to make. Consider the following *minor* premises, and the necessary conclusions (which are too obvious to require spelling out) that they would generate when taken together with the *major* premise, "One should not do evil (to anyone)":

"To abort a fetus is to do evil."
"To target non-combatants, even in conducting a just war, is to do evil."
"To use deadly force in self-defense is to do evil."
"To refuse to return a deposit kept in trust is to do evil."
"To levy a tax on income that has already been taxed is to do evil."
"To execute a convicted murderer is to do evil."

It is clear that some of these subsumptions under the broad class of doing evil are controversial. Different people affirm some of them but deny others. That does not mean, however, that the act of judgment is the expression of a merely personal prejudice. For we argue with one another about these things. And the very fact that we argue is a sufficient sign that we are convinced that reason has something to say about them. Furthermore, when, as sometimes happens, we change our minds about these things, we do so presumably because we think we have good reasons for doing so.

40. I take *nulli esse malum faciendum* as equivalent to what is expressed in the formulation *alios non offendat cum quibus debet conversari*, as I have interpreted *offendere* above. If the two formulations are not equivalent, the former can be deduced from the latter *modica consideratione*.

41. I have simplified the account of this kind of reasoning that Thomas gives in his early *Scriptum super Sententiis*, though only slightly and without distorting anything essential to it. (See Lib. 2 d. 24 q. 2 art. 4, co.) What I am here calling the act of judgment Thomas there calls reason, distinguishing between higher and lower reason, both of which involve the subsuming of something particular under something more universal. Thomas recognizes that judgment is an act of reason (see *ST* 1–2 q. 100 art. 1, co.); and he holds *synderesis* itself to be the habitual knowledge of the self-evident principles of practical reason (*ST* 1 q. 79 art. 12). The whole deductive process in the practical syllogism is then the work of reason, though of reason functioning in different ways.

iii. Self-evidence

The reasoning that culminates in the presentation of the primary and properly obligatory precepts in q. 94 art. 2 is not purely deductive. It is for this reason that I speak of Thomas's *case* for natural law. The case he makes is explicative rather than demonstrative. His way of proceeding is consistent with his claim early in the *corpus* of this article that the (primary) precepts of natural law are self-evident.[42]

An example of a self-evident proposition that Thomas cites early in the *corpus* of q. 94 art. 2, is "Man is a rational animal." In this proposition, the predicate "rational" is clearly included in the *ratio* of the subject.[43] But this proposition is not an altogether adequate model for a primary precept of natural law. Steven Jensen, in a paper entitled "How are the First Precepts *Per Se Nota*?",[44] argues persuasively that the predicate of a primary precept of natural law is not included in the *ratio* of its subject, not, that is, as what he identifies as a "component part" of the subject. Consider the precept, "that

42. Note the plural in the first sentence of ST 1–2 q. 94 art. 2, co. It is not only the first principle of practical reason that is *per se notum*. The primary precepts presented at the end of the *corpus* are *per se nota* as well. A qualification is required here however. These precepts are self-evident *given the lawful ordering of things that is nature as we know it through natural reason and ordinary human experience.* Now, if Thomas is right in arguing that God's existence, wisdom, omnipotence, and (*pace* Aristotle and Spinoza) freedom of choice are demonstrable, it follows that we can naturally know that another ordering is possible (see *ST* q. 25 art. 6, ad 3.), though we cannot naturally know what its character would be. God could, however, freely *reveal* it to man. But since the particular content of what God has freely revealed or could reveal to man—assuming that it contradicts neither itself nor anything else indubitably known—is not the target of the *philosophical* critique of natural law undertaken by Strauss and his followers, it is irrelevant to any response to that critique that also assumes, as does the present study, only what is accessible to man as man. Accordingly, I shall ignore this possibility, except when I return to it briefly in Part 2, Ch. 8, *Note*: Duns Scotus on what is *per se notum* in natural law.

43. The same is true of the other examples of *per se nota* propositions that Thomas gives early in q. 94 art. 2. In this article he makes a distinction, which he also makes elsewhere, between what is self-evident in itself (*per se notum secundum se*) and what is self-evident to us (*per se notum quoad nos*). In general, a proposition is said to be self-evident whose predicate is included in the very concept, or meaning, of the subject (*cuius praedicatum est de ratione subiecti*). A proposition that is self-evident in itself, and recognized as such by those who know the meaning of the terms, is not self-evident to someone who does not know the meaning of the terms. It is not clear exactly how this distinction bears on what Thomas says later in the *corpus* of this article, since he does not explicitly advert back to it. It is unlikely that he thinks that the principle of non-contradiction is not self-evident to all, or that the first principle of practical reason is not self-evident to all, though he is aware that only those who are thoughtful are able to articulate these principles. It is equally unlikely that he thinks the primary precepts are not self-evident to all. For he says of them that they (plural) are "equally known by all," that they are "the same for all, both as to rectitude and to knowledge," and that they "cannot be abolished from the heart of man." (ST 1 q. 94 art. 4, co.; art. 6, co). However, Thomas probably thinks with good reason that the full scope of a term, such as *offendere*, included in a practical proposition might be known only to the wise. In particular, everyone knows that it is wrong to offend others, in the sense of harming them without provocation or out of proportion to prior harm inflicted by them; but only those who are wise, that is, those who are perspicacious in judgment, are apt to know what constitutes offense in complex situations.

44. Presented at the 48th International Congress on Medieval Studies, May 12, 2013. Professor Jensen generously made this paper available to me.

man avoid ignorance" (*quod homo ignorantiam vitet*). Here the predicate, if simplified as "avoids ignorance," is not a component part of the subject "man." Man *as such* is rational.[45] But man *as such* does not avoid ignorance. After all, some human beings are more or less content to live in remediable ignorance regarding knowable and important matters.[46] And yet avoiding ignorance clearly has an intimate relationship to being "rational," and thereby to being a man as well. According to Jensen, the primary precepts of natural law are *per se nota* because their predicates are related to their subjects according to what Thomas specifies as the fourth mode of *per se* predication in his *Commentary on the Posterior Analytics*, as distinct from the first mode, which governs the way in which predicates are related to their subjects in simple declarative propositions, such as "Man is a rational animal." The predicate of a primary precept of natural law, however, is included in the *ratio* of its subject as what the subject is naturally *directed toward* (as good), or, correlatively, as what the subject is naturally *directed away from* (as evil). Because, as Thomas says, we have a natural inclination to know the truth about God and because this inclination is immediately cognized by us as good, and, furthermore, because ignorance manifestly frustrates this inclination, the imperatively expressed predicate "avoid ignorance" is included in the *ratio* of the subject "man," though not as a component part of it. Jensen's analysis is carefully reasoned and well-grounded in what Thomas has to say about *per se* predication. I recommend it to the reader.

In spite of Thomas's express statement that the primary precepts of natural law are *per se nota*, it is not uncommon to hear it objected that he has not really *demonstrated* these precepts. Indeed he has not. But that he has not done so cannot count as genuine objection. For what is *per se notum* cannot be properly demonstrated; it cannot be demonstrated without begging the question. Thomas's case for natural law and its *primary* precepts does not consist in deducing one thing from another. It

45. Douglas Kries (*PNL* 143, fn. 18) finds it odd that Thomas would claim, in q. 94 art. 2, co., that the proposition, "Man is rational," is self-evident, but only to those who know what man is (compare Aristotle, *Metaphysics* 1006b20), whereas the precept "I ought to pursue truth" is, for Thomas, "self-evident and recognized as such by everyone." Kries makes an interesting point. The proposition, "Man is rational," is indeed contested now and then, though typically on the sole grounds that some men think or act irrationally. Thomas, it should go without saying, would not deny that people often fail to think and act in full accordance with reason. But that fact does not undercut his claim that man is by nature a rational animal. Nature is not what takes place always without qualification, but what takes place always *if nothing obstructs* (*Physics* 199b25). Those who question the claim that man is rational can usually be brought to understand what Aristotle and Thomas mean, and they can usually be brought to concur in it. Neither Aristotle's claim that man by *nature* desires to know (*Metaphysics* 980a23) nor Thomas's claim that it is a *per se notum* precept of *natural* law that we should avoid ignorance is seriously undercut by observations about people whose thinking is temporarily obscured by a vehement passion, or by observations about children who have not yet reached the age of reason and adults who are retarded, insane, or comatose.

46. As a rational animal, man cannot help but take notice of curiosities that crop up in his experience of the world. But briefly attending to such things does not constitute genuine avoidance of ignorance. For the latter, the effort of study is required; and man often refrains from putting in this effort.

consists—as was noted above and will be further shown below—in explicating something relatively complex albeit *per se notum*, an obligatory precept of natural law, and analyzing it in terms of its simpler elements, namely, the first principle of practical reason and the order of natural inclinations. And though primary precepts of natural law by their very nature cannot be demonstrated, inconsistencies and other aberrations follow from the denial of these precepts.[47]

iv. Love of one's neighbor

In the last sentence of the *corpus* of q. 94 art. 2, after identifying the two primary precepts that pertain to our inclinations to know the truth about God and society, Thomas refers without elaboration to other things that pertain to this inclination (*et cetera huiusmodi quae ad hoc spectant*). What he has in mind are not only such precepts as "evil is to be done to no one," but also conversions of the negatively formulated primary precepts into the positive. The connection between the negatively formulated precept, "Avoid ignorance," and the positive, "Pursue knowledge," is tight. At the simplest level they are equivalent: one cannot avoid ignorance without pursuing knowledge; and one cannot pursue knowledge without avoiding ignorance.

The case is more complicated with the precept prohibiting offense. As positively formulated, it becomes the precept mandating love (*dilectio*) of one's neighbor, a precept that Thomas introduces in a later article and, perhaps surprisingly, also presents as self-evident.[48] However, the precept mandating love of one's neighbor is not equivalent to the precept prohibiting offense. Nor can we deduce it from the precept prohibiting offense. In trying to do so, we can express the precept that one not offend others, or just that one not offend one's neighbor, as, "Do not offend thy neighbor." And we can certainly use this as a major premise for a practical syllogism. But we also need a minor premise to generate the conclusion, "Love they neighbor." Two candidates for the minor (in different figures) that come to mind are, "Not to love thy neighbor is to offend him," and, "To not offend is to love." These two propositions, however, are not only more dubious than the major, they are more dubious than the intended conclusion, "Love thy neighbor," as well. So, rather than try to *demonstrate* this precept, let

47. See Part 3, Ch. 11, below.

48. *ST* 1–2 q. 100 art. 3, arg. 1, ad 1; see q. 99 art. 1, ad 2; q. 100 art. 11, co. In *AMPLT*, John Finnis stresses the significance of this precept as a primary precept of natural law, and he makes a number of interesting observations (126–9). Regarding the imperative to love one's neighbor as oneself, Finnis says that Thomas makes "plain his conviction that in [this] master principle he has found the point where philosophical and theological sources meet in a truth evident to reason whether aided or unaided by divine revelation" (128). Since Thomas says of the precepts commanding the love (*dilectio*) of God and the love of neighbor that ". . . illa duo praecepta sunt prima et communia praecepta legis naturae, quae sunt per se nota rationi humanae, vel per naturam vel per fidem" (ST q. 100 art. 3, ad 1; see Part 2, Ch. 8, below), their relevance to Armstrong's account of the distinction between primary and secondary precepts is considerable. Armstrong cannot, however, be said to give them their due weight. See *PSP* 107–12, and note the truncated citation of q. 100 art. 1, ad 1, at the bottom of *PSP* 111.

us consider what might have led Thomas to present it, not as demonstrable, but as *per se notum*.

Our natural inclination to live in society cannot be satisfied if our relation to our fellow human beings culminates solely in not committing offenses against them. What we count on in our dealings with our fellows is some measure, however small, of support for our various undertakings (including our educational endeavors); and we count on establishing friendships in society too. These objectives are realized only when we treat others as we wish them to treat us. This could be said to be simply a matter of *quid pro quo* and to have by itself no properly moral significance. Still, cultivating the habit of treating others as we wish to be treated sustains and makes practical the recognition that the rational nature proper to our humanity is a shared nature. It is in the mutual willing of good for one another that members of a society find their natural inclination to live with one another best satisfied. Willing of the good for another, just like willing the good for oneself, involves more than merely wishing for it. It involves actively working for it. When Thomas states the first principle of practical reason as "Good is to be done and pursued, etc.," he does not limit this good to "one's own good."[49] We ought to will the good of others as well as our own good. But according to Thomas, to will the good of another is precisely to love him.[50]

To elaborate a bit further: In loving oneself, one wills the good, real or apparent, for oneself. One does so because one apprehends something in oneself that is already good and worthy of love. Not the least of the things that one finds good and worthy of love in oneself is one's rational nature, that is, one's capacity to understand and to deliberate, choose, and act. But, again, rational nature is a shared nature. It is not confined to oneself. Wherever rational nature is encountered, it is something good (which is not to deny that it can be ignored and even distorted through willful self-deception). Now, if it is *per se notum* that rational nature is a good that is worth loving in oneself—and it is—then it is *per se notum* that rational nature is a good that is worth loving in one's neighbor too. Love of one's neighbor then, is no less rational than love of oneself. But a few qualifications are in order.

According to Thomas, for a *propositio* to be *per se nota* its terms must be understood. The neighbor (*proximus*) is one who is proximate, near, or nigh. I am not obligated to love of all mankind, because the vast majority of human beings are faceless to me. In most cases I can will, actively will and work for, the good only of those relatively close by. Even on the false but common assumption that love is only a feeling, it is dubious, to say the least, that one could have this feeling for every single human

49. Early in *A Critique of the 'Straussian' Critique*, Thomas West translates the first principle of practical reason, *bonum est faciendum et prosequendum, et malum vitandum* quite literally (13), but later on somewhat more loosely and with an unwarranted gloss in brackets that significantly restricts its scope: "do good [for oneself] and avoid evil" (23; see 29–30.)

50. *ST* 1 q. 20 art. 1, ad 3; 1–2 q. 77 art. 4, co. (Compare Aristotle, *Rhetoric* 1380b35, and consider the phrase *hekeinou heneka alla mē hautou*.) On the relation between *amor* and *dilectio*, see *ST* 1–2 q. 26, art. 3, and Part 2, Ch. 8, below.

being in the world. I can engage in endeavors—for example, medical research—that I hope will improve the lot of mankind. But the neighbor, the one I happen to meet face to face, provides me with ample opportunities to will his good, that is, to will it by going out of my way to work for it. That my neighbor, in spite of the rational nature that stamps him as human, may have (as I do) all kinds of vices that are unworthy of this rational nature, does not relieve me of the obligation to love him, that is, to will and promote both his physical well-being and his intellectual and moral well-being.

Though love of neighbor is rational and obligatory, it does not follow that one is required to love one's neighbor every bit as much as one loves oneself. Thomas is quite clear on this point.[51] In saying that one must love one's neighbor as (or, in the same way that—*sicut*) one loves oneself, [52] Thomas means that one must love him not simply as a thing or a tool for use by others, but as possessing intrinsic worth—which is exactly the way in which one loves oneself.

The precept that commands loving one's neighbor, that is, willing and working for his good, expresses a wide obligation. By a wide obligation, I mean one that requires judgment in order to fulfill it adequately. The obligation to avoid ignorance is a wide obligation because it is not humanly possible to avoid ignorance entirely: no human being can become knowledgeable about everything that can be known. One has to choose what ignorance to avoid, that is, what knowledge to pursue. On the other hand, the obligation to refrain from murder, that is, deliberately taking innocent human life, is a narrow obligation. One does not have to choose whom *not* to murder.[53]

The precept that commands loving one's neighbor leaves room for discretion in determining how the wide obligation it declares is to be fulfilled. But it does not leave room for simply disregarding this obligation.[54] Because willing and working for the good of our neighbor, though rational, is so frequently at odds with the pursuit of pleasure, we can easily, and culpably, convince ourselves that we have no obligation to him other than to refrain from violating his "rights" (with the insistence that he refrain

51. *ST* 2–2 q. 32 art. 6, co; q. 64 art. 5, ad 3; art. 7, co.

52. *ST* 1–2, q. 99 art. 1, ad 2.

53. This distinction between wide and narrow obligations is developed by Kant in *Die Metaphysik der Sitten*, *Werke*, Band 7, 520–525 [English translation: 153–156]. It is anticipated in the earlier *Grundlegung zur Metaphysik der Sitten* as the distinction between perfect and imperfect duties. *Werke*, Band 6, 52, note [English translation: 30, fn. 12]. The distinction is a sensible one, even a necessary one. There is no reason to think that Thomas would reject it. On the contrary, though the terminology is not Thomas's, the distinction is implicit in his teaching, as I argue above.

54. Not only is Thomas's natural law teaching comprehensive and yet, at the same time, economical, it is also true to the familiar phenomena of ordinary moral experience. As *synderesis*, practical reason *articulates* a natural law precept that is characterized by wide latitude, such as "Love thy neighbor" (in the sense of "Will and work for the good of thy neighbor"). And, as conscience, when it is not erring, practical reason applies this precept to a concrete case. But, as conscience, it also reproaches one for ignoring the precept or, because of its wide latitude, not taking it seriously, just as it reproaches one for acting in opposition to a precept that is characterized by narrow latitude. See *ST* 1 q. 79 art. 13, co., for the range of things Thomas holds to be accomplished by conscience. I consider Thomas's account of the phenomenon of remorse in Part 2, Ch. 6, Section c, below.

from violating ours as well). In some cases we can convince ourselves that we have no obligations at all to our neighbor, that if we refrain from actively taking advantage of him, or worse, it is only out of fear. We can convince ourselves that, whereas there is no limit to our own worth, the worth of others consists chiefly or even exclusively in the use we can make of them in the pursuit of our private interests.

Man gets himself into this frame of mind, which is through and through irrational, not just by ignoring, but by rebelling against, his own reason. And he can so habituate himself to dwelling in this frame of mind that he becomes incapable of breaking out of it on his own. It is for this reason that certain precepts of natural law, the rational knowledge of which having been obscured "on account of passion, or bad habit, or a bad disposition of nature,"[55] needed to be rearticulated in the Decalogue.

v. Natural law and the moral precepts of the Decalogue

Thomas includes the moral precepts of the Decalogue in the natural law. Like the primary precepts they do not admit of dispensation.[56] That Thomas includes the moral precepts of the Decalogue in the natural law is occasionally introduced as proof positive that his natural law teaching does not, after all, derive from reason and ordinary experience alone. What is insufficiently attended to, however, is his argument that the moral precepts of the Decalogue either reproduce or can be derived at once from the primary precepts of natural law. Thomas is not appealing to revealed theology to support his natural law teaching. He is appealing to his natural law teaching to clarify a matter of revealed theology. Divine law presupposes natural law according to Thomas,[57] and the coherence of the former presupposes the coherence of the latter.

55. *ST* 1–2 q. 94 art. 4, co.: ". . . aliqui habent depravatam rationem ex passione, seu ex mala consuetudine, seu ex mala habitudine naturae." See art. 6, co ; q. 100 art. 5, ad 1.

56. *ST* 1–2 q. 99 art. 2 ad 2; q. 100 art. 1–3, 8. At q. 100 art. 3, co., Thomas says, "Illa ergo praecepta ad decalogum pertinent, quorum notitiam homo habet per seipsum a Deo." Thomas's point here is that God set forth the precepts of the Decalogue, as distinct from the other precepts of the Old Law, by himself and not through the intermediary of Moses (or the angels—compare q. 98 art. 3, co). Nonetheless, as the next sentence makes clear, some of these precepts "can be known at once (*statim*) from the first universal principles [of the natural law itself—see q. 94, art. 4, co.] with only slight consideration (*modica consideratione*)." These precepts, Thomas is saying, can be naturally known by natural reason, without the assistance of divine revelation.

57. *ST* 1–2 q. 99 art. 2, ad 1. In q. 97 art. 3, co., Thomas says that both the divine and natural laws proceed from the reasonable will of God (*a rationabili Dei voluntate*). Cf q. 97 art. 3, ad 1. They proceed, however, in different ways, the former immediately from God's reason and will (as divine positive law), the latter ultimately from God's reason and will but proximally through the natural reason of the rational creature, which is immediately created God. (*Super Sent.*, lib. 3, dist. 37 q. 1 art. 2 qc. 1, arg. 4: "Sed legis naturalis dictamen per rationem naturalem est.") God's reasonable will is, of course, the creative source of natural reason. If divine law and natural law did not proceed in these two different ways from the reasonable will of God, there would not be, contrary to what Thomas explicitly teaches, any meaningful difference between them.

When Thomas argues that there was a *need* for divine law, he points to a weakness of natural law, more precisely, to a weakness in our knowledge of natural law. Knowledge of its precepts is a matter of reason, and Thomas tells us both that the primary precepts of natural law are true and right for all and that they are equally known by all.[58] Things are different with the secondary precepts, however. It is regarding these precepts that he says, in q. 94 art. 4, "reason can be perverted on account of passion, or bad habit, or a bad disposition of nature." Since Thomas is speaking in this article from the perspective of natural reason, he cannot base this claim on the doctrine of original sin, which is bound up with the claims of revelation.[59] He may be making an allusion to it with the expression "a bad disposition of nature." But by preceding this expression with "or" (*seu*) he implies that a bad disposition of nature is only one of several possible causes whereby our knowledge of the precepts of natural law can be obscured. Thomas is on solid ground in noting that knowledge of what we ought to do can be obscured by passion and bad habits. After all, Aristotle makes the

58. *ST* 1–2 q. 94 art. 6, "Whether the law of nature can be abolished (*aboleri*) from the heart of man." Compare the following passage referred to by Russell Hittinger (in "Natural Law and Catholic Moral Theology," 7–8) from Thomas's *Prooemium* to *De Decem Praeceptis*: "Quousque enim in primo homine anima fuit subdita Deo, servando divina praecepta, etiam caro fuit subdita in omnibus animae vel rationi. Sed postquam Diabolus per suggestionem retraxit hominem ab observantia divinorum praeceptorum, ita etiam caro fuit inobediens rationi. Et inde accidit quod licet homo velit bonum secundum rationem, tamen ex concupiscentia ad contrarium inclinator . . . Quia ergo lex naturae per legem concupiscentiae destructa erat, oportebat quod homo reduceretur ad opera virtutis, et retraheretur a vitiis: ad quae necessaria erat lex Scripturae." Unless the distinctions that Thomas makes in *ST* 1–2 q. 94 art. 6 are kept in mind, this passage from *De Decem Praeceptis* could be taken for a late-in-life renunciation of his natural law teaching *in toto*. See *ST* 1–2 q. 100 art. 5, ad 1: "lex naturalis *obscurata* erat proper peccatum . . ."; and compare 2–2 q. 25 art. 6, *sed contra*: "pecatum non *tollit* naturam" (emphasis added in both quotations). Roy Deferrari lists "weaken" as one of the meanings of *destruo* (*A Lexicon of Saint Thomas Aquinas*, 296). Given what Thomas says in these other passages and what he says elsewhere, I think that "weakened" is how "*destructa*" should be understood in the *Prooemium* to *De Decem Praeceptis*. In commenting on this *Prooemium*, Hittinger says that man's moral understanding is "bent" by sin. He refrains, rightly, from saying that man's moral understanding is "annihilated" by sin.

59. Thomas's account of how there could be something like a law in the "fomes of sin" does not occur in his treatment of natural law proper. It occurs instead in an article that falls under the question of the various kinds of law. *ST* 1–2 q. 91 art. 6. What Thomas tries to show there is that his definition of law can accommodate, albeit somewhat uneasily, Paul's claim, "I see another law in my members, resisting the law of my mind." Thomas needs to show that his understanding of law as a rule and measure of reason is not simply contradicted by what Paul says. But he does not even begin to try to demonstrate, in terms of natural reason alone, that man at some point in the past was punished by the just sentence of God for an original act of disobedience. According to Thomas West (*Critique of the 'Straussian' Critique*, 32), Thomas Aquinas in this article "says that man's rationality is not strictly a law but only 'a kind of law' or 'law in a certain sense (*quodammodo lex*).'" But Thomas applies the expression *quodammodo lex* to the inclinations of sub-rational creatures in general and only by extension to man's sub-rational and frequently contra-rational sensuous impulses. Moreover, he explicitly says in this very article that the *lex* allotted by divine providence to man "according to his proper condition" (*secundum propriam conditionem*) is "that he act according to reason" (*ut secundum rationem operetur*). This law has the character of a proposition (1–2 q. 90 art. 1, ad 2), albeit a general one. It is not merely "law in a certain sense."

same point without any allusion to original sin.[60] And even Thomas's reference to "a bad disposition of nature" does not have to be interpreted as an allusion to original sin.[61] This or that man is often said, by unbelievers as well as by believers, to have a good or bad natural disposition.

Because the moral precepts of the Decalogue belong originally and properly to natural law,[62] their obligatory character does not derive from a belief that God will reward those who obey them and will punish those who transgress them.[63] Their obligatory character derives originally not from faith but from the command of natural, human reason itself, as is the case with all the precepts that belong to natural law. And to repeat, even though Thomas does hold that God is the creator of human reason, he holds that this is not a matter of faith but of demonstration. The ceremonial and judicial precepts of the Old Law, on the other hand, are held by Thomas to be revealed specifications of what natural law says in general (*in communi*) about man's relation to God and to his fellow men. These revealed specifications go beyond what can be derived from the primary precepts of natural law. Hence recognizing their obligatory character does presuppose faith. Recognizing the obligatory character of the moral precepts of the Decalogue, on the other hand, does not presuppose faith. They already belong to the natural law. They needed to be rearticulated in the Decalogue because man is able to, and often does, ignore or rebel against his own reason. One who hears the Decalogue as a command from God sees that in ignoring and rebelling against his own reason he is also ignoring or rebelling against the very reason by which the whole universe is governed—the infinite reason of which one's own reason is a finite image.[64] The rearticulating of certain precepts of natural law in the Decalogue not only brings man back to his senses, it endows these precepts with a majesty that makes him think twice about transgressing them. Still, the moral precepts of the Decalogue belong properly to natural law, not to divine, that is, revealed law. So Thomas argues.

60. *Nicomachean Ethics* 1147b16.

61. When Thomas returns to this point in his treatment of the Old Law, he says explicitly that natural reason has become obscured by sin. See *ST* 1–2 q. 99 art. 2, ad 2. But there he is speaking from the perspective of faith, whereas earlier, in q. 94 art. 4, co., he is speaking from the perspective of natural reason. In q. 99 art. 2, ad 1, Thomas says "Ratio autem hominis . . . propter consuetudinem peccandi, obscurabatur . . ." (see *ST* 1–2 q. 100 art. 5, ad 1; 3 q. 70 art. 2, ad 1). In the parallel formulation in question 94 art. 4, co., where he does not mention sin at all, Thomas writes "aliqui habent depravatem rationem . . . ex mala consuetudine." The distinction in the wording of these two passages is clear evidence that Thomas knows full well, and counts on his readers knowing, when he is speaking from the perspective of natural reason and when he is speaking from the perspective of faith. See q. 71 art. 6, ad 5.

62. *ST* 1–2 q. 100 art. 1.

63. *ST* 1–2 q. 100 art. 11.

64. Since human reason is the proper image of the eternal law, and the eternal law is the divine reason, it follows that human reason is the proper image of divine reason. *ST* 1–2 q. 19 art. 4, co.; ad 3; q. 100 art. 2, co; see 2–2 q. 66 art. 1, co.

vi. Application of the precepts of natural law

The precepts of natural law, including the moral precepts of the Decalogue, are applied to concrete circumstances through the exercise of practical judgment. "Whether this or that [occurrence] be murder, theft, or adultery" is a matter that has to be decided by human authority.[65] But Thomas also teaches that human authority is occasionally corrupt. Presumably, then, it is the prudential exercise of human authority, or prudence itself, that determines rightly whether, say, in a given case taking something from another against his will is in fact theft.[66] As far as latitude is concerned, there is plenty of it in Thomas's ethics. Judgment and prudence are indispensable.[67]

But *synderesis* is indispensable too.[68] Not only are there a number of means to a given end, there are also a number of ends too, some of which can come into tension with others, and some of which are higher, or more rational, than others. Because *synderesis* is the *habitus* whereby we know the precepts of natural law and their rank, and because natural law does not presuppose divine law, *synderesis* does not presuppose revelation. The opposite is true: revelation presupposes *synderesis* because divine law

65. *ST* 1–2 q. 100 art. 8, ad 3.

66. *ST* 2–2 q. 66. According to articles 4, 5, and 8, theft (*furtum*) and robbery (*rapina*) are both vices and sins. But according to article 7, it is lawful for a person in dire need to relieve his need by taking from the things of someone else (*ex rebus alienis*), either openly or secretly. Doing so under such conditions, Thomas argues, is not properly theft or robbery. For, as he says in the *sed contra* of this article, without citing an authority as he typically does, "in necessity all things are common." See Simon, *The Tradition of Natural Law*, 147: "To take water from the water supply of my neighbor when he is not at home and in order to reduce my own water bill is stealing. If my house is afire and the neighbor's supply is the only source of water available to put the fire out, even if I should never be able to pay him for it, that water belongs to me under the circumstances. Extreme necessity *changes* the nature of the act. It is a very crude error to say that stealing is lawful in extreme necessity. Moral skepticism thrives on such confusion, which consists simply of a failure to notice that, the externals being equal, the moral essences of the two acts may be as different as the right is from the wrong." (Emphasis in the original.) What Simon says here applies quite well to the question of theft, for the reasons that Thomas gives. It should not, however, be taken as implying that circumstances, even extreme circumstances, can justify any act whatsoever. (Note Simon's use of the word "may.") Such is not Thomas's view. See Part 2, Ch. 9, Section c, below.

67. That we are obligated to cultivate our powers of discrimination in the interest of sharpening our judgment is implied in the precept that commands us to act according to reason (ST 1–2, q. 94, art. 3; art. 4), as it is also implied in the precept that commands us to avoid ignorance (1–2 q. 94 art. 2; see q. 76 art. 2).

68. Since Thomas distinguishes *synderesis* from prudence (ST 2–2 q. 47, art. 6, ad 1), he thereby distinguishes conscience, the act of which *synderesis* is the habit, from prudence as well, contrary to what Thomas West suggests, if I understand him (*Critique of the 'Straussian' Critique*, 24, bottom; but see 25, top). Moreover, *synderesis* is not quite, as West says, "a synonym for 'the first principles of human actions" (24). What Thomas says in *ST* 1–2 q, 94 art. 1, ad 2, by way of responding to an argument that appeals to Basil, is that "*synderesis* is the *habitus* containing the first precepts of natural law, which are the first principles of human actions (*opera*)." Natural law, which contains the first principles of human actions, is not a *habitus*, as Thomas explicitly argues in the *corpus* of this article. West has previously said that *synderesis* is "nothing but the natural inclinations from which the precepts of the natural law follow" (23). Thomas quite carefully distinguishes between inclinations, *synderesis*, and precepts. West blurs these distinctions. He is not alone in doing so.

presupposes natural law or, more broadly, because grace presupposes nature.[69] And though Thomas argues in his rational theology that God is the creator of human reason, and hence the ultimate source of natural law and the obligations it establishes,[70] their proximate source is human reason itself.

Complex circumstances can disclose the limitations of the secondary precepts of natural law. Thomas gives an example. It is a secondary precept of natural law that goods held in trust be restored to their owner, and this precept holds true in the majority of cases. "But," he adds, "it may happen in a particular case that it would be injurious (*damnosum*), and therefore unreasonable (*irrationabile*), to restore goods held in trust; for instance, if they are claimed for the purpose of fighting against one's country." [71] Refusing to restore something held in trust is usually wrong, but not in every conceivable case.

One might argue that, by according judgment its proper role in the subsumption of minor under major premises and by allowing for occasional dispensation from the secondary precepts of natural law, Thomas has introduced so much latitude into his teaching that he has deprived law of its meaning as law. To this argument, Thomas would respond that he has, on the contrary, secured the meaning of law by bringing into relief primary and rationally discernible precepts that are universal in scope, that do not admit of dispensation, and that can serve as major premises in practical syllogisms.[72]

Thomas quite clearly recognizes that practical wisdom is required in order to judge correctly in complicated cases. "[A]mong men he who is most perspicacious can judge a greater number of things by his reason."[73] The perspicacity Thomas speaks of here concerns not *synderesis* but judgment.[74] It is by *synderesis* that we know, all

69. *ST* 1 q. 2 art. 2, ad 1.

70. It is in this way that what Thomas says in *ST* q. 97 art. 3, co., 1st sentence, and ad 1, 1st sentence, should be read. God is not blind will. Nor does he look to a standard of rationality apart from his intellect, inasmuch as his intellect is the primary locus of all truth and hence of all rationality as well, though his intellect, as unmoving, is not ratiocinative. *ST* 1, q. 1–16, 19; *SCG* 1 cap. 57, n. 7. See *ST* 1–2 q. 21 art. 1, co.

71. *ST* 1–2 q. 94 art. 4, co. The same example is used at 2–2 q. 51 art. 4, co., where the implication is that to return the goods would violate natural law. See also, q. 57 art. 2, ad 1. In q. 62 art. 5, ad 1, Thomas says that restitution in such a case would be gravely harmful: *graviter noxia*; similarly in q. 120 art. 1: *nocivum*. See *Sententia Libri Ethicorum* lib. 5 lect. 12 n. 1028. Concerning a related problem that comes up in the first book of Plato's *Republic*, see Part 2, Ch. 9, Section b, i, below.

72. *ST* 1–2 q. 94 art.4–6; q. 97 art. 4, ad 3. The *corpus* of q. 96 art. 6 is not contradicted by the first sentence of q. 97 art. 4, ad 3, because the former is treating human law and human lawgivers, not natural law.

73. *ST* 2–2 q. 51 art. 4, ad 3: "inter homines ille qui est magis perspicax potest plura horum sua ratione diiudicare."

74. Remembering that for Thomas law is a certain *rule* of reason (ST 1–2, q. 90 co.), what Kant says about rules and judgment—in the speculative sphere no less than in the practical—is pertinent to the matter at hand. He argues that, though judgment is a faculty of subsuming a more particular rule (or a class or even just an individual) under a more universal rule, no rule can tell us *how* to judge

of us, that we should do evil to no one. We know this as a properly moral obligation, which is expressed in a precept of natural law that does not admit of dispensation. The testimony of *synderesis* regarding what is to be done is not eclipsed, much less nullified, by judgment (or, for that matter, by prudence). *Synderesis* is complemented by judgment. Judgment in the sphere of practice is dependent on *synderesis* as judgment in the sphere of theory is dependent on the understanding of logical principles, especially the principle of non-contradiction.

The complexity of what judgment may on occasion have to take into account in making a correct subsumption supports Thomas's claim that certain secondary precepts, though derived from the primary precepts by demonstration, are so remote from them that they can be reasoned to, and applied to complex circumstances *via* correct acts of judgment, only by the wise.[75] Judgment, after all, cannot be systematically prescribed in the same way that inference can.[76] And so, even though *synderesis* is unerring in its apprehension of the major premise, a failure of judgment (for whatever reason) in advancing the minor premise can lead to a false conclusion. The result is an erring conscience.[77]

SECTION C. OBLIGATION EXPLICATED

By the end of q. 94 art. 2 we have not just the formal first principle of practical reason but concrete precepts of natural law with determinate content, which is to say, we have moral obligation as distinct from natural necessity. Thomas does not give us a definition of obligation in q. 94 art. 2. But what he says there enables us to come up with a

correctly. For we would again need judgment to employ *that* rule, and so forth *ad infinitum*. Hence "judgment is a special talent that cannot be taught, but only exercised." (KRV B 172). "Deficiency in judgment is just what is called stupidity, and for such a defect there is no remedy." (KRV B 172, note a). Kant's assessment parallels Thomas's understanding that excellence of judgment is central to wisdom. Consider in this connection Thomas's formulation that "every judgment of human reason must be derived in some respect (*aliqualiter*) from natural reason," in practical matters ultimately from what is "of the law of nature absolutely." *ST* q. 100 art. 1, co. In distinguishing between human reason and natural reason in this passage, when he often equates them, Thomas is likely including in the former the reasoning that leads to the judgments that make up human law, properly so-called, as well as judgments concerning relatively minor matters, that is, judgments at considerable remove from the primary precepts of natural law. What Thomas means by *aliqualiter* in q. 100 art. 1, co., is illuminated by the following passage: "Et secundum illa altiora principia exigitur altior virtus iudicativa, quae vocatur *gnome*, quae importat quandam perspicacitatem iudicii." (ST. 2–2 q. 51, art. 4, co.; the example given concerns a situation in which a deposit should not be returned.)

75. *ST* 1–2 q. 100 art. 1, co.; art. 3, co.

76. Armstrong cites the objection of P. M. Van Overbeke that the line drawn between the less and the more remote among the secondary precepts is not clear, resting as it does on the distinction between the wise and the unwise: "Where does the domain of the wise begin?" (*PSP* 137). The answer to this good question is that excellence in judgment is precisely what distinguishes the wise from the unwise. It is not possible to determine, with anything like a clear dividing line, exactly where the domain of those possessing good judgment begins.

77. *De Veritate* q. 16, art. 1; see *De Malo* q. 3 art. 12, ad 13.

definition, though only if we first take the time to cross a few t's and dot a few i's. The time spent doing so is well worth it. For not only is the definition of obligation that emerges true to Thomas's texts, it is true to our experience as well.

i. Freedom of choice

Because the precepts of natural law command without literally compelling, they express what ought to be, not necessarily what is or will be. The first principle of practical reason, which Thomas presents in the middle of the *corpus* of q. 94 art. 2, does not obligate, strictly speaking. But the precepts of natural law, which Thomas presents at the end of the *corpus* of the same article, do obligate. So it has to be the introduction of the natural inclinations in between that permits him to account for obligation. If all we had were a mere multiplicity of inclinations, however, there would be no obligation, even if these inclinations were considered in conjunction with the first principle of practical reason. For there would be no standard of subordination, no best to which what is second best should take second place. Instead of a mere multiplicity of natural inclinations, Thomas introduces an order, a *hierarchical* order, of natural inclinations. It is an ascending order, and at the top of this order are the inclinations that are specific to our reason. But we have not just inclinations, tendencies, desires, wants, or needs, however pressing or however lofty; we have obligations too. It is through our reason in combination with our finitude, that is, through our peculiar nature as both rational and animal, that we have obligations. What exactly is obligation?

In saying that one has an obligation, or that one ought, to do something, one implies that it would be *good* to do that thing. There are, to be sure, some uses of the word "ought" in common parlance that do not imply a moral obligation, such as "You ought to try this apple pie!" But there are also some uses of the word "ought" that do have a genuinely moral import, but which some say fall short of declaring an obligation. Those who say this typically distinguish between acts that are obligatory and acts that are supererogatory or meritorious, i.e., acts that "go beyond the call of duty." [78] However, Thomas's denial of morally indifferent human acts (*actus humani* as distinct from *actus hominis*) calls this distinction into question,[79] though without negating the distinction between obligations of wide and narrow latitude.

78. I speak to the apparent distinction between the dutiful and the meritorious, in Ch. 3, Section c, below.

79. See Butera's account, in "The Moral Status of the First Principle," of Thomas's denial of morally indifferent *human* acts, as distinct from acts that are morally indifferent *in their species*. Consider especially the statement at *ST* 1–2 q. 1 art. 3, which Butera quotes and translates as follows: "And since, as Ambrose says, (*Prolog. Super Luc*), 'morality is said properly of man,' moral acts properly speaking receive their species from the end, for moral acts [*actus morales*] are the same as human acts [*actus humani*]" (622, fn. 24). Thomas is saying here that any act a human being deliberately engages in has a moral aspect. It has a moral aspect because it is, of necessity, directed toward the good, real or apparent. ("*Moralis,-e*" does for not, for Thomas, name only a feature of our relation to *others*, as does the word "moral" for many today.) Thomas's claim here is in keeping with the opening sentences of the

In saying that someone or other ought to do something, one implies that it is possible to do it. It is frequently said these days, and it is true, that "ought" implies "*can*."[80] But it is not as frequently said, though it is also true, that "ought" typically implies "*might not*," and does so invariably when one is speaking of obligation. In saying that someone or other is obligated to do something, one implies that the sphere of the possible is wider than the sphere of the actual. This implication, as Thomas recognizes, distinguishes obligation from natural necessity.[81] When a person says, "I ought to do x," or "I should do x," he means then (1) that it would be in some respect *good* to do x; (2) that he *can* do x, and (3) that he *might not* do x. If he meant only (1) and (2), but not (3), then he would say no more than, "I can and will do x." Built into the very meaning of the sentence, "I ought to do x," is a belief in the possibility that "I might not do x." A person who makes such a statement, if he is paying attention to the meaning of his words, is affirming freedom of choice, at least momentarily.

Unlike the first principle of practical reason, the precepts of natural law are then properly obligatory, since, in spite of their rationality, one might not act on them.[82]

Nicomachean Ethics. See *ST* 1–2 q. 18 art. 9, co; ad 1; q. 19 art. 5, co.

80. There are special uses of "ought" or "should" that do not imply "can." Some express only a reluctance to affirm without qualification something that is likely but not certain. For example, "An eclipse ought to be (or should be) visible at 9:00 tonight." This sentence could easily be expressed without using "ought": "It is likely that an eclipse will be visible tonight." The case is similar when a shoe salesman says, "These shoes ought to fit you." There are also so-called "role oughts" that do not imply "can" without further qualifications. An example used to illustrate this lack of implication is "Parents ought to provide their children with a good education." But parents who are too poor to afford a good education for their children cannot do so. So a more precise formulation would be, "Parents ought to provide their children with a good education, if they can do so." Here "ought" is expressly limited to "can." For an account of "paradigm obligations" and "role oughts," see Richard Feldman, "The Ethics of Belief." Because it is possible for the above sentences to be reformulated, they do not require a significant modification of the general claim that "ought" implies "can." A sentence using "ought" or "should" that would be deprived of its intended meaning if either of these words (or the word "obligated" and its kin) were omitted is the kind of sentence that I have in mind when I say that "ought' implies "can." Even a simple sentence like, "We ought to unpack the car before it starts raining," fits the bill. The "ought" here implies (1) that it would be *good* to unpack the car before its starts raining, (2) that we *can* do so, and (3), of equal importance, that we *might not* do so. (The last criterion, "might not," is treated in the body of the text above.) This is the normal way in which we use the word "ought." Paradigm obligations and "role oughts" are exceptions to the norm, but can be re-formulated. The same is true of sentences using "should" in ways such as the following: "Should it snow today, you'll be properly dressed for it."

81. ST. 2–2 q. 104 art. 1, ad 1. See *Sententia Libri Ethicorum* lib. 3 lect. 5 n. 455; lib. 7, lect. n. 1340, 1346, and 1348. The argument in *ST* 1–2 q. 77 art. 2, co., that it is possible for reason to be overcome by a passion, though not necessarily without reason's consent, is supplemented by the following passage from art. 7, co.: "[A]liquid dicitur voluntarium directe, vel indirecte: directe quidem, id in quod voluntas fertur: indirecte autem, illud quod voluntas *potuit* prohibere, *sed non prohibit*. . . [M]embra non applicantur operi nisi per *consensum* rationis" (emphasis added); cf. 1–2 q. 15; and *Super Sent.*, lib. 2, dist. 34, q. 1 art. 3, ad 4. Even regarding infused virtue, Thomas says that "virtus infusa causatur in nobis a Deo sine nobis agentibus, non tamen sine nobis consentientibus." *ST* 1–2 q. 55, art. 4, ad 6. See *ST* 1 q. 63 art. 1, ad 4; 1–2 q. 15 art. 4, ad 1; 2–2 q. 66 art. 6, ad 3; *De Veritate* q. 25 art. 1, co.; *De Malo* q. 6 co., ad 7, ad 15.

82. *ST* 1–2 q. 99 art. 1, co.: ". . . praeceptum legis, cum sit obligatorium, est de aliquo quod fieri

Rather than simply compelling us, they command us as rational beings. And that means that they call for an essentially free compliance.[83] Compliance with the precepts of natural law is not morally optional. For we cannot act virtuously except by complying with them, as Thomas argues in the article that immediately follows q. 94 art. 2. And yet nothing, not even natural law, literally compels us to act virtuously. Natural law does not deprive us of our freedom. On the contrary, it gives meaning to our freedom.

Freedom of choice means that in the past we could have done other than what we did, and, arguably, that right now we could be doing other than what we are doing. It also means that in the future we could do one thing rather than another or vice versa. That the future in particular is not totally determined, but depends in part on what we choose to do, is an assumption that necessarily underlies all practical deliberation.[84]

The determinist, who makes the same assumption in his practical deliberations, can always respond that this assumption is a falsehood from which, because of our limited knowledge of the future, neither he nor anyone else can free himself. And, in my opinion, he cannot be refuted outright in this claim. Though free choice is a necessary presupposition of *practical* reason, *theoretical* reason cannot definitively establish its existence. But theoretical reason cannot establish the non-existence of free choice either.[85]

---

debet." See *ST* 1 q. 82 art. 1, co., for Thomas's account of a kind of necessity that is not repugnant to the will (keeping in mind that, for Thomas, will and free choice are not simply identical). Compare 1 q. 19 art. 10, co. What I am calling "moral obligation" can also be called "rational necessitation." Both expressions name what one must do of necessity *if* one is to act rationally. Kant says that an imperative expresses "objective necessitation." I prefer the expression "moral obligation" because the terms "necessitation" and "necessity," even when prefaced by the adjective "rational" or "objective," could be misinterpreted as ruling out free choice.

83. Giuseppe Butera argues that if the first principle of practical reason is a moral imperative, then the concrete precepts of natural law that Thomas presents toward the end of the *corpus* of q. 94 art. 2 are moral imperatives too ("The Moral Status of the First Principle," 615); and that if those precepts are moral imperatives, then the first principle of practical reason must also be a moral imperative (625). For the reasons given above, I think that the first principle of practical reason cannot be a moral imperative and that the connection between it and the concrete precepts of natural law, which *are* moral imperatives, is more complex than Butera realizes.

84. On the question of whether Aristotle is a determinist, compare *Metaphysics* 1072a26–30 with *De Anima* 433a10–31. See also *De Interpretatione* 19a6-b4; *Nicomachean Ethics* 1112a30-b1; 1112b10; 1139b8; *Metaphysics* 1015a33–34, 1046b5-7, 1048a10-24, 1050b31-34.

85. Thomas's arguments for freedom of choice (e.g., *ST* 1, q. 83 art. 1; 1–2 q. 6 art. 1; q. 10 art. 2) do not, as far as I can see, conclusively demonstrate that we possess it, though they do show how it can be conceived of without contradiction. Thomas states that no object whatsoever moves the will of necessity to the exercise of its act, because one is always able *not* to think of the object: ". . . voluntas movetur dupliciter: uno modo, quantum ad exercitium actus; alio modo, quantum ad specificationem actus, quae est ex obiecto. Primo ergo modo, voluntas a nullo obiecto ex necessitate movetur: potest enim aliquis de quocumque obiecto non cogitare, et per consequens neque actu velle illud. Sed quantum ad secundum motionis modum, voluntas ab aliquo obiecto ex necessitate movetur, ab aliquo autem non . . . [S]i proponatur aliquod obiectum voluntati quod sit universaliter bonum et secundum omnem considerationem, ex necessitate voluntas in illud tendet, si aliquid velit: non enim poterit velle

Persistent allegations to the contrary notwithstanding, the concept of free choice does not contain a contradiction. Nor is it incoherent. The claim that we are capable of free choice does not contradict anything we know, *indubitably know*, about ourselves or about the world we inhabit. Nor is self-determination, which is just another name for free choice, a self-contradiction, any more than is self-consciousness, self-confidence, or self-love—or self-destruction, for that matter. The causality of self-determination to one of two or more possibilities does not apply to things. And if one insists on regarding persons as things, like stones and tables, then the concept of freedom, and hence the concept of obligation too, makes no sense. Stones and tables do not have obligations. But persons are not things. They are, and experience themselves as, rational agents. The capacity to consider the future in terms of possibilities, in terms of live possibilities as distinct from unknown necessities merely, pertains to the nature of a rational being, and so does the capacity to deliberate about these possibilities. It also pertains to the nature of a rational being to choose on the basis of deliberation and to actualize one possibility to the exclusion of others that are incompatible with it. Otherwise, deliberation would be pointless. But we all engage in deliberation. We would not be rational beings if we did not do so.[86]

It is not the concept of free choice that is incoherent but the determinist's insistence that the future does not contain live possibilities when, just like the rest of us, he unavoidably deliberates and acts as though it does. The determinist may be correct in asserting that we do not possess free choice. But his assertion places him in the strange position of holding to a theory of action that he cannot act on, and must even suspend belief in, when deliberating about action. The determinist can respond that he is pre-determined to suspend belief in determinism when he is deliberating. Again, I do not think he can be refuted on this point. The determinist might add that he deliberates only to find out how he is already pre-determined to act. I do not think that he can be refuted on this point either. For we do not have direct access to how he thinks about the future. But we do have indirect access to how he thinks about the future, namely, through what he says about it. Outside the classroom and in the ordinary discourse of daily life, the determinist, just like the rest of us, uses expressions such as, "I should

oppositum." *ST* 1–2 q. 10, art. 2, co. Thomas's argument here is profound. But it is also incomplete, inasmuch as it does not speak to the question of why, in moral deliberation, one would knowingly choose *not* to think of something pertinent to moral deliberation. I have addressed this question in a paper, "Thomas Aquinas on Sin Regarded from the Perspective of Natural Reason," which I presented at the International *Congress on Intelligence and Will in Thomas Aquinas*, University of Navarra, Pamplona, Spain, in April 2018.

86. In fact, not only deliberation in the sphere of action, but also speculation in the sphere of theory considers the possible as having wider scope than the actual. "What if the combination had yielded an acid rather than a base?" "Suppose we had drawn the line tangent to the circle rather than intersecting it. What would have happened then?" "Now, if the Ice Age had not occurred when it did . . ." And so forth. It is remarkable how frequently reason, as our natural guide to what is true as well as to what is good, employs, and must employ, the principle that the possible is of wider scope than the actual.

have done x," "I should do x," "I could do x, but I'm not going to. For if I were to do x . . .," and similar expressions in the second and third persons. In using such expressions, the determinist gives every impression of thinking, if only while deliberating, that the future contains live possibilities and not just unknown necessities. The following curiosity is worth noting in this connection. When a person uses the expression "I am determined to do x" (as in, "I am determined to get to the gym today," or "I am determined to learn calculus this year"), he usually means, not that he is determined by external circumstances to do x, but that he is internally resolved to do x and not let external circumstances deter him from doing so. The expression, "I am *determined* to do x" almost always means "I am *self*-determined to do x."[87]

If we were not free then what appears to be an obligation would be an illusion than which one could hardly imagine a greater. For reason itself, through the precepts of natural law, declares obligations, and there can be genuine obligations only if there is freedom. If we were not free, reason would be declaring an impossibility. It would be totally in conflict with itself at the level of practice. Speculative reason might not be adversely affected, but practical reason would be self-destroyed, for it would be irremediably self-contradictory in its operation. It may be that we do not possess free choice and that practical reason really is irremediably in conflict with itself. But such a thing cannot be demonstrated. For all attempts to demonstrate that we do not possess free choice either employ premises that are not indubitably known, for example, that persons and things operate under identical causal principles, or they simply beg the question, for example, by asserting that self-determination is impossible since everything is either determined by another or entirely indeterminate (or random). Given that a rigorous demonstration that we are *not* free is not possible, we are rationally obligated to assume that we *are* free, or capable of self-determination.[88] For that is the only way that we can take seriously the self-evident precepts of natural law through which reason itself dictates how we *ought* to act. So, though as far as I can see, it is neither self-evident that we possess free will nor even demonstrable that we possess it, it *is* self-evident that we *believe* that we have free will, at least when we deliberate. For deliberation necessarily presupposes the belief, even if only temporary, that future events *could* turn out one way or another, and that how they *do* turn out is in some measure up to us—whatever our philosophical, physicalist, or even (as with Spinoza, among others) theological commitments.[89]

87. Cf. *ST* 1–2 q. 17 art. 5, arg. 2; ad 2.

88. It might seem that if, as Thomas teaches, a primary precept of natural law is self-evident, it follows that the existence of human freedom, without which it would be impossible to be obligated by the precept, is also self-evident. But all that really follows is that if such freedom did not exist then *practical* reason would be in conflict with itself: it would be declaring obligations that, *qua* obligations, i.e. *qua* presupposing freedom of choice, could not be fulfilled. Such a conflict—though neither demonstrable nor self-evident, and moreover counter-intuitive at the level of deliberation, choice, and action—is nonetheless a possibility that *speculative* reason, by itself, cannot definitively rule out.

89. We can surely speculate about future events, including what may take place in our own bodies,

ii. Is and Ought

Thomas would agree with those who say that the Ought cannot be strictly deduced from the Is (though he would not use these grammatically challenged expressions). But he would deny that the distinction between the Is and the Ought is equivalent to the current distinction between facts and values. The latter distinction is bound up with the claim that, whereas facts are objective, values are merely subjective, and consequently that whereas facts can be ascertained by reason, values are solely expressions of an individual sub-rational will or a sum of sub-rational wills. Thomas would, of course, deny that what we ought to do is a merely subjective preference of sub-rational will. It is, rather, an objective determination of reason in its practical operation. The underivability of the Ought from the Is does not mean that obligation is a concept of spurious origin. For it is reason itself that, *qua* practical, declares obligations through the precepts of natural law. It is by virtue of his own reason that man stands, immediately and in his very being, under obligations.

Moreover, although precepts declaring what ought to be cannot be strictly deduced from propositions that state simply how things are, it does not follow that what is good is in no way grounded in what is. For, as we have seen, the good, according to Thomas, is being, not *simplicter*, but under the aspect of the desirable. Jean Porter gives a clear account of the role of the good in Thomas's metaphysics by drawing attention to the centrality of perfection in his conception of being.[90] Perfection forms the bridge, so to speak, from being to the good. This comes out clearly in the order of Thomas's presentation. For after proving the existence and simplicity of God in Questions 2 and 3 of the *Summa Theologiae*, Prima Pars, Thomas proceeds in Question 4 to the perfection of God, and to the perfections to be found in creatures as well. Then, in Questions 5 and 6, he treats respectively the good in general and the goodness of God in particular. Porter says,

> In its most proper sense "goodness" applies to *perfected* being, to whatever is, insofar as it is what it ought to be. A good pen is one that writes well, a good desk is sturdy and even, and a good woman is healthy, wise and virtuous. Hence to be good without qualification is to be perfect, that is, to exist in the fullest degree of actuality possible to a creature of this given kind . . . But in a secondary, but nonetheless valid sense, goodness can be applied to anything whatever, insofar as it exists, since to exist at all is to be in act and therefore possess some degree of perfection . . . Correlatively, evil always has the

without assuming free will (though even here, some concept of the possible has to be employed). But mere speculation about the future differs from actual deliberation about the future inasmuch as the latter necessarily presupposes that it will come to fruition in a *choice*, even if the choice is to "do nothing" and let things happen as they will.

90. *The Recovery of Virtue*, 34–40.

> character of deficiency, since something is said to be evil [or bad—*malum*] because it lacks some perfection that a creature of its kind ought to have.[91]

What Porter says here is helpful. But a qualification needs to be made. That a pen "ought" to write well hardly means that it has an obligation, either wide or narrow, to write well. Only a rational being (a pen maker, for example) can have obligations. And a rational being has an obligation only when, in a given situation, he is confronted with two or more goods, not all of which can be chosen. Thomas's general claim is that when something lacks "the ultimate perfection it ought (*debet*) to have . . . it is not said to be perfect simply nor good simply, but only relatively (*secundum quid*)."[92] Porter sees this claim and others like it as a way of bridging what appears to be the "dreadful chasm" between what is and what ought to be in the moral sphere.[93] In her analysis of q. 94 art. 2, she rightly argues that what Thomas says there about the specifically human good is in continuity with what he says about the good in general. Porter does not show, however, how an imperative declaring what one ought to do can be logically derived from a proposition or statement about declaring what is *simplicter*. It is not clear that she intends to show such a thing, for she acknowledges that "the conclusions of a syllogism cannot include anything not contained in the premises; hence we cannot deduce moral conclusions from factual premises."[94]

What Porter does show in *The Recovery of Virtue*, and she shows it incontrovertibly, is that for Thomas, "things exist in accordance with rational principles that are intrinsically normative, and therefore, our knowledge of what things are carries with it an intrinsically normative dimension as well."[95] It is not the case that "facts" and so-called "values," or, rather, what *is* and what *ought* to be, are entirely disparate. For what man *is*, as a rational being, is a being who *ought* to both think and act in a certain way, namely, in accordance with reason. We cannot understand what man *is* unless we understand him this way.

John Searle, in his much discussed article, "How to Derive 'Ought' from 'Is,'" shows, that, from the *statement* (1), "Jones uttered the words 'I hereby promise to pay you, Smith, five dollars,'" the *statement* (5), "Jones ought to pay Smith five dollars," can be inferred by means of three intervening statements, each of which follows necessarily from the preceding one: (2) "Jones promised to pay Smith five dollars." (3) "Jones placed himself (undertook) an obligation to pay Smith five dollars." (4) "Jones is under an obligation to pay Smith five dollars." Now, Searle's statement (4), "Jones is under

91. *The Recovery of Virtue*, 37. Emphasis in the original, except for what is in the bracketed clarification that I have added.

92. ST. 1, q. 5, art. 1 ad 1.

93. *The Recovery of Virtue*, 43–48; 84 ff.

94. *Nature as Reason*, 123.

95. *The Recovery of Virtue*, 46. This observation fits nicely with Kant's understanding that reason prohibits treating persons merely as things. Knowing what a mere thing is, what a person is, and how they differ "carries with it an intrinsically normative dimension," indeed.

an obligation to pay Smith five dollars," is identical in meaning to statement (5). And statement (3) in Searle's sequence, "Jones placed himself (undertook) an obligation to pay Smith five dollars" is no more than an explication of statement (1); and the same is true of statement (2), "Jones promised to pay Smith five dollars." If statement (1) had been merely "Jones uttered the words, 'I shall pay you, Smith, five dollars," no statement about obligation, and hence no statement employing the Ought, would necessarily follow. For "I shall pay you, etc." could be interpreted as no more than a prediction by "Jones" or, alternatively, a simple lie. All Searle has shown is that the *statement* that someone placed himself under an obligation, whether by a promise or in some other way, implies the *statement* that he ought to do something. Someone hearing Jones utter the words 'I hereby promise to pay you, Smith, five dollars," would reasonably infer that Jones ought to pay Smith the five dollars, unless, Smith dies, becomes comatose, is committed to an insane asylum, or something similar in the interim. It is hard to see how anyone could quarrel with Searle on so trivial a point.

What is missing in Searle's account is an explication of what Jones is supposed to have *meant* in *his* original utterance "I hereby promise . . . etc." If, as Searle seems to think, Jones meant to place himself under an obligation, we return to the question of what an obligation *is*, and how a statement explicitly or implicitly employing the concept of obligation could be derived from a statement about a state of affairs that has no intrinsic reference, implicit or explicit, to obligation or to good more broadly construed. Since a promise is incontestably a statement that has an intrinsic reference to obligation, Searle's article does not help us answer this question.

The Ought cannot be derived from the Is because the first principle of practical reason, to which the Ought refers back, generates human action, something that the principle of non-contradiction cannot do, either by itself or in combination with any other merely declarative statements. Neither principle is derivable from the other or from any ostensibly higher or more universal principle. These two principles are equi-primordial in their respective spheres, though the first principle of practical reason presupposes both the principle of non-contradiction—as a canon, not as something from which it can be deduced—and the *ratio boni*, whereas the principle of non-contradiction does not presuppose the first principle of practical reason. The underivability of the first principle of practical reason does not mean that this principle is just arbitrary. For it is an expression of practical reason; and practical reason is reason every bit as much as speculative reason is; and nothing is less arbitrary than reason. Neither the first principle of practical reason nor the principle of non-contradiction can be demonstrated. They cannot be demonstrated because they are already *per se nota*. Each principle is as intelligible as intelligible can be.

iii. Conditional obligations

Some people grant that the word "ought" has meaning, but hold that it must be understood as something conditional, whether or not the conditions are actually spelled out: "I ought to do x, *if* I want to do (or have) y." Or, to work with a somewhat more explicit, but also more cumbersome, formulation, "I ought to do x *if* I want, or desire, to do (or have) y, *and if* I can do (or have) y only if I also do x." Such inferences, however, are one and all invalid, if for no other reason than that I might want to do both y and not-y. I often have to choose between things I want to do. Moreover, I might *want* to do y, but still think that I *ought not* to do y. I might say, "I want to do y *more than anything in the world*," and, in saying this, think that I can do y only by doing x. But it still does not follow with any necessity that I *ought* to do x. The most that follows is that I *will* do x. If I do *not* do x in such a situation, then I am guided by a concept of obligation to which I give precedence over all mere wants. This does mean, to be sure, that at the *deepest* level I must *want* to give obligation the highest priority. So giving obligation the highest priority, rather than doing y, is what I *really* want "more than anything in the world," no matter what I said. But this considerably deeper want is not a mere want: it presupposes obligation and cannot generate it. Moreover, even if I affirm that there is by nature a good for human beings, it does not immediately follow that I am obligated to seek it, unless I simply define the good as the obligatory.[96]

An obligation cannot be inferred from a mere want.[97] And, for the same reason, an obligation cannot be inferred from a mere need either. Nor can an obligation be inferred from an inclination or tendency, even a natural one. That I am naturally inclined to something does not by itself mean that I ought to follow this inclination. For, again, I have a number of such inclinations and in a given situation they may conflict with each other. If the first principle of practical reason, "Good is to be done . . . etc.," expressed a general inclination or tendency only, rather than a practical proposition, it could not generate an obligation simply by being combined with other, more specific inclinations.[98]

If neither merely wanting to do y, nor needing to do y, nor being naturally inclined to do y is a basis for validly inferring that I am conditionally obligated to do x, as *sine qua non* for y, then what would count as a sufficient reason? The answer

96. We should remember that, when the will makes a choice, pursuit of happiness is not properly obligatory but naturally necessitated: we cannot will *not* to pursue happiness. See *ST* 1–2 q. 5 art. 4, ad 2: "voluntas ad opposita se habet in his quae ad finem ordinantur, sed ad ultimum finem naturali necessitate ordinatur. Quod patet ex hoc, quod homo non potest non velle esse beatus."

97. It is possible for someone to state that he *ought*, even has an *obligation*, to do what he holds to be morally wrong, if doing so is the only way he can experience a certain pleasure. But such a statement does not bear scrutiny, and it seems unlikely that one would ever hear it outside of a classroom. Consistent hedonists do not understand the pursuit of pleasure to be obligatory, strictly speaking, but to be naturally necessitating. They typically hold the concept of obligation to be spurious.

98. That the first principle of practical reason does not express an inclination or tendency merely is manifest in its gerundive form.

is simple: I ought to do x if and only if I also *ought* to do y and cannot do y without doing x.[99] In other words, a conditional obligation, if it really is an obligation, can be validly inferred only from another, more fundamental, obligation. And assuming, in the spirit of both Aristotle and Thomas, that this process cannot continue to infinity,[100] we are led to conclude the following:

> *Conditional obligations, if they really are obligations, ultimately and necessarily presuppose an obligation that is unconditional.*

A primary precept of natural law expresses an unconditional obligation.

The sole way to avoid inferring an unconditional obligation from conditional obligations is, as Nietzsche saw with unsurpassed clarity and spelled out with unparalleled candor, to deny that we have even conditional obligations: we have no obligations whatsoever.[101] When a Nietzschean says, "I *ought* to do x," he has to mean (lest he becomes a "moralist") either "I will x," or, "I will x in order to get y, which I also will." But since "I will x" is as easy to say as "I ought to do x," Nietzsche's response leaves unanswered the question of whence the ostensibly superfluous and misleading, though ubiquitously employed, language of "ought" derives meaning, since this language is naturally understood by everyone who can think and speak coherently. One can of course counter, less in the spirit of Nietzsche than of certain schools of contemporary philosophy, that the word "ought" is just a *meaningless* expression. This evasion will not work, however. For it is incontestable that the word "ought" (unlike, for example, the sound "garzuxy") is meaningfully, and quite naturally, employed in ordinary language, all the time. Such a thing would not be possible if the word "ought" were truly meaningless, that is, if it meant nothing at all.

As already noted, not every Ought is intended to express a genuinely moral obligation, that is, a duty. For example, I can say, "I ought to take a nap now," or "I ought

99. If two obligations (or grounds of obligation, to use a Kantian formulation) make conflicting claims on the will, and practical reason on moral grounds judges one obligation to take precedence over the other, then that is obviously the obligation that one is morally bound to fulfill. However, if neither obligation is judged on moral grounds to take precedence over the other, then what would tip the balance in favor of fulfilling one rather than the other would not be—indeed could not be—a properly moral assessment. It could be a utilitarian consideration merely or a flip of the coin. Needless to say, in determining which, if either, of two conflicting obligations should take precedence over the other, both *synderesis* and judgment must be exercised.

100. See Aristotle *Metaphysics*, 994b14–16. (Aristotle says something similar about desire at *Nicomachean Ethics* 1094a20). Commenting on this passage from the *Metaphysics*, Thomas says that an infinitude of final causes, or reasons for doing something, would eliminate practical reason. *In Duodecim Libros Metaphysicorum Aristotelis Expositio*, Lib. 2 Lect. 4.319.

101. See *Also Sprach Zarathustra*, *Sämtliche Werke*, Vol. 4, 29–31 [English translation: 25–27]. See also *Jenseits von Gut und Böse*, *Sämtliche Werke*, Vol. 5, § 36 [English translation: 35–36]. Nietzsche seems to have realized that calling the authority of practical reason into question is inseparable from calling the authority of speculative reason into question as well. See, for example, *Götzen-Dämmerung* [English translation: 166–170], *Sämtliche Werke*, Vol. 6, 74–79 and 86–87. Cf. Leo Strauss, "Relativism," 24–26, *Spinoza's Critique of Religion*, 30, and *PR* 99–100.

to take advantage of the sale they are having on Saturday." Still, just like sentences expressing genuinely moral obligations, these sentences too have the three implications we considered earlier. To consider only the first sentence, I mean by it the following: (1) it would be *good* (in some respect) to take a nap now; (2) I *can* take a nap now; and (3) I *might not* take a nap now. Such sentences can be said to express the Ought in the broad sense of the word.[102] But here the Ought is conditional, whether the condition is expressed or not. "I ought to take a nap *if*..." or "I ought to take advantage of this sale *if*..." Construed as conditional obligations, they refer back to a quasi-unconditional obligation, namely, the obligation to preserve oneself, which includes doing what enhances the prospects of self-preservation. The precept commanding self-preservation is a precept of natural law. But I call it "quasi-unconditional" because it loses its obligatory character in circumstances where acting on it would be at odds with the good of reason (*bonum rationis*), for example, if the only way I could preserve myself were by bearing false witness against an innocent human being.[103] Then the precept that prohibits offense of others, which is a precept pertaining to our higher and specifically rational nature, would override the precept commanding self-preservation.

iv. Unconditional obligations

Because there are a number of inclinations, not all of which can be followed in every case, the formal first principle of practical reason, "Good is to be done and pursued, and evil avoided," is implicitly transformed into the precept "The best is to be done and pursued and evil avoided." Thomas does not spell out this transformation in q. 94 art. 2, but it is clearly at work there. There is a distinction between "Good is to be done," and "The best is to be done." The former necessitates naturally. The latter obligates morally. Thomas recognizes that, though we can choose only what appears to us as in *some* respect good,[104] it does not follow, without significant qualification, that we can choose only what appears to us as best.[105]

But what *is* the best that is to be done? Natural reason has something to say about this. The best that is to be done is to act—in the broad sense of the word, in which even

102. No less austere a moral philosopher than Kant can say, "To assure one's own happiness is a duty (at least indirectly)." *Grundlegung zur Metaphysik der Sitten*, *Werke*, Band 6, 25 [English translation: 12]. Kant's idea of happiness is much narrower or, rather, much more hedonistic, than Aristotle's and Thomas's. Neither virtue nor rectitude of the will is a constituent of it.

103. I shall return to Thomas's understanding of the *bonum rationis* in Ch. 3, Section d, below.

104. *ST* 1–2 q. 77 art. 2, co.: "cum voluntas sit boni vel apparentis boni, nunquam voluntas in malum moveretur, nisi id *aliqualiter* rationi bonum apparet..." (emphasis added).

105. The significant qualification is that when we are confronted with a number of goods that, from different perspectives, appear equally attractive but which cannot all be chosen, we are able to convince ourselves that one of them (pleasure most conspicuously) is *the* best while, at the same time, strongly suspecting, if not actually convinced deep down, that it is no better than *second* best. See *ST* 1–2 q. 78 art. 1; see q. 58 art. 2. Consider, in this connection, Kant, *Kritik der Praktischen Vernunft*, *Werke*, Band 6, 238–241 [English translation, 92–95].

thinking is a kind of acting—according to reason. This precept, too, is operative in q. 94 art. 2. And though, like the precept, "The best is to be done, etc.," the precept, "Act according to reason," is not spelled out in this article, it is stated explicitly two articles later: "Among all men this is right and true, *that* [*one*] *act* according to reason."[106] From the perspective of natural reason these two principles are in fact equivalent: the best to be done is acting according to reason, and vice versa. To the possible objection that by effectively defining, from the perspective of practical reason, "the best" as "the rational" we have somehow narrowed the meaning of "best," the following question can be posed: How else, from the perspective of practical reason, can we define "best" (other than just nominally as "the superlative of good")? It is practical reason itself that declares itself to be the standard of the best and of how one ought to act.

Such is how things are from the perspective of natural reason in its practical employment. If, from the perspective of revelation and divine law, one holds that a voice distinct from that of natural reason can rightly declare, or reveal, that doing x (for example, partaking of Holy Communion) is better than not doing x, even though doing x goes way beyond what natural reason by itself can establish as obligatory, then this voice has to be understood as possessing an authority higher than our natural, finite reason, supplementing it but without contradicting it. According to Thomas, this higher, or rather highest, authority is also reason. But it is supernatural, infinite reason. It is God himself, addressing us through divine, or revealed, law.[107]

But to return to the perspective of natural reason and to natural law, we see that the precept, "Act according to reason," just like the precept, "The best is to be done, etc.," morally obligates. It does not necessitate in any other way. Though we ought to act according to reason, we might not do so. Moreover, unlike the first principle of practical reason, "Good is to be done, etc.," the precept, "Act according to reason," is not merely formal. It has concrete content. Its content is articulated, at the most fundamental level, in the two primary precepts of natural law identified in q. 94 art. 2: "Avoid ignorance" and "Do not offend others among whom one has to live."

The obligation to act according to reason is not vacuous. It requires that one act according to precepts or universal rules, since natural reason as such makes its pronouncements only in universal terms. Reason is no more a respecter of persons when it is directed to action than when it is directed to speculation. The interest of reason is the *common* good, which is that for the sake of which there is such a thing as law, natural or otherwise, in the first place. The obligation to act according to reason does not mean that everything we do must either spring out of reason or be mandated by reason. It does mean that what we do must not be in opposition to reason.[108]

106. *ST* 1–2 q. 94 art. 4, co.

107. See *Super Sent*., lib. 3, dist. 24, q. 1 art. 2, qc. 2, ad 3; *ST* 1–2 q. 19 art. 4, co.; q. 91 art. 1; art. 2; art. 4; q. 97 art. 1, ad 1; q. 99 art. 4, ad 2.

108. *ST* 1–2 q. 94, art. 2, ad 2: ". . . omnes inclinationes quarumcumque partium humanae naturae, puta concupiscibilis et irascibilis, *secundum quod regulantur ratione*, pertinent ad legem natuaralem,

The first principle of practical reason, the gerundive "Good is to be done, etc.," expresses only an incipient or potential obligation. It spans the realms of the Is and the Ought without being wholly situated in either.[109] The formulation, "The best is to be done," however, expresses an actual obligation. Like the formulation, "Act according to reason," to which it is equivalent, the formulation, "The best is to be done," also expresses an unqualified obligation. It is, then, an imperative in the strict sense of the word. And it is self-evident as well: doing what is *best* is in every case *better* than doing what is worse or less good. No one who grants that there is an order of goods can rationally take issue with the claim that it is the best of these that is to be done and pursued, assuming of course that it really can be done and pursued.[110] For what *reason* could one possibly give for doing or pursuing what appears to be only second or third best when one can instead do what appears to be, so to speak, "first best"? If reason says unequivocally that it is best to do x, then it thereby says that one should or ought to do x. Reason cannot at the same time say that one is permitted *not* to do x.

Because the proposition, "The best is to be done," is self-evident, it cannot be demonstrated. It cannot be deduced by way of a syllogism from the first principle of practical reason in conjunction with a proposition expressing the hierarchical order of our natural inclinations. The following argument, construed as a syllogism, is formally invalid:

> Good is to be done [and pursued, and evil avoided].
> Among our natural inclinations, one of them is best [namely, to act in accordance with reason].
> The best is to be done.

There is no way of logically deducing the conclusion from the first two premises, whichever way one orders them as major and minor. For in the shift from "good" to

et reducuntur ad unum primum praeceptum" (emphasis added). This reply corrects a possible misunderstanding of what Thomas says in the body of the article. The inclinations that we share with sub-rational animals, although natural, pertain to the natural *law* only in so far as they are regulated by reason. As a minimum, they cannot be in opposition to reason, since "participatio legis aeternae in *rationali creatura* lex naturalis dicitur" (emphasis added). Cf. q. 90 art. 2, ad 3; also q. 94 art. 3, co., where Thomas spells out more fully what is meant by saying that a thing is inclined to something according to its nature: "Inclinatur autem unumquodque naturaliter ad operationem sibi convenientem secundum suam formam . . . Unde cum anima rationalis sit propria forma hominis, naturalis inclinatio inest cuilibet homini ad hoc quod agat secundum rationem."

109. Whereas a gerundive *can* express an obligation—see below, Ch. 3, Section b—it *need not* do so. As I argue above, the gerundive expressing the first principle of practical reason does not do so. In *ST* 1–2 q. 17 art. 1, co., Thomas says of a different gerundive, "This is to be done by you" ("Hoc est tibi faciendum"), that it is a statement employing a verb in the indicative mode, not in the imperative mode. It is then a declarative sentence. But it is not simple declaration, expressing, as it does, an obligation proper.

110. Nor can he rationally take issue with the claim that if there is an order of evils, and not all can be avoided, it is the worst of these that is to be avoided, assuming that it really can be avoided.

"best" we lose the middle term that would connect the two premises.[111] And yet the third proposition is certain as certain can be. It is a self-evident proposition that arises in light of, without being deducible from, two distinct and more elemental propositions, the first principle of practical reason and the statement declaring the hierarchical order of natural inclinations.

But what about the two primary and concrete precepts that emerge in q. 94 art. 2. The following syllogism is manifestly valid:

> Evil is to be avoided. (Included in the first principle of practical reason.)
> Ignorance is evil.
> Therefore, ignorance is to be avoided.[112]

So the conclusion, which is a primary precept of natural law, seems to be demonstrable after all. And the same is true of the other primary precept given in q. 94 art. 2:

> Evil is to be avoided. (Included in the first principle of practical reason.)
> Offending others is evil.
> Therefore, offending others is to be avoided.

However, in both these valid syllogisms, the second premise depends on the articulation of the order of natural inclinations that we find in q. 94 art. 2. Given that articulation, the minor premise is true, and the syllogism is sound as well as valid. But the explication of obligation, which characterizes the precepts of natural law, in terms of the first principle of practical reason and the order of natural inclinations obviates the need for a syllogism. For the syllogism only restates what the explication has *already* brought to light.

There is, however, a more serious problem that Thomas's procedure avoids. The following syllogism is also manifestly valid.

> Good is to be pursued.
> Self-preservation is good.
> Therefore, self-preservation is to be pursued.

The problem here is that the conclusion of this syllogism, which is true in almost all cases, becomes false if self-preservation can be pursued, in a particular and atypical case, only by grossly offending someone else, for example by murdering and eating him in a time of famine. And we can construct other valid syllogisms concerning procreation and educating one's offspring, which are true in almost all cases but would

111. The very fact that the practical proposition, "the best is to be done," cannot be deduced from the practical proposition, "good is to be done" accounts in no small measure for the fact that one can deceive oneself into not acting in accordance with the former, though each *propositio* is *per se nota*.

112. This syllogism can be restructured as follows:
Offending others is evil.
Evil is to be avoided. (Included in the first principle of practical reason.)
Therefore, offending others is to be avoided.
The second and third syllogisms given above can be restructured in the same way.

become false in particular and atypical cases. In brief, the above syllogisms by themselves do not establish which conclusions are primary and unconditional precepts of natural law, and which are secondary or conditional.[113] We could of course, construct other syllogisms with other premises that would establish which conclusions are unconditional and which are conditional. But doing so would become cumbersome, and also unnecessary in light of the articulation of the order of natural inclinations that Thomas presents in q. 94 art. 2, which these other syllogisms would have to appeal to in any case.

It is for these reasons, I surmise, that Thomas chose not to treat the precepts, "Avoid Ignorance" (or "Ignorance is to be avoided"—here they mean the same thing) and, "Do not offend others," as conclusions of a demonstrative syllogisms. He could have done so, but such a procedure would have undercut his fundamental claim, at the beginning of the *corpus* of q. 94 art. 2, that the (primary) precepts of natural law are *per se nota*, hence more evident than what can be demonstrated.

The logical peculiarity in Thomas's case for natural law is that what he offers is not a proof of the proposition that the best is to be done, or that one should act in accordance with reason, or that one should avoid ignorance and not offend others. (They are all on the same epistemic level inasmuch as they are all indemonstrable but naturally known.) What Thomas offers us, as I read him, is something better than a proof, namely, an explication of what constitutes the core meaning of these propositions, and thereby what constitutes the core meaning of obligation as well. This interpretation alone makes sense of Thomas's claim in q. 94 art. 2 that the primary and morally obligating precepts of natural law, and not just the absolutely necessitating first principle of practical reason, are *per se nota*, assuming, as he says, that the meaning (*ratio*) of the terms is understood. If their meaning is not understood, explication, and not proof, is what is required. For the rest of this study I shall continue to speak, as Thomas does, of the primary precepts of natural law as self-evident.[114]

113. To the objection that Thomas does not consider a possible conflict between the two primary and unqualified precepts given in q 94 art. 2—avoid ignorance and do not offend—his reply would be that these two precepts can never come into an unavoidable conflict with each other. Ignorance can always be avoided by attempting to think clearly about important matters, and attempting to think clearly never requires us to offend others (for example, by stealing books from them). Nor does refraining from offending others ever preclude us from attempting to think clearly. Quite the contrary. I return to the question of a possible conflict between primary precepts in Part 2, Ch. 9, Section c, below.

114. Nothing crucial would have been lost in Thomas's case for natural law had he advanced the two primary precepts of natural law given in q. 94 art. 2 as conclusions of demonstrative syllogisms (though more extended and complicated than the syllogisms I presented above), rather than as *per se nota*. For the crucial point would not be undermined: knowledge of the precepts of natural law, and of their obligatory character, does not depend on a proof of the existence of God, much less on the claims of revelation. Earlier in this chapter, I suggested a way in which the distinction between *per se notum secundum se* and *per se notum quoad nos* might have a bearing on the *corpus* of q. 94, art. 2. To what I said there, I add here that Thomas may have thought that, though the first principle of practical reason and the primary precepts of natural law are self-evident in both senses of *per se notum*, the meaning of obligation that underlies the latter, though self-evident *in itself*, just might not be self-evident *to*

Thomas's solution to the problem of where our knowledge of obligation comes from consists in identifying it neither with our knowledge of the first principle of practical reason solely, for this principle is absolutely necessitating, nor with our knowledge of the order of natural inclinations solely, for the distinction between human and subhuman inclinations, need not, by itself, be interpreted as a moral distinction.

> *Our knowledge of obligation consists in the conjunction of our knowledge of the first principle of practical reason with our knowledge of the hierarchical order of our natural inclinations.*

The three *implications* of what is meant in use of the word "ought"—good to do, can be done, might not be done—do not amount to a *definition* of obligation. But Thomas's account of natural law does yield as clear, defensible, and common sense a definition of obligation as one could ask for.

> *Obligation is the effect of reason's command in the presence of two or more goods not all of which can be chosen.*[115]

In light of this explication we can see that the question, "Why ought I to do what *reason* commands me to do?" makes no more sense than the question, "Why ought I to do what I *ought* to do?" It is reason itself that commands us to act according to reason. To the possible objection that the command of reason is therefore *partial*, it can only be repeated that the command of reason is a practical proposition expressed in *universal* terms, even when it is applied in an act of judgment to specific circumstances. The command of reason *as such* cannot be partial.[116]

everyone. After all, some people, academics in particular, will occasionally say (though rarely outside an academic setting) that they have no idea what is meant by the word "obligation," or even by "ought." For them, explication of its meaning is required.

115. Some of these goods may, of course, be only apparent. A bodily good, for example, is a real, though limited, good in most situations; but it is only an apparent good in situations when it cannot be obtained except by acting in opposition to a precept of natural law or, if we bring revelation into the picture, in opposition to a precept of divine law. On the other hand, when confronted with two or more goods, not all of which can be chosen, and when, additionally, none of them is either a good pertaining to our rational nature or in conflict with a good pertaining to our rational nature—e.g., hot tea with lemon or with milk—reason does not command. In such a case, there is no obligation.

116. Those who ask why we have to accept *reason* as a canon seem not to realize that they are, if only tacitly, asking for a *reason* why we have to accept reason as a canon.

Chapter 3

Reason Commanding

SECTION A. NATURAL LAW AND ROMAN CATHOLICISM

In the Introduction I drew attention to a tendency among Thomas Aquinas's coreligionists to advertise his natural law teaching as a Roman Catholic teaching. This advertisement, which Straussians take note of but tend to misinterpret, is true only in the sense that integral to the tradition of Roman Catholic theology in its scholastic elaboration is the attempt to demonstrate what can be known by natural reason concerning the relation of God to the world and man's place within the world. The demonstrations of these matters fit within a whole of theology, a whole that consists of both rational theology and revealed theology. Thomas attempts to demonstrate that the articles of faith, though they cannot be demonstrated by natural reason, are nonetheless self-consistent and irrefutable. He also tries to show that Christianity, for which these articles of faith are central, makes more sense of certain pervasive features of our experience, of life as actually lived, than does any purely philosophical account. Finally, Thomas tries to show that the specifically Roman Catholic version of Christianity is both more self-consistent and more in harmony with the writings of the church fathers, with the proclamations of the early church councils, and with the Bible, than are alternative versions of Christianity.

Thomas's writings serve, then, as an arsenal for Roman Catholic theologians who are engaged, as many of them are at one time or another, in disputations, not only with unbelieving philosophers and their followers, but also, and more frequently, with Christians who are straying from the Roman Catholic fold or who were never Roman Catholics in the first place. In the latter disputations, where belief in the event, if not in the exact content or interpretation, of revelation, can be taken for granted, the distinction between natural and revealed theology—constitutive though it is for Thomas's endeavor as a whole—does not loom large. It can get blurred. There is, furthermore, a proprietary interest in emphasizing that Thomas's rational theology forms part of Roman Catholic theology, which is understandable given the solidity of its premises, the coherence of its demonstrations, and its scope. But if Thomas's rational theology is independent of his revealed theology, then it can be appropriated in varying degrees by believers who are not Roman Catholics. It can be appropriated by Orthodox Christians who do not distrust all things Western, by Anglicans who do not distrust all things Roman, and by Protestants who do not distrust all things rational. It can also be appropriated by Jews and Muslims, as Thomas himself appropriated what he found true in Maimonides and Avicenna. Thomas's rational theology can even be appropriated by unbelievers, that is, by people who have no faith at all, for it neither presupposes faith nor entails faith.

To be sure, one who becomes convinced that Thomas's rational theology and natural law teaching are sound may also become more receptive, that is, more open, to the possibility of revelation, even to the fundamental doctrines of Catholic Christianity, than one who thinks that natural reason has nothing substantive to say about God or moral obligation. Nevertheless, any ascent from rational theology and natural law to revealed theology cannot be propelled by natural reason alone. There is nothing in Thomas's rational theology, as distinct from his revealed theology, that is specifically Roman Catholic, or more generally Christian, from a doctrinal perspective. How could there be if the preambles to the articles of faith, which are the concern of rational theology, are knowable by natural reason apart from revelation, as Thomas not only says but sets out to prove?

In spite of the fact that Thomas presents his natural law teaching without appeal to revelation, some Roman Catholic scholars speak as though it is inextricably bound up with the articles of faith. For example, Servais Pinckaers, OP, writes, "It is absolutely impossible . . . to separate the moral section [of which the questions on natural law are a part] of the *Summa* from the study of God in the first part, which stresses his [T]rinitarian dimension, and from the third part, which gives us the [C]hristological and sacramental dimension."[1] Now, it is incontestable that the *Summa Theologiae* is a carefully constructed whole. To focus on what Thomas has to say about the preambles to the articles of faith without considering what he has to say about the articles of faith themselves, and to focus on what he has to say about natural law without considering what he has to say about divine law, that is the Old Law and the New Law, does meager justice to the sweep of his thought. But sometimes one has to restrict one's focus. And what we can know by natural reason is most definitely distinguishable from what can be accepted only through faith. After all, such distinguishing is required in order to understand why Thomas can so confidently hold that "faith presupposes natural cognition, as grace presupposes nature, and perfection the perfectible." [2]

Earl Muller, S.J., goes somewhat further than Fr. Pinckaers, when he writes, "The natural law, inherent to humanity, is the law inherent in the Body of Christ . . . [The Church can] speak authoritatively about natural law since she is fundamentally talking about herself . . . [N]atural law theory can only be successfully pursued by someone

1. *Sources*, 222.

2. *ST* 1 q. 2 art. 2, ad 1.

who has been converted to Christ."[3] What Fr. Muller presumably means is that the church alone integrates Thomas's natural law teaching into a fully comprehensive view of human nature—an altogether reasonable claim for a Roman Catholic theologian to make. But Fr. Muller's formulation reinforces the view, pervasive among Straussians, that Thomas's natural law teaching is inaccessible to man as man, a view that is seriously at odds with how Thomas presents that teaching. Human beings have a natural knowledge of natural law whether they are believers or unbelievers, or unbelievers moving toward belief, or believers moving away from belief. This knowledge persists in man whatever position he takes on the existence of God or on the nature of the church. How else could Thomas argue, as he does, that the primary precepts of natural law cannot be abolished from the human heart?

For Thomas, revealed propositions, that is, the articles of faith proper, are neither premises nor conclusions of the arguments he develops in his rational theology. If they were premises of his rational theology, then rational theology would not be, as he presents it as being, knowable by natural reason. And if revealed propositions were conclusions of his rational theology, then the articles of faith proper would be knowable by natural reason, which he explicitly denies.

Thomas's rational theology and the foundational principles of his natural law teaching are Roman Catholic only because, in the tradition of Roman Catholic theology, which reaches its height in scholasticism, the first order of business is to get clear what can be demonstrated about God, the world, and man, without appeal to the indemonstrable claims of revelation. Getting these things clear assists in defending the claims of revelation against those who would argue that they are at odds with what we demonstratively know and that a man cannot assent to them without abandoning his reason. And it serves the further purpose of showing that there is a natural appetite or desire for a supernatural end and a natural need for supernatural assistance to reach it. Only by keeping these purposes in mind, can we appreciate the full force of Thomas's claim that "faith presupposes natural knowledge, just as grace presupposes nature and perfection the perfectible."

Not only are Thomists who do not give full weight to Thomas's careful distinction between faith and knowledge, and between grace and nature, unable to understand how the former could be perfections of the latter. Of equal importance and greater urgency, they are unable to speak convincingly to unbelievers about moral matters that, according to Thomas, lie fully within the competence of natural reason to pronounce upon. As a consequence, Thomas's voice cannot effectively enter the broader ethical conversation of our times, where it badly needs to be heard and considered.

Theologians who appreciate the distinction between Thomas's rational theology and his revealed theology might, however, claim that, though his natural law teaching is not based on his revealed theology, it is based on his rational theology. If it were so based, we would expect Thomas to argue along the following lines.

3. "The Christological foundation of Natural Law, 107–109.

1. God exists and governs his creation providentially through the eternal law.
2. God divinely gives natural law to man, who is one of his creatures.
3. Man is obligated to obey natural law, because it is divinely given by his creator.

But this is not how Thomas reasons. From the perspective of rational theology, the first premise is true. But the second premise is equivocal: it is not natural law but divine law that is "divinely given," in the strict senses of that expression. Man existed for a long time without divine law. He received it only by way of divine intervention in human history, in an act of grace that goes beyond nature. On the other hand, man never existed without natural law, however much he may have deceived himself into ignoring it. For man is a rational animal and natural law is an expression of natural reason itself. Thomas does not think that man can act rationally except by acting in accordance with natural law, since it is reason itself that commands him to act this way.[4] Thomas's natural law teaching is not, then, an instance of what in contemporary meta-ethics parlance is called the "divine command theory," nor is it vulnerable to the criticisms launched against that theory.

In the context of his rational theology Thomas does, to be sure, define natural law not only as an expression of reason commanding but more properly as "the participation in the rational creature of the eternal law." So to fully understand what natural law means for Thomas we do have to turn to his rational theology. No doubt about that. But if, for whatever reason, one refused to accept Thomas's *definition* of natural law, the first principle of practical reason and the actual precepts of natural law would continue to be known, and known as self-evident.[5] In such a case one might redefine

4. The opposite view could hardly be put more directly, and more paradoxically, than it is put by David Hume: "Reason is, and *ought* only to be the slave of the passions, and can never pretend to any other office than to serve and obey them" (emphasis added). *A Treatise of Human Nature*, 415. (There is no comma after "only to be" in the text.) The view that reason exercises rule and command within the soul, on its own initiative and not at the urging of the sub-rational passions, can be traced back to the ancients. See, e.g., Plato, *Republic* 442c1–10; also 428a1–429a4; 439c1–440e10; 443c6–445a1. (Consider Allan Bloom's notes 13 and 25 on pages 456–457 of his translation, *The Republic of Plato*.) See also Plato, *Protagoras* 352b3–c2; and Aristotle, *Nicomachean Ethics* 1102a24–1103a4; 1143a8–10; 1177a15. The ruling and commanding function of human reason is not a fabrication of Christian Scholasticism. Even a thinker as distant from the Scholastics as Spinoza acknowledges and emphasizes it, in his own way of course. *Ethica* 3, Prop. 59, Schol.; 4, Prop. 18, Schol.; Props. 61–66.

5. Clifford Kossel rightly points out that, in the relation between the eternal law and natural law, the order of discovery reverses the order of causality ("Natural Law and Human Law," 172). Russell Hittinger writes, correctly enough, "Natural law is never (and I must emphasize *never*) defined in terms of what is first in the (human) mind or first in nature" ("Natural Law and Catholic Moral Theology," 6). But Hittinger should also have emphasized that, for Thomas, how natural law, as consisting of self-evident precepts of practical reason, is *originally known* is distinct from how it is *subsequently defined*. Human beings have a natural knowledge of the principle of non-contradiction, and they know it without demonstration. But that does mean that every human being can say what is meant by self-evident, or even what is meant by a demonstration, much less that this principle is the *ratio entis*. The case is analogous with the primary precepts of natural law. I emphasize this point because it is a common error, among both admirers and detractors of Thomas Aquinas, to say without the appropriate qualifications that natural law presupposes rational (or natural) theology. However, as self-evident,

natural law simply as the principle and precepts that are constituted by natural reason for choice and action. This would not be as rich a definition as Thomas's, but it would be adequate for meeting the objection that one cannot believe that there are precepts of practical reason unless one first believes in the existence of God. After all, uncertainty or disagreement about the definition of something, such as knowledge, light, life, or natural law does not necessarily entail uncertainty or disagreement about the existence of that thing. It is hardly an accident of omission that Thomas does not so much as mention his definition of natural law in the foundational argument for our knowledge of the first principle of practical reason and the primary precepts of natural law in q. 94 art. 2. Moreover, in the *sed contra* of that article he does not appeal to an authority as is his typical though not invariant practice. Instead, he presents an argument there in his own name. These are further signs of how determined Thomas is to develop his foundational argument independently even of what he thinks he has already demonstrated in his rational theology. "[For] Aquinas . . . the first principles of natural law are self-evident but . . . the existence of God is not self-evident to the human mind."[6]

The criticism I made above of some of Thomas's followers, namely, that they do not sufficiently emphasize the natural and fully rational character of the knowledge we have of natural law, does not apply to all of them by any means. In particular, it does not apply to a group of thinkers sometimes spoken of as "the new natural law theorists." The new natural law theorists are sometimes criticized by more traditional-minded Thomists for not trying hard enough to keep Thomas from sounding like Kant. I think, on the contrary, that the new natural law theorists try too hard to keep Thomas from sounding like Kant.

SECTION B. THE NEW NATURAL LAW THEORY

Proponents of the new natural law theory address a range of contemporary issues, including some, such as natural rights (in the plural), concerning which Thomas has nothing to say. But these thinkers ground their point of departure for dealing with contemporary issues in a carefully worked out interpretation of Thomas's natural law teaching. In what follows, my concern will be not with the new natural law theory as the foundation of a comprehensive account of the human good, but only with how the proponents of this theory interpret certain crucial claims that Thomas makes concerning the obligatory character of the primary precepts of natural law.

From the perspective of more traditionally minded Thomists, the interpretation of Thomas's natural law teaching that I have proposed above could appear to be only

the primary precepts themselves are naturally known independently of the demonstrations of natural theology. They are naturally known even by those who deny that there is natural law. How could it be otherwise, on Thomas's understanding?

6. John Finnis, *Natural Law and Natural Rights*, 48.

a variation of the interpretation proposed by the new natural law theorists. There are points of agreement indeed, but there are significant differences as well. Because these differences have a bearing on how Thomas's teaching can be best defended against the Straussian criticisms, to which we shall turn in Part 2, it is worth spelling them out in some detail.

One of the chief representatives of the new natural law theory is Germain Grisez. His article, to which I referred earlier, "The First Principle of Practical Reason: A Commentary on the *Summa theologiae*, 1–2, Question 94, article 2," is something of a founding document for the new theory. Grisez convincingly shows that Thomas's first principle of practical reason, "Good is to be done and pursued, and evil avoided," is neither a declarative statement nor deducible from a declarative statement or from a combination of such statements. "[A] statement is an expression of reason asserting, whereas a law is an expression of reason prescribing."[7] According to Grisez, the first principle of practical reason is not really an imperative. It is merely "prescriptive."[8] I have argued above that, for a command, imperative, precept, or practical principle to obligate, the following conditions must be met: (1) doing what is commanded is good; (2) it is possible for one to do what is commanded; (3) one might not do what is commanded, even when the command is issued by one's own reason. The first principle of practical reason does not obligate, strictly speaking, because it does not meet the third of these conditions. General as it is, there cannot be the slightest motive or inclination to act in opposition to it. In one's deliberations, choices, and actions, one aims as a matter of natural necessity at some good, an apparent good at least, if not a genuine good. Grisez's adjective "prescriptive" to describe this principle is then a bit ambiguous, as it suggests, or could be thought to suggest, the possibility of not following the prescription, and there is no such possibility. Grisez recognizes that everyone who acts, the bad man as well as the good man, acts for the sake of something that, rightly or wrongly, he is convinced or has convinced himself is good in some respect or other.[9] Genuine obligation, as distinct from the natural necessitation established by the first principle of practical reason, cannot enter the picture unless there are both a hierarchy of goods and situations in which not all of them can be done or pursued. Though Grisez seems to think that obligation is already established by the first principle of practical reason,[10] he also realizes that one lacks the freedom or ability to

7. Grisez, 191.

8. Grisez, 190.

9. Grisez, 187–9.

10. This is speculation on my part. But it is based on Grisez's quick transition from an emphasis on the underivability of the Ought (Grisez, 194, bottom) to an emphasis on the underivability of the first principle of practical reason "and other self-evident principles of natural law" (195, top), followed by a paragraph in which he seems to equate the practical and prescriptive work of reason in general (and hence also its constitution of the first principle of practical reason) with "the *ought* rul[ing] its own domain by its own authority, an authority as legitimate as that of any *is*." Furthermore, Grisez says, ". . . natural law imposes *obligations* that *good acts are to be done* . . ." (182, emphasis added) which

act in opposition to this principle. It is difficult, then, to understand exactly what he means by obligation. The matter is considerably complicated by his claim, not only that the first principle of practical reason is not an imperative, but that the primary precepts of natural law are not imperatives either, in spite of his understanding that "precepts oblige," even that "they are concerned with duties."[11] Grisez cites the following passage from Thomas in support of his position.

> A precept of law, since it is binding (*obligatorium*), is about something that ought to be (*debet*) done. That something ought to be done arises from the necessity of some end. Hence it is manifest that it pertains to the concept of a precept that it implies order to an end, insofar as what is commanded (*praecipitur*) is necessary or expedient to an end.[12]

Precepts defined this way—as involving obligation and command, as well as orientation to an end—would seem to be imperatives. Grisez disagrees. Precepts, even defined this way, are not yet imperatives.

> Human and divine law are in fact not merely prescriptive but *also* imperative, and *when* precepts of the law of nature were incorporated into the divine law they *became* imperatives whose violation is contrary to the divine will as well as to right reason.[13]

Grisez is saying here that imperatives as such can be imposed upon one only through the will of someone else, a human or a divine ruler. However, his suggestion that not just the first principle of practical reason but all the precepts of the natural law were merely prescriptive until their incorporation into divine (or human) law is not adequately supported by Thomas's text. And it is at odds with Thomas's striking claim that "the moral precepts [of the Decalogue] have their efficacy from the very dictate of natural reason, even if they had never been stated in the [Old] Law."[14] To be sure, Grisez is correct in saying that, when incorporated into divine law, the precepts of natural law acquired a new character such that their violation was understood to be contrary to the divine will as well as to right reason. But that did not cause them to *become* imperatives. Man's natural reason expressed them as precepts of natural law before God re-expressed them as the moral precepts in the Old Law. After all, precepts

---

sounds like little more than a rewording of the *necessitating* first principle of practical reason itself.

11. Grisez, 182.

12. *ST* 1–2 q. 99 art. 1, co: "Respondeo dicendum quod praeceptum legis, cum sit obligatorium, est de aliquo quod fieri debet. Quod autem aliquid debeat fieri, hoc provenit ex necessitate alicuius finis. Unde manifestum est quod de ratione praecepti est quod importet ordinem ad finem, inquantum scilicet illud praecipitur quod est necessarium vel expediens ad finem."

13. Grisez, 192 (emphasis added). See 193, fn. 64.

14. *ST* 1–2 q. 100 art. 11, co.: "[P]raecepta moralia ex ipso dictamine naturalis rationis efficaciam habent, etiam si nunquam in lege statuantur." See 1–2, q. 98 art. 5, co; q. 104 art. 1, co.

as such articulate duties.[15] To resist this conclusion is simply to redefine an imperative as a command coming *from without*. Perhaps something might be gained by acceding to such a redefinition. But then another passage from the *Summa Theologiae* that Grisez also appeals to invalidates it.

> To command (*imperare*) is indeed essentially an act of reason. The one commanding (*imperans*) directs him whom he commands (*imperat*) to doing (*ad agendum*) something by intimation or declaration; but to order thus by mode of intimating [something] to someone belongs to reason. But reason [!] can intimate or declare something in two ways. In one way, absolutely: which intimation is indeed expressed in the indicative mode; as when someone says (*aliquis dicat*) to someone, "This is to be done by you." But sometimes reason intimates something to someone by moving him to this; and such intimation is expressed by a verb in the imperative mode; namely when it is said (*dicitur*) to someone, "Do this." But the first mover in the powers of the soul to the performance (*exercitum*) of an act is the will, as was said above. Since, therefore, the second mover does not move except through the power of the first mover, it follows that the very fact that reason moves by commanding (*imperando*) is due to the power of the will. Whence it follows that to command (*imperare*) is an act of reason, presupposing an act of the will, through whose power reason moves by a command (*imperium*) to the performance of an act.[16]

Even if we take the passage beginning with "But the first mover . . ." to refer only to commands in the imperative mode as distinct from gerundives, we see that Thomas is speaking of an *interior* dynamic: "But the first mover among the powers of the soul (*in viribus animae*) to the doing of an act is the will." This act of the will leads reason to *command* the performance of the act.[17] Reason itself issues imperatives.

15. *ST* 1–2 q 100 art. 5, ad 1: "Praeceptum autem habet rationem debiti." *ST* 2–2 q.122 art. 1, co.: "Manifestissime autem ratio debiti, quae requiritur ad praeceptum, apparet in iustitua, quae est ad alterum."

16. *ST* 1–2 q. 17 art. 1, co. "Imperare autem est quidem essentialiter actus rationis; imperans enim ordinat eum cui imperat, ad aliquid agendum intimando vel denuntiando; sic autem ordinare per modum cuiusdam intimationis, est rationis. Sed ratio potest aliquid intimare vel denuntiare dupliciter. Uno modo, absolute: quae quidem intimatio exprimitur per verbum indicativi modi; sicut si aliquis alicui dicat, 'Hoc est tibi faciendum.' Aliquando autem ratio intimat aliquid alicui, movendo ipsum ad hoc: et talis intimatio exprimitur per verbum imperativi modi; puta cum alicui dicitur: 'Fac hoc.' Primum autem movens in viribus animae ad exercitum actus est voluntas, ut supra dictum est. Cum ergo secundum movens non moveat nisi in virtute primi moventis, sequitur quod hoc ipsum quod ratio movet imperando, sit ei ex virtute voluntatis. Unde relinquitur quod imperare sit actus rationis, praesupposito actu voluntatis, in cuius virtute ratio movet per imperium ad exercitium actus." Cf. *Nicomachean Ethics* 1143a9.

17. 1–2 q. 17 art. 1, co; see 1–2, q. 9 art. 1, ad 3. Cf. q. 17, art. 2, ad 2: "non est ibi [i.e., in sub-rational animals] ratio imperantis et imperati [as there is in man] sed solum moventis et moti"; art, 2, ad 3: unlike man, sub-rational animals "non . . . ipsa seipsa ordinant ad actionen"; q. 90 art. 1, ad 3: "ratio habet vim movendi a voluntate . . . ex hoc enim quod aliquis vult finem, ratio imperat de his quae sunt ad finem"; q. 91. art. 3, ad 1; q. 92 art. 1, co.; q. 94, art. 3 co: ". . . omnes actus virtutum sunt de lege naturali: dictat enim hoc naturaliter unicuique propria ratio, ut virtuose agat"; q. 100 art. 5, ad 4:

Grisez's apparent assumption that an imperative can only be communicated from without, by one person (divine or human) to another, is undermined earlier in this text too. Thomas uses the personal expression and the active voice, "someone says to someone," when describing the *gerundive*. But he uses the impersonal expression and the passive voice, "it is said to someone," when describing the *imperative* mode. Nothing in this passage supports the notion that genuine imperatives (as allegedly distinct from precepts of natural law) are issued only from one person to another person.

Though the distinction that Thomas draws in the above passage between commands issued absolutely and commands issued in the imperative mode is interesting, it is a grammatical rather than a moral distinction. Thomas does not bind himself to it when speaking of moral obligations.

> For there are certain things that each man's very reason naturally judges are to be done or not to be done (*esse facienda vel non facienda*): such as, "Honor thy father and thy mother," and "Thou shalt not kill," "Thou shalt not commit theft." And such things belong absolutely to the law of nature.[18]

These precepts can be expressed indifferently as gerundives or imperatives. In either case they are part of natural law, just as Thomas says. They would be part of natural law, with full obligatory and imperative force, "even if they had never been stated in the [Old] Law."

Grisez says that "the prescription expressed in gerundive form . . . merely offers rational direction without promoting the execution of the work to which reason directs."[19] The first principle of practical reason, which is expressed in gerundive form, promotes doing good and pursuing good with such necessity that no human agent can resist it. At the more concrete level, execution is surely promoted in a command such as, "This is your mission, and it is to be accomplished by twelve o'clock tonight," in spite of the fact that it is expressed as a gerundive rather than in the imperative mode. In Thomas's analysis of the structure of command and execution, the elemental and paradigmatic relation is between reason and will within the soul of a single individual.[20] This paradigmatic relation does not presuppose a hierarchical command struc-

". . . statim ratio naturalis homini dictat quod nulli iniuriam faciat"; q. 91 art. 3, co: "lex est quoddam dictamen practicae rationis." Cf. *SCG* lib. 3 cap. 139 n. 3; *ST* 1–2 q. 61 art. 3, co.

18. *ST* 1–2 q. 100, art. 1, co.

19. Grisez, 192.

20. Grisez concedes that, at the very beginning of his "Treatise on Law," Thomas "refers to his previous treatment of the imperative." (Grisez, 192) He even cites passages where Thomas underscores the way in which reason itself commands (*imperat*—192, fn. 63). Grisez adds, however, that "these passages should not be given too much weight" because they refer back to q. 17 art. 1, an article that, for reasons given above, I think Grisez misinterprets. I think that John Finnis, too, misinterprets this article. Apparently contrasting the gerundive with the imperative, Finnis says that the former, "as [Thomas] says in explaining the point, *directs* {*ordinat*} someone *to* something to be done" (*AMPLT* 102, note y). But Thomas means by *ordinare* to ordain something to an end; and this can be accomplished by way of commands, however they are expressed: "imperans enim ordinat eum cui imperat

ture holding sway between two or more individuals though, to be sure, commands can also be issued within such a structure.

In articulating the primary precepts of natural law (though not the first principle of practical reason) Thomas uses neither the gerundive nor the imperative mode. As we have seen, he speaks descriptively, employing the subjunctive. "It pertains to natural law . . . *that man avoid* ignorance, *that he not offend* others . . ."[21] "All acts of the virtues belong to natural law; for each one's reason naturally dictates [!] *that he act* virtuously."[22] "Among all men this is right and true, *that* [*one*] *act* according to reason."[23] But these propositions are clearly intended to express obligations. Nothing of significance is lost, and nothing questionable is introduced, by reformulating them in the imperative mode: "Avoid ignorance!" "Do not offend others!" "Act virtuously!" Thomas refers to a secondary precept of natural law in the gerundive mode. "Deposits are to be restored."[24] But that does not mean that this precept could not have been expressed in the imperative mode. According to Thomas, that "no one is to be slain" (*non esse occidendum*) is derived at once from the general principle of natural law that "evil is to be done to no one" (*nulli esse malum faciendum*). Similarly, Thomas says that "justice is to be preserved" (*justitiam esse servandum*) is a principle that never fails, whatever concrete situation is under consideration.[25] These formulations are intended to express obligations, hence imperatives or commands, constituted by practical reason itself. They can be expressed indifferently in the gerundive, as they are here, or in the imperative mode.[26] The prohibition against slaying another human being and the injunction to preserve justice are not merely "prescriptive" as distinct from imperative.

A threefold distinction can surely be drawn between: (1) the first principle of practical reason, (2) the properly obligatory precepts of natural law; and (3) commands given by one individual to another in the imperative mode. It seems as though Grisez has such a threefold distinction in mind: the first principle of practical reason differs from the other precepts of natural law in that no one can act in opposition to

ad aliquid agendum." Thomas says this *before* distinguishing between the two modes of command. See 2. 17 art. 2 co: "imperare nihil aliud est quam ordinare aliquem ad aliquid agendum, cum quadam intimativa motione." See also, 1–2, q. 91 art. 4, co. (and note the nuance of difference there between *ordinare* and *dirigere*); q. 100 art. 2, *sed contra* and co.; art. 7, arg. 1, co., ad 1; q. 108 art. 3, co.

21. *ST* 1–2 q. 94 art. 2, co.

22. *ST* 1–2 q. 94 art. 3, co.

23. *ST* 1–2 q. 94 art. 4, co.

24. *ST* 1–2 q. 94 art. 4, co.

25. *ST* 1–2 q. 95 art. 2, co. (and see 2–2 q. 40 art. 1, and q. 64 art. 2, art. 6, and art. 7, for the pertinent qualifications); 1–2 q. 100 art. 8, ad 1.

26. A second person imperative almost invariably expresses obligation, though there are exceptions, e.g., "Go to hell!" The third person imperative, "Let there be light," does not express an obligation, though the third person imperative stage direction, "Enter the king," does express an obligation, of sorts. A gerundive, though it can express obligation, need not do so. Such is the case with Thomas's first principle of practical reason in ST 1–2 q. 94 art. 2, co.

the former; while the precepts of natural law differ from imperatives because they are not yet incorporated into divine or human law. But Grisez also seems to collapse the distinction between (1) and (2), as though the difference of both of these from (3) were the decisive thing. I think, on the contrary, that the distinction between (2) and (3) is slight, and that the distinction of both from (1) is the decisive thing: though the first principle of practical reason does *not* impose obligations, the precepts of natural law, both before and after their incorporation within human or divine positive law, *do* impose obligations. Exactly *how* natural reason commands and imposes these obligations, that is, whether it does so through gerundives or in the imperative mode, is not nearly as important as the fact *that* reason does so. As we shall see in Part 2, Strauss and his students also assume that natural reason does not command categorically, that it does not impose unconditional obligations. It is largely on the basis of this assumption that they deny that there is such a thing as natural law. Grisez's claim that, for Thomas, the precepts of natural law became imperatives only when they were incorporated into divine law or human law is then in keeping with the Straussian criticism, though it is not in keeping with Grisez's own intention.[27]

Thomas uses *imperat* and *dictat*, as well as *praeceptum*, all over the place when he is speaking of how natural, human reason determines choice and action. Grisez's odd reluctance to speak of reason as issuing imperatives while nonetheless granting that reason imposes obligations, reflects, I suspect, a resolve he shares with many Thomists to make sure that Thomas's conception of practical reason does not get confused with Kant's.[28]

John Finnis develops some of the points made by Grisez.[29] Finnis's interpretation of Thomas's natural law teaching is comprehensively developed, and he is persuasive on a number of points. Though Finnis does not systematically confront the Straussian criticisms of Thomas's teaching, what he says goes part of the distance toward blunting those criticisms. Anyone who thinks that Thomas's teaching is not fully rational and accessible to man as man would be well served by attending carefully to Finnis's interpretation, along with the ample citations from all parts of Thomas's *oeuvre* that he offers in support of it.[30]

27. See Grisez, 182; cf. 187, fn. 45.

28. We shall consider the pertinent differences between Thomas and Kant in the next section.

29. *AMPLT* Chapters III and IV especially.

30. Russell Hittinger, in *A Critique of the New Natural Law Theory*, takes both Grisez and Finnis to task on a number of points. Some of Hittinger's criticisms strike me as right on target, others as missing the point. I am especially puzzled by his dismissal of the concept of intuitive knowledge (158–175). Hittinger does not show what is so problematic about this concept, apparently assuming that this has been done by others (Jacques Derrida and Richard Rorty? See 168). As noted in Part 1, Ch. 2, above, Thomas follows Aristotle in holding that the principles of understanding, in particular the principle of non-contradiction, are self-evident and hence indemonstrable; and he maintains that the same is true for the first principle of practical reason and the primary precepts of natural law. The *intellectus principiorum* is a mode of knowledge that could be called "intuition," and the same is true of *synderesis*, if all that "intuition" designates is knowledge of what is *per se notum*. See *ST* 1–2 q.

A defect in Finnis's interpretation, however, is that it does not adequately account for where obligation first emerges in Thomas's presentation. Nor does it clarify just what obligation is. Finnis's understanding of a threefold relationship between the first principle of practical reason, precepts of natural law, and imperatives closely follows Grisez's, with some qualifications. Finnis is rightly impressed by Thomas's distinction between the way mind rules the body, namely, as a slave that cannot resist, "unless impeded by some internal or external factor" (for example, a neurological defect or chains), and the way reason rules the emotions, or passions, which can resist.[31] Since Thomas compares the latter rule to that of a king over free citizens, Finnis infers that just as free citizens can on occasion rightfully resist the king's rule, so the emotions can also on occasion rightfully resist reason's rule.

But on what occasion? Free citizens can rightfully resist the king's rule when he rules unjustly. But unjust rule on the king's part is rule in opposition to reason.[32] Staying with the analogy, the emotions can rightfully resist the rule of reason when reason rules in opposition to reason. Though this statement has a paradoxical ring to it, one can easily imagine the faculty of reason functioning in a defective manner, for example, by insisting on an undue mortification of body. In such a case when, as Finnis puts it, "reason's . . . directives are going presumably beyond . . . their proper scope,"[33] the emotions might rightfully protest, resist, and attempt to, so to speak, remind reason of its proper scope. Finnis commends Thomas's "opposition to any rationalistic downgrading of human feeling, of emotional desires and satisfactions, or of the inclinations or other motivating factors which underlie consciousness and feelings."[34] The analogy between the emotions and free citizens does not, however, support the notion that the emotions can disobey reason when reason is functioning not defectively but properly. Finnis clarifies this point somewhat with an appeal to Thomas. "The fact that one's emotions [in genuinely fearful circumstances] resist (*repugnant*) one's reason 'does not prevent them from obeying it'"[35] Finnis recognizes

74 art. 10, ad 2. If Hittinger does not think that anything is *per se notum*, his quarrel is not just with Grisez and Finnis but with Thomas himself, and with Aristotle too. Hittinger writes, "Intuitionism does not necessarily imply any theistic or supernatural content; but once again, to the extent that it supplies the foundational evidence for principles and norms, intuitionism differs from fideism only by denomination" (158–9).Thomas would surely take issue with this reduction if Hittinger is using the word "intuitionism" to name the position that we know some things both independently of and prior to demonstration, for that is exactlyThomas's position; and it is not fideism. Hittinger's failure to give due emphasis to the indemonstrable but self-evident character of the first principle of practical reason and the primary precepts of natural law, in relation to the merely demonstrable, and hence not self-evident, character of the proofs in Thomas's rational theology, compromises much, though not all, of his critique of the new natural law theory.

31. *AMPLT* 72–73.

32. *ST* 1–2 q. 95 art. 2, co; q. 96 art. 4, co., arg. 3, ad 3.

33. *AMPLT* 73.

34. *AMPLT* 75.

35. *AMPLT* 76; *ST* 1 q. 81 art. 3, ad 2.

that when there are several options, none of which are opposed by reason and none of which are required by reason, emotion or a sub-rational inclination can decide the matter. This sort of thing happens frequently. Reason guides us only so far, and in countless matters sub-rational inclinations, emotion, passion, and feeling can determine action without being in opposition to reason.

Though Finnis recognizes that there are a multitude of inclinations, and hence of ends and goods as well,[36] he does not focus on the way in which this multitude gives rise to moral conflict on those occasions when the ends cannot all be pursued. Though he realizes that the rule of reason is central to Thomas's understanding of sound choice and action, he seems reluctant to rank the inclinations proper to our rationality above the inclinations we share with sub-rational beings. Finnis says that the expression, "integral good" (*bonum integrum*—also, *bonum perfectum et completivum sui ipsius*) is used by Thomas "presumably to signify that the perfection is of a good made up of many goods . . . which stand to the integral good somewhat as parts stand to a whole." This sounds right, unless the parts-whole formulation is meant to suggest that all the parts are equal in their goodness, for they are not. When the natural inclinations that belong to the irascible and concupiscible parts of human nature are not ruled by reason—as happens often enough—they do not pertain to natural law.[37] The goods aimed at by these natural but sub-rational inclinations, when they are ruled by reason, do pertain to natural law. But the goods aimed at by these natural but sub-rational inclinations, when they are not ruled by reason, do not pertain to natural law—where natural law is understood as participation of the eternal law in the *rational* creature. The inclinations are not ruled by reason when they are acted on in opposition to the inclination to good that is according to the nature of reason and proper to it.[38]

Finnis would not deny any of this.[39] His view may be that the sub-rational inclinations have an equal standing with the inclinations proper to our rational nature when, and only when, the sub-rational inclinations are ruled by reason. [40] But this is not so. The natural inclination to procreate, for example, even within the rational in-

36. ". . . one's reason puts before one *more than one reason* for action, and more than one way of acting (option) that is good in some intelligible respect." *AMPLT* 70 (emphasis in original); see fn. 39 on p. 70.

37. See *ST* 1–2 q. 94 art. 2, ad 2.

38. *ST* 1–2 q. 94 art. 2, co: "inest homini inclinatio ad bonum secundum naturam rationis, quae est sibi propria."

39. Finnis quotes Thomas as saying that "[t]here is in us a natural inclination towards what is appealing to bodily feelings against the good of practical reasonableness." (*AMPLT* 93; cf. *De Malo* q. 16 art. 2 co.) He comments: "[T]he object of that 'natural' inclination is not a basic human good or reason for action." Being natural (with or without quotation marks) does not, by itself, make an inclination pertain to natural law. For that to be the case, the inclination must be ruled by reason. *ST* 1–2 q. 94 art.2, ad 2.

40. *AMPLT* 80. Note Finnis's use of the word "equally" in the last sentence of this page. A less problematic word here would have been "also"—unless, as seems to be the case, Finnis thinks that the basic human goods are *not* hierarchically ordered.

stitution of marriage, is not for Thomas as lofty as the natural inclination to know the truth about God. Whereas Finnis speaks of contemplation as "*one* of the basic goods to be pursued and realizable by practically reasonable choices and actions," Thomas says that "imperfect happiness, such as can be had here, consists *first and principally* in contemplation," to say nothing of the beatific *vision* in which perfect happiness in the next world consists.[41] Finnis refers to acting according to reason as "*another* distinct natural inclination."[42] But it is in fact *the* inclination that underlies all specifically rational precepts.

Finnis is interested in the "possible unitary or integral directedness of the first principles when taken, not one by one, but all together."[43] There are, after all, "many precepts of natural law, all of them unified . . . by their relationship to . . . the first precept 'good is to be done and pursued and evil avoided.'" Finnis is right. They are certainly *unified* by this reference. But they are also *ranked* in terms of the order of our natural inclinations. These inclinations do not all have the same dignity. In keeping with his general approach, Finnis says that "it is obviously desirable to make all one's choices, actions, states of mind, and feelings harmonize with *all* the first practical principles taken integrally, i.e., in their *combined* guiding force."[44] Again, he should have emphasized that the integration is not just a sum but an ordering that includes higher and lower principles. The multiple goods to which we are directed through our natural inclinations are not in a relation of parity to one another.

According to Thomas "the perfection of virtue principally consists in withdrawing a man from improper pleasures, to which men are principally prone."[45] Though Finnis grants that reason has a legitimate rule over sub-rational inclinations, emotions, and feelings, many of them bodily, his opposition to a "rationalistic downgrading of human feeling," leads him to formulations in which reason's rule is deemphasized. The happiness we can have in this life is "a kind of synthesis of [the basic human goods]: satisfaction of all intelligent desires and participation in all the basic human goods (whatever they are), and thus a fulfillment which is complete and integral (integrating all its elements and participants)." The only problem with this formulation is that Finnis does not specify exactly what kind of synthesis he has in mind. Thomas would say that the synthesis is effected by the rule of reason. Finnis almost brings reason into this formulation when he speaks of "intelligent desires." But many of our desires are

41. *AMPLT* 110; *ST* 1–2 q. 3 art. 5, co (emphasis added in both passages quoted above). For a critique of the new natural law theorists on this point see Lawrence Dewan, O.P., "St. Thomas, John Finnis and the Political Good," 303–8, and 582, note 59.

42. *AMPLT* 83 (emphasis added). Though Fr. Brock distinguishes his interpretation of how we know the natural inclinations from Finnis's interpretation ("Natural Inclination and the Intelligibility of the Good,"77–78), he does not give the actual order of these inclinations the same emphasis that I do.

43. *AMPLT* 124.

44. *AMPLT* 106–7 (Finnis's emphasis).

45. *ST* 1–2 q. 95 art. 1, co.

simply not intelligent. Whatever intelligence they participate in consist only in their subordination to reason's rule.

William E. May also seems to doubt that there is a genuine hierarchy of human goods. For him, lesser goods and higher goods are only "so-called lesser goods" and "so-called higher goods." [46] May is concerned that an emphasis on a hierarchy could lead one to infer falsely that the lower goods, including self-preservation, or health and life—are merely instrumental in relation to the higher goods. But this false inference does not follow. To be sure, as May points out, Thomas regards health and life as intrinsically good and enjoyed in their own right. But this does not mean that they cannot be misused, that is, put in the service of vice, malice, and irrationality in general. The distinction between lower and higher inclinations is not a distinction between mere means and genuine ends, respectively, but between inclinations that are not specifically rational or human, and hence need to be governed by reason, and inclinations that are rational by their very nature.

Because Finnis and May do not focus on this subordination they are no more able than Grisez to appreciate how early in Thomas's presentation properly moral imperatives come to the fore. According to Finnis,

> the moral sense of ought [presumably its emergence in the form of an imperative] is reached when the absolutely first practical principle is followed through, in its relationship to all the other first principles, with a reasonableness which is unrestricted and undeflected by any subrational factor such as distracting emotion. In that sense, the 'ought' of the first principles [note the plural here] is incipiently or 'virtually', but not yet actually, moral in its directiveness or normativity.[47]

If what Finnis means here is that the "other first principles"—which I have called the primary precepts—must be reasonably, that is, judiciously, applied, he is certainly right. But that which must be judiciously applied, say the precept not to offend, is already a moral precept. It does not become moral by means of its application, which is simply the work of judgment.

Like Grisez, Finnis insists that "practical principles" are not imperatives. "They are directive."[48] If he were speaking exclusively of the first principle of practical reason he would be essentially correct, though, again, this principle is so "directive" that it cannot be resisted. But his use of the plural implies that he is not speaking exclusively of this principle but of the precepts of natural law too. Like Grisez then, Finnis also considers these precepts to be somehow obligating as well as directive, but still not quite imperative. They express an "*ought* . . . in a sense that is not moral."[49] Now this

46. "Contemporary Perspectives on Thomistic Natural Law," in STANLT, 128; see 140.

47. *AMPLT* 87.

48. *AMPLT* 86.

49. *AMPLT* 86. Contrast Thomas's claim that the concept of duty is essential to a precept: "iustitia

is certainly not true of the precept not to offend others. Even the precept to avoid ignorance is a moral precept in that it commands us to forgo stupefaction in idleness, entertainment, and distraction for the sake of a more rational and properly human employment of our leisure.

Finnis claims that it is not until the article on the precepts of the Old Law that Thomas explains "the unmistakably moral ought."[50] His point, however, is undercut by the fact that Thomas explicitly argues that the moral precepts (as distinct from the ceremonial and judicial precepts) of the Old Law were already present as precepts of natural law. It is hard to see how the moral precepts of the Old Law could have been present in natural law other than as moral precepts of natural law. As Thomas says, "[T]he *moral* [precepts of the Old Law] . . . are from the dictate of the law of *nature*."[51] The moral precept of the Old Law forbidding murder is directly deducible from the precept of natural law that one not offend others. Both are moral, and both belong to natural law. It is, Thomas says, self-evident to natural reason that "man ought (*debet*) to do evil to no one."[52] What Finnis understands by the moral Ought—though it is not present in the first principle of practical reason itself, which is merely formal—is most definitely present in the concrete precepts of natural law that Thomas founds on this principle in conjunction with the order of natural human inclinations.

A hierarchy of inclinations, and hence of goods, is implied not just by Thomas's presentation of an ascent from inclinations that man shares with inanimate things, through inclinations that he shares with sub-rational animals, to inclinations pertaining to his specifically rational nature, but also by his claims that (1) whatever contributes to the preservation of life is good for man, though it is not the supreme good since he can abuse it; that (2) the inclinations even of the irascible and concupiscible powers belong to natural law, though only insofar as they are ruled by reason; and (3) that a bodily good, though it really is good, is not equivalent to, but falls short of, the good of reason.[53] The over-arching precept that one act according to reason might require one under certain conditions to forgo self-preservation or, at least temporarily, procreation and education of one's children. But under no circumstances could this precept require one to be indifferent to truth or to commit an offense, that is, an unequivocal injustice, against another human being, since the precepts to avoid ignorance and not offend express the minimum of what is involved in acting according to reason.[54]

tamen principalius respicit rationem debiti, quod requiritur ad praeceptum . . ." *ST* 2–2 q. 56 art. 1 ad 1. cf. art. 2 co; q. 122 art. 1, co.

50. *AMPLT* 127.

51. *ST* 1–2 q. 99 art. 4, co.

52. *ST* 1–2 q. 100 art. 3, co; see q. 100, art. 5, ad 4; art. 7, ad 1.

53. *ST* 1–2 q. 59 art. 3, co; 94 art. 2 ad 2; 2–2 q. 123 art. 4, co.

54. The avoidance of ignorance entails cultivating prudence to the extent possible. This is one of the reasons why the avoidance of ignorance is commanded in the very first concrete precept of natural law that Thomas mentions. The other reason is that the avoidance of ignorance leads to distinguishing between what one knows, what one believes as a matter of faith, and what one merely opines (*ST* 2–2

We have seen that the reluctance to give adequate weight to the hierarchy of natural inclinations, and hence to the corresponding hierarchy of precepts, is what keeps Grisez, Finnis, and May from identifying just where obligation emerges in Thomas's treatment of law. On this point, however, Finnis seems to take issue with Grisez, though without singling him out for criticism. Certain precepts, "indubitably moral [!] in type," against murder and adultery for example, "appear in the Decalogue of Jewish and Christian faith, but Aquinas is clear that (if true) they are in any case truths of practical reason, of natural law knowable in principle by anybody without appeal to any divine revelation."[55] The preeminent moral principle, according to Finnis, is the precept, which Thomas thinks is a precept of natural law, that one love one's neighbor as oneself. Finnis is surely right that this is the primary moral principle governing our relation to other human beings, but it is not the first moral principle that Thomas has advanced. To repeat, the very fact that one *can* offend others distinguishes the properly moral and imperative character of the precept forbidding offense from the first principle of practical reason, "Good is to be done, etc." And even if the former is construed, wrongly, as a pre-moral, so-called "merely prudential" prescription or directive, it is still obligatory, as Finnis and Grisez both seem to recognize.

Finnis says that "the 'ought' of first practical principles is not deducible from 'is', whether from 'is willed by God' or from 'has been prescribed by me myself.'"[56] The problem with this claim is that his expression, "first practical principles," in the plural, again seems to include both the first principle of practical reason and the primary precepts of natural law. At any event, Finnis does not sort them out, and so I infer—as I inferred in the case Grisez—that he understands obligation to be present in the first principle of practical reason, the original gerundive, "Good is to be done and pursued, and evil avoided," as well as in the actual precepts of natural law.[57] But this cannot be the case for reasons that I have given earlier. So where does obligation—even if it is understood in some non-moral or pre-moral sense[58]—really come into the picture? I have argued that, for Thomas, this happens when among the multiplicity of goods

q. 1 art. 4. co.). Both achieving clarity about these speculative matters, on the one hand, and cultivating one's practical reason, on the other, are obligations, *moral* obligations. The precept commanding us to avoid ignorance is a precept of wide latitude. It does not command us to avoid ignorance, or, to put the matter positively, to acquire knowledge, regarding every *possible* subject of inquiry. But the latitude of this precept does not deprive it of its obligatory character in the least. The precept categorically commands us to think seriously, to the extent that we are able to, about serious matters—about how we are to live, about the whole of which we are a part, about whether this whole has a principle, and, if it does, whether this principle is one or many, intelligent or blind, free in some respects or necessitated in every respect, and so forth.

55. *AMPLT* 125.

56. *AMPLT* 90.

57. This inference is supported by Finnis's claim that "the Latin gerundive form 'faci*endum* et prosequ*endum* et vit*andum* exactly captures this directiveness to what '*is-to-be* done . . . pursued. . . . avoided' in the sense, not of 'will be' but of 'ought to be.'" *AMPLT* 86.

58. *AMPLT* 86–87.

corresponding to the multiplicity of inclinations some are declared by reason to be better than others and therefore as *the* goods to be done or pursued in circumstances when one cannot do or pursue them all. At that point free choice comes into play and one decides whether to follow the inclinations we share with sub-rational animals or to follow the inclinations proper to our rational nature. In such a choice one freely determines one's character, for worse or for better. It is because Finnis and Grisez do not emphasize the hierarchical character of the order of natural inclinations that they are unable to say clearly where and how obligation emerges in Thomas's presentation, or even what obligation is. As a consequence they cannot make good sense of moral freedom either.

Finnis speaks of "the long way from first principles to specific norms and choices." I think that the way from first principles to specific norms is actually quite short and can be found within a single article, q. 94 art.2. The natural law precepts commanding us to avoid ignorance and to refrain from offending others, with which the *corpus* of this article concludes, are specific norms. These two precepts hold sway throughout the spheres of contemplation and action respectively, and all the natural law precepts that Thomas later presents are derivations or enrichments of them.

The preceding analysis of the claims made by the new natural law theorists regarding precepts, imperatives, and obligations may strike the reader as nitpicking and unnecessarily prolix. I have undertaken this extended critical analysis—in spite of my conviction that there is much of enduring value in the new natural law theory—because I want to remove avoidable ambiguities and achieve the greatest possible clarity regarding Thomas's understanding of the commanding function of natural reason. Achieving this clarity is absolutely necessary for responding effectively to the Straussians criticisms. The reluctance of the new natural law theorists to recognize that the precepts of natural law are imperatives of practical reason and carry with them morally obligatory force, and their efforts to draw a sharp distinction between precepts and imperatives, rather than to distinguish both of these sharply from the first principle of practical reason, stem, I suspect, from an even deeper reluctance, long-standing among Thomists, to acknowledge any affinity of Thomas's natural law teaching with the moral philosophy of Kant. [59]

SECTION C. THOMAS AQUINAS AND KANT

I have made passing reference earlier in this study to points of correspondence between the moral teachings of Thomas and Kant. In this section I address these points

59. Alan Donagan, who acknowledges his debt to Grisez regarding the latter's interpretation of the first principle of practical reason, stands out among moral theorists of the last fifty years by virtue of his deep understanding of, and his willingness to employ, the insights of both Thomas Aquinas and Kant in his investigation of the fundamental principles of morality and their application. In his article "The Scholastic Theory of Moral Law in the Modern World," Donagan briefly makes some of the points that I argue for at greater length in the present study. See also his *The Theory of Morality*.

of correspondence thematically. But I have no intention of making the absurd claim that the differences between the *doctor angelicus* and official theologian of the Roman Catholic Church and the free-thinking secularist philosopher of the Enlightenment are superficial. The differences are profound, and I shall speak to them in due course.

Kant gives several formulations of the categorical imperative. The formulation that has the closest affinity to Thomas's primary precepts of natural law is the one that commands us to act in such a way that we treat humanity—both in our own person and in the person of another—always as an end, that is, as possessing intrinsic worth, and never as a means, or instrument, merely.[60] According to Alan Donagan,

> St. Thomas's recognition of subordination in nature, and his doctrine that "man is the end of the whole order of generation," suggests that he might have accepted Kant's principle that "man, and in general every rational being, exists as an end in himself, not merely as a means for arbitrary use by this or that will." The principle . . . must not be interpreted as implying that man is not ordered towards anything higher, as Thomas held that he is ordered to God, but rather as implying that if he is so ordered, it must be in a way consistent with his nature as an end. This is, of course, amply acknowledged in Christian theology.[61]

When we give arguments for or against a certain position, we take reason as an authoritative standard. If the premises of an argument are self-contradictory, or if they contradict what is self-evident, or if the inference from premises to conclusion is fallacious, then we feel under no necessity to accept the argument (though we may accept its conclusion on other grounds). We attempt to avoid inconsistency in articulating our convictions, regarding both speculative and practical matters. We think and speak

60. *Grundlegung zur Metaphysik der Sitten*, *Werke*, Band 6, 61: "Handle so, dass du die Menschheit, sowohl in deiner Person, als in der Person eines jeden andern, jederzeit zugleich als Zweck, niemals bloss als Mittel brauchest." [English translation: 36.] What Kant means in speaking of humanity as an end is essentially the same thing that Thomas means in his striking formulation that "man is naturally free and existing for himself." See following footnote.

61. "The Scholastic Theory," 337. Thomas would agree with Kant in part, but would also disagree with him in part, regarding the extent to which man cannot be used as a means for the arbitrary use of others: the gross abuse of freedom has consequences. "[H]omo peccando ab ordine rationis recedit: et ideo decidit a dignitate humana, prout scilicet homo est naturaliter liber et propter seipsum existens, et incidit quodammodo in servitutem bestiarum, ut scilicet de ipso ordinetur secundem quod est utile aliis." *ST* 2–2 q. 64 art. 2, ad 3. Kant does not go quite this far. But he does say in one place, with surprising severity, that "the infringement of self-regarding duties [i.e., duties to oneself] takes *all* worth from a man . . . ." *Lectures on Ethics*, 123 (emphasis added). Hugh Curtler says that later in these lectures, when speaking of duties to others, "Kant seems to renege on his earlier position." (*Ethical Argument*, 46). Curtler refers to a passage where Kant says, "There is, however, a distinction to be drawn between the man himself and his humanity. I may thus have a liking for the humanity, though none for the man. I can even have such liking for the villain, if I separate the villain and his humanity from one another; for even in the worst of villains there is still a kernel of good will. There is not one of them unable to perceive or distinguish between good, and so humanity must be loved, even in [the villain]. Hence it can rightly be said that we ought to love our neighbors. I am not only obligated to well-doing, but also to loving others with well-wishing, and well-liking too." *Lectures on Ethics*, 181.

this way because we naturally recognize, even if we do not explicitly assert it, that reason is an authoritative standard, a canon the violation of which is evidence that thought has gone astray. Not everyone thinks and speaks consistently, but virtually everyone who has, as we put it, "reached the age of reason" and who possesses normal mental powers uncompromised by congenital defects, illness, or injury, can be led to see that he should think and speak consistently.

Boethius defines a person as an individual substance of a rational nature, and Thomas accepts this definition.[62] Given that reason is recognized by all rational beings as an authoritative standard in both speculative inquiry and practical deliberation, and as an authoritative arbiter in disputations on various matters as well, it is recognized, at least implicitly, as worthy of respect. From this it follows that beings naturally possessing reason—which is to say, persons—are worthy of respect too. To be sure, many of them may not make good use of their reason. But we respect their reason, and we insist that they respect it too, when we attempt to reason with them. Moreover, we can see at once that any reason we might give for why other human beings should treat *us* as persons and not as things merely serves at the same time as a reason for why we should in turn treat *them* as persons and not as things merely. A given individual may deny that he insists on others treating him as a person rather than a mere thing. But his expressions of indignation when he thinks he is being treated as a mere thing, and his expressions of outrage when he thinks someone else whom he cares about is being treated as a mere thing, undercut his denial. And he cannot convincingly maintain that his indignation and outrage are but momentary expressions of a "spiritedness" (Gr. *thymos*) welling up from the sub-rational part of his soul. For, if pressed, he can be led to recognize that it is his very reason that is offended by an injustice done to him or someone else whom he cares about. A sub-rational animal, a dog for instance, can become enraged in response to being kicked. But only a rational being can be angered by a malicious lie. His anger in such a case is the consequence—it is hardly the ground—of his reason's recognition of mistreatment.

There are countless situations in which I have to treat another human being as a means. This happens, for example, when I have a taxi driver take me to the airport. I am clearly treating him as a means. But I am not permitted to treat him as a means *merely*, which I would be doing if I tried to avoid paying him, or to pay him less than I owed him. Treating rational beings as ends, however, involves more than not treating them as means merely. The principle of treating rational beings as ends and never as means merely, which Kant expresses in the *Groundwork of the Metaphysics of Morals*,

62. "Persona est rationalis naturae individua substantia." *ST* 1 q. 29 art. 1, arg. 1, co., ad 1, ad 2, ad 4. By accepting Boethius' definition, Thomas is able to speak not only of human beings but, in accordance with Christian theology, also of the members of the Trinity as persons. In elaborating his second version of the categorical imperative, Kant speaks of rational nature in general, and not only humanity, as an end in itself. According to Kant, a man has duties even to himself by virtue of his rational nature. The first of Thomas's two primary precepts of natural law, that one avoid ignorance, is a duty that man has to himself by virtue of his rational nature. *ST* 1–2 q. 94 art. 2, co.

is expanded in the *Metaphysics of Morals* proper into the principle of beneficence (*Wohltätigkeit*), which for Kant means making the permissible ends of other rational beings my own ends as well.[63] This obligation has to be, as he acknowledges, of wide latitude. For it is physically impossible for me to make the permissible ends of every rational being my own end. Any attempt to do so would result in paralysis. But when, for example, I see someone nearby with an armful of packages drop one of them, I have an obligation, not just to refrain from treating that person as a mere means, but to go out of my way and pick up the package for him. This practical, or active, benevolence is not love in the fullest sense of the word.[64] But it is a case of willing, indeed working for, and not just idly wishing for, the good of another; and so it squares with Thomas's general understanding of love.[65]

Kant's expansion of the second statement of the categorical imperative into the positive virtue of beneficence closely parallels Thomas's expansion of the negatively expressed obligation not to offend into the positive obligation to love others as one loves oneself. In fact, both of Kant's two overarching "ends that are also duties," namely, (1) self-perfection, the cultivation of our rational faculties in particular, and (2) beneficence, parallel Thomas's positive expansion of the two primary precepts of natural law identified in q. 94 art. 2. Neither thinker relies on the claims of revelation in the case he makes for the existence and content of these foundational moral principles.

To return to our example, though I have an *obligation* to help someone nearby who is struggling to keep from dropping an armful of packages, he does not have a *right* to my help. The current tendency to regard obligations as founded on rights, and as standing in a one to one correspondence with them, is an ominous development in ethical thought, excessively expanding, as it does, the sphere of rights while simultaneously contracting the sphere of obligations. Ernest L. Fortin perspicaciously notes that "modern rights theory [is] concerned only with the perfection of the social order as distinguished from that of the individual . . ." [66] Something like a principled disregard for the perfection of the individual is arguably entailed by modern rights theory. Of course, an ethics grounded in the concept or rights, as distinct from duties,

63. *Die Metaphysik der Sitten, Werke*, Band 7, 514–25 [English translation: 149–56].

64. A love that consists in *acts* of willing and working for the good of the other is all that natural law seems to dictate. Consider 1–2 q. 94 art. 3, co.; q. 100 art. 1–2; 9–10. Such acts, though obligatory from the perspective of natural reason, and often difficult as well, are worth comparing with the dutiful but somewhat grudging beneficence that Kant depicts in the *Grundlegung zur Metaphysik der Sitten, Werke*, Band 6, 24–25 [English translation: 11–12]. See *ST* 1–2 q. 24 art. 3, co., and ad 1. Thomas recognizes a more profound love that transcends what is dictated by natural law. See 1–2 q. 62, art. 1–2 (cf. q. 26 art. 1–3); q. 94 art. 4 ad 1; q. 107 art. 1, co., ad 2; art. 4; q. 109 art. 4. On the distinction between *dilectio* and *amor* when directed to God, see Part 2, Ch. 8, below

65. On Thomas's distinction between negatively and positively expressed precepts, see Armstrong, *PSP* 171–3.

66. "Natural Law and Social Justice," 234. See also Fr. Fortin's article "On the Presumed Medieval Origin of Individual Rights, *CCPO* 243–257.

leaves *room* for one to perfect oneself, though only if doing so happens to be one's "preference."

In this connection, the claim that one has some kind of fundamental, and not just civilly legislated, right *not* to do x, even if one is convinced that it is *best* to do x, is, absent major qualifications, untenable. For it implies either that one is not obligated to do what one thinks is best, or, more or less equivalently, that one has a right not to do what one is convinced one ought to do. In either case, reason, presumably the source of rights as much as of obligations, would be in conflict with itself. One might try to support this way of thinking by making a distinction between the obligatory and the meritorious: doing what is best is often meritorious or supererogatory; and so in these cases doing what is best cannot be obligatory. But, again, if one holds to this distinction, then the question, "Ought I to do what I think is best?" would often have to be answered with, "Not necessarily," which has a rather strange ring to it.[67]

Kant manages this issue with his distinction, which we considered earlier, between duties of narrow obligation, or duties of right, and duties of wide obligation, or duties of virtue.[68] There is no merit in fulfilling duties of right, such as refraining from murder and suicide, but there is merit in fulfilling duties of virtue, such as cultivating one's faculties and talents, on the one hand, and performing acts of beneficence on the other. For Kant, a meritorious act goes beyond the call of strict duty, but not beyond the call of wide duty, and the latitude involved in fulfilling the latter does not deprive it of its obligatory character. Meritorious acts do not transcend the realm of the obligatory for the very fact that this realm is articulated into duties of both narrow and wide *obligation*. Reason cannot without contradiction simply exempt one from fulfilling a duty that reason itself articulates, even if this duty is characterized by wide rather than narrow obligation.[69]

67. Of course, reason can say that one has an obligation to do x while something else, namely, the law of the land says that one has a (civil) right not to do x. But neither natural law nor practical reason is in tension with itself. The tension, such as it is, is between the higher standard of natural law and the lower standard of human law. Human law is, like all law, a rule of reason, but of reason functioning within constraints that do not hold in the case of natural law. *ST* 1–2 q. 96 art. 2, art. 3. Thomas, of course, recognizes that custom (*consuetudo*) plays a role in the respect that citizens have for human law. He recognizes that custom can even come to have the force of law. For that reason, though human law can be changed, it should not be changed lightly, lest respect for it be weakened (1–2 q. 97 art. 2–3). But in certain cases human laws can and should be changed. Additionally, the rulers of political communities can grant dispensation from human law in certain cases (q. 97 art. 1; art. 4), though not from the primary precepts of natural law or from the secondary precepts deduced from them *modica consideratione*.

68. *Die Metaphysik der Sitten, Werke*, Band 7, 520–5 [English translation: 153–6.]. Cf. *ST* 1–2 q. 94 art. 3, co.

69. "A wide duty is to be understood as containing, not a permission to make exceptions to the maxim of actions, but only a permission to limit one maxim of *duty* by another (e.g., love of one's neighbor in general by love of one's parents) . . ." *Die Metaphysik der Sitten, Werke*, Band 7, 520; emphasis added. [English translation: 153.]

I have argued that the distinction between duties of wide and narrow obligation, though not expressed in these Kantian terms, is present in Thomas's natural law teaching. Consider again the first two concrete precepts of natural law. The precept commanding that one avoid ignorance is characterized by wide latitude: one cannot avoid every kind of ignorance since the more thoroughly one studies one subject, the less thoroughly one can study other subjects. So the intensive study of natural science, for example, is not a narrow duty. It contributes toward filling the wide duty of avoiding ignorance, but other studies do so as well. The precept commanding that one not offend others, however, is characterized by narrow latitude. Although intensive study of one subject can prevent an equally intensive study of other subjects, treating one person justly does not rule out treating other people justly, not in Thomas's understanding any more than in Kant's understanding. Whereas one has to pick and choose what subjects one will study, one does not have to pick and choose those to whom one will act justly. But Thomas would not accede to the notion that, because avoidance of ignorance is a duty of wide obligation,[70] one has some kind "right" to be ignorant about everything or to give up trying to understand anything.

Having referred above to Kant's second statement of the categorical imperative, we should take a brief look at his first statement, which is frequently denigrated by Thomists and Straussians alike as an empty formalism: "Act only according to that maxim through which you can at the same time will that it become a universal law."[71] The function of the categorical imperative, as we can see from Kant's own treatment, is not to prescribe specific acts, which it cannot do in any case, but to serve as a canon for determining which maxims one can, and which maxims one cannot, act on rationally. A maxim always aims at a achieving some particular good, a good that is material and not only formal. This good might be an obviously moral good, such as alleviating the misery of those who are in financial distress, or a good that is not so obviously moral, such as providing for one's own financial well-being. In either case, one's maxims should be of such a kind that they could be adopted universally without

70. Duties of wide obligation do not, for Thomas, coincide with works of supererogation. Thomas treats the latter in the context of specifically religious vows. (*SCG* lib. 3 cap. 130; see *Super Sent.* lib. 4 d. 38 q. 1 art. 1, qc. 2, co.; *ST* 2–2 q. 12 art. 1, co. *Contra impugnantes Dei cultum et religionem*, pars 2 cap. 1, ad 1). Works of supererogation fall under the guidance of counsel (*Super Sent.*, lib. 3 d. 34 q. 1 art. 6, expos: "praecipue consilio indigemus in operationibus supererogationis . . ."), including the counsel of a private individual (see 1 Corinthians, 7:25, a text Thomas quotes on this matter, e.g., *Super Sent.* lib. 4 d. 15 q. 3 art. 1, qc. 4, ad 2; 1–2 q. 92 art. 2, ad 2). In one sense counsel is not divided against precept, but in another sense it is (*De Veritate* q. 17 art. 3, ad 2). And it is in the latter sense that Thomas usually speaks of counsel (e.g., *Super Sent.*, lib. 4 d. 15 q. 2 art. 1, qc. 4, ad 1; *ST* q. 108 art. 4, co.). As divided against precept, counsel concerns a more complete good than what is mandated by the former (*Super Sent.* lib. 4 d. 38 q. 1 art. 1, qc. 2, co.; *ST* 1, q. 19 art. 12, co.; ad 4.) But only a few, clerics and religious in particular, are called to this more complete good. (*Super Sent.* lib. 1 d. 45 q. 1 art. 4, co.; *ST* 2–2 q. 85 art. 4, co.)

71. *Grundlegung zur Metaphysik der Sitten*, *Werke*, Band 6, 51: "[H]andle nur nach derjenigen Maxime, durch die du zugleich wollen kannst, dass sie ein allgemeines Gesetz werde." [English translation: 30.]

thereby generating a practical contradiction, that is, without cancelling themselves out. The maxim of writing bad checks, to take an obvious example, would cancel itself out if universalized: no one would accept checks at all if everyone wrote bad checks. If adopted universally, the maxim of writing bad checks could not achieve the end it aimed at, namely, getting cash or some item of monetary value. The maxim of writing bad checks, because it cannot be universally acted upon and still achieve the end it aims at, shows itself to be contrary to practical reason, and hence immoral. This is not Thomas's argument. But Thomas does say,

> [A] man's will is not right in willing a particular good, unless he refers it to the common good as to the end . . . Hence in order that a man will some particular good with a right will, it is necessary that that particular good be willed materially, and yet [at the same time] that the common, divine good be willed formally.[72]

There are differences between Thomas and Kant on this point, but there are similarities too.

Thomists refer to Kant frequently. But they rarely engage with his thought in a productive manner. While they often object to what they regard as the excessively formal character of the first version of the categorical imperative that Kant presents in the *Groundwork*, they do not often object to the equally formal character of Thomas's first principle of practical reason. Some Thomists object to Kant's use of the language of autonomy, failing to recognize that he does not mean the autonomy of the individual in his individuality but the autonomy of reason itself. They do not object to Thomas's own formulation that "*homo constituitur dominus sui ipsius per liberum arbitrium*."[73] Thomas would surely find little to quarrel with in the following formulation of Kant's: "Everything in nature operates according to laws. Only a rational being has the ability

72. *ST* 1–2 q.19, art. 10, co: Non est autem recta voluntas alicuius hominis volentis aliquod bonum particulare, nisi referat illud in bonum commune sicut in finem . . . Unde ad hoc quod aliquis recta voluntate velit aliquod particulare bonum, oportet quod illud particulare bonum sit volitum materialiter, bonum autem commune divinum sit volitum formaliter." Mary Keys rightly observes that in this passage Thomas "posits at least a 'formal,' implicit direction of the will to the common good in general as an essential condition for moral rectitude." "Keys" 119, and footnotes 5 and 6 on that page. See *ST* 1–2 q. 19 art.3, co.

73. *ST* 2–2 q. 64 art. 5, ad 3; see *ST* 1 q. 19 art. 12, ad 3; q. 103 art. 5, ad 3; 1–2 q.1 art. 1, co.; 2–2 q. 122 art. 1, co; q. 158 art. 2 ad 3. In discussing how eternal law differs from human law, Thomas says that "nullus, proprie loquendo, suis actibus legem imponit" (1–2 q. 93 art. 5, co.). The qualification *proprie loquendo* here must be understood to mean that no one *by virtue of his particular individuality* imposes a law on his own acts. However, man's reason—which *qua* reason is not individual but universal, even though it is instantiated in the individual human being—does impose a law on his acts. This is exactly what happens in the case of natural law: "omnes actus virtutum sunt de lege naturali: dictat enim hoc unicuique propria ratio, tu virtuose agat" (q. 94 art. 3, co.). Human reason is the proper image of the divine reason (*ST* 1–2 q. 19 art. 4, co.; ad 3; q. 100 art. 2, co). Hence man, by acting according to natural, human reason, is also acting in accordance with the divine reason, whether he realizes that he is doing so or not.

to act *according to the idea* of law, that is, according to principles, or a *will*."[74] This formulation captures some of Thomas's understanding that through natural law the rational creature participates in the eternal law in an altogether unique way. Thomists occasionally express uneasiness about Kant's claim that human beings, as rational beings, are ends and not mere means, perhaps because they think this claim implies that man is not ordered to something infinitely higher than himself, that is, to God.[75] But such an implication does not follow of necessity from Kant's claim any more than it follows of necessity from Thomas's similar claim that "*homo est naturaliter liber et propter seipsum existens*."[76] Some Thomists think that Kant overemphasizes the good will, and does so at the expense of virtue. They are apparently not troubled by Thomas's claim that "a good will makes man good *simpliciter*."[77]

Although morality has a high place in Thomas's scheme of things, he does not regard it as the complete human good. But neither does Kant, contrary to the common misunderstanding, which Thomists have played a role in perpetuating. For Kant, the complete human good is happiness awarded in proportion to moral worth. This good, Kant insists, can be attained only in a hereafter and only through divine agency. Making the possibility of the complete human good intelligible requires not only arguing for freedom of the will but postulating the existence of God and the immortality of the soul as well.[78] Kant and Thomas are by no means in simple agreement in their understanding of the place of morality in the broader human good. But they do not stand in simple opposition to each other on this point either, though, unlike Kant, Thomas understands happiness *per se*, that is, both imperfect happiness and perfect happiness, as actually including a moral component.[79]

74. "Ein jedes Ding der Natur wirkt nach Gestetzen. Nur ein vernünftiges Wesen hat das Vermögen, *nach der Vorstellung* des Gesetze, d.i. nach Principien, zu handeln, oder einen *Willen*." *Grundlegung zur Metaphysik der Sitten, Werke*, Band 6, 41; emphasis in the original. [English translation: 23.] The *ability* to act according to the idea of law is also the *ability* not to do so. Consider, in this connection, John Finnis, *AMPLT* 70–71, and fn. 38–39 on page 70.

75. For example, in *Written on the Heart*. J. Budziszewski writes, "Kant says each of us is an end in himself . . . Kant says we belong to ourselves . . . Kant makes us out to be little gods" (106). Budziszewski seems to think that, though Kant explicitly says that we should not treat each other as means *merely*, Kant somehow meant to say that we should not treat each other as means *at all*. Budziszewski is understandably critical of what he calls "the mere idea of Not Using Others" (199), but this is not an idea that can be attributed to Kant.

76. *ST* 2–2, q. 64 art. 2, ad 3. See *ST* 1–2 q. 58 art. 2 ad 3.

77. "Simpliciter autem et totaliter bonus dicitur aliquis ex hoc quod habet voluntatem bonum, quia per voluntatem homo utitur omnibus aliis potentiis. Et ideo bona voluntas facit hominem bonum simpliciter." *De Virtutibus* q. 1 art. 9, ad 16. See *ST* 2–2 q. 81 art. 6, ad 1.

78. *Kritik der Praktischen Vernunft, Werke*, Band 6, 234–283 [English translation: 90–122].

79. *ST* 1–2, q. 3 art. 5, co. Though Thomas says that *perfect* happiness consists in an operation of the speculative rather than the practical intellect, he also says that rectitude of the will is necessary for perfect happiness, not just antecedently but concomitantly as well (1–2 q. 4 art. 4, co; cf. 1 q. 19 art. 1, co.). As for *imperfect* happiness, rectitude of the will is also necessary. "Beatitudo autem imperfecta, qualis hic haberi potest, primo quidem et principaliter consistit in contemplatione; secondario vero in operatione practici intellectus ordinantis actiones et passiones humanas . . ." *ST* 1–2, q. 3 art. 5, co.

Thomists rarely give sufficient attention to Kant's transformation of the version of the categorical imperative commanding us to treat humanity (or rational animality) always as an end, and never as a mere means, into the concept of ends that are also duties. The validation of this concept serves as the entrance to his account of specific virtues in the second part of the *Metaphysics of Morals* proper. One gets the impression that few Thomists have studied this work, so infrequently do they refer to in spite of its considerable relevance to their own concerns. There are exceptions. One occasionally comes across an admirer of Thomas, such as Alan Donagan, who recognizes an affinity, though hardly an identity, between Thomistic and Kantian ethics. However, that I have not exaggerated or mischaracterized the tendency of Thomists to discount Kantian ethics can be confirmed by looking at how they treat Kant in their books and essays dealing with natural law. More often than not, Kant is brought into consideration only to serve as a whipping boy.

The case is different, and in fact worse, with how Kantians treat Thomas: they rarely bring him into consideration at all, presumably because they are under the sway of the common but false opinion that his teaching presupposes the claims of revealed theology. An interesting exception is Dieter Henrich, one of the most impressive thinkers working today in the Kantian tradition. Toward the end of his essay, "The Concept of Moral Insight and Kant's Doctrine of the Fact of Reason,"[80] Henrich writes as follows.

> Christian philosophy also suspended [the basic question concerning the nature of moral insight]. It presupposed from the beginning that God, who was understood as Being itself (*actus purus*), is also the ground of the good and of our knowledge of the good. In this way ethics became just one discipline in an ontology that had a foundation independent of it.

This succinct passage goes to the heart of things. Still, there are several things not quite right about it. In the first place, God is not merely understood by Thomas Aquinas, but actually demonstrated, to be Being itself (*esse tantum*, and hence *actus purus* too). Moreover, Thomas does not *presuppose* that God is the ground of our knowledge of the good. He *demonstrates* this by way of his more general demonstrations that God exists, of necessity, and that, through his creation of our reason as a finite image of his own reason, he is the ultimate ground of our knowledge, not only of the good but of being itself. But the proximate, or immediate, ground of our knowledge of the good is our own reason, for Thomas no less than for Kant. And God is the ultimate ground, not only of knowledge of the good, but of the good itself because he *is* the good, the common good of the whole universe.[81] God is not limited by any *essentia*

80. In *The Unity of Reason—Essays on Kant's Philosophy*, 87. That Henrich has Thomas in mind, primarily if not exclusively, in this characterization of "Christian philosophy" is indicated in a footnote to this passage, which cites Etienne Gilson and R. P. Sertillanges as authorities for his characterization.

81. *SCG* lib. 3 cap. 17 n. 6; *ST* 1 q. 3 art. 5–6; 1–2 q. 100 art. 8, co.; q. 109 art. 3, co.; q. 111 art. 5, ad 1; 2–2, q. 25 art. 1, ad 2; *Quaestiones quodlibetales* 1 q. 4 art. 3, co.

distinct from the *esse tantum* that he *is*. As *actus purus*, he can do anything that is not incompatible with the *esse* that he is. Among other things, God can create a contingent being, man, not solely for God's own good—God's good is already complete and would be complete whether he created or not—but also for man's good, granted that man's good consists ultimately in being in a kind of union with God.[82] And God can *do* good for man because he already *is* good, that is, because, according to Thomas, God's goodness and his being are not really distinct.

Regarding Henrich's last sentence in the above passage, ethics is indeed for Thomas a discipline within an ontology, or, rather, within a rational theology that has a theoretical foundation and not solely a practical one as is the case with Kant. Thomas does not think that one can understand what natural law really is except in reference to the eternal law. But, then, "moral insight," or the consciousness of natural law and its obligatory character, is as intrinsic to the operation and evidence of human reason for Thomas as it is for Kant, however sharply the two thinkers part ways regarding what can be known about the ultimate ground of this reason. A proper consideration of Thomas by the followers of Kant, and a proper consideration of Kant by the followers of Thomas—a genuinely productive encounter between both parties—requires that each party have more than a superficial understanding of the other. And that, lamentably, is just what is so rare.

Lest one think that I have downplayed the disagreements between Thomas and Kant, I shall speak briefly to these. Thomas argues that nature is created by the transcendent God. Kant argues that nature at the level of its architectonic principles, such as the principle of cause and effect, is constituted by the transcendental ego. Thomas presents five ways to prove the existence of God. Kant argues at great length in the *Critique of Pure Reason* that it is impossible to prove either the existence or the nonexistence of God. On the other hand, Kant makes an argument in the *Critique of Practical Reason* that the existence of God, though it cannot be proven, must nonetheless be postulated on the basis of our elemental moral consciousness. Although Thomas could have made a similar argument shortly after q. 94 art. 2, he refrained from doing so, not least because he had already demonstrated, and not just postulated, the existence of God some two hundred questions earlier in the *Summa Theologiae*. Thomas understands the precepts of natural law, and thereby duties also, in terms of our natural inclinations. Kant opposes duty to natural inclinations. Thomas includes rectitude of the will within happiness. Kant envisions the possibility of a tension between rectitude of the will and happiness. And so on. It is not difficult to find a great number of points on which these two giants disagree. But they agree on a few points, on a few crucial points, as well.

Thomas and Kant are most manifestly in agreement in their recognition that natural reason is, of its own nature, legislative and issues commands; or, to say the same thing in different language, that practical reason of its own nature articulates

82. *ST* 2–2 q. 45 art. 4, co.

the Ought. Since Thomas does not use the expression, "the Ought," it is worth taking a brief look at Kant's definition. Though it is only contextual, it is remarkable nonetheless.

> This [practical] rule . . . is, for a being in whom reason is not the sole determining ground of the will [but who has inclinations that can be opposed to reason], *an imperative*, that is, a rule that is designated through an Ought, which expresses the objective necessity of the act, and signifies that if reason entirely determined the will the act would inevitably happen according to the rule. [83]

Kant does not attempt to derive the Ought from the Is. But he does derive it from the conditional Would: "if reason entirely determined the will the act *would* follow, etc." Because reason is not the entire determining ground of man's will, the [practical] rule takes the form of an imperative, and it is "designated through an Ought." In speaking of the quite different case in which "reason entirely determined the will," Kant has in mind, not man, but a perfectly rational being.[84] What we *ought* to do, in spite of inclinations not to do it, is what this perfectly rational being would do. Since, for Kant, the idea of a being whose will is entirely determined by his reason is the idea of God, his contextual definition of obligation relies on the idea of God. To be sure, it does not rely on there actually existing in reality anything that corresponds to this idea. Nonetheless, the definition effectively says that what we ought to do is what God, if he exists, would do, were he in our situation or in a situation analogous to ours.[85] There is clearly an affinity, though hardly an identity, between Kant's understanding that what we ought to do is what one whose reason entirely determined the will would do, and Thomas's understanding that what we ought to do is what reason commands us to do in the presence of two or more goods, not all of which can be chosen. Quite

83. "Diese Regel ist aber für ein Wesen, bei dem Vernunft nicht ganz allein Bestimmungsgrund des Willens ist, ein *Imperativ*, d.i., eine Regel, die durch ein Sollen, welches die objective Nötigung der Handlung ausdrükt, bezeichnet wird, und bedeutet, dass, wenn die Vernunft den Willen gänzlich bestimmete, die Handlung unausbleiblich nach dieser Regel geschehen würde." *Kritik der Praktischen Vernunft*, *Werke*, Band 6, 126 [English translation: 18]. (The possibility of incorporeal but still finite rational beings, i.e., angels, is apparently not under consideration in this passage.) Compare Aristotle, *Politics* 1287a33: "law is intellect without inclination (or desire—*oreksis*)." This interesting observation of Aristotle's should not be taken as implying that reason, in making or constituting law, does so without a desire of its own. *De Anima* 432b5–433a31; *Metaphysics* 1072a28.

84. An alternative interpretation is that, by the expression "if reason entirely determined the will," Kant is thinking not of God but of a perfectly moral man, that is, a man whose sensuous inclinations are so much under the control of his reason that he never, as a matter of fact, acts contrary to reason. But this interpretation fails, since even a (hypothetically) perfectly moral *man* would experience the practical rule as an *imperative* and hence as "designated through an Ought." As Kant sees it, God, unlike man, does not stand under an imperative.

85. In fact, since the divine being that is said to have placed himself in our situation is Christ, Kant's definition in the *Kritik der Praktischen Vernunft* is implicitly saying that, in determining what we ought to do, we need to take the *idea* of the Son of God as our model. Kant says this, not just implicitly, but explicitly in *Die Religion innerhalb der Grenzen der blossen Vernunft*, *Werke*, Band 7, 712–19 [English translation: 103–108].

interestingly, Kant's understanding of obligation as expressed in the above definition—whatever else we are to make of it—is more dependent on a theological concept, the idea of a perfectly, rational being, than is Thomas's understanding of obligation as founded on the first principle of practical reason in conjunction with the order of natural inclinations, and expressed in the primary precepts of natural law.[86] Unlike Thomas, Kant cannot say what is even *meant* by obligation without bringing the idea of God—the idea of a being whose reason entirely determines his will—immediately into the picture.

The difference between these two thinkers regarding their understanding of obligation can be traced to their different assessments of man's natural inclinations. Kant distinguishes between a higher and a lower faculty of desire. The higher faculty of desire is practical reason itself. The lower faculty of desire consists of the sub-rational inclinations, that is, sensuous appetites and aversions that we share with other animals. Kant's distinction parallels Thomas's distinction between the inclinations proper to our rational nature and those we share with sub-rational nature. The chief difference between the two thinkers here turns less on their understanding of practical reason, the "higher faculty of desire," than on their understanding of the sub-rational inclinations.

Kant generally reserves the word "inclinations" (*Neigungen*) for what falls under the "lower faculty of desire." Inclinations incline (*neigen*) us away from the commands of reason. Thomas, on the other hand, speaks of rational inclinations as well as sub-rational inclinations. He is fully aware of a tension between the two, and he insists that sub-rational inclinations must be ruled by reason. So, it could look as though the two thinkers are not that far apart on this point either. But here they really are far apart. For though, as I remarked earlier, Kant on occasion employs the word "nature" in the sense of essence, he more frequently employs to it name the order of appearances, construed as governed by exceptionless determinism and, to the extent that it can be known by mathematical physics, non-teleological. It is for this reason that Kant has to locate freedom of the will in an unknowable order of things, of things not as they appear but as they are "in-themselves." He does concede, or rather he argues, that natural science, especially in the investigation of biological phenomena, cannot get

86. Etienne Gilson, in *The Unity of Philosophical Experience*, suspects the emergence of a mystical tendency in the thinking of the old Kant (239). Gilson bases his conjectures on a passage from the *Opus Postumum* where Kant speaks of God as being within him, and even identical with him. It should be remembered, however, that the *Opus Postumum* it is not a finished piece and that it was written by Kant as he was entering his dotage. Much of it has the appearance of notes and questions that he was dialectically posing only to himself. The passage that caught Gilson's eye is certainly interesting, and it indicates how far Kant remained to the end of his life from *any* form of Catholicism. Still, if one wishes to convey, however so briefly, the theological tenor of this most peculiar work, one should also note Kant's emphatic claim, repeated for pages on end, that as moral beings we must cognize our duties as divine commands, as well as his related claims that, though God dwells within us, he is also above and about us, that there is only one God, and that God must be thought of as a being who has rights, and hence as a person, though, unlike us, as a person who has no duties.

very far without employing teleological principles. But, as Kant sees it, though we know that these principles are *regulative* for the investigation of nature, we do not know that they are *constitutive* of the natural objects investigated. As a consequence it is not easy to see how natural inclinations, as occurring within the sphere of appearances, can be good at all, good having for Kant the character of an end as much as it does for Thomas. And yet Kant does concede that natural inclinations are good, and he argues that any attempt to extirpate them would be bad, and not just harmful but blameworthy too.[87] For, as Kant sees it, their complete satisfaction, which requires prudently bringing them into harmony with each other, is constitutive of happiness, as he understands happiness. But, again, since these inclinations are part of an empirical order of things that is non-teleological, their character as goods is a problem for him. And that means that happiness itself, as Kant construes it, is hard to understand as something good.

Thomas, on the other hand, is able to construe the sub-rational inclinations, to the extent that they are ruled by reason, as good for two reasons. In the first place they give rise to natural pleasures that signify the perfection of natural operations. These operations do not of necessity conflict with the ends of reason, since reason is capable of governing them. Additionally, self-preservation on the one hand, and procreation and education of offspring on the other, are conditions for the life of the human individual and the human species respectively. They therefore provide the field, so to speak, within which natural reason pursues its proper ends.[88] As noted earlier, Kant actually speaks of the pursuit of happiness as a duty, albeit an imperfect duty.[89] Nonetheless, he is determined to prescind from everything empirical in his attempt to define obligation. That determination precludes him from defining it, as Thomas does implicitly, as the effect of reason's command in the presence of two or more goods (or ends of our natural, i.e., empirically experienced, inclinations) not all of which can be pursued or chosen.

If we reformulate Kant's explicit definition of the Ought (quoted a few pages earlier) and compare it with Thomas's implicit definition, we can see the difference between the two thinkers most clearly.

> Kant: To say that I ought to do x is to say that x is what I would do if reason completely determined my will.
>
> Thomas: To say that I ought to do x is to say that x is what reason commands me to do in the presence of two or more goods not all of which can be chosen.

87. *Die Religion innerhalb der Grenzen der blossen Vernunft, Werke*, Band 7, 710 [English translation: 102].

88. Servais Pinckaers argues that, well in advance of Kant, William of Ockham develops an ethical teaching based largely on a "rejection" of the natural inclinations. *Sources*, 240–5, 332–3; cf. 348.

89. *Grundlegung zur Metaphysik der Sitten, Werke*, Band 6, 25 [English translation: 12].

Clearly the Ought, as Kant defines it in the *Critique of Practical Reason*, presupposes the existence of inclinations that are in tension with reason. This presupposition is implicit in the clause "for a being in whom reason is not the sole determining ground of the will." Kant is careful not to spell out what these sub-rational inclinations are because he does not want his definition to depend on anything empirical. In not spelling them out, he is not required to say that, natural though they are, they aim at goods. And he is reluctant to say this because he is wary of the natural teleology it implies. Consequently, it is difficult for Kant to answer the question of why a rational being would *ever* choose to do something other than what reason commands.

Thomas would say with the classical philosophers that unless what these inclinations aim at fall under the aspect of the good—not the highest good, to be sure, but good in *some* respect—one could not choose to follow them at all. And if one could not choose to follow one's sub-rational inclinations in opposition to the command of reason, if they simply overpowered one, then one would not be free. One would possess neither positive freedom, as the capacity to make a rational choice, nor even negative freedom as not being totally determined by inclinations and hence able to choose *simplicter*. Why one would ever choose to resist the commands of reason is an enormous problem on any understanding of human freedom. Kant's insufficiently appreciated study, *Religion within the Limits of Mere Reason*, contains profound insights into the problem of how a rational being could willfully incorporate an evil maxim into his will. But, for Kant, the question of what would motivate or entice a rational being into doing such a thing is unanswerable.[90]

Whereas Kant is right to distinguish categorical imperatives from hypothetical imperatives, he does not appreciate the extent to which even a hypothetical imperative expresses an obligation, albeit a conditional one.[91] For though hypothetical imperatives are *limited* by conditions, they cannot be *derived* from these conditions as they are usually stated. As I argued above, the inference, "I ought to do x if I want, or desire, to do (or have) y, and if I can do (or have) y only if I also do x," is invalid. [92] Though we speak this way all the time, doing so leaves unexpressed the indispensable premise, "I *ought* to have (or do) y," which is necessary if the inference is to be valid. Any attempt to sufficiently justify hypothetical imperatives, which have to do with our this-worldly wants or inclinations, with the inclinations that are in Kantian language "merely empirical," is going to lead back to an unstated categorical and unconditional imperative.

Kant recognizes that "the empirical"—that is, "nature" as he typically though not invariably uses the word—has a transcendental ground. But he fails to recognize that

90. *Die Religion innerhalb der Grenzen der blossen Vernunft, Werke*, Band 7, 693. "Der Vernunftursprung aber dieser Verstimmung unserer Willkür in Ansehung der Art, subordinierte Triebfedern zu oberst in ihre Maximen aufzunehmen, d. i. dieses Hanges zum Bösen, bleibt uns unerforschlich . . ." [English translation: 88]. Thomas gives us the *means* to solve this problem. *ST* 1–2 q. 10, art. 2, co.

91. See *Grundlegung zur Metaphysik der Sitten*, *Werke*, Band 6, 41–46 [English translation: 22–27].

92. *Supra*, Ch. 2, Section c, iii.

even viewed from within, and not just from without and above (the transcendental ego, its pure concepts and the pure intuitions it has at its disposal), nature cannot be a self-enclosed order of thoroughgoing determinism. For, to repeat, even a merely hypothetical "ought" (or "should') implies not only "can" but "might not," and hence freedom. Hypothetical imperatives, though emerging from "the empirical," presuppose the same freedom that a categorical imperative does. Kant's insistence on understanding nature as governed by an exceptionless determinism precludes him from locating this freedom anywhere within nature.[93] As a consequence he is incapable of showing how a hypothetical imperative can be understood as an imperative at all. This is a large though insufficiently appreciated problem for Kantian ethics.

SECTION D. THE *BONUM RATIONIS*

The will, for Thomas, is the appetite or desire of reason; and a desire is always ordered to some good, real or apparent.[94] The goods to which bodily desires are ordered are life, health, nourishment, reproduction, and their associated pleasures. The good to which the will, the appetite of reason (or the rational appetite—Thomas uses the two expressions interchangeably) is ordered Thomas calls the *bonum rationis*.

In their translation of the *Summa Theologiae*, the Dominican Fathers render this expression variously as "the good dictated by reason," "the good as fixed by reason," "the good as defined by reason," "the good as appointed by reason," as well as "the good of reason."[95] The problem with all these renderings but the last one is that they give the impression that the good in question could be merely something good about which reason has something to say; and this could be a bodily good, rather than a good proper to reason. A good *determined by* reason (*bonum determinatum a ratione*) could be, but is not necessarily, a good *of* reason, which is the literal translation of *bonum rationis*. The *bonum rationis* is a good that is as intrinsic to reason as health, even life, is to the body.[96] As we would expect, truth is intimately bound up with the *bonum rationis*. But there is more to the *bonum rationis* than truth, or knowledge of truth, alone.

93. See also *Grundlegung zur Metaphysik der Sitten*, *Werke*, Band 6, 38 [English translation: 21–22], where Kant, in alluding critically, but much too briefly, to the Thomistic conception of natural law (though not referring to Thomas by name), distinguishes between (1) the particular constitution of human nature, i.e., what is *empirically* determinable about man, which Kant thinks cannot be a source of apodictic moral principles; and (2) what pertains to the idea of a rational being in general: "[1] die besondere Bestimmung der menschlichen Natur . . . [2] die Idee von einer vernünftige Natur überhaupt."

94. *ST* 1–2 q. 61 art. 2, ad 3.

95. *ST* 1 q. 63 art. 9, ad 1; 1–2 q.55 art. 4, ad 2; q. 61 art. 2, co.; q. 68 art. 1, ad 2; 2–2 q. 123, art. 4, co

96. *Sententia Ethic.*, lib. 2, l. 7 n. 4. See *Super Sent.*, lib. 3, dist. 27, q. 2 art. 4 qc. 2, ad 1; *ST* 1–2 q. 59 art. 1, co.; q. 64 art. 2, *sed contra*; 2–2 q. 47, art. 7, *sed contra*.

Thomas uses the expression *bonum rationis* in both the singular and the plural, with a range of meanings closely connected but not synonymous. He uses it in the plural to refer to the different virtues, each of which is in its own way a good of reason, or to the works of virtue, or even, derivatively, to bodily goods that assist in acquiring the virtues.[97] He uses this expression in the singular to refer, very occasionally, to a particular virtue.[98] More often, however, Thomas uses the expression in referring, not to virtue itself, or to a particular virtue, but to something at work in virtue, something that virtue serves or to which virtue is ordered.[99] To understand what Thomas means by the *bonum rationis* in this sense, we cannot rely on a single text. We must consider a number of them.

The *bonum rationis* is not so much virtue, or *a* virtue, as it is the formal principle *of* virtue.[100] It does not exist in one and the same way in all matters pertaining to what is moral, but is diversified.[101] It is through this diversification of the *bonum rationis* that the moral virtues are themselves diversified.[102]

There is an intimate connection between the moral virtues and the virtue of prudence. Prudence presupposes a right desire for the end, with respect to which it determines the most appropriate means.[103] Accordingly, Thomas says that this virtue is to a certain extent moral (*etiam quodammodo moralis est*),[104] even though it is, strictly speaking, an intellectual virtue. Because prudence is an intellectual virtue, even a virtue of reason commanding (the best means to attain a good end), it has an essential relation to the *bonum rationis*. Because the moral virtues are ordered (or commanded—*disponuntur*) by reason, they are related to the *bonum rationis* only by participation.[105]

According to Thomas, justice is the virtue proper to the will or rational appetite. It is the moral virtue most akin to reason, and the *bonum rationis* shines forth (*relucet*) in it most clearly.[106] Truth, Thomas says, is the proper *object* of the *bonum rationis*; but justice is its proper *effect*.[107] Courage and moderation, on the other hand, are the

97. See *Super Sent.*, lib. 2, dist. 36, q. 1 art. 4, co., ad 2; *SCG* 3 cap. 106 n. 4. *Sententia Ethic.*, lib. 9, l. 8 n. 11.

98. For example, *ST* 2–2 q. 155 art. 2, ad 5.

99. *Super Sent.*, lib. 3, dist. 29, q. 1 art. 1, *sed contra*. 1; lib. 3, dist. 33, q. 1 art. 1 qc. 1, co.; *ST* 2–2 q. 123 art. 8, co.; art. 11, ad 2; q. 129 art. 3, co. See *ST* 1–2 q. 59, art. 4, co.

100. *ST* 1–2 q. 61 art. 2, co.

101. *Super Sent.*, lib. 3, dist. 33, q. 1 art. 1 qc. 1, co; *ST* 1–2 q. 50 art. 5, ad 3.

102. *Super Sent.*, lib. 3, dist. 33, q. 1 art. 1 qc. 2, co.; qc. 3, co.

103. *ST* 1–2 a. 57 art. 4, co.

104. *ST* 1–2 q. 58 art. 3, ad 1; ad 2; q. 61, art. 1, co.

105. [H]abitus virtutum moralium ex bono rationis diversificantur: quod quidem in ipso rationis judicio essentialiter consistit, quod ad prudentiam pertinet; in his vero quae per rationem disponuntur, participative, quod ad morales virtutes spectat." *Super Sent.*, lib. 3 dist. 33, q. 1 art. 1 qc. 3 co.

106. *ST* 1–2, q. 66 art. 4, co.

107. *ST* 2–2, q. 124 art. 1, co.: "[A]d virtutem pertinet quod aliquis in bono rationis conservetur.

virtues proper to the irascible and concupiscible desires, respectively. The *bonum rationis* also shines forth in these virtues—though less clearly than in justice—because it is through them that the irascible and concupiscible desires are subjected to reason.

There can be a tension between the good of life itself, which is a bodily good, and the *bonum rationis*. The virtue of courage is the virtue that is chiefly concerned with the dangers of death, and thereby with the possible loss of this bodily good. According to Thomas, if the loss of life is the consequence of adhering to the good of reason, that price must be paid.

> It is proper (*oportet*) to hold firmly the good of reason against every evil whatsoever [including death, as the context makes clear], since no bodily good is equivalent to the *bonum rationis*.[108]

Life, though good, is not itself a *bonum rationis*. If it were, then all living beings, and not rational beings alone, would possess the *bonum rationis*; and they do not. Bodily goods are good for *man* only insofar as they support or are consonant with the good of reason. On those occasions when the pursuit of man's bodily goods actually impede the good of reason, he is turned toward evil.[109]

Thomas repeatedly says that the *bonum rationis* must be preserved. It must be preserved against the bodily passions, against inordinate desires and aversions. And it is the virtues that preserve the *bonum rationis*, which is a further reason to avoid simply identifying the latter with the former.[110] The moral virtues derive their excellence, even their very sense, from the role they play in ordering the desiring part of the soul to the *bonum rationis*.[111] As the formal principle of the virtues, the *bonum rationis* is

---

Consistit autem bonum rationis in veritate, sicut in proprio obiecto; et in iustitia, sicut in proprio effectu . . ."

108. *ST* 2–2 q. 123 art. 4, co. See 1–2 q. 2 art. 5, co: Sicut autem navis committitur gubernatori ad dirigendum, ita homo est suae voluntati et rationi commissus . . . Manifestum est autem quod homo ordinatur ad aliquid sicut ad finem, non enim homo est summum bonum. Unde impossibile est quod ultimus finis rationis et voluntatis humanae sit conservatio humani esse. See also q. 61 art. 3, co.; 2–2 q. 123 art. 12, co.; q. 141 art. 2, co.; q. 146 art. 1, ad 3; q. 161 art. 2, ad 3. *De virtutibus* q. 1 art. 12, co.; art. 13, ad 13; q. 5 art. 4, co.; ad 5.

109. *SCG* 3, cap. 141 n. 6: "Cum enim bona exteriora ad inferiora ordinentur, corpus autem ad animam; in tantum exteriora et corporalia bona sunt homini bona, in quantum ad bonum rationis proficiunt; secundum vero quod bonum rationis impediunt, homini vertuntur in mala." See *Primae Redactiones—Summae contra Gentiles*, lib. 3: "totum bonum hominis esse videtur in ratione, secundum quam homo est./ cum autem bonum rationis non solum in contemplatione veritatis, sed etiam in ordinatione eorum quae sub ipsa sunt, ut/ oportebat autem eos intelligere quod bonum rationis non solum consistit in contemplatione veritatis, sed etiam in ordinatione eorum quae/ nobis/ vel in nobis sunt vel nobis adiacent./ oportet enim quod per rationem ordinentur passiones animae./ unde virtutes quibus moderantur animae passiones, et quibus providetur decenter sustentationi naturae, et quibus convenienter convivimus ad eos qui circa nos, ad bonum rationis manifestum est pertinere."

110. *ST* 2–2 q. 123 art. 12, co; 2–2 q. 136 art. 1 co.; q. 141 art. 3, co; q. 141 art. 4, ad 4; q. 146 art. 2, co.; q. 149 art. 2, co.; *Sententia Ethic.*, lib. 2, l. 10 n. 10. Cf. *Nicomachean Ethics* 1151a15–19.

111. *ST* 1–2, q. 59 art. 4, co.: "[V]irtus moralis perficit appetitivam partem animae ordinando ipsam in bonum rationis. Est autem rationis bonum id quod est secundum rationem moderatum seu

that on account of which virtue is praised.[112] What is primary in the sphere of morality is, then, not the virtues themselves but the *bonum rationis*.

Though some proponents of what is called "virtue ethics" would like to claim Thomas as one of their own, it is difficult for them to do so. Thomas follows Aristotle in holding that the moral virtues are habits and that they are formed by acting virtuously.[113] The acts of virtue, then, precede the habits of virtue and, when repeated, the acts give rise to the habits. According to Thomas, all acts of virtue, considered insofar as they are as virtuous, are of the natural law (*de lege naturae*).[114] He says this in the article following q. 94 art. 2, and he explicitly refers his argument there back to q. 94 art. 2. Thomas, of course, grants that parents, community, and tradition play a major role in helping the young acquire virtuous habits. But if this were the end of the story, we would be left with a fairly crude conventionalism. For parents and communities can get things wrong—it suffices to think of racial bigotry—and traditions can be corrupt. But, even if that were not the case, the question would still arise: from where, exactly, did parents and the community get *their* knowledge of how to act? Thomas would not accept as a final answer to this question that parents and other members of the community learned how to act from *their* parents and from *earlier* members of the community, since this is, in fact, not an answer at all but only the question restated as an answer. Nor does Thomas avoid this regress by saying that we originally learned how we should act from divine revelation. For this answer would blur his careful distinction between natural and divine law, and is moreover contradicted by his argument that the latter presupposes the former. We ultimately get our knowledge of how to act from the first principle of practical reason and the primary precepts of natural law. Natural law is then the ultimate and necessary foundation of the habit of virtue.[115] Judgment and prudence are surely required as well, but these take their

ordinatum. Unde circa omne id quod contingit ratione ordinari et moderari, contingit esse virtutem moralem."

112. *ST* 2–2, q. 155 art. 4, ad 3.

113. *Nicomachean Ethics* 1103a14–b25. Thomas Aquinas, *Sententia Libri Ethicorum*, lib. 2, lect. 1 n. 2–10. *ST* 1–2 q. 51 art. 2, co. Cf. Plato, *Republic* 444c10.

114. *ST* 1–2 q. 94 art. 3. See q. 65 art. 3, *sed contra*; q. 96 art. 3, co., ad 1–3; *SCG* lib. 3 cap. 116, n. 4; lib. 3 cap. 121, n. 3. At *ST* 1–2 q. 21 art. 1, *sed contra*, Thomas says that the goodness of a human act depends principally (*principaliter*) on the eternal law, of which, he will later say, natural law is the participation in the rational creature 1–2 q. 91 art. 2, co.; cf. q. 19 art. 4, co.

115. *ST* 1–2 q. 51 art. 2, ad 3: "[A]ctus praecedens habitum inquantum procedit a principio activo, procedit a nobiliori principio quam sit habitus generatus, sicut ipsa ratio est nobilius principium quam sit habitus virtutis moralis in vi appetitiva per actuum consuetudines generatus; et intellectus principiorum est nobilius principium quam scientia conclusionum." See also *Catena aurea in quatuor Evangelia, Expositio in Lucam* cap. 6 l.7: "Est autem nobis insita lex naturalis, per quam dignoscimus quid sit virtus et vitium . . ." Against Thomas's claims here and elsewhere, Janet E. Smith writes, "It cannot be stressed too strongly that virtue has primacy over moral norms [presumably, the precepts of natural law] in Thomistic natural law ethics" ("Character as an Enabler of Moral Judgment," 22). In the same vein, E.A. Goerner writes: "Any full understanding of Thomas's ethics and politics, both natural and supernatural, must focus primarily on his treatment of virtue *rather* than of law" ("The

bearings from rules and ends, the knowledge of which is presupposed by judgment and prudence. Rules and ends are constitutive of the precepts of natural law, and these precepts express obligations. The awareness of obligation is then necessarily prior to virtue, both to the acts and to the habit of virtue. Virtue, on the other hand, renders the precepts of natural law efficacious. We admire someone for his virtue, not for his natural knowledge of natural law. For whereas knowledge of the primary precepts of natural law is common to all human beings, virtue, *qua* excellence, is exceptional. Not everyone is virtuous. Because virtue is founded on and presupposes the natural knowledge of natural law, there is no tension at all between natural law, including its obligating character, and virtue.[116] The two are complementary, but whereas the latter is loftier, the former is prior and more fundamental.[117] The contemporary distinction between "deontology" and "virtue ethics" finds no support in Thomas's ethics when his ethics is considered as a whole.[118] The misguided attempt to detach Thomas's teaching on virtue from his teaching on natural law downplays that component of his

---

Bad Man's View of Thomistic Natural Right," 109; emphasis added). Goerner is surely right that a full understanding of Thomas's ethics and politics requires a careful consideration of his treatment of virtue. But it also requires a no less careful consideration of his treatment of law, of natural law especially.

116. Fr. Pinckaers overstates the matter when he says that "[f]or Thomas, virtues were more important than precepts" (Sources 453). For Thomas, there would be no virtues unless there were precepts. Jean Porter puts things in the proper perspective when she writes, "Aquinas can say that the natural perfection of the human person consists in acting in accordance with virtue, or alternately, in being in accordance with the norms of reason, which is of course the precondition of virtuous action." (*The Recovery of Virtue*, p. 70) The passages Porter refers to in support of this sentence are *ST* 1–2 q. 5 art. 5; 2–2 q. 47 art. 6; 1–2 q. 57 art. 5; q. 58 art. 2. What she calls the "norms of reason" are nothing less than the first principle of practical reason and the primary precepts of natural law. See also 1–2 q. 63 art. 1, co; and q. 92 art. 1, ad 2: "[N]on semper aliquis obedit legi ex bonitate perfecta virtutis; sed quondoque quidem ex timore poenae; quondoque autem ex solo dictamine rationis, quod est quoddam principium virtutis." See q. 19 art. 5, co.

117. Though a major part, but by no means the whole, of Thomas's treatment of the virtues in the *Summa Theologiae* precedes his treatment of natural law, he notes several times prior to his treatment of natural law that the virtues, both intellectual and moral, have their seeds (*seminalia*) in reason and in the will as the rational appetite. *ST* 1–2, q. 63 art. 1, co.: ". . . virtus est homini naturalis secundum quandam inchoationem. Secundum quidem naturam speciei, inquantum in ratione homini insunt naturaliter quaedam principia naturaliter cognita tam scibilium quam agendorum, quae sunt quaedam seminalia intellectualium virtutum et moralium; et inquantum in voluntate inest quidam naturalis appetitus boni quod est secundum rationem." 1–2 q. 67 art. 1 ad 3: "Unde nec huiusmodi virtutes erunt in actu nisi in radice, scilicet in ratione et voluntate, in quibus sunt seminalia quaedam harum virtutum . . ." 1–2 q. 51 art. 1, co.: "In appetitivis autem potentiis non est aliquis habitus naturalis secundum inchoationem, ex parte ipsius animae, quantum ad ipsam substantiam habitus, sed solum quantum ad principia quaedam ipsius, sicut principia iuris communis dicuntur esse seminalia virtutum." The principles of *ius commune* that are naturally known and are called the seeds of the virtues turn out to be the first principle and the primary precepts of natural law. See also 1–2 q. 27 art. 3; ad 4; q. 63 art. 1 ad 1, ad 2.

118. It is by no means clear that Aristotle himself would sharply distinguish between "virtue ethics" and "deontology." The latter means the *logos* or account of what ought to be (or should be—*to deon*). Aristotle immediately explicates his famous definition of (moral) virtue by speaking of what is binding, or right, or, arguably, obligatory (*tou deonotos*) with respect to passions and actions. *Nicomachean Ethics* 1107a4–5. See Part 2, Ch. 9, Section b, i., below.

ethics that is the most serious challenge to the Straussians, namely, the case he makes that man *as such*—the philosopher equally with the non-philosopher—stands under certain elementary obligations that are established and declared by natural reason itself.

When Thomas speaks of the *bonum rationis* as the formal principle of the virtues, and as an intelligible, rather than a sensible, good,[119] he does not mean that it is merely "formalistic." It has, in fact, the character of an end.[120] Not only is the *bonum rationis* prior to the moral virtues, it is prior to prudence as well, and presupposed by both.[121] The *bonum rationis* is not created by prudence; it is, rather, determined by prudence to the mean in actions and passions as is appropriate to the particulars of concrete circumstances.[122] It pertains not to prudence but to *synderesis* to appoint (*praestituere*) the end for the moral virtues. Prudence is concerned with the means to the end. Accordingly, "*synderesis* moves prudence just as the understanding of the [logical] principles moves science."[123] Though *synderesis* has this priority over prudence and moral virtue, it would remain ineffectual without prudence and moral virtue. The latter, on the other hand, would not even exist without the former. The relationship between *synderesis*, prudence, and moral virtue is organic. All pertain, each in its own way, to the *bonum rationis*, which for a rational being is the good *simpliciter*.[124]

Because Thomas holds that the *bonum rationis* should be preserved even, if necessary, at the cost of life itself, one might be tempted to think that he understands it to be essentially a supernatural good. This is not the case.

> [T]he theological virtues ordain man to supernatural happiness in the same way as by natural inclination man is ordained to his connatural end. Now the latter happens in two ways. First, according to reason or the intellect: in so far as it contains the first universal principles known to us by the natural light of the intellect, and from which reason proceeds both in speculative and in

119. *ST* 1–2 q. 30 art. 1, co.

120. *Super Sent.*, lib. 3, dist. 33, q. 2 art. 3, co.: "Finis autem proximus humanae vitae est bonum rationis in communi."

121. *Super Sent.*, lib. 3, dist. 33 q. 2 art. 3, co.: "[E]t ideo est intentum in omnibus virtutibus moralibus, ut passiones et operationes ad rectitudinem rationis reducantur. Rectitudo autem rationis naturalis est; unde hoc modo praestitutio finis ad naturalem rationem pertinet, et praecedit prudentiam, sicut intellectus principiorum scientiam . . . [D]iscretio eorum quibus hoc bonum rationis consequi possumus et in operationibus et in passionibus, est actus prudentiae: unde praestitutio finis praecedit actum prudentiae et virtutis moralis; sed inclinatio in finem, sive recta electio finis proximi, est actus moralis virtutis principaliter, sed prudentiae originaliter."

122. *Super Sent.*, lib. 3, dist. 33 q. 2 art. 3, co.: "Sed hoc bonum rationis determinatur secundum quod constituitur medium in actionibus et passionibus per debitam commensurationem circumstantiarum, quod facit prudentia." See ad 4.

123. *ST* 2–2 q. 47 art. 6, co., ad 2, ad 3.

124. *De Malo* q. 16 art. 2, co.: sicut concupiscentiae inclinatio, quae est in delectabile secundum sensum, quod est quoddam particulare bonum, si sit immoderata, opponitur bono rationis, quod est bonum simpliciter."

> practical matters, and second, through the rectitude of the will naturally tending to the *bonum rationis*. But these two fall short of the order of supernatural happiness.[125]

The will of its very nature is inclined to the *bonum rationis*.[126] Indeed, Thomas says that *love* of the *bonum rationis* is intrinsic to the will,[127] which has to be the case if the latter is properly understood as the *appetitus rationis*: natural reason is attracted to its own good.

The will is naturally inclined to the *bonum rationis* even when a man is threatened with death, not because he is hoping for a reward in the afterlife—though he may well hope for this—but because the will, as the appetite that is proper to reason, naturally aims at a good that is proper to reason; and, again, life is not a good *proper* to reason. Thomas is fully aware of the fact that a man, faced with the prospect of death, let us say, a violent death preceded by torture, may well abandon the *bonum rationis* and commit a gross injustice. He might, for example, give perjured and damning testimony against an innocent human being in order to preserve the bodily good of his own life. But, Thomas would insist, it is not in virtue of his reason that he is inclined to do such a thing, nor can he justify doing it by appeal to his reason. Giving such testimony is categorically forbidden by reason, no matter what bodily good one hopes to preserve by doing so, and whether one believes in an afterlife or not. For a rational being, no bodily good is the highest good; nor is it the highest good that can be attained naturally.

One might take issue with this austere conception of the *bonum rationis* and the exacting demands that it places on man who, unlike God or an angel, is not only rational but animal as well. One might grant that there is an appetite proper to reason, but deny that it is oriented toward anything other than knowledge of truth. Knowledge of truth is, to be sure, intrinsic to the *bonum rationis*. But we should not forget that, though Thomas says that truth is the proper object of the *bonum rationis*, he also says that justice is its proper effect. "[J]ustice is the making *effective* of this good (*est huius boni factiva*), inasmuch as it pertains to justice to posit the order of reason in all [!] human affairs (*in omnibus rebus humanis*)."[128] The appetite of reason is the will, and justice is the virtue proper to the will.[129]

125. *ST* 1–2 q. 62 art. 3, co. (reading *in finem sibi connaturalem*, as in the *Corpus Thomisticum*, instead of *in fidem sibi connaturalem*, as in the *Biblioteca de Autores Cristianos* text of *ST* 1–2, 1962.)

126. *ST* 1–2 q. 50 art. 5, ad 3. Something can appear to be the *bonum rationis* without actually being so: q. 80 art. 1, co.

127. *De virtutibus* q. 2 art. 2, co.: "Ad virtutem igitur requiritur amor boni ad quod virtus operatur. Bonum autem ad quod operatur virtus quae est hominis in quantum homo, est homini connaturale; unde voluntati eius naturaliter inest huius boni amor, quod est bonum rationis."

128. *ST* 2–2 q. 123 art. 12, co.

129. *ST* 2–2 q. 58 art. 4.

Because this-worldly (and imperfect) happiness "consists first and principally in contemplation but secondarily in an operation of the practical intellect directing human actions and passions," the operation of the practical intellect cannot be construed as merely securing the conditions for contemplation. The operation of practical reason is, rather, an actual constituent of happiness, although a secondary constituent. Thomas's claim that the primary constituent of such happiness as we can achieve in this life is contemplation, or philosophic activity, is not contested by his Straussian critics. So I focus on the secondary constituent.

Thomas agrees with Aristotle that happiness is the good for man, and his concept of happiness is derived from Aristotle's. Happiness, Aristotle says early in the *Nicomachean Ethics*, is "an activity of the soul in accordance with virtue . . ."[130] One should not assume too quickly that Aristotle is thinking chiefly of moral virtue here. He might not be thinking of moral virtue at all, for he continues the definition with ". . . and if there are several virtues, in accordance with the best and more perfect [virtue]."[131] Aristotle argues that there are indeed several virtues and, furthermore, that the best of them are not the moral virtues but the intellectual virtues, the virtues of contemplation in particular. So it is conceivable that he considers the moral virtues, and prudence among the intellectual virtues, to be not so much constituents of genuine happiness as conditions of it, or means toward it, whether in the individual or in the city, or in both. I shall not argue for or against this interpretation of Aristotle, other than to point out that texts can be cited both on behalf of it and against it.[132] Our concern here is with how Thomas understands Aristotle's definition of happiness and how he understands the operation of the practical intellect to be a constituent of happiness and not just a condition of it.

For Thomas, just as for Aristotle, happiness is not a feeling, not even a feeling of pleasure, though it is attended by a feeling a pleasure. Happiness is an activity. The part of happiness that consists in the operation of the practical intellect is the activity by which one governs one's actions and passions and places them in the proper order. In the proper operation of the practical intellect, Thomas says, "man is lord of his acts through the choice of reason" (*homo est dominus suorum actuum per arbitrium rationis*)."[133] And even if, in extreme circumstances, it requires great sacrifice of bodily good, and hence of bodily pleasure, the operation of the practical intellect

130. *Nicomachean Ethics* 1098a17. In this text Aristotle speaks not of happiness but of the human good: *to anthrōpinon agathon psychēs energeia . . . kat' aretēn*. But he has just argued that happiness is the human good, and a bit later he speaks as though he has defined happiness. See 1098b21; 1100b10; 1102a5.

131. ". . . *ei de pleious hai aretai, kata tēn aristēn kai teleiotatēn*."

132. Compare *Nicomachean Ethics* 1102a5 (*kat' aretēn teleian*), and the ambiguity of the word *teleia* (perfect as either the highest or the most complete of virtues) in that passage, with 1100b19 (*praksei kai theorēsei ta kat' aretēn*). Consider the plural *aretai* at 1174a4–6.

133. *ST* 2–2 q. 158 art. 2, ad 3. See 2–2 q. 64 art. 5, ad 2; *Super Sent.*, lib. 1 d. 17 q. 2 art. 3, co.; lib. 2 d. 21 q. 1 art. 2 ad 1; *ST* 1–2, q. 1 art. 1 co.; q. 6 art. 2, ad 2; q. 109 art. 2, ad 1; *De Veritate*, q. 5 art. 10.

is nonetheless attended by some measure of satisfaction, and hence of the peculiar pleasure that accompanies satisfaction. This pleasure, which is not bodily, may be experienced only faintly in the presence of intense bodily pain. Nonetheless, however so faintly felt, it naturally accompanies the consciousness of duty performed just as it naturally accompanies the consciousness of progress in knowledge. The *bonum rationis* is preserved in this directive act of reason. In the case of those who are habitually directed by reason, that is, those who are virtuous, the *bonum rationis* flourishes (*viget*) in them.[134]

It should be obvious by now that the operation of the practical intellect, as an achievement of reason, is governed by rules. The measure or rule of human works (or operations—*opera*), Thomas says, is the *bonum rationis.*[135] This formulation from the early *Commentary on the Sentences*, reminds us of the formulation from the *Summa Theologiae* that law, including natural law as the participation of the eternal law in the rational creature, is a rule and measure of acts. There is then a close relationship between the natural law and the *bonum rationis.* But their relationship is not one of simple identity. For, whereas the primary precepts of natural law are indelible, the *bonum rationis* has to be preserved. Moreover, the primary precepts of natural law are known by all human beings who have reached the age of reason and are not intellectually stunted or mentally ill. And bodily goods are similarly known. But the *bonum rationis*, because it includes truth as well as justice, is known only by a few.[136] There is a natural and immediate knowledge of the primary precepts of natural law—not necessarily immediate knowledge of them as precepts of *law*, but still immediate knowledge of them as *obligatory.*[137] There is, however, no natural and immediate knowledge of the *bonum rationis.* What knowledge we have of the *bonum rationis* is achieved through sustained reflection on the nature of human reason, reflection of the very kind that Thomas engaged in.

The *bonum rationis* and the *bonum commune* are also closely related. But their relation, too, is not one of simple identity. Thomas tells us that *bonum* and *ens* (that which is) are convertible. *Bonum* expressly emphasizes the aspect of desirable; but *ens* does not.[138] Still, whatever *is* is to *that* extent good, regardless of any defects it might

134. *De Virtutibus* q. 2 art. 2, ad 8; *ST* 2–2 q. 155 art. 4, co.

135. *Super Sent.*, lib. 3, dist. 34, q. 1 art. 2, co.; q. 2 art. 1 qc. 3, co.

136. *ST* 1 q. 63 art. 9, ad 1; see *De Malo* q. 1 art. 3, ad 17.

137. The interpretation of the obligations that we are immediately aware of as what is expressed in the primary precepts of natural law and in the secondary precepts that can be derived from them *modica consideratione* is, I think, justifiable, even necessary. I do realize that not everyone will concur in this interpretation. But I do not know what good reasons could be given for not concurring in it.

138. *ST* 1 q. 5 art. 1 co; 1–2 q. 55 art. 4, ad 2. Being is common not because it is distributed equally and indifferently over all the things that are, as is a simple class such as dog or tree, but by reference to one premier instance of being that *is* more fully than anything else. Aristotle, *Metaphysics* 1003a32-b19; 1028a10-b8; Thomas Aquinas, *In Dudoecim Libros Metaphysicorum Aristotelis Expositio* lib. 4, lect. 1; lib. 7, lect. 1. This is true of the good as well. Compare Aristotle, *Nicomachean Ethics* 1096a24–28; Thomas Aquinas, *Sententia Libri Ethicorum.*, lib.1, l. 6 n. 5–7.

have. Being, or existence, considered in itself, is a perfection, just as good is. Now God, who exists perfectly, does not participate in the *bonum commune*. Rather, Thomas says, he *is* the *bonum commune*.[139] He is the separate and final good of the whole universe, the ultimate good for everything in it. Though rational creatures participate in the *bonum commune* in a preeminent way, all creatures, inasmuch as they *are*, participate in the *bonum commune* to some extent. But only rational creatures participate in the *bonum rationis*.

Natural reason is teleological. It *aims*, in both its speculative and its practical operation. It aims at both truth and justice (under the aspect of the good), as the proper object and the proper effect, respectively, of the *bonum rationis*. Kant claims that it pertains to the very nature of reason to *seek* the unconditioned ground of what is conditioned.[140] Thomas would concur. This seeking is not reducible to any psychological state or process, such as fear of death or "flight from finitude." Natural reason has interests *of its own*. These are the true and the good and, correlatively with them, knowledge and justice respectively. These two pairs constitute the *bonum rationis*.

Natural reason, that is, reason as it exists in man as distinct from reason as it exists in God, directs man toward ends through universal principles. These principles are articulated as propositions, namely, the logical principles and the precepts, or commands, of natural law. The logical principles and the primary precepts of natural law are not the *bonum rationis* in its fullness, though thinking and acting in accordance with them, or thinking and acting consistently, is constitutive of integrity.[141] Consistency is, to be sure, not the fullness of truth and justice. But it is indispensable for the movement toward truth and justice, minimizing, as it does, unnecessary detours, wandering down blind alleys, and the need to backtrack.

One might object that Thomas's conception of the *bonum rationis*, because it prescinds from what is personal and particular, prescinds from what is most fundamentally real. Thomas is hardly indifferent to the personal. For him, as for all Catholic Christians, God exists not as an impersonal principle or type, such as a law of nature or a Platonic idea, but as a Trinity of persons. The doctrine of the Trinity is, however, a matter not of rational but of revealed theology. And the personal encounter with God "face to face" is constitutive not of natural, this-worldly happiness, but of supernatural happiness in a life beyond this one. In this life, what we can know and what we ought to do are determined through the principles that reason naturally employs (which is not to deny that in this life supernatural revelation can supervene upon the operation of natural reason). Thomas leaves plenty of room for private interests and desires to play a role in thinking and action. But these interests cannot override the *bonum rationis*, which is the good of man as man.

139. *SCG* lib. 3 cap. 17 n. 6.

140. *KRV* B 364–5.

141. "Bonum rationis est quod homo faciat ordinate unumquodque quod facit." *Super* Sent., lib. 3 d. 29 q. 1 art. 1, *sed contra* 1.

But, one might continue to object, I am not man *as man*. I am, first and foremost . . . *myself*! Can't I love myself more than the good of reason? To this question Thomas would answer that I can surely subordinate love of the *bonum rationis* to love, in some sense of the word, of bodily goods, including life and physical well-being. But this subordination is prohibited by reason. And reason, not these other things, is what is best in man *as* man. Genuine love of oneself, or willing the good for oneself, is inseparable from love of the *bonum rationis*. According to Thomas, those who subordinate the good of reason to bodily goods actually hate themselves more than they love themselves. Thomas reaches this conclusion without any appeal to revelation. Aristotle reaches a similar conclusion. [142]

We have surveyed and considered Thomas's use of the expression *bonum rationis* in order to set it in relief against the assertion sometimes made by Straussians, typically with little in the way of elaboration, that *the* good is essentially if not exclusively one's *own* good.[143] Thomas's response to this assertion is that one's own (*proprium*) good is not essentially life, physical well-being, pleasure, or any other bodily good. One's *own* good, to the extent that one is a rational rather than sub-rational, is precisely the *bonum rationis*. This is the good *proper* to man as man. [144]

* * *

Thomas Aquinas's rational theology and natural law teaching are extensive and highly developed, and his revealed theology is extensive and highly developed too. In his two

142. *De virtutibus*, q. 2 art. 12, ad 6: "[C]um in homine sit duplex natura, scilicet intellectiva, quae principalior est, et sensitiva, quae minor est, ille vere seipsum diligit qui se amat ad bonum rationis: qui autem se amat ad bonum sensualitatis contra bonum rationis, magis se odit quam amat, proprie loquendo." See *Sententia Ethic., lib. 9, l. 8 n. 11; lib. 9, l. 9 n. 1.* Cf. Aristotle, *Nicomachean Ethics* 1168b12–1169a14.

143. Thomas West proposes that by "the human good" Thomas himself means "ultimately one's own good" (*Critique of the 'Straussian' Critique*, 30). Since West does not spell out what he means by this expression, we are left to surmise that he means something *essentially* private, perhaps one's own physical well-being, rather than something common (Cf. *ST* 1–2 q.19, art. 10, co.; *SCG* 3 cap. 16–18; and *ST* 1–2 q. 109 art. 3.). West does not, in any event, connect this expression, as Thomas does, with the *bonum rationis*. Speaking to a passage in the *SCG* (3 cap. 122 n. 2), West says that, "in a frank defense of self-interest properly understood, Aquinas writes . . . 'we do not offend God except by doing something contrary to our own good'" (*Critique of the 'Straussian' Critique*, 53, *supra*). One would need to know what West means by "self-interest properly understood" to determine whether this sentence from *SCG* really supports his interpretation. The sentence that West translates is, "Non enim Deus a nobis offenditur nisi ex eo quod contra nostrum bonum agimus." For what Thomas means by *nostrum bonum* see cap. 108 n. 6 of the same work, where he connects it with the *bonum proprium*. Cf. *Super Sent.*, lib. 1 d. 18 q. 1 art. 5, co., and *ST* 1–2 q. 32 art. 6, co.

144. *De Virtutibus* q. 2 art. 2, co.: "Nam proprium bonum hominis in quantum homo, est bonum rationis, eo quod homini esse est rationale esse." See *Sententia Ethic.*, lib. 10, 1. 33 n. 6; *ST* 2–2 q. 129 art. 3; *De Veritate* q. 13 art. 1, arg. 5. Compare *Nicomachean Ethics* 1168b35. In one formulation, occurring in the context of revealed theology, Thomas goes so far as to say that those who are perfect "follow principally the example of Christ, the precepts of God, and [!] the *bonum rationis*." *Super Sent.*, lib. 4, dist. 38, q. 2 art. 3 qc. 1, co.

great *Summas*, and elsewhere as well, Thomas takes his time in developing what natural reason can know about God, the world, and man. He turns to revealed theology proper only later on, and even then he does not always introduce the specific claims of revelation as soon as one would expect. As Servais Pinckaers puts it, "[E]thicists who approach the *Summa* are amazed to see that in Thomas's chief treatises on morality, such as those on happiness, actions, virtues and vices, law and so forth, he never mentions Christ."[145] Earl Muller notes that "[t]here has always been an awkwardness felt in the treatment of grace in the *secunda* [i.e., *ST* 1–2] without any explicit mention of Christ."[146] Thomas's procedure, clearly intentional, is to postpone treating the claims of revelation until he has given as purely rational an account of theological and moral matters as is possible. Only after doing so does he show the essential incompleteness of the rational account, and hence its need to be supplemented by revelation.

Bringing in the claims of revelation only after he has exhausted what reason has to say about the things that matter most to us crowns Thomas's entire presentation. It disposes even the unbeliever to take seriously the possibility that it is only by accepting these claims that one can have a comprehensive and rationally consistent account of the whole, in spite of the fact that the revealed component of this account, though internally consistent, is neither self-evident nor demonstrable but has to be accepted on faith. Thomas's procedure is manifestly designed to lead one towards acknowledging what might appear to be, but is not, a paradox. Natural reason *necessitates* neither belief nor unbelief. However, because belief is more in accord than unbelief with the demonstrable *limits* of natural reason and, at the same time, with the self-evident *teleology* of natural reason, belief is more rational than unbelief—assuming, of course, that reason is not able to refute the very possibility of revelation.[147]

145. *Sources*, 168–169.

146. Earl Muller, "The Christological Foundation of Natural Law," 107. Christ explicitly comes under consideration in 1–2 q. 114 art. 6, co.

147. See *NRH* 75.

Part 2

Straussian Criticisms

Leo Strauss and his closest followers agree with Socrates, Plato, and Aristotle in holding that philosophy is the most choiceworthy way of life for those who are able to live it. But philosophy, so understood, is challenged by an old opponent and by a new one, both formidable and neither of which Socrates, Plato, or Aristotle knew anything about: biblical revelation and Heideggerian historicism. In order to defend philosophy against the challenge of the Bible, Strauss undertakes a critique of the idea of law, which is at the center of a critique of the possibility of revelation. And in order to defend philosophy against the challenge of Heidegger, he undertakes a re-validation of the classical concept of nature as an uncreated order of intelligible necessity. The massive obstacle to Strauss's twofold undertaking is the natural law teaching of Thomas Aquinas.

Chapter 4

Criticisms Advanced by Leo Strauss

SECTION A. MEDIEVAL PHILOSOPHY VS. CHRISTIAN SCHOLASTICISM

In his Introduction to *Persecution and the Art of Writing*, Strauss contrasts Jewish and Islamic medieval philosophy with what he studiously refrains from calling "Christian medieval philosophy," but instead calls "Christian scholasticism" throughout.[1] Strauss understands philosophy to be a way of life that accepts as true only what is accessible to reason and ordinary experience, without appeal to revelation. It is a way of life that is governed by an ideal of autonomous understanding.[2] Hence it is always in some tension with the religion or the ideology of the society in which it is lived. According to Strauss, a genuinely philosophical life was easier to live within medieval Jewish and Islamic communities than within medieval Christendom, for two reasons in particular.

The first reason is that Jewish and Muslim communities were constituted in large measure by their members' observance of a comprehensive law, believed to be revealed by God through a prophet. The unbelieving philosopher is not persuaded that this law is of divine origin, but he can see its salutary effect on public life, its contribution to political order and tranquility, from which both he and his fellow citizens, unbelievers

1. *PAWr* 8. See also Strauss, "How to Begin to Study Medieval Philosophy," 221–4 (see however *PR* 116, where Strauss speaks only of "so-called Jewish medieval philosophy"); and "Preface" to Isaac Husik, *Philosophical Essays*, 252. I do not know of any place where Strauss uses the expression "Christian philosophy," although he does speak of a contemporary for whom he had considerable respect, Gerhard Krüger, as being "a very philosophic interpreter [of Plato]" (Strauss, *Plato' Symposium*, 39); and Strauss knew that Krüger was a Christian. (See, in this connection, the opening paragraph of his letter of August 18, 1934 to Krüger, *GS* Band 3, 439.) In one of his lectures, Strauss interestingly refers to Thomism as "a philosophic position." (*IE* 29/305. When I refer to this particular lecture here and elsewhere, the first of the two page numbers that I give is in accordance with the version found in *The Rebirth of Classical Political Rationalism*. The second page number is in accordance with the version given as the second of the "Two Lectures" in *Interpretation—A Journal of Political Philosophy*. When the two version differ, I quote from the latter one.) Strauss also makes a distinction, though only in passing, between Thomas's theology and his philosophy (*GS, Band 3,* 451).

2. *PR* 104. See also Strauss, "Thucydides," 72; *NRH* 74 and 76.

and believers alike, benefit. Observance of the law, of its letter, is possible for an unbelieving philosopher.[3] Christian communities, on the other hand, are unified primarily by a shared belief, that is, by confession of a common creed. It is impossible for a philosopher to participate in this belief without abandoning his commitment to the ideal of autonomy that Strauss understands to be constitutive of philosophy.

This difference between Judaism and Islam on the one hand and Christianity on the other can, however, be exaggerated. The law in Judaism and the law in Islam command not only outward deeds but belief in God and in the reliability of prophecy.[4] And Christianity—traditional Catholic Christianity, at least—requires, if not exactly observance, still a certain practice. And it requires not just a moral practice, but a liturgical practice too: attending services, participating in the sacramental life of the church, following a prayer rule, fasting, and so forth. Still, in Catholic Christianity, the centrality of the Nicene Creed and ecclesiastical pronouncements on what are, and what are not, permissible *theologoumena*, the emphasis on the "spirit" of the law as opposed to its "mere letter," the contrast between "living faith," which saves, and "dead works," which do not—to say nothing of the sacrament of confession—all these things call for a greater conformity of the inner life of the individual Christian to the inner lives of fellow Christians around him than one finds in Jewish communities (though not so obviously a greater conformity than one finds in Islamic communities). An exemplification of this difference is the familiar case of the contemporary Jew who proclaims himself, understands himself, and is understood by others, to be an atheist as well as a Jew. A Christian who understands himself to be an atheist is an impossibility. Such a being cannot exist.

The second reason why, according to Strauss, a genuinely philosophic life was easier to live within, albeit at the margin of, Jewish and Islamic communities turns somewhat paradoxically on the fact that, whereas philosophy was of little interest and of less value in a theological tradition whose chief focus was on the interpretation of law, it was of great interest and value in a theological tradition whose chief focus was on the interpretation of articles of faith. Thomas Aquinas and other scholastics treated what can be naturally known, including the existence of God and a number of other things pertaining to him, not as articles of faith but as rationally demonstrable preambles to the articles of faith. Since, as they were fully aware, philosophy has quite

3. "The Law of Reason," 139; "How to Begin to Study Medieval Philosophy," 222, bottom. See Strauss's letter of June 23, 1934, to Jacob Klein, *GS* Band 3, 516.

4. Consider Strauss's statement (which could seem on first hearing to be in tension with itself) that "what first came to the sight of the Islamic and Jewish philosophers in their reflections on Revelation was *not a creed or a set of dogmas*, but a social order, if an all-comprehensive order, which regulates not merely actions, but *thoughts and opinions as well*." *PAWr* 9–10 (emphasis added). What Strauss likely means here is that the Islamic and Jewish philosophers were not especially interested in the *particular content* of religious belief ("a creed or a set of dogmas"), since as philosophers they did not believe in it. But they were quite interested in the *general and politically salutary regulation* of "thoughts and opinions," along with actions, by those who ruled or might come to rule authoritatively in these communities, whether as (alleged) prophets or as master statesmen.

a bit to say about what can be naturally known, they realized that they had to study it carefully. As Strauss says,

> [I]t is obvious that while no one can be learned in the sacred doctrine of Christianity without having had considerable philosophic training, one can be a perfectly competent Talmudist without having had any philosophic training.[5]

This apparent compliment paid to Christianity is not unqualified. With the word "training," which he also uses in the preceding paragraph, Strauss is suggesting that there was little philosophic *education*, properly so-called, and therefore little philosophy as such in scholasticism. The respectability of philosophical studies in the Christian middle ages, Strauss claims, was purchased at the price of the independence of philosophy.

> The official recognition of philosophy in the Christian world made philosophy subject to ecclesiastical supervision. The precarious position of philosophy in the Islamic-Jewish world guaranteed its private character and therewith its inner freedom from supervision.[6]

Once again, however, there is a danger of exaggeration. Though there was some ecclesiastical supervision of philosophy in the Christian world, it was still possible for heterodox opinions to get a hearing. In scholastic practice it was essential that heterodox opinions get a hearing. What one could even call the scholastics' "art of writing," paradigmatically exemplified by Thomas Aquinas, but not only by him, involved placing at the very beginning of a treatise or article, not just *statements of* heterodox counterclaims, but *arguments for* heterodox counterclaims. These arguments are not "straw men," and they are always interesting. The scholastics' art of writing guaranteed that the case against the theological positions approved by ecclesiastical authority would be preserved and considered right along with the case for the approved positions. Strauss calls attention to the initially bewildering character of this mode of presentation.[7] But he seems not to have appreciated how far the scholastics succeeded,

5. Introduction to *PAWr* 19. See "How to Begin to Study Medieval Philosophy," 221–2.

6. *PAWr* 21. For a similar formulation, see "How to Begin to Study Medieval Philosophy," 223. Cf. *PR* 99: "[T]heology was the authority for philosophy in the middle ages" (240); and "The Mutual Influence of Theology and Philosophy" in *Faith and Political Philosophy*, 223: "[P]hilosophy was certainly in the Christian Middle Ages deprived of its character as a way of life and became just a very important compartment." Allan Bloom writes similarly, "[S]cholasticism, the use of Aristotle by the Roman Catholic Church, was the phantom of philosophy . . ." (*The Closing of the American Mind*, 264.) If by "philosophy," Bloom means something like atheism arising out of an ostensibly sober reflection on the (alleged) tension between the just and the good, then scholasticism, to its credit, is not *even* a phantom of philosophy. But if by "philosophy," Bloom means, more broadly, "rationalism," as is suggested in the sentence preceding the one from which I just quoted, then his statement reflects only the comic strip version of scholasticism that is widely subscribed to by contemporary academics, especially in America.

7. Book Review of Anton Pegis, ed., *The Basic Writings of Thomas Aquinas*, in *WhPPh* 284–285.

through the way in which they presented their teachings, in protecting free inquiry from an ecclesiastical supervision that might otherwise have stifled it completely. By the way in which they wrote, the scholastic thinkers guaranteed that heterodox arguments would be considered and re-considered as long as their own books were read. If what Strauss means by "inner freedom" is freedom of the *mind*, there is no reason to suspect that there was any less of it in medieval scholasticism than in Jewish and Islamic philosophy. After all, the ecclesiastical supervision given voice in the notorious condemnations of 1270 and 1277 was a reaction to considerable outer freedom, to freedom of *speech*, which springs from inner freedom, from freedom of *mind*, which is not susceptible to ecclesiastical supervision in any case.[8]

In his essay, "How to Begin to Study *The Guide of the Perplexed*," Strauss says of Maimonides's book that "[t]he *Guide* as a whole is not merely a key to a forest but is itself a forest, an enchanted forest, and hence also an enchanting forest . . ."[9] Because one does not usually need a key to enter a forest, I infer that, as Strauss sees it, Maimonides's *Guide* is an unusual forest not only because it is enchanted and enchanting but because it is a forest enclosed within walls, located within a city in fact, resembling a large but private courtyard garden of which most citizens are unaware and to which only those with the right key can gain admittance. I find Strauss's metaphor, which elaborates Maimonides's own metaphor, particularly apt because it helps us see how different the great writings of the scholastics are from the *Guide*.

The scholastic *summas* have been likened by the art historian Erwin Panofsky to Gothic cathedrals,[10] to which the public is admitted without keys. Panofsky sees a number of similarities between Gothic architecture and the writings of the scholastics, two of which are of particular relevance here. The structure is on the whole transparent: even the buttresses are visible. Moreover, the plan is comprehensive, and every detail is in its proper place in relation both to the other details and to the structure as a whole. Very little is concealed from public view.[11]

Compare Strauss's assertion—in disagreement with Pegis—that "Aristotle did not intend 'to leave his explanation of the origin of the world unfinished,' and did not leave it unfinished" (285), with Aristotle, *Topics* 104b5–17. See *ST* 1 q. 46 art. 1, co.

8. For a clear overview of the background, precipitating causes, and effects of these condemnations, see John Wippel, "The Condemnations of 1270 and 1277 at Paris," *The Journal of Medieval and Renaissance Studies*, 7 (1977) 2, pp. 169–201. As Fr. Wippel points out, the 1277 condemnation by the Bishop of Paris actually went beyond the papal mandate of an investigation into the *teaching*—as distinct from the mere *consideration*—of heterodox doctrines at the University of Paris (186). It was, moreover, "purely local in its binding force" (170).

9. Maimonides, *The Guide of the Perplexed*, Vol. 1, xiii-xiv.

10. Erwin Panofsky, *Gothic Architecture and Scholasticism*.

11. Panofsky, 33–36. Otto von Simson is not persuaded by the full thrust of Panofsky's thesis. (*Gothic Cathedral* xvii-xvii, fn. 3). But, like Panofsky, he too emphasizes the extent to which visibility of structure and detail was striven for and achieved in the Gothic cathedral: hardly anything is hidden (*Gothic Cathedral*, 4–6).

The analogy with the Gothic cathedral, however, works only up to a point. The cathedral is present all at once, and one can intelligently consider its structure, beginning either on the inside or on the outside, moving around more or less at random. In the case of a book like the *Summa Theologiae*, the situation is different. It is possible to simply open the book to any chance page and begin reading. But because arguments advanced later in this book depend on arguments advanced earlier, it is best to begin at the beginning. Otherwise the full demonstrative force of its argumentation is not going to be appreciated. There is, additionally, the following problem, to which Thomas draws attention.

> In the beginning [of the learning process] a man is imperfect (or incomplete—*imperfectus*) in cognition. In order that he attain the perfection of scientific knowledge, he needs an instructor, who will lead him to the perfection of scientific knowledge . . . At the beginning of [the instructor's] teaching . . . he transmits (*tradit*) to [the learner] some things, the reasons for which, at the time when the learner is first instructed, the learner does not know; but which he will know after progress in scientific knowledge.[12]

The difficulty in learning, however, is not limited to the beginning of the learning process. For not everyone is properly disposed for theological studies. Thomas gives two reasons why, in teaching certain divine matters, the instructor should moderate what he says or writes and even employ a measure of concealment.[13] (1) Non-believers (including philosophical non-believers), or adherents of other religions, who oppose the faith of the church may deride her doctrines. This was a real problem in the early church when she was persecuted by non-Christians who distorted her theology and sacraments, by claiming, for example, that in celebrating the Eucharist Christians were engaging in cannibalism.[14] (2) Even when and where, as in Thomas's own time

12. *De Veritate* q. 14, art. 10, co.

13. Thomas Aquinas, Commentary on the *De Trinitate* of Boethius q. 2 art. 4, co.

14. In *Philosophy Between the Lines*, Arthur Melzer draws attention to a number of places in the New Testament where Christ speaks in various ways about concealing some of his teachings (98–99). These passages are striking and worthy of consideration. But in none of them does Christ suggest or so much as hint that he has a properly philosophical teaching, least of all a philosophical teaching that calls into question the very possibility of revelation and needs to be expressed, if at all, only obliquely or between the lines of books, which of course he never wrote. See Kevin White, "Aquinas on Oral Teaching." In *ST* 3 q. 42 art. 3, Thomas speaks to the question, "Whether Christ should have taught all things openly?" His answer is that Christ *did* teach all things openly. But he notes that when Christ taught before the crowds he employed parables, so as not to reveal certain spiritual mysteries to the unworthy, i.e., his opponents, or to the simple among his followers who were unable to apprehend these mysteries except through parables. Nonetheless, by using these parables Christ managed to communicate to the crowds some knowledge of spiritual matters. And, Thomas adds, Christ expounded the open and unveiled truth of the parables to his disciples, so that they might expound them to others who were worthy and capable of receiving it. See *ST* 1 q. 9, ad 2, where Thomas gives another reason for the employment of metaphors in Scripture. See also Acts 1:3. Melzer is right to speak of this mode of teaching as a kind of "esotericism." But it cannot count as *philosophical* esotericism. Melzer concurs in Strauss's distinction between the practice of Thomas Aquinas and that of Maimonides and Averroes

and place, the church was not particularly exposed to persecution by non-believers, sincere but uneducated believers could be confused, and their faith shaken, by certain theological teachings that they could not easily understand. These believers may be startled to discover that God, who is not subject to passions, does not grieve when they grieve, say, over the death of a family member. Moreover, some teachings, such as the identity of being and essence in God and the distinction between being and essence in creatures, are too subtle for those who do not have the ability or the leisure required to comprehend them. Thomas says, quoting Augustine, that such teachings "are to be concealed by obscuring words" (or "by the obscurities of words"—*sunt occultanda verborum obscuritatibus*). Thomas comments on this formulation of Augustine's: "And by this procedure no one is burdened (*gravatur*), because those who understand are engaged by what they read (*lectione detinentur*), whereas those who do not understand are not compelled to keep reading." Then Thomas quotes Augustine again: "This is not a failure of duty [on the part of those of us who write on such matters] as long as we bring truths, even though very difficult to understand, to the understanding of others."[15]

Thomas is not speaking in these passages of a teaching that calls into question the moral and religious convictions of the community in which he is teaching, or of the need of the teacher to protect himself from the possibility of persecution. Of course, one can entertain the possibility that, since Thomas explicitly says that certain theological doctrines should not be taught openly to everyone, he may be hinting that he himself did not sincerely intend certain theological doctrines that he openly taught. Such a thing cannot be simply ruled out. However, Thomas gives arguments for these doctrines; and before assuming that he did not intend them seriously, one would need to identify the flaws in his arguments. Strauss writes, "If a master of the art of writing commits such blunders as would shame an intelligent high school boy, it is reasonable to assume that they are intentional, especially if the author discusses, however incidentally, the possibility of intentional blunders in writing."[16] The apodosis of this sentence could be extended to include "or the possibility of intentional concealment in writing." However, the apodosis is governed by the protasis: "If a master of the art of writing commits such blunders as would shame an intelligent high school boy . . ." Leaving to one side the question of whether Thomas was "a master of the art of writing," as Strauss understands such a master, one would be hard pressed to find Thomas committing "such blunders as would shame an intelligent high school boy."[17] One

(148). See, in this connection, *Persecution and the Art of Writing*, 20: "The reasons which Maimonides adduces in order to prove that certain *rational* truths about divine things must be kept secret, were used by Thomas in order to prove that the *rational* truth about the divine things was in need of being divinely *revealed*." (Emphasis added.)

15. Thomas Aquinas, Commentary on the *De Trinitate* of Boethius q. 2 art. 4, co. See *ST* 1 q. 1 art. 9.

16. *PAWr* 30.

17. It is possible that somewhere in Thomas's gigantic *oeuvre*, wide-ranging and composed over

cannot safely infer that, because Thomas speaks in the above passages of intentional concealment, he is hinting that he has a daring and dangerous *philosophical* teaching—say, a teaching calling into question the very possibility of revelation—that he presents only "between the lines." Such an inference would be as unwarranted as the inference that because I myself am speaking, right here, of intentional concealment, I too am hinting that I have a daring and dangerous philosophical teaching that I am presenting only "between the lines." And I have no such thing.

As for the tension between philosophical teachings, which Thomas was aware were being taught secretly, even in his own time, and the theological teachings of the church—which, in the case of the preambles to the articles of faith, he attempts to demonstrate conclusively, and, in the case of articles of faith proper, he attempts to show are non-contradictory, even though according to their nature they are not demonstrable—consider the following passage from the conclusion of his treatise *De Unitate Intellectus Contra Averroistas.*

> These are the things that we have written to destroy the aforesaid error, not by means of the teachings of faith, but by means of the arguments and words (*per rationes et dicta*) of the philosophers themselves. If, however, there be anyone glorying in his so-called knowledge (*scientia*) who wishes to say something against what we have written here, let him not speak in corners, nor in the presence of boys who do not know how to judge about such difficult matters; but let him write against this treatise, if he dares.[18]

the course of many years, one might find something he says in one passage quite difficult, perhaps impossible, to square with something he says in another passage. But, I suspect, attention to differences between the contexts in which the two passages occur or the times of their composition would account for the inconsistency, mitigate it, or remove the appearance of it. Thomas is reported to have customarily dictated several works at one sitting to several secretaries. His memory astounded his contemporaries. See O'Reilly, "The Superb Memory of Thomas Aquinas."

18. I quote, with slight modifications, the translation of this passage in *Saint Thomas Aquinas—On the Unity of the Intellect Against the Averroists*, 75. Robert Sokolowski cites this passage, to good effect, in his book, *The God of Faith and Reason*, 162–3. The Latin text, in *Opuscula Philosophica et Theologica*, 491, reads: "Haec igitur sunt quae in destructionem praedicti erroris conscripsimus, non per documenta fidei, sed per ipsorum Philosophorum rationes et dicta. Si quis autem gloriabundus de falsi nominis scientia velit contra haec quae scripsimus aliquid dicere, non loquatur in angulis, nec coram pueris, qui nesciunt de tam arduis iudicare; sed contra hoc scriptum scribat, si audit . . ." (The image of the philosopher talking in corners with boys is an old one. See Plato, *Gorgias* 485e1.) Thomas West is struck by the use of "Respondeo dicendum" to preface the *corpus* of every article in the ST. As he sees it, *dicendum* "could mean either that it 'should be said' because it is true, or it 'should be said' because of moral or prudential considerations . . . [O]ne might wonder if Aquinas thought it would be harmful to the good that he was seeking to accomplish if he challenged too openly the prevailing prejudices in the church leadership." (*Critique of the 'Straussian' Critique*, 94). Christian Scholastics as diverse as Albertus Magnus, Bonaventure, Henry of Ghent, Scotus, and Ockham use "dicendum" just as Thomas uses it, and with comparable frequency. Are we to conjecture that these thinkers, too, might be hinting that they do not subscribe to what they use this expression to introduce? Thomas uses "dicendum" around 30,000 times in his writings (see the *Corpus Thomisticum*). Assuming that he is not *always* using this expression to introduce a doctrine that will pass muster with prejudiced church leaders (while subtly dissociating himself from it), one can question whether he *ever* uses it

This passage should be kept in mind by those Straussians who are tempted to think that, because Thomas is so manifestly intelligent, he must be secretly siding with the philosophers against the theologians.

In addition to their writings, the scholastic thinkers also engaged regularly in the open theological disputation, "a public performance in which—in contrast to writing—one's position could not remain concealed, and in which objections had to be answered and not deflected."[19] Many of these public disputations were on quodlibetal ("anything you will") questions and hence could not have been easily stage-managed by ecclesiastical authorities.

It seems to have been Strauss's view that Christian *scholasticism* was so intellectually compromised by its acceptance of biblical revelation and its deference to ecclesiastical authority that, unlike Islamic and Jewish *philosophy*, it ended up saying virtually nothing both original (that is, non-Aristotelian) and of importance to man as man. The uncritical acceptance of this view on the part of many Straussians has kept them from paying much attention to the Scholastic tradition. And that is a great pity. For how certain questions get treated in this tradition has no small bearing on matters that are of abiding interest to Straussians.[20]

There is hardly any so-called "secret teaching" of import in classical political philosophy or in the writings of their Jewish and Islamic followers that is not placed in full view in the writings of the Scholastics. The assertion that God does not exist, or that, even if he does exist, he cannot know us and hence cannot take an interest in our moral strivings, the denial of transcendent exceptionless law, the denial of free will, divine and human, and the reduction of *the* good to one's *own* good—all these claims are on open display in the writings of the scholastics.[21] Not only that, they are argued *for* with great perspicacity before they are argued *against*, whether with equal

---

this way. I do not claim that there were no tensions at all between Thomas's thought and that of other 13th Century theologians. I do claim, however, that his use of "Respondeo dicendum" provides no clue as to what these tensions were. It does not even indicate that there were tensions.

19. Sokolowski, *The God of Faith and Reason*, 162.

20. Consider the titles of the following essays in McGrade, et al., eds., *Cambridge Translations of Medieval Philosophical Texts*, Vol. 2: "Is it rational for someone without hope of a future life to die for the commonwealth?" (Henry of Ghent); "Does a human being following the dictates of natural reason have to judge that he ought to love God more than himself?" (Godfrey of Fontaines—followed by the response of James of Viterbo, and then by Godfrey's counter-response); "Is a subject bound to obey a statute when it is not evident that it promotes the common utility?" (Henry of Ghent); "Is it better to be ruled by the best man or by the best laws?" (James of Viterbo; this question is also considered by Giles of Rome in the selection presented from *On the Rule of Princes*).

21. To limit ourselves only to Thomas Aquinas, and only to the *Summa Theologiae*, and only to a few passages even there, see 1 q. 2, art. 3, arg.1–2; 1 q. 14 art. 10, arg. 1–4; art. 11, arg. 1–3; art. 13, arg. 1–3; 1–2 q. 94 art. 4, arg. 1–4; art. 5, arg. 1–3; 1 q. 19 art. 10, arg. 1–2; 1–2 q. 10, art. 2, arg. 1–3; q. 13 art. 6, arg. 1–2; 1 q. 60 art. 5, arg. 2–3; 2–2 q. 26 art. 3, arg. 1–3 (cf. 1 q. 93 art. 4). For an illuminating account of how Thomas understands the love of God to be natural, see Thomas M. Osborne, Jr., *Love of Self and Love of God*, 69–112. See also Jean Porter, *Nature as Reason*, 203–20, for thoughtful reflections on Thomas's understanding of the relation between self-love and the virtue of justice.

or greater perspicacity being left entirely to the judgment of the reader. The advantage of this architectural plan is that the actual reasoning in support of both sides of a difficult question is available for careful inspection.

The disadvantage of the more circumspect presentation that Strauss and his followers admire is that, whereas it is comparatively easy for an author to *indicate* a secret teaching between the lines, it is much more difficult for him to *argue* for a secret teaching between the lines. The reader on his part runs the risk of losing his way (to say nothing of becoming "enchanted" along the way) in a forest of numerology, intimations, sly hints, and rhetorical winks, while trying to determine which, if any, of the artfully spaced and apparently contradictory claims he comes upon express the deepest thoughts of the author. The reader too often gets deflected from confronting head on the much more important question of whether what the author says or indicates is adequately supported with reasons. When the reader is uncertain as to what the deepest thoughts of, say, Plato, Xenophon, Aristotle, Al Farabi, Avicenna, Averroes, Judah Halevi, or Maimonides are, he is tempted to infer that they are the same as his own deepest thoughts, which may be superficially arrived at and altogether conventional (materialist monism and situation ethics, for example). The art of writing practiced by the scholastics reduces such uncertainty and shallow thinking to a minimum. It does not simply eliminate these things, to be sure. But it does require the reader to give more weight to open and rational argumentation than to veiled indication, and hence to give more weight, rightly, to truth than to secret intention, about which one can never be entirely certain in any case.

Scholasticism, the tradition of which Thomas is arguably the greatest, though not the only great, representative, is a tradition of rationalism in the best sense of the word. It is a tradition that delights in the activity of reason, in identifying the presuppositions of an argument, in searching for the most evident premises, in distinguishing between what is self-evidently known, what is not self-evident but can be demonstrated, and what must be taken on faith, and in constructing proofs of exemplary validity. The project of scholasticism is carried out in three stages: (1) articulating the structure of reality to the extent that it is accessible to natural reason and ordinary human experience alone; (2) showing that this very articulation points to dimensions of reality that are not fully accessible to human reason and experience;[22] and (3) demonstrating the internal consistency and, to a certain extent, even the plausibility of what Catholic Christianity holds regarding these mysterious dimensions. The subject matter and the standards of evidence of the first stage and, with qualifications, even of the second stage are identical with those of philosophy, of which Aristotle is for the scholastics the great representative. At this level, scholasticism differs from philosophy only in its motivation. It aims at establishing by demonstrations accessible to natural reason certain things, though by no means all things, that believers hold to be true, chief among them that God exists, indeed that God is properly and uniquely "he who *is*."

22. *ST* 1 q. 1, art. 5.

That scholasticism is motivated to demonstrate much, though by no means all, of what believers believe is often criticized as its prejudice. In fact, this criticism is itself a prejudice. For it crudely assumes that anyone who is a believer is incapable of bracketing his belief long enough to consider what natural reason by itself has to say about first principles and ultimate causes. Accordingly, any argument that the believer offers for what he already believes is thought to be so tainted by the motivation that gives rise to it that non-believers can justly exempt themselves from paying more than fleeting attention to it. But, though what motivates an argument can be a matter of some interest, whether the argument achieves what it aims at is something that has to be assessed in its own terms, in terms of the evidence of its premises and the validity of the deductive process that leads to its conclusion. An attorney, motivated at first by mere belief, or by just the hunch and the hope, that his client is innocent—and perhaps motivated by the desire to enhance his own legal reputation and amplify his wealth as well—may undertake an investigation that ends up confirming this belief with an unimpeachable proof of his client's innocence. Being aware of the attorney's motives, we should scrutinize his proof with particular care. But an otherwise sound proof is not compromised in the slightest by whatever belief may have motivated the inquiry that led to it. Believing something on the basis of revelation, say, that God is supremely good, does not in principle prevent one from subsequently seeking and finding a purely rational argument for it.[23] It is a gross error to think that an argument or sequence of arguments, even an entire theory, can be invalidated by pointing to the motives that might have given rise to the advancing of it.

In the case of the scholastics, the first two stages of their project, though plenty interesting in themselves, also prepare, on the basis of reason and ordinary experience alone, the third part. In that sense, one can surely say "*Philosophia ancilla theologiae est.*"[24] Philosophy, more precisely, the rational theology of the scholastics, is the

23. See *ST* 1 q. 6, art. 2. "Aquinas's Christian faith opens up for him new panoramas and possibilities for *philosophic* questioning and development . . ." ("Keys" 120, emphasis in the original). If a development proceeds logically and in sole reliance on premises that are fully accessible to natural reason, then it is philosophical, in the broad sense of the word, whether the questioning that sets it in motion emerges out of a theism that is merely believed or out of an atheism that is merely believed. According to Keys, natural law has "an inherently religious dimension . . . it regards or reflects, even if unconsciously, a reverence toward God 'as the first principle of the creation and government of things'" (193). An understanding of God as the first principle of the creation (even if the world is eternal) and government of things is surely implied in the definition of natural law, given the reliance of this definition on the eternal law. However, our awareness of natural law is not founded, even "unconsciously," upon reverence. Our awareness of natural law, of its first principle and its primary precepts, precedes and gives rise to the search for an adequate definition of it, and may well turn out to be conducive to reverence. But neither the definition of natural law nor reverence gives rise to the original awareness of the first principle of natural law and its primary precepts. That awareness, for Thomas, is knowledge. It is a knowledge that is natural to us as rational beings.

24. See *ST* 1 q. 1 art. 5, ad 2. Purely philosophical, i.e., purely rational, concepts and distinctions, such as being, essence, and nature, can also be employed in elaborating the articles of faith (consider the Nicene Creed and the Chalcedonian Definition) within *revealed* theology, and not only in the development of a *rational* theology. And there too philosophy serves as a handmaid. But even there,

handmaid of revealed theology because it clears the way for revealed theology. This it does by addressing and refuting allegedly rational arguments that God does not exist or that he exists in a way—for example, as the prime matter of the universe—that is incompatible with what the Catholic faith holds. To succeed in this project, the scholastic theologian has to work from ground that is common to him and to non-believing philosophers.[25] Scholasticism is incontestably animated by the desire to prove something already believed. It is *fides quaerens intellectum*. But something similar could be said of the anti-theological philosophers and their followers, who have their own beliefs and desires.[26] (Pascal's *apercu*, "*Le cœur a ses raisons, que la raison ne connaît point*," applies no less to unbelievers than to believers.) Rather than dismissing scholasticism because they are repelled by the third stage of the scholastic project, philosophically minded unbelievers should engage with scholasticism at the level of the first two stages. At that level, the standard of reason and ordinary human experience that unbelieving philosophers and their followers pride themselves on adhering to is equally adhered to by the great scholastic thinkers.[27]

Strauss's claim that the medieval philosopher living dangerously at the margin of an Islamic or Jewish community was more likely to live a genuinely philosophic life than the medieval master of philosophy fulfilling his academic responsibilities within a Christian university follows from his conviction that there is an essential tension, or rather a frank incompatibility, between philosophy and belief in revelation. [28] Thomas Aquinas does not recognize any essential tension, much less a frank incompatibility, between philosophy—the rational dimension of it, at least—and belief in revelation. Philosophy, as such, is committed only to demonstrating, to the extent possible, those

philosophy is reduced to a *humble* handmaid (Strauss, *RR* 173) only if the theologian deprives these concepts of their rational sense. The scholastic theologians were grateful for the refined conceptual apparatus bequeathed them, however unintentionally, by non-believing philosophers.

25. See *SCG* 1 cap. 2.3; *ST* 1 q. 1 art. 8, co.

26. See Strauss's letter of December 27, 1932, to Gerhard Krüger, *GS* Band 3, 420.

27. I assume that philosophy does not, at the very outset, claim to *know* that God does not exist and that revelation is impossible. For if it did, philosophy would have to appeal to a pre-philosophical proof to justify this claim. We would then be left with an *ad hoc*, and unconvincing, distinction between philosophy and pre-philosophy. See *RR* 147.

28. *RR* 150; cf. 179. Consider "The Law of Reason," 105, fn. 29, the last sentence especially, and 107: "[T]he philosophers whom Halevy knew [including Aristotle, 105, fn. 29, and perhaps Plato too, 107 fn. 33] went so far as to deny the very possibility of . . . Divine revelation in the precise sense of the term. That denial was presented by them in the form of what claimed to be a demonstrative refutation." In his letter of February 25, 1951, to Eric Voegelin, Strauss writes, "The classics [i.e., the great Greek philosophers] demonstrated that truly human life is a life dedicated to science, knowledge, and the search for it." (*Faith and Political Philosophy*, 78.) It is hard to see how, from Strauss's perspective, they could have *demonstrated* such a thing if they did not also have, as a complement, a demonstrative refutation of the "possibility of . . . Divine revelation in the precise sense of the term." On what is at stake for philosophy if it is compelled to grant that revelation is possible, see *RR* 176; *NRH* 75; "*PR*" 131; *Spinoza's Critique of Religion*, 29–30.

truths that are most worthy of being known. A genuine tension arises only when the philosopher attempts to argue that there can be no such thing as revealed truth.[29]

For Thomas, as we have seen, there is one complex of truth, part of which is either self-evident or demonstrable and part of which is neither self-evident nor demonstrable. An important item of demonstrable truth is that human reason cannot on its own resources apprehend what it most longs to apprehend and that it would have to be supplemented by revelation to apprehend it. Among the multiple claims that have been advanced as revealed truths by believers of different religious traditions, there is, as Thomas sees it, one body of doctrine that is preeminently self-consistent and thoroughly in accord with, though not derived from, what we know on the basis of natural reason. It is a body of doctrine that makes sense of certain things in the world that natural reason alone, even the natural reason of the greatest thinkers of antiquity, cannot make sense of, among them the human capacity for evils so unspeakably vicious that they cannot be plausibly attributed to simple and ultimately innocent ignorance.[30] That body of doctrine is, for Thomas, the deposit of the Catholic faith.

Strauss recognized that Thomas remains a force to be reckoned with and that his influence was not limited to Roman Catholics alone. "Whatever we might have to think of neo-Thomism, its considerable success among non-Catholics is due to the increasing awareness that something is basically wrong with modern philosophy."[31] Strauss surely named one of the reasons for the success of neo-Thomism, or rather

29. If, as Thomas holds, truth is being *qua* intelligible, then revealed truth, as well as self-evident truth and demonstrable truth, must be intelligible. The intelligibility of revealed truth, however, is qualified. It is not a matter of knowledge, strictly speaking, but of faith. But, for the believer, it is not a matter of blind faith. For the claims of revelation, as articulated in the doctrines of the Catholic faith, are not only internally self-consistent and logically irrefutable, they make more *sense* to the Catholic Christian of his own experience, both of himself and of the whole of which he is a part, than does any account of things that dismisses these doctrines. And the believer—the unbeliever no less so—is the final authority on what makes most sense to him of his own experience.

30. "Man in classical thought is in a precarious position, since he can act contrary to his nature. His nature, though this is not its essence, is to have the capacity to act against his own nature. He can sin . . . Medieval theory did not maintain that the classical tradition was wrong. It did insist that it needed to be completed by revelation, because classical thought was unable adequately to respond to questions that arose in political experience." James Schall, S.J., *At the Limits of Political Philosophy*, 188–9.

31. "How to Begin to Study Medieval Philosophy," 216. Strauss made this remark in 1944. Since then Thomism has lost much of the influence it was gaining among non-Roman Catholics, for three reasons in particular. First, there has been a growing distrust of reason itself, a distrust that originated in academia and has infected the wider public. Second, on the heels of Vatican II, many Roman Catholic bishops and academics have attempted to divest the image of their church, as much as possible, of all things medieval. As a consequence, a smaller number of Roman Catholics than previously are able to articulate and defend Thomas's teaching. Third, and in response to these developments, Thomists tend to direct their general presentations of Thomas's teaching to fellow Roman Catholics who have ceased paying attention to it, and to address their specialized and more tightly argued investigations to each other, or to Scotists and adherents of other schools. This state of affairs has led believers who are not Roman Catholics—and unbelievers even more so—to infer mistakenly that Thomas Aquinas has nothing of importance to say to them.

Thomism, among non-Catholics. But he seems not to have recognized that its considerable success among non-Catholics was also due to the fact that both Thomas's theoretical and his practical teaching have a rational foundation and core that is accessible to non-Catholics, even to non-believers, who choose to part way with Thomas only when he begins, typically quite late in his great systematic works, to appeal to revelation and ecclesiastical authority.

It must be stressed here that though Strauss and many, perhaps the majority, of his followers side with philosophy rather than biblical revelation, with, as they put it, the alternative of Athens rather than that of Jerusalem, they not only treat the Bible with considerable respect but speak of biblical religion (albeit of Judaism much more than Christianity) as *the* great alternative to philosophy, classically conceived. They seem to regard theological arguments that admittedly presuppose belief in revelation as more worthy of consideration than theological arguments that, like the rational theology of the scholastics, are based—or, in the view of many Straussians, pretend to be based—solely on reason and ordinary human experience. Straussians tend to regard the conflict between philosophic unbelief and religious belief as a conflict between reason and revelation. The scholastics would say that expressing the conflict in these terms is tendentious: it asserts from the outset that unbelief at its peak is more rational than belief at its peak.[32] The scholastics would say that whether thoughtful unbelief or thoughtful belief is ultimately more rational, that is, more self-consistent, more in accord with the evidence and operation of human reason, and truer to human experience, can be decided only by the kind of inquiries that they themselves undertake, with exemplary though insufficiently appreciated probity, and by a thorough and vigorous engagement with the questions raised by both parties to the disputation.

SECTION B. THE CRITICISMS IN *NATURAL RIGHT AND HISTORY*

Strauss's express criticism of Thomas Aquinas is not that what he says is actually false but that much of what he presents as naturally knowable is not grounded in reason and ordinary experience; it is not grounded in what is accessible to man as man. Strauss tries to establish a logical connection between Thomas's natural law teaching

32. Strauss himself recognizes that the conflict has to be understood, at least initially, as a conflict, not between *reason* and revelation, but between *philosophy* and revelation (*RR* 141)—or, to speak with greater precision, between philosophy and *belief* in revelation. It is loose-speaking to say that religion presupposes revelation. For if that were true, then, from the incontestable existence of religion, one could validly infer that revelation has taken place. And few people, least of all Straussians, will make that inference. The most that religion presupposes in this connection is *belief* in revelation. But even this belief is not absolutely necessary for religion. For something of a case can be made for a "religion within the limits of mere reason," as Kant showed. Such a religion, he argues, presupposes neither an actual demonstration of God's existence and providence nor belief in revelation. I shall speak to Thomas's conception of religion as a moral virtue, as distinct from a theological virtue, in Ch. 8, below. In this connection, see *PR* 117, where Strauss himself speaks, though without elaboration, of "philosophic[!] teachings . . . which even admit prayer."

and his rational theology, and then to establish a logical connection between Thomas's rational theology and both a discredited Aristotelian physics and revealed theology. Some of Strauss's followers have continued this line of criticism. If Strauss and his followers had an independently developed critique of theology, rational or revealed, their critique of law might carry some weight. The problem is that their critique of theology, to the extent that one can get it in focus, appears to presuppose their critique of law, or to presuppose the claims of post-Aristotelian physics, claims that are utterly irrelevant to the foundational argument for the existence of God that Thomas's presents in *De Ente et Essentia*.

Strauss alleges with little elaboration that there exists an "inseparable connection between Thomas' physics and his rational theology."[33] He was perhaps misled by the emphasis that Thomas and his successors give to his First Way—the argument for a first mover—in the *Summa Theologiae*. But there is not a single theological proposition that Thomas builds on his argument for a first mover that cannot be built equally well, indeed better, on his argument for a first efficient cause. Nowhere, to my knowledge, does Strauss acknowledge that Thomas has such an argument. Nor, as far as I know, does he ever refer to pertinent passages from *De Ente et Essentia*, where the argument is solidly grounded and developed.

There is not, then, an inseparable connection between Thomas's rational theology and his physics. Thomas's proof of the existence of God as the first efficient cause is independent of his proof of the existence of God as the first moving cause. Of the two, only the latter depends on his physics. But is there an inseparable connection between Thomas's natural law teaching and revealed theology? Strauss speaks briefly of Thomas's natural law teaching in *Natural Right and History*. He summarizes his criticism of it as follows.

> Thomas . . . virtually [contends] that, according to natural reason, the natural end of man is insufficient, or points beyond itself or, more precisely, that the end of man cannot consist in philosophical investigation, to say nothing of political activity. Thus natural reason itself creates a presumption in favor of the divine law, which completes or perfects the natural law. At any rate, the ultimate consequence of the Thomistic view of natural law is that natural law is practically inseparable not only from natural theology—i.e., from a natural theology that is, in fact, based on belief in biblical revelation—but even from revealed theology.[34]

33. Book Review of *Basic Writings of Thomas Aquinas*) 285–6. See also "Jerusalem and Athens" 151, where Strauss speaks of "the victory of science over rational theology." Modern science certainly calls Thomas's First Way, and the conception of motion on which it is based, into question. It does not, however, call his Second Way, much less the argument in *DEE*, into question. Natural science, whether ancient or modern, lacks the wherewithal to address an argument based on the metaphysical distinction between *esse* and *essentia*, much less refute it.

34. *NRH* 164. In *CM*, Strauss speaks in passing of "the kind of natural laws which a certain Aristotelian tradition sought, *i.e.*, 'normative' laws, laws which can be transgressed and which perhaps

A quick reading of this passage might lead one to think that Strauss's criticism could be paraphrased along the following lines:

1. Thomas's natural law teaching is based on his rational theology (= natural theology).
2. His rational theology is based on revealed theology.
3. Revealed theology is based on claims that natural reason cannot establish.
4. Therefore, Thomas's natural law teaching is based on claims that natural reason cannot establish.

If this were an accurate recasting of Strauss's reasoning, its weaknesses could be exposed on the basis of what has already been shown. Although the proof is formally valid, it is unsound. The first premise is misleading, and the second premise is false.[35] The passage in question, however, is obscure and it must be scrutinized more closely.

We are struck right away by Strauss's use of ambiguous terms and even an unusual hesitancy of expression: "Thomas *virtually* contends . . . the natural end *points* beyond itself . . . Natural reason creates a *presumption* . . . *At any rate* . . . the natural law is *practically* inseparable . . ." (emphasis added). The hesitancy of expression in this passage cannot be convincingly said to be dictated by political prudence, pedagogical tact, or a desire to avoid shaking too violently the religious convictions of unphilosophical readers. Strauss's hesitancy of expression here seems, instead, to reflect an uncharacteristic hesitancy of thought, as though he was aware that he might not have a firm grasp of Thomas's reasoning.

Strauss is essentially right on the first point: Thomas does contend, though really and not just virtually, that "according to natural reason, the natural end of man is insufficient, or points beyond itself." Thomas leans heavily on Aristotle here. Man by nature desires to know. In particular, he desires to know the cause or causes of things, to know them essentially, to know them as they are in themselves.[36] Thomas's ratio-

are more frequently transgressed than observed." (44). A few lines later he refers back to these as "the normative laws preached up [!] by the tradition." In the concluding sentence to his 1971 Preface to *NRH* Strauss distinguishes natural law not only from natural right but also from divine law. We know how Thomas Aquinas distinguishes the two kinds of law. It is not clear how Strauss intends to distinguish them. Perhaps he thinks, in 1971, that there really is something accessible to man as man that can be called "natural law," even that it declares obligations, but that it has restricted scope and admits of all kinds of exceptions in varying circumstances. It seems unlikely that late in life he finally repudiated the view, which he attributes to Plato and Aristotle, that "there are no universally valid rules of action." *NRH* 162.

35. See supra, Part 1, Ch. 1, Section a. One might think that the second premise of the argument could be replaced with "His rational theology is based on an Aristotelian theory of motion" in order to argue toward the conclusion, "Therefore Thomas's natural law teaching stands refuted by modern natural science." But this will not work either since the argument Thomas advances in *DEE* for a first *efficient* cause—as distinct from his argument for a first *moving* cause—is not based on *any* theory of motion, Aristotelian or otherwise.

36. Aristotle, *Metaphysics* 980a1; 982a5–982b11; 983a24–983b6; 993b23; 994b29; *Physics* 194

nal theology demonstrates that there is a single ultimate cause and that it is properly called "God"; and it shows both that and how God is responsible for the world. Rational theology, however, cannot yield knowledge of what, or rather who, God is, in himself and essentially. Even a rational theology as solid and extensive as the one Thomas develops cannot fully satisfy man's natural desire to know the essence of the ultimate cause or causes of things.

Because the natural end of man consists in the less than perfectly satisfying activity of *philo-sophia*, even when it culminates in rational theology, it is "insufficient." It "points beyond itself" to a supernatural end that would consist in *sophia* pure and simple,[37] the natural longing for which gives rise to philosophy at its inception and constitutes it throughout. Thomas's argument is based largely on an Aristotelian understanding of the character of our knowledge. According to Aristotle, the human intellect makes use of images derived from sensory experience in knowing the forms and, one can infer, in knowing the essence of anything, with the possible exception of itself.[38] Thomas concurs with Aristotle on this matter, and he concurs in Aristotle's express teaching that God is the very act of his immaterial intellect (*noēsis noēseōs*).[39] Thomas does not understand God's intellect to be a part, or a feature, or a transcendental dimension of man's intellect; and he does not think that any image could be adequate to God's essence. For Thomas then, there is no way for us, in this life, to know God as he is in himself. By natural reason alone we cannot know *what* he is *essentially*, but only *that* he *is* and that he is the first cause—necessary in his being but, for Thomas, free in his causality—of the contingent beings with which we are familiar, including both ourselves and the world around us. This knowledge of God as the first and necessary cause of all other things does, however, allow us to apply names to him substantially and properly, and not just negatively or metaphorically. But it still does not amount to knowledge of God as he is in himself, independently of his causal responsibility for the world. For us to have, in this life, a true conception of God as he is essentially, natural reason must be supplemented by divine revelation.[40]

One can, to be sure, take issue with Thomas's argument that the natural end of man, the imperfect happiness "that consists first and principally in contemplation"[41]

b16–195a3; 195a21; 195b23.

37. Thomas's argument that man, through the natural longing of his own soul, i.e., through the natural operation and natural limitations of his own reason, is oriented toward a supernatural end occurs within the context of his rational theology, not just in his revealed theology: *SCG* 3–1 cap. 25–26; *ST* 1–2 q. 1–5, especially q. 3, art. 8.

38. *De Anima* 431b1: "*ta men oun eidē to noētikon en tois phantasmasi noei.*" Compare 430a10–25. (See Thomas Aquinas, *In Duodecim Libros Metaphysicorum Aristotelis Expositio*, Lib. 2 Lect. 1.285; and *ST* 1 q. 12, art. 2, co.) In interpreting the cited passage from *De Anima* it should be kept in mind that Aristotle does not call his god "form." See Eugene Ryan, "Pure Form in Aristotle." Consider in this connection *Metaphysics* 983a2–10, and compare *De Anima* Book 3, Chapter 5.

39. *Metaphysics* 1071b21; 1074b34.

40. *SCG* 3, cap. 47–48, 50–52; *ST* 1 q. 12, especially art. 11–13; q. 13.

41. *ST* 1–2, q. 3, art. 5, co.

but does not amount to wisdom *simpliciter*, points beyond itself. But taking issue with Thomas's argument requires showing either that the knowledge of causes that is within our natural power is itself *sophia*, that is, perfect knowledge of the ultimate cause or causes; or that our natural desire to know the causes can be perfectly satisfied with imperfect knowledge of causes; or that the perfection of our knowledge is impossible even with supernatural assistance from God; or that perfection of our knowledge is impossible because supernatural assistance is impossible, that is, because God, understood as a being capable of freely revealing himself to man, does not exist.

One cannot be entirely certain which of these tacks Strauss would be inclined to take, since he himself says, earlier in *Natural Right and History*, that

> . . . man is so built that he can find his satisfaction, his bliss, in free investigation, in articulating the riddle of being. But . . . he yearns so much for a solution of that riddle and human knowledge is always so limited that the *need* for divine illumination cannot be denied . . . [42].

The free investigation of which Strauss speaks is satisfying only because it is experienced as progress toward wisdom, even if it is only incremental progress and never culminates in wisdom.[43] But this progress is motored throughout by the natural longing for wisdom.[44] Thomas follows Aristotle in holding that man naturally desires to know (Gr. *eidenai,* Lat. *scire*), and not just to articulate a riddle.[45] It is hard to see how man could find his satisfaction in merely articulating a riddle if, as Strauss says, he also "yearns so much" for its solution.

Strauss cannot be unaware of the difficulty here. Perhaps by choosing the expression "articulating the riddle of being," as opposed to, say, "attempting to solve the riddle of being," he meant to suggest that being is essentially a riddle,[46] that it does not admit of a solution, and that the genuine philosopher does not long for a solution to the riddle, as most men in their ignorance do, because he has a proof of its essential insolubility. A question arises at once, however: is the insolubility of the riddle rooted in the nature of things or in the limitations of the human cognitive faculties? It is hard to know what a proof of the former, of the objectively enigmatic character of being, would look like, since for such a proof one would have to know being well enough to know that it is essentially unknowable by anyone (God included, if he exists).[47] The

42. *NRH* 75 (emphasis added). There is a similar formulation in *RR*: "Human knowledge is always so limited that the possibility of revelation cannot be refuted, and the *need* for revelation cannot be denied" (172 emphasis added). Compare *Philosophy and Law* 31 [*GS*, Band 2, 20]. See also Strauss, "What is Liberal Education?" 7: "[W]isdom is inaccessible to man, and hence virtue and happiness will always be imperfect."

43. Strauss, *On Tyranny*, 101–2.

44. Aristotle, *Metaphysics* 980a22–983a23.

45. Aristotle, *Metaphysics* 983a14–19.

46. See *NRH* 29–30

47. In the *Note* appended to Ch. 13 of Part 3, below, I speak to Strauss's claim that being is

most carefully worked out attempt at a proof of the latter, of the enigmatic character of being as apprehended by the human subject, is found in the *Critique of Pure Reason*. The upshot of Kant's argument is that we simply do not and cannot know what the ultimate ground of things is. But if that is so, then we do not and cannot know that it is not the omnipotent God after all, who, as omnipotent, would presumably be able, freely and at his own initiative, to reveal himself and communicate his will to human beings of his own choosing, and not just to philosophers.

If being is essentially a riddle to us, then it is a wide-open question whether or not revelation is possible—unless one has a rigorous demonstration that there is no other life and no supernatural assistance from God, however otherwise omnipotent he might be, that would compensate for the natural finitude of human reason and experience. Strauss does not give us such a demonstration. One could try to construct a demonstration of the impossibility of revelation in light of Strauss's critique of the moral convictions that are essential to belief in revelation, at least to belief in revelation as revelation is presented in the Bible. But, again, essential to that critique, as Strauss attempts to develop it, is a demonstration of the ultimate untenability of the idea of transcendent law, natural or revealed. And that is exactly the matter that is under dispute.

According to Thomas, natural reason can establish that a supernatural end, in which the natural desire to know the causes would be consummated, is possible—in the sense of thinkable without self-contradiction or contradiction of anything we know without qualification—though natural reason cannot establish that any of us will receive the grace necessary to attain that end.[48] A "presumption in favor of divine law," of a law that would adequately direct us to this super-natural end, is then indeed generated by "natural reason itself," just as Strauss, interpreting Thomas, says.[49] But it must be emphasized that this presumption in favor of divine law is not a *presupposition* that natural reason begins with, but a *conclusion* that it ends up with, consequent to thinking through the limitations of natural reason and thereby of natural law as well. And this conclusion, to repeat, is not that there *is* a divine law because of these limitations, but only that there is a *need* for divine law.

Only in this way is natural law "inseparable" from revealed theology: it cannot by itself adequately direct man to the *supernatural* end, to knowledge of the essence of the first cause or causes, that man longs for *by nature*. Strauss may have recognized that his word "inseparable" was not quite right, for he modifies it with the ambiguous adverb, "practically": natural law is "practically inseparable . . . from revealed theology." But it is difficult to determine what Strauss means by "practically inseparable," since "all but inseparable," would deprive his criticism of its force; and "inseparable as a matter of practice" is false: one does not have to assent to revelation, to such things

characterized by "noetic heterogeneity."

48. *ST* 1 q. 12 art. 1, co.; art. 5, co.; See 1–2 q. 91 art. 4, co.; q. 99 art. 2, co; art. 6, co.; q. 100 art.1, co.

49. *NRH* 164.

as, for example, the Trinity and the Incarnation, or even to the non-eternity of the world, in order to act in accordance with the precepts of natural law. One definitely has to take the concept of obligation seriously, for this concept is inseparable from the concept of natural law. But we have already seen that our consciousness of obligation, as Thomas understands it, does not presuppose revelation or divine law. Because, as he expressly says, divine law presupposes natural law, it therefore presupposes obligation too, and not the other way around.

Strauss asserts that Thomas's natural, or rational, theology "is, in fact, based on belief in biblical revelation." This assertion comes out of nowhere. It is backed up neither by argument nor by textual evidence. Additionally, it is not even clear what Strauss has in mind, since in this passage his explicit criticisms of Thomas's natural theology *per se* are limited to saying that it necessarily presupposes, not biblical revelation, but Aristotelian physics. If all Strauss means with this assertion is that Thomas's rational theology was motivated by his belief in biblical revelation, then the assertion is not much of a criticism. In fact, it is not a criticism, at all. For Strauss surely understood (better than some of his followers it must be said) that wanting to prove something does not by itself invalidate a proof. So we have to assume he thought that Thomas's rational theology was not just motivated by belief in divine revelation but that it was based on belief in biblical revelation, that is, that one or more of its fundamental premises logically presupposes the claims of revelation. If this is what Strauss thought, he was mistaken.

Strauss may have suspected that he was mistaken. For his clause "At any rate," appears to undercut the preceding sentences, although they are presumably needed as support, as *some* support, for the most questionable conclusion that the phrase, "At any rate," announces.[50] A few lines later, Strauss writes that the efforts of the proponents of modern natural law

> were partly based on the premise, which would have been acceptable to the classics, that the moral principles have a greater evidence than the teachings even of natural theology and, therefore, that natural law or natural right should be kept independent of theology and its controversies.[51].

50. If, as Strauss says in interpreting Thomas, "according to natural reason [!], the natural end of man is insufficient, or points beyond itself . . . etc.," then natural reason really does, or should, open one up to the possibility of receiving supernatural assistance to attain that end, assistance that could well take the form of divine, or revealed, law. I think that this is Thomas's view, and it is my view too, as I indicated at the end of Part 1, above. But how does, or would, that accomplishment of natural reason support Strauss's claim that Thomistic natural law "is practically inseparable not only from . . . a natural theology that is, in fact, based on belief in biblical revelation—but even from revealed theology"? What is the meaning of "inseparable" here, with or without the adverb "practically": inseparable as a premise, as a conclusion, as a motive, or inseparable in some other way?

51. *NRH* 164. See Strauss, "The Crisis of Political Philosophy", in *The Predicament of Modern Politics* (edited by Harold J. Spaeth, Detroit: University of Detroit Press, 92): "Political philosophy is an actuality in the West today only in Thomism. This creates a difficulty, however, even for the Thomists, because it gives rise to the suspicion [!] that it is the Christian Catholic faith, and not human reason,

The phrase, "even of natural theology," seems to be a concession to the possibility that Thomas's rational theology, or perhaps someone else's rational theology, might *not* be reducible to, or based on, revealed theology. At any event, "the premise that the moral principles have a greater evidence than the teachings even of natural theology" is a premise that is as "acceptable" to Thomas as to the ancient and modern political philosophers, given his unambiguous teaching that the moral principles are self-evident whereas natural theology rests on a premise, namely, the existence of God, that is not self-evident, though it does admit of demonstration.[52]

Strauss claims that "there cannot be true justice if there is not divine rule or providence."[53] This claim is ambiguous. If it means that the unjust would not, or would not always, get their just deserts unless there were divine providence, it is true. But if the claim means that no one could act justly unless there were divine providence (beyond God's creation of the natural order in the first place), it is false. Even for someone who merely goes through the motions of acting justly, and does so solely with a view to an envisioned reward in the hereafter, there obviously need not *be* divine providence but only a *belief* in divine providence. Strauss, however, may not mean either of these things, but, given the context of the claim, something more interesting: divine providence is needed to prevent conditions of extreme scarcity. "One would not reasonably expect much [!] virtue or much [!] justice of men who live habitually in a condition of extreme scarcity so that they have to fight with one another constantly for the sake of mere survival." There is nothing to quarrel with here. But, significantly, Strauss does not say that, "One would not reasonably expect *any* virtue or *any* justice . . . etc." That is, even in a situation of extreme scarcity it is possible for a human being to act justly, or more generally, to act in accordance with reason, that is, to act in accordance with the primary precepts of natural law.[54]

In fact, in his teaching on theft, Thomas makes a distinction that, taken in conjunction with his teaching on just war, enables us to infer a Thomistic response to the concern that Strauss raises in this passage from *Natural Right and History* and in a similar passage from *Thoughts on Machiavelli*.[55] What is the right course of action

which supports this political philosophy." Strauss does not try to show whether or not this "suspicion" is justified. Instead, he immediately begins to make the case for a reconsideration of Aristotelian political philosophy.

52. *ST* 1–2 q. 94 art. 2; 1 q. 2 art. 1; art. 2.

53. *NRH* 150, fn. 24.

54. See Strauss "Jerusalem and Athens," 155: "If human life had been needy and harsh from the very beginning, man would have been compelled or at least irresistibly tempted to be harsh, uncharitable, unjust; he would not have been fully responsible for his lack of charity or justice." (155). Why Strauss bothered to make the disjunction in the first part of this sentence is puzzling, for there is a pertinent difference between compulsion and temptation only when the latter is resistible. Strauss only suggests, he does not demonstrate, that in times of great scarcity a rational being cannot resist the temptation to be "harsh, uncharitable, unjust."

55. *Thoughts on Machiavelli*, 191–2. What Strauss has to say about the exigencies caused by famine in this passage is harsher than what he says in the passage that we have been considering from

for a statesman when he finds that the population of his country is threatened with extinction due to a famine? Let us consider three cases. (1) If country A is threatened by famine, and a neighboring country B is in the same predicament, then A has nothing to gain by invading B. It would be a foolish waste of energy for it to do so. (2) If both A and B are threatened by the famine, but B, unlike A, has enough, though only enough, to survive it, then A does have something to gain by invading B. But to do so would be unjust, since B is under no obligation to give A what is essential to its own survival, and is not at fault in refusing to do so.[56] (3) If A is threatened with extinction due to the famine, while B has an abundance, then B is under an obligation to share what it has with A, certainly if A promises to reciprocate once it is able to. If B refuses to share, then B is at fault and deserves to be invaded; and A does not sin in doing so. This conclusion follows from Thomas's claims that in cases of dire need all things are common property, that in such a case one man may take, openly or by stealth, the property of another who has more than he needs, and that doing so is not properly speaking robbery or theft.[57] It is by no means self-evident, nor is it demonstrable, that famine "compels men to *sin*."[58]

Strauss himself acknowledges that "the extreme situation does not reveal a real necessity."[59] As long as the extreme situation does not simply deprive man of his reason, he is capable of choosing and acting according to it, and is in fact obligated to do so. And yet if Strauss is not saying that it is utterly impossible but only that it is very

NRH. But one has to be cautious in attributing to Strauss himself observations that he makes without attribution in *Thoughts on Machiavelli*. For in the last analysis he distances himself much further from Machiavelli than from, say, Plato, Xenophon, Aristotle, Al Farabi, and Maimonides. On the other hand, in expatiating on Machiavelli's teaching, he can occasionally seem to be advancing his own opinion, for example, when he speaks as follows: "Tutored [!] by Machiavelli, we [!] must [!] assume that Cato's good conscience in acting as he did is indistinguishable from his envy of Scipio's fame" (192). Strauss could easily have written the following instead: "Machiavelli would say that Cato's good conscience in acting as he did was indistinguishable from his envy of Scipio's fame." Perhaps by the expression, "Tutored by Machiavelli," Strauss means "If we are tutored by Machiavelli," rather than "Because we are tutored by Machiavelli." One cannot be sure from the sentence as it stands which alternative captures Strauss's (secret?) intention.

56. *ST* 2–2 q. 40 art. 1 co. If, as Thomas argues in 2–2 q. 66; art. 7, ad 2, it is permissible for one man to *take* from another what he needs for the support of his own life (when the other has more than he needs, as is evident from the context), it follows *a fortiori* that a man is not obligated to *surrender* to another what he needs for the support of his own life. And the same can be said of one country in relation to another country. Cf. 2–2 q. 26, art. 4; art. 6; q. 64 art. 5.

57. *ST* 2–2 q. 66 art. 4, arg. 1; co.; ad 1; art. 7, co. In this last article, Thomas goes so far as to say that what people have in superabundance (*superabundanter*) is due by natural right (*ex iure naturali*) to the sustenance of the poor. He supports this claim by arguing that inferior things (such as the fruits of the earth) are ordained by divine providence to meet human needs. This statement does not introduce revelation into the argument, since Thomas holds that natural reason can demonstrate not only that God exists but that he is providential too (ST 1 q. 22 art. 1). Without appeal to theology of any sort, Aristotle makes a similar, though far from identical, claim about providence, property, and human needs: *Politics* 1253a10; 1256b8–27.

58. *Thoughts on Machiavelli*, 192 (emphasis added).

59. *NRH* 196, fn. 39.

difficult to act justly in difficult times, then he leaves us with no more than a simple tautology: it is very difficult to act justly when it is very difficult to act justly, an analytic truth that in no way undermines Thomas's case for natural law.

Strauss's statement that "[T]here is a profound kinship between the notion of natural law and a perfect beginning: the golden age or the Garden of Eden,"[60] could leave one with the impression that he thinks that the concept of natural law rests upon belief in something like the *Genesis* account of man's first condition, that is, upon a claim of revelation. But this is not true, certainly not in the case of Thomas Aquinas. Nothing in the foundational argument contained in q. 94 art. 2 presupposes or implies anything like a golden age or a Garden of Eden. The only thing resembling a "perfect beginning" in Thomas's natural law teaching is the understanding that man as such, hence man from the beginning, possesses the faculty of reason, which can free him from, and elevate him above, the kind of necessitation that reigns elsewhere in nature. And to repeat yet again (because much depends on it), whereas according to Thomas the existence and providence God are demonstrable but *not* self-evident, the foundational principles of natural law *are* self-evident. Therefore, these principles *cannot* derive their evidence from the existence and providence of God. Much less, then, do they derive their evidence from revealed theology, including belief in "a perfect beginning: the golden age or the Garden of Eden."

A further sign that Thomas's case for the foundational principles of natural law is independent of his rational theology is that neither his definition of natural law, taken just by itself, nor any proposition about God that he argues for in his rational theology, singly or in combination, leads one to conclude that there are actual precepts of practical reason rooted in the rational nature of man, much less what they are. The evidence for the existence of these precepts and for their content is presented in the *corpus* of a single article,[61] in the course of which Thomas does not make a single theological assertion. His statement that man has a natural inclination "to know the truth about God" is not a theological assertion. As noted earlier, until ruled out by reason or by revelation, the truth about God might be that he does not exist. Thomas's point is that whatever the truth about God may be, man has a natural inclination to know it. Thomas could have said in this article simply that man has a natural inclination "to know God." He chose instead to say something that was theologically noncommittal. His case for natural law is centered on the concept of good and the order of man's inclinations, that is, on the structure of practical reason and its relation to inclinations that are manifestly natural to man as we know him to be.

In an earlier lecture of Strauss's, which anticipates some of what is said in *Natural Right and History*, Strauss writes, "Thomas can afford to assert the immutability of the principles of natural right *merely* because he admits a *divine* right in addition

60. *NRH* 150.

61. *ST* 1–2 q. 94 art. 2.

to natural right."[62] By his use of the expression, "principles" here, I take Strauss to be referring to natural law as well as, if not more pointedly than, to natural right. But Thomas does not assert the immutability of these principles merely because he admits divine right in addition to natural right.[63] Rather, he asserts the immutability of these principles because he recognizes the immutability of natural reason and the immutability of human nature.[64] It is this recognition that manifestly guides the argumentation in *ST* 1–2 q. 94 art. 2.

SECTION C. THE CRITICISMS IN "ON NATURAL LAW"

In 1968, sixteen years after publishing *Natural Right and History*, Strauss contributed an article entitled "On Natural Law" to an encyclopedia dealing with the social sciences.[65] Strauss's presentation of Thomas's natural law teaching in "On Natural Law," is free of the hesitancies and ambiguities that characterize his treatment in *Natural Right and History.* It is, on the whole, a fair and succinct summary of what is distinctive about this teaching. Strauss notes that, for Thomas,

> [m]an is by nature inclined toward a variety of ends which possess a natural order; they ascend from self-preservation and procreation via life in society toward knowledge of God."[66].

Strauss's interpretation of the *ordo* as an ascent is essentially correct.[67] But the passage in the *Summa Theologiae* where Thomas speaks of this order occurs in the very article

62. "Natural Right (1946)," 247. (Emphasis as in the original.)

63. On natural *right*, as distinct from natural *law*, see ST 2–2 q. 57, especially art. 2. In this article, divine (i.e., revealed) right is brought into the picture only with the third objection, and Thomas replies to it: ad 3. (For the sake of convenience, I follow common practice in referring to the arguments that Thomas presents at the beginning of an article as "objections" and as advanced by an "objector." Thomas himself does not use this terminology.) Divine right, however, plays no role at all in the *corpus* of this article. It is not advanced to support "the immutability of the principles of natural right." The reply to the first objection in 2–2 q. 57 art. 2, has to be interpreted in light of what Thomas said earlier, in 1–2 q. 94 art. 4–6.

64. In the passage from "Natural Right (1946)" quoted above, Strauss is commenting on how Thomas can allow for divine dispensation from certain precepts of natural law. This is indeed a difficulty though, I think, one that can be resolved. See the *Note* appended to Ch. 8 below. But, however this difficulty is regarded, it does not justify Strauss's emphasized word "merely." See *ST* 1–2 q. 94, art. 2. I find Strauss's reasoning in the quoted passage obscure. In fact, given his reference to *ST* 2–2 q. 64 art. 6, ad 1, it seems that "mutability"—albeit only *via* divine dispensation—would have been a better word than "immutability." Cf. NRH 163. In any case, I am not aware of another place where Strauss criticizes Thomas in these terms.

65. "On Natural Law," 137–46. This essay appeared earlier in *International Encyclopedia of the Social Sciences*, Vol. 2, 80–90. (Regarding the pagination of "On Natural Law," the careful reader will note that Strauss's two-page treatment of Thomas straddles the two *central* pages of the article. In *NRH*, Strauss's two-page treatment of Thomas straddles the two *central* pages of the book.)

66. "On Natural Law" 142; cf. *WhPPh* 215.

67. There are only two problems with passage. The first, a minor problem, is that Strauss's

in which, a few lines earlier, he transforms the declarative, "Good is that at which all things aim," into the gerundive, "Good is to be done, etc."[68] Strauss says nothing about this transformation, and one is at loss in trying to figure out how he would argue against it, or even *if* he would argue against it. But then the gerundive and the ascending order of natural inclinations *taken together* are constitutive of the primary precepts of natural *law* and the secondary precepts deduced *modica consideratione* from them—and thereby of obligations too—as distinct from natural *right* simply. It is for this reason that, as Strauss himself says, speaking of Thomas's teaching, "Natural law directs men's action toward . . . ends by commands and prohibitions." Since Strauss does not take issue with Thomas's claim that there is an order (or rank, *ordo*) of natural inclinations, and since he elsewhere says in his own name that there is a natural order of wants,[69] which are a subspecies of inclinations, he would need to take issue with the gerundive in order to avoid generating precepts of natural law as Thomas does. But taking issue with Thomas's gerundive would be particularly difficult for Strauss if he also concurs in the claim of both Plato and Aristotle that reason, or what is rational in us (*to logistikon*), rules or should rule. It rules presumably by commanding what is not rational, or not fully rational, in us, since the latter, as Plato and Aristotle (just like Thomas) recognize, does not automatically follow reason.[70]

Though Strauss does not speak of the gerundive in his actual treatment of Thomas, he does make a passing reference to it, along with a parenthetical reference back to Thomas, in his treatment of Marsilius of Padua one page later. For Marsilius,

> the dictates of right reason regarding the things *to be done* (i.e. natural law in the Thomistic sense) . . . are not as such universally valid because they are not universally known and observed.[71].

Thomas holds that the most general dictates of right reason, that is, the primary precepts of natural law, are universally known. That they are not universally observed he would readily grant. Knowing what natural law dictates (as properly obligatory) does not necessitate observance of it by man, just as knowing what the civil law dictates does not necessitate observance of it by the citizen. Even the principle of noncontradiction is not universally observed. People can reason speciously in speculative

---

expression "toward knowledge of God" should be, in order to be true to Thomas's formulation in q. 94 art. 2, "toward knowledge of the truth about God." (The former expression presupposes that God exists; the latter does not.) The second problem is somewhat more serious: Strauss fails to note that man's natural end includes not only this knowledge but also an "operation of the practical intellect directing human actions and passions" (ST 1–2 q. 3, art. 5, co.), a matter we considered in Part 1 and to which we shall return in Ch. 10 below. .

68. *ST* 1–2 q. 94, art. 2, co. (emphasis added).

69. *NRH* 126.

70. See *Republic* 439d 2–440b4; 440e3–441b2; 441c2–5; 441e3–5; cf. 435e1–3; *Nicomachean Ethics* 1098a4–5; 1102b13–18; b26–28; cf. *Politics* 1254b4–10.

71. "On Natural Law," 143 (emphasis added). Compare *NRH* 162.

matters as well as in practical matters. What is most interesting in this passage, however, is Strauss's parenthetical reference to the gerundive and his recognition that it is intrinsic to "natural law in the Thomistic sense," which suggests that he really may have considered the actual case that Thomas makes, without appeal either to revelation or to Aristotelian cosmology, for the existence of natural law.[72] It is most regrettable that Strauss did not isolate the case that Thomas actually makes and identify what he thought were its weaknesses. He says that in Thomas's presentation "the Christian natural law teaching reached its theoretical perfection,"[73] but he does not show what is specifically Christian about this teaching. He does not show, and he cannot show, that this teaching presupposes specifically Christian doctrines such as the Trinity or the Incarnation, virgin birth, passion, and resurrection of Christ.[74] Strauss quickly adds that, in Thomas's presentation, "natural law retains its status as rational," which would seem to be the critical concession. But then he seems to retract this concession at once, or at least cast some doubt on it, by pointing out that natural law "is treated within the context of Christian (revealed) theology," as if to suggest that the context within which Thomas's argument is developed, rather than its internal validity and soundness, was a sufficient indication of whether it needs to be taken seriously by non-Christians. But it is not a sufficient indication. If the case for natural law had been made by Thomas within the context of, say, a treatise on infant baptism, but was not based on anything having to do with baptism, or on anything other than what is accessible to man as man, it would still need to be inspected and evaluated in its own terms, by unbelievers and believers alike. Context is not equivalent to premise.

Strauss says rightly that, according to Thomas, God instructs men by law. He does not say (also rightly) that, according to Thomas, God instructs men, not just regarding the good, but regarding the true more generally. Thomas, in fact, goes so far as to say that "every truth by whomsoever it is spoken is from the Holy Spirit." But he adds at once that this happens simply by virtue of God's "bestowing the *natural* light, and moving us to understand and speak the truth" (emphasis added), and not by grace or a gift superadded to nature. [75] On Thomas's understanding, the latter happens only

72. If Strauss wrote "On Natural Law" not long before he had it published in 1968, it is conceivable that he had read Grisez's article, "The First Principle of Practical Reason." Since the latter article originally appeared in 1965 in a journal entitled *Natural Law Forum*, it quite likely would have caught Strauss's eye. Grisez's article, if not flawless in all its particulars, has nonetheless the great and enduring merit of challenging anyone who wishes to criticize Thomas's natural law teaching to come to terms with the actual argument on which it rests.

73. "On Natural Law," 141.

74. In Part 1, above, I argued that the conscience, as Thomas understands it, is not a concept that presupposes revelation or revealed theology. I return to this issue in Part 2, Ch. 9, below.

75. 1–2 q. 109 art. 1, ad 1: "Omne verum, a quocumque dicatur, est a Spiritu Sancto sicut ab infundente *naturale* lumen, et movente ad intelligendum et loquendum veritatem. Non autem sicut ab inhabitante per gratiam gratum facientem, vel sicut a largiente aliquod habituale donum *naturae* superadditum . . ." (emphasis added; see also the *corpus* of this article; and 1–2 q. 62 art. 1 co. for a similar argument). The following commentary on a scriptural passage is a specification of what is said in the

when man is led by revelation to faith. Man's knowledge of natural law, of its primary precepts and of secondary precepts deduced from them *modica consideratione*, is not due to this kind of supernatural assistance. [76]

Toward the end of his treatment of Thomas in "On Natural Law," Strauss writes,

> [Thomas] does say that sin is considered by the theologians chiefly in so far as it is an offense against God, whereas the moral philosophers consider sin chiefly in so far as it is opposed to reason. These thoughts could lead to the view of some later writers according to which natural law strictly understood is natural reason itself, i.e., natural law does not command and forbid but only "indicates": natural law thus understood would be possible even if there were no God . . . [77]

Strauss comes close here to expressing, not just the view of some later writers, but, unintentionally it seems, the view of Thomas himself, dissociating it for once not only

above passages: ". . . quasi lumen rationis naturalis, quo discernimus quid sit bonum et malum, quod pertinent ad naturalem legem, nihil aliud sit quam impressio divini luminis in nobis." (q. 91 art. 2, co.)

76. Thomas holds that grace is required not only for the theological virtues but for the *perfection* of the moral virtues as well. Man's nature has become so corrupted that he needs grace in order to compensate for his obscured knowledge of certain *secondary* precepts of natural law (the *primary* precepts are indelible—ST 1–2 q. 94 art. 6) and to be able to fulfill *all* the divine commandments (q. 109 art. 4, co.; cf. art. 8 co.). Since these aspects of Thomas's teaching are unquestionably bound up with his religious commitments, Peter Ahrensdorf and Thomas Pangle "begin to wonder whether there is in the *Summa Theologiae* a strictly natural basis for morality." *Justice Among Nations*, 85. But, as Thomas argues without either open or covert appeal to revelation, natural law is a purely rational law and it is *the* natural basis for morality. A precept of natural law is a dictate of natural reason (ST q. 100 art. 11, co. cf. q. 92 art. 1, ad 2) not a dogma of faith, whether one needs the assistance of grace to act upon it all of the time, or some of the time, or not all. In no sense, then, would denying the availability of grace to man—and that it is available is, to be sure, a claim of revelation, not a proposition of natural reason—entail denying, or even doubting, the intrinsic rationality of natural law and its precepts. Cf. *ST* 1–2 q. 100 art. 11, co. When Thomas, speaking of divine right in *ST* 2–2 q. 57 art. 2, ad 3, says that what is divinely promulgated is in part "de his quae sunt naturaliter iusta, sed tamen eorum iustitia homines latet," he does not mean that human nature is so corrupt that the whole of natural right is hidden from man and needs to be revealed by God. See not only q. 94 art. 4–6, but also ad 1 of this very article: ". . . id quod naturale est homini potest *aliquando* deficere" (emphasis added). Finally and of decisive importance, one does not need to *believe* in grace—even if one is, unbeknownst to oneself, *assisted* by grace—in order to know the primary precepts of natural law, i.e., to avoid ignorance and not offend others, or to know what can be deduced from them *modica consideratione*, or to recognize their obligatory character, or to act in light of them.

77. "On Natural Law," 142. (Strauss continues the last sentence with citations, which I omit, from Suarez, Grotius, Hobbes, Locke, and Leibniz.) The text that Strauss has in mind in the first sentence of this passage is *ST* 1–2 q. 71 art. 6, ad 5: "a theologis consideratur peccatum praecipue secundum quod est offensa contra Deum; a philosopho autem morali, secundum quod contrariatur rationi." For Thomas, not only are the theologian and the moral philosopher both right in their own realms, but what is *contra Deum* and what is *contra rationem* are largely the same. See *ST* 1–2 q. 68 art. 1, ad 2, where Thomas is speaking from the perspective of revealed theology: "vitia, inquantum sunt contra bonum rationis, contrariantur virtutibus, inquantum autem sunt contra divinum instinctum, contrariantur donis [of the Holy Spirit]. Idem enim contrariatur Deo et rationi, cuius lumen a Deo derivatur." See also *ST* 2–2, q. 150 art. 3, arg. 2: "dicitur aliquid esse peccatum quod bonum rationis excludit." Thomas does not disagree with this part of arg. 2.

from revealed theology but from rational theology as well. Thomas, however, would make two major qualifications. In the first place, by expressing natural law, reason *does* command and forbid. It does not "indicate" merely. In the second place, natural law would be possible even if there were no God only on the supposition, denied by Thomas, that human reason would be possible even if there were no God. As I have argued, denying God's governance of the world in general, and of man in particular, would have consequences no more and no less grave for speculative reason than for practical reason.

So a consideration of the *evidence* for the primary precepts natural law, just like a consideration of the *evidence* of the principles of speculative reason, can indeed be "kept independent of theology and its controversies," exactly as Strauss recommends. If, however, one wishes to give an account of how man comes by this extraordinary faculty of reason, an account that ascends to a sufficient cause of it, and if one wishes furthermore to give an account of the astonishing agreement of the world with human reason, rather than simply refer these things to "the riddle of being," one will have to engage, one way or another, with theology and its controversies.[78]

Since natural reason articulates its principles, regarding both what is and what ought to be, in universals, it is hard to see how there can be a good of *reason* that is not a *common* good. And here we come to the pervasive problem: reason and rationalism, like nature, are invoked with great frequency by Strauss and his followers. But they do not say clearly what they think reason is, just as they do not say clearly what they (as distinct from Aristotle) think nature is. And so they have little to say, with any clarity, about how either can serve as a principle of human deliberation, choice, and action.

Strauss's criticisms of Thomas's natural law teaching turn out on careful inspection to be weak, indeed insubstantial, based as they are on a failure to come closely to terms with the foundation of that teaching exactly as Thomas presents it, above all in *Summa Theologaie* q. 94 art. 2, though elsewhere as well. Nevertheless, Strauss's criticisms have achieved something like a dogmatic standing among his followers: *Magister dixit. De dictis eius non est disputandum.*

78. *ST* 1 q.1 art. 5, ad 2. I return to this matter in Part 3, Ch. 13, below.

Chapter 5

CRITICISMS ADVANCED BY HARRY JAFFA

IN 1952, STRAUSS'S STUDENT Harry Jaffa published a book entitled *Thomism and Aristotelianism: A Study of the Commentary by Thomas Aquinas on the Nicomachean Ethics.* Though the book, as the subtitle announces, primarily treats Thomas as a commentator on Aristotle, it also speaks substantively to Thomas's natural law teaching.[1] The thrust of Jaffa's criticism is the same as Strauss's: natural law as distinct from natural right is a concept that cannot be validated without appeal to revelation.

Jaffa is sometimes spoken of these days not just as a proponent of natural right but as a proponent of natural law. He was a young man when he wrote *Thomism and Aristotelianism*, and, since then, he may have abandoned some of his earlier views about Thomas.[2] I am not aware, however, of an actual recantation of his early critique.[3] *Thomism and Aristotelianism* is widely read by Straussians, and many of them

1. How well Thomas understood and represented Aristotle's ethical teaching is a question that lies outside the scope of the present study. On this question see John J. Schrems's "A Reexamination of Harry V. Jaffa's *Thomism and Aristotelianism*." Schrems argues that Jaffa, in his attempt to drive a wedge between Aristotle and Thomas, ends up misinterpreting Aristotle in a number of places where Thomas interprets him correctly. I think that Schrems is persuasive both at the general level and in matters of detail. I also think he occasionally overstates his case. For example, I am not persuaded that "the doctrine of natural law is to be found in the second book of Aristotle's *Physics*" (179). There is much more to the *doctrine* of natural law, its foundational principles as well as its elaboration, than can be found in the second book of the *Physics*, or anywhere else in the Aristotelian corpus for that matter. I think Schrems similarly overstates his case when he says that "Aristotle himself has demonstrated in the opening sentence of the *Ethics* and the *Politics*" that "there exist first principles of the practical intellect" (180). As I noted in Part 1, the second sentence of the *Ethics* is a declarative statement that "the good has been well declared to be that at which all things aim," not the properly practical gerundive, "Good is to be done . . . etc." that Thomas calls the first principle of practical reason. Much less is it a precept with properly obligatory force. The same is true of the phrase in the first sentence of the *Politics* that "all men do all things for the sake of what seems to be good." These overstatements by Schrems detract only slightly from what is an otherwise powerful rebuttal of the presuppositions and conclusions of *Thomism and Aristotelianism.*

2. See below, Section c of the present chapter.

3. According to Thomas West, Jaffa changed his mind about some of what he wrote in *ThAr*, but

speak of it as demonstrating the superior rationality of Aristotle's teaching when compared with Thomas's. *Thomism and Aristotelianism* contains much that is original, interesting, and true regarding points on which Thomas parts company with Aristotle in his commentary on the *Nicomachean Ethics*. But Jaffa's critique of Thomas in this book also exhibits misunderstandings, some of which it shares with Strauss's critique in *Natural Right and History*. In addressing these misunderstandings, and related misunderstandings exhibited by other Straussians in the following chapters, I shall have to reiterate points that I have made before, for which I ask the reader's indulgence in advance.

SECTION A. THOMAS'S DEPARTURES FROM ARISTOTLE

According to Jaffa, "the foundation in natural reason . . . upon which [Thomas's] Natural Law teaching . . . is said to rest is, substantially, the moral and political philosophy of Aristotle."[4] This is an overstatement. In the presentation of his natural law teaching in the *Summa Theologiae*, Thomas refers to Aristotle only to show that an objector's appeal to him is off the mark, or to introduce an analogy that Aristotle himself does not make, or to note a relationship that Aristotle does not take note of. An example of a reference to Aristotle by an objector to whom Thomas responds by referring to Aristotle in turn can be found in the very first argument and the reply to it in the "Treatise on Law."[5] An example of a non-Aristotelian analogy that Thomas introduces with a reference to Aristotle is the analogy that holds between speculative reason and practical reason, and the dependence of both on self-evident principles.[6] This analogy does not rely on the authority of Aristotle, except for the claim that *theoretical* reason necessarily makes use of self-evident principles, a claim that Jaffa presumably does not dispute. An example of a relation that Aristotle does not take note of, but that Thomas does, is the relation between Aristotle's simple declarative, "Good is that at which all things aim," and the gerundive that Thomas calls the first principle of practical

never published his reasons for doing so. *Critique of the 'Straussian' Critique*, 23, fn. 45. A chapter of Jaffa's 1965 book, *Equality and Liberty*, is entitled "A Defense of the 'Natural Law Thesis'" (190–208). The title is somewhat misleading, inasmuch as Jaffa argues in this chapter only for the possibility of rational judgments regarding such things as goodness and justice. In his first endnote Jaffa points out that there is a distinction between natural law and natural right, but he does not elaborate on this distinction (205). In the last paragraph of the chapter he says, "[A] command in the imperative mood proper . . . belong[s] to positive [!] law, whether human or divine. The imperatives of natural right are . . . hypothetical, not categorical" (204–5). With this division, Jaffa rules out the possibility of natural law in the Thomistic sense. Jaffa says nothing about natural law in the final paragraph of this chapter, and he says next to nothing about natural law in the paragraphs that precede it.

4. *ThAr* 6; see 168, 192, 200 n. 20, 225 n. 44. On 221–2, n. 9, Jaffa appeals to the authority of Aristotle—rather than taking issue with Thomas's argument as Thomas presents it—in support of the claim that a divine concern for the moral order is an "untrue opinion."

5. *ST* 1–2 q. 94 art. 1, arg. 1; ad 1.

6. *ST* 1–2 q. 94 art. 2.

reason, "Good is to be done and pursued, and evil avoided."[7] This principle can be denied, though only at the price of rendering unintelligible how we think of what is to be pursued and what is to be avoided, and of rendering unintelligible not just the concept of obligation, but even the very words "ought" and "should," however they are used; and Straussians, like the rest of us, use these words too. Jaffa has no more to say about this dimension—the fundamental dimension—of Thomas's presentation than Strauss does.

What Jaffa fails to appreciate is the reason why Thomas and the other scholastics take so great an interest in Aristotle. In their view, Aristotle's philosophy is the exemplar for anyone who is attempting to determine what can be known by natural reason about the world and man's place in it. As I have argued in the preceding chapter, this attempt is intrinsic to the first and foundational part of the trifold project that constitutes scholasticism. The scholastic thinkers are interested in Aristotle, not in spite of the fact that he did not have access to biblical revelation, but precisely because of this fact. His philosophy serves as what one could call their intellectual conscience.[8] Knowing that Aristotle disagrees with them about something that they think can be known by natural reason gives them pause. But it does not just bring them to a stupefied halt. They know that they must have good reasons for disagreeing with Aristotle in the first and foundational part of their trifold project. If they find such reasons, they state them carefully, in their clear and measured way, and continue with their thinking. Aristotle is not for them the final authority regarding what can be naturally known.[9] The final authority for what can be naturally known is natural reason itself.

Jaffa ignores the relationship between being and essence that is the solid metaphysical ground of Thomas's rational theology. He also fails to appreciate the metaphysical ground of Aristotle's moral and political philosophy.

> [W]hether the Aristotelian doctrine of species is true or false is of no immediate practical importance, because the problem of morality exists quite independently of it . . . [T]he metaphysical knowledge of the existence of a

7. *ST* 1–2 q. 94 art. 2.

8. "To assert an a priori opposition between philosophy and revelation on the grounds that the former is equivalently reason and the latter is antithetic to reason is to propound a prejudice, not to advance an analytically self-evident proposition." Frederick D. Wilhelmsen, *Christianity and Political Philosophy*, Athens, GA: The University of Georgia Press: 1978, 222–3.

9. On the relation of Thomas's expositions of Aristotelian texts to his own thought, see Mark Jordan, "Thomas Aquinas' Disclaimers in the Aristotelian Commentaries. "Thomas could write literal expositions of seemingly opposed works—Aristotle's *Metaphysics*, for example, and the *Liber de causis*. The literal commentary as such does not assert that the text under explication is true. It asserts only that the text merits careful reading" (104). Mary Keys notes that, since Thomas's calling Averroes "the Commentator" does not preclude his taking issue, sometimes sharply, with Averroes's commentaries, so Thomas's calling Aristotle "the Philosopher" should not be taken as implying that he agrees with Aristotle on all philosophical matters, i.e., on all matters of which we have natural knowledge. ("Keys," 71) See, in this connection, Jenkins, "Expositions of the Text: Aquinas's Aristotelian Commentaries."

> foundation for moral certainty is not a substitute, or even a basis for, a practical knowledge of the basis for moral certainty.[10].

The problem of morality does indeed exist quite independently of the doctrine of species. But Aristotle's solution to this problem presupposes that there is such a thing as a species, in particular, that there is a human species, which is to say, a permanent human nature. Jaffa, like most Straussians, speaks of nature, repeatedly though obscurely. He suggests at one point, taking issue with Thomas, that "a desire for what is beyond man's nature" would not "be admitted by [Aristotle] to be a natural desire."[11] And he repeatedly refers to the "natural capacity" of man in the immediate sequel. Jaffa even claims that "[t]he nature of man, as a determinate species (apart from all individual men as such) exists of necessity." Thomas would essentially agree with this claim, saying that the ideas of things, including man, exist in the mind of God from all eternity, even prior to the actual existence of things.[12] But without introducing metaphysics, or something more like metaphysics than political philosophy, it is hard if not impossible to make sense of the assertion that "the nature of man . . . exists of necessity," to say nothing of Jaffa's even more sweeping assertion that "reality in the strict sense is what is of necessity, what cannot be otherwise."[13] Though political philosophy is incapable of fully clarifying or validating the concept of nature—not even the remarkable Chapter 3 of *Natural Right and History* accomplishes these things,[14]—neither Jaffa nor any other Aristotelian can dispense with this concept. For how otherwise could man be said to be a political animal by *nature*?[15]

It needs to be stressed that Jaffa's confidence regarding the independence of political philosophy from knowledge of the whole, a confidence shared by other Straussians, was not shared by their teacher. According to Strauss, "[T]he period between Hooker and Locke had witnessed the emergence of . . . nonteleological natural science, and therewith the destruction [!] of the basis of traditional natural right."[16] Political philosophy is not self-grounding. "The nature of man cannot be understood without

10. *ThAr* 24.

11. *ThAr* 152.

12. *ST* 1 q. 15.

13. *ThAr* 153. Thomas would agree with this assertion if "reality in the strict sense" is taken to refer exclusively to the *esse subsistens* that is God. (God cannot *not* be.) But this does not seem to be what Jaffa means by "reality in the strict sense."

14. *NRH* 8. Strauss writes in his letter to Kuhn, "I myself regard [*Natural Right and History*] as a preparation to an adequate discussion rather than as a treatise settling the question."

15. Aristotle, *Politics* 1253a3.

16. *NRH* 7–8; also 321: "Prudence and 'this lower world' cannot be seen without some knowledge of 'the higher world'—without genuine *theoria*." Consider *WhPPh*: "The theoretical or cosmological basis [!] of [Machiavelli's] political teaching was a kind of decayed Aristotelianism" (47). Strauss does not elaborate on this interesting observation. But he seems to be implying that, not only Machiavelli's political teaching, but the teaching of every political philosopher has some kind of theoretical or cosmological basis, a basis distinct from, and presupposed by, his political teaching.

some understanding of nature as a whole."[17] There is, however, no understanding of nature as a whole without metaphysics. For even apart from the possibility, arguably the necessity, that nature depends on something that is not within nature,[18] a deep understanding of what *eidos*, *to ti ēn einai*, and *ousia* are, and of the role they play within Aristotelian physics, requires a properly metaphysical investigation.[19] A metaphysical investigation is then required to make full sense of the claim that man is by nature a political animal.

It is possible that Jaffa does not address the metaphysical ground of Thomas's rational theology because he is unaware of it. Jaffa is convinced that "in Thomas' own system theology, or, more correctly, revealed theology, takes precedence over the teaching of natural reason."[20] If by "natural reason" Jaffa means natural science, he is to a certain extent right. Revealed theology does take precedence over the generalizations from experience that are constitutive of natural science. For these generalizations always carry with them a measure of uncertainty.[21] Accordingly, Thomas does not think that they can be woven together into a definitive refutation of the possibility of miracles performed by an omnipotent God. Nor does Strauss think this.[22] And whereas natural science can offer alternative accounts of what revealed theology understands to have happened miraculously, such as the parting of the Red Sea, it cannot even begin to speak to the claims that revealed theology makes about God, for example, that there are personal relations in God. So, in this sense revealed theology does take precedence over natural science.

If, however, by "natural reason" Jaffa means, as Thomas does, the self-evident principles of logic, the first principle of practical reason, and the knowledge we have of the order of our own natural inclinations, then he is wrong to say that revealed theology takes precedence over natural reason for Thomas. To repeat, Thomas quite explicitly states that faith, the response to revelation (or what is believed to be revelation) presupposes natural knowledge.[23] Jaffa says that Thomas "assumes the impossibility of any real conflict between reason and revelation . . ."[24] The word "assumes" is problematic at best. The assumption in question is not logical but heuristic only. So far from dogmatically laying down this assumption as a first principle, Thomas sets out to demonstrate, rigorously and with extraordinary thoroughness, that no tenet of the Catholic faith is in conflict with natural reason, that is, that no tenet of the Catholic

17. Strauss, *CM*, 159.

18. Aristotle, *Metaphysics* 1072b13–15.

19. Aristotle, *Physics* 193b1–13; 194b27; *Metaphysics* 983a28; 1028a10 ff.

20. *ThAr* 19. Compare *ST* 1 q. 2, art. 2, ad 1. In the context of this article, Thomas is speaking of what can be known by natural reason about the existence of God and similar things pertaining to him.

21. See Aristotle, *Metaphysics* 995a16. Thomas Aquinas, *In Duodecim Libros Metaphysicorum Aristotelis Expositio*, Lib. 2 Lect. 5.336.

22. *PR* 100, 128.

23. *ST* 1 q. 2 art. 2, ad 1.

24. *ThAr* 8.

faith is self-contradictory, contradicts another tenet of faith, or is contradicted by anything we know to be true beyond the shadow of a doubt. Whether Thomas succeeds in this venture is a question that can be decided only by analyzing his demonstrations, one by one.

Jaffa seems to think that, because Thomas's rational theology reaches conclusions that one does not find in Aristotle, Thomas should have realized that the arguments in support of them are either invalid or derived from premises that are inaccessible to natural reason. Jaffa at one point lists six Thomistic propositions that he calls "principles of revealed theology." In fact, every one of them is *argued for* in Thomas's development of his rational theology.[25] In a note to this passage, Jaffa offers a major qualification, a qualification that would almost count as a retraction, were the qualification not itself qualified in a most peculiar manner.

> It is true that Thomas might consider some, if not all, of these [propositions] as knowable by natural reason. But the fact that they were not known by Aristotle—as we believe has been shown—would certainly suggest that their value as principles of *unassisted* human reason, from Thomas' own point of view, would be negligible."[26].

Jaffa concedes in the first sentence that Thomas might consider at least some of the propositions in question as "knowable by natural reason." And yet, in spite of this concession, Jaffa says in the second sentence that their "value as principles of *unassisted* human reason, from Thomas' own point of view, would be negligible." But how could their value as principles of unassisted reason be negligible if they are knowable by natural reason? The coherence of this passage could be salvaged after a fashion by a reference, which Jaffa does not make, to Thomas's claim that "every truth by whomsoever it is spoken is from the Holy Spirit." But, again, all Thomas means by this formulation is that God bestows the *natural* light upon us and so moves us to understand the truth. This bestowal of the natural light upon us is not an act of grace, as Thomas understands grace, but is simply a consequence of God's creating us as rational beings. Human reason did not create itself. Moreover, like everything else created by God, it continues to be sustained in its existence by God's ongoing creative act. So, in this sense, it can be said that human reason is never "unassisted."

It is unlikely, however, that Jaffa is making this point. By "*unassisted* human reason," he seems to mean reason functioning without the assistance of revelation. But precisely because Thomas thinks that these propositions are "knowable by natural reason," he has to think that they are knowable without the assistance of revelation.

25. *ThAr* 187. See James Lehrberger, "Crime without Punishment," 251 n. 4, for a gentle correction of Jaffa's misunderstanding. As Fr. Lehrberger says in this note, and in fact demonstrates in his article, "An adequate analysis of the basis of Thomas's natural law teaching requires an in-depth knowledge of his metaphysics and anthropology." I am indebted to Nate Sheely for bringing this fine article to my attention. It deserves to be better known.

26. *ThAr* 225, n. 44, emphasis in the original.

That man arrives at truth by virtue of a natural light that God bestowed in creating him as a rational animal does not mean—certainly not for Thomas—that every truth is thereby a revealed truth. The critical question regarding the propositions Jaffa names is whether they are cogently argued for without appeal to revelation. Jaffa does not attempt to show how the arguments that Thomas develops for them are compromised, in terms either of their proof structure or of the premises on which they are based.

Jaffa is right that Thomas invokes the authority of Aristotle with great frequency. Thomas does so not only because of his own high estimation of Aristotle, but because of the comparably high, if not higher, estimation in which Aristotle's authority is held by those with whom Thomas is frequently disputing, particularly Averroes and the so-called Latin Averroists. Thomas, however, departs from Aristotle not only in minor matters but also in matters of the greatest import, and not only in his natural law teaching but also in his rational theology, particularly in the metaphysical distinction he draws between *esse* and *essentia*, in the philosophical argument for a first efficient cause (as distinct from the argument for a first unmoved mover) that is grounded in this distinction, and in the elaborate rational theology he builds on the conception of God as the first efficient cause.

Jaffa does acknowledge that Thomas, in addition to straying from Aristotle's own teaching on this or that point, also attempts to correct Aristotle, not just from the perspective of revelation but from the perspective of natural reason itself.[27] But that acknowledgement makes all the stranger what seems to be Jaffa's guiding assumption, namely, that if he can locate a discrepancy between the positions of Thomas and Aristotle on a matter determinable by natural reason—and it is not hard to do this—then he has accomplished either a virtual refutation of Thomas's position or a reduction of it to a tenet of revealed theology in disguise. The following passage, which speaks to the issue of man's natural desire to know the causes of things as they are essentially and in themselves, an issue we considered in the preceding chapter, is representative of Jaffa's approach.

> A man may desire many things that are beyond his natural capacities . . . He may desire to fly like a bird, or run like a deer. And anyone who became obsessed by any such desire would as surely be frustrated as someone who became possessed of a desire to see God in his essence, *if* such a desire exceeded the natural capacity of man. To wish for what is beyond our capacity is, from the point of view of natural reason, as represented by Aristotle, to wish for what is impossible, to wish that reality be different from what it is. But as knowledge is an actualization of what is real, a wish for reality to be different from what it is, in order that we may know it, is a wish that can lead only to insanity.[28]

27. *ThAr* 26.

28. *ThAr* 152–3.

Jaffa does not address Thomas's argument that we have a natural desire to know the causes, including especially a desire to know the ultimate causes (or cause), to know them as they are in themselves, hence as they are essentially, and not just as they are in relation to what they cause. He does not address Thomas's argument that there is only one first cause and that this cause is God.[29] He does not address Thomas's argument that knowledge of God attained this way, though real knowledge, is limited and does not satisfy the natural desire to know the first cause as it is in itself. Jaffa's assertion that to wish for what is beyond our natural capacity amounts to "a wish for reality to be different from what it is" simply begs the question.[30] Since he assumes that "natural reason [is] represented by Aristotle," Jaffa can conclude that any departure from Aristotle is a departure from natural reason. Jaffa has armed himself with an assumption that disburdens him from identifying the flaws in Thomas's actual arguments or demonstrating the superiority of Aristotle's rational theology to Thomas's.

SECTION B. THE NATURAL DESIRE FOR A SUPERNATURAL END

On the particular question of whether man has a natural desire to behold the essence of the first cause, the positions of Aristotle and Thomas may not actually be quite as far apart as Jaffa apparently thinks. It is Aristotle's claim, and not just Thomas's, that man naturally desires to know, that wisdom is the highest knowledge and the knowledge that we seek, that wisdom consists in knowledge of the causes, that one of the causes is the final cause, and that another cause is the essence (*to ti ēn einai*). From these claims we can infer that, for Aristotle no less than for Thomas, we naturally desire to know the essence of the final cause, which according to Aristotle's express teaching is God.[31] It is not even certain that Aristotle would deny the possibility of this natural desire of ours being ultimately satisfied.[32]

29. In a later article, and in agreement with Thomas in many though not all respects, Jaffa writes, "Because God is separate [from the universe he created], reasoning about the universe (going from effects to causes) will not lead to the first cause." "Leo Strauss, the Bible, and Political Philosophy," 208. Jaffa does little to justify the connection between the two clauses in this sentence. Thomas would respond that going from effects to causes cannot lead us to knowledge of the first cause as it is in itself. But, he argues, it can and does lead to knowledge of the existence of a first cause that is properly called God, (see Part 1, Ch. 1, Section a, above; cf. *ST* 1 q. 2 art. 2, co.), as Aristotle also argues in *Metaphysics* XII.

30. As John Schrems notes in a criticism of this passage from *ThAr*, "it is not irrational to desire perfect happiness after the present life" ("Reexamination," 179). It would be irrational if one were convinced on the basis an airtight proof that happiness after the present life was impossible. But Jaffa does not provide us with such a proof, nor does he direct us to where he thinks it can be found.

31. *Physics* 194b16–33; *Metaphysics* 980a20–983b8; 1072a20–b31; 1074b15–35. *Nicomachean Ethics* 1141a29–b3. Consider also the following observation of Strauss's. "The philosopher's dominating passion is the desire for truth, i.e., for knowledge of the eternal order, or the eternal cause or causes of the whole." *On Tyranny*, 197–8.

32. See *Nicomachean Ethics* 1101a 2022; 1178a8, a23; *De Anima* 430a13, a23–25.

Jaffa finds support for his view that man's desire to know the essence of the first cause is not a natural desire in a passage from *De Veritate* that is referred to by Frederick Copleston.[33] In that passage, Thomas says that man has a natural end in the contemplation of the divine, though only as first cause, and that he has both a natural appetite and a natural capacity to attain this end. Thomas additionally says, here as elsewhere, that man also has a supernatural end, which consists in contemplating the divine according to its very essence, and that this supernatural end exceeds man's natural capacity. But, according to this passage from *De Veritate*, man does not have even a natural inclination toward it. The passage in *De Veritate*, then, is clearly in some tension with the passage in the *Summa Theologiae* where Thomas quite explicitly says, and argues, that man has a natural desire not only to know *that* there is a first cause, but to know *what* it is, that is to know it according to its essence.[34] Fr. Copleston's resolution, which Jaffa heartily endorses, is that "when in the *Summa Theologiae* and the *Summa contra Gentiles* [Thomas] speaks of a natural desire for the vision of [the essence of God] he is not speaking strictly as a *philosopher*, but as a philosopher and theologian combined."[35] What Fr. Copleston presumably means by the last phrase is that Thomas is speaking in those passages not from the perspective of rational theology alone, but from the perspective of faith and revealed theology.

Fr. Copleston's attempted resolution of the tension between these passages is unconvincing. For how could Thomas argue in the *Summa Theologiae* that man has a *natural* desire to know the essence of the first cause only from the perspective of faith and revealed theology? A natural desire to know something, whatever it may be, can be located only in natural reason itself. It seems that natural reason would be aware of this desire—its own desire—without the special assistance of revelation. And if it is not aware of this desire, then some kind of explanation is needed for why it is not. It is striking that in the *corpus* of the article from the *Summa Theologiae* (1–2 q. 3 art. 8) where Thomas argues for the existence of this natural desire, he mentions neither faith nor revelation. Nor does he need to do so, since the argument there, based exclusively on natural reason, is convincing by itself. The only authority Thomas appeals to in his argument is Aristotle, and there is no good reason to doubt that Aristotle himself would concur in it.

De Veritate (1256–59) was written before the *Summa Theologiae* (1265–72).[36] So it seems only reasonable to take the arguments of the later work, and not those of the earlier one, as expressing his mature view when they cannot be harmonized. Fr. Copleston takes issue with the conclusion of the argument in the *Summa Theologiae* that man has a natural desire to see the essence of God. But no more than Jaffa does

33. *A History of Philosophy*, Book 1, 400–405. Cf. *De Veritate* q. 27 art. 2.

34. See *ST* 1–2 q. 3 art. 8, co.; cf. 1, q 12 art. 1, co.

35. *A History of Philosophy*, Book 1, 405.

36. The *Summa Contra Gentiles* (1259–64) is also later than *De Veritate*.

he show that the argument is invalid or show where it relies, implicitly or explicitly, on the claims of revelation.

Fr. Copleston is not only struck by the tension between the passages in *De Veritate* and the *Summa Theologiae*. He is also aware that, for Thomas, the assistance of divine grace is needed for the attainment of a supernatural end. But Thomas also holds that nature does not work in vain (*inane*).[37] So, in the claim that there can be a natural desire for a supernatural end, Fr. Copleston senses an implication that this grace would be "in some sense due to man," which would be contrary to the very meaning of grace.[38] The implication that Fr. Copleston senses, however, is not there. Thomas hardly argues that man, because of his natural inclinations and limitations, *deserves* grace. Furthermore, anyone who was convinced that natural reason establishes the existence of God as first cause would naturally long for knowledge of God as he is *in himself* and apart from his causal responsibility for everything else. If, moreover, he thought on Thomistic grounds that he could not attain knowledge of God as he is in himself and essentially, he would naturally long for supernatural assistance leading him to this knowledge, granted that, apart from revelation, he would not have the slightest understanding of how such assistance could be vouchsafed him.[39]

When Thomas argues from the perspective of natural reason that there is a natural desire to behold the essence of God and that this desire is not in vain, he is arguing that this desire is only for something that *can* be, for something that is possible, not for something that *is* or *will* be: "*Utrum aliquis intellectus creatus posit Deum videre per essentiam.*"[40] Natural reason can refute the claim that it is intrinsically impossible for a created intellect to see God as he is. But natural reason cannot prove that any created intellect actually has seen, does see, or ever will see God as he is.

37. Compare Aristotle, *Politics* 1253a12; see *De Anima* 432b21.

38. *A History of Philosophy*, Book 1, 404

39. A natural desire to see God as he is does not by itself generate hope as *Thomas* understands hope, namely, as a theological and infused virtue that presupposes divine promises. ST 2–2 q. 22 art. 1, ad.1.

40. *ST* 1 q. 12 art. 1. A natural desire would be empty (*inane*), Thomas says in *SCG* 3 cap. 48 n. 11, if it *could never* be fulfilled. (*Esset autem inane desiderium naturae si numquan posset impleri. Est igitur implebile desiderium naturale hominis. Non autem in hac vita, ut ostensum est.*) He does not say that a natural desire would be *inane* if, in fact, it *is not* fulfilled. See *SCG* 3 cap. 51, n. 1, where Thomas again speaks, from the perspective of natural reason, of seeing the essence of God only as something that is *possible*. This possibility suffices to keep the natural desire from being *inane*. Thomas does conclude the *corpus* of *ST* 1 q. 12 art. 1 by saying that "the blessed" (*beati*), not just *can*, but *do* see the essence of God. In this article, however, he has advanced two arguments, one from faith and the other from natural reason. The argument from natural reason, by itself, does not establish that any created intellect really does see God as he is, but only that it is false to claim that it could not do so. On the other hand, the concluding sentence of the *corpus* clearly presupposes that some are, in fact, blessed. So Thomas is definitely speaking at that point from the perspective of faith and revealed theology, relying on the concept of grace in particular. But his doing so, momentarily, does not at all compromise the exclusively rational character of other arguments about God in this part of the *ST*. For a somewhat stronger application of the principle "nature does nothing in vain," consider the *supplementary* argument at the end of *ST* 1 q. 75 art. 6, co.

There is a special way in which the natural desire to see God as he is is not in vain. For this desire is initially just the natural desire to know the first cause or causes of things as they really are. As such, this desire is prior to and independent of a proof of the existence of God. It is prior to and independent of even belief in the existence of God. The natural desire to know the causes of things leads natural reason finally to run up against its own limits. This experience of running up against the limits of reason makes man more open to the possibility of revelation than he would be were he convinced that he could know without further assistance everything that he naturally desires to know. The natural desire that leads man to this experience is then anything but "in vain": by providing man with this experience nature does a great service to man.

Although the argument in the *Summa Theologiae* that man has a natural desire to see the essence of God contradicts the claim in *De Veritate* that he does not have such a desire, a consideration of the different contexts in which the two claims occur suggests a more satisfactory resolution than what Fr. Copleston proposes. The arguments in the passages that Fr. Copleston cites from the *Summa Contra Gentiles* and the *Summa Theologiae* occur in the context of rational theology. The claim in *De Veritate* occurs in a treatment of the relation of grace to charity.[41] The context there is obviously revealed theology. In spite of the elaborate rational theology that Thomas works out, it yields not so much knowledge of the way in which God *is*, as, by Thomas's own admission, knowledge of the way in which God is *not*.[42] The desire to see God as he is is simply what rational theology and metaphysics understand to be the intellect's natural inclination to know the causes *for what they are*. But if this desire is motivated by the theological virtue of charity, then more than nature is at work. Grace is at work. So, from the perspective of rational theology, we can say that man's natural desire to know God as he is is a natural desire for a supernatural end. But from the perspective of revealed theology, we must add that this natural desire is not properly inclined to its supernatural end except through the grace of infused charity. To be properly inclined we need not just philosophical wonder but specifically theological virtues.[43]

But just what bearing, we must now ask, does the issue of a supernatural end for man have on Thomas's claim that we have natural knowledge of the first principle of practical reason, or on his claim that there is a natural and knowable order of human inclinations toward ends, or on his explication of how man has obligations springing out of his nature as a rational animal and his argument that these obligations are declared broadly in the primary precepts of natural law that one avoid ignorance and not

41. *De Veritate* q. 27, art. 2: *Utrum Gratia Gratum Faciens sit idem quod Caritas.*

42. *ST* 1 q. 2, Prologue.

43. *ST* 1–2 q. 62 art. 1, ad 3; see q. 109 art. 3, ad 1. Consider the following formulation by Bernard Lonergan, S.J. "The best that natural reason can attain is the discovery of the paradox that the desire to understand arises naturally, that its object is the transcendental, *ens*, and that the proper fulfillment that naturally is attainable is restricted to the proportionate object of the finite intellect." *Collection*, 87.

offend others? It is not the case that these foundational elements of Thomas's natural law teaching in some obscure way logically presuppose, and are thereby epistemically compromised by, the religious belief that man really will attain a supernatural end. The epistemological point here is simply that natural reason recognizes that it cannot know, on its own, all that it naturally desires to know. By recognizing the limitations of what it can accomplish on its own, natural reason establishes a need for supernatural assistance, which, as we have seen, even Strauss acknowledges. Thomas gives rational arguments for this need. But even if one is not persuaded by his arguments, one has not refuted in the least his case, independently arrived at, for the existence of natural law and for the content of its primary precepts.

Thomas's argument that man needs supernatural assistance can be resisted only by showing that man does not really have such a need or that, if he does, it is a need for something that is not possible. Since Jaffa's teacher himself frankly acknowledges that "the need for divine illumination cannot be denied," he, or one of his students, needs to demonstrate that divine illumination is impossible. One could show such a thing only by definitively disproving the existence of the biblical God, who is said to reveal himself in human history to human beings of his own free choosing, at times and places of his own free choosing, and to the blessed in a life a beyond this one. But, according to Strauss, a conclusive disproof of the existence of the biblical God cannot be achieved by relying on the question-begging premises of natural science and the equally question-begging premises of the literary-historical critique of the Bible, or by constructing a mere alternative, metaphysical or otherwise, to the biblical account. Such a proof, if possible at all, presupposes a sustained inquiry into man's moral self-understanding or self-misunderstanding, as the case may be. For this moral self-understanding or self-misunderstanding is *sine qua non* for belief in revelation, at least for belief in biblical revelation, which addresses man as a moral being and not only as a speculative being. That, however, is where the inquiry has to come to terms with Thomas's natural law teaching—and not just with the conclusions of that teaching, but with the reasoning that leads to the conclusions.

SECTION C. NATURAL LAW AND THE AMERICAN FOUNDING

In 2000, almost a half century after *Thomism and Aristotelianism* was written, Jaffa's study, *A New Birth of Freedom—Abraham Lincoln and the Coming of the Civil War*, appeared. Commenting on the Declaration of Independence's formulation that "all human beings are endowed by their Creator with the rights that belong to them by nature," Jaffa writes, "Republican government understands itself to be in accordance with a natural order that is itself in harmony with the divine government of the universe."[44] In an endnote to this sentence Jaffa elaborates as follows.

44. *NBFr* 123.

> In this, the perspective of the Declaration is in agreement with Thomas Aquinas's conception of the natural law as the rational creature's participation in the eternal law, the law by which God governs the universe. The Declaration also assumes the existence of an eternal law when it speaks of an appeal to the 'supreme judge of the world' and of 'the protection of divine Providence.' The voice of right reason in the natural law, therefore, is as much the voice of God as is divine revelation. Also, since every member of the human species has the potentiality to participate in the natural law, in this decisive respect, all men are created equal.[45]

It is gratifying to see Jaffa point out, if only in an endnote, these points of correspondence between the founding document of the United States and the natural law teaching of Thomas Aquinas. There is, however, a significant difference. The Declaration *assumes* that there is an eternal law—"the laws of nature and of nature's God"—which it appeals to before stating "these truths to be self-evident, that all men are created equal, that they are endowed by their Creator with certain unalienable rights . . . [46] Thomas, on the other hand tries to *prove*, successfully I think, that there is an eternal law.

Jaffa validates the concept of human equality guiding the signers of the Declaration with an argument that is essentially Thomistic. All men are created equal not by virtue of lineage, physical strength and coordination, or native intelligence—for all these things vary—but by virtue of standing under natural law, that is, by virtue of the rationality proper to their species.[47] Man has knowledge of the primary precepts of natural law because he is a rational animal.[48] To be sure, application of these precepts in complex situations requires judgment, and this too is variable. Thomas would not argue that all who are endowed with reason are equally fit either for philosophical inquiry or for political office. Still, recognition of the primary precepts of the natural law through the habit of *synderesis* indeed "explains why the natural law can always be duly promulgated to all men and hence be universally obligatory."[49] This recognition stamps man as such. Only criminals and sophists deny that man has no obligations whatsoever. And the sophists' discourse about action—which, like any meaningful discourse about action, cannot dispense with expressions such as "ought" and "should"—is inconsistent with this denial, as is their anger at being treated differently

45. *NBFr* 509, n. 84.

46. It is interesting that Jefferson does not write that the truth that all men are created equal and the truths about unalienable rights are self-evident, or that we know them as self-evident. He writes only that we "hold" these truths to be self-evident, a formulation that would seem to undermine his claim for their self-evidence.

47. *NBFr* 167. "No difference of intelligence or of the skill with which reason or speech are employed is a ground for asserting different natural rights in those possessed of reason or speech."

48. *ST* q. 94 art. 6, co.; ad 2.

49. *NRH* 163.

from the way they think they ought to be treated. Natural obligations are deeper than, and are the sole possible foundation for, what Jefferson calls "unalienable rights."[50]

In *A New Birth of Freedom* Jaffa more than once invokes the concept of natural law without any explicit criticism of it.[51] It seems to be Jaffa's view in this book, as much as it is Thomas Aquinas's view, that natural *law* and not just natural *right* is an expression of reason.[52]

> If we consult the laws of nature and of reason . . . we can say with Locke and Madison that majority rule exists to protect property, not to confiscate it. Those who suffer arbitrary loss of property, whether from a thief or from a government, have a right to appeal for redress to the laws of nature and to the right of revolution.[53].

What might appear in the first clause to be two different sources of laws, "the laws of nature and of reason," seems in the last clause to be not two but one, "the laws of nature." Nature—human nature, at any event—and human reason cannot be separated from one another. With the expression "laws of reason," Jaffa presumably means laws of practical reason, for it is hard to see how the logical principles of speculative reason have much to say about property. Here and elsewhere in this book, Jaffa is speaking the language of Thomas Aquinas.[54]

Moreover, Jaffa seems to be conceding both that reason has a divine source—"the voice of right reason in the natural law . . . is as much the voice of God as is divine revelation"—and that natural law is naturally knowable by reason without the supernatural assistance of divine revelation. These things are assumed by the language of the Declaration. Now the Declaration does not appeal to divine revelation. So in speaking

50. *NBFr* 89. "Those principles of lawful behavior, or of the laws of nature, instructed the American people before they adopted the Constitution. The American people were bound by their consciences . . ." See *ST* q. 94 art. 1, ad 2.

51. "Jefferson's doctrine, which is the American doctrine in its pure form, is a doctrine of natural rights under natural law . . . It is in the defining characteristics of the doctrine of natural rights under natural law, the doctrine of the naturally right or just, that we must seek the relation of the principles of revolutionary republicanism to free elections" (*NBFr* 26–27).

52. Commenting on a formulation of Jefferson's that speaks of "rights as derived from the law of nature," Jaffa notes that "Jefferson is explicit that he is asserting the equal rights of human nature under the laws of nature . . . 'The great principles of right and wrong'. . . are accessible to man as man, by virtue of the reason that defines man's nature" (*NBFr* 25). Commenting on a passage from Locke, Jaffa writes, "Instruction by the law of nature, which is reason, can take place anywhere and at any time . . ." (*NBFr* 417). "When properly consulted by reason, nature therefore directs the use of human freedom and enables us to distinguish its proper from its improper uses" (*NBFr*. 106). "It is against the law of reason and nature to think that the questions that divided Protestants and Catholics (or Christians, Jews, and Muslims) could be decided by a vote" (*NBFr* 421). Commenting on a passage from J. S. Mill, Jaffa says, "Recognition of the law of reason and nature, condensed into the proposition that all men are created equal, is the necessary condition for being capable of improvement through free and equal discussion" (*NBFr* 421).

53. *NBFr* 427.

54. *ST* 1–2 q. 90 art. 1; q. 91 art. 2; q. 94 art. 2; 2–2 q. 66.

of nature *and* of nature's God, it seems to be appealing to rational theology. Since, furthermore, the God that the Declaration speaks of is providential, he cannot be the God of Aristotle or the God of Spinoza. He has to be the God of Thomas's rational theology, or of a rational theology similar in its essentials Thomas's. The providential God of the Declaration is God as knowable by natural reason apart from faith.

On the face of it, then, Jaffa seems to be much more sympathetic with both Thomas's rational theology and his natural law teaching in *A New Birth of Freedom* than he was in *Thomism and Aristotelianism*. Yet he has nothing to say about the actual arguments that Thomas advances in his rational theology. And he has nothing to say about Thomas's natural law teaching, aside from the endnote quoted above and an endnote touching on the issue of polygamy.[55] One of Jaffa's central assertions in *Thomism and Aristotelianism* is that whatever role right reason may be playing in Thomas's natural law teaching, the claims of revelation are there too and cannot be excised from that teaching without wrecking it. According to *Thomism and Aristotelianism*, right reason articulates natural right; it does not articulate natural law. It does not, then, articulate the concept of natural law about which the Declaration of Independence and Thomas are "in agreement." I am not aware of any place where Jaffa explicitly renounces his claim in *Thomism and Aristotelianism* that Thomas's natural law teaching is dependent on revelation. But if Thomas's natural law teaching depends on revelation, then the same is true of the Declaration's appeal to "the laws of nature and [!] of nature's God" and its "firm reliance on the protection of Divine Providence." If this appeal presupposes religious belief, if—contrary to what Thomas teaches—it cannot be shown to be grounded in a rational theology elaborated by natural reason apart from faith, then how can the Declaration expect full assent from those who do not adhere to a religion that teaches that God is a divine lawgiver, including those who do not adhere to any religion at all?

A possible answer is that such assent is prudential. Both unbelievers and believers of all stripes benefit from living under a government animated by the principles that the Declaration asserts. But then not only an assent to, but a defense of, the perspective of the Declaration, a defense such as Jaffa undertakes, is prudential: the principles of the Declaration must be defended as rational because of the good things that they make possible, not because they are self-evidently true, or true by demonstration, or true at all. I have no idea where Jaffa finally stands on this important matter.[56] He may fully concur in what the Declaration and Thomas's natural law teaching hold in common, including the propositions that there is an eternal law by which God governs the universe and that natural law, as distinct from divine or revealed law, is the

55. *NBFr* 521, endnote 50.

56. "Whether the doctrine of equality in the Gospels was knowable by unassisted reason as a doctrine of the natural law, apart from divine revelation, is not a question that needs to be decided here." *NBFr* 152. Contrast this sentence with what Jaffa says about equality at the bottom of page 421 in the same book.

participation of the eternal law in the rational creature. If Jaffa does concur, then he does so as either a matter of knowledge or of faith. That is, either he is persuaded that Thomas's or someone else's case for these theological propositions—Jefferson does not make much of a case for them—is rationally compelling, or he concurs as a matter of religious belief.

Or maybe Jaffa does not concur at all. He may think that these propositions constitute a noble falsehood, though one whose defense is more pressing now than it seemed to be half a century ago. Wherever he finally stands on this matter, it is striking that, though he can credit Aristotle with some features of the understanding that was shared by the signers of the Declaration, in order to make full sense of that understanding he has to appeal to propositions that he earlier argued Aristotle did not accept—propositions that receive their comprehensive defense in the rational theology and natural law teaching of Thomas Aquinas.

Chapter 6

Criticisms Advanced by Ernest Fortin

Some of the criticisms of Thomas Aquinas that were made by Strauss and Jaffa were developed further by Ernest Fortin. Fr. Fortin, a traditionally educated Roman Catholic priest, had a broad familiarity with Thomas's work as a whole. He did not think that Thomas's proof of the existence God was based on belief in biblical revelation. And he did not think that Aristotle was, for Thomas, the final authority on what could be known by natural reason. Fr. Fortin recognized that Thomas's rational theology rests on the distinction between *esse* and *essentia* in worldly entities.[1] He also recognized that creation *ex nihilo*, as Thomas understands it, is fully compatible with the eternity of the world. Fr. Fortin writes that "Thomas rethinks the Christian notion of Natural Law on the basis of Aristotle's *Physics*."[2] But all he seems to mean, as far as can be gathered from the follow-up to this statement, is that for Thomas there actually is an order of nature both distinct from and presupposed by the order of grace. So, with this observation, Fr. Fortin is not repeating Strauss's criticism that Thomas's teaching of natural law relies directly on a rational, or natural, theology that has been discredited by natural science, and (somehow) indirectly on revealed theology. Fr. Fortin's criticism is more pointed: Thomas's natural law teaching depends directly on revealed theology. It presupposes that revelation has already taken place and it is grounded immediately in what has been revealed.

SECTION A. PROVIDENCE AND NATURAL LAW

In his article, "On Natural Law," Strauss made the oblique remark that "[a] sufficient sanction is supplied by divine punishment for transgressions of the natural law but it is not entirely clear whether human reason can establish the fact of such punishment."[3]

1. Ernest Fortin, "Thomas Aquinas," 269–70.

2. Ernest Fortin, *ATAP* 192.

3. "On Natural Law," 142. Strauss's recurring formulation, "It is not *entirely* clear whether *p* is the case," is often code for, "*p* is not the case, but I'm not going to argue the point here." Regarding the sentence quoted above, it is unlikely (to say the least) that Strauss thought it was *partially* "clear that human reason can establish the fact of such punishment."

This criticism, also made by Jaffa, is expanded by Fr. Fortin.[4] It is defective but revealing. The criticism goes roughly as follows (combining the observations of Jaffa and Fr. Fortin, who are in basic agreement here). According to Thomas, law must be promulgated.[5] Moreover "in all laws whatsoever (*in quibuslibet legibus*), men are induced to observe the precepts by means of punishments and rewards."[6] Natural law, if it is indeed law, must meet these two criteria. But natural law, as distinct from human law, can be promulgated and imposed on men only by God, and just rewards and punishments can be meted out only by God, if not in this life then in another one. Thomas's natural law teaching therefore presupposes the existence of a providential God, and it presupposes the immortality of the human soul too. That is to say, it presupposes revealed theology. It is therefore not accessible to man as man.

Fr. Fortin tries to show that the precepts of the second table of the Decalogue, which Thomas claims belong properly to natural law, actually presuppose the precepts of the first table. Fr. Fortin argues this point in general terms: it pertains to the nature of law that it be enforceable, enforceable by God when it cannot be enforced by man.[7] But, Fr. Fortin claims, "such a view is clearly predicated on the assumption of a divine nature that is characterized by will no less than by intellect . . . [T]his view becomes intelligible only within the framework of a providential order in which the words and deeds of individual human beings are known to God and duly rewarded or punished by him."[8] In making this point, Fr. Fortin does not give due emphasis to the fact that the providence and justice of God is not a matter of revelation and faith for Thomas. If any theology is being presupposed here—and I shall argue that it is not—it is rational theology and not revealed theology. Thomas thinks he can prove that God is providential and just.

It is possible that Fr. Fortin accepts Thomas's proof of the existence of God as *esse tantum* and *actus purus*, but is not persuaded by the further arguments that Thomas makes about God. In the *Summa Theologiae* Thomas attempts to demonstrate in terms of natural reason not only that God exists, but that he knows all things, including evil things, singular things, and even future contingents, that he has will in addition to intellect, and that he is omnipotent, providential, and just.[9] Thomas's later proofs that the human soul is subsistent and incorruptible, and hence according to its nature immortal, and that man can incur a debt of punishment from God do not rely proximally or ultimately on the claims of revelation.[10] They too are demonstrated in

4. Jaffa, *ThAr* 168–71; Fortin," Thomas Aquinas," 264–5; *ATAP* 196–9.

5. *ST* 1–2 q. 90 art. 4.

6. 1–2 q. 99, art. 6 co.

7. *ATAP* 196–7.

8. *ATAP* 197.

9. *ST* 1 q. 2 art. 3; q. 14 art. 6; art. 10–11; q. 19; q. 21 art. 1; q. 22 art. 1–3; q. 25 art. 1–3. See the *Note* appended to Part 1, Ch. 1, Section a, above.

10. 1 q. 75 art. 2; art. 5; art. 6, co.; ad 2. Though, according to Thomas, the intellectual soul is

terms of natural reason. I am not aware of any place where Fr. Fortin shows how, in his opinion, these arguments break down.

There is certainly, for Thomas, a close relation between providence and natural law. It is possible to argue from natural reason's knowledge of the principles of its own operation to the providence of God, since Thomas does not think that natural, finite, human reason, whether speculative or practical, can be produced by any conjunction of sub-rational causes, or that it can produce itself. Straussians may suspect that if they grant the rational character of natural law they will be led *toward rational theology*, which is not exactly where they wish to go. It is for this reason, I suspect, that they argue, most obscurely, that Thomas's teaching on natural law is derived *from revealed theology*. They tend to ignore the actual case that he makes for the existence and content of primary *per se nota* precepts of natural law and secondary precepts that can be deduced from them *statim* or *modica consideratione*. Thomas makes this case, as we have seen in in Part 1, Chapter 2 above, without appeal to any theology, revealed or rational.

Douglas Kries makes a comparison between the starting points of ancient and Thomistic natural right theory that has a bearing on the issue of providence.

> The classical approach begins with what is said about right, with everyday opinions that are held about what is just . . . For the classical natural right theorists, one ascends to the knowledge of natural right through dialectics; for Thomas, the knowledge about what is according to nature is a descent, from God, through providence, to the law known by the human conscience, to deduced conclusions about natural law.[11]

Kries's account of the classical approach, which he develops beyond what I have quoted here, is succinct, lucid, and accurate. It could hardly be improved upon. Kries enables us to see more clearly the example that Thomas had before him, and it leads to ask why he chose not to follow it. However, Kries's account of the way in which Thomas departed from his example is misleading.

Thomas certainly gives us the means to argue from God's providence to the existence of natural law. God is providential toward rational creatures in a special way. He provides man with what he needs, including the knowledge of natural law, in order to reach his natural end, though, again, not by a special act of grace but solely by creating him as a rational being in the first place. However, Thomas refrains from making this argument in his treatment of providence in the *Prima Pars*. He seems to have thought that his case for the existence of natural law should not be separated from his account of the content of natural law. The latter would have been out of place in the question on providence, which occurs in the context of Thomas's treatment of God, not in his

naturally immortal because naturally indestructable, it can be supernaturally reduced to nothing by the divine will, just as it was supernaturally created out of nothing by the divine will.

11. "Natural Law Theory of Thomas Aquinas," 216–217.

treatment of man.[12] Moreover, knowing that God is providential does not enable us to infer anything of substance about the content of natural law, unless we spell out the order of human inclinations, which is just what Thomas does in the *Prima Secundae* q. 94 art. 2. There he makes his case for the content of natural law, as distinct from its definition, by appeal not to God's providence, nor to his authority, nor even to his existence, but to the *ratio boni*: good is what all desire (*bonum est quod omnia appetunt*).[13]

Regarding the procedure of the ancients, Thomas would say that a dialectical ascent from commonly held opinions will have to rely at least implicitly on principles, especially if, as Kries says, "such opinions when examined through friendly disputation with a philosopher, are almost always found to be self-contradictory."[14] The dialectical ascent, then, necessarily relies on the speculative principle of non-contradiction.[15] For otherwise, neither the philosopher nor the individual with whom he is in disputation would be the least bit troubled on being shown that a particular opinion leads to a contradiction. In questions of right, justice, or morality, there will likely be an implicit reliance on one or more practical principles too. There will likely be an implicit reliance on the first principle of practical reason: good is to be done and pursued, and evil avoided. And there may be even an explicit reliance on the precept of natural law that prohibits offending others. If there is place in the Platonic dialogues or in Aristotle's ethical and political writings where either of these principles, both identified in q. 94 art. 2, is explicitly called into question, I do not know where it is. And, to say the least of it, the other primary precept of natural law identified in q. 94 art. 2—that one should avoid ignorance—silently motors everything that Socrates says and everything that Plato and Aristotle write.[16] Kries is correct in calling attention to the difference between the procedure of Plato and Aristotle, on the one hand, and that of Thomas on the other. In their investigation of natural right and natural law, the ancients begin with generally accepted opinions, Thomas with identifiable principles. That one way of proceeding is superior to the other can be determined only by familiarizing oneself as thoroughly as possible with both of them.

12. Thomas could have presented his natural law teaching in the context of his treatment of man in *ST* 1, right after his account of practical reason, *synderesis* and conscience in q. 79 art. 11–13. He chose however, to postpone his treatment of natural law until after he had spoken more comprehensively about man, especially about man's happiness, will, habits, virtues, and vices, in *ST* 1–2., and in the context of law in general, which sets the stage for his treatment of grace, to which he turns immediately after his treatment of law.

13. In the following chapter, I shall compare Thomas's formulation of this principle with Aristotle's formulation in the first two sentences of the *Nicomachean Ethics*.

14. "Natural Law Theory in Thomas Aquinas," 216.

15. I have argued this point at greater length in "Socrates Exhortation to Follow the *Logos*," 118–122.

16. In Ch. 9, Section b, i, below, I show that Socrates makes ample use of the concept of obligation.

It is because Thomas's argument for God's providence and his case for natural law are advanced independently of each other that they illuminate each other. But it is because they illuminate each other that they can be easily conflated, to the detriment, especially, of a proper understanding of the latter. Thomas carefully avoids letting theological claims, including even claims that he thinks are rationally demonstrable, obscure the evidence for—indeed, the self-evidence for—the existence and content of natural law. This evidence is available to natural reason in reflecting on its own operation, granted that the full meaning of natural law as expressed in its definition cannot be fully comprehended without recourse to rational theology. Thomas's presentation of the foundational principles of natural law in q. 94 art. 2, then, presciently meets Strauss's requirement, made seven centuries later, that "natural law or natural right . . . be kept independent of theology and its controversies." Thomas knows what he is doing.

SECTION B. THE PROMULGATION OF NATURAL LAW

Fr. Fortin does not show that or how the moral precepts of the Decalogue, when construed as precepts of *natural* law, derive their obligatory character from belief in the revealed God of the Bible rather than immediately from the nature of reason itself, as Thomas attempts to show. Let us consider Thomas's full definition of law as such.

> Law is nothing else than an ordinance of reason for the common good, promulgated by him who has care of the community.[17]

Fr. Fortin remakes a point that Jaffa had made. If natural law is known by promulgation, it must be known to be promulgated.[18] Fair enough. But then both men infer that if it is known to be promulgated it must be known to be promulgated by God. Being promulgated, however, means no more than being made publicly known and, in the case of natural law, being made known to man as such. And this is just what natural reason accomplishes. After giving his definition of law, Thomas expressly responds to the objection that natural law does not need promulgation.

> Natural law is promulgated by the very fact that God instilled it into man's mind so as to be known by him *naturally*.[19]

17. 1–2 q. 90, art. 4, co., adopting the Pegis translation, but without "the" in front of "care." "Et sic quatuor praedictis potest colligi definitio legis, quae nihil est aliud quam quaedam rationis ordinatio ad bonum commune, ab eo qui curam communitatis habet, promulgata."

18. *ATAP* 197; *ThAr* 221, n. 9.

19. *ST* 1–2 q. 90 art. 4, ad 1 (emphasis added). Thomas West thinks that only "a commandment in words issued by a lawgiver" is strictly speaking a law (*Critique of the 'Straussian' Critique*, 33). A primary precept of natural law is a commandment of natural reason, which is common to all men. As such, it is not *originally* expressed in the words of any particular language, such as Hebrew, Greek, or Latin. Hence it is not literally a *sentence*. Nevertheless, in its original constitution by reason it is a *proposition* (ST 1–2 q. 90 art. 1, ad 2; q. 94 art. 1, co.). And so it can be *subsequently* expressed in

If one is not convinced by this response and insists on the public character of promulgation, Thomas has a follow-up response.

> The first common precepts of the law of nature are self-evident to one who possesses natural reason, and do not need to be promulgated (*et promulgatione non indigent*).[20]

Thomas here disposes of the first part of the criticism under consideration. Man knows of the primary precepts of natural law by virtue neither of revelation nor of the demonstrations of rational theology that are accomplished by speculative reason, but by virtue of his own reason, If we say that God, as the ultimate source of human reason, is the ultimate promulgator of natural law, we must add that natural reason is the proximate promulgator of natural law. It effects this promulgation whether man believes in God or not.

In *De Veritate*, Thomas says, "Man does not make the law for himself, but through the act of his knowledge, by which he knows a law made by someone else, he is bound to fulfill the law."[21] However, in the *Summa Theologiae*, Thomas says that "*natural* law is something established (or constituted—*constitutum*) by reason, just as a proposition is a work of reason."[22] The clarifying example in the immediate sequel refers not to God but to one who makes (or accomplishes—*agit*) an oration. That is, it refers to a *man*, and the habit of grammar by which he makes his oration. Thomas is unequivocally stating that reason, whether of God or of man, establishes natural law. God, by virtue of his care for "the community," originally establishes it by means of his reason, and man, so to speak, re-establishes it by means of *his* reason. Man does not simply receive natural law.[23] This is an important qualification of the "man does not make the law for himself" formulation in the earlier *De Veritate*. Additionally, Thomas says not

---

the words and sentences of any number of languages. West says, "[T]he law of nature is promulgated in the strict sense only to the wise . . ." (21). But later in his study (60), he quotes the passage where Thomas speaks of precepts "quae sunt prima et communia, quorum non oportet aliam editionem esse nisi quod sunt scripta in ratione naturali quasi per se nota, sicut quod nulli debet homo malefacere, et alia huiusmodi" (ST 1–2 q. 100 art. 3, co.). Thomas makes it quite clear in this article that *these* precepts are known by, indeed are self-evident to, all—hence adequately promulgated—and that it is only the conclusions deduced from them *per diligentem inquisitionem* that are known solely by wise.

20. *ST* 1–2 q 100 art. 4, ad 1.

21. *De Veritate* q. 17, art. 3, ad 1: ". . . homo non facit sibi legem; sed per actum suae cognitionis, qua legem ab alio factam cognoscit, ligatur ad legem implendam." Man as a single individual does not make a law for himself. But natural reason is common to all men. And because it is created by God, its legislation is, ultimately, God's legislation. No man, and no group of men, not even all men taken together, can override this legislation. Nonetheless, it is natural reason itself that makes or, rather, constitutes natural law, as I argue above. See also the following footnote.

22. *ST* 1–2 q. 94, art. 1, co. (emphasis added): ". . . lex naturalis est aliquid per rationem constitutum; sicut etiam propositio est quoddam opus rationis."

23. *ST* 1–2 q. 90 art. 4, ad 1. Germain Grisez states the matter well. "Aquinas does not describe natural law as eternal law passively received in man; he describes it rather as a participation in the eternal law. This participation is necessary precisely insofar as man shares the grand office of providence in directing his own life and that of his fellows." Grisez, 192.

only that all the acts of the virtues are prescribed by natural law, but that "each one's own [!] reason naturally dictates [!] this to him, that he act virtuously."[24]

If we assume a perspective that is "independent of theology and its controversies," natural law does not vanish any more than the principle of non-contradiction vanishes. It continues to be promulgated naturally. Natural law would vanish and cease to be promulgated only if we assumed a perspective independent of reason itself. Heidegger assumed this perspective, as Nietzsche did before him. It is unlikely that Strauss and his followers would wish to do the same.

SECTION C. THE QUESTION OF PUNISHMENT

Fr. Fortin's criticism is not limited to the issue of promulgation but, as noted above, focuses on punishment as well. He tries to connect the concept of punishment for infractions of natural law with an understanding of God that necessarily presupposes belief in revelation. Fr. Fortin acknowledges that Thomas does not mention punishment or rewards in his treatment of natural law.[25] In fact, Thomas does not mention punishment or rewards even in the definition of law as such. His statement that "a precept of law has coercive force" is referred back to an article entitled, "Whether the reason of any man is competent to make laws." There Thomas says that "law should have coercive force," and that this power "is held by the whole people or in some public personage."[26] The context is human law, as both the title and the *corpus* of this article make clear; and the context of the preceding quotations is the Old Law. In neither case is Thomas speaking of natural law as such.

Still, Thomas does say that punishment is bound up with the violation of the precepts of "any law whatsoever."[27] So a question indeed arises as to how this works in the case of natural law. Fr. Fortin, like Strauss and Jaffa, too quickly assumes that punishment for violating precepts of natural law, if it is not inflicted by man, can only be inflicted by God. In discussing whether the debt of punishment is an effect of sin, Thomas says something that sheds much light on how practical reason provides for a punishment, a natural punishment, distinct from both human and divine punishment.

> [M]an can be punished with a threefold punishment, corresponding to the three orders to which the human will is subject. For *in the first place* [!] a

24. See q. 94 art. 3, c: "dictat enim hoc natualiter unicuique propria ratio, ut virtuose agat." Needless to say, one man's own reason does not differ from another man's own reason with regard to the *principles* according to which it operates. The principles, whether of speculative or of practical reason, are common. Thomas, moreover, could hardly be more explicit in his insistence that law pertains to reason by virtue of the fact that reason commands. *ST* 1–2 q. 90, art. 1, *sed contra*, ad 3; q. 91, art, 3 co.; q. 92 art. 2 co. See also 1–2, q. 9 art. 1, ad 3; q. 17 art. 1, co.; art. 2, ad 2.

25. *ATAP* 196.

26. 1–2 q. 100 art. 9; 1–2 q. 90 art. 3, ad. 2.

27. 1–2, q. 99 art. 6, co.

> man's nature is subject to the order of his *own* [!] reason (*Primo quidem enim subditur humana natura ordini propriae rationis*) . . ."[28]

After speaking of the second and third orders to which the human will is subject, namely human government and divine government, and after specifying that sin is a disturbance of these orders, Thomas continues,

> Wherefore [the sinner] incurs a threefold punishment: one, inflicted by himself, namely the remorse of conscience (*unam quidem a seipso, quae est conscientiae remorsus*), another, inflicted by man, and a third inflicted by God.

Natural law does not coerce by depriving man of free choice.[29] Nonetheless it does provide for a punishment that is peculiarly its own, namely, the remorse of conscience. This provision for punishment suffices to bring natural law, considered independently of human and divine law, into perfect accord with Thomas's general claim that punishment pertains to law.[30] To be sure, some people are not deterred from violation of natural law by the prospects of a gnawing conscience.[31] But, by the same token, some people are not deterred from the violation of human law by the prospects of temporal punishment, or from violation of divine law by the prospects of eternal punishment.

One can count on an objection being raised here to the effect that remorse is just a colorful name for the fear of having incurred God's wrath. And, of course, someone who feels remorse for having done something wrong and unworthy of himself may well fear that God will punish him for his wrongdoing. But the objection gets the order of remorse and fear backwards. Such a person would not fear punishment from God unless he first thought he had done something wrong and unworthy of himself. And it is that thought that gives rise to the remorse of conscience (in a person who still has a conscience; I am not speaking of hardened criminals or *Übermenschen* who live

28. 1–2 q. 87 art. 1, co (emphasis added). See q. 72 art. 4, co., where Thomas also speaks of the threefold order in man, and argues that a man can sin against himself, as well as against God and other men. According to Thomas's terminology, sin is a bad act, an act typically springing out of vice, which is in turn a bad habit. q. 71 art. 3. Cf. q. 100 art. 5, arg. 1; ad 1. The prime instance of a sin against oneself is failing to love oneself properly. A precept has the character of a duty (*debitum*); and one has duties to oneself as well as to God and to other men.

29. *ST* 1–2 q. 58 art. 2, co. Fr. Lehrberger argues persuasively that, for Thomas, punishment pertains not to the very essence of law but, rather, to its execution, and for this reason is not included in the actual definition of law ("Crime without Punishment," 247). Although Fr. Lehrberger refers in a note to the passage we have been considering, from 1–2 q. 87 art. 1, saying that "[v]ice or sin violates the order of reason" and hence "is punished by the sting of conscience" (256 n. 43), he gives somewhat less emphasis to that passage than I do.

30. 1–2 q. 99 art. 6, co.

31. In 1–2 q. 91 art. 4, co., Thomas acknowledges that human law cannot punish all evils. One could say something similar about natural law, but with a qualification: the more stock a human being places in his natural reason, the more he will feel the pain of remorse for his transgressions of natural law, even for minor transgressions. If, for whatever cause, a human being feels no remorse at all even for major transgressions of the natural law, and cannot be brought to feel remorse for them, then he is irrational.

in Olympian serenity beyond good and evil). The person who feels remorse for having disobeyed a precept of natural law is immediately aware of having violated the order of his own reason. The awareness that he has violated God's will as well is subsequent to this immediate awareness. Even if the awareness of the one occurs at the same time as the awareness of the other, they are not the same awareness. For it is possible not to believe in God, or in a God who punishes, and still feel remorse. Remorse in the natural order of things is simply the pain that a rational being rightly feels for being in conflict with reason, with his *own* natural reason in its practical operation, whether he affirms that God exists or not.[32]

Thomas's understanding of a natural punishment that the sinner inflicts on himself by virtue of being naturally subject to the order of his own reason makes sense of a claim that we considered earlier and that Fr. Fortin must have found puzzling: "the moral precepts [of the Decalogue] have their efficacy [!] from the very dictate of natural reason, *even if they had never been stated in the* [Old] *Law*."[33] The formulation that "the good man obeys the dictates of his own reason," which is certainly Thomas's position, could appear to be undermined by his saying that "a law is imposed on others."[34] There is, however, no irresolvable tension between these two formulations. From the perspective of rational theology, natural law is simply the way the rational creature participates in the eternal law, and both laws are expressions of reason, human and divine respectively. From this perspective, God can be said to impose natural law on man by making him rational in the first place.

Even apart from the perspective of theology, rational or revealed, natural law can still be said to be imposed on others. For when Thomas elaborates his claim that "a law is nothing else than a dictate of reason in the one ruling (*in praesidente*) by whom the subdued are governed," he offers a telling example.

> Now the virtue of anything subdued consists in its being well subdued to that by which it is governed; and so we see that the virtue of the irascible and concupiscible [powers of the soul] consists in their being well obedient to reason.

32. A person can feel remorse for violating divine, i.e., revealed, law. In that case, he has to believe in divine revelation. But a person can also feel remorse for violating natural law. In that case, he need not, though he most certainly can, believe in divine revelation.

33. 1–2 q. 100 art. 11, co. (emphasis added). Fr. Fortin is aware that "for Thomas, the precepts of the Decalogue belong to the natural law and can be known without divine revelation . . ." "Natural Law and Social Justice" (223–41, in *CCPO*), 230. It is their efficacy, and perhaps their obligatory character as well, prior to being presented as divine commands that he finds dubious. See "The New Rights Theory and the Natural Law," in *Classical Christianity*, 278. Fr. Fortin does not cite a text in support of his claim that "Thomas argues that the precepts of the second table depend on the precepts of the first table for their effectiveness," a claim that is in fact undercut by the text quoted above. To repeat what was said earlier, the presentation of the precepts of the second table (at Sinai) *as divinely revealed commands* endowed them with a majesty, and hence with *increased* efficacy, for the believer. Nonetheless, even apart from this revelation they had and continue to have a measure of efficacy, as Thomas says, *ex ipso dictamine naturalis rationis*.

34. See Jaffa, *ThAr* 221 n. 9; see *ST* 1–2 q. 90, art. 4.

> And in this way, the virtue of every subject consists in his being well subjected to his ruler . . .[35]

Natural law "is imposed on others" in just this way: it is imposed by reason on the other parts of the soul. The comparison of the rule of reason over the irascible and concupiscible powers of the soul to the rule of a prince over his subjects is not a flight of fancy for Thomas, and it is not restricted to the above passage. It is a recurring analogy, in which the two types of rule illuminate each other, for Thomas as for Plato and Aristotle before him.[36]

Fr. Fortin, like Jaffa, leaves one with the impression that he thinks a human being need not feel obligated to obey even a dictate of his own reason, maybe that a human being need not feel obligated at all, unless he is convinced that he will receive some kind of extrinsic reward for doing so or punishment imposed from without for not doing so.[37] Regarding human law, Thomas says that it derives its force (*vis*) and its character as law (*ratio legis*) from being directed to the common welfare; if it is not so directed, it lacks the force of obligation (*virtus obligandi*).[38] It does not derive this force primarily, much less solely, from the promise of extrinsic reward or the threat of

35. *ST* 1–2 q. 92, art. 1, co.: "Cuiuslibet autem subditi virtus est ut bene subdatur ei a quo gubernatur: sicut videmus quod virtus irascibilis et concupiscibilis in hoc consistit quod sint bene obedientes rationi. Et per hunc modum virtus cuiuslibet subiecti est ut bene subiiciatur principanti." In commenting on *ST* 1–2 q. 90 art. 4 in *ThAr* 221, fn. 9, Jaffa gives the impression of thinking that Thomas has precluded the kind of governing that he speaks of in 1–2 q. 92, art. 1, co. At any event, he does not comment on this text in his footnote, though it is of considerable relevance to what he says there.

36. *ST* 1 q. 81 art. 3, ad 2; 1–2 q. 9 art. 2, ad 3; q. 58 art. 2, co.; q. 104 art. 1, ad 3; *De Malo* q. 3 art. 9, ad 14; *De Virtute* q. 1, art. 4, co; ad 7 (and compare, for example, *Republic* 441e–443e; note the expression "according to nature" (*kata physin*) and context at 444d5; *Nicomachean Ethics* 1102b13–1103a3; *Politics* 1254b3–10). John Finnis puts the matter well when he observes that, according to Thomas, "passion's sway over reason makes choices culpable not when emotion swallows up or sweeps away reason (rendering one's behavior non-voluntary and sub-human), but rather when emotions make reason their ingenious but corrupted servant" (*AMPLT* 72–78). See *ST* 1–2 q. 6, art. 4–5; q. 15 art. 4, *sed contra*. See *ST* 1–2 q.16 art.4, ad 3. Emotions, or passions, cannot *make* reason their servant unless reason, or the will as the rational appetite, *consents* to be their servant. *ST* 1–2 q. 77 art. 7, co.

37. Jaffa, *ThAr* 222. n. 10; Fortin, *ATAP* 196–9; "Thomas Aquinas" 264–5. I argued above for the following as Thomas's implicit definition of obligation: the effect of reason's command in the presence of two or more goods, not all of which can be chosen (Part 1, Ch. 2, Section c). If reward and, especially, punishment are situated at the core of obligation, which is where Jaffa and Fr. Fortin seem to wish to situate them, then the definition of obligation would have to modified as follows: the effect of the command of the scariest person around in the presence of two or more goods, not all of which can be chosen (or, alternatively, in the presence of a two or more evils, not all of which can be avoided). But this will not work, since it is thinkable that the scariest person around could command me to do something that reason categorically tells me I *ought not* to do. The commands of the scariest person around *simpliciter* are only conditionally obligatory and, as such, refer back to an unconditional obligation, which as such cannot be derived from, or rest on, hope of reward and fear of punishment as its ultimate ground. ("I hope, therefore I ought . . ." How does that work, from the perspective of logic?) For the same reason, obligation cannot be *defined* as that the transgression of which incurs punishment. After all, in the political sphere one can be punished by a scary and wicked ruler not for transgressing an obligation but for fulfilling an obligation.

38. 1–2 q. 96 art. 5, co.

punishment imposed from without. According to Thomas, the force of a human law depends first of all on its justice, its justice depends on its being in accordance with a rule of reason, and the first rule of reason is natural law.[39] There is, moreover, a most intimate connection between natural law and virtue.[40] Thomas recognizes that in the case of those who are "perverted and prone to vice," coercion (*coactio*) and the threat of punishment can play a role in leading to virtue, or can at least lead away from evil-doing. But he argues that, for the rest, admonition (or advice—*monitio*), which he distinguishes from "force and fear," is the better inducement to virtue.[41]

For Thomas, "the precepts of natural law are general and require to be determined . . . They are determined by both human and divine law."[42] The precepts of natu-

39. 1–2 q. 95 art. 2. In "Aquinas's Two Doctrines of Natural Law," Tony Burns argues that the *Summa Theologiae* contains two irreconcilable teachings on natural law. The first teaching is the familiar one. The second teaching is essentially that of legal positivism. According to Thomas, some human laws are just and some are unjust. The latter have more the character of violence than of laws (1–2 q. 96 art. 4). And yet it is human authority, or the positive law of the land, that determines what actually counts as murder, theft, or adultery (ST 1–2 q. 100, art. 8, ad 3). Burns sees a contradiction here because he exaggerates the scope and autonomy that he thinks Thomas accords to human authority. "Aquinas assumes that the decisions which are made by those who are responsible for the positive legislation of a particular society with respect to the specific interpretation of the secondary precepts of natural law are *quite arbitrary* when considered from the standpoint of morality . . . [F]or Aquinas the definitions of moral concepts like murder, theft and adultery which are provided by the positive law of any society are, morally speaking, *a matter of complete indifference*" (937–8, emphasis added). Burns underestimates the extent to which, in Thomas's view, human legislation—apart from such morally insignificant matters as which side of the road to drive on—is or should be guided by consideration of natural law. That is, after all, the precondition for deriving human law from natural law (1–2 q. 95 art. 2). What Burns sees as arbitrariness and complete indifference is, in fact, judgment, a better appreciation of which would not have led him to attribute to Thomas an inconsistent conception of the relationship between natural law and human law. See Part 1, Ch. 1, Section c, above.

40. 1–2 q. 94, art. 3; cf. q. 96 art. 3.

41. 1–2 q. 90 art. 3, ad 2; q. 95 art. 1, co. and ad 1. The context in both articles is *human* law. Extrapolating from what Thomas says about punishment in the *corpus* of the latter article, though without sufficiently attending to his distinction between *admonitiones*, on the one hand, and *vis et metus* on the other, E. A. Goerner writes, "Law, whether human or divine, habituates men to avoiding evil and doing good *for fear of punishment*" ("The Bad Man's View of Thomistic Natural Right," 109, emphasis in the original). This claim rests on a disjunction, "whether human or divine," that is not exclusive: natural law (eternal law, too) is not identical with either human or divine (i.e., revealed) law. Goerner's focus on punishment leads him to probe beneath the definition of natural law that Thomas gives on the surface of his text—*participatio legis aeternae in rationali creatura*—to what he seems to think is a more profound if less exalted definition, which the careful reader is meant to discern: "[N]atural law is the bad man's view of natural right" (117). Robert Sokolowski writes that "there seem to be indications in the Straussian oral tradition that Aquinas is more truly a philosopher than a believer" (*The God of Faith and Reason*, 161). In his review of Fr. Sokolowski's book, Fr. Fortin responds to this remark. "[T]o my knowledge [Strauss] never questioned the sincerity of Aquinas's religious beliefs." On noting Strauss's interest in how Thomas couched his disagreements with some of his Christian predecessors, Fr. Fortin adds, "This is not to suggest, however, that he regarded Aquinas as an esoteric writer" (311–12). For an interesting intra-Straussian dialogue regarding the relation of punishment to Thomistic natural law, see the exchange between Professor Goerner and Fr. Fortin in *The Review of Politics*, Vol. 45, No. 3 (Jul. 1983) 443–9.

42. 1–2 q. 99 art. 3, ad 2; cf. q. 91 art. 3, co.; ad 1; q. 99 art. 4, co.

ral law regarding our external acts relative to other men are either reiterated or more narrowly determined by human law. They are enforced by human law, and infractions are punished without any special supernatural assistance. But the precepts of natural law are reiterated or more narrowly determined by divine law also, and transgressors are liable to punishment by God himself. Because the acts of virtue are of the natural law, because "human law could not sufficiently curb and direct interior acts," which "pertain to the perfection of virtue," and because "human law cannot punish or forbid all evil deeds . . . it was necessary that divine law should supervene." [43]

According to Fr. Fortin, if natural law does not provide for punishment, it is not really law, and if it does provide for punishment, it is not really natural. But, in addition to the punishment for infractions of natural law that is naturally provided for by remorse, punishment is also provided for by the further determination of natural law by means of divine and human law. Determination of natural law, whether by divine law or by human law, does not compromise the naturalness of natural law considered by itself. It does not compromise the evidence in favor of its intrinsic rationality and it does not compromise its efficacy, that is, its properly obligatory force. The determinations accomplished by human law and divine law compensate for what is indeterminate in natural law. But that means that not only human law, but divine law too, presupposes natural law, just as Thomas says, and not the reverse.[44] In this way, as happens also in the natural longing for wisdom, natural reason "points to" the need for revelation, though without thereby generating a logical proof of revelation, and without logically presupposing it in the slightest.

43. 1–2 q. 91 art. 4, co. (The *necessity* of this supervening—if it means more than just a need on our part for such supervening—can only be asserted from the perspective of revelation, divine law being revealed law. We are unable to know by natural reason that there has ever *actually* been a revealed law, much less that there has *necessarily* been revealed law.) See 2–2 q. 22 art. 1, ad 1.

44. *ST* 1–2 q. 95 art. 2; q. 94 art. 6, ad 2; q. 99 art. 2, ad 1. Cf. *ST* 1 q. 2 art. 2, ad 1.

Chapter 7

Criticisms Advanced by Michael Zuckert

Michael Zuckert's task in his article, "The Fullness of Being: Thomas Aquinas and the Modern Critique of Natural Law," is "to re-open an investigation into the grounds and adequacy" of the rejection of Thomas's conception of natural law by the early modern political philosophers.[1] Given this announcement, one might be led to expect a defense of Thomas's teaching against the criticisms of the moderns. This, however, is not quite the result of Zuckert's investigation. That his real intent is not defense but, rather, criticism is signaled in the abstract that prefaces his article. There Zuckert says that, though Thomas does have a response to his modern critics, "the response pushes the ultimate philosophical question back to the issue of the validity of his natural theology." He comes to this conclusion on the basis of his interpretation of q. 94, art. 2 and what he takes to be its unstated assumptions. Zuckert is to be commended for seeing, as Strauss apparently did not, and as few if any other Straussians do, that this article has to be studied thoroughly by anyone who wishes to take serious issue with Thomas's natural law teaching.

In working through q. 94 art. 2, Zuckert makes a good case for the intrinsic evidence of the first principle of speculative reason, namely, the principle of non-contradiction, which Thomas treats in his commentary on Aristotle's *Metaphysics*, and which he briefly speaks to early in q. 94 art. 2. Zuckert also speculates cogently on why Thomas argues for the unity of natural law. In addition, he nicely frames the distinction between Thomas and his early modern critics as turning on the former's "objectivist" understanding of the good vs. the latter's "subjectivist" understanding of the good. In speaking of the difference between Thomas Aquinas's and John Locke's estimation of our natural inclinations, Zuckert correctly points out that the sub-rational desires,

1. *FB* 31.

the desires that John Locke regards as most natural to us, pertain to natural law in Thomas's understanding "only by being ordered, governed, or 'regulated by reason.'"[2]

Zuckert says that Locke, in his *Questions*, answers "No," to the question he raises, "Can the law of nature be known from the natural inclinations of man?" But Zuckert says that "Aquinas answers Locke's question in affirmative."[3] This is misleading, though only slightly so. Thomas does not hold that knowledge of the natural inclinations by themselves gives us knowledge of natural law. Knowledge of natural law, that is, knowledge of its morally obligating precepts, is constituted both by our awareness of our natural inclinations *and* our cognition of the first principle of practical reason. For inclinations as such are not precepts, and morally obligating precepts cannot be found in them considered solely by themselves. Zuckert does recognize that the precepts of natural law are commands, but he seems not to recognize that the only thing resembling a command in the corpus of q. 94 art. 2 prior to its concluding sentences is the first principle of practical reason—good is to be done and pursued and evil avoided. And even this is not actually a command, that is, a proposition declaring an obligation, since it is naturally necessitating rather than morally obligating.[4]

Zuckert makes a false distinction between the first principle of practical reason and the first precept of law.[5] He may have been misled, as others have been, by the English Dominican Fathers' translation of the *Summa Theologiae* or by Anton Pegis's revision of their translation, both of which are ambiguous on this point. As Germain Grisez makes clear, however, the Latin cannot support a distinction between the first principle of practical reason and the first precept of law.[6] The proposition, "good is what all things desire (or strive for—*appetunt*)" is not the first principle of practical reason. It is the *ratio boni*. Zuckert's repeated references to this proposition as "the first principle of practical reason" obscures much of what he has to say about it. In the interest of precision and to avoid confusion, I refer in this chapter as elsewhere to the proposition, "Good is what all things desire," as the "*ratio boni*," and I refer to the

2. *FB* 39–43; 33.

3. *FB* 31.

4. See Part 1, Chapter 2, above.

5. *FB* 36.

6. In footnote 20 of his essay, "The First Principle of Practical Reason," Grisez takes issue with D. O'Donoghue, who seems also to have identified the first principle of practical reason with the *ratio boni* rather than with the first precept of law. Grisez writes, "However, Aquinas actually says: 'Et ideo primum principium in ratione practica est quod fundatur supra rationem boni, quae est, *Bonum est quod omnia appetunt*.'S.T., 1–2 q. 94, a. 2, c. Fr. O'Donoghue must read 'quae' as if it refers to 'primum principium [neuter nominative singular],' whereas [because the relative pronoun *quae*, with *est*, is feminine nominative singular] it can only refer to 'rationem [feminine accusative singular] boni.' The *primum principium* is identical with the first precept mentioned in the next line of text, while the *ratio boni* is not a principle of practical reason but a quasi-definition of 'good,' and as such a principle of understanding." (Italics as in Grisez's text, except for those in the bracketed clarifications that I have added).

proposition "Good is to be done and pursued, and evil avoided," as the "first principle of practical reason [= the first precept of law]."[7]

Zuckert's chief criticism of q. 94 art. 2 is that Thomas's attempt "to set the phenomena of human desire and human action into the much broader context of all natural motion . . . introduces a systematic and potentially problematic equivocation in his treatment of human action."[8] Zuckert locates the "equivocation" at that point in q. 94 art. 2 where Thomas says that "good is the first thing grasped by practical reason, which is ordered to doing (*opus*), for every agent acts for an end, which has the aspect of a good (*habet rationem boni*)." Zuckert does not deny that a rational agent acts for an end, but he expresses reservations about Thomas's more general claim that all things act for an end. He then turns from q. 94, art. 2, to Thomas's interpretation, in his commentary on the *Nicomachean Ethics*, of the opening two sentences of that work. According to Zuckert, Thomas takes an Aristotelian passage, "which when most naturally read is limited to human agents, and gives it a universal meaning." Zuckert elaborates this criticism in an important paragraph that deserves to be quoted in its entirety.

> [Thomas's] universalizing interpretation is almost surely false to Aristotle's text, for Aristotle begins by speaking of human arts and human actions, which, as intentional actions, surely do posit some good as the end of action. That observation justifies the conclusion that good is what all desire if all means all men. It does not justify the related claim about all beings. Aquinas's interpretation makes Aristotle's claim equivocal and philosophically suspect. His own version in *Summa Theologiae* has the same equivocation he imports into Aristotle. Aquinas is speaking of practical reason, that is, the agent rationality of rational agents, and in that context the observation that rational agents act for some good is precisely the same as the observation with which Aristotle opens the *Ethics*. Furthermore, it has the same evidence justifying the conclusion Aristotle drew: good is what all rational agents seek. But in that form, the principle is open to the subjectivist interpretation [the object is good because it striven for] as readily as to the objectivist [interpretation—the object is striven for because it is good]. Aquinas definitively forecloses the subjectivist [interpretation] in reading: all things are guided to the good as the object of their motions and strivings. However, he has no right to this conclusion on the basis of observations about the practical reason in action; it does not follow from a phenomenology of human action."[9]

7. On the nomenclature of principles and precepts, see above, Part 1, Ch. 2, Section a.

8. *FB* 40.

9. *FB* 40–41. For Zuckert's distinction between "the 'objectivist' and the 'subjectivist' versions of the relation between love or desire, on the one hand, and the good, on the other," see *FB* 39: "is the object striven for good because it is striven for, or is it striven for because it is good, independent of its being striven for (subjective and objective, respectively)?"

Zuckert continues, "To say that the argument as presented thus far in the *Summa* is not valid is, of course, not to say that Thomas's position is simply unsupportable." If I understand him, Zuckert thinks that the argument that is not valid consists of those sentences in 1–2 q. 94 art. 2, where Thomas introduces the *ratio boni*, namely, "*Bonum est quod omnia appetunt*." Presumably, the "conclusion," to which Zuckert thinks Thomas has no right, is "all things are guided to the good as the object of their motions and strivings."

The first question that arises here is a logical one: why does Zuckert call this proposition "a conclusion"? In the article under consideration, Thomas does not present the *ratio boni* as the conclusion of an argument.[10] His formulation, "Good is what all things desire," is simply his attempt to clarify what is meant by "good." It is a further spelling out of his much earlier claim that the good is being, though under the aspect (*ratio*) of appetible (just as the true is being, though under the aspect of intelligible).[11] And the first principle of practical reason [= the first precept of law], which Thomas presents in q. 94 art. 2 immediately after the *ratio boni*, is not the conclusion of an argument either.

Zuckert is entirely right in pointing out that Thomas does not deduce the first principle of practical reason [= the first precept of law] from the *ratio boni*. He cannot in fact deduce it, nor does he try to. As I noted in Part 1, the former is a simple declarative statement, the latter a more complex gerundive (though it is not, as Zuckert says on the following page, an "Ought," for the reasons I gave in Part 1, Chapter 2, above, and have repeated several times since then). Whereas the *ratio boni* is a proposition of speculative reason describing action, the first principle of practical reason [= the first precept of law] is a proposition of practical reason generating and sustaining action. There is no way to deduce the latter from the former. Moreover, if the first principle of practical reason [= the first precept of law] could be deduced (or demonstrated) from the *ratio boni*, it would not itself be *per se notum* (hence indemonstrable) as Thomas says it is. Zuckert himself seems to recognize that this principle is self-evident, for he says quite convincingly, "when we call something 'good,' when it is a matter of action, we mean [!] nothing other than what is sought in action, or worth seeking in action."[12] If reason is going to generate and direct action, it cannot leave it at the (speculative) proposition that all things seek the good. It must also make the (practical) proposition that good is to be done and pursued, and evil avoided. The fact that, unlike the *ratio boni*, "there is nothing like the first precept of natural law [= the first principle of practical reason] in [Aristotle's] ethical thinking" indeed "pinpoints," as Zuckert says,

10. Actually, it is Aristotle who, in the first two sentences of the *Nicomachean Ethics*, makes a dubious inference. Aristotle's argument (an enthymeme) is from the teleology of human actions to the teleology of all things. This argument could, however, be more rhetorical than inferential, since the move is actually from "it seems" (*dokei*) in the first sentence to "therefore they have well-declared" (*dio kalōs apephēnanto*) in the second sentence. But see *Nicomachean Ethics* 1172b35–1173a1; 1099b21–23.

11. Part 1, Ch. 2, Section a, above.

12. *FB* 41.

"the fact that Aristotle is not a theorist of natural law."[13] It also suggests, let it be said, that Aristotle might not have thought with as much penetration about the functioning of practical reason as Thomas did.

The second question, the more serious one, is why Zuckert thinks that Thomas has misinterpreted or surreptitiously universalized Aristotle's claim in the second sentence of the *Nicomachean Ethics*. The first two sentences of Aristotle's text are as follows.

> Every art and every investigation, and likewise every action and choice, seems to aim at some good. Therefore they [impersonal] have well-declared the good [to be] that at which all things aim.[14]

In commenting on the second sentence, Thomas says that the only way an entity lacking in cognition could be said to seek or aim at something is if that entity is moved toward it by something cognitive.[15] For example, an arrow can be said to aim at, or even seek, its target—but only through the thinking agency of an archer. That is the easy case. But to make sense of how an inanimate being that is not the product of human art, say, a rock that through whatever cause has been tossed into the air, aims at returning, or seeks to return, to the earth (as the center of a finite and spherical cosmos), Thomas has to say that it does so through the cognitive agency of the divine intellect. Zuckert notes that here Thomas incorporates into his interpretation something that is not present in Aristotle's text, and may well falsify Aristotle's intention. But Aristotle's claim is problematic, since it is not easy to understand why *he* would say that "all things" (neuter plural—*panta*), including things lacking in any awareness whatsoever, aim at the good.[16] He does claim in the *Metaphysics* that the heavens and all nature, and hence all natural movement, *depend* on the divine intellect.[17] But the agency of the divine intellect, as Aristotle describes it in the *Metaphysics*, operates as a final rather than an efficient cause. And the character of that agency is in need of more explication than Aristotle offers, given his insistence that not only the heavenly bodies

13. *FB* 42.

14. *Nicomachean Ethics* 1094a2: *Pasa technē kai pasa methodos, homoiōs de praksis te kai proairesis, agathou tinos ephiesthai dokei. dio kalōs apephēnanto t'agathon hou pant' ephietai.*

15. *Sententia Libri Ethicorum.*, lib.1 lect. 1 n. 11.

16. If Aristotle had meant to say that the good is only what all *men* desire, he would likely have employed the masculine plural *pantes* (or *pantes anthrōpoi*; compare the first sentence of the *Metaphysics*), rather than the neuter plural *panta*. Similarly, if it had been his intention to restrict the good solely to what [human] art, investigation, action, and choice all aim at, he would likely have expressed this restriction by making use of the feminine plural *pasai* (which would have corresponded to the feminine singular *pasa* already occurring immediately before *technē* and immediately before *methodos*), since each of these four nouns happens to be feminine in Greek. There is a comparable use of the neuter plural *panta* (*pant' ephietiai*) in relation to *agathon* at *Nicomachean Ethics* 1172b35–1173a1.

17. *Metaphysics* 1072b14–31.

and man, but nature in general, even as operative in things devoid of cognition, acts for the sake of something.[18]

The formulation in the second sentence of the *Nicomachean Ethics* that all things aim at the good, a formulation that Aristotle says has been well-declared, calls then for a justification. Thomas tries to offer one. And because he has a powerful argument of his own for the divine intellect, not just as final cause, but as first efficient cause of the being of everything in the world, and thereby also for the motion of everything that moves, he attempts to justify Aristotle's claim in light of these arguments. What he says may not be a good exegesis of Aristotle's text. But it is arguably a good defense, it is arguably the only defense, of Aristotle's claim—assuming that Aristotle was serious when he said that "they have well-declared the good [to be] that at which all things aim."[19]

Aristotle's teleological formulation in the second sentence of the *Nicomachean Ethics* is then every bit as universal as is Thomas's. Zuckert points out that Aristotle's formulation occurs in a passage concerning human actions. But the same is true of Thomas's formulation of the *ratio boni* in both q. 94 art. 2. And his interpretation of Aristotle's formulation in the first lecture of his commentary on the *Nicomachean Ethics* is also in the context of human actions. In the paragraph quoted in full above, Zuckert actually acknowledges this sameness: "Aquinas is speaking of practical reason . . . [His] observation that rational agents act for some good is precisely the same as the observation with which Aristotle opens the *Ethics*. Furthermore it has the same evidence justifying the conclusion that Aristotle drew."[20] So it is difficult to see exactly what Zuckert is objecting to in Thomas's interpretation of the opening two sentences of the *Nicomachean Ethics*, as distinct from Thomas's attempt to make sense of how it could be true in the case not only of animate things, but of inanimate things as well, indeed of all things (*panta*), as Aristotle expressly says.

According to Zuckert, "Aquinas's interpretation makes Aristotle's claim equivocal and philosophically suspect." But Zuckert mistranslates or misstates Aristotle's claim as "good is what all rational agents seek," substituting "all rational agents" for Aristotle's "all [things]." Then he says, "But in that form"—presumably the form in which he has just presented Aristotle's "conclusion"—"the principle is as open to the subjectivist interpretation [something is good because we strive for it] as to the

18. *Physics* 199b27–200a34 and *Politics* 1253a9, to cite only two places where Aristotle speaks this way. See also *De Anima* 432b21.

19. For a particularly interesting and, what one might call, "demythologizing" interpretation of Aristotle's teleological claims, see David Bolotin, *An Approach to Aristotle's Physics*, Chapter 2, "The Question of Teleology." Thomas would concur in Bolotin's understanding of the "maturity" of a living being, its "mature form," as the goal or *telos* towards which it grows (47–48); though Thomas includes, as related *telē* in the case of animals, reproduction and care for the young. In Part 3, Ch. 13, below, I shall return to the question of whether the inclination to self-preservation or to persevering in being (Spinoza's *conatus*), in non-living as well as living entities, should also be counted as an inclination toward a *telos*.

20. *FB* 41.

objectivist [we strive for something because it is, or at least appears, good]."[21] According to Zuckert, Thomas forecloses the subjectivist interpretation with his claim that *all* things are guided to the good. In fact, however, Thomas forecloses the subjectivist interpretation with his distinction between choices based on a correct apprehension of what is good and choices based on a faulty apprehension of what is good; and, as Zuckert himself said earlier, on this point "he has the authority of Aristotle behind him."[22] Though we desire everything under the aspect (*ratio*) of good, we can mistake a merely apparent good for what is truly good. In holding this "objectivist view" of the relationship between desire and the good, Thomas does not differ from Plato and Aristotle.[23] To be sure, Thomas's "objectivist view" is reinforced by his understanding of how all things could meaningfully be said to seek, or be guided toward, the good. This general teleological understanding, however, is no more essential to his view that *rational* agents act for the sake of some good, real or apparent, than it is to Aristotle's identical view, which is also reinforced by *his* teleological understanding of nature as a whole. The first thing in the order of discovery is the incontestable fact that human action, properly so called, has a teleological orientation.

Zuckert has not identified the fallacy that he thinks is present in Thomas's case for natural law as a law governing *human* agents and immediately grounded in their natural reason, though he has made it amply clear that he thinks it has something to do with Thomas's (and Aristotle's) conception of the *ratio boni*. It is only when Zuckert turns to the natural inclinations in the latter part of the corpus of q. 94 that he begins to show how he thinks this conception compromises Thomas's case for natural law.

Zuckert takes issue with Thomas's claim that the natural inclination to self-preservation exists in all entities, inanimate entities included. He excuses Thomas for not knowing about sub-atomic particles, "which go out of existence in a nano-second," but he does not excuse him for failing to consider things he did know about, "substances like fire, whose nature it is to consume themselves and go out of being." Moreover, "all animate beings, of which man is one, persist in being for only a time." As Zuckert sees it, Thomas's claim that all entities strive to preserve their own being "is far from being true universally. Indeed it is much closer to being universally false."[24]

There are several points to consider here. In q. 94 art.2, Thomas does not say that every entity preserves its own being or persists in being but, rather, that it strives (*appetit*) to do so. How successful entities, animate as well as inanimate, are in preserving themselves is somewhat beside the point. Thomas agrees with Aristotle in holding that most entities in the sub-lunar sphere are naturally subject to corruption

21. *FB* 41.

22. *FB* 39.

23. *ST* 1–2 q. 77 art. 2, co. *Sententia Libri Ethicorum* lib. 1, lect. 1 n. 10. See Plato, *Gorgias* 466e1; *Meno* 77b8–78b2; Aristotle, *Nicomachean Ethics* 1113a23–25; *Eudemian Ethics* 1235b26–29.

24. *FB* 44.

and decay, and that they can be, and often are, destroyed by other entities.[25] But that does not undercut his claim that as long as they exist they strive to persist in their being. And leaving to one side the issue of subatomic particles—whether they are subject to laws of conservation, and, if so, how—we note that Thomas is simply following Aristotle in denying that it is the nature of fire to consume itself. [26] It is, rather, the nature of fire to consume what is combustible. When suitable material is no longer available for combustion, the fire dies out, just as when food is no longer available for an animate being that being, too, dies. But both strive to preserve themselves by consuming whatever is necessary for their conservation. Even in the case of an object that appears to have no inclination whatsoever, a stone for example, the attempt to move it is met with resistance. As modern physics likes to put it, when one pushes against a wall, the wall pushes back. The wall strives to preserve itself in being, if only in the state in which it *is*.[27] Whatever one makes of that claim, however, one cannot plausibly deny that living entities have an inclination to preserve themselves and, in the case of most animals, their offspring too. Thomas's claim that all entities, animate and inanimate alike, strive to preserve themselves in being may have to be qualified in light of quantum mechanics. It may not be universally true. But Zuckert has given us no good reason to think that "it is much closer to being universally [!] false"—unless he means that we must repudiate our natural experience of the world, including our natural experience of ourselves, in light of particle physics.[28] But this seems unlikely. For Zuckert does not explicitly take issue with Thomas's claim that there are inclinations common to man and animals, or with his claim that we have two inclinations proper to our rational nature, namely, to know the truth about God (whatever that truth is) and to live in society (rather than simply to reproduce and raise our offspring). Zuckert's tacit concession to Thomas on these two classes of inclinations—if concession is what it is—undercuts the chief thrust of his criticism.

In q. 94 art. 2 Thomas claims that man has multiple natural inclinations, that they are directed towards ends that have the character of goods, and that these inclinations and goods have a rank. It is this claim that Zuckert has to take issue with. For it is the conjunction of the ranking of natural human inclinations and goods with the first principle of practical reason (= the first precept of law) that constitutes properly obligating precepts of nature law, obligation being established by the command of

25. For Thomas, the rational soul (*anima intellectiva*) is an exception (ST 1 q. 75 art. 6), as is the active intellect for Aristotle (*De Anima* 430a23; cf. 430a13).

26. *FB* 43. According to Aristotle, fire does not consume itself. It consumes that which can be burnt (*to kauston*), and as long as this is present fire will augment indefinitely (*eis apeiron*). *De Anima* 416a10–18. Thomas follows Aristotle on this matter. *Sententia libri de Anima* lib. 2 l. 8 n. 9; cf. l. 9 nn. 9–10.

27. See Newton, *Principia*, Definition 3.

28. See Edmund Husserl, *Die Krisis der Europäischen Wissenschaften und die Tranzendentale Phänomenologie*, 48–54 [English translation: 48–56]. Cf. Aristotle, *Physics* 193a5–7; and Leo Strauss, "Philosophy as Rigorous Science and Political Philosophy," in *Studies in Platonic Political Philosophy*, 31.

reason in the presence of two or more goods not all of which can be chosen. Though Thomas says that all entities strive to preserve themselves, he does not actually need to make so strong a claim *in his case for natural law*. All he needs to claim is that the inclination to self-preservation is not a specifically rational inclination, and hence not a specifically human inclination, but one that *some* sub-rational entities have as well.

So, even if it were the case that inanimate entities, such as stones and the like, lacked inclinations of any sort, Thomas would still be able to distinguish between inclinations that we share with sub-rational animals and inclinations that are proper to our rational nature. Indeed, even if it were the case that, *per impossibile*, not only inanimate entities, but sub-rational animals too, were lacking in inclinations of any sort, Thomas would still be able to distinguish within the human being, that is, within the sphere that is actually subject to natural law, between inclinations that are sub-rational and inclinations that are rational. This distinction parallels that between physical pleasures and pleasures that are properly intellectual, such as the pleasure that accompanies the awareness that one is making progress in learning.[29]

Zuckert sets the stage for the conclusion of his argument, and justifies the title of his essay, in the following passage.

> God is the being whose essence is identical to his existence, whose being is necessary and eternal. God is the being of beings. The natural inclinations are those inclinations that incline the beings to being, as suited to their nature, including their nature as potential beings. The natural inclinations can be identified as natural because of their imitation of or tendency toward God, the eternal being, the being whose being is the fullness of being and the fulfillment of beings. The inclinations that are the truly natural inclinations are those that embody the truth that "God is the ultimate end of everything." The authentic or natural ends of those inclinations are those that reflect the fullness of being that is God.[30]

There is almost nothing to quarrel with in this passage.[31] Zuckert eloquently shows that Thomas's account of the natural inclinations *agrees with* Thomas's rational theology. He does not, however, show that what Thomas says about the natural inclinations in q. 94 art. 2, especially what he says about the natural inclinations of human beings, is deduced from or logically presupposes his natural theology. Thomas thinks that

29. The inclinations we have that are properly rational are the inclinations toward the true and the good. The satisfaction of these inclinations surely gives rise to a certain pleasure. But knowledge and morality (or integrity), not pleasure, are their proper objects. Pleasure (in varying degrees) only supervenes on the attainment of these objects.

30. *FB* 46.

31. The formulation that God is the "being of beings" could be misunderstood and requires a qualification. God, as the first efficient and exemplary cause of all other beings, is *esse tantum*, *actus purus*, and *maxime ens*. For Thomas, God *is* more perfectly than any other being. But he is not *esse commune*, i.e., being as common to, or predicable, of all beings. See *Super Sent.*, lib. 1 d. 8 q. 1 art. 2; *ST* 1 q. 3 art. 8, co., ad 1; ad 2. Cf. q. 3 art. 4 ad 1; *SCG* 1 cap. 26 n. 5; n.11.

what he says about our inclinations is evident in itself. He does not say or imply, nor does he need to say or imply, that knowing that we have both inclinations proper to our animality and inclinations proper to our rationality presupposes knowledge of, or even belief in, God. We know what our inclinations are through immediate, empirical self-inspection, not through the mediation of metaphysical or theological arguments.

After the passage quoted above, Zuckert writes, "Lying behind Aquinas's identification of the natural inclinations and their objects, therefore, is his doctrine of God . . . Those who argue that God is indispensable for Thomas's doctrine of natural law are perfectly correct." A *definition* of natural law is, as I have said before, absolutely indispensable for a *doctrine* of natural law, and Thomas's definition of natural law as the participation of the eternal law in the rational creature indeed relies on his understanding of God. So Zuckert's statement about what is "lying behind" Thomas's account of our natural inclinations is not simply false. But it is misleading. The natural knowledge we have of the precepts of natural law derives neither from rational theology nor revealed theology.[32] For, to repeat again what needs to be repeated, the precepts of natural law, the primary precepts in particular, are for Thomas *per se nota*, whereas the existence of God and related truths about him, are not *per se nota*, though they are demonstrable.[33] The statements pertaining to our inclinations that Thomas makes in q. 94 art. 2 are that good has the nature of an end; that all [ends] to which man has a natural inclination are naturally apprehended by [his] reason as good; that man's inclinations have an order or rank; that some of them are also possessed by sub-rational beings; and that some are proper to him as a rational being. Not one of these statements is the conclusion of a syllogism, implicit or explicit, that has God as a term in one or another of its premises. Thomas does hold that a comprehensive understanding of good and ends can be achieved only by bringing God into the picture. But that theological understanding of God as the *summum bonum* presupposes an initially non-theological understanding of what good and ends are. Altogether reasonably then, but no less strikingly, does Thomas devote an entire question, consisting of six articles, to the question of the good in general, *before* taking up the question of the goodness of God,[34] thereby anticipating the criticism that Zuckert is making. Again, Thomas knows what he is doing.

32. The natural knowledge we have of the precepts of natural law does not derive even from a doctrine of natural law. The doctrine is consequent to, and builds upon, this natural knowledge. The natural knowledge we have of the precepts of natural law is the genuine "first-for-us" in the practical sphere.

33. *ST* 1–2 q. 94 art. 2; 1 q. 2, art. 1 and 2.

34. Compare *ST* 1 q. 5 and q. 6. In q. 5, Thomas speaks of God only in replying to arguments, i.e., so-called "objections," that have themselves brought God into the picture (art. 2, ad 1; art. 4, ad 3), and in the *sed contra* of two articles (art. 3 and art. 5), where he appeals to authority to show that what he will *argue* for in the subsequent *respondeo* agrees with the deposit of faith. But in the actual *responsiones* of the six articles of q. 5, where Thomas argues in his own name, he does not speak of God, although by this point in the *Summa Theologiae* he has advanced demonstrations that God exists (q. 2), that he is identical both to his essence and to his being (q. 3), and that he is perfect (q. 4).

Since Zuckert holds that Thomas's statements about the natural inclinations of man in q. 94 art. 2 depend for their evidence on his rational theology, one would expect him to specify what he thinks are the weaknesses of that theology. This expectation is not fulfilled.[35] Zuckert writes, "I do not propose to follow out the complex and difficult questions raised by ["Thomas's] universal teleology."[36] But if Zuckert were correct in thinking that Thomas's account of our natural inclinations in q. 94 art. 2 could be justified only by appeal to broader teleological principles, then identifying these principles and addressing Thomas's interpretation of them, especially in Questions 5 and 6 of the *Prima Pars* of the *Summa Theologiae* is exactly what he would need to do.[37]

Zuckert seems to be impressed by "the profound questioning of natural theology" that the early modern philosophers undertook.[38] But he does not say what he finds so profound about this questioning, or even what in Thomas's teaching it was specifically directed against. For if its target was Thomas's (and Aristotle's) understanding of motion, then it failed to strike at the vital core of his rational theology, which is his understanding, not of motion, but of *esse*.

Zuckert writes, "Knowledge of the essence of man, coupled with knowledge of God, arms Aquinas with the wherewithal to secure himself from the modern critique, by allowing him the distance he needs from empirical reality."[39] Thomas would say, on the contrary, that being armed with knowledge of the essence of man *by itself* suffices to secure his teaching from the modern critique. He would say that the reason why Hobbes, Locke, and other modern political philosophers did not identify the same

Postponing his argumenat for God's goodness (q. 6 art. 1–3), and especially his subtle treatment of the question, "Whether all things are good by the divine goodness?" (q. 6 art. 4), until after he has treated of goodness in general is part of a most carefully thought-out plan. Thomas is anticipating early in the *ST* how he will make his case, much later, that the primary precepts of natural law are *per se nota*, without relying, even covertly, on the *demonstrations* of the existence and providence of God that he gives early in the *ST* (and elsewhere), to say nothing of relying on the claims of revelation.

35. Unlike Strauss and other Straussians, Zuckert does not falsely assert that Thomas's rational theology reduces to revealed theology. But he has next to nothing to say about Thomas's rational theology. "As with many other arguments of great importance (e.g. the existence of God), Aquinas treats the relation between the inclinations and the natural law in a discussion of great brevity and concision" (*FB* 34). With the parenthetical reference to Thomas's arguments for the existence of God, Zuckert is apparently alluding to Part 1 q. 2 art. 3 of the *Summa Theologiae*. Thomas gives more extensive arguments in the *Summa Contra Gentiles*, 1.13. And he presents a particularly powerful argument, prepared at some length, for the existence of God in *DEE*, an argument that I adumbrated in Part 1, Ch. 1, Section a, above. See John Wippel, *The Metaphysical Thought of Thomas Aquinas*, 400–441 for an account of, and a serious engagement with, Thomas arguments for the existence of God in texts other than in the *ST*.

36. *FB* 41.

37. This is what Jean Porter has so helpfully done. See Part 1, Ch. 2, Section c, above.

38. *FB* 47.

39. *FB* 46. I assume that Zuckert is using the word "knowledge" either loosely or ironically in this sentence. Knowledge of the essence of man cannot be *contradicted* by what experience teaches about man since it is *based* on what experience teaches about man.

human inclinations that he identified is that they did not pay sufficient attention to what man *is*, quite a apart from what these philosophers may have thought about God. It is these thinkers, not Thomas Aquinas, who have distanced their teaching from empirical reality, not least by basing it on a hypothetical state of (human) nature purportedly predating civil society and inferred from extreme situations, that is, from the abnormal and unnatural rather than from the normal and natural.[40] Thomas would say that the empirical basis on which the early modern political philosophers constructed their account of man's natural inclinations was too small. And on this point, too, he would have the authority of Aristotle behind him.[41] Neither Aristotle nor Thomas Aquinas, nor Plato for that matter, would deny that human beings often act swinishly. But how they ought to act, and, in particular, what reason has to say about how they ought to act, cannot be deduced from how they do act. What Zuckert calls the "objectivist" understanding of the relation between desire and the good, an account argued for by Plato and Aristotle as well as by Thomas, is at the core of their understanding of the role that reason can and should play in determining how men ought to act, even when men fail to appreciate fully, or deliberately ignore, what reason has to say.[42]

What could appear at first glance to be the early modern political philosophers' "subjectivist" understanding of the relationship between desire and the good,[43] turns out, on brief consideration, to be hollow. If desire were not oriented toward the good, real or apparent, then desire, all by itself, would be the foundation of the good. If that were true, then whatever one happened to desire and strive for, even in ignorance of its possibly baleful consequences, would be by definition good. But that is not true even of the pleasant, since one can desire and strive, say, to eat something on the assumption that doing so will be pleasant only to discover, on eating it, that it is anything but pleasant. Even less, then, is whatever anyone (someone sick? an addict? a fool? a lunatic?) desires and strives for, by that fact alone, good—on *any* conception of the good, whether as the pleasant, the useful, or the moral. It is hard to see how anyone in his right mind could advance the "subjectivist" understanding of the relation between desire and the good, except perhaps as a jest. No more than Plato or Aristotle does Thomas need to have recourse to a doctrine of God to counter an assertion that on the slightest examination so quickly collapses under the weight of its own vacuity.[44]

40. Aristotle *Physics* 198b35; 199b23–26; cf. *Metaphysics* 1126b33; Strauss, *NRH* 179 and 196.

41. That there are inclinations peculiar to our rational nature is expressed by Aristotle in the formulations that man *by nature* desires to know (*Metaphysics* 980a23) and that man is *by nature* a political animal (*Politics* 1253a3; a10).

42. Cf. *Phaedo* 107b7; *Republic* 394d9; *Nicomachean Ethics* 1153a10–15, a23.

43. As Zuckert presents it in the last sentence of the first paragraph on *FB* 39: "is the object striven for good because it is striven for . . . ?" See the following footnote.

44. Zuckert says that "the moderns, like Locke, endorse the subjectivist version of the relation between desire and the good" (*FB* 39). But, shortly afterwards, he presents this version in a different and more accurate form than he did earlier on the same page: "What men actually desire is *called* by

There are insights in Zuckert's essay that are valuable and worthy of more consideration than I have given them here. In keeping with my general aim, I have focused on his criticisms of Thomas's natural law teaching, especially its grounding in q. 94 art. 2. Zuckert's criticisms fall way short of refuting or even casting serious doubt on the case that Thomas makes for natural law in this article. The most puzzling feature of Zuckert's essay is that, when all is said and done, the objections to Thomas's natural law teaching that he finds in the early modern political philosophers are directed not so much against the very the idea of natural law—which is where Thomas really does part ways with Plato and Aristotle—as against Thomas's understanding of the nature of man in general and the teleology of natural reason in particular. But on this point, the objections of Locke and other moderns hold no less, and no more, against Plato and Aristotle than they hold against Thomas. Their target is virtually the whole premodern tradition of ethics and political philosophy. Zuckert gives the impression, to this reader at least, of concurring in their objections. If this impression is true, then this eminent Straussian is sharply parting ways with Strauss, and with other eminent Straussians as well; and it is strange that he does not make this disagreement more explicit. If this impression is false, then Zuckert's intention in "The Fullness of Being: Thomas Aquinas and the Modern Critique of Natural Law," seems to be little more than to emphasize the fact that Thomas's natural law teaching occurs in the *context* of his rational theology, and to cast doubt on it for this reason alone. In spite of the title of his essay and the abstract that prefaces it, Zuckert cannot be said to have adequately engaged with Thomas's rational theology and the conception of *being* upon which it is constructed. Perhaps he believes that modern philosophy and modern science in particular have relieved one of the need for such an engagement.[45] If so, this belief would go a long way toward situating Zuckert within the Straussian camp, whatever may be his own estimation of *la querelle des Anciens et des Modernes.*

them 'good'" (39, emphasis added). See Hobbes, *Leviathan*, Part I, Chap. vi [7]: "But whatsoever is the object of any man's appetite or desire that is it which he for his part calleth *good* . . ." (Cf. Spinoza, *Ethica*, 3 Prop. 9. Scholium.) Hobbes says immediately afterwards that there is nothing that is "simply and absolutely" good. The claim that there is nothing good, period—if that is what Hobbes means here—is not vulnerable to the criticisms advanced above of the formulation that "the object striven for [is] good because it is striven for." But because the claim that there is nothing good, period, reduces to the assertion that there is nothing intrinsically desirable, it is vulnerable to criticisms based on Platonic, Aristotelian, Thomistic, Kantian, and even Epicurean arguments, however much some of these arguments differ from each other.

45. Zuckert ends his essay "not with a conclusion, but with a question: Can Aquinas's God-conception hold up against the profound questioning of natural theology, which characterizes modern philosophy as much as doubt about the Thomistic theory of the natural inclinations?" Anyone who does not assume that the raising of this important question is intended to count as its own (negative) answer will expect Zuckert at some point to undertake a follow-up study of "Aquinas's God-conception." The point of departure for such a study would have to be *DEE* and whatever reasonable doubts the modern philosophers are supposed to have cast on the argument of that work.

Chapter 8

The Precept Commanding the Love and Worship of God

In their 2014 book, *Leo Strauss and the Problem of Political Philosophy*, Michael and Catherine Zuckert draw attention to the following passage from Strauss's *Natural Right and History*:

> It is reasonable to assume that these profound changes [i.e., the changes found in Thomas Aquinas's teaching on natural law when it is compared with Aristotle's teaching on natural right] were due to the influence of the belief in Biblical revelation. If this assumption should prove to be correct, one would be forced to wonder, however, whether the natural law as Thomas Aquinas understands it is natural law strictly speaking, i.e., a law knowable to the unassisted human mind, to the human mind which is not illumined by divine revelation.[1]

The Zuckerts cite this passage in a chapter entitled "Strauss on Locke and the Law of Nature." They comment on it as follows.

> The implications of that hypothesized dependence on revelation are far-reaching . . . What is at stake is nothing less than the existence of the natural law as natural, and therefore as discernible by philosophy as opposed to theology ([*NRH*] 164). In other words, Strauss makes an assumption, a "reasonable assumption," about the natural law that explodes the natural law.[2]

1. *NRH* 163.

2. *LSPPPh* 210. What Strauss seems to mean by his expression, "the unassisted human mind," is the human mind unassisted by anything allegedly above it. Thomas, however, does not speak this way, since he holds that all understanding, including the understanding that comes about through natural reasoning without either overt or covert reliance on the claims of revelation, is assisted by the Holy Spirit, whether the person engaged in such reasoning recognizes this assistance or, more likely, does not. In the present context, this is a relatively minor point and does not affect Strauss's criticism one way or the other. Nor does it compromise Thomas's case for man's natural knowledge of the first principle and precepts of natural law. God, according to Thomas, is the ultimate source of nature as

This last sentence of the Zuckerts' is intriguing, since an assumption, *qua* assumption, cannot "explode" anything, unless it is employed in a *reductio ad absurdum*, which is not how Strauss employs the assumption in question. Strauss's choice of the word "influence" in the passage referred to is also intriguing, since it could name only a motive and not a logical presupposition or premise. His statement can stand if he means only that Thomas's teaching was influenced by a desire to show that certain truths held to be revealed by God, such as his existence, providence, and so forth, and the moral precepts of the Decalogue, are also naturally knowable. If, however, Strauss's statement means that these truths can be assented to only by first assenting to revelation, then the assumption in question is not reasonable but false. To their credit, the Zuckerts recognize a difficulty here. After asserting forcefully that Strauss makes a reasonable assumption that explodes the natural law, they soften their assertion appropriately.

> But a "reasonable assumption," however reasonable, nonetheless remains an assumption and cannot be the basis for "a philosophical critique concerned exclusively with [the] . . . truth or falsehood" of philosophic doctrines.[3]

Over the next few pages of their book, the Zuckerts attempt to show that Strauss's "reasonable assumption" does, in fact, prove to be correct. They focus on Strauss's criticisms of Locke, but they also suggest ways in which Thomas might be vulnerable to the same criticisms.

The Zuckerts detect a circularity in Locke's "explicit argument" for natural law. "He seeks to prove the existence and content of natural law by proving the existence of God and God's will, assuming in doing so the very thing he is ultimately attempting to prove."[4] This circularity may well be present in the case that Locke makes for natural law. There is, however, no circularity in the case that Thomas makes for natural law, since he does *not* seek to prove the existence and content of natural law—that is, the existence and content of precepts of action constituted by a fundamental power of the human soul—by proving the existence of God and God's will.[5] The Zuckerts specify "three 'presuppositions' that Locke identified as essential to natural law," presuppositions with which they seem to think Thomas agrees or should agree. These are "a natural demonstration of the existence of God, of his will for man (the content of the natural law), and of the immortality of the soul."[6] The Zuckerts fail to distinguish between (1) the self-evident knowledge of the primary precepts of natural law, which according to Thomas everyone possesses who has reached the age of reason and whose mental faculties are not stunted or compromised by illness or injury, and (2)

well as of grace, of natural reason as well as of revelation. I go into this matter here only to clarify why I do not use the expression "unassisted reason" to characterize Thomas's conception of reason when it is functioning without appeal to, or logical reliance on, the claims of revelation.

3. *LSPPPh* 210.

4. *LSPPPh* 213.

5. See Part 1, Ch. 2, above.

6. *LSPPPh* 212.

the actual doctrine of natural law, which Thomas and those who follow him possess, and few others. The former of these two (1) does not depend on any of the three presuppositions—whether construed as demonstrated or held as a matter of faith—that "Locke identified as essential to natural law." Regarding the latter (2), the first and second of the three presuppositions are surely relied on.[7] But Thomas relies on them because he has demonstrated them.[8] The Zuckerts, like other Straussians, are so confident that what Thomas attempts to demonstrate about God cannot possibly be demonstrated,[9] that they do not feel much need to work through his actual arguments and exhibit to the reader exactly where, in their opinion, they break down.[10]

That said, the Zuckerts are to be commended for their attempt to shed much needed light on what Strauss was getting at in a reference he makes, in the course of an essay on Locke, to a statement of Thomas's regarding the love and worship of God. As Strauss translates or paraphrases this statement, "it is not reason simply but reason informed by faith which dictates that God is to be loved and worshiped." Thomas's actual statement, at *ST* 1–2 q. 104 art. 1, ad 3, is only a little different. He says that "in those things that are ordered to God, some are moral, which reason itself, informed by faith, dictates; such as God is to be loved (*amandum*) and worshipped."[11] The Zuckerts connect this statement with Locke's claim that, "'love and worship' of God are dictates, indeed 'the highest and most weighty duties prescribed by natural law.'"[12] They then say that this claim is also made, "in slightly modified form," by Thomas as well. The

7. Regarding the third "presuppostion," which concerns the apparent relation of the thesis of the immortality of the soul (demonstrated in *ST* 1 q 75, art. 2; art. 6) to the doctrine of natural law, especially as regards punishment for infractions of natural law, see Ch. 6, Section c, above.

LSPPPh 214, top of the page.

8. What the Zuckerts refer to as "the content of the natural law" is not presented by Thomas as dependent on the will of God, not, that is, in the sense of being supernaturally revealed. Man's knowledge of the content of the primary precepts of natural law, and of all secondary precepts that can be deduced from them *modica consideratione*, is achieved by natural reason, though, for Thomas, the whole universe, including nature, man, and his reason, owes its existence at every instant of its existence to the will of God. For Thomas's demonstrations of the existence and will of God, see Part 1, Ch.1, Section 1a, above, and the footnotes there that specify where Thomas works out his demonstrations.

9. *LSPPPh* 214, top of the page.

10. In Ch. 9, Section b, below, I speak to the Zuckerts' observation that "[m]oral claims are not self-evident truths, as the variety of moral claims raised by human beings indicates" (*LSPPPh* 213). In Part 3, Ch. 13, I speak to their observation that "the nontransgessible law of nature [i.e., laws of physics and the like] neither depends on nor contributes to a proof for the existence of God" (213).

11. ". . . in his [praeceptis] quae ordinant ad Deum, quaedam sunt moralia, quae ipsa ratio fide informata dictat; sicut Deum esse amandum et colendum." *ST* 1–2 q. 104 art. 1, ad 3. Thomas's expression is not simply *ratio fide informata*, but *ipsa ratio fide informata*. The expression does not mean "reason having gotten some *information* from faith" as much as "reason *itself* having received a certain *form* through faith." This is, however, a very small point in the present context; for it still holds true that human reason cannot attain this form without faith. (In the above I shall use the accusatives, *amandum* and *diligendun*, rather than their nominatives because, in the texts under immediate consideration, Thomas uses the former in infinitive-accusative constructions. I could have used *amandus* and *diligendus* instead).

12. *LSPPPh* 211.

Zuckerts are right, though one of the passages they cite from the *Summa Theologiae* in support of it, namely the crucial article 1–2 q. 94 art. 2, co., does not make this claim. As for the other passage they cite, 1–2, q. 99 (though without specifying the article[s]), they may have in mind art. 1, ad 2.[13] In any case, at 1–2 q. 100 art. 3, arg.1 and ad 1, Thomas says that the two precepts, "Thou shalt love (*diliges*) the Lord thy God" and "Thou shalt love thy neighbor" are "the first and common principles of the law of nature, which are self-evident to human reason, *either* by nature *or* by faith."[14] Before considering the relation between the statement at 1–2 q. 100 art. 3, arg.1, ad 1, and the statement at 1–2 q. 104 art. 1, ad 3, a couple of observations are in order.

First, though the precept commanding love of God is, Thomas says, self-evident, it differs from the precepts of natural law specified at the end of the *corpus* of q. 94 art. 2, in that it has an apparently conditional character. If one has a demonstration that God exists and is providential, it is immediately evident to his reason that God is to be loved. Even if one merely believes that God exists and is providential, it is still immediately evident, evident even to his reason, that God is be loved. That is to

13. *LSPPPh* 211. In *ST* 1–2 q. 99 art. 1, ad 2, Thomas, responding to an argument that appeals to sacred Scripture (arg. 1), speaks of the love (*dilectio*) of God and of neighbor, and he says that every law aims at constituting friendship either between man and man or between man and God. In q. 99 art. 4, co., Thomas says that it belongs to divine law to order, or direct, men to one another and to God. He then says, "Each of these two (*Utrumque horum*) [orderings] also belongs from a universal point of view [Pegis's translation of *in communi*] to the dictate of the law of nature, to which the moral precepts [of the Old Law] are to be referred: but it is fitting (*oportet*) that each of these two be determined (*determinetur*) by divine or human law, because principles naturally known are common (or general—*communia*), both in speculative and practical matters." (See also, q. 99 art. 3, ad 2.) This observation is in keeping with what Thomas says elsewhere, particularly in speaking of human law (q. 91 art. 3). But it cannot be taken to mean that the secondary precepts of natural law are derived exclusively or even chiefly from the *determinationes* effected by divine positive law and human positive law. Lest there be any doubt on this matter I refer again to q. 100 art. 1, co. There Thomas says that the derivation of certain secondary precepts of natural law, including the moral precepts of the Decalogue, is accomplished demonstratively "right away (*statim*), with slight (*modica*) consideration, by the natural reason of every man." An example of a precept derived this way is the precept forbidding murder (*Non occides*). Such precepts "can be known right away from the first universal principles [i.e., the primary precepts of natural law] with only slight consideration." See also his statement that "one ought to do evil (*malefacere*) to no man" (q. 100 art. 3, co.), and his statement that "the natural reason of man dictates right away that he commit injury (*iniuriam faciat*) to no one" (q. 100 art. 5, ad 4). On the distinction between *determinatio* and *demonstratio*, see Part 1, Ch. 2, Section b, ii, above. Even regarding *determinatio*, Thomas says that "certain things are judged to be observed [only] by the wise after more subtle consideration of *reason*" (q. 100 art. 1 co., emphais added; cf. q. 100 art.3). The wise can be presumed to have good judgment even if they happen not to be legislators of positive law.

14. Emphasis added: ". . . illa duo praecepta sunt prima et communia praecepta legis naturae, quae sunt per se nota rationi humane, vel per naturam vel per fidem." By *per naturam* here, as distinct from *per fidem*, Thomas means by natural reason without the assistance of revelation. This article occurs in the context of a treatment of the moral precepts of the Old Law, precepts that Thomas argues belong to the law of nature. (See also *ST* 1 q. 60 art. 5, *sed contra*: "[O]mnia moralia legis praecepta sunt de lege naturae. Sed praeceptum de diligendo Deum seipsum est praeceptum morale legis. Ergo est de lege naturae.") The article in which Thomas speaks of *ipsa ratio fide informata* (q. 104 art. 1, ad 3) occurs in the context of a treatment of the ceremonial precepts of the Old Law, precepts that do not belong to the law of nature. (See the *corpus* of q. 104 art. 1.)

say, even belief can have implications, including necessary implications. However, if someone has neither a demonstration of God's existence and providence nor belief in God's existence and providence, then it is not readily apparent that it is, or could be, self-evident to *his* reason that God is to be loved.[15] And yet, just as one can say that not being circumscriptively in a place self-evidently pertains to the concept (*ratio*) of an angel,[16] whether an angel actually exists or not, so it also pertains self-evidently to the *concept* of God that he is to be loved, just as it pertains self-evidently to the *concept* of God that he is eternal—whether he actually exists or not.[17] The proposition that an angel is not circumscriptively in a place and the proposition that God is to be loved (*diligendum*) are self-evident in basically the same way. The predicate is formally contained in the concept of the subject, or is quickly derivable from what is contained in the concept of the subject, in both cases.[18]

Second, even though the precept that God is to be loved derives its properly obligatory force, as distinct from its conceptual coherence, from assent, whether through knowledge or belief, to the existence and providence of God, it by no means follows that all precepts of natural law derive their obligatory force from assent to the existence and providence of God. We are obligated to avoid ignorance, not because we assent to the existence and providence of God, but because persisting in voluntary and remedial ignorance is incompatible with our natural inclination as rational beings to know the truth about God, whatever that truth may be. Similarly, we are obligated to refrain from offending others, not because we assent to the existence and providence of God, but because committing offenses against others is incompatible with our natural inclination as rational beings to live in society. Acknowledging the obligatory force of these two precepts, and acting in accordance with them, does not presuppose assenting to the existence and providence of God any more than does recognizing the first principle of practical reason, "Good is to be done, etc.," and the order of our natural inclinations.

15. We should remember that something's not being self-evident to everyone does not preclude its being self-evident in itself. Nor does it preclude its being self-evident to the wise. *ST* 1-2 q. 94 art. 2 co.

16. *ST* 1–2 q. 94 art. 2, co.

17. There is a further side of things that should be taken into consideration in trying to understand why Thomas says that to love (*diligere*) God is a *per se notum* precept of natural law. As will be pointed out in the sequel above, Thomas holds that religion is a moral virtue. So even if one could not *demonstrate* the existence of God—assuming, of course, that the *non*-existence of God cannot be demonstrated—one would still, according to Thomas, be obligated to *believe* in the existence of God. I have spoken to this matter in an unpublished lecture presented at the 48th International Congress of Medieval Studies in 2013. I plan to expand and publish what I said there at some point in the future.

18. In speaking of the Old Law, Thomas says that some of its precepts are so certain and manifest that they do not need publication (*editione non indigent*). Such are the commandments concerning the love of God and neighbor (*mandata de dilectione Dei et proximi*), and others like these, which he says "are, as it were, the ends of the precepts; hence regarding them no one can err according to the judgment of reason." *ST* 1–2 q. 100, art. 11, co. One can err about them, to be sure, but not "secundum iudicium rationis."

Now, to a closer consideration of the relation between the two statements cited above regarding the love of God, namely, *ST* 1–2 q. 100 art. 3, arg.1, ad 1, and q. 104 art. 1, ad 3: Thomas's perhaps surprising claim that the love of God is rational turns not only on his demonstrations, by natural reason, of God's existence, providence, justice, and so forth; it also turns on what he means by love. Among the Latin words for love are two verbs, *amo* and *dililgo*, that Thomas uses along with their derivatives. His usage is not consistent. Sometimes he means the same thing by them, sometimes something different.[19] But when he does distinguish between them, he says that it is through *amor* that man is drawn to God by God himself (though not without man's consent), whereas it is through *dilectio* that man is led to God by his own reason and will.[20] There is then a capital distinction between these two kinds of love. By attending to it we can get a consistent reading of the two passages cited above. That God is to be loved (*amandum*) with *amor* is something reason dictates only when "informed by faith," and this kind of love, like faith, is supernaturally infused by God himself. This is what is said in q. 104 art. 1, ad 3, the text to which Strauss and the Zuckerts refer. But in that passage Thomas is not speaking of natural law. The thrust of q. 100 art. 3, arg. 1, ad 1, on the other hand, is that God is to be loved (*diligendum*) with *dilectio* is something that human reason dictates independently of faith.[21] And it is this kind of love, *dilectio* not *amor*, that Thomas says in this article belongs to natural law.

In light of the distinction between *dilectio*, as dictated by reason simply, and *amor*, as dictated by reason "informed by faith," we can appreciate the contrast that Thomas makes in q. 104 art. 1, ad 3. The moral precept commanding *amor* of God, a precept of divine law presupposing both natural reason and faith, is prefigured, albeit quite imperfectly, by the moral precept commanding *dilectio* of God, a precept of natural law constituted by natural reason independently of faith. This prefiguring does not hold in the case of the ceremonial precepts, which are, of course, precepts of divine positive law *simpliciter*. The latter in their specificity have, as Thomas says, "no force of obligation apart from divine institution," that is, apart from revelation. The precept commanding *amor* of God, however, though requiring faith, and hence presupposing divine revelation too, has *some* force of obligation from natural reason itself, albeit understood as *ipsa ratio fide informata*. Divine law presupposes natural law and grace perfects nature.[22]

19. See Deferrari, *A Lexicon of St. Thomas Aquinas*, 312.

20. Thomas says that *caritas* is a perfection of *amor*, which is a passion of the soul and located in the concupiscible power. *Dilectio*, on the other hand, is located in the will only. *ST* 1–2 q. 26 art. 1 co.; art. 2, co.; and especially art. 3, co., and ad 4. The distinction Thomas draws between *dilectio* and *caritas* parallels the distinction we considered (in Ch. 5, Section b, above) between a natural inclination and a grace-infused desire for a supernatural end.

21. Faith, too, can lead one to love God with *dilectio*, as Thomas says in *ST* q. 100 art.3, arg. 1, ad 1. But natural reason itself dictates this kind of love, whether or not one has faith.

22. See *ST* 1 q. 2 art. 2, ad 1; 1–2 q. 99 art. 2, ad 1.

So Strauss is right in saying that, according to Thomas, "it is not reason simply but reason informed by faith which dictates that God is to be loved," but *only if* Strauss understands this love to be *amor* rather than *dilectio*. It is remarkable that Strauss does not connect 1–2 q. 104 art. 1, ad 3, where Thomas speaks of *amor* without reference to natural law,[23] to q. 100 art. 3, arg.1, ad 1, where he speaks of *dilectio* with explicit reference to natural law.[24] The Zuckerts say that "Strauss approaches his critique [of Thomistic natural law] in a very indirect manner—through the keyhole rather than through the front door as he once put it."[25] Still, one would have expected Strauss to refer to q. 100 art. 3, arg.1, ad 1, at least in a footnote, when citing 104 art. 1, ad 3, and leave it to the reader to draw his own conclusions.[26] He does not do this in the passage from his essay on Locke that the Zuckerts cite.[27]

The Zuckerts underestimate the extent to which, for Thomas, man's reason—by its own nature and not only when "informed by faith"—dictates that God is to be loved with the love of *dilectio*. It is precisely this love of God that Thomas says belongs to natural law. Whatever it is that gets in the way of man's loving God with the love of *dilectio*, it is not his reason, rightly functioning.

In sum, *ST* 1–2 q. 104 art. 1, ad 3, would be the "damning" admission that the Zuckerts think it is[28] only if the word translated by the English Dominican Fathers, and by Pegis following them, as "to be loved" in that article were simply a variant of the word also translated by them as "love" in q. 100 art. 3, arg. 1, ad 1. But they are two different words in the Latin text: *amandum* and *diliges*, respectively, and they

23. Because *amor* is a perfection of *dilectio*, natural law is surely in the *background* of *ST* 1–2 q. 104 art. 1, ad 3. But there Thomas is speaking of something that goes beyond, far beyond, *dilectio* and natural law.

24. The distinction in *ST* 1–2 q. 104 art. 1, ad 3, is between different kinds of precepts within divine, or revealed, law. It is not a distinction between different kinds of precepts within natural law.

25. *LSPPPh* 212.

26. With his eagle-eye for the letter of the text, Strauss may have caught sight of the distinction Thomas makes between *amor* and *dilectio*. Perhaps he did not draw attentiion to it because he did not concur in it. However, in *PR* 117, Strauss quite interestingly refers to "philosophies [as distinct from "biblical teaching"] . . . which speak of the love [!] of God and of man."

27. Strauss clearly put a lot of weight on *ST* 1–2 q. 104 art. 1, ad 3. He cites this passage not only in the essay on Locke in *WhPPh* (208) but also in in *Persecution and the Art of Writing* (133, fn. 124) and in *CM* (34, fn. 47); and he refers to it implicitly in "A Giving of Accounts," 463. In none of these places does Strauss refer to *ST* 1–2 q. 100 art. 3 arg.1, ad 1. He may have misinterpreted q. 104 art. 1, ad 3, as a telling admission on Thomas's part that natural reason cannot demonstrate that God stands in a *free* relation to the world (*PR* 117): we *believe*, as a matter of *faith*, that God is to be loved because we *believe*, as a matter of *faith*, that he did not need to create us but did so anyway, freely and out of love, which we are obligated to reciprocate. However, Thomas thinks that natural reason, without the assistance of faith, *can* demonstrate that God freely relates himself to the world. (*ST* 1 q. 19 art. 2; art. 8; art. 10.) The world is not a necessary emanation of the divine essence, but is freely created instead. Accordingly, it is a matter of natural law, of reason independent of faith, and not of reason "informed by faith", that God is to be loved (*diligendum*).

28. *LSPPPh* 211.

have different meanings. To say it for the last time, though it could be said many more times, Thomas knows what he is doing.

Regarding worship of God, Thomas argues, again on the basis of natural reason alone, that God, who can be demonstrated to exist and to be providential, should be tendered submission and honor. Natural reason does not tell us exactly how submission and honor are to be tendered, other than that sacrifice should be involved. Offering sacrifice to God, which is of course a form of worship (*cultus*), belongs to natural law.[29] Natural reason, then, dictates *that* God is to be worshipped, independently of faith and prior to revelation.[30] Where revelation is necessary is in determining *how* God is to be worshipped, and it is in *this* sense that reason has to be "informed" by faith.[31] Still, in the case not only of the love (*dilectio*) of God but also of the worship of God, natural reason has something to say. When the demonstrations of rational theology are taken into account—demonstrations that Thomas does *not* take into account when he makes his case for our natural knowledge of the precepts of natural law in q. 94 art. 2—the precepts of natural law become enriched. In light of those demonstrations, the obligatory precept that one avoid ignorance gives rise to the obligatory precept that one love (*diliget*) God. Similarly, the obligatory precept regarding justice, that one render to each his due, gives rise to the obligatory precept of rendering to God what is *his* due. All four of these are precepts of natural law. Religion is then a virtue, and it gets annexed, as Thomas puts it, to the virtue of justice.[32] This would not happen if justice were not prior in the order of knowledge, even though religion turns out to be the chief of the virtues.[33] Religion is not, for Thomas, a theological virtue but a moral virtue.[34] For if man knows by natural reason alone the things that Thomas argues can be demonstrated about God, his providence in particular, then he knows

29. *ST* 2–2 q. 85 art. 1, co.; art. 4, co. See *ST* 1–2 q. 101 art. 4, co.

30. See *ST* 3 q. 60 art. 5, ad 3.

31. *ST* 1–2 q. 99 art. 3, ad 2; 2–2 q. 85 art. 1, ad 1. Strauss cites the second of these two texts in support of his claim, "In the words of Thomas Aquinas, reason informed by faith, not natural reason simply . . . teaches that God is to be . . . worshipped" (*CM* 34, and fn.47 on that page). But Strauss's claim is not supported, it is in fact contradicted, by the words of Thomas Aquinas in this article, both in the reply to the first argument, which Strauss cites, and in the actual *corpus* of the article, which he does not cite. It is only *how* God is to be worshipped that is determined by divine positive law. *That* he is to be worshipped and that sacrifice is to be offered to him, is, to repeat, a matter of natural reason, i.e., a matter of natural law.

32. *ST* 2–2 q. 58 art. 1; art. 11; q. 80, art. 1; q. 81 art. 1–2. See 1–2 q. 60 art. 3.

33. 2–2 q. 81 art. 6.

34. 2–2 q. 81 art. 5; see 1–2 q. 62, art. 1; art. 2. Since the moral virtues are established through acts (1–2 q. 51, art. 2), and since the acts of these virtue are mandated by natural law (1–2 q. 94 art. 3), it follows that religion broadly speaking, i.e. as worship of God (whose existence, again, Thomas thinks is demonstrable and need not be taken on faith) falls under natural law, even if much of what pertains to a particular religion, Christianity in particular, falls under divine law, as with the sacraments and belief in the articles of faith properly so-called. Consequently, for Thomas, that one worship God, as well as one can, is a dictate of natural reason, whether one is the beneficiary of divine revelation or not. See 2–2 q. 81 art. 2, ad 3.

that he has obligations to God, including reverence as well as love. It is appropriate, then, that the internal act of love (*dilectio*) give rise to external acts of worship, though the specific character of these acts is not fully clear to man on the basis of natural reason alone. For full clarity, revelation is required. Here then is another argument from natural reason for the need for revelation, an argument that does not logically presuppose or conclude that this need ever has been met, is now being met, or ever will be met.

Note: Duns Scotus on what is *per se notum* in natural law.

It is worth briefly considering the opinion of Duns Scotus here, not only because of its relevance to the specific matter at hand, but also because it is bound up with a criticism of Thomas's natural law teaching that is more penetrating and much better argued for than the criticisms we have been considering. Scotus writes as follows:

> To love God above all is an act conformed to correct natural reason, which dictates that what is best must be loved in the highest degree; and hence such an act is correct of itself; indeed its rectitude, as the rectitude of a first principle of action, is self-evident.[35]

This principle, that God is to be loved, is for Scotus a self-evident precept of natural law.[36] It can be known immediately through a consideration of its terms. Such a principle, as well as any precepts that follow demonstratively from it, is then of the natural law strictly speaking (*stricte loquendo*). God can no more will an exception to it than he can will an exception to the principle of non-contradiction.

Scotus, who has his own remarkable proof of the existence of God in terms of natural reason,[37] follows Thomas in holding that God cannot do or command anything that is either self-contradictory or incompatible with his own nature, though he can do or command anything that is neither contradictory nor incompatible with his

35. "[Q]uod diligere Deum super omnia est actus conformis rectae rationi naturali, quae dictat optimum esse summe diligendum, et per consequens est actus de se rectus; immo rectitudo eius est per se nota, sicut rectitudo primi principii in operabilibus." *Ordinatio* 3, suppl., dist 27, art. 1. In Wolter, *Duns Scotus on the Will and Morality*, 424–5. Hereafter cited as "Wolter." I shall occasionally alter Fr. Wolter's translation slightly in the interest of greater literalness.

36. It is, however, more correctly expressed in the negative: God is not to be hated. "[I]llud praeceptum, 'Diliges Dominum Deum tuum,' etc., non est simpliciter de lege naturae inquantum est affirmativum, sed in quantum est negativum prohibens oppositum. Simpliciter enim est de lege naturae 'non odire.'" *Ordinatio* 3, suppl., dist. 37, "Wolter," 282–3; cf. Richard Cross, *Duns Scotus on God*, 88–89. The disadvantage of the affirmative formulation is that it could hardly be observed at *all* times, such as when one is sleeping, to take the most obvious case. (Though Thomas expresses *his* first concrete, and primary, precept of natural law in the affirmative, he does so in language that anticipates objections against affirmative formulations: "quod homo ignorantiam *vitet*"—emphasis added. *ST* 1–2 q. 94 art. 2, co.) To those who say that every so-called natural law admits of dispensation, if only in rare cases, Scotus would surely ask, "What possible exigency, political or otherwise, might be thought to warrant man's *hating* God?" *Compare* Spinoza, *Ethica* 4, Proposition 18.

37. The most fully developed version of Scotus's demonstration is to be found in *De Primo Principio*.

own nature. Whatever God commands, then, its contradictory cannot be a primary precept of natural law and, hence, *per se notum*. But, according to biblical revelation, God commands certain things that contradict the precepts of the Second Table of the Decalogue, as Thomas acknowledges.[38] Therefore, Scotus infers, these precepts are not of the natural law strictly speaking. They are, however, of the natural law broadly speaking (*large loquendo*) and by extension (*extendendo*).[39] According to Scotus then, and in distinction from Thomas, the precepts of the Second Table are not *per se nota*, nor can they be strictly deduced from what is *per se notum*. However, the precepts of the Second Table are not simply expressions of a will operating independently of reason, for excellent reasons can be advanced on their behalf. They constitute a lawful and consistent ordering of human life. These precepts are not just somewhat consonant with natural law in the strict sense but, as Scotus says, greatly consonant (*multum consona*) with it.[40]

Scotus argues that because God cannot, even by revelation, command anything that is contrary to what is *per se notum*, he cannot command any act that is incompatible with the logically consistent lawful ordering that he establishes. But, this ordering is not the only possible one. According to Scotus, God can replace one self-consistent ordering with another such ordering. He can do so permanently, as in his establishing the New Law. And he can do so temporarily, as he does in the case of the ordering in which he commands Abraham to sacrifice Isaac; for in *that* ordering, God can still lead Abraham to him.[41]

Scotus's criticism of Thomas's teaching then is that Thomas holds both (1) that the precepts of the Second Table and the primary precepts of natural law are *per se nota*, and (2) that God is able to grant exceptions to these precepts, as in his command to Abraham.[42] Scotus thinks that Thomas cannot hold both (1) and (2).

38. *ST* 1–2 q. 94 art. 5, arg. 2; ad 2.

39. See Hannes Möhle, "Scotus's Theory of Natural Law," for a good account of how different kinds of commands pertain to natural law and for the crucial background distinction between *potesta ordinata* and *potesta absoluta*.

40. *Ordinatio* 3, suppl., dist. 37, "Wolter," 278–9

41. *Ordinatio* 1, dist. 44, "Wolter," 254–61. We cannot know what commands that God might (hypothetically) give in different orders of nature would lead man to him and what commands would not. We can know, however, that a command to hate God would not lead man to him in *any* order of nature. Hence, we can know that the command not to hate God belongs to the natural law absolutely. It is *per se notum*, hence, in the language of modern modal logic, obligatory in all possible worlds.

42. *ST* 1–2 q. 94, art. 2; q. 100 art. 1–2; q. 108 art. 8. In the altogether unique case of God's command to Abraham regarding Isaac, it is significant that God does not say to him, "Take now thy son, thine only son, whom thou lovest, even Isaac, and get thee to the land of Moriah, and . . . *murder* him there." What God says is "get thee to the land of Moriah and *offer* him there for a burnt-offering." Gen 22::2.(Cohen, *Soncino Chumash*, 108–9. See the note on the translation of this passage at the bottom of 109.) The distinction between murder and offering may seem overly refined, but it is crucial to the narrative in *Genesis*. God miraculously gives Isaac to Abraham and Sarah in their advanced old age, outside the order of nature that he has established as holding "always or for the most part" (Aristotle, *Physics* 198b35). And Abraham recognizes that God can rightly command that this miraculous gift be

We can only speculate about how Thomas would respond to Scotus on this point. But we can be relatively sure that he would begin by repeating his claim that the lawful ordering that is nature, including the natural reason of man, does not adequately direct man to what, from the perspective of revelation, is his supernatural end, though it does adequately direct him to his natural end. The natural end of man is to know the first cause to the extent that speculative reason is able to naturally know it, and to direct human actions and passions through the operation of practical reason. From the perspective of revelation, however, these ends are not ultimate but relative since they are also means—though insufficient of themselves—serving in a consistent ordering that directs man *towards*, though it does not get him *to*, the supernatural end of celestial beatitude. Were Thomas to concede Scotus's distinction, characteristically subtle, between (1) God's *granting exceptions* to precepts within a lawful ordering of which he as creator is the ultimate cause and (2) God's *replacing* that ordering, permanently or temporarily, with a different ordering, he could still say that his own natural law teaching has not been essentially undermined. For natural reason *as such* functions solely within the lawful ordering that is met with in experience and articulated by natural reason. That lawful and experienced ordering is, in fact, nature as we know it. Within this ordering, which is the only ordering we have natural access to, the primary precepts of natural law are *per se nota.*[43]

returned to him as an offering. If "the ethical" is understood as Kierkegaard understands it in *Fear and Trembling*, namely, as the rule-governed sphere of man's relation to man within the sole natural order with which we are naturally familiar, and which God has established so as to lead man toward him as man's ultimate end, then Kierkegaard's interpretation of the divine command to sacrifice Isaac as a "teleological suspension of the ethical" bears an interesting relation to Duns Scotus's interpretation of this command.

43. Since it is only the *per se notum* character of certain precepts of natural law that Scotus calls into question, it is somewhat surprising to hear Straussians refer approvingly, though only in passing, to "Duns Scotus's fundamental and trenchant criticism of the Thomistic claim that there is a natural law knowable to unassisted reason" (Pangle and Ahrensdorf, *Justice*, 284, n. 39). Scotus explicates natural law differently than Thomas does, to be sure. But he does not deny that there is a natural law, knowable to natural reason without the assistance of revelation, or that it possesses morally obligatory force. Quite the contrary. See *Ordinatio* 3, suppl. dist. 37, and 4, dist. 17; compare 1, dist. 44 (in "Wolter," 254–287). Strauss himself recognizes this ("On Natural Law," 143). To repeat, according to Scotus, it is a precept of *natural* law, knowable by natural reason without the assistance of revelation and morally binding in any natural ordering that God could create and place man within, that man not hate God.

Chapter 9

The Scope of *Synderesis*

SECTION A. *SYNDERESIS* AS NATURAL

It goes without saying that Thomas's natural law teaching stands or falls with his conception of *synderesis*. But his conception of *synderesis* is easy to misunderstand. Strauss writes as follows.

> The Thomistic interpretation is connected with the view that there is a *habitus* of practical principles, a *habitus* which he calls "conscience" or, more precisely, *synderesis*. The very terms show that this view is alien to Aristotle: it is of Patristic origin.[1]

Although the term *synderesis* is indeed of Patristic origin, just as Strauss says, the actual concept of *synderesis*, as Thomas explicates it, is not derived from revelation or revealed theology. Thomas means by this term nothing more, and nothing less, than practical reason's habitual knowledge of the self-evident principles of its own operation, which is to say, its knowledge of the precepts of natural law. Natural reason as such is simply incapable of determining either what *is* or what *ought to be* except in the light of principles, logical principles in the case of the former and the precepts of natural law in the case of the latter. According to Thomas, this is simply how reasoning works: "*omnis ratiocinatio derivatur a principiis naturaliter notis*."[2] If there are not only self-evident principles of speculative reason, but self-evident principles of practical reason as well, it follows that rational beings have a natural knowledge of them, by

1. *NRH* 157–158. See *IE* 38/313. The Patristic reference to conscience that Thomas cites, at *ST* 1–2 q. 94, art. 1, arg. 2, says nothing at all about revelation: "Basilus dicit quod conscientia, sive synderesis, est *lex intellectus nostri*: quod non potest intelligi nisi de lege naturali." (See also the Patristic references in 1 q. 79, art. 12 and 13). To be sure, once divine law is revealed, *synderesis*, and practical reason in general, have a further role to play. But *synderesis* is already playing an essential role at the level of natural law.

2. 1–2 q. 91 art. 2, ad 2.

whatever term we choose to call this knowledge.[3] The existence of *synderesis* implies the existence of natural law and vice versa; neither could exist without the other. The fact that "[t]here is no *synderesis*, no *habitus* of practical principles in Aristotle," need not mean, as Strauss says it does, that Aristotle "implicitly [!] *denies* the conscience."[4] It could mean only, let it be said again, that Aristotle might not have thought with as much penetration about the functioning of practical reason as Thomas did.

Whereas Strauss limits his criticism of *synderesis* to pointing out that the *term* is of Patristic origin, almost as though nothing more need be said, Jaffa goes somewhat further. "Thomas never asks whether there is such a habit [of *synderesis*], or how we know there is such."[5] This is an overstatement. The article treating *synderesis* in the *Summa Theologiae,* is entitled, "Whether synderesis is a special power of the soul distinct from the others." This formulation echoes that of the earlier articles in the question, especially "Whether the intellect (or understanding—*intellectus*) is a power of the soul," and "Whether reason is a power different from that of the intellect."[6] Thomas's treatment of *synderesis*, the *habitus* by which we know natural law, parallels his treatment of the *habitus* that is called "the understanding of principles."[7] If

3. Mary Keys says that "[T]hrough the phenomenon of conscience . . . human beings have a vague or implicit knowledge, an intimation of the divine, transcendent source of a 'rule' that is not merely the right or even the best for them to follow, but for which they are responsible as to 'another' from whence it comes and by whose wisdom and goodness it is justified" ("Keys," 194). The word "through" is crucial here. The phenomenon of conscience, like the phenomenon of any rational act, may give rise to—it even should give rise to—an intimation of the transcendent, indeed divine, source of reason itself. But in Thomas's presentation, conscience is *qua* phenomenon not derived from this intimation. We have an immediate awareness of it when we consider moral matters rationally, since conscience is the act of *synderesis*, which is in turn the *habitus* by which we know the precepts of natural law (ST 1–2 q. 94, art. 1, ad 2); and natural law, like all law, is, as Thomas explicitly says, a rule (*regula*—q. 90 art. 1, co.; q. 91 art. 2, co.). There is furthermore the question of how the goodness, and even the wisdom, of "the other" who is the source from whence this rule comes can be recognized as such prior to our accepting the given rule, if mere accepting is all that we do. Consider Kant's answer: "Selbst der Heilige des Evangelii muss zuvor mit unsrem Ideal der sittlichen Vollkommenheit verglichen werden, ehe man ihn dafür erkennt." *Grundlegung zur Metaphysik der Sitten, Werke,* Band 6, 36 [English translation: 21].

4. Strauss's letter to Kuhn, 23 (emphasis added). If *synderesis*—not the term but the concept itself—is only of Patristic origin, as Strauss suggests it is, then it is hard to see how Aristotle could have even *denied* it, implicitly or explicitly, as distinct from never having considered it in the first place. Though Strauss seems sometimes to be working with Luther's view of the conscience (e.g., *RR* 162), his remark to Kuhn is evidence that he was familiar with Thomas's quite different view, as does the passage spanning pages 157–8 of *NRH*.

5. *ThAr* 173.

6. *ST* 1 q. 79 art. 12; art. 1; art. 8.

7. *ST* 1 q. 79 art. 9, co.; art. 12, co.; see 1–2 q. 94 art. 1, co., and *In Duodecim Libros Metaphysicorum Aristotelis Expositio*, Lib. 1 Lect. 1.34. Whereas Thomas calls the understanding of principles a *habitus*, he treats the understanding (*intellectus*), simply, as a power and one that is not, strictly speaking, distinct from reason (*ratio*—1 q. 79 art. 8, co.). Moreover, he argues that *intellectus speculativus* and *intellectus practicus* are not different powers (art. 11, co.). It is at the level of *habitus*, at the level of the two different kinds of knowledge that are possessed, that speculative and practical reason, and hence the understanding of principles—more precisely the principles of demonstrative science—and

natural law and the principles of demonstration are, as Thomas claims, both known by us and distinct from each other, then there must be distinct habits whereby we know them. Jaffa's criticism holds no more for *synderesis* than it does for the understanding of logical principles. We cannot demonstrate the self-evident and therefore indemonstrable principles of either speculative *or* practical reason, and so we cannot demonstrate the existence of habits that consist in knowledge of them. If, however, we can reason in speculative matters in such a way as to know, not just that one thing follows from another, but that something is true simply, we can do so only in light of the indemonstrable and self-evident principles of speculative reason.[8] Similarly, if we can reason in practical matters in such a way as to know, not just what we need to do if we are to satisfy our desire for this or that pleasure or private advantage, but that something is good simply, we can do so only in light of self-evident indemonstrable principles of practical reason.[9] It is by virtue of the *habitus* called *synderesis* that we know these principles, and this *habitus* is inseparable from our rational nature.

Not surprisingly, Thomas speaks of conscience in the context of revealed theology as well as in his rational theology. For example, he says in *De Veritate* that "conscience is said to bind by force of a divine precept," and he says that "a dictate of conscience is nothing other than the coming (*perventio*) of a divine precept to him who has conscience."[10] Thomas's claim that the precepts of natural law are naturally and habitually known by *synderesis* and explicitly attended to and applied in the act of conscience, does not preclude the precepts of divine law from also being known by *synderesis* and conscience, though we must always remember that, according to Thomas, divine law presupposes natural law.[11] Toward the end of his treatment of conscience in *De Veritate*, Thomas puts his earlier remarks about binding "by force of a divine precept" in proper perspective: "conscience does not bind unless by force of a divine precept, either according to written law or [!] according to the law implanted in [our] nature."[12] The "written law" is presumably divine positive law. The "law implanted in our nature" can only be natural law. Shortly afterwards, Thomas reiterates this thought. "For each is bound to examine his acts in light of the knowledge he has

synderesis, can be distinguished (1–2, q. 94, art. 2).

8. *ST* 1 q. 79 art. 12, co.

9. If we *know* that we should do something because it contributes to our private advantage, then we must also know, self-evidently and without demonstration, that our private advantage is something good. Moreover, *if* our private advantage—"one's own good"—were *the* good, we could know this only on the basis of a *habitus* that would not be easy to distinguish in terms of its epistemic character from *synderesis* itself. Those who say that the good is essentially one's own good are strangely silent about how *reason*, which, again, is not a respecter of persons, knows this alleged truth.

10. ". . . conscientia ligare dicitur in vi praecepti divini" (*De Veritate* q. 17 art. 3, c); ". . . conscientiae dictamen nihil aliud est quam perventio praecepti Dei ad eum qui conscientiam habet (*De Veritate* q. 17 art. 4, ad 2).

11. *ST* 1–2 q. 99, art. 2, ad 1.

12. ". . . conscientia non ligat nisi in vi praecepti divini, vel secundum legem scriptam, vel secundum legem naturae inditi" (*De Veritate*, q. 17 art. 5, co.).

from God, whether *natural*, acquired, or infused . . ." (emphasis added).[13] All knowledge *ultimately* comes from God, the author of nature, including that knowledge that man has by nature, independently of revelation, including *immediate* knowledge of the first, *per se nota*, principles of speculative and practical reason. And lest he leave the reader in any uncertainty about this matter, Thomas concludes this last sentence, and indeed his entire article on conscience in *De Veritate*, not by saying that "every man ought to act according to divine precepts" or "according to the divine will,"—which he certainly could have said—but by saying that "every man ought to act according to reason."[14]

Man's natural knowledge of his obligations, which he has through *synderesis*, is supplemented both by what he finds out through natural investigation and by what is supernaturally revealed or infused. Since natural law is the participation of the eternal law in the rational creature, every one of its precepts is ultimately a "divine precept," as Thomas loosely employs this expression in the above passages from *De Veritate*. But in the "Treatise on Law" in the *Summa Theologiae*, he carefully distinguishes between eternal law and divine law, and he restricts the latter to what is supernaturally revealed. In his discussion of human law in the latter work, Thomas says that "if [human laws] are just they have the force of obligating in conscience from the eternal law whence they are derived."[15] Leaving aside the determination of certain judicial precepts of the Old Law,[16] the derivation of human laws from the eternal law is not by way of divine law but by way of natural law, as Thomas devotes an entire article to showing.[17]

Against the view of Strauss and Jaffa that conscience is a concept that derives from revealed theology, consider the definition of conscience given by Kant, who hardly appeals to revealed theology.

> [C]onscience is practical reason holding man's duty before him for acquittal or condemnation in every case where law is involved.[18]

13. Article 3 in *ST* 1–2 q. 63 is entitled: "Utrum aliquae virtutes morales sint in nobis per infusionem." Thomas says in this article that, in addition to the moral and intellectual virtues that are caused in us by our own actions, certain moral and intellectual virtues need to be infused by God, so as to be proportionate to the (infused) theological virtues. (See ad 1.) Thomas does not elaborate on this observation here, but what he may have in mind are the extraordinary self-control of the saints, the extraordinary fortitude of the martyrs, and the prudence that governs such self-control and fortitude.

14. *De Veritate* q. 17 art. 5, ad 4 (emphasis added). The entire sentence is, "Unusquisque enim tenetur actus suos examinare ad scientiam quam a Deo habet, sive sit naturalis, sive acquisita, sive infusa: omnis enim homo debet secundum rationem agere." Regarding even infused knowledge, reason is at work, though in this case it is divine reason itself, and not natural reason merely.

15. "Si quidem iustae sint, habent vim obligandi in foro conscientiae a lege aeterna, a qua derivantur." *ST* 1–2 q. 96 art. 4, co. Thomas points out at the end of the *corpus* of this article that human laws opposed to the divine law, e.g., those commanding idolatry, should in no way be obeyed. See C. Kossel, "Natural Law and Human Law [Ia IIae, qq. 90–97]," 180.

16. *ST* 1–2 q. 99 art. 4; qq. 104–5.

17. *ST* 1–2 q. 95 art. 2.

18. "Denn Gewissen ist die dem Menschen in jedem Fall eines Gesetzes seine Pflicht zum

At first glance, Kant's definition has a more juridical ring to it—"acquittal or condemnation"—than does Thomas's understanding of conscience as the act of the natural habit of *synderesis*. But Thomas also recognizes that conscience can witness, accuse, rebuke, and torment, all of which fits with his argument, which we considered earlier, that the remorse of conscience is a punishment that man inflicts upon himself.[19] Kant's claim that conscience is practical reason holding a man's duty before him parallels Thomas's claim that conscience, as distinct from the habit of *synderesis*, is an act.

Fr. Fortin thinks that Thomas's teaching "expressly injects into the debate an element that is foreign to the Aristotelian view, according to which the ethical quality of human action is ultimately determined without reference to anything other than the intrinsic standard of reason alone."[20] This claim is puzzling. Presumably the "foreign element" that Fr. Fortin has in mind is belief in the divine judge, without which, he mistakenly thinks, natural law would be deprived of its obligatory character. But even if Fr. Fortin were right on this point, he would not have shown that Thomas, in his natural law teaching, refers the ethical quality of human action to any standard other than natural reason itself. That is to say, even *if* Thomas had to introduce a divine judge to make sense of how punishment for infractions of natural law could take place—and I have argued that his account of remorse *already* makes sense of this—the first principle of practical reason and the precepts of natural law would remain the standard to which ordinary human conduct should conform. (I am not speaking here of human conduct within the order of grace under the New Law.) Fr. Fortin does not try to show that the evidence for the first principle of practical reason and the precepts of natural law lies outside what is accessible to natural reason.[21]

The above claim of Fr. Fortin's is puzzling for a further reason. Though he suggests that it is Aristotle, and not Thomas, for whom the standard of human conduct is reason alone, he does not spell out in what way reason *is* a standard for Aristotle. On the contrary, he calls attention to a problematic circle in Aristotle's reasoning, though without endorsing natural law, which alone affords a way to exit the circle without appeal to revelation.

Lossprechen oder Veruteilen vorhaltende praktische Vernunft." *Die Metaphysik der Sitten, Werke*, Band 7, 531. [English translation: 160.]

19. *ST* 1, q. 79 art. 12, co; art. 13, co.

20. *ATAP* 192. The context of this remark, as well as the title of the essay itself, suggests that the teaching Fr. Fortin is referring to is Thomas's natural law teaching and not his teaching on law more generally.

21. Richard Kennington, one of Strauss's finest students, speaks of a "doubt" as to whether natural law is "a law knowable to the human mind, unassisted by divine revelation" (*SNRH*—79). But rather than spell out exactly what is doubtful about this matter, he refers the reader instead to one of the articles by Fr. Fortin that we have been considering. No more than Strauss, Jaffa, or Fr. Fortin, does Kennington analyze the actual case that Thomas's makes in *ST* 1–2 q. 94 art. 2 for the knowability of natural law independently of divine revelation.

> One can easily imagine a situation in which virtue itself might counsel that one act in a manner that is contrary to the prevailing or generally approved standards of conduct. A question immediately arises, however, as to the *principle* in the light of which a decision of this kind is made . . . The [*Nicomachean*] *Ethics* does state expressly that the mean of reason is the mean such as a prudent man, who is, as it were, a law unto himself, would determine it. But although this solution may be deemed adequate for purposes of action, it obviously leaves something to be desired from a theoretical point of view and actually *begs the question* since it does little more than suggest that the right mean is the mean as established by a prudent man, who is himself defined as a person who habitually chooses the right mean.[22]

Exactly! With his choice of the word "principle" in connection with prudence, Fr. Fortin puts his finger right on the nerve of the matter. He makes a similar observation regarding Aristotle's account of the relation of right reason in practical matters to right appetite. "[T]he whole argument, as Aquinas rightly points out, would again appear to be circular: truth or right reason in practical matters is contingent on the agreement of a particular action with the rectified appetite, which is itself determined by the fact that it agrees with right reason."[23]

In light of these perceptive observations, it is curious that in another context Fr. Fortin writes, somewhat disparagingly, of the "typically modern preoccupation with the foundations of morality."[24] Presumably, as Fr. Fortin sees it, Plato and Aristotle were not preoccupied with the foundations of morality. But a preoccupation with the foundations of morality is the natural interest that a fully rational man, ancient or modern, takes in the functioning of his own reason, both in the sphere of practice and in the sphere of theory. It was nothing less than Thomas Aquinas's preoccupation with the foundations of morality that led him, a pre-modern thinker, to the identification and explication of the principles that constitute this foundation. An interest in the foundations of morality is a philosophical interest of the first order, however far it may be from the interests of political theory.

Straussians do not avoid the language of principles and rules, but they tend to employ these terms obscurely and without elaboration. For example, Thomas Pangle

22. "St. Thomas Aquinas," 263 (emphasis added). See *Nicomachean Ethics* 1107a1 and 1144a29–36; also 1176a16.

23. "St. Thomas Aquinas," 263. Moral virtue is a habit. And a habit, as I noted in Part 1, is a readiness to act in a certain way. This readiness is formed by committing certain acts repeatedly. The habit follows and is formed by the acts. If these acts are acts of virtue, they are of the natural law. See, again, *ST* 1–2 q. 94 art. 3, co.: "omnes actus virtutum sunt de lege naturali: dictat enim hoc naturaliter unicuique propria ratio, ut virtuose agat." John Finnis says rightly that, for Thomas, "principles, propositional practical truths, are more fundamental than virtues." *AMPLT* 124; see footnote 104 on that page. See also Clifford Kossel "Natural Law and Human Law [Ia IIae, qq. 90–97]," 176–7. For a general critique of "virtue ethics," see Robert R. Louden "On Some Vices of Virtue Ethics," *American Philosophical Quarterly*, 21 (1984).

24. "Natural Law and Social Justice," 233.

speaks approvingly of Raymond Aron's assessment of *Natural Right and History* "as an elaboration of principled prudence" (which Pangle distinguishes, as one would expect, from "natural-law moralism").[25] But Pangle does not say what the principle is, or how principled prudence differs from unprincipled prudence. Similarly, Jaffa speaks of "rules of prudence," though without distinguishing the rules from the prudence they presumably inform.[26] Strauss faults contemporary social science for insisting that "we cannot have any knowledge regarding the ultimate principles of our choices,"[27] but Strauss himself can hardly be said to have given an unambiguous statement of what these ultimate principles are.

What Fr. Fortin calls the "foreign element" that Thomas "injects into the debate" is actually the first principle of practical reason, which in conjunction with the order of human inclinations is the foundation of all the concrete precepts of natural law. The prudent man, in negotiating the often uncertain terrain of human action and interaction, sets his sights by ultimate, common, and articulable principles of natural reason rather than by some unprincipled and/or ineffable quasi-standard, such as "one's own good" (construed as private advantage solely) or "what is required by the circumstances." If Aristotle were to disagree with Thomas on this matter, then it would be in the natural law teaching of Thomas Aquinas, more obviously so than in the philosophy of Aristotle, that the ethical quality of human action is determined by what Fr. Fortin calls "the intrinsic [!] standard of reason alone."

We should not assume too quickly that Aristotle would disagree with Thomas that practical reason makes use of ultimate principles, even principles that do not admit of dispensation. For, though Aristotle does not speak of natural law in the *Nicomachean Ethics* and says moreover that all natural right is changeable, he also says, unequivocally, that adultery—along with several other vicious acts—is wrong, indeed, that it is *always* wrong,[28] a claim that, if true, is immediately expressible in an injunction of natural law. It is possible that Aristotle is dissembling in this passage, though it is hard to know why he would bother to do so, since he could easily have expressed himself less emphatically and with greater circumspection.

Some have argued that the prohibition against adultery might in certain extreme situations have to be waived, and that Aristotle, being a prudent man, must have recognized this in spite of what he explicitly says.[29] A king, convinced that he needs

25. "Introduction" to *The Rebirth of Classical Political Rationalism*, ix.

26. *ThAr* 170

27. *NRH* 4. See Strauss's remarks on Aristotle, whom he apparently follows on this matter, in *CM* 25–26, and in "Marsilius of Padua," 292–293.

28. 1107a9–18: *ouk estin oun oudepote peri auta katorthoun, all' aei hamartanein*. "Concerning these things [adultery among them] it is never possible to be right; rather, one always errs."

29. See, e.g., *ThAr* 208, n. 84. Thomas West cites Aristotle's claim that adultery is *always* wrong; but he thinks that this claim might have to be qualified by the context in which Aristotle makes it, namely, his discussion of virtue as a mean. There "Aristotle is not discussing the question of whether an action that is *normally* wrong might be permissible in rare circumstances to achieve a great good or

to leave a male heir to the throne so as to reduce the prospects of a civil war after his death, might be justified in adulterating his marriage, if this was the only way he could get a male heir. The obvious example is that of Henry VIII, who was unable to beget a male heir through his lawful wife, Catherine of Aragon. After breaking with the Church of Rome, he divorced Catherine on his own authority. He then proceeded to marry a series of wives. His sole lawful male heir, Edward VI, a Protestant, died too young to accomplish anything. The accession to the throne of his daughter Mary, a Catholic, and afterwards of his daughter Elizabeth, a Protestant, was attended in both cases by bloody persecutions, of Protestants and Catholics respectively. Henry's ostensibly prudential deviation from "natural-law moralism" had the consequence of introducing into his kingdom divisions of the very sort he was trying to avoid by that deviation. One can never be sure that violating natural law for the sake of political exigency is the best means of addressing the exigency, even according to the questionable standards of those who denominate themselves "prudential realists."

Strauss and Jaffa's attempt to discredit the concept of conscience as a rational concept, not by carefully analyzing it but simply by calling attention to the origin of the term "*synderesis*" in Patristic writings, is not only ineffectual but beside the point. For the moral awareness that the term designates—whether it is a genuine awareness, as Thomas thinks, or a deluded awareness, as Strauss and his followers seem to think—is not derived from belief in revelation. On the contrary, it is a condition for belief in revelation, as Strauss himself recognizes.[30] Moral man is man shaped by the conviction that he is obligated in the core of his being. Such a conviction—whether true or false—is the accomplishment of *synderesis*, prior to belief that God has revealed himself, prior to belief in God as the divine lawgiver, prior to belief in God at all. It is not, as is sometimes said, that man has a deep but obscure and ultimately nonrational, if not irrational, attachment to morality, to justice especially. Man is attached to morality, *naturally* attached, because he is attached to his own reason.

Unlike Nietzsche, neither Strauss nor Jaffa tries to spell out what it would mean to live or attempt to live without *synderesis*. In *Thomism and Aristotelianism*, Jaffa seems not only to acknowledge the existence of conscience—though he does not call it by this name—prior to belief in revelation, but even to consider it a form of knowledge. For he says that we "know intuitively," that is, we have indemonstrable knowledge, that some things are good by nature. Jaffa mentions bodily health and, citing Aristotle, "intelligence, sight, certain pleasures, and honors."[31] Now, if we know

to avoid a great evil" (*Critique of the 'Straussian' Critique*, 11, fn. 22, emphasis added). True, Aristotle is not discussing this question. But the natural reading of the word "always" (*aei*), along with "never" (*oudepote*) in the preceding clause, is that Aristotle is ruling out the possibility that West invites us to entertain. If Aristotle had wished to leave this possibility open, he could have said something like, "Adultery [along with the other vicious acts he names] is not right; one errs in committing it"—leaving it to the careful reader to point out that Aristotle does not say "*never* right" or "*always* errs."

30. "The Law of Reason," 140.

31. *ThAr* 170.

intuitively that honors are good, it seems that we would act, or should act, in such a way as to be really worthy of receiving them, and not just worthy of receiving them in the eyes of others. Jaffa does not adequately explore this possibility. If we intuitively *know* (as sub-rational animals do not) that certain things are good and to be pursued, it can only be through a rational *habitus*, whatever name we choose to give it.

Moreover, Jaffa does not speak to the question of how we are to decide between the pursuit of, say, honors and knowledge when the pursuit of the one precludes the pursuit of the other. That is, he does not explore what *ordo* may exist among these intuitively known goods. But, if there is an *ordo*, then, when considered in conjunction with the gerundive, "Good is to be done, etc.," we once again have natural law, obligation, and *synderesis*, all rooted in human reason and experience. The only undecided question would then be the content of natural law. Do the inclinations that correspond to our rational nature rank higher, as Thomas thinks they do, than the inclinations that we share with subhuman nature? And, if so, what exactly are the former inclinations? Jaffa seems to have no disagreement with Thomas's claim that the inclination to know the causes of things—whether or not God is one of the causes—pertains to our rational nature. And Jaffa presumably has no disagreement with the particular precept that is grounded in this inclination, namely, that ignorance is to be avoided, though Jaffa might resist calling it a precept. But what about the inclination to live in society, and the precept that is grounded in it? This inclination cannot be easily satisfied without the cultivation of the moral virtues, especially those that have to do with our relation to others. For Thomas, these virtues are not simply free-floating dispositions. They have an end, and it is *synderesis* that orients them to it. This end is the common good, which is the concern of law as such.

Important as the moral virtues are for Thomas, however, he still ranks them below the intellectual virtues, for he ranks action below contemplation. Jaffa accepts this ranking. But in interpreting Thomas's position he makes a fallacious inference.

> That intellectual perfection is, in itself, a-moral is testified to by Thomas . . . [He says] that prudence, or practical wisdom, cannot be, but the other intellectual virtues can be, without moral virtue. But Thomas also says that intellectual virtue is better than moral virtue, and again that wisdom (i.e. philosophic wisdom) is the greatest of the intellectual virtues. Thus we see, by Thomas' own assertion, that according to the philosophical teaching the highest natural perfection of man is possible without moral virtue.[32]

32. *ThAr* 31. The clause "according to the philosophical teaching" in the final sentence quoted above is somewhat misleading. For taken by itself, the sentence gives the impression that Jaffa is speaking not about Thomas's own teaching but about Thomas's account of a philosophical teaching in which he may not concur. This impression is dispelled, however, when Jaffa writes a few lines later, "But it remains true, as Thomas explicitly says, that as far as natural morality is concerned, the highest perfection of man is possible without moral virtue."

Jaffa should have concluded only that, for Thomas, the greatest of the intellectual virtues is possible without moral virtue.[33] He overlooks the possibility that the "highest natural perfection of man," that is, the perfection of man understood not as a mind exclusively but also as by nature a social and political animal, requires indeed the greatest of the intellectual virtues, wisdom, though in combination with moral virtue.[34] That this is the case is implied in Thomas's statements that prudence relies on moral virtue as well as vice versa, that prudence is a virtue most necessary (*virtus maxime necessaria*) for human life, and that living well consists in acting well (*bene operari*).[35] Moreover, the highest *natural* perfection of man would (absent bad luck) entail or be realized in such happiness as can be achieved *in this life*. That happiness includes, albeit as a secondary component, an operation of the practical intellect. It does not consist in contemplation solely. Finally, Thomas holds that virtue as such—and this includes moral as well as intellectual virtue—is the perfection of a power.[36] The "highest natural perfection of man," that is, the highest perfection of man as by nature a rational being, would accordingly require the perfection of all his rational powers, including those that pertain to action. Moral virtue is precisely the perfection of the rational powers that pertain to action. I am aware of no place where Thomas says, or suggests, or even hints, that "the highest natural perfection of man is possible without moral virtue."[37] His entire teaching on the virtues as perfections of man's natural powers implies the opposite.

Jaffa's fallacious inference is revealing because it is indicative of the striking depreciation of moral virtue that one finds among Straussians, a depreciation that goes so far beyond simply ranking moral virtue a notch below intellectual virtue as to leave

33. Strauss makes a similar point but limits himself to saying that "intellectual perfection"—vs. Jaffa's "the highest natural perfection of man"—does not require moral virtue (*NRH* 164). Strauss refers to this as a "difficulty" that Thomas needs to solve, but he does make clear just what he thinks the difficulty is. See, in this connection, James Schall, "A Latitude for Statesmanship?" 141–2.

34. The highest natural perfection of man would presumably culminate in this-worldly happiness. And such happiness, Thomas explicitly says, requires a "good operation," not just in speculation but in action also, including action for the benefit of others. *ST* 1–2 q. 4, art. 8, co.

35. *ST* 1–2, q. 57 art. 4, co.; art. 5, co.; q. 58 art. 3, ad 1; see q. 4 art. 4, co. The *perfect* good of the speculative intellect that Thomas speaks of in 1–2 q. 3 art. 5, ad 2, is attained neither by philosophy nor even by theology in this life, but consists in the beatific vision supernaturally bestowed only in the life to come. See art. 5, co.; 1–2 q. 5, art. 5. Cf. *Super Sent.* Lib. 3, dist. 35, q. 1 art. 3, sol. 3c (cited by Finnis, *AMPLT* 110 and 129, note a). Consider also 2–2 q. 182 art. 4, co.; ad 2. Clark Merrill, in "Leo Strauss's Indictment of Christian Philosophy," says that "Aquinas accepted the teaching that man's rational perfection and man's moral or political perfection are interdependent and, together, constitute man's natural end" (85). Merrill is basically right. But Thomas did not simply *accept* this teaching; he *argued* for it, as I showed in Part 1, Chs. 1 and 2, above. The moral perfection naturally attainable in this life is rooted in man's reason just as much as is the intellectual perfection naturally attainable in this life. Rational perfection involves the perfection of reason as a whole, of practical reason as well as speculative reason.

36. *ST* 1–2 q. 55 art. 1, co.

37. Consider *ST* 2–2 q. 51 art. 1, ad 2: "Oportet enim circa omnia humana perfici per virtutes: et non solum circa actus rationis . . . sed etiam circa passiones appetitus sensitivi. . . ."

one with the impression that they do not regard moral virtue to be a virtue, that is, an excellence, at all.[38]

SECTION B. *SYNDERESIS* AS UNIVERSAL

The Straussian criticisms of Thomas's conception of natural law, and of *synderesis* as the *habitus* whereby its primary precepts are known, are advanced from the perspective of classical political philosophy, of which Plato and Aristotle are the greatest representatives. Straussians argue that Thomas's teaching departs from Plato and Aristotle. They are right. I have tried to show that it departs from Plato and Aristotle in the direction of truth. On the other hand, there are anticipations of Thomas's teaching in Plato and Aristotle that are largely ignored or underestimated by Strauss and his students. One such anticipation is the concept of obligation itself.

In Part 1, I considered Thomas's claim that, though the primary precepts of natural law do not admit of dispensation, the secondary precepts may on occasion admit of dispensation. His example, that one should not restore goods held in trust if they are claimed for the purpose of fighting against one's country, is of special interest. For it is reminiscent of Socrates' exchange with Cephalus in Book 1 of Plato's *Republic*,[39] a refutation from which some infer that *every* law, practical rule, or precept admits of an exception.[40] Thomas says, however, that the primary precepts of natural law, and

38. See Strauss, *On Tyranny*, 202: "... political virtue, or the virtue of the nonphilosopher, is a mutilated thing." Also *NRH* 151: "From this point of view [i.e., that of the classical philosophers] the man who is merely just or moral without being a philosopher appears as a mutilated human being. It thus becomes a question whether the moral or just man who is not a philosopher is simply superior to the nonphilosophic 'erotic' man." Strauss does not answer this question. (It may be significant that he does not say that the non-philosophic "erotic" man, too, is a mutilated human being, perhaps because he regards the non-philosophic "erotic" man, e.g., Alcibiades, as more or less open to the love of wisdom, but the non-philosophic moral man as closed to it.) Nor does Strauss answer the two related questions that he asks immediately afterwards, taking leave of all three of them with a characteristic "However that may be ..." and change of focus. He leaves little room, however, for doubting that he shares the point of view he has just described. That this point of view is indeed that of the classical philosophers, or at least that of Plato, is strongly suggested by what is said about the moral but non-philosophic man in the "Myth of Er" (*Republic*, 619b6–d1. See *On Tyranny*, 182), though it should be remembered that Socrates does not say this in his own name but reports it as having been said by Er. See p. 471, note 13, of Allan Bloom's translation of the *Republic*.

39. 331c1–331d1. See Thomas Aquinas *Super Sent.* Lib. 3, dist. 37, q. 1 art. 3, co.: "Quaedam vero leges sunt quae secundum id quod sunt, habent rationem ut observari debeant, quamvis aliquibus concurrentibus earum observatio impediatur; sicut quod depositum reddatur deponenti, impeditur quando gladius furioso deponenti reddendus esset ..."

40. David Bolotin writes regarding the Cephalus episode, "Socrates' argument implies the ... important conclusion that the law does not adequately settle the question of what justice is ... [N]o law can adequately assign to everyone what is good and only what is good for him in all circumstances." "Leo Strauss and Classical Political Philosophy," 134. "No law" seems too strong here. It is hardly obvious that it applies to divine, i.e., *revealed*, laws or commandments. In what circumstances might it be good for one *not* to say the "Our Father," if only silently, once a day? And, whether prohibited by revealed law or by a precept of natural law, is it sometimes good for a man to covet his neighbor's wife?

the secondary precepts deduced from them immediately or *modica consideratione*, do not admit of dispensation—except, only in exceedingly rare situations, only by God himself, and only through a revealed command.[41] Natural reason can hardly make an exception to the principles of its own operation. What does occasionally admit of dispensation are those secondary precepts that are at some remove from the primary precepts. The precept that one restore goods held in trust is this kind of precept. It must be added, however, that whereas it would be wrong to restore borrowed weapons to a friend who has recently lost his mind, it would also be wrong to sell the weapons and keep the money for oneself, that is, in order to further "one's own good" narrowly conceived—a side of things that is not always considered in discussions of this exchange in the *Republic*.[42]

Socrates tells Cephalus that one *ought* not to—or *should* not, it makes no difference (Greek, *oute chrē*)—return weapons taken from a friend (presumably with the friend's consent) who has subsequently gone mad and demands them back. What Socrates says sounds, on the face of it, like the statement of a moral principle. To give weapons to a man whom one knows to be mad is to make oneself complicit in the offense he may commit against others. Furthermore, it is at odds with willing the good of the madman himself.

i. Seth Benardete on obligation in Greek antiquity

In his article "XPH and ΔEI in Plato and Others," Seth Benardete examines the different ways in which these two terms, both of which occasionally get translated as "ought" or "should," are used by the classical Greek authors. Benardete does not take issue with the traditional understanding that *chrē* is in some sense "subjective" and that *dei* is in some sense "objective." Instead, he aims at clarifying how this distinction plays out in the classical authors, especially in Plato "who seems more aware (and with good reason) than any other writer of the difference."[43] Benardete does not elaborate what this "good reason" is. Knowing that Benardete is a Straussian, one might suspect that he is alluding to doubts that he thinks Plato must have entertained about the concept of obligation.

If revealed law is entirely off the table, then what about Scotus's *natural* law? To raise a question raised earlier, is it sometimes good for one to hate God? (Ch. 8, *Note*, above.) Regarding Thomas's primary precepts of natural law, Bolotin's statement can stand if one gives appropriate emphasis to the word "adequately." For judgment is required to determine, e.g., what ignorance, or kind of ignorance, it is most important to avoid (if it can be avoided) and what constitutes offense in a complex situation. Judgment, however, is nothing other than the application of a general rule—in the case of action, a law, precept, or maxim—to particular circumstances. See Part 1, Ch. 1, Section c, above. We shall consider the relationship between rule and judgment further in Part 3, Ch. 11, below.

41. See the *Note* appended to Ch. 8, above.

42. See *Republic* 442e4–443a1.

43. Benardete, "XPH and ΔEI," 286.

This suspicion is not really borne out, however. For as Benardete's examples show, Plato (usually his Socrates) often states that one is under *some* kind of obligation, and he uses *chrē* to do this. On the other hand, Plato uses *dei*, according to Benardete, to express not so much obligation as need or necessity. Benardete does not, however, make fully clear what the latter necessity consists in. For Plato does not invariably use *dei* to name an absolute necessity that rules out freedom of any kind.[44] He uses it typically to name a conditional necessity, a necessity that one is under *if* one is to think or speak consistently.[45] Benardete probably has this usage in mind when he makes the following, pertinent, and exceptionally interesting observation:

> Plato . . . seems to have introduced an innovation of his own. Because *dianoia* and *nous* are for Plato not subjective, *dianoeisthai*, *noein*, and *ennoein* often take *dei*. It is simply thinking and not *one's own thinking* that these verbs express.[46]

The distinction between (1) "simply thinking" and (2) "one's own thinking" resembles—if it is not equivalent to—the distinction between (1) the operation of reason, including practical reason, which is common and makes its pronouncements in universals, or in light of universals, and (2) private opining and musing, which may or may not accord with reason. If something like that is what is meant by the distinction between "simply thinking" and "one's own thinking," then *dei* can express obligation, including moral obligation, as firmly as does *chrē*, precisely because it roots obligation in something that is *not* merely private or subjective.[47] Benardete does not draw this conclusion. Nor does he immediately develop his interesting observation. But he probably has it in mind when he writes, a few pages later,

> It is often remarked that *chrē* is 'moral' while *dei* is not, but the fact that *ta deonta* could mean what we call moral duties shows the duties were not thought of primarily as either impositions on the person or originating in a person's 'moral sense' (as with us), but as requirements of the case which were there to be fulfilled. This change in the ordinary understanding of morality is perhaps

44. Consider, e.g., the following passages cited by Benardete: *Meno* 86b7; *Crito* 47d1; *Laws* 885b3, 933e5. Compare *Cratylus* 418b1–419b4.

45. This is how Plato uses *dei* in a number of passages that Benardete himself cites: *Republic* 578d1; *Phaedrus* 270c5; *Cratylus* 399a6, *Statesman* 286d1, 292d5 and d9; *Phaedo* 61b4, 99d5; *Laws* 643b4, 716b9, 918b8. See, additionally, *Republic* 442c11–d1: the rational part (*to logistikon*) of the soul ought to rule; *Euthyphro* 8b7–e2. Consider *Nicomachean Ethics*, 1143a9, where *dei* could hardly be more literally translated than as "ought." Cf. 1144a16, where *ha dei* [*prattein*] is associated with *chrē ton spoudaion* [*prattein*].

46. Benardete, "XPH and ΔEI," 288. (The emphasis on the English words is added.)

47. Note Socrates' use of *oiomenoi dei* at *Meno* 86b7, which Benardete justifies as expressing a "rule [!] for everyone" (296). Compare Socrates' use of *chrē* at *Republic* 352d6, which hardly indicates that what is under consideration is merely subjective, i.e., a matter of personal opinion or preference only. See also the use of *chrē* at *Apology* 32e5.

> the greatest single obstacle to our comprehension of ancient ethics. Ethics, to put it paradoxically, were outside the sphere of the subject.[48]

Benardete opposes two alternatives to the classical understanding. Neither of these quite captures Thomas Aquinas's understanding (or Kant's, for that matter). For Thomas, the "imposition on a person" occurs, in the case of natural law, immediately by virtue of the operation of natural reason itself and not by virtue of a higher authority (except insofar as natural reason itself, speculative as well as practical, is created by something transcending the natural order). And natural reason is not the same thing as "a person's 'moral sense,'" for the latter carries with it the connotation of something particular rather than universal, of something that, as a mere "sense," is perhaps not rational at all. Thomas would not take the least exception to the classical conception of duties as "requirements of the case which were there to be fulfilled," if these requirements are properly determined by reason. The only question is what *principles* reason employs in its determination of the requirements to be fulfilled. Benardete, by helpfully drawing attention to Plato's distinction between "simply thinking" and "one's own thinking," has convincingly shown (though perhaps contrary to his intention) that Plato has more in common with so-called "moralists" like Thomas and Kant than one might have expected.

In this connection, when Socrates uses the expression *oute chrē* in his exchange with Cephalus, he is not alluding to some kind of natural and irresistible, but unspecified, necessitation holding man in its grip. He is articulating a straightforward obligation: one *ought* not to return the weapons in the case under consideration. But how does Socrates know this? Is it possible to give a reason (*logon didonai*) for why one ought not to return the weapons? If no reason of any kind can be given, then Socrates' claim that one ought not to return weapons lent by a friend who has gone mad in the interim is, at best, only the expression of a private and incommunicable insight that he possesses through his superior powers of discernment. But the claim is immediately concurred in by Cephalus, whose powers of discernment are not superior. Furthermore, since none of the others present in the dialogue take issue with this claim either, we can infer that they concur in it too, as does, most likely, the reader as well. It seems, then, that it should be possible to give a reason for the claim.

Thomas would say that to return weapons to a madman is to commit an offense, to contribute to the injury of the madman or of others, or of both. Since the madman is actually specified by Socrates as a friend and not an enemy, we can infer that he held that one has some kind of obligation, however minimal, not to injure or contribute to the injury of one's friends; and, by extension, not to injure or contribute to the injury of one's fellow citizens either.[49]

48. Benardete, "XPH and ΔEI," 293. The quotation marks around "moral" are in the original.

49. The cases of enemies in a war and convicted criminals is not yet at issue at this early point in the *Republic*. According to Thomas, these cases, though not exceptions to the precept not to offend, as I interpreted *offendere* in Part 1, are nonetheless governed by principles specific to them. *ST* 2–2 q. 40.

Since it is only a secondary precept of natural law, and not one derived immediately from a primary precept, that deposits are to be restored, this precept could in exceptional cases come into conflict with a primary precept. In the case under consideration, this secondary precept conflicts with the primary precept that one should not offend others, in particular, that evil is to be done to no one (*nulli esse malum faciendum*).[50] Had Plato's intention in depicting Socrates' refutation of Cephalus been to suggest that *every* moral principle admits of exceptions, he should have picked, not a rather distant secondary precept of natural law, but one immediately deducible from a primary precept, for example, that one should not send an innocent human being to the gallows through perjured testimony.[51] Then we would have been confronted with a much more intriguing criticism of "the idea of law."

Neither in his article on *dei* and *chrē*, nor in his book, *Socrates' Second Sailing—On Plato's Republic*, does Benardete raise the question of the status of Socrates' *oute chrē*, though in the latter work he employs the expression "ought not" without comment at the conclusion of his interpretation of the exchange between Socrates and Cephalus.[52] Nor does Strauss, in his interpretation of this exchange in *The City and Man*, note that Socrates' *oute chrē* implies that one is *obligated* to refrain from restoring weapons to a madman.[53] Allan Bloom does not comment on the *oute chrē*, either in his "Interpretive Essay" or in his "Notes."[54] He translates the expression as "shouldn't",[55] which is certainly all right. But then he interprets Socrates' observation as implying only that there are situations in which one is "exempted from obeying the law" [*every* law?], situations in which there are "sufficient grounds for taking away from a man what is thought to belong to him."[56] But the *oute chrē* implies not merely that there are situations where one is *exempt from* returning what one has borrowed, but that there are situations where one is *obligated not* to return what one has borrowed—situations in which there are not merely sufficient grounds for withholding the weapons from their owner, but *morally necessary* grounds for withholding them.[57] In his important

q. 61 art. 4; q. 64 art. 2, art. 6, art. 7.

50. See *ST* 1–2 q. 94 art. 4, co., where, as pointed out earlier, Thomas explicitly speaks to the question of whether one should always return goods held in trust, and answers (just as Socrates does) that there are cases where one should not do so. Cf. *ST* 1–2 q. 95 art. 2, co.; q. 100 art. 3, co.

51. See ST 2–2 q. 70 art. 4; cf. *ST* 1–2 q. 71 art. 6, ad 5. It is interesting that, whereas in the example from the *Republic* the immediate options available to the one to whom the weapons have been leant are limited to two, either to return or not return the weapons, the immediate options available to one who in a similar situation thinks that telling the *whole* truth—*panta . . . t'alēthē legein* (331c7–d1)—would be harmful are four, namely, to tell the whole truth, to tell only part of the truth, to be evasive without frankly lying, or to tell an outright lie.

52. Benardete, *Socrates' Second Sailing*, 15–16, 219.

53. *CM* 67–69. See Strauss's essay, "Plato," 34–36.

54. Bloom, *Republic*, 314–15; 442–3.

55. Bloom, *Republic*, 7; cf. 315, top.

56. Bloom, *Republic*, 315–16.

57. Note the gerundive-like formulation, *apodoteon . . . oud' hopōstioun* at *Republic* 332a2.

study, *Plato's Introduction to the Question of Justice*, Devin Stauffer does not have anything to say about the *oute chrē* either.[58] Nor does Stanley Rosen comment on Socrates' *oute chrē*, though he devotes nine pages, in *Plato's Republic: A Study*, to Socrates' three page exchange with Cephalus and makes interesting observations on the use of the related word *chrēstos* in the connection with friendship at 334e-335a, a passage that is in fact prefigured by the use of *oute chrē* in connection with friendship at 331c.[59]

Not one of these commentators—all of them careful and astute readers of the *Republic*—speculates on why Socrates did not simply say to Cephalus that it would be "unwise," "imprudent," or "stupid" to return the weapons, which would have been as readily granted by Cephalus and would have neatly anticipated Socrates' later contextual definition of justice in 442b6–444a2. These commentators might respond that Socrates, with his "moralistic" *oute chrē*, is only trying to meet the pious old moralist Cephalus where he is. But then "moralistic" language is not entirely left behind in Socrates' own account of justice.[60] It pertains to the very nature of reason that no one, not even Socrates, can argue for or against actions without employing the language of obligation, whether (in English) one indulges in an occasional "ought," or avoids this word like death itself and conscientiously restricts oneself to using the word "should"—which is nothing more than a synonym—in its stead.

In many of the examples not only of *chrē*, but of *dei* as well, that Benardete cites in Plato, all three of the necessary conditions for obligation that were identified in Part 1 above are met: (1) what is spoken of appears to be, in some respect, *good* to do; (2) it *can* be done (or at least it appears to be something that can be done); and (3) it *might not* be done (even if it is a necessary condition for doing something else).[61] These three components are clearly present in Socrates' exchange with Cephalus: it is good to refrain from returning the weapons in the case under consideration; one can refrain from returning the weapons; and one might not refrain from returning the weapons.

The concept of obligation is not a discovery or contrivance of the Bible. This concept is present in Greek philosophy. In fact, it is present in man as such, because his reason does not and cannot direct him either in deliberation, or in choice, or in action, except in light of all three of the above components. There is no better name

58. Stauffer, *Plato's Introduction*, 23–26, and fn. 8 on p. 26.

59. Rosen, *Plato's Republic: A Study*, 22–31.

60. To cite just a few examples, consider the use of both *dein* and *deoi* at *Republic* 433a2 and a5; the use of *dein* at 442d2, 453b2, b4, and 453c3; and, again, the use of *chrē* at 352d6. Or, to turn to another dialogue that is concerned with justice, consider Socrates' use of *dei* at *Gorgias* 507b6, and his use of *chrē* at 487e9 and 500c3. One can say that Socrates uses these expressions only to bring to light the hidden and unacknowledged "moralism" that is seething in the depths of Callicles' conflicted soul. But then one would also need to say how Socrates could have expressed *his* deepest thoughts on the question of *how one should* live without using *chrē* or *dei*, or an equivalent gerundive-like expression such as *pōs biōteon*. *Gorgias* 492d5 and d6.

61. These three components are also present in the English expression, "it behooves," which Mollin and Williamson suggest as an anything-but-"ought" translation for *chrē*. *An Introduction to Ancient Greek*, Vol. 2, 260–1.

for the *habitus* whereby reason knows what is obligatory than *synderesis*, and there is no better name for the *actus* of this *habitus* than *conscientia*, as Thomas employs these terms. There is every reason to think that Socrates, the other interlocutors in the *Republic*, and the readers of the dialogue possess this *habitus*, that through it, and only through it, they are able to recognize that one *ought not* to restore weapons to a man who has lost his mind, even after depositing them in one's trust. In fact, even if one disagrees and argues for returning the weapons, he will do so by using the common language of "ought" and obligation. There is then every reason to think that *synderesis* is universal, that man would not be what he is without it.

ii. Douglas Kries on the acquisition of *synderesis*

Douglas Kries, in *The Problem of Natural Law*, addresses the question of *synderesis* in a novel and interesting manner. Among other things, he gives a valuable overview of the history of this concept. He then argues correctly that Thomas's teaching on *synderesis* does not presuppose the claims of Christian revelation, or any other revelation, as premises. Rather, Kries shows that Thomas relied heavily on Aristotle in working out his teaching on *synderesis*, and he quotes important passages from the *Nicomachean Ethics* that Thomas was able to appeal to in support of his position.

> Aristotle did indeed use language that might imply the extension of the natural habit of first principles to the practical realm . . . The position of Albert [the Great] and Thomas on a natural habit of first practical principles cannot be dismissed as having *no* textual support. Thomas does not just posit the habit and then simply say that it is true; he has Aristotelian texts that lend support to his interpretation even if they do not prove it beyond all doubt.[62]

Kries's presentation raises the question of why the passages from the *Nicomachean Ethics* that he cites have been given so little attention by the Straussians in their criticisms of Thomas. The question is important since the *Ethics* is a capital text for them and they read it closely. But Kries does not press this question, perhaps because he

62. *PNL* 41. See 44, note 61: "Strauss and Jaffa suggest that Thomas's departure from Aristotle was based, perhaps unconsciously, on Thomas's commitment to Christianity. I see no evidence for such a conclusion, and neither does Doig ([*Aquinas's Commentary on the Ethics*] p. 192)." See also *PNL* 58: "Thomas might have recognized that he was departing from Aristotle with his teaching about *synderesis* and its grasp of the first principles of practical reasoning, but he might have thought that Aristotle needed philosophical rather than theological correction on this point . . . It is impossible to prove, ultimately, whether the teachings of Albert [the Great] and Thomas were *unconscious* products of crypto-theology. The analysis in the first part of this chapter ["The Objections of the Ancient Philosophers"] was that both understood themselves as making explicit what was implicit in Aristotle's own thought. They understood themselves as proceeding philosophically." Though Kries's attempt at a revision of Thomas's natural law teaching later on in his book is, as I argue in the sequel, both unnecessary and unsuccessful, he rightly places the burden of proof on Strauss and other critics of Thomas to validate the frequently made claim that the latter's teaching on natural law and *synderesis* "is based on belief in biblical revelation" (*NRH* 164).

knows that Straussians can always play their trump card. "Aristotle is not expressing his deepest thoughts in these passages."

Kries advances a criticism of his own against Thomas that, if not Straussian in letter, is certainly Straussian in spirit. This criticism is the central theme of his book and he develops it at length: Thomas's understanding that *synderesis* is a *universally* shared habit whereby man *as such*, and not just the philosophic few, knows the primary precepts of natural law is questionable. For Kries, the existence of *synderesis*, understood as universally possessed, can be neither proven nor disproven. He finds Thomas in some agreement with Aristotle about *synderesis*, but not fully so. If I follow his argument, Kries sides with Aristotle on the point where he finds them most markedly in disagreement. Commenting on a passage in the *Ethics*, he says

> Aristotle means to say that there is something like *synderesis* in the human reasoning process, in the sense that there are starting points of practical reason, but unlike Thomas, he denies that these *archai* are indelible and thinks instead that they must be acquired as one acquires virtue. The correct interpretation is thus that Aristotle would reject Thomas's teaching on the universal knowledge of moral principles among humankind, but not the suggestion that there are moral principles.[63]

As Kries sees it, Thomas's natural law teaching would be taken more seriously by Straussians (and by Reform Protestants as well, whom he also speaks to), if the teaching on *synderesis* was, as he says, "bracketed," which is to say, not denied outright, but removed, somehow, from consideration. Kries seems to think that this bracketing would "enable [natural law theory] to avoid many objections while preserving the advantages that have resulted in its enduring presence in philosophical and theological debate."[64]

On reading into *The Problem of Natural Law*, one becomes more and more eager to see just how much of Thomas's natural law teaching Kries is going to be able to preserve once he has bracketed the teaching on *synderesis*. One discovers, not surprisingly, that he is able to preserve very little of it.

> In the eyes of philosophy, then, if the teaching on universal apprehension of the natural law is bracketed, natural law theory will look very much like the ancient natural right theory of Plato and Aristotle.[65]

63. *PNL* 44.

64. *PNL* 95. This formulation concludes the prefatory remarks to the chapter entitled "On the Possibility of Revising Thomas's Teaching on Conscience." The title is misleading, since "revising" suggests retaining certain features of Thomas's teaching on conscience and modifying others, rather than bracketing this teaching altogether, indeed, excising it (101). A better title would be "On the Possibility of Revising Thomas's teaching on Natural Law." The problem would remain, however, since the bracketing of the teaching on conscience would entail the bracketing of the teaching on natural law itself.

65. *PNL* 104.

Kries notes in his Introduction that it is a mistake to call Aristotle a natural law thinker. A fundamental position of the Straussians—and here I am in agreement with them—is that, quite apart from the strengths or weaknesses of Thomas's teaching on natural law, this teaching is something quite different from Aristotle's teaching on natural right, whatever the former borrows from the latter. In spite of Kries's clear view of the Straussians' position on this matter,[66] and his apparent concurrence with them, there are sentences in *The Problem of Natural Law* where Kries himself blurs the distinction between natural right and natural law.[67] One is tempted to assume that this blurring is deliberate. Kries's intention seems less to revise Thomas's teaching on natural law than to decapitate it and dissolve the lifeless remnant in the ethical and political philosophy of Aristotle, to which it adds nothing of genuine substance.

As for the curious notion that the wise few may possess synderesis, and thereby conscience, but the unwise many do not,[68] Thomas would say that the difference between these two groups turns instead on their differing capacities for *judgment*, and the range and proper assessment of the experiences that inform their judgment. The wise and the unwise do not differ with respect to the *habitus* of *synderesis*. If they did, then whichever of two groups possessed this *habitus* and however they happened to come by it, they would be not just two different types of men but two different species of men, with only one of them possessing *per se nota* principles of natural law intrinsic to the operation of practical reason.[69] I doubt that Kries would wish to push the distinction between the wise and the unwise quite so far, though I could be wrong about that. In any case, it is striking that he ends *The Problem of Natural Law* with an appeal, not to Thomas Aquinas, about whom he has almost nothing to say in the closing pages of the book, but to Socrates, "the original founder of natural *right*."[70]

Rather than speculate further on Kries's underlying intention in *The Problem of Natural Law*, I shall now focus on his claim that the existence of *synderesis*, understood as the habit whereby the primary precepts of natural law are *universally* known by human beings, is dubious.

Kries makes an interesting point regarding the distinction between the two vices that Aristotle identifies as intemperance (or profligacy—Greek, *akolasia*) and incontinence (or lack of self-control—*akrasia*). Both the intemperate man and the incontinent man pursue bodily pleasure excessively. But whereas the former, in pursing bodily pleasures inordinately, presumably thinks that he is doing nothing wrong, the latter struggles against his inordinate desires but yields to them nonetheless. As

66. See *PNL* e.g., 28–29.

67. See *PNL*, the last two sentences on the page 51; and compare the last sentence of the first full paragraph on page 54 with the following paragraph. Consider the sentence spanning pages 58 and 59, and the first sentence on page 114.

68. Strauss seems to suggest the opposite: *CM* 59.

69. See Plato, *Theaetetus* 174b1–4.

70. *PNL* 179, emphasis added.

Kries sees it, the incontinent man retains knowledge of what natural law prescribes regarding temperance,[71] in spite of his transgression, whereas the intemperate man no longer has this knowledge, if he ever had it. The existence of intemperance as a vice distinct from incontinence is for Kries a telling piece of evidence in support of his suspicion that *synderesis* is not universally present in man.

Kries quotes the following passage from the *De Veritate*, which he thinks is indicative of Thomas's inability to adequately preserve Aristotle's distinction between incontinence and intemperance.

> One who has the habit of some vice is indeed corrupted with respect to the principles of activity (*circa principia operabilium*), not as to universal principles, but in their application to some particular case (*non in universali sed in particulari operabili*), in so far as through some vicious habit reason is stifled so that it does not apply the universal judgment to a particular activity when choosing.[72]

Kries is right to point out that this description does not suffice to distinguish the intemperate man from the incontinent one. Thomas, however, is not speaking to the distinction between these two vices in this particular article, but only to the general question of whether there are some men in whom *synderesis* is extinguished. He denies that this is true of the natural *habitus* whereby man, as a rational animal, knows the primary principles of action, that is, what in the *Summa Theologiae* he identifies as the first principle of practical reason and the primary precepts of natural law. But as regards the *act* of *synderesis*, that is, conscience operating in concrete circumstances, Thomas holds that it can be destroyed, at least temporarily, either by an injury to the bodily organs that reason makes use of or, more pertinently, by passions that interfere with reason—the result being an erring conscience. Assuming that, unlike the incontinent man, the intemperate man is so corrupt that he does not recognize this interference as interference, it still does not follow that in him *synderesis* has been simply extinguished. In fact, it seems likely that the intemperate man, confronted with Aristotle's definition, would concede that temperance is a mean between two vices regarding bodily pleasure, one of excess and one of deficiency. He would hardly deny that it is *ever* possible, even for *him*, to eat too much food or drink too much alcohol. He would, instead, misjudge the mean as lying much closer to the extreme of excess than it actually does. And because temperance is manifestly a virtue of wide latitude, and because intemperance, at least with respect to food and drink, does not directly harm others, this misjudgment as to where the due mean lies with respect to pleasures is relatively easy for many people to make.

Thomas makes the following observation, which is pertinent to the matter we are considering.

71. *ST* 1–2 art. 94 art. 3, co; ad 1.

72. *De Veritate* q. 16 art. 3, ad 3 (Kries's translation, *PNL* 43 and n. 59 on that page).

> If we speak of virtuous acts . . . in themselves, that is, in their proper species, then not all virtuous acts are of the law of nature. For many things are done according to virtue, to which nature does not incline at first; but have been discovered by the inquiry of reason as useful to living well.[73]

Acts of temperance fit this description. Consuming this or that amount of food and drink under varying circumstances is certainly not dictated by a primary precept of natural law. Eating and drinking in moderation is one of the things that the inquiry of reason has discovered "as useful to living well." Disagreement between the temperate man and the intemperate man about how much to eat and drink does not imply that the latter lacks *synderesis* altogether.

It is the primary and most general principles or precepts of natural law, and those secondary precepts that can be deduced from them right away, that are universally known and indelibly present in the human mind.[74] Since Thomas uses the plural (both *praecepta* and *principia*) when he argues for this tenet of his teaching, we can be sure that he is not speaking only of the naturally necessitating first principle of practical reason, but of properly obligating precepts, though, again, only the most general of these, the primary precepts that one avoid ignorance and that one refrain from offending others, the positive expansions of these two precepts, and secondary precepts that can be deduced from them *statim*.

Concerning the first of these, Aristotle himself says that all men by nature desire to know. This does not mean that all men regard their avoidance of ignorance or, expressed positively, their pursuit of knowledge as having the character of an obligation. Some say that they pursue knowledge not as an obligation but as a matter of pleasure. And the pursuit of knowledge is surely pleasant, if not always so, still often enough, especially if one is making progress in this pursuit. But just why the pursuit of knowledge is experienced as pleasant, at least in some measure, is an interesting question. For it is arguable that the pleasure in question is consequent to the realization that in pursuing knowledge one is more fully human, that one is in fact *better*, than one would be were one indifferent to truth, better independently even of the pleasure that pursuing knowledge gives rise to. If so, then this "better" is more fundamental than pleasure itself. It then becomes a question of whether this "better" can be adequately understood without reference to *some* conception of obligation. I have argued elsewhere that it cannot be adequately understood without this reference.[75] So I turn now to the second precept, that one not offend others, since this precept is even more obviously resistant to a hedonist reduction.

Do all men know that they should not offend others? That is, do all human beings who have reached the age of reason and whose intellects are not grossly and

73. *ST* 1–2, q. 94 art. 3, co.

74. *ST* 1–2, q. 94 art. 4, co.: *prima principia communia*; art. 6, co.: *quaedam praecepta communissima*. Cf. Finnis, *AMPLT* 128, footnote 122.

75. "The Pleasure of Philosophizing and Its Moral Foundation."

unusually impaired know that they should not harm others without provocation or out of proportion to prior harm received? If not, then Kries is right. Thomas's teaching on *synderesis* as a *habitus* rooted in the rational nature of man, and the related argument in q. 94 art. 2, which together constitute the foundation of his entire teaching on natural law, is seriously flawed. If, on the other hand, it can be plausibly maintained that all normal human beings know that they should not offend others, then there is no need to bracket *synderesis* from Thomas teaching on natural law and effectively replace his teaching with Aristotle's teaching on natural right.

Kries rightly says that even if everyone agreed that one ought not to offend others, this by itself would not prove the existence and universality of *synderesis* as Thomas understands it. For the pertinent claim in Thomas's teaching is not that everyone *happens* to agree that one should not offend, but that everyone *must* agree on this matter, since *synderesis* is a *habitus* of reason *per se*. One cannot be a normal human being, a rational animal, without knowledge of the principles of practical reason, just as one cannot be a normal human being without knowledge of the principles of speculative reason, whether these principles are isolated and reflected on by themselves or whether they are unstated but nonetheless at work in thinking about both what is and what is to be done. If natural law is a rule of reason itself and its primary precepts are *per se nota*, then it is, as a matter of necessity and not as a contingent fact, present wherever human reason is present. It is universally known, of necessity, by a rational *habitus*, whether we choose to call this habitus *synderesis* or not.[76] The case that Thomas makes for the coherence of natural law as a rule of practical reason and for the *per se notum* character of its indemonstrable primary precepts does not rest on fortuitous agreement, even on fortuitous *universal* agreement. It is as rational and compelling a case as any that can be made for the coherence of *speculative* reason and for the *per se nota* character of *its* indemonstrable principles.

iii. The feeling of right and wrong

Kries refers to Chapter 5 of John Stuart Mill's *Utilitarianism* as offering an alternative account of our awareness of moral principles that might equally well account for the broad agreement that exists among human beings regarding the most elementary matters of right and wrong.[77] The question, however, is not whether an alternate account of our awareness of moral principles is possible—certainly it is—but how internally consistent the alternative account is and, of equal importance, how well it agrees with the *phenomenon* of moral awareness, that is, with how obligation is actually experienced and expressed in speech. I have argued in Part 1 that there is a distinction in kind, not just in degree, between the experience of simple necessitation

76. Reason or intellect "continet prima principia universalia cognita nobis per naturale lumen intellectus, ex quibus procedit ratio tam in speculandis quam in agendis." *ST* 1–2 q. 62 art. 3, co.

77. *PNL* 96.

and the experience of moral obligation; that *ought* implies *might not* as well as *can*; and that the Ought, experienced this way, cannot be derived from the Is, not because it is of spurious origin, or a mere "value" distinct from fact, but because it is primordial in its proper sphere, the sphere of deliberation, choice, and action.

In Chapter 4 of *Utilitarianism*, Mill contrasts will with desire. But he does not introduce freedom until Chapter 5. Mill does not deny, indeed he asserts, that the "feeling of right and wrong" can be distinguished from the feeling of "ordinary expediency and inexpediency."

> The feelings concerned are so powerful, and we count so positively on finding a responsive feeling in others (all being alike interested), that *ought* and *should* grow into *must*, and recognized indispensability becomes a moral necessity, analogous to physical, and often not inferior to it in binding force.[78]

This passage might leave one with the impression that, for Mill, some feelings bind of necessity whereas others leave one with a bit of freedom to resist them. That impression, however, is weakened by his passing observation that "men imagined what they called the freedom of the will."[79] I do not think that Mill, in spite of his incontestable logical acumen, can make full sense of how even he uses the word "ought;" and he uses it all over the place in Chapter 5. He does not give us in that chapter or anywhere else in *Utilitarianism* a clear definition of obligation, as Kant does, nor does he give us the means to define it, as Thomas Aquinas does. For one cannot define moral obligation as a certain kind of feeling, a feeling distinct from that of simple necessitation, albeit "analogous to it," without defining it as a feeling of moral obligation, in which case one has not defined anything at all. Mill does not offer a sufficiently comprehensive account of why all human beings who have attained the age of reason even "feel" that they *ought* not to commit offences against others—assuming, with Mill, that at some level they all do feel this way: "all being alike interested." The problem is that a specifically moral interest is experienced as different from other interests, and not infrequently experienced as requiring a subordination of other interests. What is experienced is not so much an elemental *feeling* of right and wrong as an elemental *knowledge* of right and wrong. Thomas has identified the roots of this knowledge in q. 94 art. 2. The feeling of right and wrong is consequent to the judgment of right and wrong. It is a feeling proper to a rational being, just like, depending on the circumstances, the feelings of respect, admiration, indignation, and remorse.

78. Mill, *Utilitarianism*, 98–99.

79. Mill, *Utilitarianism*, 100.

iv. *Synderesis* in moral education

I argued in Part 1 that Thomas was right to insist on the self-evident character of (1) the first principle of practical reason, (2) the order of our natural inclinations, and (3) the primary precepts of natural law, in which (1) and (2) are conjoined.

It is often said today that conscience (or *synderesis*) is formed by "moral conditioning." But unless there is something in the soul that has the capacity to be morally conditioned, moral conditioning would not take place. Such so-called conditioning, which is more properly called education, takes place when a parent tells a young child not to do something harmful to another child, especially a sibling. The language the parent employs is typically something like, "Don't hit your little sister. How would you like it if someone did that to you?" The child is being asked to see things not just from his own perspective but from the perspective of another. He is being asked to engage in a specifically rational train of thought, to engage in a universalization that is not just theoretical, as happens when one sees that an individual is a member of a certain class, but properly practical. He is asked to imagine himself in the position of the other, and to recognize that any *reason* he might have for not wanting to be harmed, is identical to the *reason* the other would have for not wanting to be harmed, and hence that he cannot *rationally* harm the other while protesting against harm to himself. The capacity, present even in children who have not yet fully attained the age of reason, to engage in this kind of universalization attests to the presence of conscience. We expect and require someone who has attained the age of reason to engage in this kind of reasoning spontaneously.

Synderesis cannot be created by moral education, any more than the understanding of logical principles can be created by education in mathematics and science. Moral education presupposes *synderesis* just as education more generally presupposes the understanding of logical principles, though education rarely involves explicitly articulating and thematizing the elemental principles it presupposes. In the absence of some kind of rudimentary awareness of moral principles, no moral education could be accomplished. That every normal human being has this awareness is borne out by the ubiquitous presence of the language of obligation—of "ought," "should' and the like, in ordinary (that is, non-academic) discourse and deliberation. That this is the case is supported by the analysis of the meaning of sentences employing "ought" and "should" that I undertook in Part 1, where I argued that even a merely conditional obligation cannot be deduced from a mere desire, inclination, or need, but, in the last analysis, only from an unconditional obligation.[80]

This view is further supported by the following considerations. Let us assume that someone—not a child, not a moron, and not a certifiable psychotic, but an adult

80. Kries apparently thinks—wrongly as I argued in Part 1—that a hypothetical imperative, and hence a conditional obligation, can be deduced from a (non-obligatory) want or a desire. Consider *PNL* 148–57.

whose mental abilities are not *way* below average—says that he does *not* know that he should not offend, or commit an offense against, others. Take murder, for example. I leave to one side here the special cases of war, self-defense, tyrannicide, and capital punishment for the most serious crimes. For these acts are not murder according to Thomas. To be sure, murder can be committed under the cover of war or self-defense, in which case it is inexcusable. But war, self-defense, tyrannicide, and capital punishment are not murder *per se*. Murder is deliberate killing of the innocent (and, in the case of war, it is the intentional targeting of noncombatants; it is not just a collateral effect of targeting combatants). So, let us assume that an adult human being who is not mentally impaired says that he does not know that he should *not* murder another human being. And surely we can find someone, maybe any number of people, who might say this. What would Thomas's response be?

We must keep in mind that, for Thomas, the precept not to offend possesses the same self-evidence as does the principle of non-contradiction. Now, some people say that they do not know the principle of non-contradiction. It can be shown, however, that they rely on this principle even when they deny it, for they distinguish as sharply between affirmation and denial as everyone else does. Moreover, their denial forces them to say things that it is inconceivable they really believe. This is how Aristotle, who also holds the principle of non-contradiction to be self-evident, argues.[81] So the fact that someone denies that something is self-evident does not by itself mean that he does not know it to be true. It does not even mean that he does not know it to be self-evident. It means that he has not sufficiently thought through what he is saying. He denies that the principle of non-contradiction is knowable because he holds the view that for something to be knowable it must be provable, a view that, according to Aristotle, exhibits a lack of education (*apaideusia*).[82]

Something similar takes place when someone asserts that he does *not* know that he should not murder another human being—an act that is prohibited by a secondary precept of natural law deduced *modica consideratione* from a primary precept. I think that this assertion is the result of self-deception, if it is not an outright lie. In either case, there is no reason to think that a person making such an assertion is telling the truth. Conscience can be wrestled with and its testimony ignored; but it cannot be simply destroyed (except, perhaps, by someone who has transformed himself into a demon). It is not the case that all we can do when confronted with someone asserting that he does not know that he should not murder is to *insist* that he *does* know it, as Kries, among others, seems to think.[83] We can *reason* with him. We should be able to get him to concede—conditional on how deeply entrenched his eristic commitments are—that he knows it would be wrong for us to murder *him*.[84] And yet, again, any

81. *Metaphysics* 1005b35–1012b32.

82. *Metaphysics* 1006a6.

83. *PNL* 101.

84. Similarly, someone who denies the principle of non-contradiction can usually be brought to

reason that he might give for why we should not murder him ends up being the same reason for why he should not murder someone else: murder is intrinsically wrong; it is an extreme case of offense, of inflicting extreme harm on another without provocation or out of proportion to prior harm received. Injustice more generally has this basic character.

Those who claim not to know that injustice, so understood, is wrong still express outrage at injustice done to those whom they care about and indignation at injustice done to them.[85] The only reason they assert that they don't actually know that offending others is wrong is that they recognize that such a thing cannot be proven without begging the question. And yet it cannot be proven only because it is immediately known without proof. It is for this reason that those who deny knowing that it is wrong to offend others belie this denial in expressions of outrage and indignation at perceived injustices, and in their expectation that others who have the same perception will spontaneously concur in their outrage or indignation. Something similar can be said about remorse.[86]

Even philosophers who call the entire moral order into question are not immune to outrage and indignation. Take Nietzsche. No philosopher worthy of the name has ever called the moral order into question as forthrightly and forcefully as he has. And yet even Nietzsche is philosophical enough, that is to say, honest enough, to concede that Thomas is right in his claim that *synderesis* is proper to man as such. He does not say this in these very words, of course. But what he does say on the matter is remarkable.

> He who attempts [to be independent] . . . goes into a labyrinth; he increases by thousandfold the dangers that life already brings with it, not the least of which

see that denial of this principle, like the denial of any other proposition, can be distinguished from affirmation of it only if the principle is itself true and recognized as such.

85. We are often told that members of primitive societies do not have the same moral principles that are recognized in developed societies. That may be the case, but it hardly proves that they have no conception of justice and injustice at all. For example, though they may engage in "free love" in various forms, it seems unlikely that *if* they make marriage *vows* they also think there is nothing wrong with *violating* them. (Compare *PNL* 99, but cf. fn.6 and, especially, fn.7.) Adultery is not just fornication. It involves injustice. As Thomas says ". . . adulterium intemperantiam admixtam inustitiae habet" (*Super Sent.*, Lib. 2, dist. q. 3 art. 1, qc. 5, ad, 1). It is virtually certain that whatever vows members of primitive societies make to each other, they take them as seriously as others people do, if not more seriously, and are rightly offended when they are unilaterally violated (as distinct from being dissolved by mutual consent). They can be offended only if they have some awareness of justice and injustice, and possess *synderesis* as the natural *habitus* whereby they recognize this distinction.

86. Whatever Strauss's intention might have been in prefacing *NRH* with the parable that Nathan tells David in 2 Sam 12, David's reaction to it shows how a deep concern for justice persists even in someone who acts unjustly. If it is not David's conscience—by whatever name it might be called—that expresses itself in his exchange with Nathan, I do not know what it is. It is hard to believe that Strauss used this motto to suggest that David's remorse revealed only an unexamined attachment to justice (Jerusalem) that would not have survived philosophical scrutiny (Athens). But it is not impossible to believe such a thing. *City and Man*, 59.

> is that no one sees how and where he errs, goes astray, becomes isolated, and is torn to shreds little by little by some cave-minotaur of conscience.[87]

I assume that this passage is autobiographical, and that Nietzsche is comparing himself to Theseus, who entered the Cretan labyrinth in order to kill the Minotaur. But Theseus succeeded, and Nietzsche does not succeed. Nietzsche may have thought that conscience was a monster. But he does not doubt its existence. Try as he might to slay it, he admits that he is torn to shreds by it instead. If someone really were able to slay the conscience—which would mean, among other things, not only coming to feel no remorse at all about anything he has ever done, no matter what it was, but actually rejoicing in the prospect of doing all of it all over again, repeatedly *ad infinitum*[88]—such a being, for Nietzsche, would no longer be "human all-too-human" but would become, precisely through the slaying of his conscience, *over-man*. However, that a being able to slay the conscience would become, not over-man, but *under-man*, a human body with a sub-human head, something of a minotaur in fact, seems much more likely. In any event, the striking thing is that Nietzsche, the impassioned critic of morality, is in essential agreement with Thomas, the rational defender of morality, on the fundamental point: the moral law cannot be abolished from the heart of *man*.[89]

SECTION C. SYNDERESIS AS INERRANT—MORAL ABSOLUTES

Not only is *synderesis* an entirely natural *habitus*, universally present in all rational animals; it is also, according to Thomas, inerrant. The inerrancy of *synderesis* implies something fixed and invariant, or absolute, in what *synderesis* knows. What synderesis knows are the primary precepts of natural law. These have the character of moral absolutes.

It might seem unnecessary to argue that Thomas fully grasps this implication, since his explicit statements leave hardly any room for doubt on the matter. It is, however, necessary to do so. For more than a few Thomists have arrived at the view, espoused by Strauss and his followers, that there are no genuine moral absolutes, no exceptionless rules of conduct. These Thomists wish to attribute this view to Thomas because, among other things, it enables them to magnify the distance between

87. Nietzsche, *Jenseits*, § 29 (cf. § 214), [the sections in the English translation bear the same numbers].

88. Nietzsche, *Jenseits*, § 56.

89. Not all critics of morality know themselves as well as Nietzsche knew himself. Consider, in this connection, the following exchange from Evelyn Waugh's novel, *Put Out More Flags* (New York: Dell Publishing Co., 1969), which is set in the first year of World War II. "There was a young man of military age in the studio; he was due to be called up in the near future. 'I don't know what to do about it,' he said. 'Of course I could always plead conscientious objections, but I haven't got a conscience. It would be a denial of everything we've stood for if I said I had a conscience.' 'No Tom,' they said to comfort him. 'We know you haven't a conscience.' 'But then' said the perplexed young man, 'if I haven't a conscience, why in God's name should I mind so much saying that I have'" (251–2).

Thomas, whom they admire, and Kant, whom they cannot stand. Some of them have been persuaded by Strauss and his followers than insisting on moral absolutes is incompatible with a just appreciation of the latitude statesmen require for dealing prudently and expeditiously with the manifold complexities of political life, especially in extreme situations. They think—some of them—that a careful reading of the relevant texts, with special attention to the order in which Thomas presents his teaching and to what strikes them as slightly veiled hints and indications here and there, suggests, if it does not exactly demonstrate, that Thomas himself denies the existence of moral absolutes.[90]

The claim that there are moral absolutes does not mean that all moral principles are exceptionless, regardless of circumstances. Thomas does not make so extreme a claim, nor does he need to do so. The claim that there are moral absolutes means only that some moral principles are exceptionless, regardless of circumstances. And this is what Thomas explicitly teaches. The primary precepts of natural law are exceptionless, regardless of circumstances.[91] To be sure, those secondary precepts that are deduced from the primary precepts only *multa consideratione* do admit of exceptions, though only in exceptional circumstances. But the secondary precepts that are deduced from the primary precepts *statim* or *modica consideratione* are as exceptionless as the primary precepts themselves.[92]

90. "While he is critical of certain dimensions of Aquinas's natural-law theory, [Ernest] Fortin goes out of his way to defend the role that prudence plays in Aquinas's political teaching. Aquinas's natural law teaching is often faulted by politically minded thinkers for failing to take into account the latitude for statesmanship that the exigencies of political life regularly demand. In the eyes of such critics, Aquinas replaces the mutable natural-right teaching of Aristotle's *Ethics*—whose lack of fixity grants statesmen a breadth of option in acting politically—with an overly rigid and moralistic [!] natural law whose precepts brook no exception. But as Fortin convincingly shows, these criticisms are often misguided, typically conflating Aquinas's nuanced position with the absolutist, a-political interpretations he has received at the hands of *soi-disant* Thomists like John Finnis and Germain Grisez. By paying careful attention to the unfolding presentation of natural law in the *Summa Theologica*, Fortin demonstrates that unlike many of his modern-day disciples, Aquinas is not a proponent of moral absolutism. On the contrary, he is a partisan of an older approach that understands the enduring need for prudence in political life." Mark Guerra, *Christians as Political Animals*, 131–2. Guerra does not spell out how Fr. Fortin accomplishes this demonstration or where he does so.

91. According to Thomas West, "the 'natural law' contains no categorical or promulgated commandments" (*Critique of the 'Straussian' Critique*, 30, quotation marks in the original; cf. 17–18.) Consider also West's attempts to shield Thomas against the accusation of "moralism"—the incessantly repeated charge of Straussians against any thinker who argues that there are some things that one should not do under any circumstances: 38, 40, 99–100. Commenting on *ST* 1–2 q. 100 art. 8, West says that, "the only thing unchangeable in the Decalogue is 'the principle of justice'" (17). This formulation is somewhat misleading. Thomas states the obvious in this article, namely, that human law has to determine what counts as murder (homicide as the result of carelessness?), theft (taxing income twice?), and adultery (remarriage after divorce?). It is only in this way that the *determinatio* of the precepts of the Decalogue concerning murder, theft, and adultery is mutable. Otherwise, Thomas would not be able to say, as he says in this very article, that "the precepts [note the plural] of the Decalogue are in no way dispensable (*praecepta decalogi sunt omnino indisipensabilia*)," and, in particular, that "human law cannot make it lawful for a man to be slain unduly (*indebite*)" (q. 100 art. 8, co; ad 3).

92. 1–2 q. 100 art. 1, co. On the question of whether the precepts of natural law admit of

As we have seen, Thomas argues that the moral precepts of the Decalogue belong to natural law. We can leave to one side the precepts having to do with God because they are bound up with theology (though, for Thomas, with rational and not revealed theology, except for the precept regarding the Sabbath),[93] and our concern here is limited to what we naturally know of the precepts of natural law apart from any theology. We can also leave to one side the precept that forbids coveting, not because it is unknowable to natural reason—Thomas holds the opposite—but because it is a precept forbidding a kind of thought rather than an act in the ordinary sense of the word.[94] Thomas holds that the precept commanding us to honor our parents, though declaring an obligation of wide latitude, is nonetheless as binding as the precept forbidding murder.[95] But because what such honor consists in could be thought to be ambiguous, we can leave it to one side as well. This leaves us with negatively formulated moral precepts, all of them prohibiting specific acts, all of them knowable to natural reason apart from theology of any kind, and none of them admitting of dispensation: the prohibitions of theft, murder (deliberate slaying of the innocent), adultery, and bearing false witness against another.

In some respects the precept forbidding theft is the most complicated, since Thomas teaches that in situations of dire and pressing need, one may take something from another openly or secretly. But he argues, as we have seen, that doing so is not theft properly speaking.[96] Whatever one makes of his argument, Thomas took it seriously enough to say that theft *as such* is forbidden.[97] The same is true of murder,[98] suicide too,[99] adultery,[100] and bearing false witness.[101] Additionally, Thomas says that lying is always a sin, though it is not always a mortal sin.[102] Rather strikingly, he says that one is not permitted to deceive with a frank lie even the enemy of one's country in time of war: doing so "is always unlawful" (*semper est illicitum*)."[103] Moreover, though an act that is good according to its species can be rendered morally evil by being ordained to an evil end, for example almsgiving for the sake of vainglory, no act that is evil according to its species can be rendered morally good, or even permissible, by being ordained to a good end, such as murdering someone wealthy for the sake of

dispensation by God, see the *Note* appended to Ch. 5, above.

93. 1–2 q. 100 art. 4, co.

94. 1–2 q. 100 art. 5, co.

95. 1–2 q. 100 art. 1, co.

96. 2–2 q. 32 art. 7, ad 3; q. 66 art. 7, co.

97. 2–2 q. 66, art. 5, co.

98. 2–2 q. 64 art. 6, co.

99. 2–2 q. 64 art. 5, co; ad 3.

100. 2–2 q. 64 art. 7, arg. 4. In his reply to this argument, Thomas does not take exception to its premise.

101. 2–2 q. 70 art. 4, co.; cf. 110 art. 4, ad 2

102. 2–2 q. 110 art. 3, co.; ad 4; art. 4, co.

103. 2–2 q. 40 art. 3, co.

appropriating his property and using it to succor the destitute, or aborting a fetus for the sake of the mother's mental health, and so on.[104]

These unequivocal statements by Thomas are thought by some to be subtly undermined by a small number of formulations that occur here and there in his immense *oeuvre*. In the *Summa Theologiae* Thomas says at one point that

> [P]ractical reason treats contingent matters, with which human actions are concerned, and hence, although there is a certain necessity (*aliqua necessitas*) in the general [principles], the more one descends to matters of detail, the more one meets with defects.[105]

With his expression *aliqua necessitas*, Thomas could be thought to be suggesting that even the general principles of practical reason, that is, the primary precepts of natural law, can admit of occasional exceptions. But Thomas uses the adjective *aliqui, aliqua, aliquod*, to name only a certain type of something, in passages far too numerous to cite.[106] The expression *aliqua necessitas* in this passage names a certain type of necessity. The necessity characteristic of the primary precepts of natural law is different from that which characterizes the first principles of speculative reason in that the former are efficacious only through a voluntary assent of the will. The principles of speculative reason, such as the principle of non-contradiction, state the necessary conditions of being, the most elemental conditions under which something can or cannot be, and thereby the conditions of knowledge as well. The first principle of practical reason initiates and propels action with the force of natural necessity. The primary precepts of natural law express the conditions under which something ought or ought not to be done. All of these are characterized by necessity, but it is not the same type of necessity. The *aliqua necessitas* that holds for the primary precepts of natural law is not a partial necessity, much less a dubious necessity. It is a moral necessity.

Because Thomas advises generally against change in long-standing human laws even when something *better* occurs,[107] it has occasionally been suggested that he is, if not a closet conventionalist, maybe not quite as committed to the primacy of natural law over human law as one would be inclined to think from what he says elsewhere. But in the very articles where he advises against change in human laws, Thomas says that a human law *should* be changed when it contains a manifest iniquity, that is, when

104. *De Malo* q. 2 art. 4, ad 2. Thomas uses the proverbial phrase, *necessitas non subditur legi*, in the context of human law, not natural law. *ST* 1–2 q. 96 art. 6, co. Consider the example given in the *corpus* of this article.

105. *ST* 1–2 q. 94 art. 4, co.

106. Here are three examples taken more or less at random from different parts of the *ST*. 1 q. 27, art. 1, co.: "cum omnis processio sit secundum aliquam actionem . . . est aliqua processio ad extra." 1–2 q. 3 art. 6, co.: "in inferiori est aliqua participatio superioris." 2–2 q. 165 art. 1, ad 1: "supra naturam humanam est aliqua natura in qua potest malum culpae inveniri, non autem supra naturam angelicam."

107. *ST* 1–2 q. 97 art. 2, co.

it is opposed to the primary precepts of natural law or what can be deduced from them *modica consideratione*, or when its observance is extremely harmful.[108] And Thomas repeats his earlier claim, lest there be any doubts about the matter, that the primary precepts of natural law, unlike human laws proper, never admit of change.[109] The reason he says that human laws should rarely be changed, even when they are not the best possible laws—assuming that they are not manifestly iniquitous—is that he recognizes that the citizens' respect for human law owes something to the force of custom.[110] But it is not an unqualified principle that human laws should not be changed, as Thomas devotes the very first article in this question to showing.

In his commentary on the *Nicomachean Ethics* there are a few places where Thomas could be thought to concur in the following claim of Aristotle's.

> Things pertaining to actions and matters of expediency have nothing fixed (*ouden hestēkos*) about them, any more than do matters of health. The *logos* regarding what is general [with respect to actions] being this way, even more so does the *logos* regarding particulars lack precision.[111]

In his remarks on this passage from Book 2, Thomas limits himself essentially to restating what Aristotle has said.[112] He does not take issue with Aristotle here. But that does not mean that he fully concurs in what Aristotle says. In his largely word for word commentaries on Aristotelian texts, Thomas's chief task is to set out as clearly as possible what it is that Aristotle has to say about the topic under consideration.

In addressing Aristotle's claim in Book 5 that natural right and political right are *both* changeable,[113] Thomas again restates Aristotle's argument, without initially

108. See *ST* 1–2 q. 97 art. 2, co. We should not forget Thomas's assertion that a human law that is opposed to natural law is not properly speaking a law but a corruption of law (1–2 q. 95 art. 2, co; cf. q. 93 art. 3, ad 2; q. 96 art. 4, co.).

109. 1–2 q. 97 art. 1, ad 1; cf. art. 3, ad 1.

110. In *CM*, Strauss says writes, "[L]aw owes its strength, i.e., its power of being observed, as Aristotle says here [*Politics* 1268b22–1269a24], entirely to custom and custom comes into being only through a long time. Law . . . does not owe its efficacy to reason at all or [does so] only to a small degree" (22). Strauss refers the reader to *ST* 1–2 q. 97 art. 2, ad 1, apparently as support for this claim. But, in the passage referred to, Thomas (quoting Aristotle) does not make as strong a claim as Strauss does. The context, moreover, is human law proper, not natural law. It would have been helpful if Strauss had referred the reader also to the following article, where Thomas says, "nulla consuetudo vim obtinere potest contra legem divina *vel legem naturalem*" (q. 97 art. 3, ad. 1, emphasis added).

111. *Nicomachean Ethics* 1104a4–8.

112. Here is Thomas's quite faithful *expositio*: "Et hoc ideo, quia sermones sunt exquirendi secundum conditionem materiae, ut ibi dictum est, videmus autem, quod ea quae sunt in operationibus moralibus et illa quae sunt ad haec utilia, scilicet bona exteriora, non habent in seipsis aliquid stans per modum necessitatis, sed omnia sunt contingentia et variabilia. . . . Et cum sermo moralium etiam in universalibus sit incertus et variabilis, adhuc magis incertus est si quis velit ulterius descendere tradendo doctrinam de singulis in speciali." (*Sententia Libri Ethicorum*, lib. 2 lect. 2 n. 4–5.)

113. *Nicomachean Ethics* 1134b29–33.

taking exception to it. But then he introduces a crucial qualification that does not correspond to anything in the text he is commenting on.

> However, it is to be noted that because the essences (*rationes*) of changeable things are unchangeable, if something is natural to us, as pertaining to the very essence of man, it is not changeable in any way, for instance that man is an animal. But things that are consequent to nature (or follow nature—*consequuntur natura*), for example, dispositions, actions, and movements, are variable in the fewer instances. Similarly, those things that pertain to the very essence (*rationem*) of justice cannot be changed in any way; for example, theft is not to be committed, because that is to commit an injustice. But those things that are consequent [to nature] are changeable in a few cases.[114]

Returning, right after this digression, to Aristotle's text, Thomas says, "Then, at 'Those things according to composition,' [Aristotle] shows how the legally just things are indifferently changeable."[115] And, as the sequel makes clear, Thomas is referring here to conventional arrangements and secondary precepts arrived at by *determinatio*. He illustrates the latter by saying,

> And so the just things *that are not natural*, but are *posited by men*, are not the same everywhere; thus the same punishment is not imposed everywhere for theft . . . All laws are posed insofar as they agree with the end of the polity, but nevertheless only one [polity] is the best everywhere according to nature.[116]

The last sentence is an important qualification, if not a gentle correction, of Aristotle's claim that even natural right is changeable. Thomas seems confident that Aristotle (and most likely Plato, too) would grant that what the best polity is *according to nature*—clearly a matter of natural right—is *not* changeable. My guess is that Strauss and more than a few of his followers would concur in this "moral absolute": by nature the wise should (or ought to) rule the unwise, and not vice versa. They would likely balk at calling the formulation "moral," though exactly why is not clear to me. I doubt they would resist calling it "absolute."[117]

114. *Sententia Ethic.*, lib. 5 lect. 12 n. 14: Est tamen attendendum quod quia rationes etiam mutabilium sunt immutabiles, si quid est nobis naturale quasi pertinens ad ipsam hominis rationem, nullo modo mutatur, puta hominem esse animal. Quae autem consequuntur naturam, puta dispositiones, actiones et motus mutantur ut in paucioribus. Et similiter etiam illa quae pertinent ad ipsam iustitiae rationem nullo modo possunt mutari, puta non esse furandum, quod est iniustum facere. Illa vero quae consequuntur, mutantur ut in minori parte.

115. *Sententia Ethic.*, lib. 5 lect. 12 n. 15: "Deinde cum dicit: quae autem secundum compositionem etc., ostendit qualiter iusta legalia sunt mutabilia indifferenter." By "iusta legali" in this context, Thomas means just things as established by human law, not the justice that pertains to natural law.

116. *Sententia Ethic.*, lib. 5 lect. 12 n. 15 (emphasis added): "Ita etiam iusta quae non sunt naturalia, sed per homines posita, non sunt eadem ubique, sicut non ubique eadem poena imponitur furi . . . Omnes enim leges ponuntur secundum quod congruit fini politiae, sed tamen sola una est optima politia secundum naturam ubicumque sit."

117. See Strauss, *CM* 69.

Elsewhere Thomas says, in an argument, that natural justice (*iustum naturale*) fails in some cases and is changeable like human nature.[118] The argument cites the authority of Aristotle. In replying to this argument, Thomas says,

> The Philosopher is not speaking of the natural justice that contains the very order of justice: for this never fails (*nunquam deficit*), justice is to be preserved. But he is speaking in reference to determinate modes (*ad determinatos modos*) of observing justice, which in certain cases fail (or even deceive—*fallunt*).[119]

Since the argument and the reply to it occur in an article in which Thomas argues that the precepts of the Decalogue do not admit of dispensation, we must infer that he holds that these precepts, in all their specificity, are not merely "determinate modes of observing justice" but, rather, "contain the very order of justice."

In his commentary of Book 5 of the *Nicomachean Ethics*, Thomas says,

> Just as in speculative matters some things are naturally known, as indemonstrable principles and what are proximate to these, whereas some are discovered by the exertion of men, so also in matters of action (*in operativis*) some are naturally known as (*quasi*) indemonstrable principles and what are proximate to these; such as evil is to be avoided, no one is to be unjustly harmed, nor is theft to be committed, whereas others are thought out by the effort of men, which are thus called the legally just.[120]

Some have thought that Thomas's use of *quasi* in this passage might be intended to imply that the naturally known principles of action are no better than *almost* indemonstrable—though what in the world could "almost indemonstrable" be thought to mean? However, Thomas sometimes uses *quasi* not in the sense of "as if (but not really)" but rather in the sense of "just as."[121] In fact, he sometimes uses *quasi* in the sense of "as" simply. A case in point is a sentence in the passage just cited from this very *lectio*. There Thomas says "if something is natural to us, as pertaining to the very essence (*ratio*) of man, it is not changeable in any way, for instance that man is an animal."[122] The expression "as pertaining to the very essence of man" is a rendering of

118. *ST* 1–2 100 art. 8, arg. 1.

119. *ST* 1–2 q. 100, art. 8. (Whether Thomas has interpreted Aristotle correctly here is not my concern.) See also 1–2 q. 94 art. 4, arg. 2; ad 2.

120. Sicut enim in speculativis sunt quaedam naturaliter cognita, ut principia indemonstrabilia et quae sunt propinqua his; quaedam vero studio hominum adinventa, ita etiam in operativis sunt quaedam principia naturaliter cognita quasi indemonstrabilia principia et propinqua his, ut malum esse vitandum, nulli esse iniuste nocendum, non esse furandum et similia, alia vero sunt per industriam hominum excogitata, quae dicuntur hic iusta legalia. *Sententia Ethic.*, lib. 5 l. 12 n. 3; cf. *Super Sent.*, lib. 2 d. 39 q. 2 art. 2, ad 2.

121. Deferrari, *A Lexicon of St. Thomas Aquinas*. 927; cf. Lewis and Short, *Latin Dictionary*, 1507.

122. There are a number of other places where Thomas uses *quasi* in the sense of "as" rather than "as if" or "almost." To cite just one example, see the last sentence of the corpus of ST 1–2 q. 94 art. 3. "Multa enim secundum virtutem fiunt, ad quae natura non primo inclinat; sed per rationis inquisitionem ea homines adinvenerunt, quasi utilia ad bene vivendum."

"*quasi pertinens ad ipsam hominis rationem.*" To translate this expression as "as if (but not really) pertaining to the very essence of man" or "almost (but not quite) pertaining to the very essence of man" would be particularly infelicitous in light of the example Thomas uses. It is hardly the case that being an animal *almost* pertains to the essence of man; there is nothing "iffy" about it. To translate *quasi indemonstrabilia* in the passage about principles of action as "as if (but not really) indemonstrable" or "almost (but not quite) indemonstrable" would be comparably infelicitous, for three reasons in particular.

In the first place, Thomas says in q. 94 art. 2 that the first principle of practical reason, which includes the phrase "evil is to be avoided," also included in the above passage, is *per se notum*. Though it does rely on the principle of non-contradiction, and on the *ratio boni* as well, it cannot be demonstrated, or deduced, from either of these, or from both together, or from any other premise that is not its own equivalent. One might think that the reliance of the first principle of practical reason on the principle of non-contradiction and on the *ratio boni* invests it with a kind of hypothetical character. But if Thomas thought so, he would hardly have said that both the first principles of demonstration and the primary precepts of natural law are *per se nota.*[123]

In the second place, Thomas uses the expression "*quaedam principia naturaliter cognita,*" without a *quasi* between *principia* and *naturaliter*, immediately before "*quasi indemonstrabilia principia,*" the latter presumably standing in apposition with the former. Since Thomas uses the expression *naturaliter cognita* and *naturaliter nota* as equivalent to *per se nota,*[124] and uses these expressions also as equivalent to *indemonstrabilia,*[125] and moreover uses *per se nota* as equivalent to *indemonstrabilia,*[126] we have to infer that all three expressions name, for him, the same thing: what is self-evidently known, that is, known immediately and not as the conclusion of a demonstration.

Finally, in the passage from the *Commentary on the Nicomachean Ethics* that is under consideration, Thomas explicitly contrasts these naturally known principles of action with those that are arrived at by discursive reasoning. If the principles that are naturally known are not indemonstrable, then they too must be arrived at by discursive reasoning—in which case the distinction that Thomas is making collapses. For there to be *known* principles of action, some of them *must* be indemonstrable.[127]

123. "[P]raecepta legis naturae hoc modo se habent ad rationem practicam, sicut principia prima demonstrationum se habent ad rationem speculativam: utrumque enim sunt quaedam principia per se nota." *ST* 1–2 q. 94 art. 2, co.

124. *De Veritate*, q. 10 art. 8 co; *SCG* lib. 1 cap. 10 n. 5; *Super Sent.*, lib. 1 d. 3 q. 1 art. 2, arg. 1; *ST* 1 q. 2 art. 1, arg. 1. *ST* 2–2 q. 8 art. 6, arg. 2.

125. *SCG* lib. 3 cap. 46 n. 4; *Super De Trinitate*, pars 3 q. 6 art. 4, co. 1; cf. *Sententia Ethic.*, lib. 6 l. 5 n. 5. See also use of *naturaliter cognita* in *Sententia Ethic.*, lib. 5 l. 12 n. 3.

126. *Expositio Peryermeneias*, lib. 1 l. 14 n. 24; *SCG* lib. 3 cap. 46 n. 4. *Expositio Posteriorum Analyticorum*, lib. 1 l. 34 n. 11.

127. It is possible that Thomas uses *quasi indemonstrabilia*, rather than *ut indemonstrabilia*, when

I argued in Part 1 that the primary concrete precepts of natural law are the two that are advanced at the end of the *corpus* of q. 94 art. 2, namely, that one avoid ignorance and that one not offend others. It is worth revisiting these two precepts in the present context. Because the precept that one avoid ignorance first serves the operation of speculative reason, and because this-worldly happiness consists primarily (though not exclusively) in an operation of the speculative intellect, we can infer that it has a certain priority over the precept that forbids offending. On the basis of this assumption one might infer further that, if these two somewhat diverse obligations should come into tension with one another, fulfilling the former would have to take precedence over fulfilling the latter. If the only way one could avoid ignorance would be by committing an offense, even a gross injustice, against others, doing so would be permissible or, rather, obligatory. Such in an inference would be, I think, formally correct, but at the same time empty. For it rests on the false assumption that the precept to avoid ignorance and the precept not to offend could come into conflict with each other. But, as I argued in Part 1, they cannot come into conflict with each other. And here we can discern the precision and the elegance with which Thomas's formulates these two precepts. Both are unequivocally categorical, and neither admits of dispensation. But whereas the precept forbidding offense expresses an obligation of narrow latitude, the precept commanding the avoidance of ignorance expresses, as noted earlier, an obligation of wide latitude. Exactly how one is to avoid ignorance is not spelled out. How to avoid ignorance differs according to one's intellectual ability and according to the varying circumstances in which one might find oneself. For those who possess the requisite talent, natural bent, and opportunity, the avoidance of ignorance might lead to intensive studies in any number of areas. But no special talent, natural bent, or opportunity is required for reflecting on the possibility that the world in which we live is not the foundation of its own being or for attempting to gain as much clarity as possible about one's obligations and the moral requirements of a choiceworthy life. Such reasoning lies within the ability of, and is obligatory for, anyone who has reached the age of reason and whose reason is not grossly impaired. It is the minimum condition for living an examined life, which includes, it must be added, the examination of conscience. Fulfilling the obligation to avoid ignorance, because it is characterized by such wide latitude, can never entail violating the obligation not to offend. Although one can imagine circumstances in which, say, a human being would have to steal, or

speaking of the principles of action in the passage from *Sententia Ethic.*, lib. 5 l. 12 n. 3, quoted above, because the three principles he names there differ from each other in the character of their evidence. The first of these, that evil is to be avoided, is part of the first principle of practical reason presented in q. 94 art. 2. It is *per se notum* and hence, according to Thomas, indemonstrable *simpliciter*. The third is that theft (as *Thomas* understands theft) is not to be committed. It is not indemonstrable; it is, however, demonstrable *modica consideratione*. The second principle Thomas names—Straussians will note that it is the *central* one—is that no one is to be unjustly harmed. This principle is essentially a restatement of one of the two primary precepts of natural law presented at the end of the *corpus* of q. 94 art. 2. Like the first of these three principles and unlike the third, then, it is *per se notum*; but unlike the first and like the third, it is properly obligatory. See Part 1, Ch. 2, Section c, above.

cheat, or even murder in order to get money to attend college, Thomas's precept does not command one to attend college. But it does command one to live an examined life. As expressed, this precept is characterized by such breadth of latitude that one could never find oneself in a situation where compliance with it would require committing an offense against another. Fulfilling the narrow obligation not to offend is always compatible with fulfilling the wide obligation to avoid ignorance. And yet the breadth of latitude that characterizes the latter obligation does not mean that the precept that declares it is dispensable or admits of exceptions.[128]

It is natural reason itself, not instinct or pleasure-seeking, that forbids one from living an unexamined life. For a man, that is, for a rational animal, such a life would not be *worth* living. It can only be through a natural *habitus* of reason that the adherents of the classical philosophers know the *per se notum* but indemonstrable and incontestably *moral* truth that life should be examined, even if they prefer not to call this habit *synderesis*, and prefer not to call this truth "moral."[129]

128. One might object that to carry out these two precepts one has to be alive, and therefore that the truly primary and overriding precept of natural law is to preserve one's own life by any means one thinks necessary, not excluding murder. Thomas, however, is emphatic that the preservation of no corporeal good, including the preservation of life itself, takes precedence over preservation of the good of reason. And there is a further consideration. One does not have to preserve one's life, least of all by unjust means, to *refrain* from committing an offense against another. Similarly, on the assumption that only a *living* being can be ignorant—we do not usually refer to stones, trees, or corpses as "ignorant"—avoidance of ignorance does not require one to avoid death at *whatever cost*. Finally, committing injustice toward others arguably presupposes a measure of self-deception, and hence a particularly abominable form of ignorance, namely, willful ignorance. We see again the aptness of Thomas's originally stating the two primary concrete precepts of natural law in the negative rather than in the positive—as, say, "Pursue knowledge" and "Give to each his due." I cannot pursue all knowledge. And I cannot give all individuals what they are due. I cannot give what they are due to individuals whom I never encounter. And regarding those individuals whom I do encounter, I cannot give them what they are due, certainly not all that they are due, from others. In this connection, see Thomas's distinction between the habit of justice and an act of justice in *ST* 2–2 q. 58, art. 1.

129. Plato, *Apology* 38a. Note the expressions *dein zētein* at *Meno* 86b and *zētēteon* at 86c. (See H. W. Smyth, *Greek Grammar*, Harvard University Press, 1956, p. 960: paragraph 933b; and p. 480: paragraph 2152 a.) If Socrates does not *know*, by some rational *habitus*, that we are better in seeking to know what we do not know than in not seeking it, then he can hardly *know* that the philosophic life is, for those who are able to live it, the most choiceworthy life.

Chapter 10

Rational Sociability

Before concluding this part of the present study, we need to explore further and consider in greater detail the difference between two rival conceptions of human association. These conceptions play no small role in distinguishing the teaching of Thomas Aquinas (and other scholastics) from the teaching of his philosophical predecessors and those Straussians who concur in it.

According to Thomas Aquinas, the interest of practical reason *qua* reason cannot be a merely private good, given that reason necessarily employs principles of universal scope. The interest of practical reason is, instead, the common good, or that for the sake of which there is law in the first place. What is good has the character of an end or is conducive to an end. Because law is an ordinance for the common good, it must be referred to an end. Our last end, or perfect happiness, consists in the beatific vision of God, who is the common good *par excellence* and the ultimate end toward which all things aim, one way or another.[1] But the beatific vision is a supernatural end. So we need supernatural assistance to attain it. That anyone has ever attained, or ever will attain, this end is then not a matter of natural reason but of faith.

Compared to this supernatural end, the happiness that is available in this world is imperfect happiness. But it is our natural end nonetheless, and it can be attained by natural reason in its speculative and its practical operation. Imperfect happiness consists of the two components that were identified in Part 1. The primary component is contemplation, as founded on natural reason and ordinary human experience; the secondary component is an "operation of the practical intellect directing human actions and passions."[2] The secondary component is not just instrumental, or a mere means, for realizing the primary component. It is one of the things in which worldly happiness consists. According to Thomas, the proper operation of the speculative

1. *SCG* 3 cap. 16–18. See *ST* 1–2 109 art. 3.

2. *ST* 1–2 q. 3 art. 5, co.

intellect and the proper operation of the practical intellect together constitute such happiness as can be achieved in this life. Together they constitute the natural end for man.

The rational directing of human actions and passions can and often does require the forgoing of various kinds of pleasure. And happiness, though not equivalent to pleasure, is necessarily accompanied by pleasure.[3] Contemplation is obviously pleasant, if not always then often enough. But it is less obvious that rationally directing actions and passions is pleasant. And if it is not pleasant at all, it is hard to see how it could be even secondarily an intrinsic component of happiness rather than merely an extrinsic means to it. If there is no pleasure intrinsically associated with morality, the sum and substance of such happiness as man can attain through the exercise of his natural reason would consist solely in contemplation, or philosophy.

Thomas realizes that one of the great themes of classical political philosophy is the difference between types of men, in particular, the difference between philosophers and the non-philosophic, often anti-philosophic, multitude. Not everyone is capable of contemplation, and not everyone is interested in action, especially in political action. The contemplative man seems to be as little attracted to political action as the man of action—including the accomplished statesman, who according to some is non-philosophic man at his height—is attracted to contemplation. The difference in ability and interest between philosophers and non-philosophers is sometimes thought to be so great as to preclude the possibility of there being a genuine good that is common to, or can be shared in by, both types of men. To be sure, political association allows for certain shared goods, most significantly public safety, especially protection from enemies foreign and domestic. Political association also provides for such things as public roads, postal services, commerce, and garbage collection. All the citizens, philosophers included, benefit from these things. Citizens make small sacrifices in the way of taxes, equally or proportionally assessed, and some of them make large sacrifices by serving in the military and police forces. But the question remains as to whether, given the different types of men and ways of life that one can find in a political community, there is a good that is truly common and yet loftier than any of the things just mentioned. Philosophers tend to be contemptuous of the non-philosophic multitude, and the non-philosophic multitude tend to be suspicious of philosophers. The difference in types of human beings, formerly a central theme in reflections on political life and the possibility of the common good, has rarely been revisited in our anti-elitist times. The conspicuous exception is Strauss and his school.

3. *ST* 1–2 q. 4 art. 1; art. 2.

SECTION A. EXOTERICISM

For Strauss, the difference between philosophers and non-philosophers is most pronounced in their way of finding answers to ultimate questions. Philosophers take natural reason and ordinary verifiable human experience to be the criteria for what is true regarding the constitution of the world, man's place within it, and his relation to his fellow men. Non-philosophers place much greater stock in received opinions about these things, in ancestral authority, inherited traditions, and religious convention. The multitude, being generally uncritical in their acceptance of received opinion, are believers of one sort or another. Even in regimes where atheism is the official doctrine, the majority of citizens are believers. They are not exactly religious believers, but they are political believers. They are ideologues. Just as in religious regimes philosophers can provoke public opposition by calling into question the existence and nature of the divine, so in secular regimes philosophers can provoke public opposition by calling into question the sanctity of the human. In the increasingly secular and liberal democracies of the West, one can easily get away with public ridicule of religion. It is much more difficult to get away with public ridicule of belief in the essential equality of all human beings, belief in fundamental human rights, belief in the goodness of diversity, and so forth. Even asking what is *meant* by essential equality (physical, intellectual, moral?), what is *meant* by fundamental human rights (if more original than anything accomplished by positive law, who or what endows us with them?), and what is *meant* by diversity (intellectual diversity, a few fascists in our midst, people who are opposed to homosexual marriages as well as people who support them?) is likely to provoke irritation or worse. The great majority of the citizens in a liberal democracy may not think deeply about these things, but they feel deeply about them. And yet what they really mean by rights, equality, and diversity is not at all easy to say. The philosopher very much wants to know what they mean and, of equal importance, whether what they mean bears any relation to reality. From the perspective of classical political philosophy, the antagonism between the philosophic few and the non-philosophic many is a permanent tension, even if only latent some of the time. It is a tension that will exist as long as man exists.

This tension can be managed in a variety of ways. Among other things, philosophers can hold their tongues. But philosophers are not content to "articulate the riddle of being" in solitude. They wish to share their thoughts with those who are capable of following their thoughts. Moreover, the great philosophers—Socrates is here the conspicuous exception—are not content to "articulate the riddle of being" in speech only to those who happen to be near at hand. They wish to share their thoughts on the most important things with thinkers who possess minds comparable to their own. But great thinkers are rare. They are typically separated from one another by significant stretches of space and time. To bridge this spatio-temporal gap the philosopher writes books.[4] In doing so he commits his thoughts to fortune, hoping that sooner or later someone will happen upon his book and understand it just as he wished it to be understood. The writing or, more precisely, the publishing of a book is a public act. The non-philosophic multitude, and their political and religious leaders who wish to protect them from the disconcerting speculations of philosophers, have access to the books that the philosophers write. By committing his thoughts to writing, the philosopher risks being persecuted for disturbing the somnambulant tranquility of the multitude. To reduce the likelihood of such persecution, the great philosophers of the past, many of them, adopted an art of writing that enabled them to present on the surface of their texts an exoteric teaching that harmonized with the prevailing opinions, religious or otherwise, that the multitude received and lived by, while at one and the same time merely indicating on the surface, "between the lines," and detectable only by highly attentive readers, an esoteric teaching that called into question or even contradicted the exoteric teaching. Strauss is the thinker who in our times was first to demonstrate, definitively, that many of the greatest and most famous books in the history of Western political philosophy cannot be adequately interpreted without giving due consideration to the exoteric art of writing that their authors practiced and expected attentive readers to notice and see through.

Philosophers of the past fall roughly into two groups: (1) an earlier group who, thinking that the moral and religious opinions of the multitude contribute to civic order—to an order from which the philosophers themselves benefit—have no desire to undermine public confidence in these opinions; and (2) a later group who, thinking that most people are capable of something that approaches philosophical sophistication, desire to undermine the multitude's confidence in received opinion and replace it with a more enlightened view of things. Those in the first group do not believe that such a thing is possible. They worry that a weakening of public allegiance to religion will be followed by a strengthening of public allegiance to ideology, and they worry that the latter can as easily, if not more easily, give rise to obscurantism, fanaticism, and hostility toward freedom of speculation as the former.

The many will never become genuinely philosophical. Destruction of their religious beliefs will be followed by moral and political anarchy. But this anarchy will be temporary only. It will sooner or later be replaced by a hard tyranny, even if preceded by a soft tyranny—"political correctness" as the latter is called today—that will be as great a danger, if not greater, to freedom of philosophic inquiry in the future as religious dogmatism was in the past. Philosophers who do not believe that public enlightenment is possible, and these are chiefly the philosophers of classical antiquity and their Medieval followers, are not inclined to undermine the religious beliefs of the community in which they reside, but to put up with it, and even pay a measure

4. Socrates did not commit his thoughts to books. He could share them directly with thinkers of the caliber of Plato and Xenophon.

of public homage to it.[5] The second group is comprised of certain philosophers and their followers who are confident that everyone would be better off without religion, and they wish to wipe it out. These are the philosophers of the Enlightenment, some of them, and their progressivist disciples. From the perspective of the first group, the confidence of the second group is unwarranted and as dangerous as it is foolish.[6] Still, for the philosophers in both groups, religion is a fiction. They differ on the question of whether this fiction is useful or not.

For Thomas, and for the scholastics in general, there is an essential harmony, even a complementarity, between natural reason and what the Catholic faith holds to be revealed. There is nothing that a philosopher knows, or can know, that causes a serious problem for the thoughtful believer.[7] Those things philosophers claim to know that seem to cause a serious problem for believers can be refuted outright by the theologian or shown to be a matter of opinion rather than of knowledge—in either case according to the standard of reason that the philosopher himself ostensibly holds to be authoritative. Because there is no essential incompatibility between what the philosopher indubitably knows and what the believing Catholic believes, the distinction between free-thinking philosophers and the thoughtlessly believing multitude that so captivated the attention of the classical political philosophers and their Jewish and Muslim followers in the Middle Ages, and continues to captivate the attention of the Straussians,[8] is for the Christian scholastics a theme of diminished significance.[9] The scholastic understanding that man *as such* is a rational animal, and that reason, whether as practical or as speculative, operates only under the illumination of

5. One encounters this sort of thing not only in Western philosophy, but in Indian Philosophy as well. See my article, "Vedic Tradition and the Origin of Philosophy in Ancient India,"

6. "In [Jehuda] Halevi's age, the right, if not the duty, to suppress teachings and books, which are detrimental to faith, was generally recognized. The philosophers themselves did not object to it." *PAWr* 110. See 17: "The attempt to establish [the Islamic philosophers'] serious teaching is rendered . . . difficult the by the fact that some opponents of the [philosophers] seem to have thought it necessary to help [the philosophers] in concealing their teaching, because they feared the harm which its publication would cause to those of their fellow-believers whose faith was weak."

7. See Robert Sokolowski, *The God of Faith and Reason*, 157–63.

8. *RR* 146: "The radical [!] distinction between the wise and the vulgar is essential to the original concept of philosophy." Strauss, "What is Liberal Education?" 14: "[T]he philosopher and the non-philosopher cannot have genuinely common deliberations." Cf. Plato, *Theaetetus*174b1–3; *Statesman* 294a6–c4; Aristotle, *Politics* 1254b12–21.

9. Strauss is right in saying that, "[n]o doubt is left [in the Thomistic doctrine of natural right] . . . regarding the basic harmony between natural right and civil society" (*NRH* 16). One should not infer from this fact, however, that the Latin scholastics were unaware of veiled and circumspect advocacy of heterodox teachings by philosophers or followers of philosophers living in their midst. See, again, the concluding sentences of Thomas's *De Unitate Intellectus Contra Averroistas* (quoted above in Ch. 4, Section a, above). If I understand Strauss, he holds that there is *not* a basic harmony between natural right and civil society because of the sharpness of his distinction between the philosopher and the non-philosophic multitude in whose midst he has to live. Thomas would say that Strauss exaggerates the difference between the two types of men. It is infinitely less sharp, and less significant, than the distinction between man *as such*, i.e., the rational animal, and sub-rational animals.

principles of *universal* scope, renders the conception of a *common* good for man, even in this life, less problematic than it was for the classical political philosophers and less problematic than it is for Strauss and his followers.

SECTION B. THE GOOD OF OTHERS

Strauss reiterates the observation of Maimonides, without dissociating himself from it, that "governmental laws are, as such, directed toward man's physical well-being only and do not pay any attention to the well being of his soul."[10] Life in a political community is not possible without governmental laws, and a philosophical life cannot be lived entirely apart from a political community, however much it may aim at transcending, in its speculative freedom, the whole sphere of the political. So governmental laws play a role in making the philosophic life possible, as Strauss acknowledges and even insists on.[11] To be sure, governmental laws rarely if ever mandate the study of philosophy. They may even forbid the study of philosophy. Still, governmental laws can, and frequently do, mandate public education. They thereby, if only incidentally, further the cultivation of the liberal arts, which can be understood as preparatory for philosophical studies.[12]

More importantly, governmental laws pay attention to the moral well-being of man's soul inasmuch as they cultivate, within the limits of human legislation, the moral virtues of courage, moderation, and justice, which are indispensable to a healthy political community. Maimonides' observation holds true, at most, on the assumption that the well-being of the soul is limited to the well-being of the speculative faculties of the soul, that it does not include the well-being of the practical or moral faculties, and that the value of the latter is instrumental only, both in the case of the good man and the good regime.[13] Thomas would disagree with this assumption.

Man has a natural inclination to live in society. Thomas distinguishes this inclination, which is proper to our rational nature, from the inclination to know the truth about the ultimate cause or causes of things, which is also proper to our rational nature. The negatively formulated precept, that one not offend others, among whom one is bound to live, expresses the minimum standard of conduct that man must abide by

10. "The Law of Reason," 133; cf. *On Tyranny*, 199.

11. See "A Giving of Accounts," 465–66.

12. Plato *Republic*, 522c–534b. See *NRH* 151.

13. "Their [i.e., the philosophers'] whole life is devoted to the pursuit of something which is absolutely higher in dignity than any human things—the unchangeable truth . . . If striving for knowledge of eternal truth is the ultimate end of man, justice and moral virtue in general can be fully legitimated *only* by the fact that they are required for the sake of that ultimate end or that they are conditions of the philosophic life." (*NRH* 151, emphasis added). This view does not lead Strauss to conclude, as one might have expected, that there is no common good. But it does lead him to articulate it in a surprising way, if, that is, he is speaking in his own voice when he writes in *Thoughts on Machiavelli* that "the only good which is unqualifiedly the common good for all men is the truth, in particular the truth about man and society" (283; see 284). Compare *ST* 1–2 q. 92 art. 1; 2–2 q. 47 art. 10.

in order to realize his inclination to live in society,[14] just as the negatively formulated precept that one avoid ignorance expresses the minimum standard of what is involved in seeking the truth about God. In the article immediately following the one in which Thomas presents these two precepts negatively, he moves quickly to the positive and begins to enrich what he has just said.

> [I]n every man there is a natural inclination to act according to reason. And this is to act according to virtue. In this way, therefore, all the acts of the virtues pertain to the law of nature.[15]

One might object that, even if there is a natural inclination to act (broadly speaking) according to intellectual virtue, one sign of this being that progress in understanding is intrinsically pleasant, still there is no natural inclination to act according to moral virtue. For the exercise of moral virtue, at least to the extent that it sometimes involves working for the good of others at the expense of working for one's own good, narrowly conceived, is not intrinsically pleasant. Thomas has something to say about this.

> Inasmuch as we consider the good of another as our own good, on account of the union of love (*propter unionem amoris*), so we delight in the good that is done by us to others, principally (*praecipue*) to friends, as in our own good (*sicut in bono proprio*).[16]

In his commentaries on the *Ethics* and *Politics*, Thomas reproduces Aristotle's statement that "man is by nature a political animal." In the *Summa Theologiae*, however, he says that "man is by nature a political and social animal."[17] The political association is most strikingly distinguishable from other comparably authoritative associations, such as the family, but also the church and cenobitic monasteries, in that it can and does employ force even to the point of killing human beings in order to defend itself. In this way, the friend-enemy opposition is at the core of "the concept of the political," even constitutive of it according to Carl Schmitt.[18]

In attempting to understand this opposition Schmitt is led, as Strauss points out, to emphasize the enemy rather than the friend.[19] By adding "social" to "political" to name the form of animality specific to man, Thomas emphasizes the friend over the enemy, as he also does when he speaks of a natural inclination to live, not just in a political community, but in society. Thomas is not blind to the exigencies of political

14. This reasoning, which is implicit in *ST* q. 94 art. 2, co., is made explicit in q. 96 art. 2, co.

15. *ST* 1–2 q. 94 art. 3, co.

16. *ST* 1–2 q. 32 art. 6, co.

17. *ST* 1–2 q. 72 art. 4, co. See *Sententia Ethic.*, Lib. 8 l. 12 n. 18; *Sententia Politic.*, Lib. 1 l.3 n. 5. *De Regimine Principum.*, Lib. 1 cap. 1.

18. *Der Begriff des Politischen*, 26 ff. [English Translation by George Schwab, 26 ff.]

19. "Comments on *Der Begriff des Politischen* by Carl Schmitt," in *Spinoza's Critique of Religion*, 335. This article of Strauss's is also published and retranslated by G. Schwab as an appendix to *The Concept of the Political*. See fn. 9 of Schwab's Introduction to this work.

life. But he regards friendship as more natural, more *deeply* constitutive of human association, than protection from possible enemies, important though the latter surely is. Man is sociable because he is rational.

However, one might ask, even if we do delight in the good we do to our friends, even if we delight in it as intrinsic to our own good, properly understood, why would we delight in the good we do even to those who are not our friends. A little later in the article from which the above passage was cited, Thomas says,

> [D]oing good to another becomes pleasant (*delectabile*) insofar as there comes to man a certain image of the abundance of good existing in himself, from which he is able confer [good] on others.

Though Thomas illustrates this point by referring to the pleasure one takes in conferring goods on one's children, he does not limit himself to this particular pleasure any more than in the preceding passage he limited himself to the pleasure one takes in benefiting one's friends. These are simply the most obvious instances of delighting in the good of others. Regarding the "union of love" we must remember that, for Thomas, to love (*diligere*) one's neighbor, that is, to will his good, is a primary and self-evident precept of natural law.[20]

That doing good to others is natural to man does not mean that everyone does it. Very young children do not readily do good to others. They are not naturally inclined to act according to moral virtue. But then they are not naturally inclined to act according to intellectual virtue either. What is natural to man is not just what is present in him at any particular time, but what is present in him at his prime. Furthermore, as we learn from Aristotle, the natural course of development can be impeded.[21] In the case of many species of plants, more seeds get eaten by birds than end up sprouting, much less growing into mature plants. For similar reasons, the young of many species of animals never make it to adulthood, not to mention eggs that never get fertilized or, once fertilized, are spontaneously aborted. But that does not mean that coming to maturity is not the natural end of what is immature. In the case of man, the failure of many, if not most, human beings to arrive at full moral maturity, and at intellectual maturity too, does not mean that such maturity is not constitutive of man's natural end. All kinds of circumstances, including poor education and the acquisition of bad habits, can impede the doing of good to others, just as they can impede the natural desire for knowledge from becoming the actual pursuit of knowledge. We cannot look to immature human beings in order to find out what is natural to man. Instead, we have to consider man's natural faculties in their unimpeded functioning, chief among them the reason that is proper to him. And it is precisely Thomas's examination of their

20. See Part 1, Ch. 2, Section b, iv, above. Consider what Aristotle says about beneficence (*euergeia*), benevolence (*eunoia*), and wishing the good of one's friend for the friend's sake (not just for one's own sake) in *Nicomachean Ethics* 1155a1–1156b24.

21. *Physics* 199b15–26. Thomas Aquinas, *In Duodecim Libros Metaphysicorum Aristotelis Expositio*, Lib. 1 Lect. 1.4.

unimpeded functioning that leads him to the view that the directing of human actions and passions by practical reason is a constituent of man's natural end of happiness, just as contemplation is, though the latter ranks higher because it bears a greater affinity to perfect or supernatural happiness. Natural law is natural not because everyone or almost everyone complies with it.[22] Natural law is natural because it is rational. It is the standard according to which a mature and fully rational human being acts.

When Thomas begins his treatment of human law ("governmental laws"), he says that "there is in man a certain natural aptitude for virtue." [23] For this aptitude to be transformed into actual virtue, discipline, training, and education are needed, as is most obvious in the case of children. These things are facilitated and even provided for by human law, which in addition to reiterating the precepts of natural law proper effects the *determinationes* that are its specific concern.[24]

If the goals of society were limited to the mutual protection and common defense of as many of its members as possible, to arrangements that allow for commodious living, to what promotes the greatest pleasure or the "maximum preference satisfaction" of the greatest number—or, put only somewhat differently, to man's physical well-being only and not to the well-being of his soul—it would follow that, should rare but conceivable situations arise in which the only way these goals could be efficiently reached would be through unjust means, such as deliberately killing innocent human beings, committing injustice would be permissible. In fact, committing injustice would be "prudential" (in the current non-Thomistic sense of the word), if not obligatory.

The goals of society, however, are more complex. In associating with others a human being is led from an early age to put restraints on the single minded pursuit of his own pleasure. He thereby comes to discover that his own good is not easily separable from the good of others, even apart from their usefulness to him. Thomas puts it this way.

> A natural thing has not only a natural inclination with respect to its own good (or, with respect to its proper good—*respectu proprii boni*), to acquire it when it does not have it, or to rest in it when it does have it; but also to share its own good with others as far as possible . . . And so it pertains to the very concept of the will (*ad rationem voluntatis*) that one communicate the good one has to others, as far as possible.[25]

22. See *ST* 1–2 q. 100 art. 5, ad 1.

23. *ST* 1–2 q. 95 art. 1.

24. See above Part 1, Ch. 2, Section b, ii .

25. *ST* 1 q. 19 art. 2, co: "Res enim naturalis non solum habet naturalem inclinationem respectu proprii boni, ut acquirat ipsum cum non habet, vel ut quiescat in illo cum habet; sed etiam ut proprium bonum in alia diffundat, secundum quod possibile est . . . Unde et hoc pertinet ad rationem voluntatis, ut bonum quod quis habet, aliis communicet, secundem quod possibile est." Those who think that the philosophical view of the good is that it is essentially "one's *own* good" need to account for why the philosopher takes so ardent an interest in the good of at least some others, such as his

This statement expresses an overarching natural teleology that is out of favor today. But one need not accept that the inclination Thomas speaks of holds for all natural beings to recognize that it holds for the natural, rational, teleologically constituted being that is man. It is of the very nature of the will, as the rational appetite, to will what is good, real or apparent. The will cannot rest in, cannot be fully content with, a good that is an exclusively private good except on the claim, which receives no support from reason, that one's *own* good, in the narrow sense of one's own life and pleasure, is *the* good. A sign that reason aims at a common good is the natural desire we have to share a fine book, a well-composed poem, or a piece of music we love with others. The delight we take in such things is enhanced by observing others taking delight in them as well. Of its very nature the will, as the *rational* appetite, wills the common good.[26]

Thomas, of course, does not deny that we often will only a private good. This is especially true with regard to the pleasures corresponding to the lower appetites, which we share with sub-rational animals. Except when pursuing these pleasures is at odds with the good of reason there is nothing blameworthy about doing so, though there is nothing particularly commendable about it either. We are unlikely to feel admiration, much less respect, for someone solely because he got a really good massage or ate a sumptuous meal, a fact that by itself suggests that we are not disposed to regard pleasure *per se* as the good.[27] When people go so far as to commit offenses against others in order to further their private pleasure they are, according to Thomas, acting contrary to reason. They are acting irrationally. Whether they understand it or not, the will in them is conflicted because it is mistaken to be in service of the self, most narrowly conceived, exclusively. Such people cannot appeal to reason to justify acting the way they do, not even to justify it to themselves. Since practical reason enunciates its precepts, just as theoretical reason enunciates its propositions, in the language of universals, a man can rationally justify his actions only if he can regard them as being, in principle, permissible to others as well.[28]

These considerations enable us to answer an objection that one might advance against the second of the two primary precepts of natural law that Thomas identifies in q. 94 art. 2. One might grant that Thomas is right in identifying in man a natural inclination to live in society, but take issue with his holding that this inclination cannot

philosophic friends and those youths whose souls exhibit the beauty of philosophic promise.

26. It is not for nothing that Aristotle devotes two books of the *Nicomachean Ethics* to a consideration of friendship, which he says "is a virtue or accompanies virtue." *Nicomachean Ethics* 1155a2.

27. *NRH* 128–9.

28. The qualification "in principle" is essential here. A man does not have to permit others to do the *identical* thing that he himself does, e.g., to build houses on a particular piece of property that he himself happens to own and is building a house on. But he has to permit others to build houses on property that they own. And if any restrictions are placed on this permission, they too must be expressed in universal terms: no one may build houses above a certain height in certain locations, and so forth. This qualification is reflected in Thomas's qualification, *secundum quod possibile*, in the passage quote above.

be realized by committing offenses against others: Thomas's view is too high-minded. It is naïve. For surely it is possible to live in society, even to live quite comfortably in society, while committing any number of offenses against others, as long as one does not get caught. To this objection Thomas would repeat that the inclination to live in society, that is, to live *with* others as distinct from just living *surrounded by* others, is an inclination specific to our nature as rational beings. One can certainly commit offenses against others, but one cannot do so as a rational being. As noted earlier, a man cannot give a reason for why it is all right for him to commit offenses against others while holding that it is not all right for them to commit offenses against him.[29] A man cannot rationally say, "Treat me like a human being!" without recognizing that, in saying this, he is placing himself under an obligation to treat others the same way. This recognition attests to an elemental equality between human beings, in spite of incontestable variations, minor and major, variations in acuity of judgment not least among them. This elemental equality consists in our common rationality, which we appeal to without hesitation in conversations, disputations, and quarrels, day in and day out, not just with those who are inclined to philosophy, but with butchers, bakers, candlestick makers, and countless others. We cannot conceive of having these conversations, disputations, and quarrels with sub-rational animals.

When Thomas says that "all men are by nature equal" (*omnes homines natura sunt pares*),[30] he does not mean that they are equal in terms of intelligence, physical strength, and the like. Rather, they are equal by virtue of their capacity for free choice or self-determination.[31] A human being naturally desires to be treated as a human being, as a person, and not as a mere thing for the use of others. This desire is entirely natural, and it is entirely rational. For to treat a human being as a mere thing is to treat him as something he is not. To treat a human being as a mere thing is irrational, in fact stupid. And for someone who has reached the age of reason, treating a human being as a mere thing is not innocently stupid but willfully stupid. To exempt oneself from a precept that practical reason expresses universally, such as not to bear false witness against another human being, is an instance of this kind of willful stupidity. Not only can one make no appeal to one's reason to justify this exemption, one must silence one's reason to do so.

A mature man, that is to say, a fully rational man, realizes that his own good is bound up with the good of his spouse, his children, his friends, and his fellow citizens.[32] He delights in their good—including especially their intellectual and moral

29. Though a human being may tolerate others acting unjustly toward him, it is impossible for him to regard what they do as both unjust and "all right", whatever he may say. He cannot even, strictly speaking, forgive them without thereby acknowledging that what they have done to him is wrong.

30. *ST* 2–2 q. 104 art. 5, co.

31. *Super Sent.* lib. 2 d. 44 q. 1 art. 3, ad 1.

32. *SCG* 3 cap. 24; *ST* 1 q. 60 art. 5, co; 2–2 q. 47 art. 10, ad 2. Cf. *Nicomachean Ethics* 1269b15: "No one would wish to have all [!] goods by himself alone (*kath'auton*)." Strauss himself recognizes that "[t]here is . . . a natural attachment of man to man which is prior to any calculation of mutual

virtues—independently of how useful it may be in furthering his private ends. He also takes a measure of enjoyment in performing small, everyday courtesies even to perfect strangers, in the exchange of greetings and pleasantries, in opening doors for others and letting them "go first," without first asking secretly, "What's in it for me?" He regards this way of behaving towards others as worthy of a rational being, as obligatory.

A mature man realizes furthermore that his own good includes not only his own pleasure, but also his own good character. The achievement and maintenance of good character requires acting in accordance with principles. It requires subordination of the particular to the universal, subordination of individual self-interest, narrowly understood, to the dictates of practical reason, that is, to the precepts of natural law and thereby to the common good at which natural law aims. It is for these reasons that Thomas speaks of an inclination not just to live, but to live in society, as an inclination that pertains to our specifically rational nature. This is a rational inclination because, in living together with others, we are elevated above the irrational and infantile self-centeredness in which we would otherwise remain, and back to which we all too frequently descend.

The implication of all this is indeed "that every fully rational man would choose justice, as he would choose health," an implication that Harry Jaffa finds dubious.[33] The implication, however, is dubious only on the assumption that, in human deliberation, choice, and action, reason does not have an appetite of its own but functions only instrumentally and in the service of ends that are not specifically rational, ends such as self-preservation, health, and pleasure. To the assertion that reason does have an appetite of its own, but that it is only the appetite for knowing the truth, Thomas would repeat that reason has an *appetite* even for knowing the truth only because it recognizes that it is *good* to know the truth.[34] Jaffa's doubts regarding the choiceworthiness of justice are based on the indisputable fact that one often has to pay a price for being just. He speaks as though this price is worth paying solely on the assumption that one will receive a reward for paying it or will receive a punishment for not paying it, a reward extrinsically conferred or a punishment extrinsically inflicted, in either case by another human being or by God.[35]

benefit" (*On Tyranny*, 200). But he adds at once that "[t]his attachment to human beings is weakened in the case of the philosopher by his attachment to the eternal beings." Thomas would agree in part with Strauss here: our attachment to the eternal being that is God has to take precedence over our attachment to human beings, if attachment to the latter comes into conflict with attachment to the former. But he would add that genuine love of human beings, as distinct from mere attachment to them, cannot come into conflict with one's love of God. So far from being weakened by love of God, love of human beings can only be strengthened by love of God.

33. *ThAr* 170. It would have been helpful if Jaffa had specified what conception of reason informs his criterion of rationality. Man's rational nature and his social nature are more intimately connected than Jaffa seems to realize.

34. *ST* 1 q. 79 art. 11, ad 2.

35. This sometimes appears to be the view of Strauss as well. See "On Natural Law," 142, and "The Law of Reason," 140.

Regarding punishment, we have considered Thomas's argument that remorse is itself a kind of punishment. Regarding reward, practical reason certainly requires forgoing many pleasures. It requires small sacrifices on a regular basis and can occasionally require extraordinary sacrifice. Still, in subjecting one's actions and passions to the rule of reason, one is conscious of having done something good. This consciousness is accompanied by a feeling of pleasure, even if it is only slight. The feeling of pleasure that accompanies the consciousness of having done something good, and the feeling of pain that accompanies the consciousness of having done something bad, when these feelings arise in a clear-headed human being, presuppose the rational assessment that one has acted in way that is worthy of oneself or in a way that is unworthy of oneself, that what one has done was objectively right or objectively wrong.

This kind of reward and punishment is possible only for a finite but nonetheless rational being who is able to judge his own choices and actions in light of an objective standard, a rational standard, that he realizes is higher than his private interest. If a man recognized that his own reason dictated certain acts and forbade others, it is hard to see how he could not regard himself as obligated to act in accordance with these dictates. The view that man has no obligations except when faced with threats of punishment or promises of reward needs some kind of argument in support of it. It is not easy to imagine what such an argument—with premises identified and their logical interconnection spelled out—would look like.

SECTION C. PHILOSOPHY AND THE CATHOLIC FAITH

If Thomas is right about what the philosopher knows and does not know, and if he is right about what the Catholic believer believes and does not believe, then he is right to hold that philosophy poses no challenge to the Catholic faith that cannot be met. Since the unbelieving adherent of philosophy is not well positioned to argue with Thomas about what the Catholic believer believes and does not believe, the only way he can reasonably argue with Thomas is by showing that he is wrong about what the philosopher knows and does not know. To show such a thing requires, however, a thoroughgoing investigation of Thomas's rational theology, both its rational bedrock and its detailed working out. Neither Strauss nor, as far as I know, his followers have undertaken such an investigation.[36] Not surprisingly, they are much more interested in Thomas's ethical and political thought, although they quite seriously misinterpret the natural law teaching that is at the foundation of his ethical and political thought. They frequently assert that such and such is a matter of religious belief without closely analyzing the texts in which Thomas attempts to demonstrate that it is a matter of natural knowledge. What lies behind the Straussian claim that there is an essential

36. See, however, Strauss's letter to Kuhn, 24.

tension between philosophy and religious belief seems to be a conviction that the content of the believer's faith just *has* to be false. But if what believers believe is internally consistent and does not contradict anything that can be naturally known—known, that is, beyond the shadow of a doubt—then it cannot be shown to be false except by proving either that revelation, which communicates the content of belief to the believer, is simply impossible, or that belief in revelation is inextricably connected with moral convictions that are either self-contradictory or contradict something more evident than they are. Strauss and his followers seem to think that an advance along the latter line has the greater chance of success. But that is just where they run up against the imposing figure of Thomas and "the classic form of the natural law teaching," which, rather than tackle head on with an argument, they try to undermine by alleging a dependence on revelation, or to outflank with appeals to the authority of Aristotle, or—what is least excusable of all—to make magically disappear with incantations of "being led to wonder," of "a doubt being raised," and of "it not being entirely clear" whether natural reason can know the things that Thomas powerfully argues it does know.

At the end of *Thomism and Aristotelianism*, Jaffa writes as follows.

> [O]ur social science, if it is to be of any use, must be addressed to Moslems and Jews, as well as to Christians, to Buddhists and Hindus as well as to believers in the Bible; it must be addressed [and here Jaffa quotes Churchill] "not only to those who enjoy the blessings and consolation of revealed religion, but also to those who face the mysteries of human destiny alone."[37]

No one can reasonably take issue with this moving statement. But its relevance to Jaffa's criticisms of natural law is not obvious. If it is specifically Christian to hold that good is to be done and pursued and evil avoided, that one should shun ignorance and refrain from harming others without provocation or out of proportion to prior harm received, that one should will what is good not just for oneself but for others as well, and that reason should rule the passions, then Christianity is more universal than even Christians claim.

One can certainly raise the question of why, if natural law is accessible to human reason independently of revelation, the classical form of the natural law teaching emerges for the first time only in the Catholic theological tradition rather than in the philosophical tradition of Greek antiquity. An answer that suggests itself is that Catholic theologians are less inclined than philosophers of any period to quibble with the testimony of natural reason when it elaborates a natural theology that demonstrates both the existence and, especially, the free choice of God, when it articulates natural

37. *ThAr* 193. As I noted in Ch. 5, Section c, above, Jaffa now seems to be more sympathetic to the natural law teaching of Thomas Aquinas as a teaching accessible to man as man, and not just to Christians, largely because of what he perceives to be its close agreement with the perspective of the Declaration of Independence, which is meant to be accessible to man as man, including "those who face the mysteries of human destiny alone," and not just to Christians.

law as binding on all human beings, philosophers included, and when it brings fully into view the altogether natural desire for supernatural revelation.

That there is a natural desire, even a need, for revelation certainly does not by itself imply that revelation is possible. This implication would follow in conjunction with the premise that nature does nothing in vain, and hence that no natural desire is in vain. But that premise is neither self-evident nor immediately demonstrable from what is self-evident. On the question of whether Thomas's natural theology as a whole establishes the possibility of revelation Ernest Fortin writes, "Thomas will go no further than to say that the highest achievement of natural reason is to prove, not that revelation is possible—to administer such a proof would be to deny implicitly the supernatural character of revelation—but that the arguments against it on rational grounds are never such as to compel our assent."[38] The thrust of Fr. Fortin's offset clause, "to administer such a proof . . . etc." is not clear. For natural reason's establishing the possibility, as distinct from the actuality, of revelation does not deny its supernatural character in the least. Indeed, if it can be shown that the reason why the arguments against revelation, as Fr. Fortin himself says, *never* compel our assent is that they *cannot* compel our assent, then revelation as a possibility, at least in the sense of entailing no contradiction, gets established at once. Perhaps Fr. Fortin has in mind a richer notion of possibility. The possibility of revelation, in as rich a sense of possibility as one could ask for, gets established by Thomas as an implicit corollary to his demonstrations, which do not presuppose revelation, that God necessarily exists, that he is the free creator of all things *ex nihilo* by virtue of being uniquely responsible for their *esse* at every instant of their existence, and that he is omnipotent.[39] Anyone who holds that the *possibility* of revelation is not established thereby—assuming that he accepts Thomas's demonstrations—needs to show how it is thinkable that an *omnipotent* God could be *incapable* of revealing himself to his rational creatures.[40]

Strauss apparently "concluded as a young man that [the controversy between philosophy and the Bible] could not be resolved on theoretical grounds alone, since the basic premise of orthodoxy, namely that God is omnipotent, and hence stronger than any so-called natural necessity, can no more be refuted than it can be proved."[41] Now, if one had an independent proof of the impossibility of revelation, that is, a proof that did not presuppose the impossibility of an omnipotent God, then an immediate corollary of this proof would be that there is no omnipotent God. If such an independent proof established that there really is a necessity, say, in the finite nature of the

38. Fortin, "Between the Lines," 325. See "Rational Theologians," 295, for a similar formulation; and "Faith and Reason" 302, top, for an argument that appears to lead to a different conclusion.

39. *ST* 1 q. 25 art. 1–3; art. 5; q. 44; q. 45 art.1–5; *SCG* 2 cap. 15, 21–27; *De Potentia*, q. 1, art. 7. See the Note appended to Part 1, Ch. 1, Section a, above.

40. In disagreement with Spinoza (*Ethica* 1, Prop. 17. Scholium), and in agreement with Thomas (*ST* 1 q. 25 art. 5; art. 6), I understand omnipotence to imply freedom of choice: God *can* do things that he *does* not do.

41. David Bolotin, "Leo Strauss and Classical Political Philosophy," 141.

rational *creature*, that precludes the possibility of revelation, then it would establish a necessity that the infinite *creator* himself would not be powerful enough to overcome: he would be unable to create a rational creature to whom he could reveal himself. If revelation is impossible, then an omnipotent God is impossible. But then correlatively, by the principles of transposition and double negation, if an omnipotent God is possible then revelation is possible. If "the basic premise of orthodoxy, namely that God is omnipotent" *cannot* be refuted, then one who recognizes this fact must immediately concede the *possibility* of an omnipotent God, and thereby the *possibility* of revelation as well.

Part 3

Beyond Natural Law

Leo Strauss's criticisms of Thomas Aquinas's natural law teaching are part of his broader critique of the idea of law itself. Strauss understands philosophy to be one way of life, and religious piety, to which obedience to divine law is central, to be a quite different way. These two ways of life are, as Strauss understands them, incompatible. The validation of philosophy, which takes pride in grounding itself in indubitable knowledge, requires a demonstration. The same is not true of belief in revelation, which does not—or certainly should not—claim to be knowledge, but faith instead.[1] As Strauss sees it, "Revelation or faith is *not* compelled, by its principle, to *refute* philosophy . . ."[2] On the other hand, if philosophy cannot refute the possibility of revelation then it is left with taking it, if not on faith strictly speaking, still on something much closer to faith than knowledge, that its way and not the way of faith is the right way. Strauss detects an inconsistency here, one that threatens the integrity of philosophy from its inception. To remove this inconsistency, he says, philosophy must attempt to refute the very possibility of revelation.[3] For only through such a refutation can philosophy, understood by Strauss as intransigently rational inquiry, be confident that it has met the minimum criterion of rationality, the criterion of internal consistency. Philosophy cannot take it on faith, or on anything like faith, that the way of faith is inferior to its own way.

1. *ST* 2–2 q. 1, art. 4, co.; q. 2 art. 1, ad 3; see art. 9, ad 2; 1–2 q. 6 art. 4, ad 1.

2. *RR* 174 (emphasis in the original).

3. There are places where Strauss says that the possibility of revelation cannot be refuted and suggests that the disputation between philosophy and revelation could end up in a standoff, from which neither side would emerge as the clear victor. And some of his followers take this as Strauss's final view of the matter. (See, e.g., Ernest Fortin, "Between the Lines" 317–27.) But, in other places, Strauss advances an argument to the effect that the result of such a standoff would have to count as the refutation of philosophy as a way of life that can rationally and definitively validate itself as *the* right way of life for those who are able to live it. (See, e.g., *RR* 176; *NRH* 75; "*PR*" 131; *Spinoza's Critique of Religion*, 29–30.) Anyone wishing to show that this argument of Strauss's does not express his ultimate view of the matter needs to show why he would have thought, or would have come to think, that it was less than compelling. Additionally, one would need to show why the critique of morality, including the moral presuppositions of belief in revelation—a critique initiated in classical political philosophy and revived by Strauss, a critique that it is one of the aims of the present study to counter—was not understood by him to be decisive.

Thomas argues that divine law presupposes natural law. But divine law is revealed law, and, for both Thomas and Strauss, it is an essential constituent of revelation. If natural law could be shown to be incoherent—and natural law would be incoherent if it turned out to be reducible to revealed law while falsely claiming to be a presupposition of revealed law—then a big step would be taken toward refuting the possibility of revelation. It is not surprising then that Strauss and more than a few of his followers, in their attempt to vindicate philosophy, attempt to show that Thomas's natural law teaching is founded on the claims of revelation, or, to say the same thing, that so-called natural law is only revealed law disguised as natural.

When I said in the Introduction that Strauss and his followers launch an "attack" on Thomas's natural law teaching, I was not indulging in hyperbole. For Strauss says, in the whole sentence, of which I quoted only the first half two paragraphs earlier, "Revelation or faith is *not* compelled, by its principle, to *refute* philosophy—threatened by the very possibility of revelation which it cannot refute: philosophy cannot leave it at a *defense*; it *must* attack." [4] Because Thomas's natural law teaching does not rest on the claims of revelation, or even assume the possibility of revelation, it can open one up to the possibility of revelation, without, of course, establishing its actuality. It is not surprising then that philosophy, as Strauss understands philosophy, must attack Thomas's natural law teaching. The only surprise here is that the attack has been so feebly executed. One would have thought that Thomas's grounding of natural law (or morality) in natural reason, and his argument for the dependence of divine law (or revelation) on natural law, and not the reverse, would have been engaged in depth and detail by Strauss and his followers. It has not been. Their attack lacks focus, and it lacks force. It does not come to terms with the relevant texts and arguments, and so it fails to penetrate to the core of Thomas's teaching.

With the formulation that philosophy "cannot leave it at a *defense*; it *must* attack," Strauss announces the relationship of philosophy, as he understands philosophy, to revealed religion, including the moral presuppositions of revealed religion, to be a relationship that is essentially polemical,[5] whether it is conducted openly and recklessly by moderns who are intoxicated by the prospects of public enlightenment or covertly by the ancients who took a more sober view of those prospects. Strauss certainly did not aim at the actual destruction of religion. Nor do his followers, though many of them seem less committed to expressing their criticisms indirectly, or less adept at doing so, than their teacher. Straussians recognize that religion functions as a support for civic virtue, that is, for the unreflective virtue of the many, without which there cannot be a "decent" political order. They intend, like the classic philosophers whom they most admire, to discredit religion and its moral presuppositions in the eyes of the few

4. *RR* 174. The emphasis is Strauss's throughout.

5. See "Thucydides: The meaning of Political History," 72: "We speak, and we speak rightly, of the antagonism between . . . faith and philosophy; and "The Law of Reason" 107: "A merely defensive attitude on the part of the philosopher is impossible . . ."

only, that is, in the eyes of those who have an innate talent for philosophy but might be perplexed as to what way of life is most consistent and sound. The Straussians' critique of natural law is essential to this endeavor. But not only is their attack inadequately supported, it also leaves them exposed to a counter-attack, more precisely, to a firm but respectful, and long overdue, "push-back."

Chapter 11

Inconsistencies and Other Aberrations

SECTION A. THE DENIAL OF UNIVERSAL RULES

Neither Thomas's self-evident first principle of practical reason and primary precepts of natural law nor the self-evident principles of speculative reason can be demonstrated. But that does not mean that no case can be made for them at all. For it is possible to follow through the logic of denying what is indemonstrable solely because it is self-evident to a point at which inconsistencies and other aberrations emerge. Only in this way can a case be made for something that is indemonstrable *because* it is self-evident.[1]

I argued in Part 1 that a conditional Ought cannot be deduced from a desire, a want, a need, or from anything else except another Ought, and sooner or later from an unconditional Ought. A conditional Ought implies an unconditional Ought. In the same way it can be shown that a hypothetical imperative, *qua* imperative, implies a categorical imperative, and that a conditional duty, *qua* duty, implies an unconditional duty. It is transcendent law that articulates an unconditional Ought, is expressed as a categorical imperative, and proclaims an unconditional duty. If an unconditional Ought, a categorical imperative, and an unconditional duty can be discerned as such by natural reason, the principle that is their source can only be natural law, by whatever name it is called.[2]

Strauss does not shy away from using the word "ought." On the contrary, he employs it with considerable frequency. And he speaks of legitimacy and duty too. Strauss uses the language of obligation as much as Thomas does. He uses this

1. Aristotle, *Metaphysics* 1005b35–1006a28.

2. In a brief but compelling article, "Natural Law under Other Names: de Nominibus non est Disputandum," Cristóbal Orrego shows why even legal positivists have been led to acknowledge the unavoidability of moral reflection in interpreting and applying the law of the land, and that this reflection cannot be distinguished from the ostensibly unscientific "natural law thinking" with which they had earlier hoped to dispense.

language—positively, not by way of a *reductio ad absurdum*, and to all appearances not ironically either—in preparing his case against the very teaching that rationally legitimates its usage.

> [W]hen deciding what *ought* to be done, i.e., what *ought* to be done by this individual (or this individual group) here and now, one has to consider not only which of the various competing objectives is higher in rank but also which is most urgent in the circumstances. What is most urgent is *legitimately* preferred to what is less urgent, and the most urgent is in many cases lower in rank that the less urgent. But one cannot make a universal rule that urgency is a higher consideration than rank. For it is our *duty* to make the highest activity, as much as we can, the most urgent or the most needful thing.[3]

That Strauss cannot make a case against "absolutism," by which he means moral absolutism,[4] without using such morally resonant language is evidence of how inextricable the concept of obligation is from all discourse about the human good. Leaving aside Strauss's apparent equation of the "most needful" with the "most urgent" rather than with the "highest," an equation that begs the question on the whole point at issue,[5] we note that it cannot be our duty to do what Strauss so eloquently recommends

3. *NRH* 162–3 (emphasis added). For some other places in this book where Strauss uses the moral language of ought, obligation, and imperative either in his own name or by attribution to the classical political philosophers, with whom he seems to be in agreement, see 3, 36, 47, 178, 196. See *On Tyranny*, 78. *RR* 146. And consider the concluding sentence of the version of "Progress or Return" contained in *The Rebirth of Classical Political Rationalism*. In that sentence Strauss seems to recognize that "ought" means more than "can," in particular that it also means (as I argued in Part 1, Ch. 2, Section c, above) "might not." It thereby presupposes *free* choice. If one thinks that Strauss did not recognize that his use of "ought" means that the possible is of wider scope than the actual, especially in the sphere of deliberation and decision, then one would need to show what Strauss's use of "ought" in this sentence, and elsewhere, should be taken to mean (assuming that Strauss intended it to mean *something*, which I realize some of his followers might contest).

4. "Both [i.e., Plato and Aristotle] avoided the Scylla of 'absolutism' and the Charybdis of 'relativism' by holding a view which one may venture to express as follows: There is a universally valid hierarchy of ends, but there are no universally valid rules of action." *NRH* 162.

5. There is ambiguity not only in the expression "most needful" but in "needs" as well. In *CM*, Strauss says that "[t]he modern project . . . was meant to satisfy in the most perfect manner the most powerful needs of man" (7), and a little later on the same page he speaks of "the natural needs of man." In *NRH* he rightly speaks of the necessity of "a standard with reference to which we can distinguish between genuine needs and fancied needs." Strauss does not spell out on these pages what our most powerful needs, our natural needs, and our genuine needs really are, and how they are related to each other if they are not identical. David Bolotin righly raises the question of the extent to which "our deepest needs, as individuals" are satisfied in the political sphere, though without stating exactly what these deepest needs are. ("Leo Strauss and Classical Political Philosophy," 133). In speaking to the question of human needs, Thomas Aquinas would say that some are rooted in our animal nature whereas others are rooted in our rational nature, and that, when animal needs and rational needs come into irreconcilable conflict with each other, natural reason dictates that the satisfaction of the former be subordinated to the satisfaction of the latter. But, as we have seen, he expresses this difference in the language of conflicting inclinations rather than conflicting needs. (See in this connection *Republic* 493c2, where Socrates distinguishes between necessary and good.)

unless our recognition of the "highest" entails a consciousness of obligation, and that this consciousness is possible only on the basis of something like Thomas's conception of natural law. One might counter that Strauss is expressing himself loosely in the passage we just quoted. But then one must either show that the thought expressed is not Strauss's own thought—which would be a problem since the thought expressed is essential to his argument *against* natural law—or show how the thought could be expressed, *tightly* expressed, in less "moralistic" language.

Strauss illustrates his understanding of the inadequacy of rules to concrete ethical decisions with a characteristically perceptive interpretation of Socrates' refusal to escape from prison on the eve of his execution. In the course of his interpretation, Strauss says,

> [Socrates'] refusal was not based on an appeal to a categorical imperative demanding passive obedience, without if's and but's. His refusal was based on a deliberation, on a prudential consideration of what was the right thing to do in the circumstances.[6]

Strauss's suggestion that obedience to a categorical imperative, or to natural law, is "passive" is tendentious. Such obedience is voluntary. It is, to say the very least, every bit as active as being *determined* by the apparent good, which without important qualifications sounds about as passive as passive can be. What is of more immediate interest here, however, is Strauss's formulation, not that Socrates was considering what was the *best* thing to do in the circumstances, for "best" can be given a non-moral interpretation, but that Socrates was considering what was the *right* thing to do. And the word "right," when applied to action, generates moral overtones that cannot be dampened. Thomas would say that this happens not in spite of, but because of, the qualifier "prudential" that Strauss places before "consideration," since prudence, though itself an intellectual virtue, presupposes moral virtue, as Aristotle recognized.[7]

That Strauss is assessing Socrates' refusal from an essentially moral perspective is borne out by what he says a bit further on.

> Socrates preferred to sacrifice his life in order to preserve philosophy in Athens rather than to preserve his life in order to introduce philosophy into Crete. If the danger to philosophy in Athens had been less great, he might have chosen to flee to Crete.[8]

The choice of the word "sacrifice" should be a sufficient indication that, according to Strauss, Socrates did not accept the death penalty solely because he was old and ready

6. *WhPPh* 33. The mention of a categorical imperative is a sign that Strauss's principal target here is Kant. But it could as easily be Thomas, since the two thinkers are in essential agreement that there are some rules of action, or precepts, that do not ever admit of dispensation. See also *WhPPh* 280–1; 295.

7. *Nicomachean Ethics* 1144b32; 1152a8.

8. *WhPPh* 33. See Plato, *Apology* 28e–29a.

to die.[9] Moreover, Strauss's parallel purpose clauses—sacrificing life or preserving life, in either case, "in order to,"—subordinate life to something other than life. The difference between Strauss's Socrates and Thomas does not concern the question of whether there is a good to which the preservation of one's life is to be subordinated. For Socrates, this good seems to be the future of philosophy: if not in Athens, then Crete; and if not in Crete, then in Athens; in any case, the future of philosophy *somewhere*. Socrates' choice evokes our admiration because for him it was an absolute, non-negotiable principle, and not just an idiosyncratic and incommunicable preference, that philosophy be preserved, without if's or but's, even if doing so should require the sacrifice of one's own life. Strauss says that Socrates' choice not to flee Athens "did not consist in the simple subsumption of his case under a simple, universal, and unalterable rule." But Strauss's interpretation implies, correctly I think, that for Socrates the preservation of philosophy was just such a rule.

For Thomas, philosophy—understood here as speculation motored by natural reason without appeal to the claims of revelation—is as much a good of reason (*bonum rationis*) as it is for Socrates, Plato, Aristotle, and Strauss. But, for Thomas, the good of reason includes the good of practical as well as of speculative reason, and the former is inseparable from acting in accordance with precepts, the highest of which do not admit of dispensation. We should never forget that the first concrete precept of natural law named by Thomas is that one avoid ignorance. It is then a dictate of practical reason that one pursue wisdom to the extent that one has the ability and opportunity to do so. This pursuit is not simply an operation of speculative reason, for it is, like every human *pursuit*, animated not just by the concept of being (*ratio entis*) but by the concept of good (*ratio boni*), in this case by the good as it really is,

9. Strauss intimates this suggestion here and there, and expresses it frankly in a letter of Dec. 12, 1938, to Jacob Klein (GS, Band 3, 562). He may well be right in saying that Socrates' age "played no mean part" in his decision not to escape from prison and flee to Crete. (*The Argument and the Action of Plato's Laws*, Chicago: The University of Chicago Press, 1975, 2.) Socrates was probably concerned, even decades before his trial, that if he lived into advanced old age he would lose his virtue, i.e., in particular, the excellence of his intellect (see *Protagoras* 345b; *Apology* 17c–d, 34e, 38c, 39b; *Laws* 928e, 929d). But Plato does not present Socrates' intellectual powers as being on the wane in the dialogues that he situates at the end of his life, namely, the *Theaetetus*, *Euthyphro*, *Apology*, *Crito*, and *Phaedo*. Far from it. Socrates is not the central interlocutor in the *Sophist* or *Statesman*, which are dramatically situated between the *Euthyphro* and the *Apology*. But his age and health do not seem to be the reason for that. Plato himself is reported to have lived more than a decade longer than Socrates did. He wrote his longest dialogue, the *Laws*, in advanced old age and, for all we can tell, in full possession of his intellectual powers. Strauss himself finished his commentary on the *Laws*, as well as his late works on Xenophon ("die ich für meine beste Sache halte"—letter of September 6, 1972, to Gershom Scholem, *GS* Band 3, 762), when he was several years older than Socrates was at the time of his execution. And Strauss, too, seemed to be in full possession of his intellectual powers during those years, as those of us who attended his study groups at St. John's College, Annapolis, can attest. Strauss argues persuasively that the Athenian Stranger in the *Laws* is none other than Socrates as he would have been had he fled to Crete. In choosing to present the Stranger as an old man, but one intellectually alive, fully so, Plato undermines the notion that, for a philosopher, life over the age of seventy is barely worth living.

as it is in truth, and not just as it appears to be.[10] Moreover, philosophy is a common good (*bonum commune*). It can be participated in with others who are equipped for it, without any loss to oneself or to them, and with benefit to both. And its survival is worth risking the great, but still lesser, good of one's own life for its sake. That Socrates' thought this to be true is borne out by his whole adult life and fate. Even if one holds that the future of philosophy was essentially Socrates' "own good"—a projection of his *eros* or will to power, let us say, the founding of a school, the attainment of the only quasi-immortality that is available to him, and so forth—Strauss's response, as we shall see, is that the reduction of the good to one's own good—narrowly conceived as one's own life and pleasure—is not the classical understanding of the matter. Nor does it appear to have been Strauss's understanding of the matter either.

Though the proposition that the good is essentially one's own good, conceived about as narrowly as possible, can be asserted, it cannot be rationally defended. The proposition can be denied without the slightest contradiction, so it is not self-evidently true. And it is not demonstrably true either, since there are no premises from which it could be deduced that are not as questionable as it itself is. The proposition could be advanced simply as a definition: the good is essentially one's own good. But such a definition would be logically defective since the term, "good," appears in both the subject and the predicate of the proposed definition. If this logical defect is remedied by rephrasing the proposed definition as, "the good is one's own life and pleasure," the definition becomes immediately contestable, again without contradiction: "No, the good is *not* one's own life and pleasure." A more straightforward formulation of the thought lying behind the assertion that the good is essentially *one's own* good is that the good is essentially *my* own good, or to avoid the barbaric circularity, that the good is essentially *my* own life and pleasure (and not, with all due respect, *yours*). One cannot expect to hear a publicly accessible and rigorous proof of this singular proposition, with a specification of the premises that would justify it, or even an explication of exactly what is meant by it. Such a proposition hardly mirrors the view of the classics or the view of Strauss. If indeed "there is necessarily a tension between one's own and the good," if indeed "the good is higher in dignity than one's own," a view that Strauss ascribes to the classics, then the good is presumably higher than the preservation of one's own life, to say nothing of the pursuit of one's own pleasure.[11] If the view of the classics is that the good is, additionally, higher even than the preservation of one's own particular political community (at any cost), then the view of the classics approaches the view of Thomas Aquinas.

10. "[V]erum est bonum intellectus." *ST* 2–2 q. 1 art. 3, ad 1. We must keep in mind that the pursuit of wisdom is not as good as the actual attainment of it, but remember that, for Thomas, the attainment of perfect wisdom, which would consist in knowing of the first cause as it is *in itself*, exceeds man's natural capacity.

11. *WhPPh* 36–37; see *NRH* 107–9, 126, 151. Cf. *Gorgias* 512e1, 521d9–e1; *Nicomachean Ethics* 1120a6–8.

One sentence in the first passage that I quoted from *Natural Right and History* near the beginning of the present chapter stands out by virtue of *not* explicitly employing the moral language that occurs in the sentences that surround it: "[O]ne cannot make a universal rule that urgency is a higher consideration than rank."[12] Actually, one *can* make a universal rule that urgency is a higher consideration than rank, and the "prudential realists" do exactly that. But one cannot make such a rule rationally. So even this apparently non-moral sentence requires a more precise reformulation: "one *ought* not to make a universal rule that urgency is a higher consideration than rank." Only understood this way can Strauss's sentence support the connection he wishes to establish with the sentence that immediately follows: "For it is our duty to make the highest activity, as much as we can, the most urgent or the most needful thing." This sentence, too, looks like a universal rule, even if—as is no less the case with Thomas's primary precepts "avoid ignorance" and "do not offend others"—its application requires practical judgment.

In developing his capital claim that "there are no universally valid rules of action,"[13] while at the same time stating that "[w]hat is most urgent is legitimately [!] preferred to what is less urgent," Strauss can hardly avoid setting a trap for himself. He avoids falling into it, however, by saying that one cannot make it a universal rule that urgency is a higher consideration than rank. For if urgency is in all cases a higher consideration than rank, then we have both obligation and a universal rule: one ought to preserve the political community, or perhaps oneself, at any cost. In either case, preservation of the community or self-preservation, we have a rule that admits of no exceptions. That is to say, we have a primary precept of natural law.[14] The dispute between Thomas and the "prudential realist"—*not* Strauss—who makes it a universal rule that urgency is a higher consideration than rank, concerns only the content of natural law, not whether there is a natural law, obligatory and exceptionless as regards its most general principles.

One might counter that if we were to pay closer attention to Strauss's language we would see that, so far from falling into a trap, he has not even set one. For he has left open the unexpressed analytic truth that urgency, while not higher than rank—how could it be?—is certainly more urgent than rank. Because successfully dealing with

12. *NRH* 163.

13. *NRH* 162. In defense of this claim, it has been said that practical reason does make use of rules, not universal, exceptionless rules such as we find in the Decalogue, in Thomas, and in Kant, but something more like "rules of thumb." Strauss writes, "All [!] laws, written or unwritten . . . are crude rules of thumb." ("Plato," in *History of Political Philosophy*, p. 75. Strauss may not be speaking in his own name here, but only presenting the view of the Eleatic Stranger in Plato's *Statesman*.) But however reasonable, balanced, or prudential this assertion may sound at first hearing, it comes to sound increasingly unreasonable as one tries to fathom what it might mean. Calling a municipal law that forbids, say, jaywalking, a "rule of thumb" sounds sensible enough. But to call such things as the natural law prohibitions against murder, rape, adultery, and false accusation, to say nothing of genocide, "rules of thumb" has an odd ring to it, to my ears at least.

14. Consider Hobbes's definition of *lex naturalis* in *Leviathan* Part 1, Chapter 14.

the more urgent is the *sine qua non* for striving toward the higher, the more urgent should always be given precedence over the higher. But then the identical question re-emerges, even at this low level: what notion of obligation lies behind the word "should" here? One cannot deflect this question by saying, not that one *should*, but that one *must* give precedence to urgency, or that one *will* give precedence to urgency, because neither natural necessitation nor prophecy is at issue. Contrary to what some seem to think, there is no irresistible force of nature that compels man to give priority to urgency over rank.[15] For it is simply a fact that, wisely or foolishly, rightly or wrongly, some humans beings have given rank precedence over urgency. They have regarded the highest, and not the most urgent, as the most needful. One cannot argue against them that urgency *should* take precedence over rank without employing the language of morality—obligation and universal rules—and thereby, *aut volens aut nolens*, the language of natural law, whatever one's reservations about the idea of law.

Strauss avoids falling into the trap he has set, not only by saying that "one cannot make a universal rule that urgency is a higher consideration than rank," but by actually suggesting a situation in which the urgent in its most acute form, namely, self-preservation—and not just self-preservation of the individual as in the Socrates example, but self-preservation of the political community itself—is *not* a higher consideration than rank, a situation in which apparently there is no force of nature compelling even the political community to give urgency priority over rank. Strikingly, Strauss makes this most interesting suggestion on the heels of an assertion of what seems to be a rule to the contrary. He thereby manages, intentionally it seems, to undermine the seeming universality of the rule.

> The city may and must demand sacrifice from its citizens; the city itself however cannot sacrifice itself; a city may without disgrace accept even under compulsion the overlordship of another city which is much more powerful; this is not to deny of course that death or extinction is to be preferred to enslavement proper.[16]

15. Strauss explicitly denies that there is such a force. See *NRH* 196, fn. 39: "Yet Carneades did not contend that in such a situation [two men at sea clinging to a plank too small to support both] one is compelled to kill one's competitor (Cicero, *Republic* iii. 29–30): the extreme situation does not reveal a real necessity." Strauss gives the impression of granting here that we possesses the freedom to resist the most powerful physical inclinations and that, in the realm of human choice and action, even in the extreme situation, consciousness of moral obligation can override what could be misinterpreted as a simple necessity of our nature. Perhaps this impression is incorrect, however. The footnote in *NRH* is in some tension with the thrust of the comment in *Thoughts on Machiavelli* that "it suffices to think of the two shipwrecked men on a raft" (192, and context).

16. *CM* 189. (The "even" in this sentence looks to me like a minor error.) In both this passage and in the passage from *WhPPh* 33, Strauss carefully speaks of *preference* rather than *obligation*. But one has to ask whether, for Strauss, the city's preference and Socrates' preference in these two cases are grounded in rational principle as distinct from unaccountable idiosyncrasy. A third possibility might be prudence. But genuine prudence takes its bearings from rational principle. If it does not do so, it degrades to cleverness merely. (See above, Part 1, Ch. 1, Section c; Ch. 2, Section b, vi; Ch. 3, Section d; *Nicomachean Ethics* 1144a23–36.) In any case, cleverness would hardly account for the city's

The "must" in this most complicated sentence seems not to mean simple necessitation, since it is paired with "may." The "must" probably means obligation, and the "cannot" certainly means obligation. So the problem of an implicit but inadequately grounded "absolutism" resurfaces. Strauss navigates around it in the final clause, which suggests that extinction of the entire political community might be better than enslavement proper. He does not come right out and say this. I recognize that his introductory "this is not to deny" is not the same as "this is to affirm." [17] And so Strauss might be thought to leave a little bit of room for artful interpretation by the careful reader. But if interpretation artfully reverts to the claim that self-preservation should always take precedence over all other goods, including avoidance of enslavement proper, then we are once again back with a universal rule. And, needless to say, if the right interpretation is that avoidance of slavery proper should always take precedence over survival, then we simply get a different universal rule.

Perhaps Strauss wished to leave open the possibility that slavery proper might, not always, but in some rare circumstances, be preferable to extinction. It suffices to think of the Babylonian captivity. In that case enslavement proper was preferable to extinction lest, along with extinction, remembrance of what Jerusalem stands for vanish from the mind of man. But what does Jerusalem stand for? [18] It stands for God's Covenant, to be sure. But it thereby stands just as much for the Law. If enslavement proper is preferable to forgetting the Law, might it not also be preferable to transgressing the Law? And if extinction is preferable to enslavement proper, might not both extinction and enslavement proper be preferable, *always* preferable, to transgressing the Law, in particular, preferable to committing a gross injustice? [19] Thomas's unequivocal answer to this question is contained in a text we considered earlier.

---

preference and Socrates's preference in the passages under consideration. Even if one resists the notion that prudence takes its bearings from rational principle, one has to grant that it discerns the means to a *good* end. In these two passages the good end can hardly be life, since that is what is being sacrificed. What life is being sacrificed *to* can only be something higher than life. Thomas would say that one cannot make sense of this "higher" without reference to the *bonum rationis*.

17. Consider, however, Strauss's discussion of voluntary martyrdom in "Why We Remain Jews," 322–3. See also *NRH* 144–5. In his "Introduction" to Herman Cohen's *Religion of Reason*, xxi, Strauss says that Cohen "does not speak of the moral obligation not to desert one's people especially when they are in need—and when are Jews not in need?—because for him this went without saying." Maybe, *just maybe*, this did *not* go without saying for Strauss himself. But Strauss gives no indication of disagreeing with Cohen about this particular "moral obligation"—yet another principle that is hard to interpret as a "rule of thumb."

18. *WhPPh* 9–10.

19. Lest it be objected that, by speaking of *the* Law, i.e., *revealed* law, at this point, I am compromising Thomas's defense of *natural* law, it should be remembered that, for Thomas, the moral precepts of the Decalogue reiterate precepts already contained in natural law.

> It is proper (*oportet*) to hold firmly the good of reason against every evil whatsoever [including death, as the context makes clear], since no bodily good is equivalent to the good of reason.[20]

The good of reason (*bonum rationis*) is promoted by natural law, and justice is a good of reason. The loss of life and liberty, both of the individual and of the entire political community, is a price that should be paid if the only alternative is committing a gross injustice.

It is not obvious where Strauss stands on this matter other than that he will not justify his stand by appeal to an exceptionless rule of any stripe. He does grant that "in all concrete decisions general principles are implied and presupposed."[21] These "principles," however, are not precepts of natural law. Though Strauss acknowledges that these principles are somehow at work in what Aristotle called commutative and distributive justice, he does not describe how they are at work there. Perhaps he does not need to since "[p]rior to being the commutatively and distributively just, the just is the common good."[22] Strauss does not state here exactly what the common good is. Though it is normally determined by commutative and distributive justice, or by other moral principles like them, Strauss notes that these principles may have to be waived in extreme situations, especially situations "in which the very existence or independence of a society is at stake." In such cases, though only in such cases, "it can be justly said that the public safety is the highest law." And what constitutes such extreme cases? This cannot be specified in advance, least of all by the application of rules. In a war against "an absolutely unscrupulous and savage enemy . . . there are no assignable limits to what might become just reprisals."[23]

Thomas would disagree. There are assignable limits: one may not deliberately target non-combatants; one may not make promises, even to an enemy in war, with the intention of breaking them; one may not bear false witness against the enemy, that

20. *ST* 2–2 q. 123 art. 4, co.

21. *NRH* p. 159.

22. *NRH* 160; see *WhPPh* 41.

23. *NRH* 160. James Schall understandably finds what Strauss has to say about these matters "almost chilling." But he is nonetheless convinced that "[n]either Strauss, nor Aristotle, nor St. Thomas would hold that a clearly evil act ought to be done in any circumstances" ("A Latitude for Statesmanship?" 134). Fr. Schall may be right about this, but only if Strauss holds that certain acts, evil in situations that are not extreme—for Thomas these acts would be violations of the primary precepts of natural law or of those secondary precepts that are demonstrable *modica consideratione*—cease to be evil, indeed, become even just, in extreme situations. And this does seem to be Strauss's position: "[I]n extreme situations the normally valid rules of natural right are justly changed, or changed in accordance with natural right; the exceptions are as just as the rules" (*NRH* 160). We assume that Strauss concurs in what he takes to be the position of Aristotle: "there is not a single rule, however, basic, that is not subject to exception." Because Fr. Schall recognizes that "St. Thomas 'suffers no exceptions' in principles," i.e., in the primary precepts of natural law, it is a bit surprising to hear him say, "I see nothing in Strauss's concern for latitude to deal with particular complexities of action that would prevent him from agreeing with St. Thomas here"—where "here" seems to refer to how practical reason directs our acts without assistance from divine revelation.

is, accuse him of things he has not done, so as to win over a third party as an ally.[24] Or, to be a bit more concrete, a statesman may not authorize the rape, torture, and execution of an innocent child, even in the interest of obtaining vital military information from his mother or father who is perhaps being held as a prisoner of war. One may not do such things even to preserve "the very existence or independence" of one's society. For some acts are so abominable that a rational being would take little satisfaction in a life that could be preserved only by committing them or by knowingly acquiescing in their commission. Strauss does emphasize that the true statesman "reluctantly deviates from what is normally right only in order to save the cause of justice and humanity itself."[25] But since he indicates, albeit in general terms only, how very extreme this deviation may have to be, it is hard to imagine what, if anything, he thinks is left of the "cause of justice," nay, the cause of "humanity" itself, when secured by measures to which "there are no assignable limits."[26]

Strauss's integrity as a thinker leads him to press his point about reason's inability to assign limits in extreme situations. Since "war casts its shadow on peace" and "societies are not only threatened from without," extreme measures may have to be applied to deal with "subversive elements *within* society."[27] After making this suggestion, Strauss adds at once, "Let us leave these sad exigencies covered with the veil with which they are justly covered." We shall not follow Strauss's advice here. In taking a peak beneath this veil, to which he has drawn our attention, and from which he has immediately tried to draw our attention away, we behold not just a few sad exigencies but a veritable abyss, toward which the denial of exceptionless rules was leading all along.

Strauss identifies as one of the salient features in the founding of modern political philosophy a tendency to give primacy to the extreme situation. And although he has reservations about this tendency,[28] he himself gives primacy to the extreme situation—the situation in which "there are no assignable limits"—in making his case

24. *ST* 2–2 q. 40, art. 3 co.; 2–2 q. 64, art. 6. See 1–2 q. 100 art. 8, ad 3.

25. *NRH* 162.

26. *NRH* 160. See "The Law of Reason," p. 140, fn. 141. Even if we momentarily set aside the requirements of justice, we still have to ask how a statesman can be sure that certain actions, normally unthinkable, can alone save the political community from destruction by the enemy. How can the statesman be sure that such actions will not actually strengthen the resolve of the enemy to persevere and cap off victory with a furious and merciless extermination of everything that the statesman had hoped to save?

27. *NRH* 160 (emphasis added). In his letter to Kuhn, Strauss writes, "[I]n considering natural right and its changeability I consider not merely the relation to foreign enemies but the relation to domestic enemies as well; and not only the relation to enemies . . . I emphasize the relation to foreign enemies only because this is the most obvious and common case in which noble statesmen are not blamed for actions which under normal conditions would be unjust" (25; the puzzling ellipsis between the words "to enemies" and "I emphasize" occurs in the letter as published). See, in this connection, Werner J. Dannhauser, "Leo Strauss in His Letters," 359; and Hans Jonas, *Memoirs*, 161.

28. *NRH* 179 and 196.

against natural law. So we are justified in posing a question about an extreme situation in making the case for natural law. Though Strauss addresses natural law primarily in the context of political legislation, exigencies, and decisions, its precepts are binding not only on statesmen but on private citizens as well. They too can find themselves in extreme situations. Consider the following scenario, which concerns not so much the common good or public safety as one's own life.

A tyrant wishes to do away with a rival, let us say a highly successful and widely admired general. The tyrant knows that he cannot simply have the general murdered without risking a popular uprising. So he has him arraigned on a trumped up charge of treason. To support this charge, the tyrant approaches a young man—not seventy years old like Socrates at his trial, but like Socrates in philosophical aptitude and passion—and asks him to give perjured testimony against the general. The tyrant informs the young man that if he refuses to give the perjured testimony, which will send the general to the gallows, then the young man himself will be executed, out of public view. (And we could vary the scenario, such that the young man is asked by the tyrant to give perjured testimony not against a popular general but against some other innocent human being, for example, his next door neighbor, his friend, his brother, a philosopher.) The young man realizes that if he himself goes unnoticed into the night and mist, no serious problems will result for the tyrant. He has to make a decision, and his options are limited to two.

Our question here is not what Strauss and his followers would say the young man should do. One can be virtually certain that they would both think and say that he ought not to give the perjured testimony, that it is better for him to die an early and unjust death than be complicit in sending an innocent man to the gallows.[29] After all, they have before them the example of Socrates who, at an earlier age than seventy, incurred a risk to his life on at least two separate occasions rather than commit or acquiesce in an injustice less grave than bearing false witness against an innocent man that would send him to his death.[30] Our question, instead, is how the conduct recommended to our hypothetical young philosopher, and the conduct Socrates exhibited, can be rationally defended without appeal to a rule that does not admit of dispensation, that is, without appeal to a primary precept of natural law. And it is not enough to say that the young man should refuse to perjure himself because of the shame he would otherwise feel, shame in his own eyes even if not in the eyes of the public. For he would not feel shame, or remorse, unless he thought he was violating a principle of justice, a principle that ought not to be violated.

29. One can also be virtually certain that Strauss and his followers would both think and say that genocide, the deliberate extermination of an entire people, is always wrong. It is wrong whether it is committed against Jews, Armenians, Tsutsis, or any other racial, ethnic, or religious group. But genocide cannot be asserted to be *always* wrong without appeal to a universal rule.

30. Plato, *Apology* 32a–d; cf. 28b, 29b; *Symposium* 220d–e.

It would be inexcusable to say that Strauss is indifferent to justice. But he has doubts about its scope and how it relates to concrete situations.

> Aristotle seems to suggest that there is not a single rule, however basic, which is not subject to exception. One could say that in all cases the common good must be preferred to private good and that this rule suffers no exception. But this rule does not say more than that justice must be observed, and we are anxious to know what it is that is required by justice or the common good.[31]

Justice is not an empty concept. It requires, minimally, that one not offend, as *offendere* was interpreted in in Part 1, Chapter 2, Section b, above. Before deciding what he is going to do, the young man in our example has to ask himself whether bearing false witness against another human being, an innocent human being, is a form of offense. This judgment is easy and can be made by anyone who has reached the age of reason: a lying accusation that will send an innocent human being to his death is an offense, grossly so. It is intrinsically unjust. He ought not—no if's or but's—to make a lying accusation that will send an innocent human being to his death. *Synderesis* and a simple act of judgment generate this conclusion at once. And there is no latitude for judging that, though false accusation is unjust in general, it is not unjust in the present situation. The consequence of acting on the conclusion, that is, refraining from bearing false witness, is terrible for the young man. And so he may, with great reluctance, decide to bear false witness. But he cannot appeal to *reason* to justify doing so, not if, as Thomas holds, no precept, or maxim, based on the inclinations we share with subrational beings takes precedence over a precept proper to our rational nature. "The good of reason is man's good." There is no denying that "fear of the dangers of death is more effective than anything else in making man recede from this good."[32] Nonetheless, as we noted above, Thomas holds that one should hold firmly to the good of reason even if one has to lose one's life in doing so, "for no bodily good is equivalent to the good of reason." Something within a man can surely say, "It is better for me to send an innocent man to his death through false accusation than to suffer an unjust death myself." But his reason cannot say such a thing. For this "better" does not accord with the *bonum rationis*, which, because it is "of reason," can only be expressed in the language of universals.

SECTION B. CIRCUMVENTING THE PRACTICAL SYLLOGISM

Action involves particulars. So practical reason in the service of action has to issue in singular propositions, or rather prescriptions, of the form, "This is to be done," "This is not to be done," or "Do this," "Do not do this," where "this" stands for some particular concrete act. Reason arrives at these singular prescriptions, which can be expressed

31. *NRH* 160–1. *Nicomachean Ethics* 1107a9–18.

32. *ST* 2–2 q. 123 art. 12, co.

indifferently as gerundives or in the imperative mode, by means of a practical syllogism. The major premise is a rule, a precept of law in fact; and the minor premise is a singular proposition, like the conclusion, though expressed neither as a gerundive nor in the imperative mode, but as a simple indicative. Here is an example of the three step practical syllogism.

> Do not bear false witness against another human being.
> To say x (in this particular situation) is to bear false witness against another human being.
> Do not say x.

The syllogism moves deductively from a universal imperative known by *synderesis* to a singular imperative through a singular indicative reached by an act of judgment.[33] Practical reason is able to direct us, to command us, not just in a general way but specifically and concretely. To do so, it must indeed take into account the actual situation, which is stated declaratively in the minor premise as a simple matter of fact. But the minor premise cannot by itself or in combination with any other merely declarative statements about the Is, whether expressed in universal or singular propositions, generate, much less necessitate, the imperative conclusion. No matter how many declarative statements one assembles in deliberating about what to do, one will never reach an imperative conclusion without reliance on a major premise expressed in the imperative mood, or as a gerundive, or as a sentence containing the words "ought," "should," or "good" construed as something to be pursued. Without such reliance one can say nothing about the Ought; and however "practical" the thought process might be in its intention, it is not reason.

Even in the extreme situation, practical reason, if it is to function at all, must proceed through an express or implicit practical syllogism.[34] Some kind of universal proposition—if only "Always do what feels good"—has to function as the major premise, no matter how elevated it is beyond good and evil. Otherwise, practical reason, *qua* reason, is silent. To be sure, speculative reason can still speak: "If one does x, then y will follow; y is disagreeable; so doing x will lead to something disagreeable." But speculative reason cannot conclude that x is to be avoided. To reach such a conclusion practical reason needs employ a gerundive such as, "What is disagreeable is to be avoided," or an equivalent imperative such as, "Avoid what is disagreeable," that will

33. *ST* 1–2 q. 76 art. 1, co. See q. 90 art. 1, ad 2; q. 94 art. 4, co.; *Nicomachean Ethics*, 1144a33. Cf. *De Anima* 434a18. One rarely articulates such a practical syllogism in speech, because thought moves much more quickly than speech. But if asked to justify what one thinks in such a situation, a practical syllogism can be articulated, and the putative truth of its premises and their relation to the conclusion can be scrutinized.

34. Even if practical reason is going to *set aside* a quasi-universal principle, lower order rule, or secondary precept of natural law, it has to proceed through a practical syllogism, e.g.: (1) Never do x. (This prohibition has the character of a higher order rule or primary precept of natural law that cannot be set aside.) (2) Not to set aside rule A (a lower order rule) in this particular situation would amount to doing x. (3) Set aside rule A in this particular situation.

of necessity have a universal form. Even when speculative reason determines that this or that particular desire is most expeditiously satisfied in this or that way, or that this particular event follows from that particular event, it has to appeal to a universal rule to say that necessity of any kind is involved in such consecution.

In the process of giving reasons, one reason is conditioned by or subordinated to another. If this process does not at least implicitly ascend to, or explicitly descend from, an unconditioned reason, or set of reasons, that conditions all the rest, then it is less a process of practical reasoning properly so-called than one of asserting "values," declaring preferences, or making excuses, that is to say, "rationalizing." As Kant argues, it is the very nature of reason, practical no less than speculative, to aim at or take its bearings from something unconditioned. Thomas agrees with him on this matter. Reason has, one can say, a life of its own. So little is reason merely instrumental that, as conscience, it resists being pressed into the service of "prudential realism," an outlook that, on the basis of an impoverished conception of reality, reduces prudence to cunning merely.

Strauss would hardly contest the structure of the practical syllogism or the bearing it has on concrete decisions. Instead, he denies the unrestricted scope of the major premise. Such premises have for Strauss only a qualified universality: most of the time they can be appealed to, but not always. In the extreme situation they may have to be set aside. As I noted earlier, Socrates' refutation of Cephalus in Book 1 of the *Republic* is sometimes misinterpreted as implying that there is no such thing as a primary precept of natural law, a precept that never admits of dispensation, and hence that there is no such thing as natural law at all. We humans, it is said, make use of rules, but none of them are absolutely inviolable. An extreme situation can require the waiving of any rule, no matter how authoritative it might seem to be. Let us consider formally how this is envisioned to play out.

I have two rules of conduct, A and B, and these two rules rarely come into conflict with each other. However there is an unusual situation, p, in which they do come into conflict, and in this conflict I find it more reasonable to follow rule A than to follow rule B. But then I encounter or imagine another unusual situation, q, in which I find it more reasonable to follow rule B than to follow rule A. Now, assuming that it is really reason that leads me to give rule A precedence over rule B in situation p, and yet to give precedence to rule B over rule A in situation q, I should be able to state the reason. The only way I can do so rationally is to say that, in situation p, following rule B rather than rule A would be incompatible with following some third rule, C, but that, in situation q, following rule A rather than rule B would be incompatible with following rule C. In other words, C is a higher-order rule that determines whether one should follow lower-order rule A or lower-order rule B in those situations when one cannot follow both. And if there are some situations in which even C should not be followed, it must be because following C would be incompatible with some yet higher rule.

Only in this way is it possible to give a *reason* for why one rule rather than another is to be followed in situations where they come into conflict. And, as I argued in Part 1 above, lest thought lose itself in an infinite regress, one is sooner or later going to have to appeal to a rule that admits of no exceptions. Such a rule, even it is only "Preserve thine own life at any cost!" is going to have, for the person who adopts it, the character of a primary precept of natural law. The only question remaining is whether this ostensibly primary precept is itself fully grounded in natural reason. Thomas would argue that it is not so grounded, for reasons we have already considered.

It may be countered that extreme situations can present one with alternatives in the face of which practical reason as such has nothing helpful to say. But if this is really so, it follows that in such situations the choice of one alternative cannot be said to be more rational than the choice of the other. We do not have to argue that reason is adequate to every imaginable situation, but only that if choice and action are determined by reason they are determined ultimately by some rule or rules that do not admit of dispensation. There may be some account of the operation of practical *reason* that avoids this conclusion, though I doubt it. In any case, neither Strauss nor his followers have, as far as I know, given such an account.

In response to the Straussian view that discerning the full particulars of the concrete situation reveals, at most, only what *quasi*-universal rule should come into play, we must again, even at the risk of overkill, press the question of just how this is supposed to work. If one surveys the most feasible courses of action and then says, "I should apply this quasi-universal rule rather than that one," the question reemerges of exactly where *this*, so to speak, *higher order* Should—"I *should* apply . . . etc."—comes from. To blunt this question one might reformulate the above sentence: "I *will* apply this quasi-universal rule rather than that one." And that reformulation is not open to the particular logical difficulties I have sketched. Nietzsche seems to have recognized that practical reason can set aside an obligatory precept only by appealing to a higher obligatory precept. It was probably to avoid going down, or rather up, this path that he entertained expunging the vocabulary of obligation—ought, should, duty, "thou shalt," etc.—from precise discourse about action, and replacing the "thou shalt" with "I will." Doing so does mean saying farewell to reason, but that was a consequence Nietzsche was apparently willing to accept.

Strauss, however, thought it would be unwise to say farewell to reason, and so he did not follow Nietzsche's lead.[35] He thinks that reason is fully operative only in pre-modern "rationalism,"[36] and he reminds us of what he calls "a rational morality, the heritage of Greek philosophy."[37] He refrains, however, from spelling out what is specifically moral about this morality, not in its presumably exoteric presentation—as, for example, in Plato's *Gorgias*—but in the philosopher's deepest, own-most, and

35. *Spinoza's Critique of Religion*, 31.

36. *Philosophy and Law*, 21–22, and 135, fn. 1. [*GS* Band 2, 9–10, and 9, fn. 1.]

37. *PR* 100.

only cautiously indicated thoughts. Strauss also refrains from spelling out what is specifically rational about this morality. He seems to think that reason is most truly sovereign when it recognizes that the exigencies of decision and action in the extreme situation require transcending the sphere of rules altogether. I do not see how this could possibly be true of reason. It might be true of will on certain interpretations, or of resoluteness, but not of reason.

What is required for rational, human action is a Should or an Ought. Either the concrete situation reveals only an Is, or, if it reveals an Ought as well, that is only because it is a situation involving rational beings already governed by natural law. What is missing from Straussian criticisms of natural law is an analysis of the structure and functioning of practical reason, including especially the distinction between *synderesis* and judgment. The absence of this analysis is one of the two most conspicuous lacunae in Strauss's teaching. The other lacuna is the absence of a validation, or even a transparent explication, of the concept of nature. Strauss was fully aware of, and rightly concerned about, the second lacuna. As far as I can see, he was not fully aware of the first, in spite of his repeatedly expressed deference to reason as a standard—to say nothing of his students' characterization of their teacher's philosophical project as a rehabilitated "rationalism."

SECTION C. COMPETENCE AND CONSCIENTIOUSNESS

I have argued that Strauss's undeveloped appeal to prudence and judgment does not remove but only obscures the difficulties inherent in his critique of natural law. In the following passage from *Natural Right and History*, he seems to bring something else into the picture.

> What cannot be decided in advance by universal rules, what can be decided in the critical moment by the most competent and most conscientious statesman on the spot, can be made visible as just, in retrospect, to all . . . [38]

It is striking that Strauss does not say only that the statesman must be competent, but also that he must be conscientious. Thomas would point out that the conscientiousness of which Strauss speaks here is nothing other than *synderesis*. Conscience—again, the act of which *synderesis*, or conscientiousness, is the habit—is the act of attending to the precepts of natural law in the critical moment. And Thomas fully recognizes that knowledge of rules, however broad or narrow, is not a substitute for judgment but must be complemented by judgment. He would insist, however, that any "conscientiousness" operating in total isolation from rules would reduce ultimately to irrational decisionism.

Perhaps Strauss did not intend to distinguish between competence and conscientiousness. Perhaps he intended merely to place the latter in apposition to the former:

38. *NRH* 161 (emphasis added). See also Strauss, "The Crisis of Our Time," 48.

properly understood, they are two different names for the same thing; they are just two different names for prudence. Because on Strauss's understanding—as distinct from Thomas's—prudence functions independently of exceptionless rules, it is, he might say, practical reason *par excellence*. But not only is this conception of prudence subject to the charge of circularity and ultimate unintelligibility that Fr. Fortin makes and which we considered in Part 2, Chapter 9, Section a, it is hard to distinguish this conception from the familiar, but decidedly *non*-Thomistic, conception of conscience itself, construed as a faculty of moral discernment, if not moral feeling, that also functions independently of rules.

Heidegger once startled his students by saying of prudence, in reference to one of its features specified by Aristotle in the *Nicomachean Ethics* (1140b29): "That is the conscience!" Hans-Georg Gadamer, who relates this anecdote, is quick to point out that Heidegger's remark was something of a pedagogical overstatement.[39] Nonetheless, the dissociation of prudence both according to Heidegger's non-Thomistic interpretation and according to the Straussian interpretation—each being presumably a *habitus* of practical discernment—from universal rules makes it difficult to distinguish the Heideggerian interpretation from the Straussian. Strauss might say that they differ in that the approval of conscience, just like its promptings, is essentially private, whereas the excellence of prudence is publicly manifest. And yet what is decided without any appeal to universal rules can be "made visible as just, in retrospect, to all"—to *all* and not just to the statesman's fellow countrymen and their allies—only if it happens by chance to agree with a universal rule. Had Hitler's decision to have allied commandos executed in the closing months of World War II actually saved Germany from defeat, that action too might have been "made visible as just, in retrospect," to the Germans and their allies perhaps, but hardly "to all." Something similar could be said about the Allied firebombing of Dresden.

One might suspect that Strauss's indications on these matters could be reduced to a secret teaching that morality, or justice, is in the last analysis a theoretically insupportable construct, but one that must be publicly defended in the interest of the decent politics that even philosophy requires for its own security.[40] But this reduction does not rise to the full complexity of Strauss's thought. For, apart from his use of both moral terminology and moral reasoning in his criticisms, not only of decisionism and hedonism, but of natural law as well, Strauss makes the moral claim that justice has not solely a political but also a natural and trans-political dimension.

39. "Martin Heidegger und die Marburger Theologie," 85. [English translation, 201]. More than *pädogogische Übertreibung* seems to have been involved in Heidegger's statement. See his study, *Plato's Sophist*, § 8, (c) p. 39; and consider *Nicomachean Ethics* 1143a9.

40. Plato *Republic* 368b3–c2. Cf. "A Giving of Accounts," 463.

> To say nothing of the relations between parents and children, the relation of justice that obtains between two complete strangers who meet on a desert island is not one of political justice and is nevertheless determined by nature.[41]

Strauss writes similarly to Helmut Kuhn, though with a qualification.

> Plato and Aristotle granted that there are obligations of every human being to every human being as such. They did not think however that these minimum obligations can be the root of all obligations: the end cannot be deduced from the beginning.[42]

Given Strauss's regard for Plato and Aristotle, and taking this quotation together with the preceding one, we can infer that he too thought there were obligations, trans-political obligations, of every human being to every human being as such. But then Strauss calls these obligations "minimum obligations." They are not "the root of all obligations." They are not where obligations begin; they are only where they end. But then what is that root? From what do obligations *per se* originate? Strauss does not say.[43] Since, however, he does say, on behalf of Aristotle and in apparent concurrence with him, that "political right . . . is the fullest form of right," he may have thought that obligations to strangers could be deduced from obligations to fellow citizens.[44] It is not easy to see how this could be the case, unless the former obligations or so-called obligations are just maxims of self-interest employed in the service of realizing the latter obligations, or so-called obligations: a community that deals harshly with strangers may find itself attacked by the strangers' fellow countrymen. However, a more convincing deduction can be made by way of specification or determination to concrete circumstances, *from* obligations of every man to every man, *to* obligations of every citizen to every citizen. And that is, in effect, the Thomistic determination of natural law by human law. But such determination presupposes just the kind of universal rule that Strauss wishes to reject.

And yet, it must be reemphasized, Strauss does not just employ the language of obligation ironically. He indirectly argues for its legitimacy by reducing to absurdity the denial of what the term "obligation" expresses. His most extended argument along these lines is contained in the second chapter of *Natural Right and History*, "Natural Right and the Distinction between Facts and Values." There Strauss clearly establishes that even apparently "value free" science, natural science as well as social science,

41. *NRH* 157. See Strauss's letter to Kuhn, 25: "The relation of right between a citizen and a stranger is of necessity less full or rich [than that between citizen and fellow citizen]. By this I do not mean that it is beyond the distinction of right and wrong . . ."

42. Strauss's letter to Kuhn, 26.

43. "If man's ultimate end is trans-political [presumably philosophy, for those who have what it takes to engage in it], natural right would seem to have a trans-political root. Yet can natural right be adequately understood if it is directly referred to this root? Can natural right be deduced from man's natural end? Can it be deduced from anything?" *NRH* 145.

44. Strauss's letter to Kuhn, 25.

is necessarily guided by the value conviction that science is *good* and that it *ought* to be preferred to superstition, prejudice, and simple ignorance.[45] Though Strauss himself does not take issue with this value conviction, he does not say what might justify it from his perspective. Thomas would say that the justification is contained in the reasoning that culminates in the first concrete precept of natural law that he names, namely, that one avoid ignorance. Strauss cannot avail himself of this reasoning because of his doubts about the preeminent rationality of natural law. He does say at one point that "the philosophers would deny that the rules which are called obligatory by the societies, are in fact obligatory strictly speaking."[46] This sentence leaves open the possibility that the philosophers, and for that matter Strauss himself, might regard something else as "obligatory strictly speaking" and hence the root, or close to the root, of all obligations. The problem is that Strauss does not spell out what might be meant by "obligatory strictly speaking." He does not even spell out what might be meant by "obligatory loosely speaking." If the latter, or for that matter the former as well, consists of conditional obligations, then again we cannot specify the conditions without being led sooner or later, necessarily and irresistibly, to an unconditional obligation, that is, to a precept of natural law. The concept of an ethical order constituted exclusively by conditional obligations, if they really are obligations, is intrinsically incoherent.

SECTION D. SCIENCE AND VALUES

According to Strauss, "Science and History, those two great powers of the modern world" are widely held to have destroyed the very possibility of political philosophy, especially as conceived by the ancients.[47] They have done this through a relentless critique of the conception of nature that informs the political philosophy of Plato, Aristotle, and their medieval followers, as well as through their promotion of a conception of history unknown to Plato, Aristotle, and their medieval followers.

"Natural right in its classic form," Strauss says, "is connected with a teleological view of the universe."[48] The implication of this formulation is not only that natural

45. Strauss undertakes a similar but briefer analysis in *WPPh*, 18–23.

46. "The Law of Reason," 140, fn. 141. (I am assuming that the "which" clause in this sentence is restrictive because "which" is not immediately preceded by a comma, though the comma after "societies" complicates things. One of the very few infelicities in Strauss's English prose, which is exceptionally well-crafted, is the frequent use of "which" instead of "that" to introduce restrictive clauses.)

47. *WhPhP*, 18.

48. *NRH* 7. Strauss seems to be referring here to natural right not only as understood by the Stoics and Thomas Aquinas, but as understood by Aristotle (and perhaps also by Plato) as well. Richard Velkley, in "Roots of Rationalism," says of the passages from Aristotle's *Physics* that Strauss cites in this connection (196a25ff; 199a3–5) that they "argue that causality in the heavens is not 'for the sake of an end' but necessary causation" (254). Something can indeed happen of necessity without being for the sake of an end, at least not for the sake of a readily apparent end. See *Physics* 198b18–23. Aristotle's example is rain falling of necessity rather than for the sake watering plants. But necessity as such is not

right in its classic form stands or falls with the claim that man has natural ends, but also that those ends were viewed as comprehended within a universe of ends. Man is comprehended within nature. Human teleology is not an anomaly but a local, if most interesting, instance of natural teleology. And nature places limits on human freedom and self-assertion. As Strauss puts it, "if man is not by *nature* ordered toward virtue or perfection, if there is no *natural* end of man, man can set for himself almost any end he desires."[49] Strauss recognizes that modern science has called the teleological view seriously into question, but he may not be fully persuaded that modern science has unequivocally refuted it: "the issue between the mechanical and the teleological conception of the universe . . . seems [!] to have been decided in favor of the nonteleological conception of the universe." [50] Strauss, however, does not argue for a revalidation of the teleological conception of the universe, as distinct from a teleological conception of man. Whether such a conception can, in fact, be revalidated is a matter we shall consider in Chapter 13, below. Our present question concerns the bearing of the non-teleological commitment of modern science, not on the so-called "hard sciences," such as astronomy, physics, chemistry, biology, but on the social sciences, and on political science in particular.

Strauss criticizes contemporary value-free political science for denying that "man has natural ends—ends toward which he is naturally inclined."[51] With this formulation Strauss comes quite close to the position of Thomas himself, and only a bit less so when he says in this connection that "man possesses a certain latitude; he can *choose* not only from among various ways of overt behavior . . . but from among values; this latitude, this possibility, has the character of a fact."[52] Thomas would have been somewhat puzzled by the use of the word "values" in this context, but he would have recognized in the latitude of which Strauss speaks the very freedom that he argues is

incompatible with teleological causation: something can be necessitated to act for the sake of an end, i.e., it can act for the sake of an end without having any choice in the matter (note the *amphō* clause at *Physics* 196b19). Man is necessitated to act according to the first principle of practical reason: he cannot choose *not* to act according to this principle. Whatever man does deliberately or "on purpose," and not accidentally, he does because he thinks that it is in some respect good to do. Otherwise, he could not deliberately do it at all. And yet the first principle of practical reason is emphatically a teleological principle. In the case of causality in the heavens, necessity (*anagkē*) is present (*Metaphysics* 1073a26; a33); but Aristotle does not present this necessity as incompatible with being for the sake of an end. Quite the opposite (1074a18–31; 1075a18–19). Chance (*automaton*) is incompatible with being for the sake of an end, to be sure. And yet, according to Aristotle's argument, neither chance nor luck (*tychē*) can be understood for what it is except in contrast to, and even in the context of, teleological causality (*Physics* 197a33–35).

49. *WhPPh* 42

50. *NRH* 8. Fr. Fortin writes similarly, "One of the major difficulties facing the natural law theorist is that his understanding of human nature was originally bound up with a teleological view of the universe which has *seemingly* been destroyed by natural science" (emphasis added). "The New Rights Theory and the Natural Law" (265–86 in *CCPO*), 266.

51. "An Epilogue," 127.

52. "An Epilogue," 126 (emphasis added).

bound up with man's specifically rational nature. Strauss underscores this freedom by denying that man's choice of values is simply determined by his desires.

> The fact that someone desires something does not make that something his value; he may successfully fight his desire, or if his desire overpowers him, he may blame himself for this as a failure on his part; only choice, in contradistinction to mere desire, makes something a man's value.

In the first two parts of this sentence, Strauss comes close to summarizing how Thomas himself understands man's free choice to manifest itself; he comes close, as well, to the critique, which I advanced above, of any attempt to derive an Ought, conditional or otherwise, from a want or a mere desire.[53] But in the third part of the sentence, Strauss begins to make a distinctively non-Thomistic turn. In the sentence that follows it appears to be a distinctively Nietzschean, if not Heideggerian, turn.

> Choice does not mean here the choice of means to pre-given ends; choice here means the choice of ends, the positing of ends, or rather of values.[54]

It is certainly possible, likely even, that at some point in the paragraph from which these sentences are taken Strauss ceases to speak in his own voice. But it is not obvious at what point this happens.[55] If the "positing of values" springs out of the will *alone*, it is a decisionist act and not a rational one, and Strauss has no use for decisionism. After all, he "could not stomach . . . 'resoluteness' without any indication as to what are the proper objects of resoluteness."[56] The "proper objects" are understood by Thomas to be ends that are not so much "posited" by man as read off his very nature.[57] And Strauss seems to agree with Thomas on this as well.

> We conclude that the "relativism" accepted by the new political science, according to which values are nothing but objects of desire, is based on an insufficient analysis of the Is, that is, of the pertinent Is, and furthermore that one's opinion regarding the character of the Is settles one's opinion regarding the

53. Part 1, Ch. 2, Section c, iii.

54. "An Epilogue," 126

55. Strauss leads into the first of the passages that I have quoted from this paragraph as follows, "Let us assume that a man's 'values' . . are fully determined by his heredity and environment . . . In this case the Ought would be determined by the Is or derivative from it. But the very issue as commonly understood presupposes that this assumption is wrong: man possesses a certain latitude . . . etc." It is possible that Strauss is not speaking in his voice in any part of this passage, though when he rightly says "A man lacking this latitude . . . is a defective man," it certainly sounds as though he is speaking in his own voice.

56. "A Giving of Accounts," 461.

57. Ernest Fortin writes that "one cannot give an adequate account of the end or ends of human existence by conceiving of them as posited by desires or impulses . . ." "Natural Law and Social Justice," in *CCPO* (232). Fortin is right about this. But, though these ends are not posited by the desires, they are signaled by the desires, though, according to Thomas, the choice to act in accordance with this desire rather than that one is—with the exception of the desire for happiness—free.

> character of the Ought. We must leave it open here whether a more adequate analysis of the pertinent Is, that is, of the nature of man, does not lead to a more adequate determination of the Ought, or beyond a merely formal characterization of the Ought.[58]

It is most regrettable that Strauss left this last question open. For it is on this very point that he seems to disagree with Thomas's natural law teaching, in spite of the fact that his three formulations, (1) "a merely formal characterization of the Ought," (2) "the pertinent Is, . . . the nature of man," and (3) "a more adequate determination of the Ought," strikingly parallel the three themes of q. 94, art.2, that we considered in Part 1, Chapter 2, above: (1) the formal first principle of practical reason, (2) the order of natural inclinations, and (3) the concrete and properly obligatory precepts of natural law.

Strauss has certainly inquired into the nature of man. But in doing so he has not exposed the root of obligation. In particular, he has not shown how obligation can exist in the absence of universal rules of conduct, imperatives, or natural law.[59] We are left then with an apparent inconsistency in his position, since obligation and imperatives are inseparable from each other. It is possible that Strauss did not speak to this apparent inconsistency because he harbored uneasy doubts about whether a

58. "An Epilogue," 127. In his Review of C. B. Macpherson's *The Political Theory of Possessive Individualism*, Strauss writes that "Macpherson's defense of Hobbes's derivation of right and obligation from fact against the strictures of present-day logicians belongs to the most valuable parts of the book" (*Studies in Platonic Political Philosophy*, 231). Doubting that Strauss himself can derive the Ought from the Is, I turn to Macpherson's book for illumination. Macpherson writes, "[Hobbes] believes that . . . once a man has transferred rights to another 'then he is said to be OBLIGED, or BOUND, not to hinder those, to whom such Right is granted . . . from the benefit of it: and that he *Ought*, and it is his DUTY, not to make void that voluntary act of his own.' In short, Hobbes believes that he has deduced moral obligation from fact, ought from is" (Macpherson, 71). In the sequel to this passage Macpherson argues for the soundness of Hobbes deduction. Without reproducing his argument or evaluating its cogency, I list here only a few of the propositions that are essential to it. Obligations are founded on rights (Macpherson, 70–72; Hobbes, *Leviathan* XIV 7 [though consider the use of "*ought*" in XIV 4]; cf. *NRH* 181 ff.). But a right for Hobbes is nothing but a liberty, or absence of external impediments; and in the state of nature it has no opposite: there is no natural wrong (*Leviathan* XIV 1–2. cf. XIII 13). Hobbes's deduction rests on "the postulate of the equality of man" (Macpherson, 74), which in turn presupposes "his original postulate of mechanical materialism" (Macpherson, 76; cf. Strauss *The Political Philosophy of Hobbes*, Chapter 2). In this scheme of things "there is no question of a hierarchy of wants" (Macpherson, 78; cf. *NRH* 126). The preceding claims and postulates are not those of Plato or Aristotle, nor, as far as I can tell, does Strauss concur in them. It is not clear, then, how Macpherson's interpretation of Hobbes's concept of political obligation, valuable as Strauss may have found it in other respects, could be of much use to him in attempting to derive the Ought from the Is, or in defending such an attempt "against the strictures of present-day logicians."

59. Whatever Strauss's intention may have been in referring to "a sacred awe . . . a kind of divination that not everything is permitted . . . this sacred fear" as what "we may call . . . man's natural [!] conscience" (*NRH* 130), this reference does not sufficiently expose the root of what, if anything, "the philosophers" might regard as "obligatory strictly speaking."

convincing analysis of the nature of man was possible. For such an analysis presupposes that human nature is part of nature as a whole, and that nature persists through history without being modified by history. This presupposition has been called into question by Heidegger.

Chapter 12

Philosophizing in the Shadow of Heidegger

SECTION A. NATURE AND WORLD

The concept of nature, according to Heidegger, is derivative from the more primordial phenomenon of the world. So he argues in *Being and Time*,[1] where he attempts to show that Being-in-the-world (*das In-der-Welt-sein*) is a fundamental state (*Grundverfassung*) of man. Man is distinguished from other things that *are* insofar as his Being is an issue for him. Man, considered in his openness to and concern with Being, is *Dasein* (existence, or literally "Being-there").[2]

In *Being and Time* Heidegger characterizes nature as *a* being, as *an* entity (*ein Seiendes*), that is itself encountered within the world.[3] The so-called discovery of nature, which for Strauss inaugurates philosophy as distinct from myth or religion,[4] is according to Heidegger less a discovery than an abstraction, and this abstraction is an event, an *historical* event. It is a choice of attitude and turn of thought that deprives the world of its worldhood.[5] It can be objected that nature is objective reality and that what Heidegger calls the world is merely a subjective interpretation, or misinter-

1. *SZ* 45–50, 31. This work first appeared in 1926 as a special edition of the *Jahrbuch für Philosophie und phänomenologische Forschung*, Vol. 8. [The English translation by John Macquarrie and Edward Robinson, includes the pagination from *SZ* in the margins. It is to this pagination, or to the sections designated as §, that I shall refer in citing passages from *SZ*.] Heidegger's infinitive *Sein* is the German equivalent of the Latin *esse*. As others have done, I shall generally translate Heidegger's *Sein* as "Being," capitalized, in order to distinguish it from the ordinary English participle "being" and from a being (or an entity—*ein Seiendes*). I shall do something similar with compound expressions in which *Sein* occurs.

2. See "Einleitung zu 'Was ist Metaphysik'" in *Wegmarken*, 201–204. [English translation: 282–5.]

3. *SZ* 63; see 9, 95; 211.

4. *NRH* 82; see *RR* 145.

5. *SZ* 65; see 70; 112; 361.

pretation, of objective reality. But, according to Heidegger, this presumed objectivity is a spurious objectivity. Nature is not what is first for us. What is first for us is a context of concerns that are constitutive of Being-in-the-world. Our pre-philosophic understanding of the world predates any understanding we might have of nature. And nature is only supposedly (*vermeintlich*) independent of the standpoint of the observer.[6] If anything, nature is more subjective than the world. For nature is a theoretical construct, whereas the world is the concrete, complex, and elemental field of man's comportment, interest, and engagement, both prior to and independent of supposedly disinterested *theoria*.

The world then, and not nature, is the background out of which *theoria* emerges and, at the end of the day, back into which it fades. Essential to this background is history, which is the past that is still having its effect, pressing right through the present and into the future. Empty time is an abstraction. Strictly speaking it is not even a possible object of experience. Time is history, and history is concrete. History encompasses whatever happens in time, which is everything that happens. In this sense, not only the discovery of nature, but nature itself, belongs to history.[7] As a theoretical construct that deprives the world of its elemental meaning, the concept of nature is of little avail in illuminating and comprehending either the world itself or *Dasein* in its Being-in-the-world. Nature, so understood, is too abstract to serve as an unambiguous standard and source of pre-given ends for human choice and action.

Though Heidegger speaks of nature in *Being and Time* as a being (*ein Seiendes*), in a later essay, "On the Essence and Concept of *Physis* in Aristotle's *Physics* B. 1,"[8] he says that, for Aristotle, nature is the being-ness (*die Seiendheit*—Heidegger's translation of the Greek *ousia*) of a limited realm of what-is, the realm of things that, unlike works of art (*technē*), have a principle of motion within themselves, essentially so and not accidentally. Heidegger knows that, for Aristotle, nature understood this way is not simply identical to Being (*Sein*). He knows that according to Aristotle there are separate *ousiai*—the unmoved movers—that are eternal, outside of and unaffected by time, and permanently present. Hence, for Aristotle, they alone *are* without qualification. However, Heidegger also hears in Aristotle's treatment of nature in *Physics* B.1 an "echo" of an earlier, pre-Socratic understanding, in which nature, as the immanent principle of coming to be and passing away, is itself Being. Heidegger places great emphasis on the togetherness of "presence-ing" and "absence-ing" in Aristotle's account of nature, and in doing so he leans heavily on the arresting formulation, at the end of the *Physics* B.1, that absence (or privation—*sterēsis*), too, is somehow form

6. *SZ* 152.

7. *SZ* 378–9; 388.

8. "Vom Wesen und Begriff der *Physis*: Aristoteles' Physik B, 1, in *Wegmarken*, 309–71. [English translation, "On the Essence and Concept of *Physis* in Aristotle's *Physics* B, 1," 183–230.] See also Heidegger, *The Fundamental Concepts of Metaphysics*, 25–26.

(*eidos*). Heidegger regards Aristotle's concept of nature as incalculably richer than the derivative concept that he deflates in *Being and Time*.

If one were to shear off the theology of separate *ousiai* in Book 12 of the *Metaphysics* as an exoteric accommodation—as some of Strauss's followers are inclined to do—then little difference would remain between the Aristotelian and the pre-Socratic conception of nature.[9] In the case of both, nature would be solely an immanent principle of motion, of presence-ing and absence-ing. In fact, Strauss's marvelously concise and precise characterization of Heidegger's *Sein*—"[I]t is a synthesis of Platonic ideas and the biblical God: it is as impersonal as the Platonic ideas and as elusive as the biblical God"—is applicable to nature, conceived this way, as well.[10] For, in the famous formulation of the pre-Socratic philosopher Heraclitus, a formulation that Heidegger quotes toward the end of his essay, "Nature loves to conceal" (*physis kryptesthai philei*). Nature, so understood, is too enigmatic to serve as an unambiguous standard and source of pre-given ends for human choice and action.

SECTION B. STRAUSS'S STRUGGLE WITH HEIDEGGER

However repellant Strauss may have found Heidegger's historicism, to say nothing of "the straight line which leads from Heidegger's resoluteness to his siding with the so-called Nazi's in 1933,"[11] he recognized that "Heidegger surpasses all his contemporaries *by far*," that he is "the *only* great thinker in our time."[12] On the basis of intermit-

9. *NRH* 8: "From the point of view of Aristotle—and who could dare to claim to be a better judge in this matter than Aristotle?—the issue between the mechanical and the teleological conception of the universe is decided by the manner in which the problem of the heavens, the heavenly bodies, and their motion is solved." Aristotle's express teaching is that the problem is solved theologically. *Physics*, 267a17–b27; *De Caelo*, 288a28–b8; *Metaphysics*, 1072b3–1075a11.

10. *IE* 46/318. Catherine Zuckert interprets this formulation as a reduction of Heidegger's understanding of Being to a hybrid of "two elements [that] are, in fact, fundamentally contradictory, incommensurable, and incoherent." "Leo Strauss: Jewish, Yes, but Heideggerian?" 98. In support of her interpretation, Zuckert refers the reader to two articles by Strauss, "Jerusalem and Athens" and "Progress or Return." These two articles do not explicitly address Heidegger's understanding of Being. They do argue that various attempts at a synthesis of biblical religion and Greek philosophy have proved inferior to the original elements of the synthesis. Such is manifestly the case with those attempts that try to preserve the *whole* of each element in the synthesis. Thomas Aquinas is not guilty of this error, though some think he is. But neither, as far as I can see, is Heidegger guilty of this error. Nor do I think that Strauss intended, in the formulation under consideration, to imply that Heidegger was guilty of it. As Strauss would surely have recognized, synthesizing only *parts* of the two elements, the elusiveness of the biblical God but without his personhood, and the impersonality of the Platonic ideas but without their (rational) accessibility, need not result in a contradiction at all—assuming, of course, that elusiveness does not imply personhood and that impersonality does not imply accessibility. Consider, in this connection, *WhPPh* 38–39: Socrates' knowledge was "knowledge of the *elusive* character of truth, of the whole . . . [H]e viewed man in the light of the unchangeable ideas, i.e., of the fundamental and permanent *problems*" (emphasis added).

11. "Kurt Riezler," 246.

12. *IE* 29/305 and 30/306, for this quotation and the following two quotations (emphasis added throughout). Though Strauss was free of conceit, he was also free of false modesty.

tent but careful reading Strauss says, "The more I can see what Heidegger is aiming at, the more I see how much still escapes me." For these reasons Strauss adds, "The *most* stupid thing I could do would be to close my eyes or reject his work."

i. Choice of ends

If Heidegger is right in holding that nature—whether understood as the abstraction that natural science busies itself with or as Being itself in its impersonal elusiveness—is not a source of pre-given ends even to man, then choice is no longer choice of the means to pre-given ends, but choice of the ends themselves: "the positing of ends, or rather of values." Value is projected from the particular will of the evaluating subject. Ends being reduced to values, no chosen end is, objectively considered, any better or worse than any other. The sole criterion for evaluating meaningful choice or decision would be what any thinker other than Heidegger would call "subjective": the strength of will that lies behind the choice, the unflinching resoluteness and follow-through of the decision itself, fidelity to oneself and one's own. This criterion is the *terminus a quo* of the "straight line" that, according to Strauss, leads to Heidegger's siding with the National Socialists.

Strauss says that "Heidegger . . . explicitly denies the possibility of ethics because he feels that there is a revolting disproportion between the idea of ethics and those phenomena which ethics pretended to articulate."[13] With his choice of the word "feels," rather than, say, "realizes," Strauss dissociates himself from Heidegger's position. The word "pretended" in the subordinate clause is worrisome, but it can be interpreted as merely a fleeting attempt to enter Heidegger's frame of mind and express it. Strauss makes this statement in his memorial piece on Kurt Riezler. In his lecture "An Introduction to Heideggerian Existentialism," Strauss says essentially the same thing, but this time without the qualifications one might expect. Heidegger "declared that ethics is impossible and his whole being was permeated by the awareness that this fact opens up an abyss."[14] Perhaps "this fact" could be interpreted as referring only to Heidegger's *declaration* that ethics is impossible. But such an interpretation would be a stretch. The more natural interpretation is that the impossibility of ethics opens up an abyss. On the face of it, then, Strauss seems to be conceding to Heidegger that ethics is impossible. Strauss may well be speaking loosely here. I entertain the possibility that he was not speaking loosely only because I cannot find a crystal clear and solidly grounded statement from him "regarding the ultimate principles of our choices,"[15] and because his explicit and repeated denial of universal rules, of natural law, and of categorical

13. "Kurt Riezler," 246. Whereas rational ethics as a special region determined by principles of its own is of little interest to Heidegger, his ontological inquiries were connected to properly ethical concerns from the start. See James D. Reid, "Ethical Criticism in Heidegger's Early Freiburg Lectures."

14. *IE* 28/304.

15. *NRH* 4.

imperatives makes it difficult to see how he, any more than Heidegger, could have thought that an ethics based on objective principles was possible. And an ethics not based on objective principles is not an ethics at all but a value system merely.

It is striking that Strauss does not explicitly take issue with Heidegger on the question of the possibility of ethics, though he devotes an entire essay to him and explicitly takes issue with him on other points. To be sure, Strauss frequently adopts the voice of the thinker he is interpreting. It is almost impossible to avoid doing so from time to time in the course of any exposition of someone else's thought, if the exposition is to proceed beyond a few sentences. Moreover, Strauss also frequently adopts a dialectical mode of presentation. He will make a strong case for one position, say, that of belief in divine revelation, then state the case for the opposing position, that of philosophical unbelief, and continue alternating between the two, strengthening each position, until finally concluding with an ambiguous statement that puts the ball in the reader's court and requires him to think for himself. This mode of presentation is pedagogically efficacious; and it also allows the writer to express his own thoughts on a controversial matter with circumspection, between the lines, or not at all.

Strauss had grave reservations about Heidegger's thought. In his published works and letters he expressed his reservations about Heidegger both as a thinker and as a man. But Heidegger is hard to argue against. His thought is remarkably consistent, in spite of the fact that more than any other great philosopher, with the possible exception of Nietzsche, he depreciates the importance of logical consistency as the canon for serious thinking about the most important questions the mind of man can entertain. Many who excoriate Heidegger for the conclusions he drew from his historicist premises embrace even more extreme historicist premises, but draw no conclusions from them at all, or draw conclusions, after a fashion, that are at odds with the premises themselves. Not Strauss. He resists historicism from start to finish in all its forms. It is historicism that is the implacable foe of reason, of speculative reason and practical reason equally.

ii. Historicism

Heidegger's historicism is not arbitrary. It is grounded in phenomenological descriptions and analyses that, as Strauss says on more than one occasion, disclose the roots and articulation of human experience more adequately than do even those of Husserl, the founder of phenomenology. Heidegger's account of human finitude, especially in *Being and Time*, is compelling to almost anyone who takes the time to think it through and does not view it against the background of eternity.

Strauss tries to make a case for eternity, not for the supra-temporal divine that Thomas argues for, but for an eternal within time. Strauss tries to make the case for something like the classical conception of nature, in full appreciation of the challenge posed to this conception by modern natural science and historicism. But what Strauss establishes is only a pallid version of the classical conception: "The fundamental problems . . . persist or retain their identity in all historical change."[16] If this claim can be sustained, then it can be inferred that these problems present themselves as problems at all times only because there is a permanent human *nature* that recognizes them, or is capable of recognizing them, as problems at all times. Whether the claim that justifies this inference can, in fact, be sustained is a question we shall turn to shortly. But first we need to consider how Strauss understands history

Strauss seems to find the classical conception more defensible than the modern conception. The word itself, *historia*, originally meant inquiry. And so Aristotle could entitle one of his books *History of Animals*. It treats, not how animals used to be or came to be what they are now—after all, Aristotle argues that the species (*eidē*) are eternal—but how they are now. Its themes are comparative anatomy, physiology, and ethology. Every inquiry is by definition *historia*. But among the various kinds of inquiry, one in particular, the inquiry into human customs and events, including especially political institutions and wars, is of such preeminent interest that it came to apply the single word "history" to itself. This modification appears to have encountered little resistance, in part because even in this case "history" continued to name the inquiry simply. Only later did "history" come to name both the inquiry and the object of the inquiry. The notion that there is an object investigated by the historian and called "history," comparable to the object called "nature" that is investigated by the natural scientist, would have made little sense to the classical philosophers.[17] And yet that there is such an object is taken for granted by almost everyone today. Historicism is the view that this object is the decisive determinant of human thought. Thought is true, if true at all, only for its own time. There can be no trans-historical thought.

Historicism seems easy to refute. The refutation goes like this: If thought is true only for its own time, then this very thought—that thought is true only for its own time—is true only for its own time. This thought was not true in the past and it will not be true in the future. And yet this thought is advanced as a permanent characteristic of thought, of thought at any time. The very thought that there is no trans-historical thought understands itself to be a trans-historical thought. Historicism, like other forms of relativism urging as absolutely true that nothing is absolutely true, cancels itself out. It is absurd.

Strauss sees that there are two versions of historicism that resist so neat a refutation. We meet these two versions in Hegel and Heidegger. In both thinkers there is an "absolute moment" in which the essential historicity of thought becomes manifest.

In the case of Hegel, this moment is a culminating one. History is the long, laborious, and often violent struggle of humanity (or, to use Hegel's word, spirit—*Geist*) toward a point at which human beings finally come to recognize one another mutually and, in principle, universally. It is at this culminating point of history that absolute

16. *NRH* 32. See *On Tyranny*, 196; *WhPPh* 39. Cf. *Thoughts on Machiavelli*, 14.

17. Aristotle, *Poetics* 1451a36–1451b7; cf. *Posterior Analytics* 87b19–88a8.

knowledge, including but by no means limited to absolute knowledge of history itself, is achieved, by Hegel in particular. Absolute knowledge of history presupposes that history as a whole has come into view. As Alexandre Kojève has demonstrated, Hegel understood history as a whole to have come into view by virtue of coming to an end, not as a stop—human events will continue to occur—but as a consummation. Absolute knowledge of history, realizable at the end of history and only at the end of history, is not so much trans-historical as post-historical.

Strauss points out that there is in Heidegger's conception of history a comparable absolute moment. Unlike Hegel, however, Heidegger does not construe this moment as a culminating one, nor does he understand the events preceding it to be directed toward it by the hidden activity or "cunning" of reason. Hegel grounds actual historical development in the necessary dialectic to which consciousness is subject, and he makes this dialectic the theme of his great work, the *Phenomenology of the Spirit*, which he designated on the title page of the first edition as the "First Part" of the "System of Science" (*System der Wissenschaft*). Heidegger sees no comparable necessity in history. History is no more a rational process for Heidegger than it was for the classical philosophers. Heidegger differs from Hegel by holding that history does not come to an end; and yet he differs from the classical philosophers by holding, as Hegel does, that history decisively shapes human thought. And so Heidegger could appear at first glance to be only the finest flower of the *relativistus vulgaris* that abounds in our time.

Like Hegel, however, Heidegger holds that there is an absolute moment. The absolute moment is the moment in which the essential and inescapably fate-laden historicity of thought becomes manifest for the first time, and quite possibly for the last time. This manifestation occurs in our time, the distinctive and disorienting features of which are unforgettably described by Heidegger as "the darkening of the world, the flight of the gods (*die Flucht der Götter*), the destruction of the earth, the transformation of human beings to a mass, the hatred and suspicion (*der hassende Verdacht*) of everything creative and free."[18] It is as though a flash of lightning in the gathering darkness grants one an insight into the utter finitude not just of human thought but of Being itself. There is no good reason to think that this ontological insight will be preserved and its implications thought through, especially if, as seems increasingly probable, it is Nietzsche's "last man" who will inherit the earth. Though historically conditioned, insight into finitude is genuine insight nonetheless. The absolute

18. *Einleitung in die Metaphysik*, 29. [English translation: 38.] Transient breakdowns in the referential structures that constitute everyday life, which Heidegger describes in *SZ* § 16, have taken place as long as man has existed, though they have received little attention by philosophers in the past. The ontological significance of such breakdowns may have suggested itself to Heidegger by virtue of the unprecedented magnitude and moment that they have assumed in the present historical epoch, where they are commonly designated as "crises" of various sorts. "Heidegger's understanding of the contemporary world is more comprehensive and more profound than Marx's . . . In all [!] important respects Heidegger does not make things obscurer than they are." L. Strauss, "The Problem of Socrates" (1970), 330.

moment allows one to see that human thought always has been, is, and always will be under the sway of forces that are not rational. It is this understanding that keeps Heidegger from simply contradicting himself. No more than Hegel's historicism, then, does Heidegger's historicism immediately reduce to common, self-referential, and self-annulling relativism. Strauss recognizes this.[19]

Catherine and Michael Zuckert say, "In his later work Heidegger admitted that the analysis of human existence he had presented in *Being and Time* was true only in and of our time."[20] The Zuckerts do not cite where Heidegger makes this admission, so that one could consider its exact wording and context. For the admission as the authors report it would undercut Strauss's argument that for Heidegger, no less than for Hegel, there is an "absolute moment" in history, granted that it is quite differently understood by these two philosophers. Not all historicism reduces at once to simple relativism. There is an immediately detectable contradiction in the statement, made without qualification, that all truth is relative. For this statement implicitly presents itself as a non-relative and unqualified truth. There is not an immediately detectable contradiction in the qualified statement that thinking is always historically conditioned. The thinking that comes to this realization is indeed historically conditioned, in the sense that thinking cannot *always* come to this realization. But it does not follow that *everything* about thinking varies.[21] For that would lead ultimately to the absurd conclusion that thinking is always historically conditioned, totally so, but sometimes it is not. Heidegger does not reach this conclusion, nor need he do so. If Heidegger is right, the deepest truth about being has not always been accessible; it is partially accessible in our times, and it may well become inaccessible again in the future. It may become forever inaccessible, if man continues down his current path of self-degradation. I am not claiming that Heidegger is right on these points, only that they do not sum up to a variation of the Cretan liar paradox.

As we shall see, the conception of truth as un-anticipatable un-concealment is fundamental to Heidegger's philosophy. Anyone who wishes to take issue with his peculiar form of historicism has to come fully to terms with this conception. I know of no place where Strauss does this.[22] In "The Problem of Socrates," he makes reference

19. See Strauss's letters of February 26 and May 14 in his Correspondence with Gadamer, 7 and 11; *NRH* 29; 315; "Philosophy as Rigorous Science and Political Philosophy," 33. See also Alexandre Kojève, "Note sur l'éternité, le temps, et le concept" in *Introduction*, 337–8, and note 1 to page 338. [English translation: 101–102, and note 1 to page 102.]

20. *The Truth about Leo Strauss*, 100. Zuckert, C., "Leo Strauss: Jewish, Yes, but Heideggerian?" 103; cf. 96.

21. Something similar, though hardly identical, can be said regarding the biblical conception of revelation: the deepest truth about God is not accessible at all times. Access to this truth is historically conditioned, in the sense that it is revealed only at certain un-anticipatable points in time, and perhaps adequately revealed only in an un-anticipatable "fullness of time." But it does not follow that *everything* that can be known about God, or about revelation, varies.

22. Strauss may be alluding to this conception with his observation about revelation in *IE* 32 /308 (top). If so, he does not develop this observation.

again to the necessity, for Heidegger, of an "absolute moment [in History]." He says, "The historicist insight remains true for all times . . . Historicism is an eternal verity."[23] This last sentence is followed immediately by: "[That of course is impossible.] According to Heidegger there are no eternal verities: eternal verities would presuppose the eternity or sempiternity of the human race." That man is neither eternal nor sempiternal is surely half the story for Heidegger, but it is only half. The other half is that there is no eternal or sempiternal un-concealment.[24] There is not even an ongoing un-concealment coterminous with finite man and accessible in principle at any point in human history, at least to philosophers. So Strauss's claim that there are, for Heidegger, no eternal verities, is, with qualifications, certainly true. However, the fact (to speak loosely) that the deepest truth about Being is, in principle, accessible only at certain exceptional and un-anticipatable times could be a fact co-extensive with, and in large measure constitutive of, finite human history.[25] In that qualified sense, there would indeed be no *eternal* truths, though this particular truth about man's relationship to un-concealment would hold for man *as long as he exists*, even if he were only rarely able to apprehend it. This, I take it, is Heidegger's view. It is not my view, but I do not regard it as a simple self-contradiction.

iii. The Struggle with Heidegger in *Natural Right and History*

In the first chapter of this book, "Natural Right and the Historical Approach," Strauss discusses the challenge to the classical conception of natural right that is posed by historicism. Though, quite interestingly, Strauss does not mention Heidegger by name, he clearly has Heidegger in mind when, toward the end of the chapter, he lists certain theses that have the greatest possible bearing on the understanding of nature that is indispensable to classical philosophy in general, including any attempt to validate the concept of natural right in its classical form.

> [W]hat is called the whole is actually always incomplete and therefore not truly a whole; the whole is essentially changing in such a manner that its future cannot be predicted; the whole as it is in itself can never be grasped, or it is not intelligible; human thought essentially depends on something that cannot be anticipated or that can never be an object or that can never be mastered by the subject; "to be" in the highest sense cannot mean—or at any rate, it does not necessarily mean—"to be always."[26]

23. "The Problem of Socrates" (1970), 327. Regarding the brackets, see the editorial introduction, 321.

24. There are, for Heidegger, no eternal truths in the full sense of the word because there is for him no eternal and infinite God from whom nothing is concealed, who knows eternal verities, and even reveals some of them to finite man.

25. Again, a comparison with the biblical conception of revelation suggests itself.

26. *NRH* 31.

On reading this passage the naive reader of Strauss whose education, interests, and taste have been formed by the allegedly senescent and moribund tradition of Christian scholasticism eagerly anticipates a point by point rebuttal—*ad primum*, *ad secundum*, etc.—or at least a close analysis of these theses that would show, not only that "we cannot assume that the issue [of natural right] has been finally settled by historicism"—of course we cannot *assume* that—but that historicism is, in fact, indefensible; or, failing that, that historicism is markedly less plausible than classical philosophy. Instead, Strauss immediately says, "We cannot even attempt to discuss these theses," provoking our uninitiated reader to ask in astonishment, "What kind of *responsio* is *this*?" Strauss does not say why he cannot even *attempt* to discuss these theses. Instead, he makes a series of observations.

In the first place, he insists on the necessity for an "unbiased consideration of the most elementary premises whose validity is presupposed by philosophy," that is, by "philosophy in the full and original meaning of the term." No one in his right mind could quarrel with this insistence. But then a truly unbiased consideration requires thinking through these premises—which Strauss says are merely "presupposed"—not only as they are present in classical antiquity but also as they are radically called into question by Heidegger.

Strauss, great thinker that he is—and he *is* great—knows that he cannot simply turn his back on Heidegger and seek refuge in the company of the ancients. Instead, he makes a second observation.

> The "experience of history" and the less ambiguous experience of the complexity of human affairs may blur, but they cannot extinguish, the evidence of those simple experiences regarding right and wrong which are at the bottom of the philosophic contention that there is natural right. Historicism either ignores or else distorts these experiences.[27]

I agree with Strauss's assessment here. But the matter is complicated, and Strauss does not elaborate on the "simple experiences" to which he refers. Elsewhere he briefly alludes to "the riddle posed by Heidegger's obstinate silence about love or charity on the one hand and about laughter and the things which deserve to be laughed at on the other."[28] The implication seems to be that Heidegger has not given sufficient attention to the alternatives of Jerusalem, where love or charity is central, and Athens, where, according to Strauss, philosophy is closer to comedy than it is to tragedy.[29]

27. *NRH* 31-2. Heidegger, it must be added, is not the only great thinker to ignore or distort these experiences.

28. "Kurt Riezler," 260.

29. See *CM* 61; "On the Euthyphron," in *The Rebirth of Classical Political Rationalism*, 206; also, "Preface", 9: "Heidegger's new thinking led far away from any charity as well as from any humanity." By disassociating charity from humanity here, Strauss may be alluding to another feature of the Jerusalem-Athens opposition, as he understands it.

Heidegger would respond that it is only because man is finite that he can be *beholden* to God (Jerusalem) or *desire* wisdom (Athens). He would add that neither the Bible nor Greek philosophy supplies us with a sufficiently deep understanding of the character of this finitude. He would reiterate what he repeatedly says in *Being and Time*, namely, that the "Analytic of *Dasein*" is not a philosophical anthropology in which the variety of human attitudes and experiences is investigated in its plenitude but, rather, fundamental ontology.[30] Just as Husserl undertakes a phenomenological reduction, which transforms man into transcendental subjectivity, so Heidegger undertakes what one could call an "existential reduction," which transforms man into *Dasein*. The latter transformation is in the interest of keeping firmly in view, and thinking through, the unsettling intimations of ultimate finitude, of the absence of unqualified necessity anywhere, that occur in transient moments of anxiety as Heidegger understands anxiety.[31] In opposition to both the rational theology of Thomas Aquinas and the phenomenology of Husserl—different as these two thinkers most definitely are from each other—Heidegger teaches that the peculiar way in which *Dasein* is held out into "the Nothing" is the genuine, in fact, the only, transcendence.[32]

After his brief assessment of the limitations of historicism's comprehension of the sphere of the human, Strauss turns with equal brevity to what he seems to think are the limitations of Heidegger's understanding of Being, and he makes a third observation.

> [T]he most thoroughgoing attempt to establish historicism culminated in the assertion that if and when there are no human beings, there may be *entia* but there cannot be *esse*, that is, that there can be *entia* while there is no *esse*. There is an obvious connection between this assertion and the rejection of the view that "to be" in the highest sense means "to be always."

However Strauss may have intended this passage, Heidegger would understand it not as a criticism, but as a succinct statement of the ontological import of the investigations in *Being and Time*. Moreover, though Heidegger himself does not understand Being to be a mere concept, an abstract construct of human thought, a number of thinkers understand it just this way, and for them too, let alone nominalists of every stripe, there could in principle be particular *entia* without there being a universal *esse*. We know how Thomas Aquinas would respond, comprehensively and unambiguously, to these thinkers and to Heidegger regarding this matter and also regarding the inextinguishable "evidence of those simple experiences regarding right and wrong which are at the bottom of the philosophic contention that there is natural right." But I cannot locate a comprehensive and unambiguous response by Strauss. Nor can I construct one on Straussian grounds.

30. *SZ* 45–50, 31, 131.

31. "Was ist Metaphysics," 8–9. ["English translation," 88–89.]

32. "Was ist Metaphysik?", 15; "Vom Wesen des Grundes," in *Wegmarken*, 33–36. ["What is Metaphysics?" 93; "On the Essence of Ground," 107–10.] See *SZ* 363–6.

The fault may be mine. The thrust of the concluding pages of this first chapter of *Natural Right and History* is that an adequate response to Heidegger can be found by way of the attempt to understand philosophy in its original sense, that is, as it was understood by the ancients. But then one would expect an explicit and sustained confrontation with Heidegger toward the end of one of Strauss's studies of Xenophon, Plato, or Aristotle. I am not aware of any place where this happens. A Straussian might say that Strauss presents his sustained criticism of Heidegger implicitly, by way of hints and between the lines. But why Strauss would criticize Heidegger (the Nazi!) with such caution would then have to be accounted for. If anything, it would make more sense to praise Heidegger obliquely than to criticize him obliquely. It is hardly the case that anyone was in danger of persecution in the second half of the twentieth century for *criticizing* Heidegger.

Strauss makes a fourth and final observation, and it is not brief. He develops it over the course of the last several pages of this first chapter of *Natural Right and History*, and he continues to develop it over the course of the whole book. A representative passage, from which I cited a fragment above, is the following.

> [T]he fundamental problems, such as the problem of justice, persist or retain their identity in all historical change, however much they may be obscured by the temporary denial of their relevance and however variable or provisional all human solutions to these problems may be. In grasping these problems as problems, the human mind liberates itself from its historical limitations. No more is needed to legitimize philosophy in its original, Socratic sense . . .[33]

Strauss says that the classical thinkers "agree in regard to the most fundamental point: [they] admit that the distinction between nature and convention is fundamental. For this idea is implied in the idea of philosophy." "The first philosopher was the first man who discovered nature."[34] Taking these passages from *Natural Right and History* together we can infer that, for Strauss, man's discovery of nature consists principally if not exclusively in the discovery that he has questions, questions regarding the fundamental problems, to which he does not have fully satisfying answers. Lack of knowledge is man's permanent, and hence *natural*, condition, a condition that history neither effaces nor, *pace* Hegel, allows man to transcend.

But the "nature" that gets disclosed in this discovery is only a ghost of *physis* as Aristotle defines it in *Physics* B. 1, and interprets it over the rest of the book. Man's recognition of his ignorance is not equivalent to the discovery of the first things.[35] It does not even imply that there are first things, unless the fundamental problems are

33. *NRH* 32; *NRH* 35: "The possibility of philosophy does not require more than that the fundamental problems always be the same . . ." See "On a Forgotten Kind of Writing," 229.

34. *NRH* 11, 82.

35. *NRH* 81–84.

themselves the first things.[36] The quest for the first things as philosophy understands them, and presupposes them to be, is the quest for principles of the whole and not just of human thought; they are eternal, they are necessary, and they are the ultimate *causes* of "beings that are not always."[37] It would be hard to argue that the fundamental problems are themselves the fundamental principles of the whole without recourse to some dialectical variant of a fundamental, typically modern subjectivism, with which Strauss seems to have little sympathy.

Knowledge of ignorance is hardly the preserve of philosophy. The recognition that one does not know does not legitimize philosophy as Strauss conceives philosophy, for the same thing legitimizes belief in revelation, the possibility of which, according to Strauss, philosophy must attempt to rule out for its own validation. After all, the believer understands himself to be a *believer* rather than a *knower* because he too recognizes that he does not know. Not only can a recognition that one does not know lead as easily to belief as to a quest for knowledge, an unconsummated quest for knowledge can as easily lead to belief as to unbelief.

Regarding fundamental problems, there are two of them that have neither persisted nor retained their identity in all historical change. One of these is the problem that the Bible poses for philosophy. Strauss may have thought, by following up on a clue of Avicenna's, that Plato anticipated the essential claims of biblical revelation in his *Laws*. Not understanding how Plato could have done that, and not even being sure that Strauss really thought Plato had done it,[38] I turn to the second problem, which is not unrelated to the first; and that is the problem that Strauss himself acknowledges is posed to philosophy by historicism. For it seems to have been Strauss's view, altogether justifiable I think, that "the existence and even the possibility of natural right must remain an open question as long as the issue between historicism and nonhistoricist philosophy is not settled."[39] This is certainly a fundamental problem. But it is certainly

36. See Kennington, *SNRH* 67.

37. See *NRH* 89–90. In light of the criteria Strauss lays out in those pages, it is not easy to see how he could have identified "the unchangeable ideas" in Plato with "the fundamental and permanent problems" (*WhPPh* 39). The latter could perhaps be argued to be causes of transiently existing *thought*, but hardly of transiently existing *things*, unless one takes the giant step of identifying things with thoughts And there is a further problem: can nature, if it is construed solely as the persistence of fundamental problems, meaningfully be said to exhibit *grace*? (*WhPPh* 40.)

38. "A Giving of Accounts," 463; "How to Begin to Study Medieval Philosophy?" 224. Compare *RR* 167: "Objection c."

39. *NRH* 33. Richard Kennington writes, "If philosophy is impossible, the case for natural right is hopeless; if possible, the question of natural right remains open. Strauss's book moves back and forth . . . between two planes, the possibility of philosophy, and the still further question of natural right and its 'sufficient condition'" (*SNRH* 63). These are indeed two separate "planes," but they intersect. Historicism, with its denial of a trans-historical nature, poses a problem not just for natural right but for philosophy itself. As Strauss puts it, "[T]he discovery of nature is identical with the actualization of a human possibility which, at least according to its own interpretation, is *trans-historical* . . . The distinction between nature and convention . . . is . . . coeval with the discovery of nature and hence with philosophy" (*NRH* 89, 90; emphasis added; see also Strauss's letter of November 22, 1960, to

not one of the problems that "persist or retain their identity in all historical change." Aristotle did not have to contend with the problem of historicism in developing his account of natural right, any more than he had to contend with the problem of a rival and extensively worked out non-teleological natural science. Plato did not have to contend with the problem of historicism either. But Strauss, living in a much later epoch, most definitely had to contend with it.

> [T]he problem [!] of historicism must first be considered from the point of view of classical philosophy, which is nonhistoricist thought in its pure form . . . We need, in the first place, a nonhistoricist understanding of nonhistoricist philosophy. But we need no less urgently a nonhistoricist understanding of historicism, that is, an understanding of the genesis of historicism that does not take for granted the soundness of historicism.[40]

The last sentence in this passage is revealing. Strauss speaks as though an understanding of the genesis of historicism in general and, most urgently, of Heideggerian historicism in particular might count as an adequate confrontation with it. *Natural Right and History* is a magnificent book. Even when one disagrees with Strauss, one learns something of importance in virtually every paragraph. But though the range of matters dealt with in the book is unusually broad, its argumentative thrust is rather narrowly circcumscribed. Consider the following sentences on the last page of the first chapter.

> It was a predicament peculiar to eighteenth-century political philosophy that led to the emergence of the historical school . . . Historicism is the ultimate outcome of the crisis of modern natural right.

Natural Right and History does not conclude with the confrontation with Heidegger that the first chapter leads one to expect. It concludes instead with a confrontation with Edmund Burke. In declining to directly treat Heidegger's analyses as he develops them, and by referring these analyses instead to their historic antecedents, Strauss comes precariously close to historicism itself, not, to be sure, to the *theory* that all thought is in the decisive respect historically conditioned, but to the *practice* of considering an author's teaching less in its own terms than as the reflex of historical forces external to his arguments and analyses proper.[41]

We have already seen Strauss take a similar tack in his confrontation with Thomas Aquinas, in whose teaching "no doubt is left . . . regarding the immutable character of the fundamental propositions of natural law," and for whom "[t]he doctrine

Gershom Scholem, *Gesammelte Schriften*, Band 3, 743, bottom). To this it must be added that even if the bare *possibility* of philosophy can be established independently of natural right, the *justification* of philosophy as *the* right way of life (for those who can live it) cannot be established independently of natural right. See *NRH* 127, 152–3, 156.

40. *NRH* 33.

41. Strauss is generally critical of this practice. See "Political Philosophy and History," 64.

of *synderesis* or of the conscience explains why the natural law can always be duly promulgated to *all* men and hence be *universally* obligatory." [42] Rather than attempt to exhibit defects in the reasoning that led Thomas to these conclusions, Strauss says immediately, "It is reasonable to assume that these profound changes were due to the influence of the belief in divine revelation."

But "influence" is much too vague a term, whether it names, in the case of Thomas Aquinas, belief in divine revelation or, in the case of Heidegger, belief in the historical school. As argued earlier, whatever beliefs motivate a thinker to make a case for certain claims, if the case itself is presented exclusively in terms of what is accessible to man as man, then it must be evaluated in these terms, and not in terms of what influenced the making of it.

In *Being and Time* Heidegger tries to show first of all, without appeal to the historical school or to any other authority, that *Dasein* by virtue of its essential temporality is historical in its essence. Only toward the end of this book does he address claims made by the historical school. As Hegel attempts to ground actual history in his description of the necessary though dialectical development of consciousness itself, so Heidegger attempts to ground actual history in his description of the "historizing" (or happening—*Geschehen*) of *Dasein*. On the basis of this analysis, Heidegger can then say that "the historicality" (*Geschichtlichkeit*) of *Dasein* is the basis for a possible historical (*historisches*) understanding."[43] Heidegger's historicism is not a logical presupposition of the "Analytic of *Dasein*" but a consequence of it, as the very structure of *Being and Time* bears out. A confrontation with Heideggerian historicism, which Strauss himself recognizes is not intrinsically self-contradictory, requires showing that the "Analytic of *Dasein*," the analysis of existence, construed not as a philosophical anthropology but as fundamental ontology, is essentially defective. [44] One might

42. *NRH* 163 (emphasis added). To begin to gauge the extent of Strauss's reservations about what "the doctrine of synderesis" in Thomas's natural law teaching, or anywhere else, accomplishes, one should ponder and re-ponder the following, unusually long sentence from *CM*, to which I alluded in Part 2, Ch. 9, above. "[O]ne must consider Macbeth's utterance in the light of the play as a whole; we might thus find that according to the play as a whole, life is not senseless simply, but becomes senseless for him who violates the sacred law of life, or the sacred order restores itself, or the violation of the law of life is self-destructive; but [!] since that self-destruction is exhibited in the case of Macbeth, a human being of a particular kind, one would have to wonder whether the apparent lesson of the play is true of *all* men or *universally*; one would have to consider whether what appears to be a natural law is in fact a natural law, given the fact that Macbeth's violation of the law of life is at least partly originated by preternatural beings" (59, emphasis added).

43. *SZ* 332; see § 75.

44. See the concluding sentence of "Political Philosophy and History," in *WhPPh* 77, where Strauss says that historicism is "inevitable on the basis of modern philosophy." Strauss may be right about this. But even if he is right about this, the inevitability he speaks of hardly proves that Heidegger's attempt to ground his historicism in the "Analytic of *Dasein*"—and not in the inadequately justified assumptions of the historical school—is itself unsuccessful. It only alerts us to this possibility. To consider the matter logically, that a later theory is inevitable on the basis of an earlier one, even if the earlier one is false, does not preclude the later one from being true, especially if argued for in its own terms and without logical reliance on the earlier one. Richard Velkley pushes Strauss's point further:

think that Strauss was so unimpressed by Heidegger's analysis of existence that he felt no need to grapple with it. Not so. Strauss writes that it is Heidegger—and not, say, Socrates, Plato, Xenophon, Aristotle, Al Farabi, or Maimonides—who "has thought through most clearly the problem of 'existence.'"[45]

Strauss says that Heidegger's "analytics of existence appears still to partake of modern subjectivism."[46] Indeed it does. Heidegger's orientation in *Being and Time* is professedly phenomenological. In spite of crucial modifications, he is working on ground prepared by Husserl, as he generously acknowledges.[47] If one could show that the whole phenomenological orientation that Husserl opened up was unsound, then one could make a beginning at criticizing Heidegger.

Strauss does not attempt such a thing. In his short article on Husserl, "Philosophy as Rigorous Science and Political Philosophy," he devotes only about five pages (out of nine) to Husserl. Strauss limits himself to commenting on Husserl's 1911 essay, "Philosophy as Rigorous Science." He observes that, in connection with the critique of naturalism (or psychologism), phenomenology takes the form of a "study of essences" as distinct from natures "and in no way of existence."[48] It is not obvious that Strauss intends this observation to be a criticism, except perhaps as a special instance of his more general criticism that the moderns depreciate nature. In any event, he

"radical historicism [i.e., Heidegger's philosophy] is undermined by its failure to have adequate historical awareness of its own premises" ("On the Roots of Rationalism," 248); Velkley seems to endorse this "genealogical critique of Heidegger" (249), though he says that "in a significant pair of speeches given at the University of Freiburg in August 1934 . . . Heidegger shows awareness of the sources of his thought—and of current political realities—in the historical school" (248, fn. 4). Strauss says in his letter of July 17, 1935, to Karl Löwith, that "the necessity of Hegel can only be radically understood from the foundation of modern philosophy in the 17th Century." As regards "necessity," perhaps. But radically understanding, or even undermining, the foundation of modern philosophy in the 17th Century cannot substitute for a close and sustained engagement with Hegel unless it can be convincingly shown that he built uncritically upon it. Strauss responds in a similar vein to Helmut Kuhn's charge that "the bulk of [*NRH*] is devoted to the causal genesis of the error [historicism] rather than to its frontal criticism" (Letter to Kuhn, 23). Strauss manages to temporarily deflect Kuhn's charge with an appeal to Aristotle: "it is necessary to state not only the truth but the cause of the error." The problem is that *NRH* does not conclusively demonstrate that mature and refined historicism, either in its Hegelian or in its Heideggerian form, *is* an error, however questionable its inchoate and crude precursors.

45. Letter of December 17, 1949 to Eric Voegelin, in *Faith and Political Philosophy*, 63. See *IE* 38/312: "The great [!] achievement of Heidegger was the coherent [!] exposition of the experience of *Existenz* . . ." In light of these strong assertions, one cannot be sure that Strauss does *not* agree with Heidegger's repeated claim in *Being and Time* that *Dasein* is constituted by having *possibilities*, hence that it is *not determined* across the board. (See, for example, *SZ* 259, conclusion of the second paragraph on that page; cf. *SZ* 266).

46. *IE* 39/313.

47. *SZ* 38: "Die folgenden Untersuchungen sind nur möglich geworden auf dem Boden, den E. Husserl gelegt, mit dessen *Logische Untersuchungen* die Phänomenologie zum Durchbruch kam." See also the note to that page.

48. "Philosophy as Rigorous Science and Political Philosophy," 35. See Husserl, *Ideen*, Erstes Buch, [English translation: *Ideas*, First Book] § 51.

does not develop the observation. The explicit criticism is that, in drawing a sharp distinction between philosophy as a rigorous science and the much less rigorous *Weltanschauungsphilosophien* (literally, world-view philosophies), Husserl

> did not go on to wonder whether the single-minded pursuit of philosophy as a rigorous science would not have an adverse effect on *Weltanschauungsphilosophie* which most men need to live by and hence on the actualization of the ideas which that kind of philosophy serves, in the first place in the practitioners of philosophy as rigorous science but secondarily also in those who are impressed by those practitioners. He seems to have taken it for granted that there will always be a variety of *Weltanschauungsphilosophien* that peacefully coexist within one and the same society. He did not pay attention to societies that impose a single *Weltanschauung* or *Weltanschauungsphilosophie* on all their members and for this reason will not tolerate philosophy as a rigorous science.[49]

In brief, Husserl (in 1911) was not as sensitive to the precarious place of philosophy within society as were Socrates and those who learned from the teaching of Socrates or at least from his fate. True. But this criticism of the *practical* consequences of Husserl's single-minded focus on the constitution of meaning and objectivity does not speak at all to the question of whether there was or was not sufficient *theoretical* warrant for his radicalization of the Cartesian turn to subjectivity and his attempt to show that subjectivity properly understood is the field within which all meaning and objectivity are constituted.[50]

Strauss recognizes Husserl's greatness.[51] Moreover, he says that, in order to understand Heidegger—to say nothing of refuting him—"one must not neglect the work of his teacher Husserl."[52] There is no doubt about that. But Husserl's *oeuvre*, like Heidegger's, is comparable in bulk and density to Thomas Aquinas's (though it should be remembered that Husserl and Heidegger outlived Thomas by about 30 and 40 years respectively). One cannot fault Strauss for failing to advance comprehensive interpretations of every thinker he commented on. His reading was wide by any standard, and

49. "Philosophy as Rigorous Science and Political Philosophy,"37. In the last paragraph of this essay, Strauss acknowledges that Husserl later "modified the reflection we have been speaking about, under the impact of events which could not be overlooked or overheard [*sic*]." The passage that Strauss quotes in that paragraph he identifies as being from Husserl's Prague lecture of 1935. It occurs in "The Vienna Lecture," which is appended to David Carr's translation of *The Crisis of the European Sciences and Transcendental Phenomenology*, p. 288. According to Carr, the "Vienna Lecture" was given six months before the Prague lecture. See p. 269 n. 1. The quoted passage is so striking that one might suspect that Husserl had become aware, if only at second hand, of Strauss's own investigations.

50. For a comparable criticism of the practical consequences of Heidegger's thought, see *WhPPh* 26–27.

51. See, for example, Strauss's lecture, "Living Issues in German Postwar Philosophy," in *Leo Strauss and the Theologico-Political Problem*, 137, and his letter of May 9, 1943, to Eric Voegelin in *Faith and Political Philosophy*, 17.

52. "Philosophy as Rigorous Science and Political Philosophy," 31.

he advanced comprehensive interpretations of a number of philosophers, interpretations that are original and are interesting at almost every point. Still, given the importance he explicitly assigns to the challenge that Heidegger's thought poses to nature as classically conceived,[53] and the prominence that he himself gives this concept, it is puzzling that he did not leave behind a full-blown critique of Heidegger's thought, including especially its Husserlian presuppositions, similar in comprehensiveness and acuity to his studies of Plato, Xenophon, Aristotle, Maimonides, Machiavelli, Hobbes, Spinoza, and others.

iv. The Struggle with Heidegger in "Introduction to Existentialism"

What is most praiseworthy about this lecture is Strauss's fair-minded and generally successful attempt to restate the essentials of Heidegger's thought within a small compass. There are a few critical observations, but they are not developed. Hence they do not succeed in casting serious doubt on Heidegger's thought except for those who would rather find a reason to dismiss it than expend effort in trying to understand it. Strauss says,

> Heidegger demanded from philosophy that it should liberate itself completely from traditional or inherited notions which were mere survivals of former ways of thinking. He mentioned especially concepts that were of Christian theological origin. Yet his understanding of existence was obviously of Christian origin (conscience, guilt, being unto death, anguish).[54]

Again, Strauss substitutes an attribution of influence for an actual engagement with the thought of a thinker as the thinker presents it. Strauss does not engage with Heidegger's detailed attempt to show that these phenomena are primordial, accessible to description and philosophical conceptualization, and—something one would think would be of special interest to Strauss—seriously misinterpreted by Christianity itself.[55] Strauss continues with another criticism, which is limited to a single sentence.

> The fact that [Heidegger's] analytics of existence was based on a specific ideal of existence made one wonder whether the analysis was not fundamentally arbitrary.

Strauss invites us to wonder whether something might not be the case instead of giving us an actual argument that it is the case. Even the invitation is problematic here because Strauss does not clarify how the Analytic of *Dasein* was based on a specific ideal of existence. He does not specify the character of the base—a premise or a heuristic

53. See Strauss's letter of March 15, 1962 to Karl Löwith, *GS* Band 3, 685–6.

54. *IE* 38/313.

55. See *SZ* 48–50, 180, 230, 270–95. See also Heidegger's acerbic attribution of the continued philosophical interest in eternal truths and in "an idealized absolute subject" to residues of Christianity that have not yet been "radically driven out" (or "exorcised"—*ausgetrieben*; *SZ* 229).

assumption? a motivation? one influence among several? He does not even say here what the specific ideal is supposed to have been. Strauss may be alluding to something he said earlier in his lecture.

> Existentialism appeals to a certain experience (anguish) as the basic experience in light of which everything must be understood. Having this experience is one thing; regarding it as the basic experience is another thing. Its basic character is not guaranteed by the experience itself. It can only be guaranteed by *argument*. The argument may be invisible because it is implied in what is generally admitted in our time. What is generally admitted may imply, but only imply, a fundamental uneasiness which is vaguely felt but not faced . . . Yet this vaguely felt uneasiness is distinctly a present-day phenomenon.[56]

Perhaps anxiety, which Strauss here calls "the basic experience" (in Heidegger's scheme of things), is what he later refers to as the "specific ideal of existence" on which Heidegger "based" his Analytic of *Dasein* in *Being and Time* (though "ideal" hardly seems to be the right word for a "basic experience," especially if the experience is one of anxiety).

To evaluate Strauss's criticism we must begin by noting that Heidegger is about one hundred pages into the Analytic of *Dasein* before he speaks of anxiety. At that point, at the end of Section 29, in which he has been treating what gets translated as "state-of-mind" (*Befindlichkeit*) in a general way, Heidegger announces that anxiety as *an* existential-ontologically significant, basic state-of-mind will become a theme some forty pages further on, in Section 40.[57] The title of Section of 40 is "*Die Grundbefindlichkeit der Angst als eine ausgezeichnete Erschlossenheit des Daseins.*" Anxiety is *a* distinctive (or capital) way in which the Being of *Dasein* as *care* gets disclosed; and Heidegger devotes Section 42 of *Being and Time* to arguing that care was recognized as the Being of *Dasein* even in classical antiquity. Anxiety, then, is not the only way in which the Being of *Dasein* as care is disclosed, though it is particularly suitable for this disclosure.[58] Heidegger does later on specify anxiety as *the* (and not just *a*) state of mind in which *Dasein*, in its Being-towards-death, finds itself in the present facing the ultimate nothingness of its future.[59] More generally, it is the fundamental mood in which man is brought before "the Nothing" that, according to Heidegger, is at work within—and by no means functions merely as a negative placeholder and

56. *IE* 32/307–308.

57. *SZ* 140.

58. *SZ* 185: Die Möglichkeit, in interpretierenden Mit- und Nachgehen innerhalb eines befindlichen Verstehens zum Sein des Daseins vorzudringen, erhöht sich, je urspruenglicher das Phänomen ist, das methodisch als erschliessende Befindlichkeit fungiert. Dass die Angst dergleichen leistet, ist zunächst eine Behauptung.

59. *SZ* 265.

counter-concept of—Being itself.[60] So Strauss's designation of anxiety as, for Heidegger, "the basic experience" is, with the above qualifications, essentially on the mark.

Yet we have seen that Strauss himself says later in "Introduction to Existentialism" that anguish—by which he presumably means anxiety or *Angst*—is a concept of Christian provenance. Anxiety is, then, hardly "a present day phenomenon" exclusively. Nor is it even a concept of Christian provenance exclusively.[61] What may be specifically modern is the vagueness with which this uneasiness is felt, although that too can be doubted. But if Strauss is right about this, then he has simply reinforced his point that, for Heidegger, there is an absolute moment in history, in the very midst of our vexed times, when Being, or *Sein*, in its truth and as inseparable from the history of *Da-sein*, comes to the fore for the time being with an unprecedented vividness. He has not refuted Heidegger on this point.

Strauss makes another criticism, or rather a critical observation. It is particularly interesting.

> The highest form of knowledge was said [by Heidegger] to be finite knowledge of finiteness; yet how can finiteness be seen as finiteness if it is not seen in the light of infinity?[62]

We can assume that Heidegger would answer by granting at once that the concept of finitude is logically inseparable from the concept of infinitude; but he would add that this merely logical connection has no ontological implication. Heidegger is unimpressed with attempts, such as Descartes's, to demonstrate the existence of an infinite, perfect, and eternal being, or God, from the mere concepts of infinitude, perfection, and eternity. I am aware of nothing in Strauss's works suggesting that he was any more impressed with such attempts than Heidegger was.

Strauss does say elsewhere of Heidegger, though without naming him, that "[m]odern thought reaches its culmination, its highest self-consciousness, in the most radical historicism, i.e., in explicitly condemning to oblivion the notion of eternity," and that this oblivion amounts to the "estrangement from man's deepest desires and therewith from the primary issues."[63] Strauss presumably thinks, not without reason, that man's "notion of eternity" serves as an *entré* to the primary issues, one of which is the contrast between the philosophical conception of an eternal, or at least persisting, nature and the biblical conception of the eternal, freely creating God. Strauss presumably thinks—I am not entirely sure about this—that the former conception is the more coherent of the two. But then he also realizes that the former conception, as well as the

60. "Was ist Metaphysik?" 10–19. [English translation: 89–96.]

61. See for example Hans Jonas, *The Gnostic Religion* (Boston: Beacon Press, 1963), 62–68. Consider also Heidegger's treatment of the famous *polla ta deina* chorus from Sophocles' *Antigone* in his *Einleitung in die Metaphysik*, 112–26. [English translation: 146–65.]

62. *IE* 38/313.

63. *WhPPh* 55; see *NRH* 176.

latter, has been rendered deeply problematic by Heidegger. Heidegger's condemnation of the notion of eternity, including nature as classically conceived, to oblivion is hardly an offhand condemnation, as Strauss fully realizes. It is the consequence of his thinking through the problem of existence. And Heidegger is the man who, according to Strauss himself, "has thought through most clearly the problem of 'existence.'"

Finally, though Strauss and others have detected in the prominence that Heidegger gives to resoluteness (*Entschlossenheit*) in *Being and Time* a portent of his later decision for National Socialism, it has to be recognized that resoluteness is not the sole ethical or cypto-ethical principle that appears in *Being and Time*. Far in advance of his introduction of resoluteness in Section 54 of that book, he dwells in Section 26 on the phenomenon of Being-with-others in what he takes to be both its inauthentic and its authentic modes, with special attention, respectively, to indifference and solicitude. Solicitude (*Fürsorge*) is clearly a specification of care (*Sorge*), for Heidegger the very Being, the *Sein*, of *Dasein*. Solicitude provides a wealth of content in advance to the otherwise merely formal and content-less concept of resoluteness.[64] Indifference to others, and especially being inconsiderate (*rücksichtlos*) toward them, produces, according to Heidegger, a kind of blindness. It keeps one from seeing the *Sein* that is there (*da*) in them as well as in oneself. It thereby prevents one from adequately understanding one's own *Dasein*. To that extent, it occludes one's apprehension of Being in its truth. To be sure, Heidegger does not criticize indifference to others and being inconsiderate toward them as violations of a precept of natural law, the categorical imperative, or any other objective moral principle. But though he does not criticize indifference and inconsiderateness on exactly moral grounds, he does criticize indifference and inconsiderateness on theoretical grounds: they are obstacles to clear seeing. That is to say, they are obstacles to knowledge, and hence to philosophy.[65]

Heidegger's accounts of care, solicitude, indifference, and even resoluteness do not compel anyone who is persuaded by them to side, or even move towards siding, with Nazism. No one has ever demonstrated such a thing. Even if Heidegger's accounts of these things in light of his understanding of our "having been thrown" into our particular and contingent situation lead to the placing of inordinate weight on "one's own" and "the "fatherland,"[66] and thereby on some kind of patriotism, this patriotism could as easily induce one to resolutely join forces with those who tried to assassinate Hitler as to resolutely join forces with those who supported him. The *real* problem is that Heidegger's accounts of Being-in-the-world and Being-with-others do not *rule out* siding with Nazism. His understanding of what goes by the name of

64. Compare *IE* 36/311, conclusion of the paragraph that starts, "Existentialism begins then . . ."

65. The German word *Rücksicht*, which can be translated as "consideration," contains the word *Sicht* which means sight, and so is similar to the English word "re-spect," itself another translation of *Rücksicht*. If one finds "inconsiderate" too tepid a way of characterizing the viciousness that man can exhibit to his fellows, it should be noted that *rücksichtlos* can also be translated as "ruthless."

66. *WhPPh* 35–36.

"ethics"—leaving aside the execrable way he put this understanding into practice in the critical moment[67]—is in fact not so far from that of Nietzsche and other philosophers for whom, unlike Thomas Aquinas and Kant, the moral virtues "are understood only as subservient to philosophy and for its sake."[68]

Strauss has more in common with Thomas and more in common with Heidegger than Thomas and Heidegger have in common with each other. But these two thinkers pose, in diametrically opposed ways, more radical challenges to Strauss's attempt to rehabilitate classical political philosophy than do a small host of other thinkers whom he treats with admirable thoroughness and penetration. I have argued that Strauss's response to the challenge posed by Thomas was uncharacteristically superficial because he did not appreciate it. But Strauss did appreciate the challenge posed by Heidegger. The uncharacteristic superficiality of his express response to that challenge, in that challenge's own terms, is inexplicable to me. Strauss's followers might say that I have failed to recognize that Strauss's whole impressive intellectual project can count as response to Heidegger. But to make that claim good, they would have to show not only how Strauss managed to correct Heidegger's "great achievement . . . the coherent exposition of the experience of Existenz,"[69] but also how, absent an unambiguous and convincing revalidation of the concept of nature that animated classical philosophy, he managed to retrieve "the notion of eternity" from the oblivion to which Heidegger condemned it.[70]

SECTION C. TOWARD A THOMISTIC RESPONSE TO HEIDEGGER

Not only does Heidegger pose a radical challenge to Strauss's attempt to rehabilitate classical political philosophy, he poses an equally radical challenge to Thomas Aquinas. In fact, Heidegger poses a more radical challenge to Thomas than does Plato, Aristotle, Spinoza, Kant, Hegel, Nietzsche or any other thinker in the philosophical tradition, Strauss included. After having spoken at such length about the challenge that Heidegger poses to Strauss and his followers, and their failure to meet it, it would be unfair of me not to say something about the challenge that Heidegger poses to Thomas and his followers, and how they might meet it. The radicality of Heidegger's challenge turns, not on his historicism,[71] but on his depreciation of natural reason, and the principles that are proper to its operation.

As Heidegger sees it, taking *ratio* and its principles as a canon for thought has always led metaphysical thinking astray and will always do so.[72] His view resembles

67. *WhPPh* 27.

68. See "A Giving of Accounts," 465, and "The Law of Reason," 114.

69. *IE* 38/312.

70. *WhPPh* 35.

71. See the *Note* appended to this section.

72. See *Einführung in die Metaphysik*, Tübingen, 18–19 [English translation, 23–25]. And consider

that of Kant. But whereas, for Kant, the problem lies on the subjective side, where speculative reason attempts to transcend the limits of its proper employment and can never penetrate to the heart of things, for Heidegger the problem lies equally on the objective side, in the unpredictably concealing and disclosing history of Being itself. As intrinsically non-rational,[73] Being does not conform to the ways in which our reason works, more or less satisfactorily, with individual entities in everyday life.

Heidegger's depreciation of logic shields his teaching from a logical refutation. But it also prevents him from mounting a logical offensive against an alternative account. Thomas's rational theology and natural law teaching is an alternative account. Or rather, I think, it is *the* alternative account—comprehensive, consistent, and accessible to man as man. Since logical refutation is ruled out from the start, the contest between these two thinkers has to be decided on the plausibility of the conflicting premises that shape their thinking and their comparative success in making sense of human experience. In essaying even a sketch of what a Thomistic response to Heidegger would look like, we must heed Strauss's admonition that the influence of Husserl on Heidegger not be underestimated. For not only does Heidegger dedicate *Being and Time* to Husserl, he explicitly announces his own investigation as phenomenological.[74]

i. Problems in the Husserlian background

With his phenomenological reduction, that is, with the "bracketing" of the naïve belief in the world as existing independently from consciousness, Husserl systematically rules out any attempt to account for what is phenomenally present to consciousness by appeal to what is not phenomenally present. Husserl replaces accounts that purport to explain the given world with an essentially descriptive account of the given world. And this means that he replaces accounts that appeal to an ultimate and wholly *transcendent cause*, accounts that necessarily go beyond the sphere of the given, with an account in terms of *immanent constitution*, an account that ostensibly confines itself to the sphere of the given. The phenomenological reduction is supposed, at one stroke, to rule out of consideration anything that cannot be made intuitively present to consciousness. God, construed as ultimate cause, is certainly not given this way, nor can he be made present this way. He is not a phenomenon, a "datum" of

the final sentence of Heidegger's essay "Nietzsches Wort, 'Gott ist tot,'" in *Holzwege*, 247: "Das Denken beginnt erst dann, wenn wir erfahren haben, dass die seit Jahrhunderten verherrlichte Vernunft die hartnäckigste Widersacherin des Denkens ist." Strauss writes to Erik Voegelin that, in *Holzwege*, Heidegger, though he gets some things "simply right," also "says many *adunatotata*" (*Faith and Political Philosophy*, 76). And to Alexandre Kojève he writes, "Most interesting, much that is outstanding, and on the whole bad: the most extreme historicism" (*On Tyranny*, 250).

73. Though, for Kant, speculative reason cannot ascend to an unconditioned in the realm of what *is*, practical reason actually constitutes an unconditioned in the realm of what *ought* to be, i.e., the moral law. To that extent, Kant's unconditioned is not as "elusive" as Heidegger's Being.

74. *SZ* § 7.

consciousness.[75] He is inferred from the data of consciousness. Such an inference, for Husserl, is unwarranted when working within the confines of the phenomenological reduction where alone, according to him, one can achieve clarity and certainty.

On the other hand, Husserl himself seems to make inferences that are unwarranted when working within the confines of the phenomenological reduction. Some of Husserl's most thoughtful followers hold that neither his hyletic data nor his transcendental ego are phenomenally given, either before or after the reduction, and hence are not accessible to description.[76] These things are inferred, without phenomenological justification, from what is phenomenally given. Invoking them to account for phenomena is at odds with the most fundamental methodological tenet of Husserlian phenomenology.[77] If one is permitted to infer descriptively inaccessible hyletic data in order to account for the facticity of particular phenomena, why should one not be permitted instead to infer Kant's allegedly "absurd" thing-in-itself to account for the same facticity? In fact, why should one not be permitted to infer Thomas's descriptively inaccessible God, rather than Husserl's descriptively inaccessible transcendental ego, as the cause of both the lawful structure *and* the facticity of phenomena, that is, as the cause of the world in its entirety?[78] There is nothing intrinsically unreasonable about an attempt to account for what is given by appeal to what is not given. But such an attempt is no longer phenomenological and, according to Husserl's own criteria, lacks the level of certainty that can be obtained by limiting oneself to describing the phenomenally given exactly *as* it is given.

The phenomenological reduction and the commitment to describing only what is phenomenally given, can seem innocent enough, seemingly serving the purpose solely of an "intuition of the essence" (*Wesenschau*) of what is phenomenally given without regard to its being, focusing on *essentia* in isolation from *esse*, a Thomist might say.[79] There is, for Husserl, only one thing whose being is not and cannot be bracketed out of consideration by the phenomenological reduction, and that is consciousness itself.[80]

75. See Strauss's anecdote in "A Giving of Accounts," 461.

76. See Aron Gurwitsch, "A Non-egological Conception of Consciousness," 287–300; 253–7, and Dorion Cairns, "The Many Senses and Denotations of the Word *Bewusstsein*," 27–29. Consider also Alfred Schutz's letter of August 19 to Gurwitsch in *Philosophers in Exile*, 6–10.

77. See, e.g., Husserl's *Logische Untersuchungen* (Sixth Edition, Tübingen: Max Niemeyer, 1980), VI, § 15, concluding paragraph, 63. [English translation: 718.]

78. Consider, in this connection, the highly interesting but obscure "*Anmerkung*" to *Ideen I* § 51, and also § 58, "The Transcendency God Excluded". See Rudolph Boehm's commendable attempt—I think not entirely successful—to clarify how Husserl, in *Ideen I*, approached the question of God from a phenomenological perspective. "Husserl's Concept of the 'Absolute,'" 183–7; 190, n. 88. Compare Husserl's letter of May 4, 1933 to Dietrich Mahnke, quoted by Ronald Bruzina in his Introduction to Eugen Fink's *Sixth Cartesian Meditation*, xlviii. See also Fink's "Phenomenological Philosophy," 136.

79. It would, however, be more accurate for the Thomist to say "focusing on *quidditas* (what-ness) in isolation from *esse*" inasmuch as, "per [essentiam] et in ea ens habet esse" (*DEE* 4 [English translation, 32]).

80. *Ideen 1*, § 33. One might say that, from the perspective of phenomenology, it is transcendental subjectivity, and not God, whose *essentia* necessarily includes *esse*.

For this reason and others, Husserl is led to the assertion that only phenomenology can lay claim to being first philosophy,[81] which is an anticipation of Heidegger's assertion in *Being and Time* that only as phenomenology is ontology possible.[82]

Husserl's phenomenological reduction, which at first appears performed merely as a matter of method, ends up ruling out metaphysics—as it was classically conceived from the time of Plato through the period of high scholasticism and beyond—as an unrecognized absurdity. For metaphysics assumes that it can know, or at least think, an ultimate cause that, though somehow an object of consciousness, is not constituted by consciousness. Moreover, Husserl's attempt to apprehend the essence of knowledge solely in terms of how *we* acquire it from pre-predicative, essentially perceptual experience, leads him to conclude that this genesis is inseparable from the essence, from the very meaning, of knowledge. And so Husserl concludes that an intellectual intuition not founded in perceptual experience, that is, an intellectual intuition such as Thomas and others ascribe to God, is also an absurdity.[83]

A Thomistic response to these and related theses will begin by raising the question of what occurs within the "natural attitude" that, if it does not motivate, nevertheless occasions the phenomenological reduction and the full panoply of strictures and puzzles that it entails, including the "paradox" of communication between the phenomenologist working within the reduction and the non-phenomenologist who remains within the natural attitude but attends to what the phenomenologist has to say.[84]

I shall not argue at length here against the claim that, instead of God, the human mind, as reduced by Husserl to transcendental subjectivity, is itself the source of all objectivity, including not only the intelligibility and meaning of the world but the very existence of the world. I limit myself instead to noting that in perceiving, which for Husserl is the necessary foundation for higher order acts of understanding, the human mind necessarily makes use of the sense organs of the human body with which it is manifestly, and at the same time mysteriously, associated. The human mind perceives the world not just by beholding it but by interacting kinesthetically with it. Now, the human body is incontestably in the world. So, in its presumed constituting of the world, the human mind must constitute the very body through which it constitutes the world. The constitution of the human body would also have to be by way of kinesthesia, which presupposes the human body. On this interpretation, the human

81. *Ideen 1*, § 63. Heidegger has his own take on this issue. See the following footnote.

82. *SZ* 35; 42: "Das 'Wesen' des Daseins liegt in seiner Existenz" (42). Karl Löwith recognizes that this claim is an extreme, anti-theological transformation of the claim of the scholastics that God is the *ens* whose *essentia* (or *Wesen*) is uniquely *esse* (or *Existenz*). See Löwith, "Heidegger."

83. *Logische Untersuchungen*, Investigation VI, § 60 and *Ideen 1*, § 43; see *Cartesianische Meditationen*, § 28.

84. This problem is acknowledged within the phenomenological movement itself. See Fink, "Phenomenological Philosophy," 134–5; and Alfred Schutz, "On Multiple Realities," 256–9.

body has to play a role in its own constitution, which sounds as though it has to be present before it can be present.

Nietzsche caught sight of this problem,[85] and Husserl and his school have been much preoccupied with it. Drawing attention to the problem hardly counts as a refutation of phenomenology. But the problem is an enormous one, and it cries out for a definitive solution by anyone who holds that the world and all within it, including the human body, is constituted in and by a transcendental dimension of the human mind, rather than created *ex nihilo* by the transcendent God. Without a definitive solution, there is no way for the followers of Husserl, or for the followers of Kant, to refute those who, like Thomas Aquinas and Duns Scotus, hold that we are not locked up within consciousness and that an ascent from the phenomenal and empirical order of things, that is, the given world, to the existence of a cause truly transcending the world is both possible and demanded by natural reason itself.

Heidegger works generally within a phenomenological framework in spite of his significant departures from Husserl. It is within this framework, and only within it, that he can speak of the history of how Being is variably understood at different times, not as the history of an understanding merely, but as the history of Being itself.[86] Not unrelated to this way of regarding things, though isolatable from it, is Heidegger's conception of what he calls "the ontological difference."

ii. The ontological difference between Being and beings

According to Heidegger, there is a fundamental difference between Being (or to-be, *Sein*) and beings (or entities—*Seienden*).[87] The difference is so fundamental that no being, not even the highest being, God, can properly be called Being itself. To the Thomistic response that Heidegger, in his interpretation of *Sein*, is conflating a mere concept, *esse commune*, with the act, *esse*, whereby a being *is*, and that it is the latter and not the former that is meant when God is understood as *esse subsistens*, Heidegger would assert that no individual being is the *act* whereby it *is*. God construed as *esse subsistens*, that is, as Thomas Aquinas understands him, is incoherently construed.

85. *Jenseits von Gut und Böse*, *Sämtliche Werke*, Vol. 5, § 15 [the section number is the same in the English translation].

86. See *SZ* 35 (and compare 63), where Being (*Sein*) is spoken of as a phenomenon, and even as meaning (*Sinn*). This conception is already a significant departure from Husserl's "subjectivism," but at the same time a radicalization of it (*SZ* 212). Truth is no longer timeless. It is the historically conditioned, varying, unpredictable, and radically contingent un-concealment of *Sein*, i.e., the emergence of Being from concealment. Heidegger develops this theme in *Being and Time*, § 44, and in a number of shorter works. Of special interest in connection with the problem of historicism is his essay "Plato's Doctrine of Truth." According to Alfred Schutz, "Strauss says [of this essay] that it is the most brazen thing he has run into." *Philosophers in Exile*, 97.

87. In writing of Kurt Riezler's ontology, Strauss notes that for Riezler, just as for Heidegger, the difference between *esse* and *entia* is fundamental and admits of no exceptions. Strauss does not take issue with Riezler on this point, nor with Heidegger either. "Kurt Riezler," 247–50.

Neither God (if he exists) nor anything else that *is* can be coherently construed as Being, as that whereby entities *are*. The ontological difference between Being and beings, including even God, is absolute and does not admit of exceptions.[88]

If we restrict our attention to what is phenomenally given, this assertion of Heidegger's is justifiable. We have no direct experience of anything that is its own act of being, its *esse*. *Dasein,* in contradistinction to Husserl's transcendental ego, is not only essentially finite but is essentially constituted by its awareness, however so fleeting it may be, of this finitude. Thomas of course would grant, he even insists, that in the case of each thing we encounter in the world, including ourselves, *what* the thing is, its *essentia*, is distinct from the act, *esse*, whereby it is. Our direct experience is of things that could *not-be*, of *entia* that *need* not *be*. So far, then, Thomas and Heidegger are fundamentally in agreement. All worldly things, including the world itself, are non-necessary. *Esse* does not pertain to the *essentia* of a single worldly *ens*, and so no worldly *ens*, not even the world itself as the sum and system of worldly *entia*, can be its own *esse*. In attempting to give an account of how worldly *entia* come by their *esse*—since they cannot bring themselves into being nor, according to Thomas, sustain themselves in the contingency of their being—Thomas is led to infer that there *must* be something that is its own *esse*, something whose essence is identical to the act of being whereby it is. It is natural reason itself that leads to the conclusion, unexpected perhaps, but not contradictory in the least, that there really is a being, an *ens*, that is its own act of being (*actus essendi*, *esse subsistens*, *esse tantum*).

Thomas calls God an *ens*.[89] But God is an *ens* utterly different from any of the *entia* in this world. In the case of God, and God alone, *essentia*, *esse*, and *ens* are all simply identical. There is no distinction whatsoever between what he is, the act whereby he is, and the entity that he is. To the objection that there is nothing in the world that is its own act, that the act of any entity, including its act of being, is different from the entity of which it is the act—and this is essentially Heidegger's objection—it can be responded: (1) that God is not in the world, but transcends it altogether; (2) that there is no contradiction at all in the assertion that God is pure act, only an inability to imagine or think of him as a worldly entity; and (3) that we are compelled to conceive

88. In "The Problem of Socrates" (1970), Strauss says regarding Heidegger's understanding of Being (*Sein*), "The ground of all beings, and especially of man, is Sein—this ground of grounds is coeval with man and therefore also not eternal or sempiternal. But if this is so, Sein cannot be the *complete* ground of man: the *emergence* of man, in contradistinction to the *essence* of man, [would require] a ground different from Sein." (329; cf. 337, n. 65.) Heidegger is aware of the difficulty that Strauss identifies, and his conception of a "dif-ference" (*Aus-trag*) holding sway between Being and beings, deeper than and somehow grounding the ontological difference (*Differenz*) whereby Being and beings are only, so to speak, formally distinguished, is apparently intended to address it. I shall return to this conception below, in Subsection iii of the present section.

89. E.g., *Super Sent.* lib. 1 d. 2 q. 1 art. 1, *sed contra*; *SCG* lib. 1 cap. 21 n. 5; *ST* 1 q. 3 art. 8, co. Thomas speaks of God not as *ens* but as *supra ens* when he is using *ens* to name what finitely participates in *esse*. See *In de Causis*, l. 6, n. 175. See Caputo, *HA* 144. I shall shortly consider Caputo's treatment of the difference between Thomas and Heidegger.

of God as pure act by an *argument*, the argument of *De Ente et Essentia*, which takes its point of departure from a consideration of worldly entities. We are compelled to conceive of God as pure act by natural reason itself.[90]

Heidegger recognizes this. His response is to call into question the adequacy of natural reason for dealing with the question of Being (*die Seinsfrage*) and to substitute for natural reason an ostensibly deeper mode of thinking. This deeper mode of thinking reveals, he holds, that all worldly things, and the very world itself, are contingent, not in the sense that they *depend* on something else and finally on something necessary in itself, but *only* in the sense that they need not *be*. The contingency of the world consists in the fact that it *is*, that (like God) it is *uncaused*, and that (unlike God) it is *non-necessary*. There is no *reason* why the world is. It just . . . is.

Heidegger's assertion of the impossibility of *esse subsistens*, however, presupposes the phenomenological tenet that we must restrict our attention to what is phenomenally given. How else could Heidegger infer from the finding that nothing *phenomenally given*, that nothing worldly, not even the "given" world itself, is its own *esse*, to the conclusion that nothing *whatsoever* could be its own *esse*? Heidegger is committed to dealing exclusively with phenomenal, that is, this-worldly, *entia*, which is to say finite *entia*, and to penetrate, to the extent possible, into how *they* are related to their *esse*, from which they are nonetheless distinct. He is prohibited by his phenomenological commitment to speculate about an *ens* that is not related to its *esse* by way of difference but by way of identity.

90. I said in Part 2, Ch. 4, above, that I was not aware of Strauss's ever undertaking a consideration of *De Ente et Essentia*. I could certainly be wrong about that. In "The Problem of Socrates" (1970), Strauss writes. "'Sein' would be translated in the case of every writer other than Heidegger by 'being'; but for Heidegger everything depends on the radical difference between being understood as verbal noun and being understood as participle" (328). The radical difference: "Sein is *einai*, *esse* [!], *être*; Seindes is *on*, *ens*, *étant*." Strauss may have recognized that for Thomas, just as for Heidegger, there is a distinction between *Sein/esse* and *Seindes/ens*, but may have thought the distinction is more "radical" for Heidegger than it is for Thomas. Strauss writes, "One is tempted to say in Platonic language that Seiendes is only by participating in Sein but in that Platonic understanding Sein would be a Seiendes." The brief comparison with Plato is interesting, but a comparison with Thomas here would have been much more apposite. That Strauss did not make such a comparison, even one unfavorable to Thomas, reinforces my suspicion that he was not familiar with *DEE*. This suspicion receives further reinforcement from what Strauss says a paragraph later. "This [the summary of what Heidegger means by Sein that Strauss offered in the intervening paragraph] is misleading insofar as it suggests that Sein is *inferred*, *only* inferred. But of Sein we know through *experience* of Sein; that experience [however] presupposes a *leap*; that leap was not made by the earlier philosophers and *therefore* their thought is characterized by oblivion. They thought only of and about Seiendes. Yet they could not have thought of and about Seiendes except on the basis of some awareness of Sein. But they paid no attention to it—this failure was due, not to any negligence of theirs, but to Sein itself." No one who had given any consideration at all to *DEE* (or even to *ST* 1 q. 3 art. 4) could say of Thomas that he "thought of and only about Seiendes" (*ens*) and not of *Sein* (*esse*). One might respond that Strauss was not thinking here of Thomas as an earlier *philosopher*. Fair enough. But Struass's point seems to be about earlier thinkers more broadly: *none* of them paid attention to *Sein*. Perhaps Strauss intends to be speaking here only of Heidegger's understanding of his predecessors, and not his own. If so, he still should have made some reference to Thomas in the above passages, even if he thought, as Heidegger did, that Thomas failed to appreciate the radicality of the difference between *Sein/esse* and *Seiendes/ens*.

iii. Metaphysics and mysticism

The challenge that Heidegger poses to Thomas is considered at length by John Caputo in *Heidegger and Aquinas—An Essay on Overcoming Metaphysics*. Caputo's treatment is well-informed and a model of fair-mindedness. I shall not point out all the places—and there are many of them—where I am persuaded by what Caputo has to say. Instead, I shall restrict myself to sketching how he interprets the ontological difference that Heidegger highlights, noting some of the places where I am not persuaded by what he has to say, and stating why I think that neither Heidegger nor anyone else has ever succeeded in "overcoming" metaphysics, or will ever be able to do so.

Metaphysics is the accomplishment of natural reason. It makes use of principles that are *per se nota* and immediately known by *intellectus*, and it makes use of the general findings of ordinary human experience (for example, that the things that are "first for us" are caused). Basing itself on this solid foundation, it aspires as *ratio*, in the narrow sense, to move validly, that is to say, necessarily—the critic of metaphysics will say, rigidly—from premises to conclusions, ultimately to conclusions regarding the ultimate cause or causes of the given world. As Heidegger and Caputo see it, metaphysics is constrained, both by the rigidity of its procedure and, of equal importance, by its aspiration to account for what is given in terms of causes. Metaphysics, as they see it, precludes thought from opening itself up, from attuning itself, to a dimension of Being, the fundamental dimension, that cannot be apprehended logically or in terms of causes.

Caputo sees more at work in the ontological difference than a simple and straightforward distinction between Being and beings, exceptionless as Heidegger holds this distinction to be. He quotes the following passage from Heidegger's *Nietzsche* book:

> The distinction [*Unterscheidung*] as a difference [*Differenz*] means that a dif-ference [*Aus-trag*] exists between Being and beings. Whence and how it comes to such a dif-ference is not said. Let difference be for the moment only named as the occasion and impulse for the question into this dif-ference."[91]

Caputo comments:

> Dif-ference (*Austrag*) names what is differing in the difference (*Differenz*), the way in which Being and beings are borne or carried outside of one another yet at the same time borne toward one another. The dif-ference is somehow [!] deeper than the more straightforward ontological difference [i.e., the difference between Being and beings], or better, is the depth dimension in it.

Though Thomas would not take strong issue with Heidegger's understanding of the ontological difference as it holds sway throughout the phenomenon that is the world, he would be puzzled by Heidegger's invoking of a yet more primordial dif-ference at work within the ontological difference. For this dif-ference seems, even and especially

91. *HA* 148.

on Heidegger's terms, to be neither Being nor a being. What is it then? How can Heidegger, and presumably Caputo also, be so confident that what "makes" and "opens up"[92] the ontological difference holding sway throughout the world is not God's very act of creating a (necessarily) finite order of existence, with man living and thinking in the midst of it, an order of existence in which Being (*esse*) and beings (*entia*) possessing *essentiae* that are never reducible to *esse* must always differ? Heidegger's and Caputo's confidence on this matter stems from their conviction that if one suspends natural reason something comes to the fore that natural reason is blind to, and it is not God, construed metaphysically as the first efficient cause of worldly beings.

Heidegger speaks of a "step back [that] moves out of metaphysics into the essence of metaphysics."[93] As Caputo understands it, "[This] step back moves from a naïve acceptance of the difference between Being and beings to the origin of that difference, to that which makes the difference possible." [94] The origin of the ontological difference Caputo also calls its source, but certainly not its cause[95]—though one has to ask, "Why not?" The answer, it seems, is that invoking a causal principle at this level of thought is essentially misleading. It is a case of trying to account for the given, the phenomenal, in terms of what is not given, an inferred cause. Since any putative cause of the ontological difference is not itself a phenomenon, it has to be, as Husserl would say, "bracketed" out of consideration. Here, Thomas would say, Heidegger's phenomenological commitment to describe the phenomenally given, what one might call the insufficiently appreciated surface of things, paired with his arguably non-phenomenological determination to think beyond the phenomenally given into the depth of things leads him, and Caputo with him, into obscurity. For example,

> the *Austrag* is the dif-fering in the difference between Being and beings, that which makes the difference between them, that which opens up the difference, holding them apart and sending them to one another in the appropriate manner, so that Being revealingly conceals itself in beings."[96]

This formulation is intriguing, even fascinating, momentarily. But just what is the *Austrag* [dif-ference]? It is, Caputo says, "the hidden source of metaphysics."[97] It is

92. *HA* 151.

93. This formulation occurs in *Identity and Difference*. See *HA* 150.

94. *HA* 150.

95. *HA* 150, 155.

96. *HA* 151–2. To point to just one oddity in this formulation, it is not clear how the *making* of a difference relates to the *opening up* a difference. The *Austrag* is said to accomplish both, though they do not seem to be the same. There can hardly be a difference prior to the difference's being *made*, unless "makes the difference" is used equivocally for recognizing the difference *in mente* as well as for producing the difference *in re*. On the other hand, there could be a difference prior to its being *opened up*—existing *as* a difference, though initially closed off from view. Caputo's suggestion may be that from a phenomenological perspective there is no difference between making and opening up. If so, it would have been helpful if he had spelled this out, and then explicated its implications for the phenomenological perspective within which, or finally out of which, Heidegger is attempting to think.

97. *HA* 152.

the source of the ontological difference between beings and Being; and at the same time it is the source of human thought about Being. The ontological relation between the dif-ference and the ontological difference makes possible an (for the lack of a better expression) epistemological relation between the mind and what, in the history of metaphysics, the mind should have taken as its theme but did not. Caputo notes that what Heidegger calls the *Austrag* (dif-ference) he also calls the *Unter-Schied* (scission, distinction, or difference; lit. "under-severing"). "The *Unter-Schied* is the 'between' which opens up the difference between Being and beings, which opens up the ontological difference."[98] Thomas would say that to speak of any "between" this way is not only obscure but meaningless too. He would say that Being and beings are not themselves "borne or carried outside of one another yet at the same time borne toward one another," except in thinking and speaking about beings, more precisely in thinking and speaking about worldly beings. In no sense is there a motion, as Caputo's formulation suggests, between worldly beings and their individual acts of being, as distinct from the motion that is present in thinking about such things.

According to Caputo,

> there can be no more ultimate framework for Thomas than the distinction between *esse subsistens* and *ens participatum*. Now, from Heidegger's point of view, St. Thomas moves within the horizon of this difference without questioning the source from which this difference opens up, without questioning the difference itself, the "between" in the distinction between *esse* and *ens*.[99]

There is indeed an ontological difference (*Differenz*)—an ontological relationship and not just a logical one—between Being and beings. But the relation of this difference *itself* to the two *relata*, Being and beings, gives every appearance of being a merely logical relationship, and a rather trivial one at that. According to Caputo, this difference is not to be so naively interpreted. Instead, we must attend to the dif-ference (*Aus-trag*) that is its deeper origin or source. If we elevate, or deepen, the difference to the dif-ference, then we introduce not merely a *logical* relationship between (on the one hand) the ontological difference *itself* and (on the other hand) the two members of this difference (Being and beings), but rather a newly disclosed *ontological* relationship between origin (the dif-ference) and originated (the difference).

But why should we stop here? Once we interpret the relationship between, on the one hand, the ontological difference and, on the other hand, its two members as an ontological relationship, we have to ask about the character of the relationship between the dif-ference and the ontological difference. Is it at bottom merely logical, or is it ontological? Perhaps Heidegger and Caputo would say that we should not ask this question: "Whence and how [the ontological difference] comes to such a dif-ference is not said." It is, however, altogether natural to ask this question. If we answer that the

98. *HA* 160.

99. *HA* 155–6.

relationship between the difference and the dif-ference is merely logical, then we have not said much. If, on other hand, we answer that the relationship between the difference and the dif-ference is also ontological, then we have to ask further whether *this* relationship itself has a source. In that case we would be led either to a variant of the famous "third man" dilemma,[100] or to an arbitrary stopping point, or to God exactly as Thomas understands him, that is, as source, origin, or cause that exists neither contingently nor historically but necessarily and eternally—self-sufficient and independent of any deeper, or higher, source, origin, or cause.

Whereas Thomas interprets *esse*, in the privileged case of the first cause, as *esse subsistens*, prior to and independently of its causal activity, Heidegger interprets *Sein* as *Ereignis* (event, appropriation, or, perhaps, the event of appropriation). Caputo correctly says that "any confrontation of Heidegger and Aquinas must in the end be a confrontation of *esse* and *Ereignis*."[101] *Ereignis* is essentially temporal. As Thomas sees it, *esse*, though temporal in the case of worldly *entia*, is not temporal in the case of God. The divine *esse* cannot rest upon, much less arise out of, the dif-ference, because it is the source or origin. It is the first cause, both of the ontological difference between Being and (finite) beings, and of the dif-ference, such as it is. There is no way that Heidegger can refute Thomas on this point except, again, by demanding that all meaningful discourse about Being be restricted to the given, phenomenal, temporal world. This demand precludes discourse about ultimate causes.

Instead, adherence to this restriction gives rise to claims of a Heideggerian cast that Caputo formulates as follows: "The *Ereignis* is the 'and' in *Being 'and' Time*."[102] "[T]he *Ereignis* not only delivers Being and time into their own nature, but also delivers them over to one another. It is the *Ereignis* which holds (*hält*) the two *Sachen*, time and Being, together in a single state of affairs (*Sachverhalt*)."[103] "The *Ereignis* is the dif-fering in the dif-ference."[104] Note that this last formulation goes beyond Caputo's earlier formulation that "Dif-ference (*Austrag*) names what is differing in the difference (*Differenz*)."[105] It also goes beyond his related but not quite identical formulation that, "*Austrag* is the dif-fering in the difference between Being and beings."[106] For now we have a dif-fering, not just in the difference (Differenz), but in the dif-ference (*Austrag*) itself; and this new, and apparently deeper, dif-fering receives a name of its own: *Ereignis*. This is "the original saying (*Sage*) in virtue of which language itself speaks (*Ereignis der Sprache*)."[107]

100. See Plato, *Parmenides* 132a1–b3; Aristotle, *Sophistical Refutations* 178b37–179a8; *Metaphysics* 999b18; 1038b34–1039a3.

101. *HA* 168.

102. *HA* 168.

103. *HA* 172.

104. *HA* 167. Heidegger's binding of Being to language, "the house of Being," is likely motivated by his phenomenological commitment.

105. *HA* 148.

106. *HA* 151.

107. *HA* 167.

Now, although these formulations are obscure, and obscurely related to one another, one has to entertain the possibility that Heidegger, and Caputo following him, are onto something. The problem is that one has to leave reason behind, rather far behind, in order to entertain this possibility seriously. For otherwise one will say in agreement with Thomas, and with Aristotle too, that neither difference (*Differenz*), nor dif-ference (*Austrag*), nor *Ereignis* (construed as a dif-fering), can be rationally conceived other than as a relationship. And a relationship cannot be prior to, or the source of, *both* its *relata*, whether Being and beings, Being and time, or any other related members. *Ereignis*, as the dif-fering in the dif-ference, is a *relatio* and cannot by itself "give" or "deliver" *anything*. Heidegger and Caputo are, of course, fully aware of this objection, but they are not troubled by it. The trouble lies not in the *Ereignis* but in the attempt to comprehend it though *ratio* and the metaphysical categories that are devised by *ratio*.

What then is the alternative to *ratio*? For Caputo, the alternative is *intellectus*. Caputo discerns a "silent call which speaks in St. Thomas's works to suspend *ratio* and enter into the intuitive unity of *intellectus*."[108] He wishes to show that there is a "critique of *ratio*" in Thomas, not just in the sense that natural reason needs to be supplemented by divine revelation, but in the sense that—apparently without the assistance of revelation—man can achieve a "unity of *intellectus* and *esse* in which metaphysics [as the accomplishment of *ratio*] can be overcome." Caputo concedes that "Thomas does not say this with explicit clarity."[109] Indeed Caputo concedes that, though angelic cognition has an intuitive character, such cogntion is "an ideal which human cognition can only vainly approximate." He cites two passages from the *Summa Theologiae* where Thomas contrasts *intellectus* with *ratio*.[110] Here is another one, part of which we considered earlier, from the article in the *Summa Theologiae* titled "Whether *ratio* is a different power [of the soul] than *intellectus*."

> Reason (*ratio*) and understanding (*intellectus*) in man cannot be diverse powers. This can be clearly recognized if the acts of both are considered. For to understand (*intelligere*) is to apprehend intelligible truth (*veritatem intelligibilem*) simply. But to reason (*ratiocinari*) is to proceed from one thing understood (*uno intellectum*) to another, [and so] to the knowing of intelligible truth. And hence the angels, who perfectly possess, according to the mode of their nature, the cognition of intelligible truth, have no need to proceed from one thing to another; but simply and non-discursively apprehend the truth of things. . . . Men, however, arrive at the knowing of intelligible truth by proceeding from one thing to another . . . and hence they are called rational. It is evident, therefore, that reasoning is compared to understanding as moving to resting, or as acquiring to having; of which one pertains to the perfect

108. *HA* 249.

109. *HA* 260.

110. *HA* 261–2. *ST* 1 q. 58 art. 3, co.; art. 4, co.

> and the other to the imperfect. And because motion always proceeds from something immobile and terminates in something at rest, so it is that human reasoning (*ratiocinatio*), according to the way of inquiry or discovery, proceeds from certain things simply understood (*intellectis*), which are the first principles; and, again, according to the way of judgment, returns by analysis (*resolvendo*) to the first principles, with respect to which it examines what has been discovered.[111]

Ratio and *intellectus* are not two powers of the human soul but complementary parts of one power. *Intellectus* is intuitive apprehension of the logical principles, such as the principle of non-contradiction, that animate *ratio* in its discursive movement. That is, *intellectus* actually *grounds* the very *ratio* that Caputo contemns.[112] Moreover, *intellectus* is not left behind once *ratio* begins to move. It is present throughout, and its principles are explicitly appealed to when what *ratio* discursively discovers is examined. Caputo is critical of *ratio*, but as far as I can tell his only criticism is that *ratio* precludes access to Heidegger's insight, if that is the word for it.

Ratio, and hence *intellectus* as well, are at work in Thomas's arguments for the existence of God, including the powerful argument in *De Ente et Essentia*, and in the other arguments advanced in his rational theology (and, of course, in the case he makes for natural law as well). Caputo does not show where these arguments break down. If they break down at all from Caputo's perspective, it can only be that they lead to a conception of God that Caputo finds problematic. According to Caputo, following Heidegger, the conception is the conception of God as cause, which is how Heidegger and Caputo interpret Thomas's conception of God as pure act. As Heidegger sees it,

111. *ST* 1 q. 79, art. 8, co. The whole passage (quoted only in part earlier) reads in the original as follows: "Respondeo dicendum quod ratio et intellectus in homine non possunt esse diversae potentiae. Quod manifeste cognoscitur, si utriusque actus consideretur. Intelligere enim est simpliciter veritatem intelligibilem apprehendere. Ratiocinari autem est procedere de uno intellecto ad aliud, ad veritatem intelligibilem cognoscendam. Et ideo Angeli, qui perfecte possident, secundum modum suae naturae, cognitionem intelligibilis veritatis, non habent necesse procedere de uno ad aliud; sed simpliciter et absque discursu veritatem rerum apprehendunt, ut Dionysius dicit, VII cap. de Div. Nom. Homines autem ad intelligibilem veritatem cognoscendam perveniunt, procedendo de uno ad aliud, ut ibidem dicitur, et ideo rationales dicuntur. Patet ergo quod ratiocinari comparatur ad intelligere sicut moveri ad quiescere, vel acquirere ad habere, quorum unum est perfecti, aliud autem imperfecti. Et quia motus semper ab immobili procedit, et ad aliquid quietum terminatur; inde est quod ratiocinatio humana, secundum viam inquisitionis vel inventionis, procedit a quibusdam simpliciter intellectis, quae sunt prima principia; et rursus, in via iudicii, resolvendo redit ad prima principia, ad quae inventa examinat. Manifestum est autem quod quiescere et moveri non reducuntur ad diversas potentias, sed ad unam et eandem, etiam in naturalibus rebus, quia per eandem naturam aliquid movetur ad locum, et quiescit in loco. Multo ergo magis per eandem potentiam intelligimus et ratiocinamur. Et sic patet quod in homine eadem potentia est ratio et intellectus."

112. For Caputo, *ratio* is largely a matter of noise: "the clatter of syllogisms and *respondeos*" (*HA* 249), "the chatter of discursive reason" (254), "the outer rattle of Scholastic machinery" (256), "the noisy machinery of . . . elaborate and clever ratiocination" (264). *Intellectus* is closer to silence (*HA* 249) and presumably more central than *ratio* to "Heidegger's conception of language, according to which it is not so much man who speaks but language itself speaking in and through him, or, alternately put, in which human speaking is more a response to a word addressed to man by Being." *HA* 88.

Thomas's "*esse* means to be actual, *wirk-lich,* and so belongs within the horizon of effecting, *wirken.* As such it is a falling away from the primordial Greek experience of presencing."[113] Caputo speaks of "the profoundly causal character of the metaphysics of St. Thomas."

Now, it is surely the case that Thomas understands the pure act that is God to be causal *with respect to the world.* But Caputo goes way too far in saying, in agreement with Heidegger whom he cites, "In Thomas Aquinas . . . where presence is determined as *actus*, it is thoroughly subjected to the categories of causing and making."[114] For God is pure act independently of his creating the world. He is pure act in himself, according to his very essence, prior to creation. He is pure act in creating, but he would have been pure act even had he never created. This is the conclusion of the argument in *De Ente et Essentia*, and it is adverted to throughout Thomas's rational theology as developed in the *Summa Theologiae*, in the *Summa Contra Gentiles*, and in other works as well. To be pure act does not mean to *cause*. It means to *be*, without qualification and limitation, even to *be present* without qualification and limitation, though for this very reason it includes the power to cause. It is not the case that, for Thomas, pure *esse*, pure *actus*, or pure presence is "thoroughly [!] subjected to the categories of causing and making." As for created *esse*, though it is caused or made by God, it is not itself necessarily a causing or a making. A stone has *esse*, and it need not be causing or making anything else in order to be. The same holds for the world taken as a whole. These claims about *esse*, however, are metaphysical claims.

What then is the alternative to metaphysics? For Caputo, the alternative is mysticism. Though he recognizes that, for Thomas, intuitive *intellectus* informs discursive *ratio*, even makes *ratio* possible, he also recognizes that, for Thomas, the human *intellectus* can function independently of, unrelated to, and utterly transcendent of discursive *ratio*. This happens in the beatific vision.[115] But the beatific vision occurs in the hereafter. Nonetheless Caputo thinks that, for Thomas, something analogous to the beatific vision, or approximating it, can occur in this life. He has in mind Thomas's treatment of rapture (*raptus*).[116]

In the passages on rapture that Caputo cites from the *Summa Theologiae*, though Thomas makes a brief mention of Moses, his focus is on Paul and the experience he recounts of "having been caught up (*raptum*) into the third heaven."[117] These

113. *HA* 96; See also 90, 87, 169, 200–201.

114. *HA* 170.

115. *ST* 1 q. 12 art. 1.

116. *HA* 269–70. (Caputo says that Thomas devotes two important questions to *raptus*, and he cites these as *De Veritate* q. 9 and *ST* 2–2 q. 175. The first citation might be an error. *De Veritate* q. 13 treats rapture; q. 9 treats the communication of angelic knowledge. This is a very small point, however, since Caputo focuses on *ST* 2–2 q. 175.).

117. Second Corinthians 12:2. The expression Paul uses here is *harpagenta*, the 2nd aorist passive participle of *harpazō*, which in turn means to steal or snatch away—it is cognate with the word "harpy" (as *raptus* is with "raptor")—but also to carry off without meeting resistance. (Thomas recognizes that

two experiences are exceptional, to say the least. They are understood by Thomas to be, as Caputo correctly puts it, "an exertion applied to a nature by an *external agent* which impels that nature beyond the limits of what it is capable of by its own natural powers."[118] The external agent is God.[119] "Mystical rapture," Caputo says, occurs "when the soul is impelled or elevated to a level of intellectuality which exceeds that of which it is of itself capable, although it tends naturally in that direction." What Caputo apparently means by "tends naturally" is that, though natural reason cannot know the first cause, God, as he is in himself, it naturally desires such knowledge. This too is exactly Thomas's teaching.

However, even before reading what Caputo has to say about *raptus*, even in just wondering why he introduces this topic, the suspicion arises that he is going to conflate an altogether supernatural experience visited by a *personal* agent, that is, by God, upon an individual human *chosen* by him, with the silent attending to the *Austrag*, an experience that Heidegger surely does not understand to be supernatural in the way that Thomas does. This suspicion is quickly confirmed.

> This [mystical] experience is the most perfect fulfillment of *intellectus*, its most complete and total actualization. On earth one can have, if not the habit, at the least the act, the transient share, of the beatific vision.
>
> Now, I do not think that one must read these questions [on rapture] as if it were Thomas's opinion that one must be a Paul or a Moses to enter into mystical experience. St. Thomas is seeking to explain here the fact of evident mystical experiences recorded by the Scriptures. But the conditions under which these experiences were possible apply to all men and can be realized by everyone to a greater or lesser extent—if not to the "third" heaven," then to a lesser heaven.[120]

It may not have been Thomas's opinion that one had to be a Paul or a Moses to have the experience of mystical rapture, but it was certainly his opinion that the experience is brought about by God, not by man. The "conditions under which these experiences were possible" do *not* "apply to all men," *nor* can they "be realized by everyone to a greater or lesser extent"—not that is, *unless God so chooses*. There is no reason to think that, for Thomas, such experience is available to just any human being who sets out to "suspend *ratio* and enter into the intuitive unity of *intellectus*."

there are different kinds of rapture: *ST* 2–2 q. 175, art. 1.) It is in the last sense that Paul presumably uses the word *harpagenta*. He describes his rapture, his being rapt away, as something that is *done* to him, not something that he *does*: he will not boast of it. Paul speaks of his rapture in the context of revelation. 12:1.

118. *HA* 270 (emphasis added).

119. *ST* 2–2 q. 175, art. 1.

120. *HA* 271. When Caputo quotes Thomas as saying that, in *raptus*, "the soul is borne totally into God (*totaliter fertur in deum*)," he does not, in my opinion, give sufficient attention to the passive syntax of this formulation. The soul is borne into God by God himself.

Caputo writes of the famous incident that is reported to have occurred when Thomas, late in his relatively short life, was celebrating Mass on the feast of St. Nicholas.[121] He had some kind of experience that led him to say, "All [i.e., all things—*omnia*, in the plural] that I have written appear to me as straw compared to those things that I have seen and that have been revealed to me." Caputo slightly mistranslates this latter part of this sentence—*in respectu eorum, quae vidi et revelata sunt mihi*—as "what I have seen and what has been revealed to me." Shortly afterwards he retranslates the latter part of the sentence more correctly as "those things which I have seen and which have been revealed to me." But the momentary mistranslation of *eorum* as "what," in the singular, enables Caputo to say, before he corrects his mistranslation, that "Thomas underwent an experience of Being itself (of *ipsum esse subsistens*) in comparison with which his metaphysical-theological writings appeared to him as straw."[122]

Thomas may well have had this very experience. There is no way of knowing. But it is misleading to suggest, as Caputo seems to be doing, that Thomas's mystical experience was something like that which Heidegger calls his readers to be open to. Among other things, Thomas speaks specifically of revelation, and of revelation of things (*eorum*) in the plural. His mystical experience is reported to have occurred in church, not in a *Hütte* nor on the *Holzwege* of the *Schwarzwald*.

There is indeed a point of comparison between Thomas's understanding of divine revelation and Heidegger's understanding of Being's emergence out of concealment into un-concealment (*Unverborgenheit*) or uncovered-ness (*Entdeckheit*)—which is how Heidegger, taking his bearings from the Greek word, *alētheia*, understands truth.[123] Both divine revelation and the un-concealment of Being are understood to occur in history, and both are un-anticipatable. But here the comparison ends. In the case of revelation, God chooses to reveal himself. In the case of un-concealment, Being does not choose to emerge from concealment. At any event, it is hard to see how anything as impersonal as Heidegger's Being could choose.[124] The emergence of Being into un-concealment is an event (*Ereignis*), and the only person involved is the thinker who is open to it.

Caputo writes,

> There is a tendency within metaphysics to pass beyond itself, to overcome itself, and to become a simple vision . . . But this remains forever impossible

121. *HA* 252–6.

122. *HA* 253.

123. *SZ* § 44. See "Platons Lehre von der Wahrheit," in *Wegmarken*.

124. A qualification may be in order here. Though Heidegger's Being cannot choose, as we typically understand choice, it may play some kind of role in decision, though not as we typically understand decision: "Whatever comes to pass with historical man always ensues from a previously made decision about the essence of truth, a decision that never rests with man alone." (Was immer sich mit dem geschichtlichen Menschen begibt, ergibt sich jeweils aus einer zuvor gefallenen und nie beim Menschen selbst stehenden Entscheidung über das Wesen der Wahrheit." "Platons Lehre von Wahrheit," *Wegmarken*, 143—emphasis added).

> for metaphysics as long as metaphysics is a *scientia* practiced by men whose characteristic mode of thinking is "rational." What is needed to carry out this inner tendency of metaphysics, of which metaphysics itself remains incapable, is for man to take up an altogether new way of thinking, that of *intellectus* itself.[125]

Heidegger, as Caputo sees it, has overcome metaphysics. Thomas has not. "[W]hat is clearly lacking in St. Thomas is a doctrine, or doctrinal analogue to, the dif-ference in the sense of the *Austrag*, the setting outside of one another of *esse* and *ens*."[126] Caputo is right. But, such a doctrine or doctrinal analogue is lacking in Thomas because, for him, there is no exceptionless "setting outside one another of *esse* and *ens*." They are identical in God, who creates the *ens* that is the world and all the *entia* that are within it, not one of which is identical to its own *esse*. Worldly beings possess *esse* by virtue of being created, and it is for this reason that they cannot be identical to their *esse*. Such an understanding of being is the achievement of natural reason. To "overcome metaphysics," then, would be to overcome natural reason itself. But natural reason pertains to the essence of man, and it cannot be overcome. It can only be ignored.

iv. Logic, ontology, and *theoria*

Heidegger correctly says that Thomas and the scholastics generally regard the world as *ens creatum*. But, as he knows full well, they have logical arguments, which cannot be just brushed aside, for why they regard the world as *ens creatum*.[127] There can be little doubt that it was their belief that motivated them to search for such arguments. But, again, such motivation does not invalidate their arguments in the slightest. Heidegger knows this too, and so he confronts their arguments. The confrontation does not consist exclusively of Heidegger's assertion of the ontological difference on the heels of his insistence that only as phenomenology is ontology possible. He seems to recognize that Thomas's argument for the existence of God as *esse subsistens* is formally valid. At least he does not call the formal validity of this argument, which is the argument of *De Ente et Essentia*, into question.[128] Instead he tries to show that this argument is unsound, that it rests on a false premise.

125. *HA* 264–5. It is not clear why Caputo places "rational" in quotation marks here, since his general claim is not that the mode of thinking of those who engage in metaphysics as *scientia* is spuriously or deficiently rational but that it is all but monmaniacally rational.

126. *HA* 155.

127. Heidegger also knows full well that, for the scholastics, *creatum* does not necessarily mean brought into being at some finite point in the past. *Creatum* means, for them, the ongoing and total dependence of the world's existence at every moment on existence on the will of God, whether it has always existed or has existed for only a finite period.

128. Caputo's admiration for Heidegger does not keep him from noting that he relies too heavily on Giles of Rome in his interpretation of Thomas's *esse—essentia* distinction. In doing so, Heidegger comes up with "a garbled version of Thomas's teaching." *HA* 68.

A premise of Thomas's argument is a variant of the principle of sufficient reason, though not named by him as such: if something *is* that need *not* be, there must be a reason, or cause, outside that thing, for why it is.[129] Heidegger fully agrees with Thomas that worldly things need not be. So to prevent the inference from contingent beings to a necessary being, he has to reject the principle of sufficient reason. Things *are*, they *need* not be, and there is *no reason* for why they are. For Heidegger, the question, "Why are there beings rather than nothing at all?" is *essentially* a question: it must be asked, and yet in principle it cannot be answered.[130]

Heidegger does not shrink from thinking through this apparent insight to its startling implication. Being, because it is non-necessary, has "the Nothing" at work within it. "The Nothing itself nihilates" (*Das Nichts selbst nichtet.*)[131] It nihilates within beings and it nihilates within Being itself—hence the irreducibly temporal character of both. Heidegger realizes that in speaking this way about "the Nothing" he is endowing it with an efficacy that logic does not acknowledge. It is for this reason that he denies that logical thinking, or *ratio*, is able to shed much light on the nature of Being.[132]

Logical thinking operates in accordance with principles, with fundamental truths such as the principle of non-contradiction, with principles that are not just postulated to see what follows from them—as though one could just as reasonably posit their contradictories—but are brought into relief by inspecting how reason operates. Heidegger takes issue with those who would say that the truths of logic are eternal. "That there are eternal truths will be sufficiently proven only when a demonstration has succeeded [in showing] that *Dasein* has been and will be throughout all eternity."[133] How truth exists apart from *Dasein* is a meaningless question for Heidegger, just as how truth exists apart from consciousness, transcendentally reduced, is a meaningless question for Husserl.

Heidegger holds that the conception of truth as un-concealment is deeper than the conception of truth as the adequacy of the intellect to what the intellect considers. Being as true is, for Heidegger, Being as having emerged out of concealment. Now, the Thomist can grant, he will even insist, that truth is not permanently cognized by us humans. It is hidden from us much of the time, some of it most of the time. Truth can be known by us, up to a point, through the proper operation of natural reason. But the truth about God, the most important truth, cannot be known by us in its fullness without divine assistance, beginning in this life by way of revelation and consummated

129. Simply showing that this premise is dubious would, if possible, be sufficient to call into question the soundness of Thomas's argument. But Heidegger tries to show that it is not just dubious but false.

130. See *Einführung in die Metaphysik*, Chapter 1.

131. "Was ist Metaphysik?" 11. [English translation: 90.]

132. *SZ* § 13, § 44, and page 437; "Was ist Metaphysik?", 14 [English translation: 92.]; *Einführung in die Metaphysik*, 19, 92–94 [English translation: 25, 120–122.]. See Heidegger, *Nietzsche*, Erster Band, 474–80 [English translation: Vol. 3, 48–52]; and Heidegger, *Metaphysical Foundations of Logic*, 103–7.

133. *SZ* 227.

in the hereafter, for the blessed, in the beatific vision. However, the Thomist will also insist that the truth that is hidden from us is eternally present to God. It is the content or correlate of his eternal intellect. The thrust of the sentence quoted in the preceding paragraph is that, for Heidegger, there are no eternal truths because there is no eternal intellect, neither divine nor human.[134] Truth as the un-concealment of Being is as historical as is human thinking.

There is, however, a problem in Heidegger's conception of truth. For in speaking of Being as emerging into un-concealment, or un-concealedness, he cannot help implying that prior to this emergence Being somehow *was*, albeit concealed, even that Being *is*, whether it happens to be concealed from us or not. Heidegger would resist this way of speaking. Being "is" only in its emergence for us. Independently of this emergence for us there may be beings (*entia*, *Seiendes*), but there cannot be Being (*esse*, *Sein*).

Heidegger's determination to refrain from speaking of how anything, including Being itself, *is* apart from its relation to human *Dasein* is of a piece with Husserl's determination to refrain from speaking of how anything *is* apart from its relation to consciousness, transcendentally reduced. In both cases, this determination "partakes of modern subjectivism." The phenomenological commitment, and subjectivism more generally, are at odds with the operation of natural reason, which resists confinement to the sphere of what is subjective and phenomenally given and naturally infers from this sphere, that is, from what is first "for us," to what is first "by nature," or first "in itself."

Husserl and Heidegger are on solid ground in insisting that we adequately describe the phenomenally given before attempting to explain it, much less explain it away, by reference to what is not phenomenally given. But if what is phenomenally given is given as contingent, which is to say, given as having an *esse* that is not identical with its *essentia*, then natural reason will naturally ascend from the contingent to the unqualifiedly necessary, to an unconditioned ground of the conditioned, or to a first cause of the world that is not itself the effect of anything else. I have noted that even Husserl is led to speak of what is phenomenally given in terms of what is not phenomenally given, and that he thereby transgresses a fundamental principle of phenomenology.[135] The same is true of Heidegger: the un-concealed, which is phenomenally

134. In that sentence, Heidegger dismisses without mention the possibility of a divine intellect. Plato, or his Socrates, is sometimes interpreted as holding that there could be eternal truths—truths pertaining to the forms, or *eidē*—quite independently of any intellect. However, if the *eidos* is regarded etymologically as "looks," then it would seem to have an essential relation to an intellect *to which* it would "look" the way it does, i.e., to "look" as it *is* in *truth*. See *Republic* 508d2–509a6; 510b2–511c2. If the *eidē* really do have an *essential* relation to an intellect, even to just a *possible* intellect, and if they are, moreover, eternal in their being, then it would seem to follow that, if time is infinite, an intellect would *have* to be or come into being, sooner or later. Consider, again, the undeveloped observation that Socrates makes at *Republic* 526e4 about "the happiest part of that which is" (*to eudaimonestaton tou ontos*).

135. See above, Subsection i of the present section.

given, is necessarily referred to the concealed, which is not phenomenally given. (The question resurfaces: how can he be sure that the concealed is not the elusive God himself?) If Heidegger had spoken of the truth of Being, not as a historically varying and unpredictable emergence from concealment, but as trans-historical intelligibility, he would not on this point have transgressed a fundamental principle of phenomenology. But in speaking of the truth of Being this way he would have been led by natural reason back to the Medieval, even the classical, understanding of Being as, in its highest instance, permanently present, or eternal. Heidegger refuses to "follow the *logos*" that far.[136]

Heidegger's refusal is bound up with his critique of *theoria* as classically understood. The theoretical attitude of beholding the world, contemplating it, and attempting to cognize it dispassionately requires, Heidegger says, that the world be "dimmed down" (*abgeblenden*) to something merely present at hand (*Vorhandensein*). The world, however, is not a mere correlate of perception and thought. It is, *fundamentally*, the full complex context of concerns and *pragmata* in the midst of which we originally find ourselves, from which we attempt to detach ourselves in *theoria*, but with which we again become engaged when we suspend, as sooner or later we must, our purely theoretical attitude and return to dealing with things and persons in concrete, highly particularized situations, including situations in which things are not going quite right: the broken hammer, the burnt out light bulb, the lost car keys, the malfunctioning computer, the sick child.[137] As Heidegger sees it, ostensibly disinterested *theoria*, the preoccupation with logic, hypostasized universals, seemingly timeless structural principles of various sorts, and, especially, the search for a transcendent cause or causes—all this, just like considerably less sophisticated ways of Being-in-the-world, has its source in an attempted flight from finitude, a fleeing in the face of Being-towards-death that is anything but disinterested. By orienting us toward an apparent realm of trans-temporal truth and thereby speaking to, even encouraging, our longing for eternity, *theoria* tends to tranquilize us and distract us from squarely facing up to our mortality.

Heidegger's critique of *theoria* in general, and of logic in particular, is problematic. For Heidegger does not merely *deal* with *pragmata*. As a philosopher, he attempts to *understand* what it *means* to deal with *pragmata*, just as he attempts to understand the disclosure of *Sein*. In thinking and speaking about *pragmata* and *Sein*, he cannot avoid using logical principles. He advances propositions—though he might be uneasy about calling his utterances "propositions"—and he assumes with good reason that, true or false, they retain their identity when reiterated. That is to say, Heidegger employs the principle of identity, and hence the principles of non-contradiction and

136. According to Heidegger, *logos* primarily means letting-something-be-seen as un-concealed. Only in a derivative sense does *logos* mean *ratio*, *Vernunft*, or reason. See *SZ* § 7 B. It is, however, only in this allegedly derivative sense that *logos* could be *followed*.

137. *SZ* 61, 135, 138, 358.

the excluded middle as well—all three being logically equivalent. Heidegger employs these principles in every paragraph that he writes, as does everyone else who tries to write something that is consistent enough to be intelligible to his reader.

Heidegger is not unaware that he employs logical principles. He would say that he never intended a blanket denial of their validity. It is only when thinking defers to these principles as an inviolable canon for genuinely probing inquiry into Being that thinking goes astray. But, then, it is not easy to determine when a Heideggerian sentence that speaks of Being is to be taken as self-identical and excluding its contradictory, and when it is to be taken as losing its identity when reiterated and including its contradictory. Heidegger would respond that he never claimed that thinking about Being was easy. Hermeneutical tact and attentiveness to the context of his utterances about Being will disclose their meaning to the sympathetic and thoughtful reader. Logical principles are necessarily utilized in thought and discourse about Being, as they are utilized in all thought and discourse. But, Heidegger thinks, the limitations of these principles in thought and discourse about Being will sooner or later be recognized by anyone who is not committed in advance to insisting on their unqualified self-evidence and infallibility. This response, however, is not going to impress those who note that logical principles typically get called into question by Heidegger only when thought about Being, about *esse*, is about to take a theological turn.

v. Conscience phenomenologically considered

Though Heidegger does not develop what one could easily call an ethics, he does have something to say about conscience. He develops his account of conscience over a number of pages, characteristically gripping throughout. I limit myself here to noting its salient features.

Heidegger treats conscience from an ostensibly phenomenological perspective. "All experiences and interpretations of conscience agree in this, that the 'voice' of conscience (*'Stimme' des Gewissens*) somehow speaks of guilt."[138] This observation is relatively uncontroversial as it stands. But Thomas Aquinas would say that it must be qualified: conscience can and often does speak of guilt, but its role is by no means limited to speaking of guilt.[139] Conscience is the act of which *synderesis* is the habit. *Synderesis* is habitual knowledge. Conscience is a focused act of knowledge. *Synderesis* is the *habitus* containing the primary precepts of natural law. In the act of conscience this habitual knowledge is applied to concrete situations. Without knowledge or moral principles, Thomas would say, there is no way that conscience could render a verdict of guilty, or of innocence for that matter. For in such a case conscience would not know what it was declaring. Declaring guilt is a secondary, founded, and even contingent act of conscience. The primary, founding, and necessary act is the act of knowing what one ought to do in the concrete situation. Guilt cannot be meaningfully declared

138. *SZ* § 57, page 280.

139. See *ST* 1 q. 79 art. 13, co.

absent knowledge of moral principles, and these, for Thomas, have the character of law.

Heidegger sees things differently. According to him, guilt is deeper than any real or alleged knowledge of moral principles, so much so that, "[t]he idea of guilt (*Schuld*) must be detached from reference to an ought and law (*ein Sollen und Gesetz*)."[140] Having detached guilt from this reference, Heidegger can "determine the formally existential idea of 'guilty'" in a novel and surprising way. It is, "Being-the-basis for a Being that is determined through a Not (*Grundsein für ein durch ein Nicht bestimmtes Sein*)—that is, *Being the basis for a nullity* (*Grundsein einer Nichtigkeit*)."[141] "The Nothing nihilates" here as everywhere else. "If natural reason has a problem with that," Heidegger would say, "then so much the worse for natural reason."

Heidegger allows a place for moral responsibility, or something like moral responsibility, as we have seen in the case of solicitude. But moral responsibility is not, for him, what is primary. "Being-guilty (*Das Schuldigsein*) does not first result from indebtedness (*Verschuldung*), but vice versa: the latter [i.e., indebtedness] first becomes possible 'on the basis of'' (*'auf Grunde'*) an original Being-guilty."[142] As Heidegger sees it, being guilty is not based on one's willful choice to rebel against the moral order articulated by one's own natural reason (whether this moral order is reinforced by divine commandment or not). Being guilty, for Heidegger, is itself the basis: it is not just a *possibility* of human finitude; it *is* human finitude. Man is essentially guilty, not through any so-called sinful choice, but from the experienced fact of his finite existence.

A Thomist can respond that, however gripping one may find Heidegger's account, it nonetheless distorts the actual phenomenon of guilt. One experiences guilt, not as having been *thrown* into existence, but as having *chosen* to do something one did not *have* to do and *should not* have done. What Heidegger has described is not the experience of guilt, but only the awareness of being finite. It makes no sense at all, nor does it correspond to our experience, to say that we are guilty, or feel guilty, simply by virtue of being finite or of being aware that we are finite (or created, for that matter). Heidegger's account of guilt does not do justice to the phenomenon. It is a construct, certainly ingenious, but compelling only to those who are determined to find some way, *any* way, to rise above or get beneath "moralism" in particular and natural reason in general.

It is because Heidegger calls natural reason, and thereby logic, itself into question that he cannot be logically refuted by Thomas.[143] On the other hand, it is because

140. *SZ* § 58, page 283.

141. *SZ* § 58, page 283 (the latter of these two phrases is italicized in the original).

142. *SZ* § 58, page 284 (The entire sentence is italicized in in the original).

143. Husserl and Heidegger both root reason, and hence logic, in a pre-rational, or pre-predicative, consciousness. For Husserl, as for Aristotle (*Posterior Analytics* 99b15–100b18), this more original consciousness is perception. For Heidegger it is care. For Husserl, reason arises teleologically out of its pre-rational origin. (See *Formal and Transcendental Logic*, § 23 b, § 60.) For Heidegger, reason reacts

Heidegger advances a description of conscience and guilt that Thomas would not recognize as minimally faithful to the phenomena that Thomas cannot be refuted by Heidegger. Thomas can only offer his own description of conscience and guilt, and leave it to the reader to decide for himself which description is more faithful to the phenomena. So we have what appears to be a standoff. To be sure, Thomas offers a comprehensive and consistent alternative to Heidegger. But then Heidegger offers a comprehensive and, in its own most peculiar way, consistent alternative to Thomas. Because Heidegger's assertion of the exceptionless character of the ontological difference, his denial of logic as an inviolable canon for speculative thinking, his depreciation of *theoria*, and his alternative description of the phenomena of conscience and guilt are consequences of the idiosyncratic way in which he radicalizes Husserlian phenomenology, a truly effective Thomistic response would require a thoroughgoing critique of phenomenology, its fundamental tenets, its orientation and commitment, the cogency of its analyses, and its fidelity to the phenomena. In this section I have highlighted some of the points on which I think Husserl and Heidegger are vulnerable to criticism. Phenomenology, both as originated by Husserl and as radicalized by Heidegger, has to count as a significant challenge not only to the rational theology of Thomas Aquinas but more generally to metaphysics as classically conceived. If Thomists are to be taken seriously by thoughtful non-believers in the contemporary world, they will have to rise to that challenge. They are capable of doing so.

Note: Language and history.

The argument for history as the decisive determinant of human thought turns in part on the nature of language. For Heidegger, thought is inextricable from language.

> Thinking accomplishes the relation of Being to the essence of man . . . [I]n thinking Being comes to language (*Sprache*) . . . Language is the house of being.[144]

The attempt to speak of Being or *esse*, as distinct from beings or *entia*, strains the resources of a given language, not only its vocabulary but its grammar also, to the limits.[145] The original source and meaning of most of the words employed in philosophical discourse, as in all discourse, is obscure. Even terms and expressions specifically selected or coined for philosophical employment tend over time to lose not only their vividness, but something of their original meaning as well, through carelessness, overuse, and forgetfulness.[146] Their meaning becomes "sedimented," to use Husserl's

stubbornly against its pre-rational origin. It reacts even against thought itself. See, again, the final sentence of "Nietzsches Wort, 'Gott ist tot.'"

144. "Brief über den Humanismus," in *Wegmarken*, 145. [English translation: 239.]

145. *SZ* § 7 C, concluding paragraph.

146. A case in point, noted earlier, is the English word "substance." It derives from the Latin *substantia*, which was a good translation of Greek *hypostasis*, but came to be used in the speculative tradition as a translation—and very poor translation it is—of the Greek *ousia*, as Aristotle used that

expression. Every individual language is historical, and the metaphysical tradition of the West courses through several languages. The terminology of Being, that-which-is, entities, reality, what-ness, essence, and the like, obviously differs from one language to the other, and it can be exceedingly difficult to capture in Latin, German, or English the original meaning and the grammar of such Greek expressions as *to einai*, *to on*, *ta onta*, *hē ousia*, *to ti esti*, and especially *to ti ēn einai.*

Translation is possible, however. The denotative sense of foreign terms and expressions, though not always their connotative sense, can be captured by the skilled translator, especially by use of periphrasis rather than one-to-one translations. The most striking example of this kind of work is, in fact, provided by Heidegger himself. Whatever one may think of his translation of this or that Greek term into German, his etymological investigations and painstaking renditions of Greek terms and expressions into German must count as evidence that we are not simply incarcerated within a single language, or within a single historical epoch, and that we can gain access to the thought of those who came long before us. In translation we become aware that, though thinking is expressed in *sentences* of a particular language, the sentences themselves refer back to *propositions* that transcend the peculiarities of the language in which they happen to be expressed. Propositions, Thomas tells us, are the work of reason.[147] Propositions are more fundamental than the particular sentences in which they are expressed, as reason is more fundamental than any particular language in which it is at work.

We are historical beings, for sure. But, in studying the history of philosophy and theology with care, our thinking can become trans-historical. For reason itself is trans-historical. The claim that history in general and historical languages in all their contingency are the decisive determinant of human thought is undercut by the example of Heidegger himself.[148]

term. This translation gave rise to well-known disputations between Greek and Latin theologians, particularly regarding whether *consubstantialem* is an adequate translation of *homoousion* in the Nicene Creed. The scholastics in their metaphysical writings usually use *substantia* as a simple substitute for Aristotle's *ousia*. Keeping this in mind, one can make tolerable headway in understanding what they are saying. In our time, "substance" more and more frequently names a special kind of chemical composition like marijuana, cocaine, or heroin—as in "substance abuse," an expression the Scholastics would have found perplexing.

147. *ST* 1–2, q. 94 art. 1, co.

148. In the oral presentation, "A Giving of Accounts," that Jacob Klein undertook jointly with Strauss, the former expressed his debt to Heidegger as follows. "[W]hat preoccupied me mostly during those years [i.e., in the 1920's when Klein and Strauss formed their friendship] was this: whatever thought I might have, and whatever interest I might have in anything, seemed to me to be located completely within me, so that I always felt that I could not really understand anything outside me, could not understand anything uttered or written by another person. I felt that I was in a kind of vicious circle out of which I could not escape . . . When I heard [Heidegger] lecture, I was struck by one thing: that he was the first man who made me understand something written by another man, namely, Aristotle. It broke my vicious circle. I felt that I could understand. Then I began studying seriously, not superficially." (458).

Chapter 13

Natural Teleology Revalidated

That nature is governed by teleological principles, or exhibits teleology at any level, is generally denied by modern natural science. Strauss recognizes that the critique of natural teleology causes serious problems not only for pre-modern physics but for the pre-modern understanding of man a well. Classical ethics and political philosophy understand man to be teleologically constituted, to aim naturally at ends that are not just posited as "preferences" or "values," more or less arbitrarily by the will, but are pre-given by nature. If the concept of natural teleology is hollow, the claim that man possesses ends pre-given by nature is untenable. Strauss sees that there is a problem here, and he does not minimize it. In the "Introduction" to *Natural Right and History*, he writes as follows.

> The fundamental dilemma, in whose grip we are, is caused by the victory of modern natural science. An adequate solution to the problem of natural right cannot be found before this basic problem has been solved. [1]

The jettisoning of a teleological conception of nature has led some

> to accept a fundamental, typically modern dualism of a nonteleological natural science and a teleological science of man. This is the position which the modern followers of Thomas Aquinas, among others, are forced to take, a

1. *NRH* 8. See Jaffa, *NBFr.* 508 n. 60: "The Aristotelian conception of nature, and its logical and moral embodiment in the idea of species, is fundamental to the doctrine of the Declaration." Cf. 101–2. Ernest Fortin observes critically that "it has been decided [by Germain Grisez and John Finnis] that nature has nothing to do with ethical behavior" (Review of Russell Hittinger, *A Critique of the New Natural Law Theory*, "in *CCPO* 362). Fortin's criticism is not quite fair. Grisez and Finnis do, after all, recognize that natural inclinations have *something* to do with ethical behavior, even if, as I argued in Part 1, Ch. 3, section b, above, they do not give appropriate emphasis to the *ordo* of these inclinations. The strange thing, however, is that, in the course of his criticism of these thinkers, Fortin does not spell out how exactly how *he* conceives nature—against the background of what his teacher Strauss calls "the victory of modern natural science"—or how *his* conception of nature might shed light on ethical behavior.

> position which presupposes a break with the comprehensive view of Aristotle as well as that of Thomas Aquinas himself. [2]

It is unclear whether Strauss includes himself in the "others" to whom he alludes since, on the one hand, he seems not to be drawn to the opposite conclusion that he mentioned a few lines earlier, namely, acceptance of "a nonteleological conception of human life," and since, on the other hand, he does not directly take issue with non-teleological natural science as, incidentally, some Thomists do.[3] One might respond that Strauss and his followers succeed in avoiding "a fundamental, typically modern, dualism of a non-teleological natural science and a teleological science of man" by not embracing natural science of any kind, teleological or non-teleological. But such a response would only raise, yet again, the question of what the Straussians hope to accomplish with their frequent but vague invocations of "nature," invocations that can sound to the puzzled outsider more like expressions of piety than of thought.

John Finnis writes, "So far as I can see, Strauss . . . makes no attempt to justify his prominent but vague assertion that 'natural right in its classic form is connected with a teleological view of the universe.'"[4] In his essay on *Natural Right and History*, Richard Kennington replies to Finnis by arguing that Strauss's consideration of the Stoic form of natural right "substantiates the claim of the introduction that 'natural right in its classic form is connected with a teleological view of the universe.'"[5] Kennington may be implying that, as Strauss sees it, there is an earlier and deeper conception of natural right—perhaps a conception of Plato's, maybe even a conception of Aristotle's faintly detectable between the lines—that is *not* connected with a teleological view of the universe.[6] But if, according to a pre-Stoic alternative to the Stoic form of classical natural right, man is viewed as teleological independently of a teleological view of the universe, then this pre-Stoic alternative would not differ in principle from the "typically modern . . . dualism" that Strauss attributes to "the modern followers of Thomas Aquinas, among others." In any event, whatever we are to make of the possibility that there is a pre-Stoic conception of natural right that does not presuppose a teleological view of the universe, we must remember that Thomas's case for the knowledge of natural law, and for the order and content of its precepts, does not presuppose a

2. *NRH*. 8. Fr. Fortin speaks similarly of "the meretricious dualism of a nonteleological natural science and a teleological science of man that became prevalent in Neo-Scholastic or Neo-Thomistic circles" ("Natural Law and Social Justice," 233).

3. Consider, for example, Glenn Coughlin's "The Final Cause in Nature" and "A Brief Note on Inertia," both of which are appended to his translation, *Aristotle's Physics, or Natural Hearing* (South Bend, Indiana: St. Augustine's Press, 2005), 240–5 and 274–7.

4. *Natural Law and Natural Rights*, 52.

5. *SNRH* 78.

6. Consider Kennington's description of what he calls "the second ascent." *SNRH* 79–80.

teleological view of the universe either, certainly not of such a kind that includes a teleological conception of "the heavens, the heavenly bodies, and their motion."[7]

Early in his essay, Kennington says that among the "distinguished conservatives [of the middle of the last century] who pointed to the necessity of a 'higher law' . . . the protagonists of Thomistic natural law possessed the greatest clarity."

> The exposition of natural law within the architectonic of Thomas's thought was and remains their greatest strength. It proves also a ground for reservation of assent. It leads one to wonder whether the ultimate grounds of the doctrine were accessible to human reason. It forces one to ask whether the "nature" of the Thomistic doctrine, clearly of mainly Aristotelian origin, could withstand the claims of "nature" presumably established for all to see by the victory of modern natural science.[8]

It would have been helpful if Kennington had tried to answer the questions he was led to wonder about and was forced to ask. He does not develop his reservations. They may be the same as Strauss's, but Strauss's reservations are not developed either.

Kennington says that "the modern followers of Thomas . . . fail adequately to realize that modern science has never been able to deliver a comprehensive and intelligible account of nature—if indeed that was ever its promise."[9] Whereas Kennington is surely on target in his characterization of modern science, he does not say why he thinks contemporary Thomists are under its spell and, more importantly, what bearing he thinks the status of modern science has, or perhaps must have, on their conception of natural law. Nasser Behnegar repeats Strauss's claim that natural right is bound up with a teleological conception of the universe, and seems to agree with him that this causes a problem for "the contemporary followers of Aquinas."[10] Kennington and Behnegar, like Strauss, fail to see that the foundational principles of Thomas's natural law teaching can be detached from Aristotle's physics and astronomy with no loss whatsoever to their evidence and inner coherence.

Thomas's case for natural law does presuppose that man shares certain inclinations with sub-rational animals, and that he has inclinations that pertain to his specifically rational nature; or, put more simply, that man is both animal and rational. There is not much reason to think that Strauss and his followers would take issue with this presupposition, given their generally high regard for Aristotle, who understands man in just these terms. Interestingly enough, a non-teleological conception of sub-human

7. *NRH* 8.

8. *SNRH* 57–58.

9. *SNRH* 61. The relation between modern science's theoretical limitations and the technological promise that it really does deliver on is a guiding theme in the studies that are contained in Kennington's book, *On Modern Origins*, edited by Pamela Kraus and Frank Hunt, Lexington Books: Lanham MD, 2004.

10. *Leo Strauss, Max Weber, and the Scientific Study of Politics* (Chicago: University of Chicago Press, 2003), 60.

nature would actually strengthen an important claim that Thomas makes. For if man *is* teleologically constituted, but the rest of nature is *not*, then—unless non-teleological causality can give virgin birth to teleological causality—man cannot be understood to have an exclusively natural and subhuman origin. He has to be brought into existence by a supernatural and superhuman being, that is, by God.[11] The alternative is that the core of man's being is itself supernatural and without origin, a transcendental subjectivity that constitutes nature *a priori*, inaugurates history, enters history, and teleologically ascends to a grasping of its own true self as the origin and locus of all meaning.[12]

It seems unlikely that Strauss would accept the latter alternative. Among other things he says by way of contrast to "the anthropocentric character of modern thought" that "even the atheistic, materialistic thinkers of classical antiquity took it for granted that man is subject to something higher than himself, e.g., the whole cosmic order, and that man is not the origin of all meaning."[13] It is possible, maybe even likely, that Strauss himself did not accept the mechanistic alternative to the teleological conception of the universe, since he suggests, although without elaboration, that the decision in favor of the non-teleological conception of the universe may have been premature.[14] And yet he does regard the scientific challenge to the teleological conception of the universe as grave. Whereas Strauss greatly exaggerates the challenge that modern natural science poses to the followers of Thomas Aquinas, he does not exaggerate the challenge that it poses to himself and to his followers. For there is no way that nature as it is understood by modern natural science can serve as an objective standard with respect to which subjective decisions must take their bearings. If the modern understanding is correct, then an analysis of the nature of man has to lead to the conclusion that man, like everything else in nature, can and must be understood without appeal to pre-given ends. Choose what he may, man's choice cannot be judged in terms of objective ethical principles.

One might seek a way out of the fundamental dilemma that Strauss describes by replacing objective ethical principles—that is, natural law—with prudence, the worth

11. Similarly, man's freedom, and contingency in general, cannot be understood as originating from an underlying necessity that is not itself also free—free enough, that is, to produce contingency. When Strauss writes that "all freedom and indeterminacy presuppose a more fundamental necessity" (NRH 90), he does not say how the necessity he has in mind (which presumably is *not* for him, as it *is* for Thomas Aquinas, the necessarily existing God) can give rise to freedom.

12. See Husserl, *Krisis*, 83–84, 100– 101, 102, 155–156, 187, 189–190, 208–210 [English translation: 81–82, 98, 99, 153, 183, 185–186, 205–206]. Eugen Fink's essay "The Phenomenological Philosophy of Edmund Husserl and Contemporary Criticism," which was certified by Husserl as containing nothing he could disagree with (71), presents a remarkable account of how transcendental subjectivity, though not a transcendent reality above man, must still be distinguished from man as a natural being living within the world and naively accepting the world as existing independently of its correlation with consciousness (102–4, 119, 126, 136). Cf. *Ideen 1*, § 27—§ 33.

13. *PR* 102.

14. *NRH* 7–8.

of which could seem at first glance to be unaffected by the victory of modern natural science. After all, prudence is just excellence of deliberation. And excellence of deliberation is not about ends; it is about means. But prudence is about means to an end. And prudence as a virtue presupposes a true conception of the end.[15] If there are no pre-given ends, then prudence (*phronēsis*) cannot be distinguished from mere cleverness (*deinotatē*).[16] It cannot be distinguished from excellence in deliberation about the means that are most conducive to one's self-given ends, that is, to the realization of one's own idiosyncratic preferences or values. Strauss seems to reject this conclusion, for he says of "natural right in its classic form," with which he seems to be in sympathy, and in a formulation that could have been lifted right out of the *Summa Theologiae*, "[R]eason determines what is by nature right with ultimate regard to man's natural end."[17] Regarding this ultimate end, Strauss expresses it, conditionally, as follows.

> If striving for knowledge of the eternal truth is the ultimate *end* of man, justice and moral virtue in general can be fully legitimated only by the fact that they are required for the sake of that ultimate *end* or that they are conditions of *the philosophic life*."[18]

The problem raised by this formulation, and the likely reason Strauss chose to present it conditionally, is the character of the end. Is it natural and pre-given? And if so, how so?

In grappling with this problem under Strauss's guidance, we find ourselves repeatedly thrown back to square one. We can move forward more successfully if we take Thomas as our guide. In doing so, we shall discover that a traditional conception

15. *Nicomachean Ethics*, 1142b35. Prudence also presupposes universals of some sort. 1141b14–16: *oud' estin hē phronēsis tōn katholou monon, alla dei kai* [!] *ta kath' hekasta gnōrizein*. Cf. 1144a35.

16. *Nicomachean Ethics*, 1144a23–b17. On the concern of prudence with the common good, as distinct from one's own good merely, see *ST* 2–2 q. 47 art. 10. Thomas advances not only an argument from revelation but one from right reason (*ratio recta*) as well: reason *as such* judges that the common good, by virtue of being what is most good, is better than the good of the individual merely. Reason necessarily projects the individual man beyond himself, both in the sphere of contemplation and in that of action.

17. *NRH* 7. The following passage from Strauss's 1941lecture "*German Nihilism*" could also have been lifted right out of the *Summa Theologiae*: "Human reason is active, above all, in two ways: as regulating human conduct, and as attempting to understand whatever can be understood by man; as practical reason and as theoretical reason" (365). Strauss is not using the word "regulating" loosely, for he adds a couple of sentences afterwards, "By morals we understand the *rules* of decent and noble conduct, as a reasonable man [and not just a "decent" man] would understand them; those rules are by their nature [!] applicable to *any* human being, although we may allow for the possibility that not all human beings have an equal natural aptitude for decent and noble conduct" (emphasis added). Strauss asserts the universality of the rules, calling into question this time, not their applicability to all men, but an equal capacity in all men to measure up to them fully. And Strauss recognizes that on the latter point he is in some measure of agreement with Thomas (though less so with Kant): *CM* 38–41. But maybe we will be told that Strauss is not expressing his deepest thoughts in this passage.

18. *NRH* 151 (emphasis added). The latter part of this sentence, beginning with "justice . . ." is quoted by Kennington at *SNRH* 80.

of nature, a conception of nature that is invulnerable to the criticisms of modern natural science, that is more fundamental than the idea of history, and that is richer than the persistence of the fundamental questions, can *in its essentials* be revalidated. By taking Thomas as our guide we shall also discover that what is thought to be least convincing about the classical conception, namely, that nature exhibits an overarching teleology, can be revalidated as well.

Thomas says, in agreement with Aristotle and with almost every other great philosopher apart from Nietzsche and Heidegger, that what most profoundly distinguishes human nature from subhuman nature is human reason. So we can tighten up Strauss's statement that "reason determines what is by nature right with ultimate regard to man's natural end." Human reason determines what is by nature right with ultimate regard to the end or ends *of human reason itself.*

It is incontestable that man's reason is employed in two distinct though related spheres, speculation and action. For Thomas, as for Kant, speculative and practical reason are not two different reasons, but one single reason employed in the different but not unrelated spheres of theory and practice. Natural reason operates in terms of principles, that is to say, rules, in whichever sphere it is employed. The first principles of speculative reason, which are employed in thought about what *is*, are also employed in thought about what *is to be done*. But, by themselves, the first principles of *speculative* reason cannot generate action. They cannot even generate speculation, since speculation itself is a kind of act, end-directed, and occurring under the direction of the *practical* precept that ignorance *is to be avoided.*[19] Accordingly, if reason is to direct acts of any sort, it must do so in terms of principles specific to its practical employment, which for Thomas are, of course, the first principle of practical reason and, when this principle is viewed in relation to the experienced order of our natural inclinations, the primary precepts of natural law.

For Thomas, natural reason *qua* natural is a part of nature, though not exactly in the way Aristotle understood nature. According to Thomas, and in distinction from the grand constitution accounts of Kant and Husserl, the human intellect in its pursuit of truth is measured by things. There is a measure of things, but it is not the human intellect, not even when transcendentally reduced. The measure of things is the divine intellect.[20] Thomas justifies these claims in his rational theology. That the divine intellect is the measure of things is demonstrable by natural reason, though, as demonstrable, it is less certain than what is self-evident simply.

Man's *awareness* of the principle and precepts of natural law does not presuppose a teleological conception of nature as a whole. However, it is possible to comprehend man's teleological constitution, of which this awareness is indicative, within a teleological conception of nature as a whole. To do so we need not embrace all the particulars of Aristotle's conception of natural teleology, according to which all natural

19. *ST* 1 q. 20, art. 1, ad 1; 1–2 q. 94, art. 2. Cf. Husserl, *Formal and Transcendental Logic* § 7.

20. *ST* 1–2, q. 93 art. 1, ad 3.

things, inanimate as well as animate, sub-human as well as human, exhibit particular *telē* and nature itself is compared to a doctor healing himself. What we need, instead, is a conception of natural teleology that is not, and in principle cannot be, called into question by natural science, modern or otherwise.

We find this conception in the *Summa Theologiae*, right in the "Treatise on Law," in fact. To validate it, however, we have to move beyond Thomas's natural law teaching proper and enter into his rational theology. We have to take seriously his claim that the human intellect, in pursuing a natural knowledge of things—that is, in the pursuit of natural science—and adjusting itself to things as distinct from constituting them, is thereby adjusting itself to, and thereby in varying degrees catching sight of, though without a full comprehension of, the divine governance of things through eternal law.[21] Because the eternal law is a "sovereign type" (*summa ratio*) existing in God, human reason in spite of its finitude participates in the divine reason not only in moral action but also in its investigation of nature. That is to say, natural law as "the participation of the eternal law in the rational creature" functions not only in the sphere of action but in the sphere of speculation too.

It is because the world is governed by divine reason through the eternal law that it so remarkably accords with our own human reason. Man discovers that the world is rationally constituted. He does not, however, discover that the world is constituted by or in himself, even at the level of transcendental, as distinct from merely empirical, subjectivity, though he can develop extensive and divergent philosophical systems in support of the view that it is constituted in just this way.[22] Man's discovery of the world's intrinsically rational constitution precedes any awareness he might have, or be thought to have, of constituting it himself, either alone or in community with other human beings, whether as transcendental subjectivity or as transcendental intersubjectivity. It pertains to the very meaning of discovery, to discovery as a phenomenon, that what is discovered—in this case the natural and intelligible constitution of the world—exists prior to and independently of the discovery.

21. See *ST* 1–2 q. 93 art. 2.

22. Husserl's understanding of constitution is complex and much controverted. At the foundational level of perception and pre-predicative experience, constitution is accomplished *passively*, automatically, and, so to speak, *in* transcendental subjectivity; whereas at the founded and higher, categorial level, constitution is accomplished *actively* and *by* transcendental subjectivity. See Robert Sokolowski, *The Formation of Husserl's Concept of Constitution* 214–7, and Dorian Cairns, "Some Results of Husserl's Investigations," 148, #10—#18. The difference between passive constitution *in* subjectivity and active constitution *by* subjectivity, though of great significance, should not be taken as implying that subjectivity is not responsible for passive constitution. For, according to Husserl, not only does passive constitution take place *in* subjectivity, it takes place *only* in subjectivity. For this reason, we are justified in saying broadly that, for Husserl, transcendental subjectivity, in its passive as well as in its active syntheses, constitutes whatever it is conscious of, including the very world itself. See Husserl's *Cartesian Meditationen*, 63–64, 88 [English translation, 62, 85]. See also Fink's account of constitution in "Phenomenological Philosophy," 124–31: "The world in its entirety, formerly the universal theme of all philosophy, can, through the reduction, be known as the result of a transcendental constitution: it is expressly taken back into the life of absolute subjectivity" (130).

Without abandoning my earlier claim that animate nature, both human and subhuman, is teleologically constituted, I now note that whether the rationality of the world manifests itself in *particular* cases (apart from man, who directly experiences himself as teleologically constituted) as teleology or as mechanism is a secondary matter. For mechanism, as the very word suggests, manifests reason just as much as teleology does: machines are intelligible, and they do not make themselves. According to Thomas then, the world as we encounter it has already been constituted by a supreme lawgiver, not at random but in accordance with reason, more precisely, in accordance with the supreme reason of the supreme lawgiver. As a consequence of the original constitution of the world by divine reason, human reason can discover rational principles in the world. It discovers them in the form of regularities or rules (*regulas*), indeed, as laws of nature, of physics, chemistry, and so forth. This process of discovery is ongoing, mixed with many false starts and false conclusions, and acknowledged by the thoughtful scientist to be an infinite task.

Kant attempts to interpret the world as constituted, not by the divine reason, but by human reason itself, functioning as transcendental subjectivity or, in his language, the transcendental ego. The "Transcendental Aesthetic" and the "Transcendental Analytic" of the *Critique of Pure Reason* are an attempt to account for the lawfulness of the world in terms of what Kant takes to be the human mind's original prescribing of laws *a priori* to nature, without the human mind's even realizing that it is doing this. But Kant realizes that his constitution account is revolutionary—a kind of "Copernican Revolution"—that it is at odds with the way we naturally understand our relation to the world. Husserl, too, realizes that his own constitution account—which can be called, not altogether misleadingly, a variation of Kant's—is revolutionary, that it is at odds with what he tellingly calls "the natural attitude."[23] Thomas views nature as teleological, not only because he understands man to be oriented to ends by virtue of the reason that is intrinsic to his nature, but also because he understands the world in which man lives to exhibit God's governance. Governance is always for the sake of an end, and the world in its lawfulness, its rationality, gives every impression of being ordered with reference to, of being *purposive* for, man's rational investigation and

23. Cf., e.g., *Ideen 1*, § 32; § 50.

understanding of it.[24] It is not only natural *reason* that is teleological. Nature *itself*, by virtue of its intelligibility, is teleological as well.[25]

Thomas's treatment of the way in which God governs the world contains claims about particular natural entities and their operations that have been called into question by modern natural science. But though modern science can raise questions about the way in which God governs the world, it cannot prove that God does not govern the world, that is, that there is no eternal law. (What would such a proof look like? From what premises would it proceed?) On the contrary, the very rationality of the world—of the physical world that we see and touch, and that scientists are perpetually and rightly fascinated with—its thoroughgoing lawfulness, implies reason and legislation at its foundation.

Natural science cannot make the slightest sense of *why* the world is rational and lawful; it can only find more and more evidence *that* it is rational and lawful. Even the discovery of anomalies in nature, for example, indeterminacy in quantum mechanics, is, *qua* discovery, an act of the intellect that finds at least some degree of intelligibility

24. As I pointed out earlier, Thomas's example of the inclination to self-preservation that he finds in inanimate entities, though understood by him as teleological, nonetheless has something in common with Spinoza's *conatus*. Spinoza, of course, does not advertise his *conatus* as a teleological principle. Indeed, he seems to deliberately posit it in opposition to Aristotle's natural tendency to change (*emphytos hormē metabolēs—Physics* 192 b18). But Spinoza's *conatus* must be construed, even if contrary to his intention, as a teleological principle, because it is an *inclination* that, when opposed by something else, manifests itself as an *exertion*. To be sure, Spinoza does not speak of self-preservation as aiming at anything *beyond* itself; but then neither does Thomas in q. 94 art. 2, though what he says there can be comprehended within the general teleology he argues for elsewhere, e.g., in *SCG* 3 cap. 16–22. Spinoza's *conatus* is obviously oriented toward *continuous* self-preservation, hence *future*, self-preservation. This *conatus* is not oriented solely toward a *present* self-preservation. A striving toward self-preservation solely in the pure, i.e., instantaneous, present (vs. the specious present) is not even possible for a temporal being. Continuous, hence future as well as present, self-preservation is a *telos* that cannot be separated from *conatus*. Nietzsche (hardly a Thomist, but very much an admirer of Spinoza) saw that a construal of the *conatus* for self-preservation as "inertia" is belied by the phenomena. It is for that reason that he introduces, not an intrinsic appetite for good, much less any guidance of a divine intellect, but will to power as *the* basic principle of being, including inanimate being. (*Jenseits von Gut und Böse*, *Sämtliche Werke* Vol. 5, § 36; cf. §§ 9, 19, 211. See Martin Heidegger, *Nietzsche*, Stuttgart, Neske 1961, Erster Band, 2 [English translation Vol. 1, 3–4].) Will necessarily orients itself *toward* something. What it orients itself toward has then the character of a *telos*, in Nietzsche's view, the *telos* of power. In understanding this *telos* as power, rather than as good in a more substantial sense, Nietzsche may hope to forestall a teleological interpretation of his principle. If so, he does not succeed. For power always has an intrinsic reference to what it can and cannot accomplish, to future obstacles to be overcome, to obstacles that can be quite formidable. If, *per impossibile*, there were not such a reference, all power would be . . . *equal*, a proposition that Nietzsche would be the first to deny. Power is intelligible to us only in terms of what falls under its scope. If Spinoza's *conatus* and the power that is the object of what Nietzsche calls "will" did not have a future orientation, there would be temporal chaos rather than temporal nature, and this chaos would be *entirely* unintelligible.

25. Bertrand Russell asserts that science exhibits the world not only as "purposeless" but as "devoid of meaning" ("Free Man's Worship" III [47]). Russell overlooks the fact that science itself is evidence of meaning in the world, that is, of the world's intelligibility. If the world were truly devoid of meaning, science would be meaningless too. In fact, science would not exist at all.

in its otherwise anomalous object.[26] The question of why the world is rational, lawful, and intelligible can be addressed only by rational theology or by philosophy—though not, let it be said, by *political* philosophy.

Interesting as is the question of whether the cause of a given thing is best understood as teleological or as non-teleological, it is not as interesting by a long shot as the question of why things are intelligible *at all*. For Thomas, the accord between the human intellect and the intelligible causes at work in the world is due to the divine intellect that, through the act of creation, is responsible for both the human intellect and the intelligible world, and of nature as comprising both.[27] Thomas anticipates the modern notion that the ultimate ground of the intelligibility of the world is the mind itself, but with the all-crucial qualification that this ultimate ground is not the mind of man but the mind of God.

Thomas, on the one hand, and Kant and Husserl on the other, are in agreement that the correspondence between human reason and the rest of the world is too thoroughgoing to be construed as fortuitous, as, say, the happy but transient result of random genetic mutations in the nervous system of apes.[28] Natural science is constitutionally incapable of demonstrating that nature is not teleological in the broad sense that Thomas's rational theology legitimates. To the extent that it refrains from making "value judgments," natural science cannot account even for its own presumed goodness, since goodness is, according to the scientist, just a "value." And, to the extent that natural science regards matter and its properties as what alone is

26. Similarly, as Aristotle remarks, though the geometrician wonders at the incommensurability of the diagonal of a square with its side, he would wonder even more if the diagonal *was* commensurable with its side. *Metaphysics* 983a15–21. Book X of Euclid's *Elements* is a rational account (*logos*) of what is irrational (*alogon*) in geometry, the existence of such an account by itself demonstrating that the irrational in geometry is not *entirely* irrational.

27. Though the human intellect is the image of the divine intellect, the difference between image and original is, to say the least, vastly greater than we can comprehend. It is because the human intellect is an image, and yet only an image, of the divine intellect that natural science is both possible and an infinite task.

28. Consider Husserl's repeated references in the *Krisis* to the "enigma" (*Rätsel*) of the world's agreement with reason, e.g., 82, 91, 96, 100, 208 [English translation, 80, 89, 93, 96–97, 204]. Husserl thinks that only phenomenology, by appeal to the constitutive performances of transcendental subjectivity, can effectively solve this enigma—and do so without recourse to theology. Kant, on the other hand, recognizes that transcendental subjectivity can convincingly account for only so much. We can know the architectonic principles or laws of nature *a priori* because our cognitive faculty prescribes these laws to nature. But the same is not true of particular empirical laws. Though we can know *a priori* that empirical laws must conform to the architectonic laws, we cannot know *a priori* what the former are (*KRV* B 165), for then they would not be properly empirical. We cannot even know *a priori* that the empirical laws of nature will form a systematic whole. And yet we must *a priori* assume that they will do so. *Kritik der Urteilskraft, Werke,* Band 8, 256–7 [English translation: 19–20]. The consequent empirical discovery—which resists being interpreted as constitution by the human mind—that the empirical laws of nature do in fact form a systematic whole is "the ground of a quite noticeable pleasure, often even of an admiration (*Bewunderung*)" (261). This systematic connection of the empirical laws, unknowable by us *a priori*, is the purposiveness (*Zweckmässigkeit*) of nature for our cognitive faculty.

real, something it does not need to do, it cannot account for its own presumed truth, since truth is neither an empirically observable property of matter, nor a property that can be meaningfully derived, much less logically deduced, from the empirically observed properties of a material entity, even one as complex as the human brain or a computer.[29]

Thomas's rational theology can account for both goodness and truth. The taken-for-granted but truly astonishing agreement between the world and its laws on the one hand, and the finite reason of man on the other, as due ultimately to the creative agency of the infinite reason of a divine lawgiver who transcends both, seems to anyone whose thought is not driven by anti-theological aspiration, or by simple anti-theological ire, to be about as plausible as plausible can be. The attempt to explain this correspondence by invoking an original incarnation of transcendental subjectivity into carnal man, and a subsequent apotheosis of carnal man back into transcendental subjectivity, in which, alone, the world—including especially the very body employed in constituting the world—is constituted, is somewhat less plausible than plausible can be.[30]

In outlining the case for a broadened conception of natural teleology that is invulnerable to the criticisms of modern science, I have gone beyond natural law and its self-evident principles, and I have appealed to Thomas's rational theology.[31] But I have not relied on his revealed theology or on the claims of revelation at all. In the light of Thomas's rational theology we can see that what Strauss called "a fundamental, typically modern dualism, of nonteleological natural science and a teleological science of man," is encompassed within this broadened conception of natural teleology. In no way need this dualism be, as Strauss suggests, an embarrassment for "the modern followers of Thomas Aquinas." It is, however, an embarrassment for the modern followers

29. If truth were a material entity like a particle, a dirt clog, or a neuron, it would have to possess something like mass, volume, and/or a velocity; and it would have to be present, either at rest or in motion, in a specifiable region of space. Regarding truth, such things can be neither imagined nor conceived. Moreover, if truth were a material entity, falsehood would have to be a material entity too—if, on the thesis of materialism, it were even possible to make a meaningful distinction between them. One might reply that truth and falsehood are just abstractions. But an abstraction is not a material entity either.

30. Strauss calls attention to the fact that "man's soul is somehow [!] 'all things': man is the microcosm," and that "[t]here is a natural [!] harmony between the whole and the human mind." (*CM* 41). I know of no place where Strauss speculates on the cause, source, or ground of this harmony which, if *natural*, hardly seems *fortuitous*.

31. Some contemporary scholars working in the Thomistic tradition think that the tensions between modern natural science, including the theory of evolution in particular, and, on the other hand, the scholastic conception of teleology have been overstated and that they share more common ground than is generally supposed. For an overview of the controversies, and their perceived bearing on the question of natural law, see Jean Porter, *Nature as Reason*, 82–125. While not retracting the claim I made in Part 1, above, that non-teleological and anti-teleological reductions of the *subhuman* sphere of life get tangled up in problems of their own, I emphasize that a definitive refutation of these reductions is not essential to a defense of Thomas's natural law teaching, concerned as it is with the *human* sphere of life, i.e., the participation of eternal law in the *rational* creature.

of Aristotle, since Aristotle does not conceive of God as governing the world through the *summa ratio* that is eternal law.[32] It is, *a fortiori*, an embarrassment for Straussians who will have nothing to do with theology of any kind and who do not attempt to account for the accord between the intelligibility of the world and the intellect of man in Kantian or Husserlian terms. "An adequate solution to the problem of natural right cannot be found before this basic problem has been solved," just as Strauss says. But neither Strauss nor his followers advance such a solution. Nor, as far as I can tell, do they clearly state what form they think a solution to the problem would have to take.

The root of the problem for Strauss and those of his followers who do not depart very far from him is that they do not engage frontally with the rational theology of Thomas Aquinas or with that of the other great scholastics, because they mistakenly think that it surreptitiously presupposes the claims of revelation and openly presupposes, of necessity, the physics and cosmology of Aristotle. They mistakenly think that rational theology has been deflated, directly by modern natural science or indirectly by their own politico-theological critique of the moral presuppositions of belief in revelation. A work such as Thomas Aquinas's *De Ente et Essentia* or Duns Scotus's *Tractatus de Primo Principio* is not even "on their radar." The problem, moreover, is exacerbated by the suspicion with which many Straussians view, not just rational theology, but metaphysics more generally (epistemology too, in some case even logic). There are exceptions, to be sure: in the first generation of Straussians, Richard Kennington, Seth Benardete, and Stanley Rosen come quickly to mind; and there are notable exceptions in the second and third generations. But far too many Straussians ignore or dismiss the metaphysical inquiries of Plato and Aristotle, figures whose works are otherwise canonical for them, as little more than accommodations to the exigencies of political life, that is, as noble lies or disguises that the careful reader is expected to see through. Or they interpret these inquires as pedagogically motivated detours, undertaken to wean philosopher-puppies from their immature attachment to the idea of eternity by indulging, for a while, their adolescent propensity to engage in "big talk" about matters that neither they nor anyone else can understand. They fail to see that it is the teaching regarding God that emerges in the metaphysics of Aristotle, in particular, and in its elaboration with modifications by the Islamic philosophers—and not classical political philosophy with its alleged exposure of an intractable "tension" between the good and the just—that poses the greatest challenge to the scholastics, a challenge that thinkers of the caliber of Thomas and Duns Scotus met head on and, in my opinion, decisively.

Thomas's broadened concept of teleology makes full sense of why the inclination to know the truth is a natural inclination. It accords with the teleologically constituted nature of man, which is not a product of anything else in the world, but is immediately

32. For Aristotle there is no eternal law. His god, *noēsis noēseōs*, is not a lawgiver, but a self-contemplator, who moves as *object* of love and does not so much as even *think* of the world. *Metaphysics* 1072b4, 1074b22–34.

created by God, and created with a purpose. Strauss's view is certainly that man is teleological. He cannot, however, find teleology anywhere in nature as understood by modern natural science or as understood by Heidegger. He does, as we have seen, find a residue of teleology—the persistence of the fundamental problems—in the modern world. But aside from the thinness of this residue, it leaves us at best with "a typically modern dualism of a nontelelogical natural science and a teleological science of man."

Strauss refers to Thomism, or rather to "neo-Thomism," in his essay on Heidegger. In a perhaps unguarded moment, he even calls it, as noted earlier, a "philosophic position."[33] Along with "Marxism crude or refined," it is, according to Strauss, one of the two sole philosophic positions that are still in existence. Strauss does not mention Husserl in this connection, perhaps because he is convinced that Husserl has been surpassed by Heidegger in his very allegiance to Husserl's most striking insights. But because Heidegger regards nature as having been eclipsed by history, Strauss is reluctant to speak of him as a philosopher or as occupying a philosophic position: "no one has questioned the premise of philosophy as radically as Heidegger."[34] The premise in question is the existence of nature as necessary, unchanging and permanently present, within time but not passing away in time, and certainly not eclipsed by history.

In *Natural Right and History*, Strauss speaks of the discovery of nature as the event that inaugurates philosophy as distinct from the religious way of interpreting "the first things."

> Nature was discovered when man embarked on the quest for the first things in the light of the fundamental distinctions between hearsay and seeing with one's own eyes, on the one hand, and between things made by man and things not made by man on the other . . . [I]t can be said that the discovery of nature is identical with the actualization of a human possibility which, at least according to its own interpretation, is trans-historical, trans-social, trans-moral, and trans-religious.[35]

It is impossible to discover something that, even after being discovered, cannot be known, *indubitably known*, to exist. And yet in the very sentence following the above passage, Strauss writes,

> The philosophic quest for the first things presupposes not merely that there are first things but that the first thing are always and that the things which are always or are imperishable are more truly beings than the things which are

33. *IE* 29/305. For another observation that seems to have been made in a unguarded moment, see Strauss's essay "Relativism," 22: "[P]resent day positivism deviates from Hume . . . Hume was still a political *philosopher*. More particularly, he *still* taught that there are *universally valid rules* of justice and that those rules are not improperly called *Laws of Nature*" (emphasis added).

34. "An Unspoken Prologue to a Public Lecture at St. John's College in Honor of Jacob Klein," 450. Intriguingly, in light of the sentence quoted above, Strauss says only a few lines later, "as a philosopher [!] Heidegger was not a Christian." See also *WhPPh* 17.

35. *NRH* 88–89.

> not always. These presuppositions follow from the fundamental premise that no being emerges without a cause . . . One may express the same fundamental premise also by saying that "omnipotence" means power limited by knowledge of "natures," that is to say, of unchangeable and knowable necessity; all freedom and indeterminacy presupposes a more fundamental necessity.[36]

Strauss understands these presuppositions as bound up with, if not identical to, the premise that there is such a thing as nature, as nature was understood by the Greek philosophers. For not only does Strauss speak of the discovery of nature in the final sentence of the first of these two passages, he begins the paragraph that immediately follows the second passage with, "Once nature is discovered . . ." and ends with, "The distinction between nature and convention, between *physis* and *nomos*, is therefore coeval with the discovery of nature and hence with philosophy." If I understand him, Strauss is saying both that the existence of nature is discovered by philosophy and that it is presupposed by philosophy. But if nature is really discovered, then its existence is not just a premise or a presupposition.[37] There is manifestly a tension here. In fact, there appears on the face of it to be, not just a tension, but a contradiction. The appearance of a contradiction can be removed if the presupposition is shown to be a true presupposition. But Strauss does not show, not directly and unequivocally, that the presupposition that nature (as he construes it) exists is true. In fact, in the first passage quoted above, Strauss's qualification, "at least according to its own interpretation," could be read to suggest that what is allegedly discovered is only interpreted as having existence. But if that were the case, then philosophy itself, as the "actualization of a human possibility which . . . is trans-historical . . . etc." would be grounded not in what is incontestably evident but on a presupposition, a presupposition that the non-philosopher does not have to grant.

That with his choice of the word, "presupposition," Strauss is not speaking loosely in *Natural Right and History* is confirmed by the following passage from his "Restatement on Xenophon's *Hiero*" in *On Tyranny*.

> Philosophy in the strict and classical sense . . . presupposes that there is an eternal and unchangeable order within which History takes place and which

36. Regarding, the limitation of [divine] omnipotence by knowledge of natures, Strauss refers the reader to *Odyssey* 10, lines 303–6. In this passage Hermes shows Odysseus the nature (*physis*) of a plant that will protect him from the charms of Circe. Hermes knows of this plant, and can pull it out of the ground more easily than a man can. But he is not presented as creating the plant or as able to alter its nature. Strauss's depiction of the discovery of nature in the above passage consists of more than a discovery of the persistence of the fundamental problems. One might assert, cryptically, that the fundamental problems are themselves "the first things." But that hardly seems to be what Strauss is getting at in these passages.

37. Aristotle, who devotes an entire book to *physis*, and invokes it throughout his writings, does not speak of its existence as presupposed, or even as demonstrable, but as manifest (*phaneron*) and known through itself (*di' auto gnōrimon*), or as Thomas says, *per se notum*. Aristotle, *Physics* 193a3–8; cf. Thomas Aquinas, *In Octo Libros de Physico Auditu sive Physicorum Aristotelis Commentaria*, pp. 74–74, § 306.

> is not in any way affected by History. It presupposes in other words that any 'realm of freedom' is no more than a dependent province within 'the realm of necessity.' It presupposes, in the words of Kojève, that 'Being is essentially immutable in itself and eternally identical with itself.' This presupposition is not self-evident.[38]

If the presupposition is not self-evident, then it needs to be rigorously demonstrated, *if* philosophy is to fully justify its claim to be *the* right way of life for those who are able to live it. I am aware of no train of reasoning anywhere in Strauss's writings that would count, in his own eyes, as a rigorous demonstration.

One might respond on Strauss's behalf that his whole life and thought testifies to the existence of philosophy—of philosophy in the concentrated classical sense of the word, not in its diluted contemporary and academic sense. If Strauss is right that there can be philosophy only if nature exists, then his whole life and thought testify to the existence of nature as well. But such a response, though perhaps attractive, does not survive scrutiny. For apart from the fact that Strauss repeatedly refused to call himself a philosopher, the "radical" questioning of "the premise of philosophy" by Heidegger must have led Strauss to wonder, if only for a while, whether philosophy itself might not be fundamentally deluded.

Things are not so dark, however. For the shadow that Heidegger cast upon the existence of nature, and thereby upon the theoretical life, including the philosophic life, is, I propose, removed by the Thomistic revalidation of the concept of natural teleology advanced in the present chapter. Strauss says that "neo-Thomism" has been shown to be "inadequate."[39] And yet he knows that Thomists are neither mesmerized nor cowed by Marxism, by positivism, by existentialism, or by any of the other developments that have attracted the attention and allegiance of the contemporary mind. Thomists keep doing their own thing, as they have been doing since the thirteenth century. Strauss knows that Thomists take a stand, and he seems to respect them for doing so.

> Someone might say that science by itself as well as poor and stupid positivism are . . . helpless against the Existentialist onslaught. But we do not have a rational philosophy which takes up the thread where science and positivism drop it, and for which poetic, emotional Existentialism is no match. I have looked myself for a long time—where do I find that rational philosophy? If I disregard [!] the neo-Thomists, where do I find today the philosopher who dares to say that he is in possession of the true metaphysics and the true ethics which reveal to us in a rational, universally valid way the nature of being and the character of the good life?[40]

38. *On Tyranny*, 212.

39. *IE* 29/305.

40. *IE* 34/309. (See "How to Begin to Study Medieval Philosophy," 216.) For Strauss, if not for all his followers, a rational philosophy aims at shedding light on the nature of being itself (and not just on

In a letter to his friend, the refined Marxist Kojève, Strauss writes, "I am glad to see, once again, that we agree about what the genuine problems are, problems that are nowadays on all sides either denied or trivialized."[41] Below this sentence, in the letter as published, is written "Existentialism Marxism and Thomism" without punctuation. An arrow is drawn from the word "denied" in the preceding sentence to "Existentialism," and a second arrow is drawn from the word "trivialized" to "Marxism." It is curious that no third arrow is drawn to Thomism. Perhaps Strauss intended the second arrow, the one drawn to "Marxism" to be aimed at what he may have understood to be a conjunction, "Marxism and Thomism." If so, we have to ask in what way Strauss thought that Thomism, with or without the prefix "neo-", has been shown to be inadequate or has trivialized the genuine problems such that it could be justly disregarded. The only answer I can think of is that he remained captive to the assumption that Thomas's thinking regarding the genuine problems is dependent upon the claims of revelation, an assumption that is false regarding Thomas's natural law teaching, and can be shown by even a cursory reading of *De Ente et Essentia* to be equally false regarding Thomas's metaphysics and the rational theology that he builds on it. It is a pity that Strauss did not realize this, since he would have found in Thomas Aquinas the comprehensive "rational philosophy" that he was looking for and seems never to have found.[42] He would have found in it the broadened conception of teleology that brings the two members of the "typically modern dualism," human nature and subhuman nature, together without blurring the difference between them. Man is finite but intelligent; what is beneath man is finite but intelligible; the two are teleologically related by virtue of their dependence on the infinite, creative intellect that is God. Thomas's rational theology no more *proves* that revelation has actually occurred than it *presupposes* that it has actually occurred. Accordingly, one could assent to the whole of it while refusing to assent to the claims of revelation. One could not, however, assent to the whole of it while refusing to assent to the possibility of revelation.

Strauss read Thomas, widely if selectively—there is a whole lot of Thomas to be read. Strauss often cites Thomas. He even cites Thomas with approval, though typically as collateral support for claims advanced by Aristotle and others. But knowing that Thomas was a believer, Strauss mistakenly assumed that there was little of a truly substantive nature that he could learn from him concerning the fundamental questions. It is for this reason that Strauss did not—as far as can be concluded from what he published—isolate and engage in depth with the exclusively rational part of Thomas's

"the beings") as well as shedding light on the character of the good life.

41. *On Tyranny*, 244.

42. "Naturally we can sit at the feet of the great philosophers of old, of Plato and Aristotle. But who can dare to say that Plato's doctrine of ideas as he intimated it, or Aristotle's doctrine of the *nous* that does nothing but think itself and is essentially related to the eternal visible universe, is the true teaching?" *IE* 34/309. See *NRH* 20.

teaching. He did not identify its fundamental premises, and he did not analyze the actual arguments that lead to the conclusions he rejects.

Note: Richard Velkley on noetic heterogeneity.

Strauss undertook no sustained metaphysical (or epistemological or logical) investigations in his published works. In one place, he says that political philosophy in its original form—not metaphysics, much less rational theology—is "the first philosophy."[43] In another place, he indicates that discourse that is exclusively "about Being" can occlude one's view of matters closer at hand and of more immediate philosophical, as well as political, urgency.[44] Yet Strauss, as we have seen, also says that "man is so built that he can find his satisfaction, his bliss, in free investigation, in articulating the riddle of being."[45] And there are a number of other passages, some of which have also been quoted in the present study, that show he had an ongoing interest in metaphysics, particularly regarding the whole of which man is a most interesting part, even a "citizen," though not, as in "modern subjectivism," somehow the source.

One of Strauss's most intriguing formulations, a formulation that definitely has a metaphysical ring to it, is "noetic heterogeneity."[46] In his probing study, *Heidegger, Strauss, and the Premises of Philosophy—On Original Forgetting*,[47] Richard Velkley attempts to shed much needed light on this formulation. Velkley sees an affinity between Strauss' concept of noetic heterogeneity and his understanding of man as dyadic. Velkley regards this affinity as the clue to properly interpreting and evaluating claims such as we see in the following striking passage from Strauss's 1958 lecture, "The Problem of Socrates."

43. *CM* 20. Compare Aristotle, *Metaphysics*, 1003a20–32; 1025b8–17; 1026a16–32; 1064a33–b6; 1071b4 ff.

44. *On Tyranny*, 212

45. *NRH* 75.

46. See Strauss's letter of May 28, 1957 to Alexandre Kojève, in *On Tyranny*, 276–80; "The Problem of Socrates," 142; *WhPPh* 39; *CM* 19.

47. There is much more to Velkley's book than his treatment of noetic heterogeneity. I restrict myself above to stating what in his book is most pertinent to the question of natural law. Velkley is in general agreement with Strauss. He does not question Strauss's verdict that Thomas's natural law teaching depends on "the authority of revelation" (161). The attempt to articulate natural law is futile (16, 72, 107). Laws are of human origin and are dependent on the regime (60). Velkley does not take seriously the possibility of a law that is of human origin because, quite independently of the peculiarities of this or that regime, it is grounded in the evidence and operation of human, natural reason. Velkley does speak of "law based on rational inquiry" as distinct from "law grounded in ancestral custom" (149). The former turns out to be "universal nature as standard," a standard that is discovered by Greek philosophy and is not quite the same thing as Thomas's *lex eterna*. I understand Velkley to be saying that universal nature functions as a standard by way of *eros*, which is in tension with law (23). Philosophical *eros* enables one to transcend the salutary pieties of the city (72, 108, 172, n. 40), ordinary human "attachments" (12, 17), and, of course, "moralism" (60). But Velkley also seems to agree with Strauss that nature is a problem (16–17), that its very existence is not self-evident (58). If so, then it remains an open question whether nature as *eros*, even as philosophical *eros*, situates one closer to the most important truths than does ordinary morality, or faith for that matter.

> The human or political things are indeed the clue to all things, to the whole of nature, since they are the link or bond between the highest and the lowest, or since man is a microcosm, or since the human or political things and their corollaries are the form in which the highest principles first come to sight, or since the false estimate of human things is a fundamental and primary error. Philosophy is primarily political philosophy because philosophy is the ascent from the most obvious, the most massive, the most urgent, to what is highest in dignity.[48]

A quick reading of this passage might lead one to assume that Strauss is suggesting here only what he states, implies, or suggests elsewhere. Political philosophy, as engaged in preeminently by Socrates, through its intransigent questioning of received opinions, discovers (allegedly) that the moral convictions of ordinary non-philosophical human beings—moral convictions that are of great political utility, that are, indeed, indispensable for decent politics—are less than fully coherent. These moral convictions, especially regarding free choice, the character of justice, the intrinsic worth of courage and moderation, and the nobility of dedication to the common good, give rise to, and in turn are reinforced by, religious convictions. They are reinforced, in particular, by the conviction that what is highest is a personal being, a god (or gods) of immense power, intelligence, and providence, who takes an acute interest in human affairs and reveals his will through oracles, prophets, and divinely inspired legislators who in turn codify it in the *nomoi* of the city. This personal being then rewards and punishes citizens in a hereafter in proportion to how lovingly they have, in simple unquestioning piety, lived in accordance with the divinely sanctioned *nomoi*. In (allegedly) discovering that the moral convictions of ordinary non-philosophical human beings are less than fully coherent or, rather, that they are ultimately inconsistent, the political philosopher (allegedly) discovers that there is no reason to believe that what is highest reveals itself freely, or contingently, to this individual rather than to that one, to this city rather than that one, or to this people rather than that one. There is, in fact, no reason to think that what is highest reveals itself at all. The only access to what is highest is through philosophy—though even that access is only partial, since being is, in the last analysis, a riddle. If the possibility of revelation cannot be simply disproven, it can still be shown to be a possibility that the philosopher has no good reason to take seriously or wake up at night worrying about. The political things are "of decisive importance for understanding nature as a whole,"[49] because the philosophical scrutiny of the political things reveals the limits of the political and thereby projects the philosopher beyond the political toward nature as a whole, toward impersonal and unfree nature as a whole, that is, toward a necessity more fundamental than any freedom.[50]

48. "The Problem of Socrates" (1958), 133; cited and commented on by Velkley in *HSPPh* 138; cf. 140, 160–2, and 172, endnote 40.

49. "The Problem of Socrates" (1958), 126.

50. *NRH* 90.

All this is familiar territory to anyone who has done a little reading around in the works of Strauss and his followers. But Velkley understands Strauss to be saying something that is more interesting than all this. For Strauss's statement that "man is a microcosm" must be interpreted in light of his understanding that man is a dual entity, if only by virtue of being in the whole while open to the whole.[51] If man the microcosm is dyadic, then the macrocosm, or the whole, is dyadic as well. Regarding the microcosm, Velkley writes.

> To restate Strauss's central insight: the *knowledge* of human dyadic openness to the whole, or the knowledge that access to the fundamental problems (including the problem that revelation claims to answer) is available only through an erotic ascent from the moral-political realm, is the root trans-historical insight. Hence "the political things and their corollaries are the form in which the highest principles first come to sight" and "they are the link between what is highest and lowest." The political things are the key to all things since man as political is the microcosm.[52]

Velkley characterizes the dyadic character of the human in variations on the same theme: "the duality of the human as political and transpolitical"; "the human dyadic openness and closedness of the 'cave' [= the city]"; an "unbridgeable dualism: the city and man"; "the duality of the human, the tension between law and *eros*"; "the tension between philosophy and politics. . . the necessary duality in human ends." [53] As Velkley interprets Strauss, "Morality or law is the primary way in which the human exists as the dualism 'of being a part [of the whole] while open to the whole, and therefore in a sense being the whole itself.'"[54] Even the ordinary non-philosophical human being under the (alleged) illusion that morality or law has absolute significance is "open to the whole,"[55] though his transcendence towards it is limited by his attachment to an inadequately examined conception of justice that does not free him for philosophy but imprisons him within the (alleged) superstition that is religion in every one of its forms. The philosopher's openness to the whole consists primarily in his transcendence of,

51. Reflecting philosophically on this peculiar duality leads to the recognition "that the political things, the merely human things, are of decisive importance for understanding nature as a whole" "The Problem of Socrates" (1958), 164. Strauss justifies his claim that "[t]he human or political things are indeed the clue to all things, to the whole of nature" (133) in four clauses, the first beginning with "since," and the last three preceded by "or since." As connoisseurs of Strauss's exotericism will note, that "man is a microcosm" is one of the two central alternatives that Strauss names. It is hence not as "exposed" as the first and fourth alternatives. And as the first of the two central alternatives it is likely the first to be lost sight of. Velkley expands Strauss's statement that "man is a microcosm" to "man as political is the microcosm." *HSPPh* 161.

52. *HSPPh* 160–1.

53. *HSPPh* 15, 21, 22, 61, 172, endnote 40; 160; 17, 79, 143; 23, 147; 64. Cf. 77.

54. *HSPPh* 153. The phrase in single quotations marks is Strauss's. "The Problem of Socrates" (1958), 164. The bracketed phrase is added by Velkley for clarification.

55. *HSPPh* 77.

or erotic ascent from, "moralism."[56] The philosopher, of course, needs the city for the leisure it provides, for friendship with other philosophers or potential philosophers, for a measure of safety (though only if he is prudent enough to express his thoughts circumspectly to non-philosophers), and for a specifically human life in general.[57] But unlike the non-philosophic multitude, the philosopher is not *fully* at home in city.[58]

The claim that man by virtue of his thinking about the whole somehow contains the whole is a familiar trope.[59] But Velkley interprets Strauss as making a stronger and more intriguing claim. Man by virtue of his duality mirrors a duality that exists in the whole itself. But what is the character of this supra-human ontological duality: the One and the indeterminate dyad? same and other? being and becoming? motion and rest? form and matter? the rational and the sub-rational? the unmoved mover and the moved cosmos? creator and creature? All these are possible answers. But they are hardly answers that one could arrive at solely or even chiefly by reflecting on the dualism that is found in man as political. An answer that one might divine by concentrating on this dualism is that the macrocosm, or the whole, exhibits a duality that mirrors the duality between the wise few and the unwise many holding sway in the political microcosm. For such an answer, which is astonishing in more ways than one, to be persuasive, it has to be comprehensively articulated and rigorously argued for. Velkley writes,

> For Socrates political life offered "the link between the highest and the lowest," between mind and body, and therefore was "the clue to all things, to the whole of nature." In Strauss's provocative readings of Plato and Xenophon, the Socratic innovation of looking to speeches or "ideas" for uncovering the "noetic heterogeneity" of the beings was the same as the discovery of the cosmological significance of the political.[60]

Velkley states here and elsewhere that nature as a whole becomes illuminated by philosophically comprehending the full significance of man *as political.* Man as political exhibits a duality of high and low, and this is the duality between the philosopher and

56. *HSPPh* 21, 66, 76–77, 139, 160.

57. Aristotle, *Politics* 1253a25–29.

58. "The structure of the relationship of philosophy to the city is an indeterminate dyad: philosophy must distinguish itself from the city but it cannot exist apart from the city." *HSPPh* 157.

59. Strauss's claim that man is "in a sense . . . the whole itself" ("The Problem of Socrates" (1958), 164; *HSPPh* 153) would seem to be open to the charge he levels against Heidegger's analytics of existence: it "appears still to partake of modern subjectivism" (*IE* 39/313). Perhaps Strauss would respond that the problem is not subjectivism *per se*, but only modern subjectivism, and that he has rediscovered an ancient subjectivism that is more solidly grounded in what is authentically "first for us," namely, the political in its full complexity, and hence is more defensible than modern subjectivism, the latter starting not with the *polis* or with *societas*, but with the individual, whether construed transcendentally as consciousness or existentially as *Dasein*.

60. *HSPPh* 138. The formulations that Velkley places within quotation marks in this passage are Strauss's.

the non-philosopher. By attending carefully to the duality in the microcosm that is man, an analogous duality in the macrocosm comes to light. The whole, too, exhibits a duality of high and low. But Velkely does not, as far as I can tell, disclose exactly what the high and the low in the macrocosm actually are.[61] That, however, is the very thing he needs to do in order to make good his claim that Strauss has discovered the *cosmological* significance of the political. As for the distinction between mind and body, it is hard to see how it gets discovered by political philosophy *per se*, least of all by political philosophy's focus on the dual and divergent ways in which philosopher and the non-philosopher are within the whole while open to it.

A bit later in his book, Velkley writes,

> [T]he Socratic turn to political philosophy is centrally a recognition that being is heterogeneous, articulated into knowable classes or kinds; this awareness of "noetic heterogeneity" is above all the recognition of the distinctiveness of the political. The political is a realm between body and mind, partaking of both; its heterogeneity from the rest of nature depends on the source of its precarious unity: *thumos*. The Socratic turn to the ideas is first of all a turn to the significance of *thumos* as the ground of a decisive heterogeneity in being. The intrinsic relation between *eidos* and *thumos*, in other terms, consists in the fact that the core of Socrates's philosophic revolution is the uncovering of the political as an *eidos* or class.[62]

Velkley interprets Socrates's turn to *logoi*, and thereby his discovery of *eidē*, as the same as his discovery of political philosophy. As Plato has Socrates describe this turn, however, it was not primarily, much less exclusively the political that he turned to but rather the causes of coming to be, passing away, and being, to the extent that these causes are accessible to *logos*.[63] To be sure, Socrates' discovery of the *eidē* had considerable bearing on his inquiry into the political. But Plato's Socrates does not describe this discovery as originating out of his inquiry into the political.[64]

61. Velkley explicitly disassociates the illumination of the whole by Socratic political philosophy, as rediscovered by Strauss, from classical metaphysics. (*HSPPh* 23, 140, 156.) But he does not make sufficiently clear what he finds problematic about classical metaphysics, which is to say, Aristotelian metaphysics and the varied and rival medieval metaphysics that are of Aristotelian provenience. Velkley sometimes gives the impression of thinking that Heidegger's critique of classical metaphysics is simply unanswerable. At other times he gives the impression of thinking that, quite independently of Heidegger's critique, metaphysics as developed by Aristotle (and perhaps even as developed by Plato) was a vain quest for knowledge of timeless essences, a quest made possible only through an original forgetting of the radical insight of Socrates' that *the* clue to the whole is the political.

62. *HSPPh* 153.

63. Plato, *Phaedo* 96a4–100e5.

64. According to Aristotle, on the other hand, "Socrates was concerned with ethical matters, and not at all with the whole of nature." *Metaphysics* 987b1: *Sōkratous de peri men ta ēthika pragmateuomenou, peri de tēs holēs physeōs outhen . . .*" Cf. 1078b18. Aristotle seems not to have thought that Socrates had discovered that the political was "the clue to all things, to the whole of nature."

Velkley's book is valuable in a number ways that I have not spoken to. With regard to what I have spoken to, it is, in its thoughtful and thorough-going attempt to make sense of what Strauss meant by "noetic heterogeneity," without rivals. I am not persuaded, however, that Strauss interpreted "the Socratic innovation of looking to speeches or 'ideas' for uncovering the 'noetic heterogeneity' of the beings [to be] the same as the discovery of the cosmological significance of the political."

Strauss's prime or immediate interest is not "ontological heterogeneity," or "ontic heterogeneity," but "*noetic* heterogeneity." He seems to have chosen the expression "noetic heterogeneity" in order to refer to different kinds of knowing (*noēseis*) and different kinds of knowables (*noēta*). The way we know some things, the human things, is irreducibly different from the way we know other things, the sub-human things. Man is different from everything else in nature.[65] Hence he cannot be known in the same way that other things are known.

In a letter reflecting on the relation of Aristotle to Plato, Strauss explains what he means by "noetic heterogeneity."

> There is a realm of ideas: hence there must be a hierarchy, an organizing principle: the idea of the good. But as the highest principle it must be the ground not only of the ideas, but of the sensible as well. Hence the idea of the good is "the Good." The problem of *diareisis* is the problem of the organization of the realm of ideas, and in particular the problem of the knowability of that organization. If wisdom is not available but only philosophy, the *diairesis* as descent from the One to all ideas is not available. We live and think in the derivative and ascend to some extent, but not to the origin of things . . . [W]hat is available to us is a dualism of a hypothetical mathematical physics and a non-hypothetical understanding of the human soul.[66]

65. Noetic heterogeneity certainly presupposes some kind of ontological or ontic heterogeneity. Strauss, in fact, uses "essential heterogeneity" in apposition with "noetic heterogeneity." "The Problem of Socrates" (1958), 142. But as this passage, like others, bears out, Strauss's focus is on how we know the sphere of the human as distinct from the sphere of what is not human. "The discovery of noetic heterogeneity permits one to let things be what they are and takes away the compulsion to reduce essential differences to something common. The discovery of noetic heterogeneity means the vindication of what one could call common sense. Socrates called it a return from madness to sanity or sobriety. . . . Socrates discovered the paradoxical fact that, in a way, the most important truth is the most obvious truth, or the truth of the surface. . . [T]he fact that there is a variety of being [= essential, or ontological, heterogeneity], in the sense of kinds of classes, means that there cannot be a single total experience of being . . . There is indeed mental vision, or perception, of this or that kind of pattern, but the many mental patterns, many mental perceptions, must be connected by *logismos*, by reasoning, by putting two and two together." (142–3.)

66. Letter of May to 28, 1957, to Alexandre Kojève, in *On Tyranny*, 277– 9. In this letter Strauss says, "The difference between Plato and Aristotle is that Aristotle believes that biology, as a mediation between knowledge of the inanimate and knowledge of man is available, or Aristotle believes in the availability of a universal teleology . . ." The possibility of a "rational biology," as Strauss puts it in this letter, has in fact been demonstrated in modern times by Hans Jonas: *The Phenomenon of Life*, Chapters 1–7. The "universal teleology" that Strauss alludes to consists in the purposiveness of nature that I have spoken of above, where nature includes both the human and the sub-human inanimate,

Mathematical physics is hypothetical because it depends ultimately on postulates that are neither self-evident nor deducible from what is self-evident.[67] Understanding of the human soul is non-hypothetical because (1) we have direct, and more or less adequate, access to our own souls;[68] and because (2) opinions about the human soul, including man's concern for justice or what he understands to be justice, can be dialectically scrutinized as hypotheses, and those that disclose themselves as self-contradictory can be disregarded, or, rather, destroyed.[69] Though Strauss indeed says "the whole is characterized by noetic heterogeneity," he speaks in the passage under consideration of this heterogeneity as derivative and as having its foundation in a unity, namely, "the One," which is, however, not accessible to us.[70] As for the heterogeneity itself, it seems to have nothing to do initially with the distinction between man as philosophical and man as non-philosophical but, rather, with the distinction between man as such and what is different from man, granted that in the former case the distinction between types of human beings may become a central theme.

In his essay "What is Political Philosophy?" Strauss writes as follows.

> The knowledge which we possess is characterized by a fundamental dualism which has never been overcome. At one pole we find knowledge of homogeneity: above all in arithmetic, but also in the other branches of mathematics, and derivatively in all productive arts or crafts. At the opposite pole we find knowledge of heterogeneity, and in particular of heterogeneous ends; the highest form of this kind of knowledge is the art of the statesman and of the educator. The latter kind of knowledge is superior to the former for this reason. As knowledge of the ends of human life, it is knowledge of what makes human life complete or whole; it is therefore knowledge of a whole. Knowledge of the ends of man implies knowledge of the human soul; and the human soul is the only part of the whole which is open to the whole and therefore more akin to

and, additionally, the sub-human animate, which links the former two while keeping either of them from being reduced to the other.

67. Plato, *Republic* 533b5–c5.

68. Though see Plato, *Phaedrus* 229e2–230a8.

69. *Republic* 533c8–d2.

70. It is curious that Strauss does not mention the indeterminate dyad in this passage. He speaks instead as though the noetically heterogeneous world—comprising the human and the sub-human—might by grounded in a *single* first principle, which as far as it goes is the teaching of Thomas Aquinas himself. But it is not the teaching of Plato and Aristotle. See Aristotle, *Physics* 187a18; 191b35–192b6; 203a15; *Metaphysics*, 1053b9–15; 1059a30–35; 1071b4–5; 1083a32–35. 91–98. On the indeterminate dyad, see Jacob Klein, *Greek Mathematical Thought*, 91–98; and, by the same author, "A Note on Plato's Parmenides" and "About Plato's *Philebus*," both in *Lectures and Essays*. In the passage from "The Problem of Socrates" (1958), 142–3, some of which I quoted five footnotes earlier, Strauss does not speak as though the noetic heterogeneity or essential heterogeneity that he has in mind might be derivative from a more fundamental unity.

> the whole than anything else is. But this knowledge—the political art in the highest sense—is not knowledge of *the* whole.[71]

In this passage, we see something that supports Velkley's understanding—or, to put it more cautiously, what I take to be Velkley's understanding—that the duality of man, as philosophical and non-philosophical, is at the core of noetic heterogeneity. For here Strauss explicitly connects knowledge of heterogeneous ends with knowledge of the human soul, which is to say, with the knowledge possessed by the statesman and the educator, and, we can add, by the political philosopher. This heterogeneity within the sphere of the political consists largely, if not principally, of the distinction between philosophical man and non-philosophical man, and their different ends. For Strauss this distinction is sharp indeed.[72] But he does not say that it is a local manifestation of a more general cosmological distinction. Nor does he suggest what the cosmos would look like if it were constituted by a distinction comparable to that between man as philosophical and man as non-philosophical. The cosmos is arguably constituted by a variety of what could be called "macro-dualisms," among them inertia and extension, consciousness and matter, living and non-living, persons and things. But the dualism, philosophical and non-philosophical, is at most a micro-dualism. It exists solely *within* one member of a macro-dualism, within the class of persons as distinct from things.

Strauss uses the shorthand expression "noetic heterogeneity" to name the fact, significant to be sure, that we cannot understand the human things and the sub-human things in the same way. Nonetheless, the heterogeneity that holds between the human sphere and the sub-human sphere is bridged without being obliterated by the inseparable connection between the intellect operative in the former sphere and the intelligibility discovered in the latter, their truly marvelous concordance testifying, unceasingly and at the most elemental level, to the natural teleology of the world we inhabit: its purposiveness for our rational investigation of it. If the two spheres were separated by an unbridgeable abyss, man could not as a rational being find himself in any way at home within the world. In spite of all their differences, the two spheres do not add up to an insoluble "riddle of being." For they have as their common, originating, and, for Thomas, rationally demonstrable principle the divine creative intellect, who is himself the act of being in its purity.

71. *WhPPh* 39.

72. *On Tyranny*, 202; *NRH* 151; *CM* 59.

Chapter 14

Objections and Replies

One might object to the response that I have given to Strauss's criticisms of Thomas Aquinas: Strauss did not need to address Thomas's teaching in detail because he offered a superior alternative to it. In particular, he indicated as clearly as is possible in our egalitarian times that the natural end of man is not accessible to all men, but only to a few. That natural end is the happiness provided by philosophy, or contemplation, for the small number of human beings who are equipped for it.

Strauss and Thomas might seem to be not so far apart in this assessment of the natural end for man, setting to one side what Thomas believes about a supernatural end of man. But in fact they are quite far apart. Thomas concludes that contemplation is one of the two natural ends for man, and the higher of the two, by analyzing the nature of man, especially the activity of his reason. In the *Summa Theologiae* this conclusion is reached through two independent analyses. In the first analysis, which occurs in the "Treatise on Happiness" at the beginning of the *Prima Secundae*, Thomas appeals to his rational theology. And Strauss rejects rational theology. In his second analysis, which occurs in the "Treatise on Law" later on in the *Prima Secundae*, Thomas concludes that, stated positively and maximally, the pursuit of knowledge, or, stated negatively and minimally, the avoidance of ignorance, is a primary and obligatory precept of natural law. And Strauss rejects natural law. The argument Thomas advances in the "Treatise on Happiness" leads to the conclusion that, though the happiness available to us in this life consists chiefly in contemplation, it consists also in an operation of the practical intellect directing human actions and passions, not only as a means to contemplation but as worthwhile in its own right as well. Strauss does not reach this conclusion. Finally, Thomas's argument in the "Treatise on Law" leads to the conclusion that another primary and obligatory precept of natural law is, stated negatively and minimally, not to offend others, or, stated positively and maximally, to love one's neighbor. Strauss does not reach this conclusion either. Strauss does say, speaking of Aristotle and in apparent agreement with him, that

> human action has principles of its own which are known independently of theoretical science (physics and metaphysics) . . . The principles of action are the natural *ends* toward which man is by nature inclined and of which he has by nature some awareness.[1]

The apparent confidence with which Strauss can appeal to a *natural* teleology "known independently of theoretical science (physics and metaphysics)" is puzzling, given the doubts we have seen him raise elsewhere. Nature, as conceived by Aristotle, establishes ends. But Aristotle's conception of nature seems to have been invalidated. In any case, it has not been revalidated, certainly not *in toto*. Only Thomas's conception of nature as an expression of eternal law withstands the anti-teleological critique advanced by modern natural science without forcing reason to take refuge in a counter-intuitive theory of the subjective constitution of objectivity, including nature itself, and to succumb eventually to historicism as happens, according to Strauss, in the Kant-Husserl-Heidegger sequence. Only Thomas's conception of nature as an expression of eternal law stands as an irrefutable alternative to historicism. But then this conception opens one up to the possibility of revelation rather than closing one off to it. And Strauss seeks a disproof of this possibility.

What is of particular interest in the passage quoted above is Strauss's claim that the principles of action are ends—note the plural—given by nature (however conceived). Thomas agrees. But then Thomas says that the inclination toward these ends can serve as principles of action only in conjunction with the first principle of practical reason. It is this conjunction, I have argued, that gives rise to precepts, *obligatory* precepts, of natural law. To limit ourselves to the precept that one avoid ignorance, or pursue knowledge, since this seems to be what Strauss is chiefly interested in, we have to ask how Strauss understands the mere inclination to know the truth to be a principle. We have, after all, multiple inclinations, and they frequently come into conflict with one other. Strauss speaks to this matter in a sentence that has a Thomist ring to it. "[T]he scholarly quest for political knowledge is essentially animated by a moral impulse, the love of truth."[2] This moral impulse animates the quest for theoretical knowledge as well as for political knowledge. But how does Strauss understand the *love* of truth to be a *moral* impulse? Strauss's choice of the word "moral" here leads one to think, on first hearing, that he regards the pursuit of truth as, at least for some human beings, obligatory. That man loves truth does not deprive the pursuit of truth of its obligatory character, because man loves other things as well, some of which can be obstacles to the pursuit of truth. What then directs man, the rational animal, to the pursuit of truth in preference to other pursuits? Thomas would say that the pursuit of truth is the pursuit that is most in accord with what is highest in us, that is, with our

1. "An Epilogue," 103 (emphasis added).

2. *WhPPh* 16.

specifically rational nature. It is for this reason that the pursuit of truth is obligatory. Natural law directs us to this pursuit, and it does so by way of a command.

This is not the way Strauss argues. Perhaps he wishes to leave things at saying simply that it is *natural* for us to love truth.

> [Philosophy] is necessarily accompanied, sustained and elevated by *eros*. It is graced by nature's grace.[3]

This characteristically striking formulation of Strauss's is memorable. But it turns out to be not just memorable but problematic for anyone who is not simply charmed by it. If is to be taken as definitive, then it says only that philosophy, or the pursuit of truth, is good because it is natural, period. Now, the fact that only some people have been graced, or as is said "gifted," with a love of truth so compelling as to be, for them, erotic does not argue in the least against its being natural, since nature bestows her gifts unequally. But from the perspective of either modern science or historicism, neither of which is unequivocally refuted by Strauss, everything is natural or nothing is natural, but surely one thing, even philosophy, is not more natural than another. If Strauss's formulation is not taken as definitive, then we have to ask again why one engages in philosophy, however erotic the engagement may be. If the answer is that the pursuit of truth is pleasant, period, then we have a simple hedonistic reduction, a reduction that not only is at odds with Strauss's persistent employment of the concept and terminology of obligation, even in his criticism of natural law, but, as we shall shortly see, is emphatically rejected by him.

We cannot leave it at saying that philosophy, or the pursuit of truth, is good because it is natural, period. Man is a rational being. He does not pursue truth as a matter of blind instinct. He elects to do so. According to Kant, who has never been refuted on this point, there are only two possible motives for the pursuit of something. One motive is simply the pleasure, however loftily it may be conceived, that one expects to receive from the pursuit. The other is the intrinsic goodness, and hence the obligatory character, of the pursuit, as distinct from whatever degree of pleasure may accompany it.[4] There is no reason to think that Thomas Aquinas would find himself in essential disagreement with Kant on this particular point.[5]

The teaching of Plato and Aristotle, because it employs the concept of obligation but does not make a case for natural law, appears to be incomplete. The teaching of Strauss, because it employs the concept of obligation but tries to make a sustained case against natural law, appears to be inconsistent. There are three drastic but still ineffectual strains of thought that could seem to rescue Strauss from the charge of inconsistency.

3. *WhPPh* 40.

4. *Kritik der Praktischen Vernunft*, *Werke*, Band 6, 127–33. [English translation: 19–24.]

5. See *ST* 1–2 q. 2 art. 6, ad 3. (Cf. Plato, *Gorgias* 468a7; 499e6–500a4; *Nicomachean Ethics* 1174a4–6.)

In the first place, one might object that I have misinterpreted the Ought from the outset. The Ought is indeed not *deduced* from the Is; but might it not be just a convenient but ultimately misleading *name* for the Is, more precisely, for a certain region of the Is, the region having to do with the desire for pleasure? The inference that one *ought* to do x if one thinks that doing x will give more pleasure than not doing x is, however, invalid. It requires the supplementary inference that the pursuit of pleasure is obligatory, and that premise is neither self-evident nor deducible from premises that are self-evident. So, rather than attempt vainly to *deduce* obligation from the desire for pleasure could we not perhaps *define* obligation in terms of the desire for pleasure? To say that "one ought to do x" is perhaps to say nothing more nor less than that "one thinks that doing x will give one more pleasure than not doing x." That one ought to do something means only that one is thinking about it according to a calculus of pleasure and pain.[6] There is, then, nothing peculiarly moral about the Ought. It does not presuppose law. It does not even presuppose moral freedom. It only presupposes and gives expression to the desire for pleasure and the aversion to pain.

The problem with this reduction is not only that it would leave us with no real opposition between duty and the pursuit of one's own pleasure, but that it would leave us with no imagined opposition between duty and the pursuit of one's own pleasure either. On the basis of the proposed re-definition of obligation, the person who says, rightly or wrongly, that he should put duty before the pursuit of personal pleasure *means* only that he should put the pursuit of personal pleasure before the pursuit of personal pleasure. But that is nonsense, and it is not what he means. The case against obligation—and thereby against categorical imperatives, unconditioned duty, and natural law—cannot be sustained merely by arbitrarily proposing a redefinition of obligation in which nothing at all corresponds to the defined term as it is ordinarily used.[7] One could show the incoherence, not only of the concept of obligation, but of any concept by re-defining it that way.[8]

6. Whereas it is doubtful that Harry Jaffa. Fr. Fortin, or E. A. Goerner would ever make so crass a claim, it does fit with the emphasis they place on reward and punishment in their understanding of how obedience to law can be construed as obligatory. See Part 2, Ch. 6, Section c, above.

7. A redefinition of obligation in hedonist terms would lead to surrounding the word with quotation marks, which is not Strauss's way. In speaking of the social science prohibition against making value judgments, he says that it "reminds one of the childish game in which you lose if you pronounce certain words, to the use of which you are constantly incited by your playmates . . . To put the terms designating such things [as statesmanship, corruption, and even moral corruption] in quotation marks is a childish trick which enables one to talk of important subjects while denying the principles without which there cannot be important subjects—a trick which is meant to allow one to combine the advantages of common sense with a denial of common sense" (*NRH* 52–53).

8. It would be perverse to define obligation as "that the non-fulfillment of which incurs (or might incur) punishment." For one can be punished, say, by an unjust ruler, for actually fulfilling an obligation, i.e., for doing what one ought to do. Regarding the punishment of remorse, see above, Part 2, Ch. 6, Section c. Needless to say, one could not feel the pain of remorse, or anticipate it, unless one were antecedently convinced that one had violated one's obligations, or was about to do so. As for belief in punishment by God, this belief obviously presupposes belief in the existence of God as one who takes

Only if one could demonstrate first that the concept of obligation just as it is ordinarily understood is incoherent—and not simply that the Ought cannot be deduced from the Is—might one afterwards be justified in considering a redefinition of obligation in hedonistic terms. If, alternatively, one wishes to say that no one lives up to the Ought, even that no one can live up to the Ought, what the Ought actually *means* must first be understood, and it cannot be understood by being re-defined in such a way as to render it indistinguishable from pleasure-seeking.

Hedonistic reductions of the concept of obligation, such as the one we just considered, play no role in Strauss's criticisms of natural law. They play no role even in his criticisms of what he very occasionally calls, and what his followers very frequently call, "moralism."[9] When Strauss refers to "what might seem to be one specific danger to which German thought is exposed—moralism unmitigated by sense of humor or sense of proportion," he does not mean by "moralism" a covert hedonism of any kind, but, as he explicitly says in the context of this formulation, "non-mercenary morality."[10]

More decisively from Strauss's perspective, hedonism, crude or refined, fails to take into account the distinction between the desire for, or urge toward, pleasure and the "wants" that, Strauss says interestingly but without sufficient elaboration, are articulated according to nature: "The primary fact is not pleasure, but rather the wants and the striving for their satisfaction . . . The different kinds of wants are not a bundle of urges; there is a natural order of the wants."[11] Hedonism, however sublime the pleasure it sets its sights by, can make sense neither of excellence nor of admiration. It is an expression of moral obtuseness.

---

interest in how we live. As we have seen, Strauss himself points out that such a belief in God, which is a properly religious belief, presupposes convictions about morality, i.e., about obligations, and not the other way around. ("The Law of Reason," 140.) Hence, belief in God is not what generates these convictions. One might respond that what generates these convictions is "the city," and that it is a great failing of the present study that I have had so little to say about the sphere of the political in general, and about the best regime in particular. However, the political is but one kind of society, even if it is the most authoritative kind. Thomas says that the inclination to live in society—as distinct from a herd, a hive, or an anthill—is an inclination that pertains to our specifically rational nature. (*ST* 1–2 q. 94 art. 2, co.; cf. Aristotle, *NE* 1098a3–5; *Politics*, 1253a1–18.) Natural Reason, then, is the root of political life, as it is also the root of philosophy. Man is political, and some men are philosophical, only because man is rational. (The causality is not reversible: man is not rational because he is political, nor is he rational because he is philosophical.) Since natural reason includes practical reason as well as speculative reason, natural reason—and not "the city"—is the deepest root of our convictions about morality.

9. To take only one example, in his essay, "The Moral Basis of National Security," Thomas Pangle designates the Thomistic doctrine of just war as "moralism" four times in less than three pages (326–8), qualifying it once as "exaggerated moralism" and once as "belligerent moralism." Strauss speaks of "moralism" as "the view that morality or moral virtue is the highest." ("A Giving of Accounts," 463–4.) This is indeed Kant's view of what is highest (or loftiest—*supremum*) for man. And, for what it is worth, it is my view as well. But it is not Thomas Aquinas's view.

10. Review of John Dewey's *German Philosophy and Politics*, in *WhPPh* 280–1. A development of the central thrust of this review can be found in "German Nihilism."

11. *NRH* 126.

> From the point of view of hedonism, nobility of character is good because it is conducive to a life of pleasure or indispensable for it; it is not good for its own sake. According to the classics, this interpretation distorts the phenomena as they are known from experience to every unbiased and competent, i.e., not morally obtuse, man. We admire excellence without any regard to our pleasures or to our benefits. No one understands by a good man or man of excellence a man who leads a pleasant life.[12]

After these compelling sentences, Strauss proceeds to draw a distinction between hedonism, or "the identification of the good with the pleasant," and "the thesis of the classics," and he gives every impression of concurring in the latter. His case against the identification of the good with the pleasant is not undermined, it is in fact supported, by his related claim that

> progress toward wisdom will be accompanied by awareness of that progress. And that awareness is necessarily pleasant. This whole—the progress and the awareness of it—is both the best and the most pleasant thing for man. It is in this sense that the highest good is intrinsically pleasant.[13]

Progress in wisdom is pleasant because one is aware of it *as* progress, that is, as *in itself* good. Hence Strauss speaks of a complex conjunction, "*both* the best *and* the most pleasant thing for man" (emphasis added), rather than a simple apposition such as, "the best, that is to say, the most pleasant thing for man." That the highest or consummate human good is intrinsically pleasant—a view held not only by Strauss, but also by Thomas and even by Kant—does not mean that the highest good is simply identical to the pleasure that the consciousness of attaining or approximating it gives rise to.[14]

Strauss draws attention to what he calls "the open secret of [Plato's] *Philebus*: the highest good: *theoria* plus *hēdonē*."[15] This formulation of the highest good, or the best thing for man, differs from the preceding one by actually including the pleasant within the best thing for man rather than as a complement to it. Even so, the clear implication is both that pleasure alone is not the highest good and that *theoria* is not good simply because it is pleasant: each is good, and both together constitute the highest good. But when we try to find out why Strauss and his students think that *theoria* is a constituent of the highest good, distinct from, though surely giving rise to, pleasure, things become obscure again. We are left with little more than asseverations about its being somehow "natural," but with neither clarity nor agreement about what nature is, except that, whatever it is, it is not the created order of things governed by divine reason through the eternal law.

12. *NRH* 128 (emphasis added); see 167. Cf. *On Tyranny*, 89.

13. *On Tyranny*, 101; see 95–96.

14. *ST* 1–2 q. 2 art. 6 (cf. *ST* 1 q. 5 art. 6, ad 2); *Kritik der Praktischen Vernunft*, *Werke*, Band 6, 238–9. [English translation: 92–94.]

15. *RR* 162.

Since the tension between Strauss's employment of the concept of obligation and his denial of natural law cannot be resolved by merely redefining obligation, least of all in a way completely foreign to Strauss's own usage,[16] a second, related, yet even more drastic way of blunting the inference that Strauss's teaching is inconsistent suggests itself: Strauss thought that some people are obligated, really obligated, in the core of their being, but that others are not. Obligation expresses no more than the apprehensiveness associated with how we interpret our relation to some powerful being, real or imagined, whom we understand to be making demands upon us. We are obligated to obey the law of the land in this way. There is nothing particularly moral about it. Believers understand themselves to be obligated to obey God and what they take to be his law in an analogous way. As we obey the law of land out of fear and hope of reward, so, it is argued, we obey what we take to be the law of God out of fear and hope of reward as well. There is nothing particularly moral about it. And though officers of the law can see only how we act, and even then only some of the time, God can see how we always act, and he can see how we always think as well. He can see our intentions. The believer, then, really is obligated in the core of his being. But this obligation is founded on an error that is also in the core of his being, and that error is belief itself. The unbeliever, the unbelieving philosopher in particular, is not obligated because he does not live the error of belief. The human species, then, is divided into the non-philosophic many, who are obligated, and the philosophic few, who are not.

Though this interpretation finds some support in what Strauss wrote, it fails as a consistent interpretation of his thought. For he writes as follows.

> One has not to be naturally pious, he has merely to have a passionate interest in genuine morality, in order to long with all his heart for revelation: moral man as such is the potential believer.[17]

Man is moral before he is a believer. Otherwise, he could not be a *potential* believer. Man understands himself to be obligated prior to believing that God has placed demands on him or has made promises to him. Strauss comes very close to the position of Thomas himself here. Thomas would say that this prior understanding is *synderesis*, the entirely natural *habitus* wherein are contained the precepts of natural law.[18] Strauss rejects this account. As a consequence, his complex teaching and the way he chose to present it repeatedly gives rise to the all-important question, which he himself chose neither to answer nor even to pronounce—the question *quid sit obligatio*.[19]

16. See the passages cited above in the third footnote of Ch. 11, Section a, of the present part.

17. "The Law of Reason," 140. See *RR* 165. "[T]he foundation of belief in revelation is the belief in the central importance of morality."

18. *ST* 1–2 q. 94 art. 2, ad 2.

19. This question is inseparable from the broader question, also uninvestigated by Strauss—*quid est ratio.*

A possible answer to this question is one that we have brushed up against more than once, and it constitutes the third and most drastic way of absolving Strauss of the charge of inconsistency: he thought that obligation was . . . nothing at all. His frequent employment of terms such as "ought" and "duty," was but an exoteric accommodation to the requirements of civic morality. This reduction of Strauss's teaching, however, is even more aberrant than the inconsistencies it is trying to eliminate. For it requires hacking away not just salutary commonplaces that crop up here and there but whole arguments, including recurrent criticisms of positions such as hedonism and decisionism, from which Strauss's own teaching, so reduced, would become in its essentials indistinguishable.

There is, of course, no way of refuting the suggestion that Strauss's arguments against hedonism and decisionism do not reflect his deepest thoughts, given the emphasis he himself has placed on distinguishing between an author's genuine intention and its exoteric presentation. This suggestion, then, does resolve the appearance of inconsistency in Strauss's teaching, even if at a high price. And yet it still leaves unanswered the crucial question of what *principle* deliberation sets its sights by. Is it solely or essentially the good of one's own community? If so, that is, if one's *own* becomes the highest court of appeal, we must again ask, should not one's own *private* good, one's own life and pleasure, take precedence over the good of one's community? It is only fair to let Strauss have the last word here, though it is difficult to square with his criticisms of natural law. As we have seen, in a presentation of Aristotle's thought from which he does not dissociate himself, Strauss writes, "All human love is subject to the law [!] that it be both love of one's own and love of the good, and there is necessarily [!] a tension between one's own and the good."[20] An adequate understanding of this sentence is the key to any interpretation that would reconcile the different strains of Strauss's complex teaching on the principles of human choice and action. Lacking such an understanding, I think it does greater justice to Strauss to acknowledge the inconsistencies in his teaching as he presented it than to distort or truncate that teaching so that it becomes indistinguishable from hedonism or decisionism, both of which he held to be not only at odds with human nature but despicable to boot.

20. *WhPPh* 35.

Conclusion

I have tried in this study to raise the dispute between Thomists and Straussians above the level on which it has hitherto been conducted. I have not tried to defend at any length propositions that are generally accepted by both parties, even if not always understood by them in the same way. Among the most important of these propositions are that there is a distinction between nature and convention, that something in the nature of things corresponds to the word "soul," that human thought is not irremediably prejudiced, and that movement from opinion towards knowledge on at least some matters of fundamental and enduring significance is a human possibility. Each of these propositions, and others closely related to them, has been called into question, or denied, or ridiculed in our time, but none, as far as I know, by serious Thomists or serious Straussians.

One of the most remarkable features of Thomas's natural law teaching is the extent to which he anticipates and, centuries before the fact, responds to the very criticisms that Strauss and his followers level against it. Criticisms that Straussians take to be so bold as to be prudently expressible solely between the lines and as secret teachings communicable only to the few, were perfectly well known, even commonplace, among Thomas and his contemporaries. That Thomas felt a need to respond to these criticisms is a sufficient sign that he regarded them as non-trivial and worthy of careful consideration. Strauss and his followers can be commended for raising them again in our time when they have largely been lost sight of. But though these criticisms might work when they are directed against some thinkers, they are, I have argued, ineffectual when directed against Thomas Aquinas.

I tried to show in Part 1 that Thomas's rational theology does not rely on the claims of revelation, and that, properly understood, it does not rely on the claims of Aristotelian or any other physics either. I also argued that Thomas's case for our natural knowledge of the primary precepts of natural law does not rely on his rational theology or on any other kind of theology. For this reason, the existence and rationality of natural law can serve as the foundation for independent arguments in favor of some of the central claims of rational theology.

One can argue broadly from natural law to the existence of God by reflecting on the purposiveness of nature for our cognitive faculties, as I tried to show in Part 3. The manifest teleology of natural reason, its orientation toward ends in both its speculative and its practical employment, cannot be comprehended within the materialist and anti-teleological reductionism that characterizes contemporary natural and social science. The manifest teleology of natural reason and the correlative intelligibility of the world are best comprehended within the context of natural law exactly as Thomas defines it: *participatio legis aeternae in rationali creatura,* where *lex aeterna* is the supreme reason (*summa ratio*) existing in God, the supreme reason whereby the world is rationally created and governed. Neither speculative reason declaring what *is*, nor practical reason declaring what *ought to be*, can be understood to have been produced by chance interactions of particles, chunks, or elaborate concatenations of deaf and dumb matter. One can of course assert such a thing. It is asserted all the time these days. But one cannot even begin to render the assertion intelligible.[1] Contemporary thinkers make this unintelligible assertion only because they can do nothing else once they have foresworn and detached themselves from, not only rational theology, but the classical philosophy of Plato, Aristotle, and their medieval followers, on the one hand, and the transcendental philosophy of men like Kant, Hegel, and Husserl, on the other.

In addition to arguing broadly from natural law to the existence of God, one can also argue more narrowly, by focusing not on the nature of reason as such and the discovered intelligibility of the world in general, but on practical reason specifically. Because *ought* implies not only *can* but *might not*, reason *qua practical* testifies that we are free. From the perspective of *speculative* reason alone, we may or may not be free. Indeed, from the perspective of speculative reason alone, lack of freedom makes more sense, up to a point, than does freedom, though only because non-freedom is easier to understand than freedom, a mere thing being easier to understand than a person. But though we cannot fathom our freedom, or know beyond the shadow of a doubt that we actually possess it, practical *reason* commands us to think of ourselves as free. For that is the only way we can take the other commands of practical reason to heart.[2] Belief that we are free is then more *rational* than belief that we are not free. We think of ourselves as free, and must do so, even prior to choosing, namely, when we deliberate. For all deliberation necessarily presupposes the conviction that we have live options before us, that the future is not already determined and beyond our control, and that it can be shaped one way or another by the choices that emerge from our deliberation, whether these are properly moral choices, immoral choices, or morally neutral choices.

Practical reason is experienced as *causal*, as the unique causality of a free being. Freedom is a principle of self-determination that cannot be reduced to the

1. I have argued that materialist reductions of reason are not only unintelligible but, in fact, lead to absurdity in a lecture I presented at St. John's College, Santa Fe, in 2006, "The Privilege of Reason I—Evolution and History."

2. This is Kant's argument, not Thomas's. But I see no reason to think that Thomas would have a serious disagreement with it, except that he is more confident than Kant is (or than I am) that we can actually know, in the full sense of the word, that we possess free choice. ST 1 q. 83 art. 1, co; 1–2 q. 10, art. 2, co.

determinism of sub-rational nature, even if the latter gives way at the micro-level to some kind of indifferent indeterminism. If, *per impossibile*, we could know definitively that we were not free, that the conviction that we are free was only a deluded experience, then natural law as the law whereby practical reason imposes obligations on a free but finite being would be absurd. And so the operation of practical reason would be absurd too, contrary to how we experience its operation in deliberation—how *all* of us experience it, believers and unbelievers, saints and sinners, ordinary human beings and sophisticated intellectuals, the non-philosophic many inhabiting "the city" and the philosophic few who dwell spiritually among mountain heights and ice. We all deliberate and act on the basis of deliberation as though we possess free will, whether we use this expression or not. Anyone who disputes this claim needs to come up with an account of deliberation that makes full sense of how he regards the ontological status of the *alternatives* that he surely entertains when he deliberates.

We do not, of course, experience our will as infinite but, rather, as finite. Though freely responsible for its *choices*, our will cannot be construed as freely or in any other way responsible for its own *existence*. What is responsible for the existence of a free but finite will possessing a causality that distinguishes it from everything else in nature can only be something ultimately transcending the causality that reigns in sub-rational nature. This something has to be thought of as a cause that is not itself the effect of something else, a cause that is thereby infinitely freer than our finite free will. We must think of this ultimate cause as altogether necessary in its existence, because uncaused, and infinitely free in its acting, also because uncaused. We can consistently think of such an ultimate cause only as the free creative will of God. To resist this theological conclusion, one can deny the premise that chiefly generates it. One can deny that we possess free will. The person denying free will, however, places himself in a contradiction—not in a theoretical contradiction, to be sure, but in a practical one. He holds to a view of action that he cannot deliberate on, a view of action that he must suspend again and again, day by day, in actual deliberation.[3]

Rather than live in this practical contradiction one might decide neither to deny free will, nor vainly try to explain it away, but simply leave it as a *mysterium non explicandum* in "the riddle of being." A rational being, however, can hardly be satisfied with leaving it at this. For it is the very nature of reason to seek for a sufficient cause of whatever *is* but *need not be*. It is in seeking for the sufficient cause of the causality of our finite freedom that one is led to the central claims, and the most powerful arguments on their behalf, of scholastic metaphysics and theology.

Though our natural knowledge of the primary precepts of natural law does not presuppose rational theology, rational theology is able to integrate this knowledge into a broad account of the whole. Similarly, though rational theology does not presuppose revealed theology, revealed theology is able to answer questions that rational theology *has* to pose but can *only* pose. In particular, revealed theology can answer both how it

3. See above, Part 1, Ch. 2, Section c, i.

is that natural reason's fully natural and fully rational desire for a knowledge that surpasses its limited capacity can actually be fulfilled, and also how it is that the rational creature can rebel against his own reason so successfully as to become imprisoned in willful blindness, in a sinfulness from which he cannot extricate himself on his own, or even understand on his own, even though it is entirely of his own making.

By arguing that the natural law teaching of Thomas Aquinas is an altogether rational teaching, I do not entertain high hopes that it or any other purely rational account of moral principles will ever be as persuasive or efficacious at the public level as the moral teaching of the Bible. On the other hand, since biblical religion is on the wane in our time largely due to criticisms falsely advanced in the name of reason, it is necessary, indeed a duty, to restate the case that the moral principles of the Bible and the moral principles articulated by right reason do not contradict each other at all, but are, as I think Thomas establishes, on more than a few points essentially identical. This identity, however, has been obscured by many of Thomas's co-religionists who, in speaking of natural law as integral to Roman Catholicism, have not given appropriate emphasis to Thomas's foundational distinction between what is knowable by natural reason and what is accessible only through divine revelation. The unintended effect has been to weaken Thomas's teaching and to confirm not only Straussians, but non-believers of all stripes, and even believers who are not Roman Catholics, in the impression that Thomas has nothing of importance to say to them. The chief purpose of the present study has been to correct that impression.

If Straussians give close attention to the texts I have cited in this study, they will come to a better understanding of the subtlety, complexity, and comprehensiveness of Thomas Aquinas's thinking on the matters that matter most, or should matter most, to thoughtful human beings. If afterwards they persist in trying to refute Thomas's natural law teaching and what it points to, their attempts will take place on more solid ground than previously. They will discover that the great challenge to classical political philosophy, as they interpret it, is not modern political philosophy. It is neither hedonism nor decisionism, and it is certainly not "poor and stupid positivism." The great challenge is the natural law teaching of Thomas Aquinas, a teaching that grounds the concept of obligation in the evidence of practical reason and legitimates the use put to it both by the classical political philosophers and by Strauss himself. It grounds and legitimates this concept as it is employed naturally by every human being.

Though I have argued for the integrity and cogency of Thomas's natural law teaching, I have not tried to show that it is superior in every respect to all other accounts of the principles of human choice and action. In particular, I have not tried to show that it is superior in every respect to the moral philosophy of Kant, to which I have had occasion to make frequent reference in this study and which has not a little in common with Thomas's teaching in spite of significant differences.[4] It is a lamentable

4. Nor have I tried to show that Thomas's natural law teaching is superior in every respect to the natural law teaching of Duns Scotus, to which I have been able to make reference only in passing in

feature of the specialization characteristic of the study and teaching of philosophy at present that the adherents of the Thomist, Kantian, and Straussian schools conduct their inquiries and disputations regarding ethics primarily *intra parietes*. The concern with the ultimate principles of human deliberation, choice, and action is both too lofty and too urgent not to be considered jointly by the adherents of these three impressive schools, who, though giving divergent accounts, are nonetheless addressing common questions and should be listening carefully to each other, instead of ignoring or dismissing each other and speaking only to themselves.

this study.

Bibliography

Anastaplo, George. "On the Thomas Aquinas of Leo Strauss." http://anastaplo.wordpress.com/2012/05/02/on-the-thomas-aquinas-of-leo-strauss .

Aristotle. *"Art" of Rhetoric*. Translated by J. H. Freese, with facing Greek text. Cambridge: Harvard University Press (Loeb Classical Library), 1926.

———. *De Interpretatione*. Translated by Hugh. Tredennick, with facing Greek text. Cambridge: Harvard University Press (Loeb Classical Library), 1938.

———. *Ethica Nicomachea*. Edited by L. Bywater. Oxford: Oxford Classical Texts, 1984. [English translation by Terrence Irwin: *Nicomachean Ethics*. Indianapolis: Hackett Publishing Co., 1999.]

———. *Eudemian Ethics*. Translated by H. Rackham, with facing Greek text. Cambridge: Harvard University Press (Loeb Classical Library), 1952.

———. *Metaphysics*. Edited, in two volumes with Introduction and Commentary, by W.D. Ross. Oxford: Oxford University Press, 1924 and 1953.

———. *Physics*. Edited, with Introduction and Commentary, by W.D. Ross. Oxford: Oxford University Press, 1936.

———. *Politics*. Translated by H. Rackham, with facing Greek text. Cambridge: Harvard University Press (Loeb Classical Library), 1967.

———. *Prior Analytics* and *Posterior Analytics*. Edited, with Introduction and Commentary, by W.D. Ross. Oxford: Oxford University Press, 1949.

Armstrong, R. A. *Primary and Secondary Precepts in Thomistic Natural Law Teaching*. The Hague: Martinus Nijhoff, 1966.

Behnegar, Nasser. *Leo Strauss, Max Weber, and the Scientific Study of Politics*. Chicago: University of Chicago Press, 2003.

Benardete, Seth. *Socrates' Second Sailing: On Plato's Republic*. Chicago: University of Chicago Press, 2000.

———. "XPH and ΔEI in Plato and Others." Glotta XLIII, 3/4 (Göttingen, 1965) 285–295.

Bloom, Allan. *The Closing of the American Mind*. New York, Simon and Schuster, 1987.

Boehm, Rudolph. "Husserl's Concept of the 'Absolute.'" In Elveton, ed. *The Phenomenology of Husserl*. 180–187; 190, n. 88.

Bolotin, David. *An Approach to Aristotle's Physics: With Particular Attention to his Manner of Writing*. Albany: State University of New York, 1998.

———. "Leo Strauss and Classical Political Philosophy." In *Interpretation: A Journal of Political Philosophy*, Fall 1994 Vol. 22 No. 1, 129–42.

Brock, Stephen L. "Natural Inclination and the Intelligibility of the Good in Thomistic Natural Law." *Vera Lex*, VI.1–2 (Winter 2005) 57–78.

———. "Natural Law, the Understanding of Principles, and Universal Good." *Nova et Vetera*, English Edition, Vol. 9, No.3 (2011) 671–706.

Budziszewski, J. *Written on the Heart: The Case for Natural Law.* Downers Grove IL: InterVarsity Press, 1997.

Burns, Tony. "Aquinas's Two Doctrines of Natural Law." *Political Studies* 48, no. 5 (2000) 929–46.

Butera, Giuseppe. "The Moral Status of the First Principle of Practical Reason in Thomas's Natural Law Theory." *The Thomist*, 2007, 609–31.

Cairns, Dorion. "The Many Senses and Denotations of the Word *Bewusstsein* ('Consciousness') in Edmund Husserl's Writings." In *Life-World and Consciousness: Essays for Aron Gurwitsch*. Edited by Lester E. Embree. Evanson IL: Northwestern University Press, 1972. 29–31.

———. "Some Results of Husserl's Investigations." In *Phenomenology: The Philosophy of Edmund Husserl and Its Interpretation*. Edited by Joseph J. Kockelmans. New York: Doubleday & Co., 1967, 147–9.

Caputo, John. *Heidegger and Aquinas: An Essay on Overcoming Metaphysics.* New York: Fordham University Press, 1982.

Carey, James. "Christianity and Force: The Just War Tradition." In *Religion, Fundamentalism, and Violence*. Edited by Andrew L. Gluck, Scranton, PA: Scranton University Press, 2010, 245–84.

———. "The Pleasure of Philosophizing and Its Moral Foundation." *Interpretation: A Journal of Political Philosophy.* Fall 2013, Vol. 40, Issue 2, 253–86.

———. "Socrates' Exhortation to Follow the *Logos*." In Paul Diduch and Michael Harding, eds. *Socrates in the Cave: On the Philosopher's Motive in Plato*. Cham, Switzerland: Springer (Palgrave, MacMillan) 2018, 107–39.

———. "Vedic Tradition and the Origin of Philosophy in Ancient India." *The St. John's Review*, Volume XLIX, number 3 (2007), 5–66.

Cessario, Romanus, OP. "Why Aquinas Locates Natural Law within the *Sacra Doctrina*." In Goyette et al. eds., *St. Thomas*, 79–93.

Cohen, A., ed. *The Soncino Chumash*. London: The Soncino Press, 1976.

Copleston, Frederick, SJ. *A History of Philosophy*. Garden City: Image Books, 1985.

Coughlin, Glenn. *Aristotle's Physics, or Natural Hearing*. South Bend, Indiana: St. Augustine's Press, 2005.

Cromartie, Michael, ed. *A Preserving Grace: Protestants, Catholics, and Natural Law*. Grand Rapids, MI: William.B. Eerdmans, 1997.

Cross, Richard. *Duns Scotus on God*. Burlington VT: Ashgate, 2005.

Crowe, Michael C. *The Changing Profile of Natural Law.* The Hague: Martinus Nijhoff, 1977.

Curtler, Hugh. *Ethical Argument*. Oxford: Oxford University Press, 2004.

Dannhauser, Werner J. "Leo Strauss in His Letters." In Minkov, ed., *Enlightening Revolutions*, 355–62.

Davies, Brian, ed. *Aquinas's Summa Theologiae—Critical Essays*. Lanham, MD: Rowman and Littlefield, 2006.

Deferrari, Roy J. *A Latin-English Dictionary of St. Thomas Aquinas*. Boston: St. Paul Editions, 1960.

———. *A Lexicon of St. Thomas Aquinas*. Washington: Catholic University Press, 1948.

Deutsch, Kenneth L., and Walter Nicgorski, eds. *Leo Strauss—Political Philosopher and Jewish Thinker*. Lanham MD: Rowman and Littlefield, 1994.

Dewan, Lawrence, OP. "St. Thomas, John Finnis and the Political Good." In *Wisdom, Law, and Virtue*, New York: Fordham University Press, 2008, 279–311.

Diels, Hermann and Walther Kranz, eds. *Fragmente der Vorsokratiker*. Zürick: Weidman, 1972.

Doig, James. *Aquinas's Philosophical Commentary on the* Ethics; *A Historical Perspective*, Dordrecht: Kluwer Academic Publishers, 2001.

Donagan, Alan. "The Scholastic Theory of Moral Law in the Modern World." In Kenny, ed. *Aquinas—A Collection of Critical Essays*. 325–39.

———. *The Theory of Morality*. Chicago: University of Chicago Press, 1977.

———. "Thomas Aquinas on Human Action." In Kretzmann, Norman, Anthony Kenny, Jan Pinborg, eds. *The Cambridge History of Later Medieval Philosophy*. 642–54.

Elveton, R. O., ed. *The Phenomenology of Edmund Husserl*. Seattle: Noesis, 2000.

Fay, Thomas A. "The Development of St. Thomas's Teaching on the Distinction Between Primary and Secondary Precepts of Natural Law." *Doctor Communis* 46, 1993, 262–72.

Feldman, Richard. "The Ethics of Belief." *Philosophy and Phenomenological Research*, Vol. 60, No. 3 (May 2000) 677–95.

Fink, Eugen. "The Phenomenological Philosophy of Edmund Husserl and Contemporary Criticism." In Elveton, ed., *The Phenomenology of Edmund Husserl*, 70–139.

———. *Sixth Cartesian Meditation*. Translated by Ronald Bruzina. Bloomington: Indiana University Press, 1995.

Finnis, John. *Aquinas—Moral, Political, and Legal Theory*. Oxford: Oxford University Press, 1998.

———. *Natural Law and Natural Rights*. Oxford: Oxford University Press, 1980.

Fortin, Ernest L. "Augustine, Thomas Aquinas, and Natural Law." *Mediaevalia*, Vol. 4, 1978: 179–208.

———. "Between the Lines: Was Leo Strauss a Secret Enemy of Morality?" In *Classical Christianity and the Political Order*, 317–327.

———.*The Birth of Philosophic Christianity: Studies in Early Christianity and Medieval Thought*. Edited by J. Brian Benestad. Lanham MD: Rowman and Littlefield, 1996.

———. "Book Review of Russell Hittinger, *A Critique of the New Natural Law Theory*." In *Classical Christianity and the Political Order*, 360–2.

———. *Classical Christianity and the Political Order—Reflections on the Theological Political Problem*. Edited by J. Brian Benestad. Lanham MD; Rowman and Littlefield, 1996.

———. *Dissent and Philosophy in the Middle Ages*. Lanham MD: Lexington Books, 2002.

———. "Faith and Reason in Contemporary Perspective: Apropos of a Recent Book." (Review of *The God of Faith and Reason*, by Robert Sokolowski.) In *Classical Christianity and the Political Order*, 297–315.

———. *Human Rights, Virtue, and the Common Good—Untimely Meditations on Religion and Politics*. Lanham MD: Rowman and Littlefield, 1996.

———. "Natural Law and Social Justice," in *Classical Christianity and the Political Order*, 223–41.

———. "Rational Theologians and Irrational Philosophers: A Straussian Perspective." In *Classical Christianity and the Political Order*, 287–96.

———. "Response" to E. A. Goerner, "On the Naturalness and Lawfulness of the Natural Law: A Few Remarks on Ernest Fortin's Doubts." *The Review of Politics*, Vol. 45, No. 3 (Jul. 1983) 446–9.

———. "Thomas Aquinas." In Strauss, Leo, and Joseph Cropsey, eds., *History of Political Philosophy*. 248–75.

Gadamer, Hans-Georg. "Martin Heidegger und die Marburger Theologie." In Gadamer, *Kleine Schriften I*, Tübingen: J. C. B. Mohr 1967, 82–92. [English translation by David Linge: *Philosophical Hermeneutics*, Berkeley: Univ. of California Press, 1976, 198–212.]

George, Robert P. "Natural Law." *Harvard Journal of Law and Public Policy*, Vol. 31, No. 1, Winter 2008, 171–96.

Gildin, Hilail, ed. *Political Philosophy: Six Essays by Leo Strauss*. Indianapolis IN: Bobbs Merrill, 1975.

Gilson, Etienne. *The Unity of Philosophical Experience*. New York: Charles Scribner's Sons, 1937.

Gluck, Andrew L, ed. *Religion, Fundamentalism, and Violence*. Scranton, PA: Scranton University Press, 2010.

Goerner, E. A. "The Bad Man's View of Thomistic Natural Right." *Political Theory*, Vol. 7, No.1, Feb., 1979, 101–122.

———. "The Good Man's View of Thomistic Natural Law." *Political Theory*, Vl. 11, no.3, Aug. 1983. 393–418.

———. "On the Naturalness and Lawfulness of the Natural Law: A Few Remarks on Ernest Fortin's Doubts." *The Review of Politics*, Vol. 45, No. 3 (Jul. 1983) 443–5.

Goyette, John. "Natural Law and the Metaphysics of Creation." In Goyette et al., *St. Thomas*, 74–77.

Goyette, John, Mark S. Latkovic, and Richard S. Myers, editors. *St. Thomas Aquinas and the Natural Law Tradition—Contemporary Perspectives*. Washington, DC: Catholic University of America Press, 2004.

Grathoff, Richard, ed. *Philosophers in Exile: The Correspondence of Alfred Schutz and Aron Gurwitsch, 1939–1959*. Translated by J. Claude Evans. Indianapolis: Indiana University Press, 1989.

Green, Kenneth Hart, ed. *Jewish Philosophy and the Crisis of Modernity*. Albany: State University of New York Press, 1997.

Grisez, Germain. "The First Principle of Practical Reason: A Commentary on the *Summa Theologiae*, 1–2, Question 94, article 2." *Natural Law Forum*, Vol. 10, 1965, 168–201.

Guerra, Mark. *Christians as Political Animals*. Wilmington, DE: ISI Books, 2010.

Gurwitsch, Aron. "A Non-egological Conception of Consciousness." In *Studies in Phenomenology and Psychology*. Evanson IL: Northwestern University Press, 1966, 287–300.

Hegel, Georg W. F. *Phänomenologie des Geistes*. Hamburg: Felix Meiner, 1952.

Heidegger, Martin. "Brief über den Humanismus." In *Wegmarken*, 145–94. [English translation: "Letter on 'Humanism'" by Frank A. Capuzzi. In *Pathmarks*. 239–76.]

———. *Einführung in die Metaphysik* 3rd edition. Tübingen: Max Niemeyer Verlag, 1966 (from a lecture originally given in 1935). [English translation by Ralph Mannheim: *Introduction to Metaphysics*. New Haven: Yale University Press, 1959.]

———. "Einleitung zu 'Was ist Metaphysik.'" In *Wegmarken*, 195–211. [English translation by Walter Kaufmann: "Introduction to 'What is Metaphysics." In *Pathmarks*, 277–90.]

———. *The Fundamental Concepts of Metaphysics*. Translated by William McNeill and Nicholaus Walker. Bloomington IN: Indiana University Press, 1995.

———. *Holzwege*. Frankfurt: Vittorio Klostermann, 4th edition, 1963. [English translation by Julian Young and Kenneth Haynes: *Off the Beaten Path*. Cambridge: Cambridge University Press, 2002.]

———. *Identity and Difference*. German text with English Translation by Joan Stambaugh. New York: Harper and Rowe, 1969.

———. *Metaphysical Foundations of Logic*. Translated by Michael Heim. Bloomington IN: Indiana University Press, 1984.

———. *Nietzsche* (2 vols.). Stuttgart: Günther Neske, 1961. [English translation by David Farrell Krell. San Francisco: Harper, 1991.]

———. "Nietzsches Wort, 'Gott ist tot.'" In *Holzwege*, 193–247. [English translation: "Nietzsche's Word "God is Dead." In *Off the Beaten Path*, 157–199.]

———. "Platons Lehre von Wahrheit." In *Wegmarken*, 155–182. [English translation by Thomas Sheehan: "Plato's Doctrine of Truth." In *Pathmarks*, 109–144.]

———. *Plato's Sophist*. Translated by Richard Rojcewicz and André Schuwer. Bloomington: Indiana University Press, 1997

———. *Sein und Zeit*. Tübingen: Max Niemeyer, 1967. [English translation by John Macquarrie and Edward Robinson: *Being and Time*. New York, Harper and Row: 1962.]

———. "Vom Wesen des Grundes." In *Wegmarken*, 21–71. [English translation by William McNeill: "On the Essence of Ground." In *Pathmarks*, 97–135.]

———. "Vom Wesen und Begriff der *Physis*: Aristoteles' Physik B, 1. In *Wegmarken*, 309–71. [English translation by Thomas Sheehan: "On the Essence and Concept of *Physis* in Aristotle's *Physics* B, 1." In *Pathmarks*, 183–230.]

———. "Was ist Metaphysik?" In *Wegmarken*, 1–19 [English translation by David Farrell Krell: "What is Metaphysics?" In *Pathmarks*, 82–96.]

———. *Wegmarken*. Frankfurt am Main: Vittorio Klostermann, 1967. [English translation: *Pathmarks*. Edited by William McNeill. Cambridge: Cambridge University Press, 1998.]

Henrich, Dieter. "The Concept of Moral Insight and Kant's Doctrine of the Fact of Reason." Translated by Manfred Kuehn. In D. Henrich. *The Unity of Reason—Essays on Kant's Philosophy*. Edited by Richard Velkley, Cambridge MA: Harvard University Press, 1994, 55–87.

Hittinger, Russell. *A Critique of the New Natural Law Theory*. Notre Dame IN: University of Notre Dame Press, 1987.

———. "Natural Law and Catholic Moral Theology." In Cromartie, ed. *A Preserving Grace: Protestants, Catholics, and Natural Law*. 1–30.

Hobbes, Thomas. *Leviathan*. Edited by Edwin Curley. Indianapolis IN: Hackett Publishing Company, Inc., 1994.

Hume, David. *A Treatise of Human Nature*. Oxford at the Clarendon Press, 1965,

Husserl, Edmund. *Cartesianische Meditationen*. Edited by Elisabeth Ströker. In *Edmund Husserl—Gesammelte Schriften*, Band 8, Felix Meiner Verlag, 1992. [English translation by Dorion Cairns: *Cartesian Meditations*. The Hague: Martinus Nijhoff, 1969.]

———. *Formale und Transzendentale Logik*. Edited by Paul Jannsen. Haag: Martinus Nijhoff, Husserliana, Band XVII, 1974. [English translation by Dorion Cairns: *Formal and Transcendental Logic*. Hague: Martinus Nijhoff, 1969.]

———. *Ideen zu einer Reinen Phänomenologie und Phänomenologischen Philosophie*, Erstes Buch. Edited by Karl Schumann. The Hague: Martinus Nijhoff, 1976. [English translation by F. Kersten: *Ideas pertaining to a Pure Phenomenology and to Phenomenological Philosophy*, First Book. Dordrecht: Kluwer, 1998.]

———. *Die Krisis der Europäischen Wissenschaften und die Tranzendentale Phänomenologie.* In *Edmund Husserl: Gesammelte Schriften,* Band 8, Felix Meiner Verlag, 1992. Text according to Husserliana, Band VI, Hague: Martinus Nijhoff, 1976. [English translation by David Carr: *The Crisis of European Sciences and Transcendental Phenomenology.* Evanston: Northwestern University Press, 1970.]

———. *Logische Untersuchungen* (3 vols.). Tübingen: Max Niemeyer Verlag, 6th edition, 1980. [English translation by J. N. Findlay: *Logical Investigations.* New York: Humanities Press, 1979.]

Jaffa, Harry. *Equality and Liberty.* New York: Oxford University Press, 1965.

———. *A New Birth of Freedom—Abraham Lincoln and the Coming of the Civil War.* Lanham MD: Rowman & Littlefield, 2000. First paperback edition, 2004.

———. "Leo Strauss, the Bible, and Political Philosophy." In Deutsch and Nicgorski, eds., *Leo Strauss—Political Philosopher and Jewish Thinker.*

———. *Thomism and Aristotelianism: A Study of the Commentary by Thomas Aquinas on the Nicomachean Ethics.* Chicago: University of Chicago Press, 1952.

Jenkins, John, CSC. "Expositions of the Text: Aquinas's Aristotelian Commentaries." *Medieval Theology and Philosophy* 5 (1996) 39–62.

Jonas, Hans. *The Gnostic Religion.* Boston: Beacon Press, 1963.

———. *Memoirs.* Waltham MA: Brandeis University Press, 2008.

———. *The Phenomenon of Life.* New York: Harper and Rowe, 1966.

Jordan, Mark. "Thomas Aquinas' Disclaimers in the Aristotelian Commentaries." *Philosophy and the God of Abraham—Essays in Memory of James A. Weisheipl, OP.* Toronto: Pontifical Institute of Medieval Studies, 1991, 99–112.

Kant, Immanuel. *Grundlegung zur Metaphysik der Sitten.* Edited by Wilhelm Weischedel. In Band 6 of Kant, *Werke.* [English translation by James Ellington. *Grounding for the Metaphysics of Morals.* Indianapolis IN: Hackett, 1993.]

———. *Kritik der Praktischen Vernunft.* Edited by Wilhelm Weischedel. In Band 7 of Kant, *Werke.* [English translation by English translation by Mary Gregor: *Critique of Practical Reason.* Cambridge: Cambridge University Press, 1997.]

———. *Kritik der Reinen Vernunft.* Edited by Wilhelm Weischedel. In Band 3 and Band 4 of Kant, *Werke.* [English Translation by Norman Kemp Smith: *Critique of Pure Reason.* London: Macmillan, 1964.]

———. *Kritik der Urteilskraft.* Edited by Wilhelm Weischedel. In Band 8 of Kant, *Werke.* [English translation by J. H Bernard: *Critique of Judgment.* New York: Haffner, 1951.]

———. *Lectures on Ethics* Translated by Peter Heath, Cambridge: Cambridge University Press, 1997.

———. *Die Metaphysik der Sitten.* Edited by Wilhelm Weischedel. In Band 6 of Kant, *Werke.* [English translation by Mary Gregor: *The Metaphysics of Morals.* Cambridge: Cambridge University Press, 1996.]

———. *Opus Postumum.* Edited by Erich Adikes. Berlin: Reuther & Reichard, 1920. [English translation by Eckart Förster and Michael Rosen: *Opus Postumum.* Cambridge: Cambridge University Press, 1993.]

———. *Die Religion Innerhalb der Grenzen der Blossen Vernunft.* In Band 7 of Kant, *Werke.* [English translation George Di Giovanni: *Religion within the Boundaries of Mere Reason.* Cambridge: Cambridge University Press, 1996.]

———. *Werke in Zehn Bänden.* Edited by Wilhelm Weischedel. Darmstadt: *Wissenschaftliche Buchgesellschaft,* 1981.

Kennington, Richard. *On Modern Origins*. Edited by Pamela Kraus and Frank Hunt. Lexington Books: Lanham MD, 2004.

———. "Strauss's *Natural Right and History*." *Review of Metaphysics* 35, September 1981, 57–86.

Kenny, Anthony, ed. *Aquinas, A Collection of Critical Essays*. South Bend, IN: University of Notre Dame, 1976.

Kerr, Fergus G., OP. "Natural Law: Incommensurable Readings." In Davies, ed. *Aquinas's Summma*. 245–263.

Keys, Mary. *Aquinas, Aristotle, and the Promise of the Common Good*. Cambridge: Cambridge University Press, 2006.

Klein, Jacob. *Greek Mathematical Thought and the Origin of Algebra*. Translated by Eva Brann, New York: Dover, 1992.

———. *Lectures and Essays*. Annapolis MD: St. John's College Press, 1985.

Kojève, Alexandre. *Introduction à la Lecture de Hegel*, Paris: Gallimard, 1947. [English translation by James H. Nichols, Jr.: *Introduction to the Reading of Hegel*. Edited by Allan Bloom, New York: Basic Books, 1969.]

Kossel, Clifford. J, SJ. "Natural Law and Human Law [Ia IIae, qq. 90–97]." In *The Ethics of Aquinas*, edited by Stephen J. Pope, Washington: Georgetown University Press, 2002, 169–193.

Kries, Douglas. "On Leo Strauss's Understanding of the Natural Law Theory of Thomas Aquinas." In *The Thomist: A Speculative Quarterly Review*. Vol. 57, Number 2, April 1993, 215–232.

———. *The Problem of Natural Law*, Lanham MD: Lexington Books, 2007.

Kuhn, Helmut. "Naturrecht und Historismus." In *The Independent Journal of Philosophy*, Volume II, 1968. 13–21.

Lehrberger, James, O Cist. "Crime without Punishment: Thomistic Natural Law and the Problem of Sanctions." In *Law and Philosophy: the Practice of a Theory: Essays in Honor of George Anastaplo*. Edited by John A. Murley, Robert L. Stone, and William T. Braithwaite. Ohio University Press 1992, 237–57.

Lewis, Charlton and Short, Charles. *A Latin Dictionary*, Oxford: Clarendon, 1975.

Lonergan, Bernard, SJ. *Collection*. New York: Herder and Herder, 1967.

Long, Steven. "Natural Law or Autonomous Practical Reason: Problems for the New Natural Law Theory." In Goyette et al., *St. Thomas*, 165–93.

Louden, Robert R. "On Some Vices of Virtue Ethics." *American Philosophical Quarterly*, 21 (1984) 227–36.

Löwith, Karl. "Heidegger: Problem, and Background of Existentialism." In *Nature, History, and Existentialism*. Translated by Arnold Levinson, Evanston IL: Northwestern University Press, 1966.

Macpherson, C. B. *The Political Theory of Possessive Individualism*. Oxford: Oxford University Press, 1962.

Maimonides, Moses. *The Guide of the Perplexed*. Translated by Shlomo Pines, with an Introductory Essay by Leo Strauss. Chicago: University of Chicago Press, 1963.

McGrade, Arthur S., John Kilcullen, and Michael Kempshall, editors. *Cambridge Translations of Medieval Philosophical Texts*, Vol. 2: *Ethics and Political Philosophy*. New York: Cambridge University Press, 2001.

May, William. "Contemporary Perspectives on Thomistic Natural Law." In Goyette et al., *St. Thomas*, 113–56.

Meier, Heinrich. *Leo Strauss and the Theological-Political Problem*, New York: Cambridge, 2006.

Melzer, Arthur. *Philosophy Between the Lines: The Lost History of Esoteric Writing*. Chicago: University of Chicago Press, 2014.

Merrill, Clark. "Leo Strauss's Indictment of Christian Philosophy." *The Review of Politics*, Vol. 62. No. 1 Winter, 2000, 77–105.

Mill, John Stuart. *On Liberty and Utilitarianism*. Edited by Roger Crisp. Oxford: Oxford University Press, 1998.

Minkov, Svetozar, ed. *Enlightening Revolutions: Essays in Honor of Ralph Lerner*. Lanham MD: Lexington Books, 2006.

Möhle, Hannes. "Scotus's Theory of Natural Law." In *The Cambridge Companion to Duns Scotus*. Edited by Thomas Williams, Cambridge: Cambridge University Press, 2003, 312–329.

Mollin, Alfred and Robert Williamson. *An Introduction to Ancient Greek*, Third Edition. Lanham MD: University Press of America, 1997.

Muller, Earl, SJ. "The Christological Foundation of Natural Law." In Goyette et al., *St. Thomas*. 102–109.

Nelson, Daniel Mark. *The Priority of Prudence*, University Park, PA: Pennsylvania State University Press, 1992.

Newton, Isaac. *The Principia* (*Mathematical Principles of Natural Philosophy*). Translated by I. Bernard Cohen and Anne Whitman. Berkeley, CA: University of California Press., 1999.

Nietzsche, Friedrich. *Also Sprach Zarathustra*, *Sämtliche Werke*, Band 4. [English translation by Walter Kaufmann: *Thus Spake Zarathustra*. New York: The Modern Library, 1995.]

———. *Götzen-Dämmerung*. *Sämtliche Werke*, Band 6. [English translation by Judith Norman: *Twilight of the Idols*. Cambridge: Cambridge University Press, 2005.]

———. *Jenseits von Gut und Böse*. *Sämtliche Werke*, Band 5. [English translation by Judith Norman: *Beyond Good and Evil*. Cambridge: Cambridge University Press, 2002.]

———. *Sämtliche Werke*, Kritische Studienausgabe in 15 Volumes. Edited by Giorgio Colli and Mazzino Montinari. Munich: Deutscher Taschenbuch Verlag, 1988.

O'Connor, D. J. *Aquinas and Natural Law*. New York: St. Martin's Press, 1968.

Orrego, Cristóbal. "Natural Law under Other Names: de Nominibus non est Disputandum." *The American Journal of Jurisprudence* 2007, 77–92.

O'Reilly, Hugh. "The Superb Memory of Thomas Aquinas." https://www.traditioninaction.org/religious/h086rpMemory.html .

Osborne, Thomas M., Jr. *Love of Self and Love of God in Thirteenth Century Ethics*. Notre Dame: University of Notre Dame Press, 2005.

Owens, Joseph. *St. Thomas Aquinas on the Existence of God*. New York: State University of New York, 1980.

Panofsky, Erwin. *Gothic Architecture and Scholasticism*. Cleveland OH: The World Publishing Company, 1957.

Pangle, Thomas. *Leo Strauss: Studies in Platonic Political Philosophy*. Edited by Thomas Pangle. Chicago: University of Chicago Press, 1983.

———. "The Moral Basis of National Security: Four Historical Perspectives." In *Historical Dimensions of National Security Problems*. Edited by Klaus Knorr, Lawrence KS: University Press of Kansas, 1976, 307–73.

———. *The Rebirth of Classical Political Rationalism—An Introduction to the Thought of Leo Strauss*. Edited by Thomas Pangle. Chicago, The University of Chicago Press, 1989.

Pangle, Thomas and Ahrensdorf, Peter. *Justice Among Nations*. Lawrence KS: University of Kansas Press, 1999.

Pinckaers, Servais, OP. *The Sources of Christian Ethics*. Translated by Sr. Mary Thomas Noble, OP. Washington DC: Catholic University of America Press, 1995.

Plato. *Gorgias*. Edited by E. R. Dodds. Oxford: Oxford University Press, 1959.

———. *Opera*, in 5 vols. Edited by John Burnet. Oxford: Oxford Classical Texts, 1901–1907.

———. *Republic*. Edited by James Adam. New York: Cambridge University Press, 1963. [English Translation with an Interpretive Essay by Allan Bloom: *The Republic of Plato*. New York: Basic Books, 1968.]

Porter, Jean. *Moral Action and Christian Ethics*. New York: Cambridge University Press, 1995.

———. *Nature as Reason—A Thomistic Theory of the Natural Law*. Grand Rapids MI: William B. Eerdmans, 2005.

———. *The Recovery of Virtue—The Relevance of Aquinas for Christian Ethics*. Louisville KY: Westminster/John Knox Press, 1990.

Reid, James D. "Ethical Criticism in Heidegger's Early Freiburg Lectures." *The Review of Metaphysics* 59 (1) September 2005, 33–71.

Rosen, Stanley. *Plato's Republic: A Study*. New Haven: Yale University Press, 2005.

Russell, Bertrand. "A Free Man's Worship." In *Mysticism and Logic and Other Essays*. London: Goerge Allen and Unwin, 1917. https://en.wikisource.org/wiki/Mysticism_and_Logic_and_Other_Essays/Chapter_03 .

Ryan, Eugene. "Pure Form in Aristotle." *Phronesis*, Vol. CVIII, No. 3, 1973, 209–24.

Scotus, John Duns. *Opus Oxioniense* II, dist. 42, qq. 1–4. In *Duns Scotus on the Will and Morality*. Selected and translated by Allan Wolter, OFM. Washington DC: Catholic University of America Press, 1987.

———. *De Primo Principio*. Translated, with facing Latin text, by Alan Wolter, OFM, as *A Treatise on God as First Principle*. Chicago: Franciscan Herald Press, 1966.

Schall, James, SJ. "A Latitude for Statesmanship? Strauss on St. Thomas." *The Review of Politics*, Winter 1991, Vol 53, No.1, 126–145.

———. *At the Limits of Political Philosophy*. Washington DC: The Catholic University of America Press, 1996.

Schmitt, Carl. *Der Begriff des Politischen—Text von 1932 mit einem Vorwort und drei Corollarien*. Berlin: Dunker & Humbolt, 1963. [English Translation by George Schwab: *The Concept of the Political*. New Brunswick NJ: Rutgers University Press, 1976.]

Schrems, John J. "A Reexamination of Harry V. Jaffa's *Thomism and Aristotelianism*." *The Political Science Reviewer*, Vol. XVIII,Fall 1968: 163–93.

Schrock, Thomas. "Resistance to Punishment: Controversies Old and New." In Minkov, ed., *Enlightening Revolutions*, 91–126.

Schutz, Alfred. "On Multiple Realities." In Schutz, *Collected Papers* I. Edited by Maurice Natanson. The Hague: Martinus Nijhoff, 1962, 208–259.

Searle, John. "How to Derive 'Ought' from 'Is.'" *The Philosophical Review*, vol. 73, No. 1, Jan., 1964, 43–58.

Simon, Yves. *The Tradition of Natural Law*. New York: Fordham University Press, 1967

Simson, Otto von. *The Gothic Cathedral*, New York: Harper & Row, 1964.

Smith, Janet E. "Character as an Enabler of Moral Judgment." In Goyette et al., *St. Thomas*, 17–23.

Smith, Thomas. "The Order of Presentation and the Order of Understanding in Aquinas's Account of Law." *The Review of Politics*, Vol. 57, No. 4, Autumn 1995, 607–640.

Sokolowski, Robert. *The Formation of Husserl's Concept of Constitution*. The Hague: Martinus Nijhoff, 1970.

———. *The God of Faith and Reason*. Notre Dame: University of Notre Dame Press, 1982.

Spinoza, Baruch. *Ethica in Geometrische Ordnung Dargestellt* (*Ethica Ordine Geometrico Demonstrata*). Latin text with German translation by Wolfgang Bartuschat. Hamburg, Felix Meiner, 1999. [English translation by Edwin Curley: *Ethics*, in *The Collected Works of Spinoza*, Vol. 1, 401–617. Princeton NJ: Princeton University Press, 1985.]

Stauffer, Devin. *Plato's Introduction to the Question of Justice*. Albany: State University of New York Press, 2001.

Strauss, Leo. *The City and Man*. Chicago: Rand McNally, 1964.

———. "Comments on *The Concept of the Political* by Carl Schmitt." In *Spinoza's Critique of Religion*, 331–351.

———. Correspondence with Hans-Georg Gadamer concerning *Wahrheit und Methode*. In *The Independent Journal of Philosophy*, Volume 2, 1968. 5–12.

———. "The Crisis of Our Time." In *The Predicament of Modern Politics*. Edited by Harold J. Spaeth. Detroit: University of Detroit Press, 1964. 41–54.

———. "An Epilogue." In Gilden, Hilail. ed. *Political Philosophy—Six Essays*. Indianapolis: Bobbs-Merrill, 1975. 99–129.

———. "Existentialism." In "Two Lectures."

———. *Faith and Political Philosophy—The Correspondence between Leo Strauss and Eric Voegelin*. Columbia: University of Missouri Press, 2004.

———. "German Nihilism." Edited by David Janssens and Daniel Tanguay. In *Interpretation: A Journal of Political Philosophy*. Spring 1999, vol. 26, No. 3. 353–378.

———. *Gesammelte Schriften*, Vols, 1, 2, and 3. Edited by Heinrich and Wiebke Meier. Stuttgart: J. B. Metzler, 1996– .

———. "How to Begin to Study Medieval Philosophy." In Pangle, ed. *The Rebirth of Classical Political Rationalism*, 207–26.

———. "An Introduction to Heideggerian Existentialism." In Pangle, ed., *The Rebirth of Classical Political Rationalism*, 27–46.

———. "Introductory Essay" for Herman Cohen's *Religion of Reason out of the Sources of Judaism*. New York: Frederick Ungar, 1972, xxiii—xxxviii.

———. "Jerusalem and Athens." In Pangle, ed. *Studies in Platonic Political Philosophy*, 147–73.

———. "Kurt Riezler," in *What is Political Philosophy? And Other Studies*. 233–260.

———. "The Law of Reason in the Kuzari" in Strauss, *Persecution and the Art of Writing*, 22–37.

———. Letter to Helmut Kuhn. *The Independent Journal of Philosophy*, Volume II, 1968, 23–26.

———. *Liberalism, Ancient and Modern*. New York: Basic Books: 1968.

———. "Marsilius of Padua," In Strauss and Cropsey, eds., *History of Political Philosophy*, 276–95.

———. "Natural Right (1946)." In Colen and Minkov, eds., *Toward Natural Right and History*, 221–252.

———. *Natural Right and History*. Chicago: University of Chicago Press, 1953.

———. "On the Euthyphron." In Pangle, ed. *The Rebirth of Classical Political Rationalism*, 187–206.

———. "On a Forgotten Kind of Writing." In *What is Political Philosophy? And Other Studies*, 221–33.

———. "On Natural Law." In Pangle, ed. *Studies in Platonic Political Philosophy*, 137–46. Originally published in *International Encyclopedia of the Social Sciences*, Vol. 2. Edited by David L. Sills. Macmillan: 1968. 80–90.

———. *On Tyranny*. Chicago: University of Chicago Press, Third edition, 2000.

———. *Persecution and the Art of Writing*. Glencoe, Ill: The Free Press, 1952.

———. *Philosophy and Law*. Translated by Eve Adler. Albany: State University of New York Press: 1995.

———. "Philosophy as Rigorous Science and Political Philosophy," in Pangle, ed., *Studies in Platonic Political Philosophy*, 29–37.

———. "Plato." In Strauss, Leo and Cropsey, J. *History of Political Philosophy*. 33–89.

———. *Plato's Symposium*. Chicago: University of Chicago Press, 2001.

———. "Political Philosophy and History." In *What is Political Philosophy? and Other Studies*, 56–77.

———. *The Political Philosophy of Hobbes*. Translated by Elsa M. Sinclair. Chicago: University of Chicago Press, 1952.

———. "Preface." Added to the 1968 translation of Strauss, *Spinoza's Critique of Religion*.

———. "Preface" to Isaac Husik, *Philosophical Essays*. In Green, ed., *Jewish Philosophy and the Crisis of Modernity*, 235–66.

———. "The Problem of Socrates" (1958). In Pangle, ed., *The Rebirth of Classical Political Rationalism*, 103–83.

———. "The Problem of Socrates" (1970). In Strauss, "Two Lectures."

———. "Progress or Return?" In Green ed., *Jewish Philosophy and the Crisis of Modernity*, 87–136.

———. "Reason and Revelation." Included as an appendix to Meier, Heinrich, *Leo Strauss and the Theological-Political Problem*, 141–80.

———. "Relativism." In Pangle, ed., *The Rebirth of Classical Political Rationalism*, 13–26.

———. "Review of Anton Pegis, ed., *The Basic Writings of Thomas Aquinas*." In *What is Political Philosophy? and Other Studies*, 284–6.

———. "Review of C. B. Macpherson, *The Political Theory of Possessive Individualism*." In Pangle, ed., *Studies in Platonic Political Philosophy*, 229–231.

———. "Review of John Dewey's *German Philosophy and Politics*." In *What is Political Philosophy? And Other Studies*, 279–81.

———. *Spinoza's Critique of Religion*. Translated by E. M. Sinclair, New York: Schocken Books, 1965. [Originally published in German as *Die Religionskritik Spinozas als Grundlage seiner Bibelswissenschaft*. Berlin: Akademie-Verlag. 1930.]

———. *Thoughts on Machiavelli*. Chicago: University of Chicago Press, 1958.

———. "Thucydides: The Meaning of Political History." In Pangle, ed., *The Rebirth of Classical Political Rationalism*, 72–103.

———. *Toward Natural Right and History: Lectures and Essays by Leo Strauss, 1937–1946*. Edited by J. A. Colen and Svetozar Minkov. Chicago: University of Chicago Press, 2018.

———. "Two Lectures." Edited by David Bolotin, Christopher Bruell, and Thomas Pangle. *Interpretation: A Journal of Political Philosophy*, Spring 1995 Vol. 22 No. 3, 301–38.

———. "An Unspoken Prologue to a Public Lecture at St. John's College in Honor of Jacob Klein." In Green, ed., *Jewish Philosophy and the Crisis of Modernity*, 449–52.

———. "What is Liberal Education?" In *Liberalism, Ancient and Modern*, New York: Basic Books: 1968, 3–8.

———. "What is Political Philosophy?" In *What is Political Philosophy? And Other Studies*, 9–55.

———. *What is Political Philosophy? And Other Studies.* Chicago: University of Chicago Press, 1959.

———. "Why We Remain Jews." In *Jewish Philosophy and the Crisis of Modernity*. In Green, ed., *Jewish Philosophy and the Crisis of Modernity*, 457–66.

Strauss, Leo, and Joseph Cropsey, eds. *History of Political Philosophy*, Third Edition. Chicago: University of Chicago Press, 1987.

Strauss, Leo, and Jacob Klein. "A Giving of Accounts." In Green, ed., *Jewish Philosophy and the Crisis of Modernity*, 457–66.

Thomas Aquinas. *The Basic Writings of Thomas Aquinas*, Volumes I and II. Edited by Anton Pegis. New York: Random House, 1945.

———. *Catena Aurea in Quatuor Evangelia, Expositio in Lucam*. In *Corpus Thomisticum*.

———. *Commentary on the* De Anima. Translated by Kenelm Foster and Sylvester Humphries. New Haven: Yale University Press, 1959.

———. Commentary on the *De Trinitate* of Boethius q. 2 art. 4, co. http://www.logicmuseum.com/authors/aquinas/superboethiumq2.htm .

———. *Commentary on the* Nicomachean Ethics. Translated by C. I. Litzinger. Notre Dame, IN: Dumb Ox Books, 1967.

———. *Compendium Theologiae*. In *Corpus Thomisticum*.

———. *Contra Impugnantes Dei Cultum et Religionem*. In *Corpus Thomisticum*.

———. *Corpus Thomisticum*. Enrique Alarcón. General Editor. http://www.corpusthomisticum.com .

———. *De Ente et Essentia* (*Le "De Ente et Essentia" de S. Thomas D'Aquin*). Edited by M-D Roland-Gosselin, OP. Paris: Librairie Philosophique J. Vrin, 1948. [English translation: *On Being and Essence*, by Armand Maurer, CSB. Toronto: Pontifical Institute of Medieval Studies, 1968.]

———. *De Malo*. In *Quaestiones Disputatae*.

———. *De Potentia Dei*. In *Quaestiones Disputatae*.

———. "De Unitate Intellectus Contra Averroistas." *Opuscula Philosophica et Theologica*, Vol. 1. Edited by Michael de Maria, Rome: Desclée et Socii Editores, 1913. [English translation: *Saint Thomas Aquinas—On the Unity of the Intellect Against the Averroists*. Translated by Beatrice H. Zedler, Milwaukee, WI: Marquette University Press, 1968.]

———. *De Regno*. In *Corpus Thomisiticum*.

———. *De Veritate*. In *Quaestiones Disputatae*.

———. *De Virtutibus*. In *Quaestiones Disputatae*.

———. *Expositio Libri Posteriorum Analyticorum*. In *Corpus Thomisticum*.

———. *Expositio Peryermeneias*. In *Corpus Thomisticum*.

———. *In Duodecim Libros Metaphysicorum Aristotelis Expositio*. Edited by M. R. Cathala. Rome: Marietti, 1950.

———. *In Octo Libros de Physico Auditu sive Physicorum Aristotelis Commentaria*. Naples: M. D'Auria Pontificus, 1953.

———. *Quaestiones Disputatae* (2 vols.). Rome: Marietti, 1949.

———. *Quaestiones de Quolibet*. In *Corpus Thomisticum*.

———. *Sententia Libri Ethicorum*. In *Corpus Thomisticum*.

———. *Scriptum Super Sententiis*. In *Corpus Thomisticum*.

———. *Summa Theologica* (5 vols.). Translated by the English Dominican Fathers. New York: Benzinger Bros., 1948.

———. *Summa Theologiae, Prima Pars*. Biblioteca de Autores Cristianos, Fourth edition. Madrid, 1978. *Summa Theologiae, Prima Secundae* and *Secunda Secundae*, Third edition. Madrid, 1962.

———. *Summa Contra Gentiles*. Rome: Desclée–Herder, 1934.

———. *Super Epistolam B. Pauli ad Ephesios Lectura*. In *Corpus Thomisticum*.

———. *Super Librum De Causis*. In *Corpus Thomisticum*.

Velkley, Richard. *Heidegger, Strauss, and the Premises of Philosophy—On Original Forgetting*. Chicago: University of Chicago Press, 2011.

———. "On the Roots of Rationalism: Strauss's *Natural Right and History* as Response to Heidegger." *The Review of Politics* 70 (2008) 245–59.

West, Thomas. *Thomas Aquinas on Natural Law: A Critique of the "Straussian" Critique*. (A revised and expanded version of a paper presented at the American Political Science Association annual meeting, Philadelphia, August 31, 2006.) http://citation.allacademic.com//meta/p_mla_apa_research_citation/1/5/3/4/4/pages153448/p153448-30.php .

White, Kevin. "Aquinas on Oral Teaching." *The Thomist* 71, 2007, 505–528.

Wilhelmsen, Frederick D. *Christianity and Political Philosophy*. Athens, GA: The University of Georgia Press, 1978.

Wippel, John. "The Condemnations of 1270 and 1277 at Paris." *The Journal of Medieval and Renaissance Studies*, 7 (1977) 2, pp. 169–201.

———. *Metaphysical Themes in Thomas Aquinas*. Washington DC: Catholic University of America Press, 1984.

———. *Metaphysical Themes in Thomas Aquinas II*. Washington DC: Catholic University of *America Press, 2007*.

———. *The Metaphysical Thought of Thomas Aquinas*. Washington DC: Catholic University of America Press, 2000.

Wolter, Alan, OFM, ed. *Duns Scotus on the Will and Morality*. Latin Texts and Translations by Alan Wolter, OFM. Washington DC: The Catholic University of America Press, 1986.

Zuckert, Catherine. "Leo Strauss: Jewish, Yes, but Heideggerian?" In *Heidegger's Jewish Followers*. Edited by Samuel Fleischacker. Pittsburgh, PA: Duquesne University Press, 2008, 83–105.

Zuckert, Michael. "The Fullness of Being: Thomas Aquinas and the Modern Critique of Natural Law." *The Review of Politics* 69 (2007) 28–47.

Zuckert, Catherine and Zuckert, Michael. *Leo Strauss and the Problem of Political Philosophy*. Chicago: University of Chicago Press, 2014.

Index

Anastaplo, George, 9.
Albertus Magnus, 131 n. 18, 220.
Al Farabi, 133 , 145 n. 55.
Aristotle, 2, 9, 11 n. 2, 17, 21–22, 24 n. 51, 25 n. 53, 26–27, 28 n. 65, 30–31, 33, 34 n.85,.n. 88, 37 n. 94, 39, 40 n. 10, 41–42, 53 n. 42, 54 n. 45, 56 n. 50, 59, 66 n. 84, 73, 79 n. 102, 83 n. 4, 90 n. 30, 107 n. 83, 114, 115 n. 118, 119 n. 138, 121, 123, 127 n. 6, 128 n. 7, 133, 135 n. 28, 139–41, 145 n. 55, n. 57, 148, 151–61, 166–8, 171, 177, 180, 182–7, 190–3, 202 n. 42, 204–5, 208–11, 214, 220–5, 228, 231 n. 90, 234–6, 246–7, 249 n. 26, 253, 262 n. 4, 263–4, 269, 272, 277–80, 282 n. 58, 285–6, 289, 295, 297, 299, 301, 305, 315 n. 100, 316, 327 n. 143, 328 n. 146, 329 n. 148, 330–2, 334–5, 337 n. 24, 338 n. 26, 340, 342 n. 37, 344, 345 n. 43, 345 n. 61, n. 64, 350, 351 n. 70, 353–5, 357 n. 8, 360, 362.
Ahrensdorf, Peter, 150 n. 76, 203 n. 45.
Armstrong, R. A., 29 n. 68, 31 n. 72, 44–45, 46 n. 25, 50–51, 55 n. 48, 100 n. 65.
Aron, Raymond, 210.
Augustine of Hippo, 130.
Avicenna, 18, 81, 133, 296.
Basil of Caesarea, 63 n. 68, 204 n.1.
Behnegar, Nasser, 331.
Benardete, Seth, 215–19, 340.
Bloom, Allan, 83 n. 4, 127 n. 6, 214 n. 38, 218.
Boehme, Rudolph, 307.
Boethius, 99.
Bolotin, David, 185 n. 19, 214 n. 40, 254 n. 41, 262 n. 5.
Bonaventure, 131 n. 18.
Brock, Stephen, 43 n. 16, 93 n. 2.
Brown, Patterson, 17 n. 23.
Budziszewski, J., 104 n. 75.
Burns, Tony, 178 n. 39.
Butera, Giuseppi, 30 n. 71, 64 n. 79, 66 n. 83.
Cairns, Dorion, 307 n. 76, 335 n. 22.
Caputo, John, 310 n. 89, 312–21, 322 n. 128.
Carey, James, 24 n. 51, 25 n. 53, 48 n. 32, 171 n. 15, 224 n. 75, 284 n. 5.
Cicero, 267 n. 15.
Cohen, A., 202 n. 42.
Cohen, Herman, 268 n. 17.
Copleston, Frederick, 160–2.
Coughlin, Glenn, 330 n. 3.
Cross, Richard, 261 n. 36.
Crowe, Michael, 32, n 79.
Curtler, Hugh, 98 n. 61.
Dannhauser, Werner, 270 n. 27.
Deferrari, Roy, 13 n. 12, 59 n. 58, 198 n. 16.
Descartes, R., 303.
Dewan, Lawrence, 93 n. 41.
Diels, Hermann, 25 n. 53.
Doig, James, 220 n. 62.
Donagan, Alan, 25 n. 52, 97 n. 59, 98, 105.
Duns Scotus, John, 14 n. 12, 53 n. 42, 131 n. 18, 201–3, 215 n. 40, 309, 340, 364 n. 4.
Fay, Thomas, 45 n. 20.
Feldman, Richard, 65, n. 80.
Fichte, J. G., 2 n. 3.
Fink, Eugen, 307 n. 78, 308 n. 84, 332 n. 12, 335 n. 22.
Finnis, John, 11 n. 2, 40 n. 10, 55 n. 48, 84 n. 6, 88 n. 20, 90–97, 104 n. 74, 177 n. 36, 209 n. 23, 213 n. 35, 224 n. 74, 231 n. 90, 329 n. 1, 330.
Fortin, Ernest, 7, 27 n. 58, 35 n. 91, 100, 168–79, 208–10, 231 n. 90, 254, 257 n. 3, 277, 280 n. 50, 281 n. 57, 329 n. 1, 330 n. 2, 356 n. 6.
Gadamer, Hans-Georg, 277, 291 n. 19.
Goerge, Robert, 50 n. 37.
Giles of Rome, 132 n. 20.
Gilson, Etienne, 105 n. 80, 108 n. 86.
Godfrey of Fontaines, 132 n. 20.
Goerner, E. A., 31 n. 75, 51 n. 38, 114 n. 115, 178 n. 41, 356 n. 6.

Grisez, Germain, 40 n. 8–10, 85–91, 94, 96–97, 149 n. 72, 173 n. 23, 181, 231 n. 90, 329 n. 1.
Grotius, H. 150 n. 77.
Guerra, Mark, 231 n. 90.
Gurwitsch, Aron, 307 n. 76.
Hegel, G. W., 2 n.3, 289–91, 295, 298–9, 305, 362.
Heidegger, Martin, 8, 18, 123, 174, 277, 281, 284–328, 334, 337 n. 24, 341, 343, 345, 348 n. 59, 349 n. 61, 354.
Henrich, Dieter, 105–6.
Henry of Ghent, 131 n. 18, 132 n. 20.
Heraclitus, 25 n. 53, 286.
Hittinger, Russell, 59 n. 58, 83 n. 5, 90 n. 30, 329 n. 1.
Hobbes, T., 2 n.3, 150 n. 7, 190, 191 n. 44, 266 n. 14, 282 n. 58, 301.
Hooker, R., 155.
Hume, D., 83 n. 4, 341 n. 33.
Husserl, Edmund, 22 n. 44, 187 n. 28, 288, 294, 299–301, 313, 322–4, 327–8, 332 n. 12, 334 n. 19, 335 n. 22, 336, 340–1, 354, 362.
Jaffa, Harry, 7, 152–69, 172, 174, 176 n. 34, 177, 205–7, 208 n. 21, 210–13, 220, 251, 253, 329 n. 1, 356 n. 6.
James of Viterbo, 132 n. 20.
Jefferson, T., 164 n. 46, 165, 167.
Jenkins, John, 154 n. 9.
Jensen, Steven, 53–54.
Jesus Christ, 35 n. 91, 81–2 , 107 n 85, 121 n. 144, 122, 129 n. 14, 149.
Jonas, Hans, 270 n. 27, 303 n. 61, 350 n. 66.
Jordan, Mark, 154 n. 9.
Kant, I., 2, 6–7, 9, 18, 26–28, 32 n. 76, 33, 34 n. 85, 42 n.14, 57 n. 53, 62 n. 74, 66 n. 82, 70 n. 95, 73 n. 99, 74 n. 102, n. 10, 84, 90, 97–111, 120, 137 n. 32, 142, 192 n. 44, 205 n. 3, 207–8, 217, 226, 231, 263 n. 6, 266 n. 13, 274, 305–7, 309, 333–4, 336, 338, 340, 354, 357 n. 9, 358, 362, 364.
Kennington, Richard, 208 n. 21, 296 n. 36, n. 39, 330–1, 333 n . 18, 340.
Kerr, Fergus, 9 n. 1, 43 n. 27.
Keys, Mary, 2 n. 2, 103 n. 72, 134 n. 23, 154 n. 9, 205 n. 3.
Kierkegaard, S. 203, n. 42.
Klein, Jacob, 126 n. 3, 264 n. 9, 328 n. 148, 351 n. 70.
Kojève, Alexandre, 290, 291 n, 19, 306 n. 72, 343–4, 345 n. 46, 350 n. 66.
Kossel, Clifford, 47 n. 27, 83 n. 5, 207 n. 15, 209 n. 23.
Kranz, Walther, 25 n. 53.
Kries, Douglas, 54 n. 45, 170–1, 220–5, 227 n. 80, 228.
Krüger, Gerhard, 125 n. 1, 135 n. 26.
Kuhn, Helmut, 27 n. 59, 155 n. 14, 205 n. 4, 252 n. 36, 270 n. 27, 278 n. 41–42, n. 44, 299 n. 44.
Lehrberger, James, 157 n. 25, 175 n. 29.
Locke, J., 150 n. 77, 155, 165, 180–1, 190, 191 n. 44, 192–5, 199.
Lonergan, Bernard, 162 n. 43.
Louden, Robert, 209 n. 23.
Lincoln, Abraham, 163.
Löwith, Karl, 299 n. 44, 301 n. 53, 308 n. 22.
Machiavelli, N., 145 n. 55, 155 n. 16, 301.
Macpherson, C. B., 232 n. 58.
Madison, James, 165.
Maimonides, Moses, 81, 128, 129 n. 14, 133, 145 n. 55, 245, 299, 301.
May, William, 94.
Melzer, Arthur, 129 n. 14.
Merrill, Clark, 213 n. 35.
Mill, John Stuart, 34 n. 85, 165 n. 2, 225–6.
Möhle, Hannes, 202 n. 39.
Mollin, Alfred, 219 n. 61.
Muller, Earl, 81–82., 122.
Nelson, Daniel Mark, 50 n. 38.
Newton, Isaac, 187 n. 27.
Nietzsche, Friederich, 73, 174, 211, 229–30, 275, 281, 290, 305, 309, 334, 337 n. 24.
Ockham, 109, 131 n. 18.
O'Connor, D. J., 22 n. 44, 29 n. 69.
O'Donague, D. 181 n. 6.
Orrego, Cristóbal, 261 n. 2.
O'Reilly, Hugh, 131 n. 17.
Osborne, Thomas M., 132 n. 21.
Panofsky, Erwin, 128.
Pangle, Thomas, 150 n. 76, 203 n. 43, 209–10, 357 n. 5.
Pinckaers, Servais, 4 n. 7, 34 n. 85, 36 n. 96, 43 n. 16, 81, 109 n. 88, 115 n. 116, 122.
Plato, 22 n. 44, 24 n. 51, 26, 30 n. 70, 42, 62 n. 71, 83 n. 4, 114 n. 113, 120, 123, 125 n.1, 131 n. 18, 133, 135 n. 28, 139 n. 34, 145 n. 44, 148, 171, 177, 186, 191–2, 209, 214–19, 221, 222 n. 69, 235, 239 n. 129, 243 n. 4, 244 n. 8, 245 n. 12, 262 n. 4, 263 n. 8, 264, 266 n. 13, 271 n. 30, 275, 277 n. 40, 278–9, 282 n. 58, 286, 295–7, 299, 301, 305, 308, 311 n. 90, 315 n. 100, 323 n. 134, 330, 340, 344 n. 42, 348, 349–50, 351 n. 67–70, 355 358, 362.
Porter, Jean, 4 n. 7, 69–70, 115 n. 116, 132 n. 21, 190 n. 37, 339 n. 31.
Reid, James D., 287 n. 13.

Riezler, Kurt, 287, 309 n. 87.
Rosen, Stanley, 219, 340.
Russell, Bertrand, 337 n. 25.
Ryan, Eugene, 140 n. 38.
Schall, James, 12 n. 3, 136 n.30, 213 n. 33, 269 n. 23.
Schmitt, Carl, 246.
Schrems, John J., 152 n. 1, 159 n. 30.
Schrock, Thomas, 45 n. 23.
Schutz, Alfred, 307 n. 76, 308 n. 84, 309 n. 86.
Searle, John, 70–71.
Simon, Yves, 61 n. 66.
Simpson, Otto von, 128 n. 11.
Smith, Janet E., 114 n. 115.
Smith, Thomas, 11 n. 1.
Sokolowski, Robert, 131 n. 18, 178 n. 41, 244 n. 7, 355 n. 22.
Socrates, 123, 171, 214–20, 222, 239 n. 139, 242, 262 n. 5, 263–5, 267–8, 271, 274, 286 n. 10, 299–300, 310, 323 n. 134, 346, 348–9, 350 n. 65.
Spinoza, Baruch, 18, 29, 53 n. 42, 69, 83 n. 4, 135 n. 28, 166, 185, 192 n. 44, 201 n. 36, 254 n. 40, 301, 305, 337 n. 24.
Stauffer, Devin, 219.
Strauss, Leo, 1–10, 17 n. 22, 19 n. 30, 25 n. 51, 26, 27 n. 58–59, 39 n.7, 53 n. 42, 73 n. 101, 90, 123–52, 154–6, 163, 168, 172, 174, 178 n. 41, 180, 187 n. 28, 190 n. 35, 191 n. 40, 192–5, 198–200, 203 n. 43, 204–5, 207, 208 n. 21, 210–11, 213 n. 33, n. 35, 214, 218, 220 n. 62, 229 n. 86, 230–1, 234 n. 110, 235, 241, 243, 244 n. 8–9, 245–6, 250 n. 32, 251 n. 35, 252–4, 257–306, 307 n. 75, 309 n. 86–7, 310 n. 88, 311 n. 90, 328 n. 148, 329–61, 364.
Suarez, F., 150 n. 77.
Velkley, Richard, 279 n. 48, 298 n. 44, 345– 50, 352.
Waugh, Evelyn, 230 n. 89.
West, Thomas, 10 n. 2, 44 n. 19, 56 n. 49, 59 n. 59, 61 n. 68, 121 n. 143, 131 n. 18, 152 n. 3, 172 n. 19, 210 n. 29, 231 n. 91.
White, Kevin, 129 n. 14.
Wilhelmsen, Frederick, 154 n. 8.
Williamson, Robert, 219 n. 61.
Wipple, John, 14 n. 11, 16 n. 17, 19 n. 20, 128 n. 8, 190 n. 35.
Wolter, Alan, 201 n. 35.
Xenophon, 133, 145 n. 55, 243 n. 4, 264 n. 9, 295, 299, 301, 342, 348.
Zuckert, Catherine, 193–6, 198–9, 286 n. 10, 291.
Zuckert, Michael, 7, 180–96, 198–9, 291.

Made in the USA
San Bernardino, CA
08 May 2020